'Professor Baetens has brought a fascinating new perspective to the study of international law, looking at the role of unseen actors in various areas. While unseen, these actors are certainly not unimportant for the effective functioning of their respective institutions, and the discharge of their duties benefits parties, States and the rule of law. This volume demonstrates how the many unseen actors contribute to making international adjudication efficient and effective, and is a fresh approach to the study of international adjudication.'

Meg Kinnear, ICSID Secretary-General

'Freya Baetens has put together a stellar collection of contributions highlighting the role of multiple actors involved in the work of international courts and tribunals. Some are visible, others are less visible. Some are directly involved in the litigation process, others are involved in a more indirect manner. This lifting of the stage curtains also places a welcome spotlight on issues concerning legitimacy, neutrality or transparency.'

Laurence Boisson de Chazournes, Professor,
University of Geneva, and Director of the LLM in
International Dispute Settlement (MIDS)

'This book not only has the merit of exploring areas of international adjudication to which little attention has been paid to date, it also brings together an impressive array of experiences, information and insights from leading practitioners and researchers on essential aspects of the functioning of international courts and tribunals. By shining a light on the "unseen actors" in international adjudication, this work is a welcome and ground-breaking contribution to reflection on the role and responsibilities of these *auxiliaires de justice* in the sound administration of international justice.'

Philippe Couvreur, ICJ Registrar

'My advice to every practitioner of international law, to every advocate before an international tribunal, and to every State or private party to an international dispute is: *read this book! Legitimacy of Unseen Actors in International Adjudication* is a fascinating and well-researched study of how courts and tribunals actually function, the importance of court personnel and other behind-the-scenes actors, and the impacts they can have on outcomes. No international advocate, no matter how experienced, should step into court again without having read it.'

Paul Reichler, Partner, Foley Hoag LLP

'There are few works of international legal scholarship which shine the spotlight on the important "hinterland" of international legal adjudication – namely, the work of registries, secretariats, appointing authorities and others, which both enables and shapes international adjudication in typically unseen ways. In this volume, an impressive range of experienced and expert authors is marshalled to do just that, and to provide their perspectives on the nature, significance and, indeed, legitimacy of the work of such professionals. This will be of great interest and value to those working on international tribunals across a range of disciplines.'

Andrew Lang, Chair in International Law and
Global Governance, Edinburgh Law School

'Finally, the missing piece of the puzzle! There have been numerous books on international judges, prosecutors and the so-called international bar, but rarely has scholarship focused on the unexplored world of the people who keep the lights of international adjudication on. This is a must-read for anyone who wants to understand how international adjudication actually works, in reality.'

Cesare Romano, Professor of Law, Loyola
Law School, Los Angeles

LEGITIMACY OF UNSEEN ACTORS IN INTERNATIONAL ADJUDICATION

International courts and tribunals differ in their institutional composition and functions, but a shared characteristic is their reliance on the contribution of individuals other than the judicial decision-makers themselves. Such 'unseen actors' may take the form of registrars and legal officers, but also non-lawyers such as translators and scientific experts. Unseen actors are vital to the functioning of international adjudication, exerting varying levels of influence on judicial processes and outcomes. The opaqueness of their roles, combined with the significance of judicial decisions for the parties involved as well as a wider range of stakeholders, raises questions about unseen actors' impact on the legitimacy of international dispute settlement. This book aims to answer such legitimacy questions and identify 'best practices' through a multifaceted enquiry into common connections and patterns in the institutional composition and daily practice of international courts and tribunals.

FREYA BAETENS (Cand. Jur./Lic.Jur. (Ghent); LL.M. (Columbia); Ph.D. (Cambridge)) is Professor of Public International Law at the PluriCourts Centre, Faculty of Law, Oslo University, working on an interdisciplinary research project evaluating the legitimacy of international courts and tribunals. She is also affiliated with the Europa Institute, Faculty of Law, Leiden University. As a Member of the Brussels Bar, she regularly acts as counsel or expert in international and European disputes. She is specialized in the law of treaties, responsibility of states and international organizations, law of the sea, WTO and investment, energy and sustainable development law.

STUDIES ON INTERNATIONAL COURTS AND TRIBUNALS

General Editors
Andreas Føllesdal, University of Oslo
Geir Ulfstein, University of Oslo

Studies on International Courts and Tribunals contains theoretical and interdisciplinary scholarship on legal aspects as well as the legitimacy and effectiveness of international courts and tribunals.

Other books in the series:

Mads Andenas and Eirik Bjorge (eds.) *A Farewell to Fragmentation: Reassertion and Convergence in International Law*

Cecilia M. Bailliet and Nobuo Hayashi (eds.) *The Legitimacy of International Criminal Tribunals*

Amrei Müller with Hege Elisabeth Kjos (eds.) *Judicial Dialogue and Human Rights*

Nienke Grossman, Harlan Grant Cohen, Andreas Follesdal and Geir Ulfstein (eds.) *Legitimacy and International Courts*

Robert Howse, Hélène Ruiz-Fabri, Geir Ulfstein and Michelle Q. Zang (eds.) *The Legitimacy of International Trade Courts and Tribunals*

Theresa Squatrito, Oran Young, Andreas Føllesdal and Geir Ulfstein (eds.) *The Performance of International Courts and Tribunals*

Marlene Wind (ed.) *International Courts and Domestic Politics*

Christina Voigt (ed.) *International Judicial Practice on the Environment: Questions of Legitimacy*

Martin Scheinin (ed.) *Human Rights Norms in 'Other' International Courts*

LEGITIMACY OF UNSEEN ACTORS IN INTERNATIONAL ADJUDICATION

Edited by

FREYA BAETENS

University of Oslo

CAMBRIDGE
UNIVERSITY PRESS

University Printing House, Cambridge CB2 8BS, United Kingdom

One Liberty Plaza, 20th Floor, New York, NY 10006, USA

477 Williamstown Road, Port Melbourne, VIC 3207, Australia

314-321, 3rd Floor, Plot 3, Splendor Forum, Jasola District Centre, New Delhi - 110025, India

79 Anson Road, #06-04/06, Singapore 079906

Cambridge University Press is part of the University of Cambridge.

It furthers the University's mission by disseminating knowledge in the pursuit of education, learning and research at the highest international levels of excellence.

www.cambridge.org
Information on this title: www.cambridge.org/9781108725286
DOI: 10.1017/9781108641685

First published 2019
First paperback edition 2021

A catalogue record for this publication is available from the British Library

Library of Congress Cataloging in Publication data
Names: Baetens, Freya, editor.
Title: Legitimacy of unseen actors in international adjudication / edited by Freya Baetens.
Description: Cambridge, United Kingdom ; New York, NY : Cambridge University Press, 2019. | Series: Studies on international courts and tribunals
Identifiers: LCCN 2019019447 | ISBN 9781108485852 (hardback) | ISBN 9781108725286 (paperback)
Subjects: LCSH: Arbitration (International law) | Jurisdiction (International law) | International courts. | BISAC: LAW / International.
Classification: LCC KZ6115 .L44 2019 | DDC 341.5/22–dc23
LC record available at https://lccn.loc.gov/2019019447

ISBN 978-1-108-48585-2 Hardback
ISBN 978-1-108-72528-6 Paperback

CONTENTS

FIGURES

TABLES

CONTRIBUTORS

PHILIPP AMBACH is Chief of the Victims Participation and Reparations Section at the International Criminal Court (ICC). He previously served as the ICC President's Special Assistant, after having worked at the ICTY/ ICTR as a legal adviser in the Registry and the Appeals Chamber. Mr. Ambach holds a Ph.D. in international criminal law and has been admitted as prosecutor in the regional prosecutor's office in Cologne, Germany.

FREYA BAETENS (Cand.Jur./Lic.Jur. (Ghent); LL.M. (Columbia); Ph.D. (Cambridge)) is Professor of Public International Law at the PluriCourts Centre of Excellence (Faculty of Law, University of Oslo) and affiliated with the Europa Institute (Faculty of Law, Leiden University). As a member of the Brussels Bar, she regularly acts as counsel or expert in international disputes.

DANIEL ARI BAKER is a dispute settlement lawyer in the Legal Affairs Division of the World Trade Organization, where he advises dispute settlement panels across a range of WTO law issues. He holds a B.A./ LL.B. from the University of Melbourne and an LL.M. from NYU School of Law.

LEDI BIANKU (LL.M. College of Europe, Bruges) has been a judge at the European Court of Human Rights since 2008. He taught public international law, EU law and ECHR law at the Law Faculty in Tirana University (1993–2007) and Albanian School of Magistrates (1997–2007) and was a member of the Venice Commission for Democracy through Law (2006–2008).

GILLIAN CAHILL is a barrister, specialised in International Arbitration and European Union Law having practised in Paris, Dublin and Madrid. She has also served as a référendaire to Justices Regan and O'Caoimh at the Court of Justice of the European Union.

DAMIEN CHARLOTIN is a Ph.D. candidate at the University of Cambridge (Corpus Christi College), where he studies international dispute settlement under an empirical, data-analysis approach. He blogs on Medium (https://medium.com/@damien.charlotin) and is also a main contributor to *Investment Arbitration Reporter*.

KATHLEEN CLAUSSEN is Associate Professor of Law at the University of Miami School of Law. Her primary scholarly interests include trade and investment law and dispute settlement. Prior to joining the faculty in 2017, she served as Associate General Counsel at the Office of the United States Trade Representative in the Executive Office of the President of the United States. She received her law degree from the Yale Law School where she was Editor-in-Chief of the *Yale Journal of International Law*.

GIOVANNA MARIA FRISSO is Professor of International Law at the Universidade Federal Fluminense and coordinator of the School of the Public Defender's Office in Brazil. She developed an interest in the relationship between medicine and law within the context of international criminal tribunals during her stay as a visiting professional at the International Criminal Court. She holds degrees from the University of Nottingham (Ph.D.) and the University of Uppsala (LL.M.).

PHILIPPE GAUTIER has been the Registrar of the International Tribunal for the Law of the Sea since 2001. He is Professor of Law at the Catholic University of Louvain (Louvain-la-Neuve). He has published on the law of treaties, protection of the environment, settlement of international disputes, law of the sea and Antarctica.

CATHERINE H. GIBSON is an international arbitration and trade associate at Covington & Burling LLP in Washington, DC. She previously served as a legal adviser to the Honorable O. Thomas Johnson, Jr. at the Iran-United States Claims Tribunal, and as a trial attorney in the US Department of Justice.

GUILLAUME GROS is a research assistant and Ph.D. candidate at the Faculty of Law of the University of Geneva. Admitted to the Luxembourg and Paris bars, he has litigation experience within the field of European law and previously worked as a lecturer at the Robert Schuman University in Strasbourg.

CAROLINE HEEREN has been working as an administrator at the Registry of the General Court of the Court of Justice of the European Union since 2010, and is currently detached to serve as référendaire to Justice Bieliūnas. Previously she worked as a lawyer in private practice in Brussels.

She holds an LL.M. in International and Comparative Law from the Vrije Universiteit Brussel.

KABRE R. JONATHAN is a Ph.D. candidate in International Public Law at the University of Lausanne (Switzerland). He holds LL.M. degrees in International and Comparative Law from the University of Lausanne and in Judicial Law from University of Ouaga II (Burkina Faso). His current research focuses on the role of private lawyers in international public adjudication.

PETER KEMPEES (LL.M., University of Leiden) is a senior member of the Registry of the European Court of Human Rights, which he joined in 1992. He was seconded to the Human Rights Chamber for Bosnia and Herzegovina to serve as its Registrar in 1997–98 and 2000–01.

HANNES LENK is a Ph.D. candidate at the University of Gothenburg and holds an LL.M. from Leiden University. His research revolves around constitutional aspects of EU foreign investment policy, combining scholarship from diverse fields of international economic law with EU external relations. He has published in the *European Business Law Review* and *Transnational Dispute Management*.

GIACOMO MARCHISIO is a research associate and lecturer at McGill University's Faculty of Law, where he specializes in evidence law, comparative civil procedure and international adjudication. He holds a doctoral degree and master of laws from McGill University, and a J.D. from the University of Turin. He is a member of the International Task Force on Mixed Mode Dispute Resolution (Pepperdine School of Law) and of the ICC Task Force on emergency arbitration.

GABRIELLE MARCEAU (Ph.D.) is Professor at the Faculty of Law, University of Geneva; President of SIEL (Society of International Economic Law); and Senior Counsellor in the Legal Affairs Division of the World Trade Organization. At the WTO, her main function is to advise panellists in WTO disputes, the Director-General's Office, the Secretariat and WTO members on WTO-related matters.

BRIDIE MCASEY works in the Foreign Investment Division at the Australian Department of Treasury. Previously she was a legal adviser to the President of the Iran-United States Claims Tribunal, and an associate in a global law firm practising in investor-State arbitration.

BRIAN MCGARRY is a lecturer at the Geneva LL.M. programme in International Dispute Settlement (MIDS), where he teaches inter-state adjudication and arbitration. He is also a researcher at the Geneva Center for International Dispute Settlement (CIDS).

MARKO DIVAC ÖBERG is a legal officer in chambers at the Special Tribunal for Lebanon. He previously held the same position at the International Criminal Tribunal for the Former Yugoslavia. He has also clerked at the International Court of Justice and worked for human rights NGOs in Malawi and Palestine.

JOSEF OSTŘANSKÝ is a lecturer at the Geneva LL.M. programme in International Dispute Settlement (MIDS), where he teaches commercial and investment arbitration. He also carries out research under the auspices of the Geneva Center for International Dispute Settlement (CIDS).

PIETRO ORTOLANI is an assistant professor at Radboud University, Nijmegen. He is interested in all forms of arbitration and transnational dispute resolution. He has acted as an expert for the European Parliament and the European Commission. In 2016, he received the James Crawford Prize.

MARIE-CATHERINE PETERSMANN is a Ph.D. fellow at the European University Institute (EUI). Her publications and teaching focus on regime interactions and adjudication of conflicts between international environmental law and human rights law. Her work has appeared in numerous edited volumes and journals. In 2018, she was awarded an Honorable Mention in the Richard Macrory Prize for Best Article in the *Journal of Environmental Law* and in 2016, the IUCN Academy of Environmental Law granted her the 'Best Graduate Student Paper' award. She is a senior editor for the *European Journal of Legal Studies* and a member of the Global Network for the Study of Human Rights and the Environment (GNHRE) and the IUCN World Commission on Environmental Law (WCEL).

KSENIA POLONSKAYA holds a Ph.D. from Queen's University, Faculty of Law. She holds an LL.M. degree from University of Toronto, Faculty of Law. She was the recipient of a graduate scholarship from the Centre for International Governance Innovation (CIGI). In 2013–14, she served as Associate Editor at the *University of Toronto Law Review*.

RELJA RADOVIĆ is a Ph.D. candidate at the University of Luxembourg. He holds an LL.B. and an LL.M. degree from the University of Novi Sad (Serbia), as well as an LL.M. (Adv.) in public international law from the University of Leiden.

CHRISTINE SIM is a rising specialist in international dispute settlement. She has published and presented her work on international investment arbitration, conciliation, and UNCLOS dispute settlement. Her research is supported by several years' experience in litigation, arbitration, mediation, a public international law practice and assisting arbitrators as tribunal secretary with case management.

TOMMASO SOAVE is a researcher in international law. His work focuses on the socio-professional interactions that shape global regulations and governance. In addition, he has several years of experience in the practice of international dispute settlement, both as a counsel and as an assistant to adjudicators. A member of the New York Bar, Tommaso holds degrees from the University of Turin, Sciences Po Paris, Harvard Law School, and the Graduate Institute of International and Development Studies.

LEIGH SWIGART, an anthropologist by training, is Director of Programs in International Justice and Society at the International Center for Ethics, Justice and Public Life of Brandeis University. For more than fifteen years she oversaw the Brandeis Institute for International Judges and is the co-author, with Daniel Terris and Cesare Romano, of *The International Judge: An Introduction to the Men and Women Who Decide the World's Cases* (2007). Her academic work and publications have focused on the international judiciary, language diversity in international criminal courts and tribunals, and African sociolinguistics.

MATTHEW W. SWINEHART is the Counsel for International Trade and Financial Regulatory Policy, and Lead Financial Services Negotiator, at the US Department of the Treasury. Before joining the Treasury, he was an international arbitration and litigation associate at Covington & Burling LLP and served as a law clerk to the Honorable Patrick E. Higginbotham of the US Court of Appeals for the Fifth Circuit.

HUGH THIRLWAY (M.A, Ll.D. Cantab.) was for many years an 'unseen actor' in the Registry of the ICJ, where the post of Principal Legal Secretary was created specifically for him. He was subsequently appointed Professor of International law at IUHEI in Geneva, and has since held Visiting Professorships at various universities worldwide. His published works include *The International Court of Justice and The Sources of International Law* (2nd. Ed., Oxford University Press, 2019).

PETER TZENG is an Associate at Foley Hoag LLP, where he exclusively advises and represents States on matters of public international law and international investment law. He is a graduate of Yale Law School, a former law clerk of the International Court of Justice, and a recipient of the Diploma of The Hague Academy of International Law. He speaks all six official languages of the United Nations at varying levels of proficiency.

NATHALIE WILES is a senior legal officer (First Secretary of the Court) in the Department of Legal Matters of the Registry of the International Court of Justice. She previously worked in the international law department of Frere Cholmeley Eversheds in Paris, after having qualified in London as a solicitor of the Supreme Court of England and Wales.

ANDREAS R. ZIEGLER is Professor of International Law at the University of Lausanne. Previously he was a civil servant working for several Swiss Ministries and international organizations. He regularly advises governments, international organizations, NGOs and private clients, and has represented them before various domestic and international courts and arbitral tribunals. He is on the permanent roster of panellists of the WTO and ICSID.

FOREWORD

My role as author of the Foreword to this book perhaps needs a few words of explanation. Professor Baetens invited me to attend the conference that gave rise to it, knowing that, as a long-serving 'unseen actor' at The Hague myself, I might have valuable experience to draw on, and also honoured me with an invitation to give a keynote speech. Unfortunately, when the time came I was recovering from an operation and I had to conclude that it would not be possible to attend. I was happy therefore to be able to accept her further suggestion that I should contribute a Foreword, introducing the main themes on which the various papers elaborate. It is for me a pleasant coincidence that the planned publication date will fall almost exactly fifty years after the date on which I entered the service of the International Court of Justice (ICJ)!

Any international lawyer who has had contact with the process of international judicial or arbitral settlement of disputes, the judicial protection of human rights, or with the administration of international criminal law, even if such contact is only if from the vantage point of the study or library, will be aware that it involves more than a judge, or a bench of judges. There necessarily exists a number of occupations, comparable in some ways with those of the *auxiliaires de justice* of French law, whose purpose is to support, to provide the framework for, the decision-making process. Every court requires, at least, a secretary or registrar to record the proceedings and the decision, and to authenticate it, and this official must be supported by the appropriate clerical staff. Unless the court and the parties before it use only a single language, interpretation and translation must be provided. Access to a library, with a staff, will be necessary; particularly if the tribunal is a standing one, archives will be needed, and must be curated. The need for contributors in these categories and generally the nature and extent of the contribution they make to the final product – the decision or decisions – is determined by their pre-defined functions, and in that sense visible to the parties and to the world. That contribution is valuable, but limited and non-judicial. Even a Registrar does not, *as Registrar*, suggest how the case should be decided, or himself write any part of the judgment.

But in the actual practice of international dispute settlement the situation is frequently less simple. The role of a Registrar or secretary may in practice include confidential support; the registry may have staff specifically specified as legal staff, as is now the case of the ICJ; and the judges may have legal assistants, or there may be persons described as, for example, interns, who support the judges in unspecified ways. Not only is the contribution of such additional persons not visible to the outside world, but their presence may also not be generally disclosed. It was primarily officials such as these that formed the focus of the Call for Papers in preparation for the conference, designated 'unseen actors in international adjudication'. The stated goal of the Conference was stated as being 'to identify and analyse [alleged] common connections and patterns on the institutional makeup and daily practice of international courts and tribunals, through an interdisciplinary investigation of the functioning of "unseen actors", with the purpose of explaining and answering legitimacy challenges, for example, through the developments of codes of ethics'.

The unspoken question was whether in practice their activities always fall within proper limits – those limits being defined by reference to the unique function reserved to the international judge – reaching the decision: might judges be over-influenced by their invisible supporters? Might they even be tempted to delegate some part of their powers, where delegation conflicts with judicial duty? But once the concept of 'unseen actors' was examined, Professor Baetens and her team found that it had relevance in other contexts within the international dispute-settlement process, a number of which were enumerated in the 'Call for Papers'. As will be evident from the Table of Contents of the present publication, there proved to be even more aspects worthy of examination than then foreseen.

The conference afforded the participants many opportunities to venture on comparisons between the operation of different international tribunals, the functioning of which was presented in the various papers. Part I offers a descriptive overview of institutional perspectives: mention is made of the ICJ (Chapter 2), International Tribunal for the Law of the Sea (ITLOS) (Chapter 3), arbitral institutions (Chapter 4), the World Trade Organization (WTO) (Chapter 5), as well as the more specialized bodies such as the International Criminal

Court (ICC) (Chapter 6) and the European Court of Human Rights (ECtHR) (Chapter 7), and the Court of Justice of the European Union (ECJ)(Chapter 8). Subsequently, these international tribunals are dealt with in depth in subsequent chapters, such as the ECJ in Chapters 16 and 24, the Court of Arbitration of the International Chamber of Commerce in Chapter 13, the ICC in Chapters 15 and 21, and the International Centre for the Settlement of Investment Disputes (ICSID) in Chapters 19 and 20.

Unseen actors may be at work even before any judge or arbitrator takes up his functions. He has to be appointed by some means: could the appointment process be adjusted to ensure the presence of a favourable inclination (not to say 'bias')? How transparent is any system for the appointment of judges or arbitrators? (Chapter 9). For established bodies like the ICJ, the ICC, the ECtHR and the ECJ there are constitutional systems in place, but even for some of these 'screening bodies' exist, whose role should not be overlooked (Chapter 10).

Most fascinating on the theoretical level was, first, the group of papers devoted to the issues of 'Confidentiality and Transparency' (Part IV), and those addressing 'Ethics and Accountability' (Part V), subjects that underlay the original Call for Papers, and together perhaps may be seen as revealing the *point névralgique* of the whole. The essential quality of the persons or entities here under study is that they are 'unseen'; and this raises questions as to what extent this invisibility is justified, and what it may cloak. The deliberations of a tribunal must be confidential, and yet its workings must, from a different viewpoint, have some degree of transparency in order to generate and justify trust in the justice of the process. The problem is most marked, as already mentioned, in the case of assessment of the degree and nature of the influence exerted by secretariats, law clerks, interns, legal officers: all those officials equipped by legal training and education to think, write and speak in terms shared with judges, and working alongside them in the preparation of decisions. Might it be the case that their influence, to borrow the terms of the famous UK House of Commons motion of 1780, 'has increased, is increasing, and ought to be diminished'? The Chapters of Parts IV and V offer valuable material and reflection on these issues.

It is almost inevitable that questions of language will arise in international dispute settlement. When French and English were selected nearly a hundred years ago as the languages in which the Permanent Court of International Justice (PCIJ) would work, it was expected the candidates for the role of judges would be capable of working in one of other of these languages, and many would be fluent in both. In much of the modern world, for the purposes of litigation and adjudication, English is today the *lingua franca*,[1] except in the case of tribunals dealing exclusively with a regional group with a common language, e.g. Arabic. Interpreters and translators have already been mentioned; they may provide the bridge between party and judge, or between judge and judge. Arguably they could be left out of the classification of 'actors', inasmuch as ideally their activity does not affect the outcome: the only change effected should be to the language of expression, not the sense and purport, of the written or spoken material. However, the matter may be more complicated, in particular following the establishment of international criminal tribunals, which has made it necessary to examine witnesses (including the accused)[2] to a far greater extent than in general inter-State disputes, where provisions such as Article 70 of the ICJ Rules of Court[3] have sufficed; in such context, a wider range of languages and cultures make 'perfect' translation less practicable. Chapter 15, on the language services at the ICC, affords a picture of how problems such as this are being met in the context of, in particular, the languages of the African continent.

Finally, however paradoxical it may sound, even the international judge may be an unseen actor, in the sense that some of his or her activities may not be visible to the participants in the proceedings before him, yet may have an impact on, or at least some relevance to, those proceedings. This need not amount to conflict of interest, as normally understood; but it may, as suggested in Chapter 25, have relevance to workload management considerations.

A case can be made for the view that transparency is not necessarily the highest value to be aimed at in international judicial settlement, and that what matters is that the ideas on which the decision is built should be those that ultimately move the judge, even if for their expression, and even to some extent their suggestion, he has a debt to others which evades assessment; that in this field there is something to be said for *quieta non*

---

[1] A situation very thoroughly studied in Anthea Roberts, *Is International Law International?* (Oxford: Oxford University Press, 2017), pp. 9–10, 260–6.

[2] Involving, less obviously, medical practitioners as unseen actors: see Chapter 21.

[3] Which regulates arrangements for translation and interpretation between the official languages, and into these when a party employs a non-official language

movere. If investigation there is to be, however, it could hardly be more effectively, efficiently and discreetly done than in this collection, each contribution to which, in Blake's words, 'bodies forth the form of things unseen'.

Hugh Thirlway
The Hague, 31 October 2018

1

Unseen Actors in International Courts
and Tribunals

Challenging the Legitimacy of International Adjudication

FREYA BAETENS[1]

*They are the unsung heroes of international litigation ... their proper func-
tioning is absolutely vital for the effectiveness of the international adjudicative
process.*

Sir Arthur Watts[2]

'Unseen actors' are vital to the functioning of international courts and
tribunals, exercising varying levels of influence on the adjudicatory process and its outcome. The last few decades have witnessed an expansion
in the number of international judicial bodies.[3] Although these bodies
differ in their institutional make-up and functions, a characteristic shared
among them is their reliance on the contribution of individuals or entities
other than the judicial decision-makers themselves. Unseen actors may
take the form of registries, secretariats, law clerks and legal officers, but
they also include non-lawyers such as translators, members of the medical

[1] Special thanks are due to Andreas Føllesdal, Geir Ulfstein and the participants in the
PluriCourts seminar on 24 January 2018 and the seminar organized by the Department
for Public and International Law of Oslo Law Faculty on 30 January 2018 for their useful
comments, as well as to my research associates, Sophie Starrenburg and Sophie Schiettekatte.
This work was partly supported by the Research Council of Norway through its Centres of
Excellence funding scheme (Project number 223274).
[2] Sir Arthur Watts, 'Enhancing the Effectiveness of Procedures of International Dispute
Settlement', in J.A. Frowein, R. Wolfrum and C.E. Philipp (eds.), *Max Planck Yearbook of
United Nations Law* (Leiden: Brill, 2001), vol. V, p. 30, focusing on Members of Secretariats
in particular.
[3] Cesare P.R. Romano, 'The Proliferation of International Judicial Bodies: The Pieces of the
Puzzle', (1999) 31 *New York University Journal of International Law and Politics* 709; Karen
J. Alter, 'The Multiplication of International Courts and Tribunals After the End of the Cold
War', in Cesare P.R. Romano, Karen J. Alter and Chrisanthi Avgerou (eds.), *The Oxford
Handbook of International Adjudication* (Oxford: Oxford University Press, 2013).

profession and scientific experts. Some of these actors may be 'more unseen' than others but most remain nameless in the written decisions, and the extent of their contribution is generally unclear. The opaqueness of their role, combined with the significance of the judicial decision for the parties involved as well as for a wider range of stakeholders, raises questions about the impact of these unseen actors on the legitimacy of international adjudication as such. For example, an unseen actor's influence has formed a ground upon which an arbitral award was challenged, as substantial parts had allegedly been written by a legal assistant rather than the arbitrators themselves.[4] The domestic court adjudicating the dispute in first instance set aside the award on a different ground, so it did not address this point; the case is currently pending on appeal. This book aims to answer such legitimacy questions and identify 'best practices', where feasible, through a multifaceted enquiry into possible common connections and patterns in the institutional make-up and daily practice of international courts and tribunals.

This volume results from an interdisciplinary research project conducted over the course of 2017, culminating in an international conference on 26 and 27 October in The Hague, supported by the PluriCourts Centre of Excellence (Oslo University) and the Europa Instituut (Leiden University). In this book, scholars of legal, political and anthropological science, as well as members of adjudicatory institutions consider and scrutinise the practice of assigning unseen actors certain roles in the judicial process, as well as the implications for the legitimacy of international dispute settlement mechanisms. The individual chapters investigate the character and activities of one or more particular categories of unseen actors, with the aim of clarifying this practice and answering the legitimacy challenges it raises.

The structure of the book reflects overarching themes arising out of the analysis of a broad variety of unseen actors within international adjudication. This approach was preferred to an 'actor-by-actor' examination since many legitimacy concerns are common to the experience of several adjudicatory bodies. For example, the theme of confidentiality and transparency is relevant with respect to a range of actors in multiple fora, from

---

[4] The arbitration in question was *Hulley Enterprises Limited (Cyprus), Yukos Universal Limited (Isle of Man) and Veteran Petroleum Limited (Cyprus) v. Russian Federation*, PCA Cases Nos. AA 226, AA 227 and AA 228, Final Award (18 July 2014), which was subsequently challenged by Russia before The Hague District Court (C/09/477160/HA ZA 15-1, Judgment of 20 April 2016, ECLI:NL:RBDHA:2016:4229).

'ghost experts' to physicians in criminal trials. This introductory chapter provides a broad overview of the issues scrutinised in this book, without seeking to pre-empt the conclusions. First, it discusses why analysing the contribution of unseen actors is important for the assessment of international courts' and tribunals' legitimacy; second, it outlines the structure of the book, and highlights the sub-questions discussed across various parts and chapters; and third, it indicates for whom this research project is relevant and how future projects might build upon its findings.

1.1 The Importance of Unseen Actors for the Legitimacy of International Courts and Tribunals

In order to analyse the influence of unseen actors on the perceived legitimacy of international courts and tribunals, it is important to understand, first, the meaning of legitimacy in the context of international adjudication; secondly, the multidimensional conceptualization of legitimacy as applied to unseen actors in particular; bearing in mind, thirdly, the epistemological and methodological challenges this exercise inevitably entails.

1.1.1 The Meaning of Legitimacy in the Context of International Adjudication

As international courts and tribunals have expanded in number, so too have the areas of international law and international relations on which they adjudicate. As a result, their visibility has increased. Their growing profile is accompanied by strong challenges to their functions, competence and even existence.[5] This should come as no surprise given the volatile political environment in which international courts and tribunals operate, and the challenge they present to States' sovereignty and their law-making role.[6] International courts and tribunals are also costly institutions for States to maintain. The decision to allocate resources to them can come at the expense of non-judicial initiatives that may also

---

[5] See e.g. in relation to human rights, Johan Karlsson Schaffer, Andreas Føllesdal, and Geir Ulfstein, 'International Human Rights and the Challenge of Legitimacy', in Andreas Føllesdal, Johan Karlsson Schaffer, and Geir Ulfstein (eds.), *The Legitimacy of International Human Rights Regimes: Legal, Political and Philosophical Perspectives* (Cambridge: Cambridge University Press, 2013).

[6] Christine Chinkin and Alan Boyle (eds.), *The Making of International Law* (Oxford: Oxford University Press, 2007), p. 268.

have the potential to contribute to peace and security. As a consequence, international courts and tribunals are, and should be, held to a high standard. Their legitimacy is paramount and they must be subject to scrutiny. Arguably, what the international system needs, is not *more* international courts and tribunals, but ones that are *viewed as legitimate* in the eyes of their intended beneficiaries. The unseen actors within international courts and tribunals can function as an important bridge between international and domestic actors and audiences, and they may at times have the ability to improve or damage this relationship.

The charges of a lack of legitimacy levelled at international courts and tribunals require closer examination of what precisely the notion of legitimacy entails. Legitimacy is a concept that is widely used in a number of disciplines, and is understood differently by various groups.[7] In particular, the concept of legitimacy in the context of international law has been subject to a rich and varied scholarship,[8] in particular since the 1990s.[9]

---

[7] A point which has formed the subject of critique in relation to the ballooning of discourse within international legal academia with regards to legitimacy; see James Crawford, 'The Problems of Legitimacy-Speak' (2004) 98 *ASIL Proceedings* 271.

[8] E.g. Thomas M. Franck, 'Legitimacy in the International System' (1988) 82 *AJIL* 705; Thomas M. Franck, *The Power of Legitimacy Among Nations* (Oxford: Oxford University Press, 1990); Daniel Bodansky, 'The Legitimacy of International Governance: A Coming Challenge for International Environmental Law' (1999) 93 *AJIL* 596; Jean-Marc Coicaud and Veijo Heiskanen, *The Legitimacy of International Organizations* (Tokyo/New York: United Nations University Press, 2001); A.E. Buchanan, *Justice, Legitimacy, and Self-Determination: Moral Foundations for International Law* (Oxford: Oxford University Press, 2003); Rüdiger Wolfrum and Volker Röben (eds.), *Legitimacy in International Law* (Berlin/Heidelberg/New York: Springer, 2008); Hilary Charlesworth and Jean-Marc Coicaud (eds.), *Fault Lines of International Legitimacy* (Cambridge: Cambridge University Press, 2010); John Tasioulas, 'The Legitimacy of International Law', in Samantha Besson and John Tasioulas (eds.), *The Philosophy of International Law* (Oxford: Oxford University Press, 2010); Lukas H. Meyer (ed.), *Legitimacy, Justice and Public International Law* (Cambridge: Cambridge University Press, 2009); Steven Wheatley, *The Democratic Legitimacy of International Law* (Oxford: Hart, 2010); Jean d'Aspremont and Eric de Brabandere, 'The Complementary Faces of Legitimacy in International Law: The Legitimacy of Origin and the Legitimacy of Expertise' (2011) 34 *Fordham International Law Journal* 190; Robert Howse, Hélène Ruiz-Fabri, Geir Ulfstein and Michelle Q. Ziang (eds.), *The Legitimacy of International Trade Courts and Tribunals* (Cambridge: Cambridge University Press, 2018); Harlan Grant Cohen, Nienke Grossman, Andreas Føllesdal and Geir Ulfstein (eds.), *Legitimacy and International Courts* (Cambridge: Cambridge University Press, 2018).

[9] Bodansky, 'The Legitimacy of International Governance', 596–597; Mattias Kumm, 'The Legitimacy of International Law: A Constitutionalist Framework of Analysis' (2004) 15 *European Journal of International Law* 907, 907–908; Christopher A. Thomas, 'The Uses and Abuses of Legitimacy in International Law' (2014) 34 *Oxford Journal of Legal Studies* 729, 731. A notable early exception is Inis Claude, 'Collective Legitimization as a Political Function of the United Nations' (1966) 20 *International Organization* 367.

The legitimacy of international organisations in general has long been recognised as a layered, multi-dimensional concept,[10] although international courts have in recent years also begun to be examined through the lens of legitimacy. The concept of legitimacy is linked, inter alia, to legality, moral justification, social acceptance and compliance. As a result, legitimacy is subject to criteria that are legal, moral and social.[11]

Scholars have generally viewed legitimacy as comprising sociological and normative dimensions.[12] From a sociological perspective, legitimacy is based on perception: an institution or an actor has legitimacy if its addressees provide it with acceptance and recognition, and consider its authority to be justified.[13] In this sense, a legitimate institution can override the self-interests of its addressees, albeit only to a certain

---

[10] Silje Aambø Langvatn and Theresa Squatrito, 'Conceptualising and Measuring the Legitimacy of International Criminal Tribunals', in Nobuo Hayashi and Cecilia M. Bailliet (eds.), *The Legitimacy of International Criminal Tribunals* (Cambridge: Cambridge University Press, 2017). For an overview of the literature on the legitimacy of international organisations, see inter alia Shane P. Mulligan, 'The Uses of Legitimacy in International Relations' (2005) 34 *Millennium* 349; Allen Buchanan and Robert O. Keohane, 'The Legitimacy of Global Governance Institutions', in Lukas H. Meyer (ed.), *Legitimacy, Justice and Public International Law* (Cambridge: Cambridge University Press, 2009); Daniel Bodansky, 'Legitimacy in International Law and International Relations', in Jeffrey L. Dunoff and Mark A. Pollack (eds.), *Interdisciplinary Perspectives on International Law and International Relations: The State of the Art* (Cambridge: Cambridge University Press, 2012).

[11] Anne Peters, 'Membership in the Global Constitutional Community', in Jan Klabbers, Anne Peters and Geir Ulfstein (eds.), *The Constitutionalization of International Law* (Oxford: Oxford University Press, 2009), pp. 235–236.

[12] A range of terminology is used in the literature to refer to these two categories. See Bodansky, 'The Legitimacy of International Governance', 601; Michael Zürn, 'Global Governance and Legitimacy Problems' (2004) 39 *Government & Opposition* 287; Robert O. Keohane and Allen Buchanan, 'The Legitimacy of Global Governance Institutions' (2006) 20 *Ethics & International Affairs* 405; Lukas H. Meyer and Pranay Sanklecha, 'Introduction: Legitimacy, Justice and Public International Law. Three Perspectives on the Debate', in Lukas H. Meyer (ed.), *Legitimacy, Justice and Public International Law* (Cambridge: Cambridge University Press, 2009); Nienke Grossman, 'Legitimacy and International Adjudicative Bodies' (2009) 41 *George Washington International Law Review* 107.

[13] Legitimacy from this perspective is also known as 'descriptive', 'empirical', 'origin' and 'social' legitimacy. Sociological legitimacy has in turn been divided into source-, process- and result-oriented forms of legitimacy; see Rüdiger Wolfrum, 'Legitimacy in International Law from a Legal Perspective: Some Introductory Considerations', in Rüdiger Wolfrum and Volker Röben (eds.), *Legitimacy in International Law* (Berlin/Heidelberg/New York: Springer, 2008), pp. 6–7; Harlan Grant Cohen, Andreas Føllesdal, Nienke Grossman and Geir Ulfstein, 'Legitimacy and International Courts – A Framework', in Nienke Grossman, Harlan Grant Cohen, Andreas Føllesdal and Geir Ulfstein (eds.), *Legitimacy and International Courts* (Cambridge: Cambridge University Press, 2018).

extent: individuals or States might question an individual judgment of an international court, yet retain belief in its overall legitimacy and authority to render that judgment.[14] Sociological legitimacy is fact-based in the sense that it can be measured empirically,[15] although it nonetheless entails a normative judgment amongst its addressees, which illustrates the closely intertwined nature of normative and sociological legitimacy.[16] A normative conception of legitimacy, on the other hand, is concerned with the rightfulness of an entity's authority; that is to say, 'whether it is justified in some objective sense'.[17]

Departing from the sociological perspective of legitimacy, in the broadest sense, a legitimate court or tribunal is thus one whose authority is perceived as being justified.[18] In the case of international courts, beliefs about the authority of a court are sometimes linked to views about the organisation of which the court is a part.[19] In the context of international courts and tribunals, one of the grounds upon which this authority is constructed relates to its legality, arising from the consent of the parties involved in the adjudicatory process, also known as constitutive or legal legitimacy.[20] Some authors have expressed concerns that State consent in particular is a 'morally anaemic' perspective from which to depart in an analysis of international legal legitimacy, in light of the increasing

---

[14] Keohane and Buchanan, 'The Legitimacy of Global Governance Institutions', 410; Erik Voeten, 'Public Opinion and the Legitimacy of International Courts' (2013) 14 *Theoretical Inquiries in Law* 411, 415.

[15] Erik Voeten, 'Public Opinion and the Legitimacy of International Courts' (2013) 14 *Theoretical Inquiries in Law* 411, 414.

[16] Ibid.; Bodansky, 'Legitimacy in International Law', p. 317.

[17] Bodansky, 'The Legitimacy of International Governance', 601.

[18] Grossman, 'Legitimacy and International Adjudicative Bodies'. This definition builds upon earlier literature on legitimacy, including the work of Daniel Bodansky, as well as later literature, such as Antonio Cassese, 'The Legitimacy of International Criminal Tribunals and the Current Prospects of International Criminal Justice' (2012) 25 *Leiden Journal of International Law* 491, 492.

[19] Voeten, 'Public Opinion and the Legitimacy of International Courts', 416. To give an example: the perceived legitimacy of the WTO Dispute Settlement Body might thus be influenced by broader conceptions of the WTO.

[20] Yvonne McDermott and Wedad Elmaalul, 'Legitimacy', in William A. Schabas and Shannonbrooke Murphy (eds.), *Research Handbook on International Courts and Tribunals* (Cheltenham, UK: Edward Elgar, 2017), pp. 229–231; Kumm, 'The Legitimacy of International Law', 918; Thomas, 'The Uses and Abuses', 735. However, some authors caution that legitimacy should not be conflated with legality, as the notion of legitimacy is broader than that of legality: see Keohane and Buchanan, 'The Legitimacy of Global Governance Institutions', 406; Cassese, 'The Legitimacy of International Criminal Tribunals', 492.

importance of non-State actors within international law.[21] In addition, some may consider that non-democratic States do not enjoy normative legitimacy at the domestic level – and as such, their consent could not 'transfer' legitimacy to, say, an international institution such as the United Nations.[22]

Courts might be perceived as enjoying a greater or lesser degree of legitimacy with regard to the manner in which consent was given and the method through which the court was created.[23] Contemporary international adjudicatory practice often involves many different stakeholders other than States, such as individuals or corporations. As a result, some authors argue that legitimacy might also require, if not the consent of those not party to proceedings, at least consultation and some form of involvement of relevant stakeholders in the court's decision-making process.[24]

The scope of constitutive legitimacy might change in accordance with the purpose and function of the international court in question: thus, for example, international criminal courts derive their legitimacy from the fact that every accused person has the right to be tried by a tribunal 'established by law'.[25] A further facet of legitimacy in this regard is procedural legitimacy, which emphasises not only the outcome of the work of international courts, but the method by which this is achieved.[26] Elements of procedural legitimacy can relate to the existence of fair procedures and transparency; the degree to which the court has to answer to a higher or founding body; the participation of all parties in proceedings; and a balance of means between parties.[27] Equally, procedural legitimacy can be

---

[21] McDermott and Elmaalul, 'Legitimacy', pp. 231–232; Nienke Grossman, 'The Normative Legitimacy of International Courts' (2013) 86 *Temple Law Review* 61.

[22] Keohane and Buchanan, 'The Legitimacy of Global Governance Institutions', 413.

[23] Tullio Treves, 'Aspects of Legitimacy of Decisions of International Courts and Tribunals', in Rüdiger Wolfrum and Volker Röben, *Legitimacy in International Law* (Berlin/Heidelberg/New York: Springer, 2008), pp. 171–173.

[24] Cohen et al., 'Legitimacy and International Courts'.

[25] McDermott and Elmaalul, 'Legitimacy', p. 232.

[26] Bodansky, 'The Legitimacy of International Governance', 612; Kumm, 'The Legitimacy of International Law', 924; Jean d'Aspremont and Eric de Brabandere, 'The Complementary Faces of Legitimacy in International Law: The Legitimacy of Origin and the Legitimacy of Expertise' (2011) 34 *Fordham International Law Journal* 190; Grossman, 'The Normative Legitimacy of International Courts'; Thomas, 'The Uses and Abuses', 750; McDermott and Elmaalul, 'Legitimacy', p. 235.

[27] Wolfrum, 'Legitimacy in International Law', pp. 6–7; Treves, 'Aspects of Legitimacy, pp. 171–173; Cassese, 'The Legitimacy of International Criminal Tribunals', 493; Cohen et al., 'Legitimacy and International Courts'.

derived from the method of appointment of the organs of the court and its judges; the degree to which politics plays a role in these appointments; the type of expertise required of judges; guarantees of impartiality and independence; and the perceived quality of previous judgments of the court.[28]

A further understanding of sociological legitimacy in relation to international courts and tribunals relates to the outcomes of a court's decisions. One element of these outcomes is whether the institution in question is able to meet the goals for which it was created.[29] However, some authors have noted the often expansive and ambitious goals that international courts are expected to meet – goals which can often not be met without sincere cooperation from the States involved in the dispute.[30] Furthermore, '[p]rinciples related to outcomes only play a limited role because disagreement about substantive policy are exactly the kind of thing that legal decision-making is supposed to resolve authoritatively'.[31] As such, effectiveness should not overpower other understandings of legitimacy.

Compliance is a further method through which it is possible to determine the outcome legitimacy of international courts.[32] Other elements to take into account can include the voting record in relation to decisions rendered, whether judges issue separate or dissenting opinions, the degree to which the court's judgments are perceived to be clear and well reasoned, and whether the court addresses all arguments raised by the parties or whether it raises arguments *proprio motu*.[33] It is also possible to take into account whether a court's judgment is considered to be consistent with earlier case law or with the case law of other international courts.[34] In this regard, it is important to observe that perceptions of legitimacy in relation to these factors will likely differ across jurisdictions and between legal systems: as such, common lawyers might consider it more legitimate if a court addresses issues which were not raised by the parties, whereas an individual educated according to the civil tradition might argue the opposite.

---

[28] Treves, 'Aspects of Legitimacy', pp. 171–173.
[29] Wolfrum, 'Legitimacy in International Law', pp. 6–7; Grossman, 'The Normative Legitimacy of International Courts'; Cohen et al., 'Legitimacy and International Courts'.
[30] McDermott and Elmaalul, 'Legitimacy', p. 233.
[31] Kumm, 'The Legitimacy of International Law', 927.
[32] McDermott and Elmaalul, 'Legitimacy', p. 234.
[33] Treves, 'Aspects of Legitimacy', pp. 171–173.
[34] Ibid.

Even in the context of sociological legitimacy, it is impossible to ignore the importance of normative standards. Thus, as Antonio Cassese writes, legitimacy also encompasses the 'moral and psychological acceptance of a body'; the legitimacy of an adjudicative body is often constructed in light of whether it reflects the values of the majority.[35] This statement refers to a sociological understanding of normativity: that is to say, beliefs by the addressees of a court or tribunal with regard to the normative value of the court.

However, one can also examine the legitimacy of courts from a purely normative standpoint – in other words, from the perspective of normative legitimacy described above. Normative conceptions are concerned with whether an entity is authoritative,[36] decoupled from the views of States, the international community, or the court's addressees. Similar to descriptive legitimacy, some authors argue that consent lies at the heart of normative legitimacy, but a range of normative theories hold that actual compliance may matter for normative legitimacy also.[37] For example, numerous authors have argued that the normative legitimacy of an international court can flow from adherence to democratic standards,[38] although such claims are complicated by the movement of court activities from the domestic to the international level.[39] In addition, legitimacy can also be derived from the court's adherence to values shared by the international community as a whole, such as compliance with peremptory norms or fundamental human rights.[40] More broadly, normative legitimacy can be determined with reference to whether a court helps to achieve justice – a concept which evidently can be construed in various ways.[41]

---

[35] Cassese, 'The Legitimacy of International Criminal Tribunals', 492.

[36] Thomas, 'The Uses and Abuses', 738.

[37] Meyer and Sanklecha, 'Introduction: Legitimacy, Justice and Public International Law', p. 3.

[38] Bodansky, 'The Legitimacy of International Governance', 599; Armin von Bogdandy, 'Globalization and Europe: How to Square Democracy, Globalization, and International Law' (2004) 15 *EJIL* 885; J.H.H. Weiler, 'The Geology of International Law – Governance, Democracy and Legitimacy' (2004) 64 *ZaöRV* 547; Steven Wheatley, *The Democratic Legitimacy of International Law* (Oxford: Hart, 2010).

[39] Allison Marston Danner, 'Enhancing the Legitimacy and Accountability of Prosecutorial Discretion at the International Criminal Court' (2003) 97 *AJIL* 510, 535.

[40] Cassese, 'The Legitimacy of International Criminal Tribunals', 492.

[41] Cohen et al., 'Legitimacy and International Courts'.

1.1.2   A Multidimensional Conceptualization of Legitimacy
as Applied to Unseen Actors

In the present book, different facets of this multidimensional conceptualisation of legitimacy are addressed from a range of disciplinary perspectives, incorporating both sociological as well as normative understandings of legitimacy. The 'orthodox' approach based on the concept of legal legitimacy has its merits, given that it mirrors the discourse that international courts seek to project to the outside world, as well as the discourse into which most international lawyers have been socialised. Applying it to the exclusion of other approaches, however, runs the risk that the results will be too general, abstract and reductionist to produce an analysis which is sufficiently sophisticated and nuanced to capture the reality of the issue of unseen actors within international adjudication.

As such, a multidimensional conception of legitimacy can produce more fruitful results,[42] as it can acknowledge that these unseen actors are often explicitly or implicitly obscured within the language of the law. With regard to international courts and tribunals, an assessment of legitimacy should include an examination of their origins, function (including their day-to-day procedure), and performance (that is, the outcome and effects of its function). In this sense, legitimacy can be examined with reference to three factors: an international court's genesis; its daily execution of procedure; and the results it produces. It is these elements that the various contributions to this volume seek to address, producing a multidisciplinary view on the issue of unseen actors.

The participation of unseen actors in the adjudication process may be assessed with reference to this multidimensional conceptualisation of legitimacy. A number of contributions in this volume highlight challenges that are intrinsically tied to one of the elements of legitimacy outlined above: the genesis of international courts. In this understanding, legitimacy requires that courts function according to their mandate, whereby the actions of a court (including those of its unseen actors) are justified with reference to its role as envisaged by its founders. In other words, in the consent-based international legal order, legitimacy with reference to an international court's origins rests on whether the founders have consented to the international court's actions. Legitimacy concerns may arise when a legal assistant or tribunal secretary fully or partially drafts

---

[42] Langvatn and Squatrito, pp. 51–52.

a judgment or award as it can be debated to what extent the founders consented to (or even foresaw) the delegation of this essentially judicial function. The counterargument would be that, as unseen actors act under the instructions of the members of the bench, the bench bears the final responsibility when it adopts their work as its own.

Secondly, the functioning of unseen actors could potentially pose a challenge to the legitimacy of an international court on a day-to-day procedural basis. For example, registries and secretariats are tasked with registering cases, performing administrative functions, maintaining records, and conducting the international court's business on its behalf. In some contexts, they may even influence who adjudicates a dispute, establish the procedural steps involved, and make essential decisions that affect the scope of a case. Their mandate to take such decisions may be viewed expansively or restrictively, and the perspective adopted influences their legitimacy as actors.

Finally, unseen actors may have an effect on the legitimacy of the output and results of an international court, beyond the 'legal' aspects of the court's work and rather examining the outcome and effects of its functioning. Translators provide a pertinent example: they are responsible for conveying the meaning of a decision, which may not be readily comprehensible in all languages. In some cases, they must invent words and convey the meaning of legal concepts. Is a translator an appropriate medium for transmitting such meaning? Does the profound impact of translators on the adjudicatory process and the translation of the decision meet the high standards of legitimacy? Similar questions can be asked with regard to other non-legal unseen actors such as physicians or technical experts.

An important element to remember is that the tenure of some unseen actors may well be longer, even much longer, than that of the adjudicators for whom they work. This can be seen as a force for good, as an institutional memory may well be more efficient and create a more coherent jurisprudence. However, if such a force goes unchecked, it may cause significant legitimacy issues. Thus it has been discussed in the context of international organisations that the long periods in office of the 'neutral' members of an organisation, such as its secretariat, can lead to stagnation.[43]

---

[43] See the discussion in Henry G. Schermers and Niels M. Blokker, *International Institutional Law: Unity within Diversity*, 5th rev. edn (The Hague: Martinus Nijhoff Publishers, 2011) paras. 518–522.

It might also cause issues if long-standing members of an international court or tribunal were, for example, appointed during a period in which there was less emphasis on geographical or gender parity – which can entail that whilst the 'visible' actors of a court or tribunal are seen to be progressive, the realities of the court or tribunal might lag behind. This can lead to a mismatch between the expectations of the public served by the institution and what the institution itself deems necessary in order to carry out its functions, leading to a reduction in the perceived legitimacy of the court. In the particular context of international courts and tribunals, long periods of tenure of such unseen actors might also lead to a mismatch in the ability of these institutional factors to comprehend the effects of a court's jurisprudence beyond its walls, and thus an inability to perceive the outcome and effects of the court's function.

We are witnessing the retreat of certain States from international organisations, law-making and dispute settlement, such as the near complete absence of US diplomats from recent Conferences of the Parties of the UN Framework Convention on Climate Change and the Paris Agreement; or the withdrawal by Burundi from the Statute of the International Criminal Court (ICC), by Ecuador and Venezuela from the Convention on the Settlement of Investment Disputes between States and Nationals of Other States (ICSID Convention) or by the United States from the World Heritage Convention. In the broader context of contemporary international law as a field in crisis and of shifts from unipolarity to multipolarity, it is important to address these questions comprehensively, in order to ensure the continued legitimacy of international courts and tribunals.

1.1.3   Epistemological and Methodological Challenges

Unseen actors are often explicitly or implicitly obscured within the language of the law. As such, a work that seeks to scrutinise the activities of these actors faces a number of methodological hurdles and requires one to adopt epistemological and ontological approaches different from those usually employed within the mainstream tradition. How can scholars observe, discuss and dissect that which is 'unseen'? Precisely that which makes unseen actors interesting – their hidden character from the perspective of classic epistemological understandings of international law – also greatly complicates attempts to conduct research on their activities, a problem compounded by the fact that these actors will often be prevented from publicly disclosing information about their activities due to confidentiality requirements.[44]

One important challenge that needs to be faced in a study of unseen actors is that of access: how can members of the scholarly community access unseen actors and evaluate their conduct? As noted above, strict doctrinal approaches will often not be sufficient in this regard, as this practice is often not reflected in constitutive documents or rules of procedure of international courts and tribunals. Engaging in 'insider research' is one method through which it is possible to investigate the 'reality' of international institutions such as international courts and tribunals.[45] A quick glance at scholarly works focusing on the practice of international adjudicative bodies will reveal that the author will often have two hats: that of a practitioner in the relevant organisation, and that of a (part-time) academic – a trend which is even highlighted in the present volume in relation to the impact of outside activities on the legitimacy of international judges.[46] However, there is generally little reflection on the impact of these dual roles on the eventual shape of the research produced.[47]

Insider research can represent an advantage, as insiders can usually gain access to individuals or practices which are hard to reach for other researchers and might enjoy higher levels of trust as they understand the methods of interaction which are common to the institution in question.[48] In addition, insider researchers already possess the requisite knowledge about their topic of research.[49] However, it is more difficult for readers to evaluate whether insider accounts by court officials or those 'in

---

[44] Nicolas Lamp, 'The "Practice Turn" in International Law: Insights from the Theory of Structuration', in Moshe Hirsch and Andrew Lang (eds.), *Research Handbook on the Sociology of International Law* (Northampton, MA: Edward Elgar, 2018); Matthew Windsor, 'Consigliere or Conscience? The Role of the Government Legal Adviser', in Jean d'Aspremont, Tarcisio Gazzini, André Nollkaemper and Wouter Werner (eds.), *International Law as a Profession* (Cambridge: Cambridge University Press, 2017), pp. 358–359.

[45] Windsor, 'Consigliere or Conscience?', 358–359.

[46] Chapter 26 in this volume.

[47] Cf. Herdis Hølleland and Marit Johansson, '"… To Exercise in All Loyalty, Discretion and Conscience": On Insider Research and the World Heritage Convention' (2017) 23 *International Journal of Cultural Policy* 1.

[48] Sue Wilkinson and Celia Kitzinger, 'Representing Our Own Experience: Issues in "Insider" Research' (2013) 37 *Psychology of Women Quarterly* 251; Melanie J. Greene, 'On the Inside Looking In: Methodological Insights and Challenges in Conducting Qualitative Insider Research' (2014) 19 *The Qualitative Report* 1, 3–4.

[49] Greene, 'On the Inside Looking In', 3–4.

the know' are accurate and reliable, than, say, for them to engage in traditional doctrinal research based on publicly available legal documents.
Furthermore, insider research is sometimes critiqued for being too subjective and biased towards the object of study, as such undermining the
objectivity of the research because the researcher cannot retain a critical distance from the object of study.[50] A particular problem for insider
research on international institutions is that 'there are limits to what a
member of any bureaucracy with formal regulations can publicly articulate', and publications might tend to be less critical of the institution than
might be warranted.[51]

However, the insider/outsider distinction is often found to not form
as great a barrier to research as was once thought in the sense that 'true'
objectivity can perhaps not be said to exist,[52] so insider research need
not be dismissed outright as long as the researcher engages in reflexivity
about their dual role as researcher and 'insider'.[53] To a certain extent,
even those working outside legal practice are part of the subject matter of
this book, given that they are all part of the 'invisible college' of international lawyers.[54] Simultaneously, this does raise the question whether this
'invisible college' can capture the full diversity of perspectives on international adjudicatory practices, including those departing from Third
World Approaches to international law, feminist legal theory or critical
legal analysis.

The fact that unseen actors will often only be able to be uncovered
by those with close ties to the institution in question can also raise
difficult issues with regards to Eurocentrism. For this reason, the present volume aims to steer a middle course between authors with some
'insider knowledge' (who are often, but not always, European men) and
authors who can offer an outsider perspective. As a result, slightly over

---

[50] Ibid., 5; Teresa Brannick and David Coghlan, 'In Defense of Being "Native": The Case for
Insider Academic Research' (2007) 10 *Organizational Research Methods* 59, 60.
[51] Hølleland and Johansson, ' "… to exercise in all loyalty, discretion and conscience" ', 10;
Windsor, 'Consigliere or Conscience?', 365.
[52] D.K. Lewis, 'Anthropology and Colonialism' (1973) 14 *Current Anthropology* 581; R.
Merton, 'Insiders and Outsiders: A Chapter in the Sociology of Knowledge' (1972) 78
American Journal of Sociology 9.
[53] Brannick and Coghlan, 'In Defense of Being "Native"'; see also Andrea Bianchi,
International Law Theories: An Inquiry into Different Ways of Thinking (Oxford: Oxford
University Press, 2016), pp. 3–5.
[54] Oscar Schachter, 'The Invisible College of International Lawyers' (1977–1978) 72
Northwestern University Law Review 217.

one-third of the contributions have been authored by non-Europeans and a similar number have been written by women (with some authors falling in both categories). The contributions to the present volume highlight a variety of ways in which it is possible to assess the functioning of unseen actors in international adjudication. As already mentioned, these approaches include traditional insider accounts, in which knowledge is drawn from the author's own experiences in international courts or tribunals.[55] Similarly, insider accounts can also be drawn from domestic practice in order to illustrate best practice for international bodies;[56] such domestic accounts can be (relatively) more accessible for larger groups of scholars. Other approaches include the application of modern technology to the texts of the decisions of courts and tribunals, such as through the use of forensic linguistics or network analysis,[57] in order to uncover the involvement of unseen actors in the drafting of judicial decisions. Other examples include ethnographic research or other forms of qualitative research, through which researchers who are not insiders can nonetheless examine the practices of an international court or tribunal.[58] Furthermore, some unseen actors can be hidden in plain sight, as is the case for online court reporters and those who compile case-law databases.[59]

1.2   Structure and Underlying Legitimacy Questions

The book examines five constitutive competences or roles that determine the work of many, if not most, unseen actors, regardless of the particular international adjudicatory mechanism within which they operate: nomination and appointment (Part II); case management and deference to the bench (Part III); confidentiality and transparency (Part IV); ethics and accountability (Part V); and external influences and activities (Part VI). But first, the part on 'institutional perspectives' (Part I) provides an introduction to the registries and secretariats of the main adjudicatory bodies which form the object of the cross-regime analysis in the main body of the book.

---

[55] See the contributions in Part I of this volume.
[56] See Chapter 22 of this volume.
[57] See Chapter 20 of this volume.
[58] See Chapter 15 of this volume.
[59] See Chapter 27 of this volume.

1.2.1   Institutional Perspectives

The book starts with laying out a number of institutional perspectives on the functioning of unseen actors, in particular, the arguably most influential ones, namely registries and secretariats, through seven short chapters, written by (former) members of those institutions. This part has been inserted because the book aims to offer a comparative analysis of unseen actors across a wide range of adjudicatory bodies, types of actors and aspects of their roles and functioning. In order to engage with the in-depth analysis in Parts II to VI, it is necessary to understand the manner in which key institutions function in the first place.

More specifically, the following international courts and tribunals are addressed: the International Court of Justice (ICJ), the International Tribunal for the Law of the Sea (ITLOS), the Dispute Settlement Body of the World Trade Organization (WTO), several international arbitral mechanisms, the ICC, the European Court of Human Rights (ECtHR) and the Court of Justice of the European Union (CJEU). These chapters are considerably shorter and intentionally descriptive, so as to allow readers to acquire the necessary background knowledge without immediately being bombarded with scholarly interpretations and proposals for reform.

1.2.2   Nomination and Appointment

The process through which judges are appointed has strong implications for the procedural and output legitimacy of an international court; unseen actors are often tasked with screening potential judicial appointments, yet it is not always entirely clear which criteria dictate their decisions. Part II of this book contains three chapters that address these issues.

The overarching question to which this section seeks to respond is how to assess the competence of certain secretariats or other unseen institutional actors to appoint adjudicators. To this end, the chapters in this section seek to uncover the variety and scope of procedures which are employed in the appointment of adjudicators, including arbitrators, highlighting the important – yet often overlooked – role played by appointing authorities. Appointing authorities are often posited as a method through which the legitimacy of an international court can be strengthened, supposedly by allowing for the elimination of political considerations in the appointment process and thus strengthening the perception of procedural legitimacy by the broader public. However, closer examination of their own working procedures and membership raises a separate set of legitimacy concerns, which may not be readily visible.

In addressing the range of appointing procedures that exist across a range of areas of international legal practice, the authors of this section ask whether the power given to appointing authorities is within the scope of their original mandate – something which is at the core of orthodox conceptualisations of sociological legitimacy. This section also seeks to highlight the host of concerns which appointing authorities need to grapple with, such as conflicts of interest (for example when an appointing authority appoints itself as an arbitrator in a dispute) or what happens when an appointing authority declines to exercise its power to appoint an adjudicator or arbitrator.

This section also seeks to delineate how secretariats have evolved over time and across various institutions to carry out this appointing function, examining whether common trends – and shared best practices – can be discerned. It furthermore asks whether secretariats are equipped with the appropriate tools to provide a sense of legitimacy to their functioning, such as mechanisms of accountability or financial independence from Member States. Overall, what is at stake for secretariats in their position as 'gatekeepers' of international adjudication? On whose behalf are they exercising this gatekeeping function? Are adjudicators nominated or appointed in light of the opinion they might eventually espouse? Moreover, what are the broader implications of these developments for the legitimacy of international adjudication as a whole?

1.2.3   Case Management and Deference to the Bench

Part III of the book is, chronologically, the next step within the process of adjudication: once a court or tribunal has been constituted, and the proceedings have been initiated, how can the work of unseen actors affect the legitimacy of the proceedings? This part questions what might be considered the 'proper' role of judges: to what extent is it possible to delegate parts of the decision-rendering process to other actors? Where does a judge's duty end, and where does that of a case manager or member of a secretariat begin? When can the input of registry and secretariat staff into the drafting of decisions be considered as legitimate, and what (if any) is its legal basis? More importantly, to what extent is transparency concerning the participation of these actors a necessary criterion for the legitimacy of individual decisions and judicial institutions as a whole? These questions have implications for a range of different understandings of legitimacy, such as legal legitimacy, procedural legitimacy, and output legitimacy.

The topics addressed in this part touch upon a variety of actors and roles within the process of adjudication. This can include issues relating to case management; how do unseen actors at international courts and tribunals work with disputing parties to manage pending cases, for example through agreeing on a written submission calendar, or to seek a solution for cases that have been 'on the docket' for a considerable amount of time? How do the various allocation systems for individual cases operate? How may practices on case preparation and deference to State policy affect the legitimacy of a judicial institution?

Part III also addresses processes such as fact-finding procedures, particularly in relation to the procuring of expert evidence upon which the court or tribunal can base its judgment, focusing on how these actors can enhance the legal and procedural legitimacy of a judicial institution amongst its intended publics. Fact-finding bodies have become increasingly necessary in the context of modern international adjudication in light of the complex issues which are regulated within modern international law. Yet within most judicial institutions, little provision has been made for the scope within which these bodies should function and the manner in which they can be consulted by judges. Fact-finders are often used in an attempt to improve the perceived quality of a judicial decision, yet their use can also mean increased costs for the parties, lengthier trials, and a lack of transparency as to the factual and legal basis upon which a decision has been rendered.

Similar questions are raised with regard to interpreting and translation services, particularly in the context of the ICC, which is faced with witnesses, victims, and suspects from a wide range of linguistic backgrounds. Translation thus sits at the heart of the international judicial function for certain courts, particularly if the goal of the institution in question is to achieve broader processes of justice and peace within victimised communities. The position of an interpreter is crucial to questions of output legitimacy, as interpreters need to tread carefully when translating a text to ensure that the original meaning is conveyed in the translation – even if this original meaning is, in fact, vague. Simultaneously, there is also significant room in which increased emphasis on the importance of (linguistic) diversity can be a boon to the output legitimacy of certain international courts facing periods of crisis.

Another category of unseen actor is the scientific (technical) expert consulted in the course of a trial; the opinions which these experts produce are intended to enhance the procedural and output legitimacy of a judgment by inserting a degree of scientific 'neutrality' into the decision-making process. However, upon closer inspection the functioning of these experts raises its own questions of legitimacy, in particular from the perspective of legal and procedural legitimacy. Is it legitimate for decisions to be guided by the opinions of these experts? To what extent is it possible to mediate between the indeterminacy of legal texts through the intervention of scientific expertise? These debates show that unseen actors sit, in many ways, at the core of the legitimacy of an international court or tribunal.

In addition, expanded functions of certain managerial bodies within international judicial institutions might fundamentally change the nature of the decision-making process, contrary to the original intent of the States involved in the creation of the decision-making body in question, thus running counter to orthodox consent-based understandings of legitimacy. These developments might provide new roles to these unseen actors which can limit, rather than assist, the functions of the arbitrators or judges involved in a judicial decision. The growth of these managerial considerations can have an important impact on the sociological legitimacy of the judgment of a court or tribunal. These considerations demonstrate the importance of finding an appropriate balance between the administrative and adjudicative functions of judicial institutions.

1.2.4   Confidentiality and Transparency

Part IV looks into the legitimacy of unseen actors from the perspective of the tension between the need to protect confidentiality versus the need to provide information to agents and the broader public about ongoing and concluded proceedings. Such issues are linked to the procedural legitimacy of an international adjudicatory body. Confidentiality concerns affect a wide range of actors acting at the periphery and centre of court proceedings, such as 'ghost experts', whose contribution to a judgment is never officially acknowledged; physicians, who must strike a balance between the confidential character of their patient's medical file and the need to disclose information to a criminal court; or legal experts who are prohibited from disclosing the full extent of their contribution to the text of a judgment. The balance between the dual factors of confidentiality and transparency is a further constitutive element of the perception of legitimacy of a given judicial institution.

The chapters in this Part focus, amongst other things, on the socio-political factors which have made the 'invisibility' of certain unseen actors possible and desirable within the history of international judicial institutions. Officials are often required to maintain strict confidentiality with regard to their actual contributions to the judgments produced by the court or tribunal for which they work, often in the name of maintaining the legitimacy of a given court in the eyes of States and the broader public. In this sense, international legal practice diverges from domestic practice, where the contributions of these actors are routinely acknowledged and examined by practitioners and scholars. One technique to examine the wider range of actors implicated within the creation of international judicial decisions is the application of computer technology to the texts of the decisions of courts and tribunals, such as through the use of forensic linguistics or network analysis. As written decisions are one of the core ways in which an international judicial institution seeks to construct a sense of legitimacy with regard to its function, analyses of these written texts can shed light on broader debates surrounding the issue of legitimacy, making it possible to test unproven assumptions. To this end, transparency can thus be achieved without the direct intervention of the judicial institution in question.

Moving beyond the question of outward transparency, this section also questions whether the work of unseen actors can be legitimate if even the parties to a dispute are unaware of the (full) extent of their contribution to the eventual decision of an arbitrator or judge. Can the presence of 'ghost experts' in international dispute settlement be justified from the perspective of the law, for example by recourse to the statutes or rules of procedure of the respective adjudicative bodies? Moreover, how does the use of these unseen experts affect the perception of the adjudicative body's legitimacy by the parties who have submitted their dispute to it? This Part also explores how institutions themselves can provide a powerful counter-narrative to the perceived ills of international dispute settlement – particularly in the context of investment arbitration – with regard to a perceived lack of diversity, expediency and transparency.

1.2.5   Ethics and Accountability

Closely intertwined with issues of confidentiality and transparency are questions concerning ethics and accountability within international courts and tribunals. Whilst there are codes of conduct regulating the actions of judges and other adjudicators, these rules do not apply to unseen actors. Is it necessary to ensure accountability of unseen actors towards the disputing parties, as well as towards the international legal community? One standard by which to assess a court or tribunal's legitimacy is to examine avenues for securing its accountability. In this vein, several contributions propose methods through which to reduce perceived legitimacy problems. Some suggest *ex-post facto* measures, while others advocate systematic training, and still others argue that the best approach might be to implement structural measures that regulate the discretionary space.[60]

First, Part V examines a setting within which an appropriate, yet still disputed, balance between ethical obligations and accountability has been found: in the context of the ICC, physicians have played an important role in assessing the fitness of certain defendants to stand trial. Tasked with ensuring that defendants are not only physically, but also mentally 'present' in the courtroom, the contribution of physicians to the overall goals of institutions such as the ICC – the administration of justice by virtue of an international (and fair) trial – is thus vital. Arguably, the functioning of these actors, located at the periphery of trial proceedings, ought to be regulated within the statute or rules of procedure of a judicial institution in order to prevent conflicts of interest and ensure the legitimacy of the outcome of a trial.

Other chapters in Part V identify a number of practice areas where reform might be needed. One such area relates to the position of arbitral institutions and their ability to screen requests initiating investment arbitrations. In the exercise of these powers, due caution must be exercised that these institutional actors do not disturb the appropriate balance between executing a purely procedural analysis and engaging in substantive analysis of the merits of the claim brought. The exercise of these powers thus requires its own considerations of diligence in order to safeguard the transparency and legitimacy of the overall adjudicative process.

In drawing up reform proposals, it is possible to look at the growing body of international jurisprudence in which the attention of courts and tribunals has been explicitly drawn to the legality of the involvement of legal officers in the decision-making process. The judgments that have been rendered in these contexts have laid out the nature of these legal officers' contributions to the work of a court or tribunal and determined where the boundary lies between work which must be carried out by

---

[60] David Kosař, *Perils of Judicial Self-Government in Transitional Societies* (Cambridge: Cambridge University Press, 2016), pp. 34–36, 59–65.

a judge and that which can be delegated to other actors. The case law
has thus, in some judicial contexts, already engaged with the balancing
act between pragmatism and concerns relating to judicial integrity and
legitimacy.

Other proposals for reform include remodelling and applying judicial
management strategies to the transnational context. Practices developed
at the domestic level are often overlooked in proposals for reform. They
can nonetheless be particularly relevant in certain contexts, for example
in situations where a domestic court is required to pronounce upon the
legality of a secretary's involvement in arbitral proceedings. International
courts and tribunals can also learn from each other. Thus, the CJEU
employs *référendaires*, who play a vital role in its functioning. This raises
the question whether the role of these types of unseen actor should or can
be more or less hidden depending on whether they are acting in the context of a more permanent (CJEU) or a more ad hoc (international arbitration) system.

However, when formulating these proposals, a delicate balance needs
to be struck between independence and accountability. International
courts and tribunals must possess independence and discretion in order
to settle disputes effectively.[61] At the same time, they must be prevented
from forming a 'juristocracy', whereby autocratic judges make decisions
based on arbitrary considerations rather than the rule of law.[62] It is worth-
while analysing, therefore, whether accountability mechanisms seeking
to prevent unseen actors from 'illegitimately' influencing the adjudication process strike the right balance. Indeed, the mere fact that unseen
actors influence the adjudication process does not necessarily diminish
the usefulness of dispute settlement bodies, or the fairness or quality of
their decisions. If measures combating a perceived lack of legitimacy
are imposed on an international court or tribunal, this may impinge on
judicial independence and institutional efficiency, possibly leading to
outcomes that genuinely damage the adjudicatory process and outcomes.
For example, regulatory measures might lead to undue delays or excessive
formalism.

---

[61] Eric A. Posner and John C. Yoo, 'Judicial Independence in International Tribunals' (2005)
93 *California Law Review* 3; Laurence R. Helfer and Anne-Marie Slaughter, 'Why States
Create International Tribunals: A Response to Professors Posner and Yoo' (2005) 93
California Law Review 899.

[62] Ran Hirschl, *Towards Juristocracy: The Origins and Consequences of the New Constitutionalism* (Cambridge, MA: Harvard University Press, 2004).

1.2.6   External Influences and Activities

The previous Parts all looked at unseen actors that are 'insiders', because they work for an international adjudicatory institution on a permanent or semi-permanent basis. However, not only internal unseen actors have a stake in the legitimacy of international courts and tribunals; external actors can also play a role in the (de)construction of this legitimacy. The contributions to Part VI of the book seek to widen the scope of analysis so as to include external unseen actors, highlighting the challenges faced by courts and tribunals in securing and enacting outcome legitimacy on the international stage. This Part thus, for example, tackles how online reporters and databases such as Italaw and IAReporter can play a role in the praxis of investor-State dispute settlement. Online reporters can fulfil the function of invisible clerks; gatekeepers providing symbolic capital to the arbitral practice; as a liaison between the system of investor-State dispute settlement and society at large; and as tools which actively change the way in which investment disputes are litigated and decided. It is thus important to scrutinise their functioning in order to gain a holistic view of the practice of international dispute settlement and the actors that are involved in this practice.

This Part also draws attention to the fact that international adjudicators often take on a number of different roles within and outside international adjudicatory bodies. Thus, a permanent judge at an international tribunal might be appointed to an ad hoc arbitral tribunal and might at the same time continue to carry out research and teaching activities at one (or more) universities across the globe. These 'unseen activities' can impinge upon the legitimacy of a judicial institution to much the same extent that unseen actors can. This section thus critically examines whether limits should be placed on the outside activities that adjudicators can undertake. How can adjudicators maintain their independence, avoid conflicts of interest, and simply ensure that they have sufficient time to devote to their judicial tasks? Should international guidelines be established in this regard? Another category of unseen actors working *outside* the scope of international courts and tribunals includes the lawyers who act on behalf of States. The relationship between the State, its agents and its counsel raises a host of procedural legitimacy concerns, to which this Part seeks to draw further attention. To what extent does the proximity between the State and its lawyers influence the legitimacy of the court in question? Is there transparency in the rules governing counsel accountability, and can comparisons be made across different courts and tribunals?

Finally, it is important to consider who is shaping the legal context in which courts and tribunals operate. Thus, in the context of free trade agreements that allow for investor-State adjudication, the trade committees negotiating these agreements are an important unseen actor within the international adjudicatory process. These committees shape the decisions which are eventually made on the structure, process and substance of possible adjudication under free trade agreements. The interventions and actions of trade committees in this regard are often made in the interest of increasing the legitimacy of investor-State dispute settlement, yet might in actuality represent inadequate mechanisms for improving the overall legitimacy of the system.

1.3   Contribution to the Existing Scholarship and Building Blocks for Future Research

What the foregoing aims to illustrate is the extent to which the perceived legitimacy of international courts and tribunals is impacted by the institutional make-up of international courts and tribunals and the input of unseen actors, such as registries, secretariats and legal officers. These actors are often employed in order to counter concerns about the legitimacy of international courts and tribunals, yet, as the contributions outlined above indicate, they may also raise a new set of legitimacy concerns. The unseen character of these actors' work should not detract from its significance: when a court's administration runs smoothly and effectively, it inspires trust and confidence from its users and has a real impact on the legitimacy endowed on the institution on the world stage. The legitimacy of international courts and tribunals has previously been analysed from a variety of angles,[63] including democratic principles,[64] the proper role of such institutions,[65] the promotion of global peace and security,[66]

---

[63] See also Section 1.1 of this chapter.

[64] A. von Bogdandy and I. Venzke, 'In Whose Name? An Investigation of International Courts' Public Authority and Its Democratic Justification' (2012) 23(1) *EJIL* 7; Mortimer N.S. Sellers, 'Democracy, Justice, and the Legitimacy of International Courts', in Nienke Grossman, Harlan Grant Cohen, Andreas Føllesdal and Geir Ulfstein (eds.), *Legitimacy and International Courts* (Cambridge: Cambridge University Press, 2018).

[65] I. Venzke, 'The Role of International Courts as Interpreters and Developers of the Law: Working out the Jurisgenerative Practice of Interpretation' (2011) 34(1) *Loyola of Los Angeles International and Comparative Law Review* 99; Laurence R. Helfer and Karen J. Alter, 'Legitimacy and Lawmaking: A Tale of Three International Courts' (2013) 14 *Theoretical Inquiries in Law* 479.

[66] A. Spain, 'Examining the International Judicial Function: International Courts as Dispute Resolvers' (2011) 34(1) *Loyola of Los Angeles International and Comparative Law Review* 5.

prosecutorial discretion,[67] the legitimacy of judicial decisions[68] and effectiveness[69] to name a few. In addition, in recent years, a number of projects have come to fruition which have cast a broader lens across the legitimacy of, amongst others, international trade courts and tribunals, international criminal tribunals and human rights bodies.[70] Scholars have also devoted attention to broader issues, such as the performance of international courts and tribunals and the exercise of authority by these bodies.[71] These projects have laid the foundations for a robust analysis of legitimacy in relation to international adjudication, including unseen activities within the practice of international courts of tribunals.[72] However, there have generally been few attempts to discern common approaches across international courts and tribunals.[73] Similarly to the present volume, these approaches seek to open the 'black box' of international institutions

---

[67] Danner, 'Enhancing the Legitimacy and Accountability'.

[68] Treves, 'Aspects of Legitimacy'.

[69] J. Donoghue, 'The Effectiveness of the International Court of Justice' (2014) 108 *Proceedings of the Annual Meeting of the American Society of International Law* 114; Voeten, 'Public Opinion and the Legitimacy of International Courts', 411.

[70] Andreas Føllesdal, Birgit Peters, Johan Karlsson Schaffer and Geir Ulfstein (eds.), *The Legitimacy of International Human Rights Regimes: Legal, Political and Philosophical Perspectives* (Cambridge: Cambridge University Press, 2014); Nobuo Hayashi and Cecilia M. Bailliet (eds.), *The Legitimacy of International Criminal Tribunals* (Cambridge: Cambridge University Press, 2017); Robert Howse, Hélène Ruiz-Fabri, Geir Ulfstein and Michelle Q. Ziang (eds.), *The Legitimacy of International Trade Courts and Tribunals* (Cambridge: Cambridge University Press, 2018); Nienke Grossman, Harlan Grant Cohen, Andreas Føllesdal and Geir Ulfstein (eds.), *Legitimacy and International Courts* (Cambridge: Cambridge University Press, 2018).

[71] Yuval Shany, *Assessing the Effectiveness of International Courts* (Oxford: Oxford University Press, 2014); Theresa Squatrito, Oran R. Young, Andreas Føllesdal and Geir Ulfstein (eds.), *The Performance of International Courts and Tribunals* (Cambridge: Cambridge University Press, 2018); Karen J. Alter, Laurence R. Helfer and Mikael Rask Madsen (eds.), *International Court Authority* (Oxford: Oxford University Press, 2018).

[72] Jens Meierhenrich, 'The Practice of International Law: A Theoretical Analysis' (2013) 76 *Law & Contemporary Problems* 1; see also the contributions in Cesare P.R. Romano, Karen Alter and Yuval Shany (eds.), *The Oxford Handbook of International Adjudication* (Oxford: Oxford University Press, 2014); Mikkel Jarle Christensen, 'The Emerging Sociology of International Criminal Courts: Between Global Restructurings and Scientific Innovations' (2015) 63 *Current Sociology* 825; Windsor, 'Consigliere or Conscience?'; Gregory Messenger, 'The Practice of Litigation at the ICJ: The Role of Counsel in the Development of International Law', in Moshe Hirsch and Andrew Lang (eds.), *Research Handbook on the Sociology of International Law* (Northampton, MA: Edward Elgar, 2018). A further example is the currently ongoing research project on 'Investigating International Law Backstage' at the Vrije Universiteit Amsterdam; see www.ceptl.org/index.php/research-publications/research-projects.

[73] Cohen et al., 'Legitimacy and International Courts'.

by departing from a purely State-centric analysis of international legal practice and analysing it from the level of the individual from a range of disciplinary perspectives, in particular that of sociology.[74] However, this literature has generally not engaged in an analysis of the link between the findings regarding the practice of these individuals or institutions and normative or sociological legitimacy. Nor have works focusing on the practice of international law tended to examine unseen actors, instead electing to focus on 'major' players on the international legal stage, such as judges.

The present volume seeks to fill this gap by focusing on one important cross-sectoral element with an impact upon the legitimacy of most international courts and tribunals: unseen actors. The main objective is to explore, across the different judicial regimes, the roles and functioning of such unseen actors, so as to identify common connections and patterns in the institutional make-up and daily practice of international courts and tribunals. The book aims to encourage reflection among scholars and practitioners concerning unseen actors in international adjudication and contribute to a cross-institutional dialogue. As such, it seeks to contribute to existing debates not only in relation to the legitimacy of international law, but also more generally in relation to the 'practice' of international law, broadly understood.

A better understanding of the impact that unseen actors have on the judicial process may improve the internal functioning of international courts and tribunals but also inspire a consistent approach to legitimacy challenges emanating from the institutional make-up of international courts and tribunals across these institutions as a whole. The biggest gains are therefore to be had where the book facilitates sharing of best practices between institutions. Beyond this, international law practitioners may more effectively perform their role in the adjudicatory process of international courts and tribunals with a better understanding of the inner workings and not-so-visible challenges faced by these institutions.

The book could be used by scholars to continue the project of assessing other unseen actors within international adjudication, complementing future research and allowing the construction of a robust theorisation of the role of unseen actors within international law as a whole. For example, analyses on the functioning of unseen actors can assist scholars working on issues relating to the functioning of judges, or the broader functioning

---

[74] Messenger, 'The Practice of Litigation at the ICJ'.

of the judicial institutions. The book could furthermore form part of the continuing research agenda on the legitimacy of international institutions more generally, as well as the interplay between these institutions and domestic judicial institutions, raising the question whether different approaches need to be taken at the domestic and international levels, or whether there is room for fruitful dialogue and exchanges of best practices.

In addition, the approaches developed in the book can form a helpful theoretical lens, through which researchers working on 'orthodox' legal research questions relating to international courts and tribunals can view their topic of research, thus uncovering how certain issues in the practice of international courts and tribunals are not the result of the law, but of the wider political, economic and social context of the adjudicatory institutions under study. In turn, this sets the stage for future inter- and multidisciplinary debates on these issues, involving disciplines such as political theory, international relations and network theory. It can, moreover, feed into broader discussions on the commonality of international courts and tribunals, as well as philosophical debates on the indeterminacy of international law.

PART I

Institutional Perspectives

The International Court of Justice

NATHALIE WILES[1]

2.1 Introduction

The Registry of the International Court of Justice (ICJ) has grown and adapted to the needs of the Court over the years, but its fundamental purpose has remained the same: to provide unobtrusive support to the principal judicial organ of the United Nations.

When I joined the Registry as an associate legal officer in 2000, it was my first experience of being part of a secretariat, as I had previously worked as a lawyer in the private sector. A small part of me wondered whether the relationship between the Registry officials and the Judges would be anything akin to that between British civil servant Sir Humphrey Appleby and Minister Jim Hacker in the wonderful 1980s BBC political satire *Yes Minister* by Antony Jay and Jonathan Lynn. To those readers who may not be familiar with this series, the Machiavellian Sir Humphrey spends most of his time trying to outmanoeuvre his Minister, while claiming to stay in the shadows. Thus, Sir Humphrey explains his functions to the Minister in his inimitably obsequious manner as follows:

> Minister, the traditional allocation of executive responsibilities has always been so determined as to liberate the ministerial incumbent from the administrative minutiae by devolving the managerial functions to those whose experience and qualifications have better formed them for the performance of such humble offices, thereby releasing their political overlords for the more onerous duties and profound deliberations which are the inevitable concomitant of their exalted position.

While it is true that the purpose of our work as Registry officials is indeed to ensure that the elected Members of the Court can work in the best

---

[1] The views expressed in this chapter are personal to the author and do not necessarily reflect those of the United Nations, the International Court of Justice, or of any other particular organization.

conditions, I am happy to report that there are no Sir Humphreyesque ulterior motives! The work of the Judges and Judges *ad hoc* is at the heart of the Court's unique mandate under the United Nations Charter to bring about the peaceful settlement of disputes between States, in accordance with international law, and to give advisory opinions on legal questions referred to it by authorized United Nations organs and specialized agencies. Since the Court's inception in 1946, its Registry has provided dedicated assistance to the Judges, with a particular focus on judicial, diplomatic, administrative, financial and linguistic tasks. The Statute of the ICJ is based upon that of its predecessor, the Permanent Court of International Justice (PCIJ). The PCIJ Statute was widely considered to work well and it therefore made sense to follow it. In addition, it was deemed important to retain a sense of continuity between the PCIJ and the ICJ.

The role of the Registry is defined by reference to the functions of the Registrar. Indeed, the Statute of the Court only makes specific mention of the Registrar. This factor is key in addressing the question of the controls in place within the Court's Registry to ensure the legitimacy of the process of international dispute settlement at the Court. Put simply, the Registry derives its authority by virtue of the fact that it plays a pivotal role in carrying out, under the supervision of the Registrar, the many statutory functions which are necessary to ensure that the Court's judicial processes are underpinned by a well-structured and carefully considered set of administrative rules, which take into account practical and ethical considerations – such as possible conflicts of interest. At the risk of forcing a nautical analogy, if the Court is the ship that plots its course through legal waters, charted and uncharted, the Registry is the mainstay providing the necessary stability to ensure that the vessel reaches each port of call safe and sound.[2]

The Registry of the ICJ is headed by a Registrar (currently Mr. Philippe Couvreur),[3] who is aided by a Deputy-Registrar (currently Mr. Jean-Pelé Fomété). Traditionally, in supervising the work of the Registry as a whole, the Registrar has given priority to diplomatic and judicial matters and the Deputy-Registrar to administrative matters. Within the organization, these two senior United Nations officials are the most visible. The current Registrar was previously the Head of the Legal Department, reflecting the important role that lawyers hold within the institution. Indeed, the Court

---

[2] See, in this connection, the insightful analysis of Stéphanie Carter and Cristina Hoss in their chapter on "The Role of Registries and Legal Secretariats" in *The Oxford Handbook of International Adjudication*, 1 December 2013, edited by Cesare P.R. Romano, Karen Alter and Yuval Shany.

[3] Earlier this year, Mr. Couvreur notified the Court of his decision to step down from his functions with effect from 1 July 2019. A procedure is currently underway for the election of a new Registrar.

has always been ably assisted by lawyers of great distinction. Former Heads of the Legal Department have included the eminent international scholar and contributor to this book, Mr. Hugh Thirlway. The Court has benefited from Registrars of great academic standing since its creation, namely, Mr. Edvard Hambro, Mr. Julio López-Oliván, Mr. Jean Garnier-Coignet and Mr. Stanislas Aquarone. In more recent times, former Registrars have included renowned international lawyers Mr. Santiago Torres Bernárdez (1980–1986) – who subsequently served as Judge *ad hoc* at the Court – and Mr. Eduardo Valencia-Ospina (1987–2000) – who subsequently acted as counsel before the Court.[4] The Registry officials who perhaps fit more within the category of "unseen actors" are the lawyers who make up the Legal Department, and the officials from other departments and divisions, who all play a key role in the smooth functioning of the Court.

2.2   Organization of the Registry

So, how is the Registry of the Court organized? For a number of years after its creation, the Registry was made up a small number of "multifunctional" secretaries, much as had been the case with the Registry of the PCIJ. These ICJ Registry officials were expected to carry out a range of multidisciplinary tasks, from undertaking legal research to understanding issues of diplomatic protocol to providing translations into the two official languages of the Court, English and French. Over the years, however, the various departments and technical divisions of the Registry have become increasingly specialized, with the creation of a department-based structure in 1997. The Registry is now made up of three departments, namely the Department of Legal Matters, the Department of Linguistic Matters and the Information Department, and eight technical divisions, namely the Archives, Indexing and Distribution Division, the Finance Division, the Publications Division, the Security and General Assistance Division, the Library of the Court/ Documents Division, the Text Processing and Reproduction Division, the Information and Communications Technology Division and the Administrative and Personnel Division. In addition, there are the Registrar's office and the Deputy-Registrar's office, the Secretaries to the Judges, and a Senior Medical Officer (part-time).[5]

The tasks undertaken by Registry officials are broadly set out in the Instructions for the Registry, as drawn up and approved by the Court on 20

---

[4] Regrettably, to date, no woman has ever held the office of Registrar, neither has the Head of the Departments of Legal or Linguistic Matters ever been a woman. In this respect, the Registry and the Court as a whole still have a way to go in terms of "gender legitimacy".

[5] The Court's website contains an Organizational Chart of the Registry giving a more detailed overview.

March 2012. These instructions replaced those drawn up in October 1946
and amended in March 1947 and September 1949. Registry officials are also
subject to regularly amended Staff Regulations, which are largely similar to
the Staff Regulations of the United Nations and United Nations Staff Rules.

2.3   In What Way Is the Registry Unique?

The role played by Registry officials is unique in large part as a result of
the *sui generis* nature of the Court. The current Court is fully integrated
into the United Nations, but it is a judicial body whose independence must
be preserved. Its organization and functioning are governed by its Statute,
which is an integral part of the Charter. The Court is the only principal
United Nations organ that has a separate Registry that is not part of the
Secretariat[6] and it is the only main organ that is not located in New York –
instead, The Hague is specified as the seat of the Court.[7] Moreover, the
Court submits its own budgetary requests for each biennium to the
General Assembly, through the Secretary-General. As clearly explained by
Mr. Philippe Couvreur in an illuminating and comprehensive article on
the role of the Registrar of the International Court of Justice, the autonomy
of the Court in terms of establishing its own internal organization is a key
element in maintaining the legitimacy of the Court's judicial function:

> The administrative tasks to be performed by the Court as such are both a
> corollary and a guarantee of its independence. Those tasks are therefore of
> great importance. It is for the Court to ensure, however, that the fulfilment
> of those tasks is organized in such a way that they do not impinge on its
> Members' judicial work. With its ultimate responsibility for major admin-
> istrative and budgetary decisions, the Court cannot concern itself with
> minor issues. In this respect, everything hinges on internal organiza-
> tion: the role of the President and of the Registrar is thus essential.[8]

By extension, as noted above, Registry officials play an important role in
this process in terms of the assistance they give the Registrar in the performance of his many duties.

This judicial and administrative autonomy also requires a special
regime of privileges and immunities applicable to Judges and Registry
officials, which can be found in the 1946 Exchange of Letters between

---

[6] Article 98 of the UN Charter.
[7] Article 22 of the Statute of the Court.
[8] Philippe Couvreur, 'The Registrar of the International Court of Justice: Status and
Functions', in Carlos Jiménez Piernas (ed.), *The European Practice in International Law and
European Community Law: A Spanish Perspective* (Boston, MA/Leiden: Martinus Nijhoff
Publishers, 2005), p. 20.

the President of the Court and the Minister for Foreign Affairs of the Netherlands and in General Assembly Resolution 90 (I) of 11 December 1946, entitled "Privileges and Immunities of Members of the International Court of Justice, the Registry, Assessors, and Agents and Counsel of the Parties and of Witnesses and Experts". In particular, in his letter of 26 June 1946 addressed to the Minister for Foreign Affairs of the Netherlands, President Guerrero noted that "the Court is an organism whose members, with their small staff, perform duties of a special character and whose requirements are consequently different from those of the other organs of the United Nations"[9]. In recognition of this fact, the "General Principles" appended to the 1946 Exchange of Letters between the President of the Court and the Minister for Foreign Affairs of the Netherlands stated that Members of the Court and the Registrar of nationality other than Dutch were generally assimilated, for the purposes of privileges and immunities, to "heads of diplomatic missions Accredited to H.M. the Queen of the Netherlands", while the "higher officials" (Deputy-Registrar and Secretaries of the Court) were assimilated to counsellors and secretaries "attached to diplomatic missions at The Hague".

2.4   The Role of the Different Departments and Divisions of the Registry

A brief overview of the work carried out by each department and division (with a special emphasis on the Legal Department) provides a snapshot of the contribution made by the various different "unseen actors" of the Registry to the overall functioning of the Court.

2.4.1   The Department of Legal Matters

The Legal Department consists of a core group of lawyers providing legal assistance to the Court and to the Registrar, as well as of a contingent of law clerks who are assigned to individual Judges. In order to understand more clearly the duties of the Department of Legal Matters and our role within the Registry, it is essential to know what the statutory functions of the Registrar of the Court are, as set out in Article 26 of the Rules of Court. This is because, in fulfilling these multiple functions, the Registrar relies on the lawyers of the Legal Department (and other

---

[9] *Acts and Documents Concerning the Organization of the Court No. 6*, p. 207, reproducing the letter of 26 June 1946 from the President of the Court and the Minister for Foreign Affairs of the Netherlands.

Registry officials). Under Article 26, paragraph 1 of the Rules of Court, the Registrar's functions are listed as follows:

> (a) Communications between the Court and the outside world; (b) Keeping the General List of cases; (c) Custody and communication of declarations made pursuant to Security Council resolution 9 (1946); (d) Transmission to the parties of copies of pleadings; (e) Functions pertaining to privileges, immunities or facilities granted in connection with the work of the Court; (f) Preparation of minutes of meetings of the Court; (g) Interpretation and translation into the Court's two official languages; (h) Signature of all judgments, advisory opinions and orders of the Court, and minutes of the Court's meetings; (i) Publications of the Court; (j) Administrative and budgetary responsibilities; (k) Dealing with enquiries concerning the Court; (l) Assisting in maintaining relations between the Court and other organs and specialized agencies of the United Nations, and international bodies and conferences concerned with the codification and progressive development of international law; (m) Responsibilities in terms of making information about the Court's work accessible; and (n) Custody of the Court's seals, stamps and archives.

The Legal Department assists the Registrar in the fulfilment of his statutory functions, in particular in the following ways. It provides timely and accurate legal research, drafting and support to the Court in current judicial cases. In this regard, teams are furnished (generally composed of at least one Francophone legal officer, one Anglophone legal officer, and a team leader) to attend and assist in the work of the Court's Drafting Committees. The Court's Drafting Committees are made up of the President and usually two other Judges elected by the plenary at the close of the Court's first full deliberation in a case, on the basis that their views reflect the majority's position on the main aspects of the case. The Drafting Committee Judges, with the assistance (as necessary) of their law clerks and the assigned Legal Department team, then prepare the draft Judgment for consideration by the plenary Court. The legal issues raised by the cases before the Court are extremely wide-ranging, including, inter alia, territorial sovereignty, national and maritime boundaries, rights to natural resources, environmental rights and international human rights – such as the right to consular assistance for detained foreign nationals, the right to judicial redress for acts of racial discrimination and acts of genocide. This means that, as Registry lawyers, we have to be versatile in the legal support we bring to the Judges. We may be asked to research a strictly legal question, for example, the determination of compensation in international law; or a question relating to evidence, such as the differences in the common law and civil law approaches to the standard of proof or the rules and practice of the Court in terms of witness and expert evidence. The research we carry out is also often on procedural issues, for example, the rules and practical considerations of requests for revision and interpretation of a judgment. On occasion, our research may be on a question of ethics, for example, on conflict rules in a situation where a member of the counsel of one party has previously acted for the other party. Our research may turn on the historical or factual background of a given set of proceedings – which will always be case specific in the sense that all disputes brought for resolution by the Court, even those based on similar considerations of law and/or fact, are unique.

The Registry lawyers also prepare case-related documents in accordance with the Court's programme of work, including the procedural history of the case (also known in archaic Court "franglais" speak as the *qualités*); the summary of arguments of the parties; under the supervision of the President, the list of legal issues raised by a case and draft Orders when no Drafting Committee is elected. In addition, we undertake legal research and give drafting assistance to the Court's Rules Committee, which provides recommendations to the Court on issues of procedure.

On a day-to-day basis, the Department is responsible for preparing, for signature by the Registrar, the official judicial correspondence of the Court. In particular, Registry lawyers prepare correspondence with the Agents of parties in pending contentious cases, correspondence with representatives of States participating in pending advisory proceedings and notifications and transmissions contemplated in the Statute. Such correspondence may relate, inter alia, to the receipt of an Application instituting proceedings, the submission of a Request for the indication of provisional measures, the filing of a Memorial, Counter-Memorial, Reply or Rejoinder, the appointment of a Judge *ad hoc*, or the case-related notifications under Articles 34 and 63 of the Statute (notification to a public international organization that the construction of its constituent instrument or of an international convention adopted thereunder is in question in a case before the Court).

The Legal Department is also responsible for keeping the General List of cases, which contains the procedural history of cases before the Court – detailing, for example, the case number, title, date of filing, whether contentious or advisory, parties, any incidental proceedings, time-limits of filing of pleadings, date of hearings and final outcome. The titles of cases are chosen by the Court on the proposal of the Legal Department, with a view to ensuring as neutral as possible a description of the dispute. The General List looks like an outsized Dickensian ledger on thick cream paper, where entries until not so very long ago were handwritten. It is these small historical throwbacks to a former time that add such character to the Court.

Finally, with reference to Article 26 of the Rules of Court, the Registry lawyers prepare the minutes of the judicial and administrative meetings of the Court. When discussions relate to administrative or procedural matters, a detailed *procès-verbal* (PV) is prepared. The reason being that it is important to have a written record of the administrative decisions taken by the Court; it is also very helpful to have a record of the Court's discussions on procedural questions, as this can assist in ensuring a cogent and cohesive approach to similar procedural issues that might arise in the future. For example, the Legal Department may be asked to check the PV record for the Court's discussions on the question of the recusal of a Judge from a case, or on the question of the right of a Judge, who has been absent for part of the deliberations in a case, to record by telephone his or her vote on the operative part of a decision of the Court. When discussions relate to strictly judicial matters, the PV does not record any detail of the positions expounded by the Judges. The main reason for this is that Members of the Court and Judges *ad hoc* should feel completely free to express their opinions, which might indeed evolve in the process of the Court's deliberations in a case. Moreover, the final position of the Court will be set out in the Judgment or substantive Order in question and Judges are free to append opinions and declarations thereto should they so wish.

One of the enjoyable aspects of our work as Registry lawyers is the close collaboration we enjoy with colleagues from other departments – in this respect, we regularly liaise with the Department of Information on case-related press communications, with the Publications Division on various legal issues that arise in the course of its preparation of the Court's publications, and with the Linguistic Department in conducting parallel readings and review of case-related translations.

2.4.2   *The Department of Linguistic Matters*

Article 39 of the Statute provides that the official languages of the Court are English and French, which reflects the linguistic set-up of the Court's predecessor, the PCIJ. Unlike other international Secretariats where English has become the predominant language, the Court has placed much emphasis on maintaining a balance between the two languages, both of which, in a very real sense, are the working languages of the ICJ and its Registry. The Registry must accommodate Judges who prefer to work in French in the exact same way as Judges who prefer to work in English. This bilingualism is at the core of the Court's judicial drafting process with Judgments, substantive Orders and Advisory Opinions being prepared in both languages at each and every stage of the process, rather than the Court merely relying on a translation of a final text prepared in one language. Thus, although every judicial decision specifies whether English or French is the "authoritative language", in fact, all of the deliberations, readings and redrafts of the text are meticulously carried out in both languages. This bilingualism also improves the quality of the legal drafting, as the meaning and structure of each paragraph of a decision must pass muster in both languages. That said, parties to cases before the Court increasingly tend to communicate and file pleadings more in English than in French, and this means that the Court employs noticeably more French-speaking translators than English-speaking ones.

Simultaneous interpretation is provided at all of the Court's private meetings, as well as during public hearings. Currently, two Registry linguists are trained interpreters and regularly assist at meetings and hearings. The majority of the highly skilled Registry linguists prepare translations of all official Court documents and many internal documents. They also assist in the preparation of the Court's bilingual decisions. In my experience, the process of preparing a bilingual legal text certainly leads to improvements in the quality of the drafting. The contribution of the Department of Linguistic Matters to the work of the Court is therefore very precious.

2.4.3   The Information Department

The Information Department also plays a key role in the work of the Court. It is responsible for ensuring that the work of the Court is properly publicized, while taking care to protect the confidentiality of the Court's judicial processes prior to the final outcome of a case. This Department is in constant contact with the media and the public, imparting information (often through press releases) about the progress of pending cases. It responds to requests for information from diplomatic, legal and academic sources, as well as from the general public. It assists in maintaining relations between the Court and other organs and specialized agencies of the United Nations, and international bodies and conferences concerned with the codification and progressive development of international law. The Department also acts as the Court's protocol department, and is responsible for the organization of public hearings and official visits by high-ranking dignitaries, including Heads of State, Royalty and the Secretary-General of the United Nations. During my time at the Court, the Department has organized visits for Their Majesties the King and Queen of Jordan, the Emperor and Empress of Japan, Her Majesty Queen Elizabeth II, and the Heads of State of France, Romania, Mexico, Madagascar, Brazil, the Netherlands, Sri Lanka, Vietnam, the Russian Federation and others.

The Information Department is, in addition, responsible for the Court's website, which has just been updated. The new website provides an excellent resource for people interested in the work and history of the Court. It also contains details about Members of the Court, Judges *ad hoc*, the Registry, publications, basic documents and the Court's jurisdiction. Finally, it is thanks to the energy and initiative of this Department that the Court's museum has recently been renovated with new exhibits and a video presentation of the Court has been made in over fifty languages.

2.4.4   *The Technical Divisions*

The technical divisions are made up of small teams who bring vital backstage support to the Court.

The *Information and Communications Technology Division* ensures the smooth functioning of the electronic resources of the Court and all of its computer systems. In liaison with the Information Department, it provides the technical maintenance of the Court's website, making sure that it is an easy-to-access platform containing information about all of the proceedings before the Court.

The *Finance Division* plays a key role in preparing the Court's draft budget proposals, which are then presented by the Registrar to New York. In accordance with the Instructions for the Registry, the Finance Division not only prepares the budget estimates, but also ensures that the budget is properly implemented, including in terms of providing oversight of the expenditure of funds and for the charging of such expenditure to the proper items of the budget, making sure that no expenses are incurred that are not provided for in the budget. Day-to-day, the Finance Division keeps the financial accounting books, carries out financial reporting, manages vendor payments and payroll, pays pensions to retired Members of the Court and maintains regular contact with the tax authorities of the host country.

The *Publications Division* is responsible for the bilingual publication of various series and editions – Judgments, Advisory Opinions and

Orders; Pleadings, Oral Arguments, Documents; Acts and Documents; Yearbook; Bibliography; Handbook on the Court and coffee-table books explaining, with illustrations, the Court's role and function to the general public. Many of these series are now available electronically on the Court's website.

The *Archives, Indexing and Distribution Division* is responsible for the storage and digitalization of the Court's documents, including case files and correspondence. This Division plays a key role vis-à-vis document retrieval and storage, including with regard to documents from the PCIJ. It is constantly seeking to apply new technologies to complement its paper records.

The *Security and General Assistance Division* has responsibility for all security-related matters, often liaising, in this respect, with the Carnegie Foundation, which owns the Peace Palace building. It also provides general assistance to Members of the Court and Registry staff in regard to messenger, transport and reception services.

The *Library of the Court* has its origins in the Library of the PCIJ. Since its creation, the Library's collection has expanded considerably and now contains some 60,000 volumes. One of the Library's tasks is to maintain the Archives of the International Military Tribunal of Nuremberg, which were entrusted to the ICJ by a decision of the Tribunal of 1 October 1946. The Library's main role is to assist Members of the Court and staff of the various departments of the Registry – in particular the Legal and Linguistic Departments – with their research.

The *Text Processing and Reproduction Division* provides indispensable support to all Departments and Divisions of the Registry. It is in charge of the production of all of the Court's documents in both official languages, in accordance with the required quality standards and often having to deal with competing deadlines.

The *Administrative and Personnel Division* has a wide range of duties, including planning and implementation of staff recruitment, appointment, promotion, training and separation from service.

2.5   Conclusion

The Registry of the Court is unique in many ways. Unlike the vast United Nations Secretariat, which covers the main headquarters in New York as well as duty stations in Geneva, Nairobi and Vienna, the ICJ Registry staff is modest in number – comprising 116 personnel at the time of writing. There is a strong unified purpose to the Registry of the Court, by virtue of the Court's mandate. The ICJ is not a large institution split into multiple sections with different, complementary functions, neither is it a criminal court with a prosecutor's office and/or a victim support unit, etc. The combination of these factors has a real impact on the way in which Registry lawyers and other officials carry out their duties. In particular, there is a palpably close connection between the work of the Registry lawyers and the work of the Judges, and a cohesive working environment among Registry officials in general, which reflects the historically interdisciplinary duties of Registry staff from the early years of the ICJ. From a statutory viewpoint, the Registry derives its authority by virtue of the fact that it plays a pivotal role in ensuring that the Court's judicial processes and general functioning are supported by a sound constitutional structure. The work and dedication of the unseen actors of the Registry of the Court finds reward in itself in the laudable mandate of the ICJ to deliver peaceful solutions and settlements of international disputes.

The International Tribunal for the Law of the Sea

PHILIPPE GAUTIER

3.1 Introduction

In addressing the role of unseen actors in international adjudication, one could be tempted, at first sight, to state that those persons who, behind the scenes, are serving international courts and tribunals should simply remain unseen. To give credit where credit is due, judges or arbitrators have been elected or selected by States to deal with international disputes. They are the ones deciding on cases submitted to the court or tribunal. Clerks, legal assistants, cartographers or other experts may assist the judges but there should be no doubt: the ultimate responsibility for adjudication rests with the members of the bench.

That would be a brief statement and one could stop there but this would not be very satisfactory for the reader. In bringing up the topic 'unseen actors in international adjudication' – and furthermore in questioning the legitimacy of their functioning or the potential effect of their work on the legitimacy of the entire judicial system – the editor certainly had something else in mind. This 'something else' cannot relate to inside stories of how a judgment is arrived at. The golden rule applicable to all civil servants and judges prescribes a duty of reserve and of confidentiality as regards the deliberations of the Tribunal.[1]

That said, there is a perfectly legitimate goal in addressing this topic. Those who are examining the work of international courts and tribunals, or more broadly, are affected by any of their decisions, would like to know how they function – for the sake of transparency – and be assured that decisions are truly the result of the judges' work. Keeping this objective

---

[1] Pursuant to Article 42, para. 1, of the Rules of the Tribunal, '[t]he deliberations of the Tribunal shall take place in private and remain secret.' Rules of the Tribunal (ITLOS/8), adopted on 28 October 1997 (amended on 15 March and 21 September 2001, on 17 March 2009 and on 25 September 2018) [hereinafter 'Rules'].

in mind, this chapter explains the role of the Registry of the International Tribunal for the Law of the Sea (ITLOS or 'the Tribunal') in the handling of a case and the drafting of a judgment. To that end, the following questions are addressed: who are the unseen actors? What are their functions and what is their contribution to the work of the Tribunal, in particular with respect to judicial decisions? And finally, what mechanisms are in place to preserve their neutrality and ensure their legitimacy?

3.2   Who Are the Unseen Actors at ITLOS?

It is interesting to observe that the Statute of the Tribunal (Annex VI to the United Nations Convention on the Law of the Sea ('the Convention'))[2] is somewhat reticent as regards the role of persons other than judges in the functioning of the Tribunal. This appears justified, since judges alone are responsible for deciding on cases submitted to the Tribunal. The only reference to actors other than judges may be found in Article 12, paragraph 2 of the Statute which states that '[t]he Tribunal shall appoint its Registrar and may provide for the appointment of such other officers as may be necessary'.

One needs to consult the Rules of the Tribunal, adopted by the Tribunal in 1997, to find a set of Articles (Articles 32 to 39) relevant to the topic of unseen actors, in a section entitled 'the Registry'. Besides specific provisions applicable to the election of the Registrar, the Deputy Registrar and the Assistant Registrar, these Articles specify that '[t]he Registry consists of the Registrar, the Deputy Registrar, the Assistant Registrar and such other staff as required for the efficient discharge of its functions,'[3] and contain rules regarding the recruitment of the staff members of the Registry.[4] Currently, the Registry consists of 38 posts (20 in the General Service category and 18 in the Professional and higher categories). Every

---

[2] United Nations Convention on the Law of the Sea, Montego Bay, 10 December 1982, in force 16 November 1994, 1833 UNTS 3.
[3] Article 38, para. 1 of the Rules.
[4] Article 35, paras. 1 and 2 of the Rules:
　1. The staff of the Registry, other than the Registrar, the Deputy Registrar and the Assistant Registrar, shall be appointed by the Tribunal on proposals submitted by the Registrar. Appointments to such posts as the Tribunal shall determine may, however, be made by the Registrar with the approval of the President of the Tribunal.
　2. The paramount consideration in the recruitment and employment of the staff and in the determination of the conditions of service shall be the necessity of securing the highest standards of efficiency, competence and integrity. Due regard shall be paid to the importance of recruiting the staff on as wide a geographical basis as possible.

year, the list of staff members is made available to the States Parties to the Convention, as an annex to the Tribunal's annual report.

That said, unseen actors are not invisible and those attending a public hearing will note the presence of some of them in the courtroom. The Registrar supervises the organization of the hearing and sits on the bench with the judges. In front of the bench, the Deputy Registrar and the Legal Officers sit at a desk which faces the parties and the public. Among other tasks, they will make sure that documents produced during the hearing have already been duly filed with the Tribunal and that each party complies with the time allocated to it. They will also listen to the simultaneous translation to verify that no interpretative errors are made in the process and go through advance copies of statements to be delivered, taking note of the arguments made and of any new issue raised. At another desk sits the team of précis-writers, whose task is to transcribe the oral statements made during the hearing. On that basis, they will prepare the draft minutes of the sitting which, after a first check, will be made available to the parties and the judges, at the end of each day. Less visible – but no less important – is the task of interpreters, translators and technicians, who, respectively, ensure that statements made in one official language are properly understood by those listening to them in the other official language, verify the accuracy of the minutes of the hearing, and check whether the equipment (e.g. for displaying maps or a PowerPoint presentation) is functioning properly.

3.3   What Are the Functions of Unseen Actors at ITLOS?

The Registry fulfils a wide range of functions which are listed in Article 36 of the Rules.[5] This Article refers to the functions of the Registrar but, obviously, even though the Registrar bears the ultimate responsibility to

---

[5] Article 36 of the Rules:
  '1. The Registrar, in the discharge of his functions, shall:
  (a) be the regular channel of communications to and from the Tribunal and in particular shall effect all communications, notifications and transmission of documents required by the Convention, the Statute, these Rules or any other relevant international agreement and ensure that the date of dispatch and receipt thereof may be readily verified;
  (b) keep, under the supervision of the President of the Tribunal, and in such form as may be laid down by the Tribunal, a List of cases, entered and numbered in the order in which the documents instituting proceedings or requesting an advisory opinion are received in the Registry;

ensure the efficient functioning of the Registry, the discharge of all those tasks can only be the result of teamwork.

The list of tasks contained in Article 36 of the Rules mainly refers to action to be taken in relation to cases before the Tribunal. However, upon closer examination of the list, one may note that it comprises two different categories of tasks. In addition to the functions related to the judicial

(c) keep copies of declarations and notices of revocation or withdrawal thereof deposited with the Secretary-General of the United Nations under articles 287 and 298 of the Convention or Annex IX, article 7, to the Convention;

(d) keep copies of agreements conferring jurisdiction on the Tribunal;

(e) keep notifications received under article 110, paragraph 2;

(f) transmit to the parties certified copies of pleadings and annexes upon receipt thereof in the Registry;

(g) communicate to the Government of the State in which the Tribunal or a chamber is sitting, or is to sit, and any other Governments which may be concerned, the necessary information as to the persons from time to time entitled, under the Statute and the relevant agreements, to privileges, immunities or facilities;

(h) be present in person or represented by the Deputy Registrar, the Assistant Registrar or in their absence by a senior official of the Registry designated by him, at meetings of the Tribunal, and of the chambers, and be responsible for preparing records of such meetings;

(i) make arrangements for such provision or verification of translations and interpretations into the Tribunal's official languages as the Tribunal may require;

(j) sign all judgments, advisory opinions and orders of the Tribunal and the records referred to in subparagraph (h);

(k) be responsible for the reproduction, printing and publication of the Tribunal's judgments, advisory opinions and orders, the pleadings and statements and the minutes of public sittings in cases and of such other documents as the Tribunal may direct to be published;

(l) be responsible for all administrative work and in particular for the accounts and financial administration in accordance with the financial procedures of the Tribunal;

(m) deal with inquiries concerning the Tribunal and its work;

(n) assist in maintaining relations between the Tribunal and the Authority, the International Court of Justice and the other organs of the United Nations, its related agencies, the arbitral and special arbitral tribunals referred to in article 287 of the Convention and international bodies and conferences concerned with the codification and progressive development of international law, in particular the law of the sea;

(o) ensure that information concerning the Tribunal and its activities is accessible to Governments, the highest national courts of justice, professional and learned societies, legal faculties and schools of law and public information media;

(p) have custody of the seals and stamps of the Tribunal, of the archives of the Tribunal and of such other archives as may be entrusted to the Tribunal.

2. The Tribunal may at any time entrust additional functions to the Registrar.

3. In the discharge of his functions the Registrar shall be responsible to the Tribunal.'

activities of the Tribunal, the Registrar is 'responsible for all administrative work and in particular for the accounts and financial administration in accordance with the financial procedures of the Tribunal'.[6] This refers to a broad range of activities covering, inter alia, maintenance of premises, staff matters, budget and contributions, library services, information technology services and archives.

Given the overarching topic of this book, the present chapter only focuses briefly on tasks closely linked to the judicial functions of the Tribunal. The staff of the Registry who are involved in those tasks are mainly the legal officers (four legal officers under the direct supervision of the Head of the Legal Office), the Deputy Registrar and the Registrar. As regards the role of these officials in the judicial process, the practice of the Tribunal is well established and their work may be divided into five categories. First, the Registrar, Deputy Registrar and the legal officers assist the President and the Judges in the conduct of the case and the administration of the procedure (such as the organization and schedule of the case, preparation of correspondence with parties and judges, *procès-verbaux* of consultations with parties, organization of the hearing, administration of evidence and records of judicial deliberations).

Second, they draft research notes on procedural issues relating to the conduct of the case or on legal issues raised by cases submitted to the Tribunal. The objective is not to write an academic paper but rather to give an overview of positions previously adopted by the Tribunal and other international courts, or views expressed in the legal literature on specific issues (e.g., joinder of proceedings, exhaustion of local remedies, *forum prorogatum*, preliminary objections, registration of vessels). Research papers are also prepared on the factual background of the cases, pointing out facts which are disputed between the parties. Third, they assist in the preparation of the President's working paper, which serves as a guide for the deliberations. This working paper, which is referred to in the Resolution on internal judicial practice of the Tribunal,[7] is prepared

---

[6] Article 36, para. 1(1) of the Rules.
[7] Article 2, para. 3 of the Resolution on internal judicial practice of the Tribunal: 'On the basis of the written pleadings and the judges' notes, the President draws up a working paper containing: (a) a summary of the facts and the principal contentions of the parties advanced in their written pleadings; and (b) proposals concerning: (i) indications to be given, or questions to be put, to the parties in accordance with article 76 of the Rules; (ii) evidence or explanations to be requested from the parties in accordance with article 77 of the Rules; and (iii) issues which, in the opinion of the President, should be discussed and decided by the Tribunal.'

on the basis of the written pleadings. It is further revised and updated at the end of the oral proceedings, in light of the arguments presented by the parties.

Fourth, they assist the Drafting Committee. Usually, the first part of the judgment, giving a description of the procedure as well as a short factual background of the case, is prepared by the Registry. Upon request, assistance may also be provided in the drafting of specific paragraphs of a judgment. The text of the judgment – in English and in French – will also be carefully reviewed by Registry staff in order, for example, to ensure consistency between both official languages, to correct clerical errors, to verify the accuracy of texts quoted and the consistency in the manner in which references are inserted. Fifth, Registry staff may also provide assistance in technical matters. For example, external translators may be recruited during the hearing in order to enable the Registry to issue a daily *procès-verbal* of the public sitting. The drawing of charts may also be done by a cartographer who is recruited on a temporary contract for that purpose. Likewise, the review of invoices submitted as part of a compensation claim could be done by an accountant hired on a temporary basis.

3.4 How Is the Neutrality of Unseen Actors at ITLOS Ensured and Their Legitimacy Preserved?

Staff members of the Registry are international civil servants who are subject to certain rules intended to ensure their neutrality and integrity. Those rules are important to preserve the legitimacy of the judicial process. First, all staff recruitment has to comply with a number of requirements under the Tribunal's Staff Regulations and Rules. The selection of staff has to be made on 'a competitive basis'[8] and 'on as wide a geographical basis as possible'[9] with the objective of 'securing the highest standards of efficiency, competence and integrity.'[10]

Second, members of staff – including staff engaged on a temporary basis – have to make a solemn declaration before the President of the Tribunal, in the presence of the Registrar, before taking up their duties. By this oath, staff members declare that they will 'perform [their] duties as an official of the International Tribunal for the Law of the Sea in all loyalty,

---

[8] Regulation 4.3 of the Staff Regulations of the Tribunal.
[9] Article 35, para. 2 of the Rules.
[10] Ibid.

discretion and good conscience and that [they] will faithfully observe all the provisions of the Statute and of the Rules of the Tribunal'.[11] The importance of the oath should not be underestimated as it triggers a set of obligations applicable to all staff members involved in judicial activities.

Third, these obligations are incorporated in the Staff Regulations of the Tribunal in order to preserve the neutrality and integrity of staff and to avoid the possibility that any doubt may be cast on their functioning. For example, pursuant to Regulation 1.3 of the Staff Regulations of the Tribunal, members of the Registry, '[i]n the performance of their duties ... shall neither seek nor accept instructions from any government or from any other entity external to the Tribunal'. Regulation 1.5 requires staff members to 'exercise the utmost discretion in regard to all matters of official business' and prohibits the communication 'to any person [of] any information coming to their knowledge by reason of their official position which has not been made public, except in the course of their duties or by authorization of the Registrar'. The same Regulation also specifies that '[t]hese obligations do not cease upon separation from the Registry'. Likewise, Regulation 1.6 provides that no staff member shall 'accept any honour, decoration, favour, gift or remuneration from any source external to the Tribunal, without first obtaining the approval of the Registrar'. It adds that such approval is 'granted only in exceptional cases and where such acceptance is not incompatible ... with the individual's status as an international civil servant'. Prior approval is required, for example, whenever a staff member participates in an academic activity – such as the writing of the present chapter – which relates to the work of the Tribunal. These rules are binding on all staff members and their breach may lead to the adoption of disciplinary measures in accordance with the Staff Regulations and Rules.

Fourth, Article 52 of the Rules, which preserves the confidentiality of the Tribunal's deliberations, also contains provisions regarding the presence of Registry staff members during deliberations of the Tribunal. Pursuant to Article 52, paragraph 2, '[o]nly judges and any experts appointed in accordance with article 289 of the Convention take part in the Tribunal's judicial deliberations. The Registrar, or his Deputy, and other members of the staff of the Registry as may be required shall be present. No other person shall be present except by permission of the Tribunal.' This Rule

---

[11] Ibid. For the solemn declaration of the Registrar and the Deputy Registrar (to be made at a meeting of the Tribunal), see Article 34 of the Rules.

is also applicable to the meetings of chambers of the Tribunal and to the meetings of the drafting committee.

3.5 Conclusion

To conclude, the role of the Registry is to assist the judges in the fulfilment of their judicial functions on the basis of the Rules and the established practice of the Tribunal. The tasks performed by the Registry are clearly defined and delimited so as to avoid compromising the legitimacy of the judicial process. A corpus of rules has been developed which intends to preserve the neutrality and integrity of the Registry's staff and to prevent undue interference with the judicial process, which remains the sole responsibility of the judges of the Tribunal.

4

International Arbitral Institutions

BRIDIE MCASEY

4.1 Introduction

This chapter provides an insight into the work of the unseen actors within various international arbitral institutions, describing their functions, organisational structures and applicable rules and regulations. Because the unseen actors work within the frameworks of these arbitral institutions, this overview provides the necessary context and background for the discussion in subsequent chapters of the legitimacy of unseen actors. This chapter focuses on *how* arbitral institutions regulate the behaviour of unseen actors, or provide transparency as to their actions, as well as providing a general description of the work of each institution. This chapter makes no argument as to whether or not regulation or transparency are panaceas for legitimacy, but recognises that it is at least a possibility.[1]

The discussion in this chapter is structured as follows. For each institution, the chapter provides a brief overview of the work of the institution (that is, the type of cases it deals with), followed by a discussion of who the unseen actors in each institution are, what they are doing and how they are regulated. Of course, the degree to which the actors are unseen may in some cases be debatable. For the purposes of this chapter, unseen actors are those involved in arbitration but who are not arbitrators. That is, they are not the primary decision-makers in a dispute as traditionally understood. In several instances discussed below, the unseen actor is the secretary general of a given institution. Obviously, such individuals are very much seen in several respects (their identity and background is known, for example). However, applying a broad concept of an 'unseen actor',

---

[1] See, e.g., Allen Buchanan and Robert O. Keohane, 'The Legitimacy of Global Governance Institutions' in Rüdiger Wolfrum and Volker Röben (eds.), *Legitimacy in International Law* (Springer, 2008), pp. 51–55.

they are unseen because they are not one of the arbitrators deciding a dispute, but have the ability to influence a dispute to some degree. Further, in some instances what is unseen is *how* the actor is taking decisions and performing their functions.

Discussion of *what* the unseen actors are doing and how this is regulated is in each instance organised around the different phases of a typical arbitration: initiation of the claim; constitution of the tribunal; and the determination phase (written submissions; hearings; and issuance of an award and/or other decisions). As this chapter aims merely to provide an overview, the discussion of what the unseen actors are doing is not exhaustive.[2] Arbitral institutions may engage in a range of work, such as promotional activity and policy development, but this chapter will focus on the work of institutions that relates to the administration of arbitrations (that is, case-related work).

The arbitral institutions covered in this chapter range from those that deal or have dealt with a mix of arbitrations between private parties, claims against a State by private entities or State–State disputes (Permanent Court of Arbitration (PCA)), to institutions that predominantly administer investor-State disputes (the International Centre for the Settlement of Investment Disputes (ICSID)), to those dealing with primarily international arbitrations between private parties (the London Court of International Arbitration (LCIA); the International Chamber of Commerce's (ICC) International Court of Arbitration; the Hong Kong International Arbitration Centre (HKIAC) and the Arbitral Institute of the Stockholm Chamber of Commerce (SCC)), grouped under the heading 'commercial arbitration institutions'.

4.2   The Permanent Court of Arbitration (PCA)

4.2.1   *The Work of the PCA*

The PCA's caseload comprises a range of cases, most involving a State in some way. The PCA's 2016 Annual Report records that it administered 148 cases in the course of 2016, including inter-State arbitrations and conciliations, investor-State arbitrations, and one arbitration between private parties.[3]

---

[2] For a more complete discussion of the roles and functions of arbitral institutions, see Remy Gerbay, *The Functions of Arbitral Institutions* (Kluwer Law International, 2016).

[3] Annual Report 2016, available at https://pca-cpa.org/en (last accessed 26 February 2018) 7.

4.2.2   Who Are the Unseen Actors?

The PCA's founding documents established an International Bureau that was to act 'as registry for the Commissions which sit at The Hague' and would 'place its offices and staff at the disposal of the Contracting Powers for the use of the Commission of Inquiry'.[4] The International Bureau is headed by the Secretary-General of the PCA and is staffed with legal counsel and administrative staff.

4.2.3   What Is the Role of the Unseen Actors and How Is the PCA regulated?

It is important to make a clarification at the outset regarding regulation. The PCA can and does administer arbitrations under a range of procedural rules. For the sake of brevity, the discussion below will focus on the 2012 PCA Arbitration Rules (PCA Rules),[5] with some discussion of other rules where warranted.

4.2.3.1   Initiation of a claim

In terms of the formal process of initiating a claim, the role of the PCA's unseen actors is limited. Initiation of a claim under the PCA Rules is by way of a notice of arbitration. The PCA Rules make it clear that any question over the adequacy of a notice of arbitration or response is a question for the arbitral tribunal and does not impede the initiation of proceedings.[6] Unlike some other institutions, the PCA has no power to reject a claim because the document initiating proceedings is deficient, because the claim is defective, or because a prima facie question of jurisdiction has arisen.[7]

One area in which unseen actors at the PCA *can* have an impact on initiation of a claim is through the administration of the Financial Assistance Fund for Settlement of International Disputes. This fund can assist qualifying States[8] with costs associated with *initiating* a claim. As such, a decision whether or not to provide funding could arguably materially

---

[4] Convention on the Pacific Settlement of International Disputes of 1907, The Hague, 18 October 1907, in force 26 January 1910, 1 *Bevans* 577, Article 15.

[5] Available at https://pca-cpa.org/en/documents/pca-conventions-and-rules/ (last accessed 26 February 2018).

[6] PCA Rules, Articles 3(5) and 4(3).

[7] See the discussion at Section 4.3.1 below.

[8] To qualify, a State must be a party to one of the PCA's founding conventions and be listed on the 'DAC List of Aid Recipients' prepared by the Organization for Economic Cooperation

impact whether or not a State proceeds with a case.[9] The International Bureau administers the fund, but decisions on whether or not to grant funding are made by a 'Board of Trustees' under 'Terms Of Reference and Guidelines' ('Fund Guidelines').[10] The Fund Guidelines lightly regulate disbursement decisions, specifying only that the Board of Trustees 'shall be guided, inter alia, by the financial needs of the requesting State and the availability of funds'.[11]

There are limited transparency requirements on the operation of the fund. The Fund Guidelines require the PCA's Annual Report to summarise the activities of the Fund. Reports in recent years contain information about which States have contributed to the fund, but a limited amount of information about States that have been recipients of the Fund. The PCA's 2012 Annual Report, for example, indicated that '[i]n previous years, assistance grants were given to two Asian States, a Central American State, and five African States. In 2012, the PCA was able to offer a Latin American State a grant'.[12] No information is provided about *how* decisions are taken to award funds or how the Board of Trustees is guided by financial needs or the availability of funds, or whether and how often applications are rejected.

4.2.3.2   Constitution of the Tribunal

The Secretary-General of the PCA is named as appointing authority under the PCA Rules, a role that is activated when the parties have failed to appoint arbitrators themselves. The PCA Rules regulate this role by specifying that the Secretary-General must allow the parties

---

and Development (Terms of Reference and Guidelines, para. 5, available at https://pca-cpa.org/en/documents/pca-conventions-and-rules/ (last accessed 26 February 2018)).

[9] Arbitration proceedings are costly and there are an ever-increasing number of them. See Brooks W. Daly and Sarah Melikian, 'Access to Justice in Dispute Resolution: Financial Assistance in International Arbitration' in K. Nadakavukaren (ed.), *Poverty and International Economic Law: Duties to the Poor* (Cambridge University Press, 2013), pp. 212–13 noting that '[a]lthough varied resources exist in national contexts, as more disputes become international, domestic resources may not be available or equipped to assist parties in an international setting ... parties with limited financial resources consenting to arbitral jurisdiction will find no generally established system of assistance' and p. 222, noting that in some instances a grant from the Financial Assistance Fund will be enough to cover a substantial part of a State's costs.

[10] Available at https://pca-cpa.org/en/documents/pca-conventions-and-rules/ (last accessed 26 February 2018).

[11] Fund Guidelines, para. 12.

[12] PCA, 112th Annual Report (2012), available at https://pca-cpa.org/wp-content/uploads/sites/175/2015/12/PCA-Annual-Report-2012.pdf (last accessed 1 November 2018), p. 20.

or arbitrators an opportunity to present their views, and must have regard to securing the appointment of 'an independent and impartial arbitrator' and 'the advisability of appointing an arbitrator of a nationality other than the nationalities of the parties.'[13] As well as appointing specific arbitrators, the Secretary-General in his or her appointing authority capacity under the PCA Rules may be called upon to determine whether appointment of a sole arbitrator is appropriate 'in view of the circumstances of the case.'[14]

The Secretary-General also has a specified role in constituting tribunals under the UN Commission on International Trade Law's arbitration rules ('UNCITRAL Rules').[15] Under the UNCITRAL Rules, the Secretary-General is named as a potential appointing authority or authority to designate an appointing authority. With respect to the designating authority role, the PCA is the default authority in certain circumstances (for example, failure by the parties to agree an appointing authority).[16] If acting as appointing authority under the UNCITRAL Rules, the PCA's Secretary-General can also constitute a tribunal with a sole arbitrator or in a reconstituted state,[17] deprive a party of its right to appoint a substitute arbitrator and authorise a truncated tribunal to proceed.[18] Unlike the ICC, which has published appointment data to improve transparency, there is no specific record of appointments made by the PCA's Secretary-General.

Arguably, the PCA Secretary-General is not really an unseen actor because his or her function is clearly stipulated by the relevant arbitral rules and his or her role is a highly visible one. However, *exactly* how the appointing function is carried out is only lightly regulated and the function is arguably 'unseen' to some extent because both the PCA Rules and the UNCITRAL Rules offer little by way of a framework as to *how* the Secretary-General should make appointments.[19]

---

[13] PCA Rules, Articles 6(2) and 6(3).
[14] PCA Rules, Article 7.
[15] Available at www.uncitral.org/uncitral/en/uncitral_texts/arbitration/2010Arbitration_rules.html (last accessed 26 February 2018).
[16] UNCITRAL Rules, Article 6(1).
[17] UNCITRAL Rules, Article 7(2).
[18] UNCITRAL Rules, Article 14(2). *See also* Sarah Grimmer, 'Expanded Role of the Appointing Authority under the UNCITRAL Arbitration Rules 2010' (2011) 28(5) *Journal of International Arbitration* 501.
[19] This is further reflected in the 'Q&A' on the PCA website, which states that '[w]hen the PCA appoints an arbitrator, it is not restricted to appointing individuals on any particular list. The PCA will appoint the individual it considers most appropriate, subject to

4.2.3.3   Determination Phase

Regulation of activities that unseen actors at the PCA may carry out in the determination phase is light. The PCA website indicates that 'a staff member of the International Bureau may be appointed as registrar or administrative secretary for a case and carry out administrative tasks at the direction of the arbitral tribunal'. An enumeration of the type of administrative tasks an International Bureau member might carry out concludes with the arguably very broad 'carrying out *any other tasks entrusted to it by the parties or the arbitral tribunal*' (emphasis added).[20] More generally, the work of the International Bureau is governed by a four-page document issued in 1900, which, in terms of regulation, speaks only of the requirement of confidentiality:

> The Staff of the International Bureau are forbidden to communicate to persons outside the Bureau, either by word of mouth or in writing, any information concerning the business entrusted to them in the course of their work, or to allow such persons any access to the documents pertaining to the work of the Bureau.[21]

Other unseen actors may be involved in PCA cases, but because they are not PCA staff, they are not regulated by the PCA's rules or the PCA itself. Tribunals, or presiding members of tribunals, sometimes appoint an assistant to the tribunal in addition to the Secretary to the tribunal or Registrar who is taken on by a member of the PCA's International Bureau. This was famously the case in the arbitration brought by Yukos Universal Limited (Isle Of Man) against Russia,[22] and Russia sought to set aside the final award partly on the basis that the tribunal assistant exceeded his remit.[23] The Russian Federation's set-aside application was unsuccessful

---

the parties' agreement and the rules governing the arbitration. Nor are parties to PCA arbitrations required to appoint arbitrators from any given list.'

[20] 'Case Administration', available at https://pca-cpa.org/en/services/arbitration-services/case-administration/ (last accessed 10 August 2018).

[21] Rules Concerning the Organization and Internal Working of the International Bureau of the Permanent Court of Arbitration (18 December 1900), Article V, available at https://pca-cpa.org/en/documents/pca-conventions-and-rules/ (last accessed 5 March 2019).

[22] *Yukos Universal Limited (Isle of Man) v. The Russian Federation*, UNCITRAL, PCA Case No AA 227.

[23] Dmytro Galagan and Patricia Živković, 'The Challenge of the Yukos Award: An Award Written by Someone Else – A Violation of the Tribunal's Mandate?' (27 February 2015), *Kluwer Arbitration Blog*, available at http://arbitrationblog.kluwerarbitration.com/2015/02/27/the-challenge-of-the-yukos-award-an-award-written-by-someone-else-a-violation-of-the-tribunals-mandate/ (last accessed 26 February 2018).

on this ground, but if the Yukos example nonetheless reflects a genuine issue, it is one with a potential regulatory gap at present.

Another area where the Secretary-General of the PCA (again in his or her capacity as appointing authority) may impact the determination phase is if a challenge is mounted against an arbitrator. The PCA Rules specify that a challenge can be made 'if circumstances exist that give rise to justifiable doubts as to the arbitrator's impartiality or independence.'[24] There is no strict requirement for the appointing authority to give reasons for his or her decision on a challenge, but he or she may do so.[25] Although it is not specified as part of the challenge procedure in the rules, the PCA website indicates that 'depending on the circumstances of the case, [the Secretary-General] may make the decision directly or after consultation with a special committee, consisting of three persons, a majority of whom will be of nationalities different from that of any party.'[26]

4.3 The International Centre for the Settlement of Investment Disputes (ICSID)

4.3.1 The Work of the ICSID

The ICSID is established under a multilateral treaty as a forum for investor-State dispute resolution and at the time of writing was administering over 250 investor-State arbitrations.[27]

4.3.2 Who Are the Unseen Actors?

The ICSID maintains a Secretariat that is headed by the Secretary-General. ICSID also has an Administrative Council, and this body plays a role in the administration of cases, specifically with respect to the appointment of arbitrators, as discussed below. Unlike the other arbitral institutions discussed in this chapter, in the ICSID the resolution of challenges is determined by the unchallenged tribunal members.[28]

---

[24] PCA Rules, Article 12.
[25] PCA Rules, Article 13(5).
[26] 'PCA Secretary-General as Appointing Authority,' available at https://pca-cpa.org/en/services/appointing-authority/pca-secretary-general-as-appointing-authority/ (last accessed 26 February 2018).
[27] See https://icsid.worldbank.org/en/pages/cases/pendingCases.aspx?status=p (last accessed 26 February 2018).
[28] See ICSID Convention, Article 58.

4.3.3   What Is the Role of the Unseen Actors and How Is the ICSID Regulated?

Generally speaking, the work of ICSID's Secretariat as it relates to arbitral cases is regulated by the ICSID Convention; the ICSID Convention Arbitration Rules, or if applicable, the Arbitration (Additional Facility) Rules which permit access to ICSID when a State not party to the ICSID Convention is involved; and the ICSID Administrative and Financial Regulations.[29]

4.3.3.1   Initiation of a Claim

The ability of the ICSID as an institution to impact the initiation of a claim sits at the more interventionist end of the spectrum. Under the ICSID Convention, a request for arbitration must be addressed to the Secretary-General. That request must be registered (and dispatched to the respondent) unless the Secretary-General determines that the dispute subject of the request is 'manifestly outside the jurisdiction of the Centre'.[30] In carrying out this screening function, the Secretary-General will have regard to the jurisdictional requirements in Article 25 of the ICSID Convention.[31]

The Secretary-General's power under Article 36 is arguably one with teeth and quite far from a purely administrative function. As Sergio Puig and Chester Brown have highlighted:

> some critics have argued that it is becoming more difficult to persuade the Secretary-General to register a request for arbitration than it is to persuade a tribunal to exercise jurisdiction over a claim, and have noted that this is troubling, given that there is no appeal open to a putative claimant should the Secretary-General refuse to register a request for arbitration.[32]

The exercise of this screening function arguably lacks transparency. Although it is relatively clear that Article 25 provides the criteria for exercise of the Secretary-General's power under Article 36, the

---

[29] All of these documents are available on the ICSID website at https://icsid.worldbank.org/en/pages/icsiddocs/overview.aspx (last accessed 26 February 2018).

[30] ICSID Convention, Article 36.

[31] 'Screening and Registration – ICSID Convention Arbitration,' available at https://icsid.worldbank.org/en/Pages/process/Screening-of-Request-and-Registration-Convention-Arbitration.aspx (last accessed 26 February 2018).

[32] Sergio Puig and Chester Brown, 'The Secretary-General's Power to Refuse to Register a Request for Arbitration under the ICSID Convention' (2012) 27(1) *ICSID Review* 172, 173.

Secretary-General's decisions are not made public.[33] This means that the Secretary-General's practice must be inferred, and is 'unseen', which could result in uncertainty for claimants.[34] Against these concerns is the fact that a refusal to register has no lasting impact on the claim, because a claimant is not precluded from resubmitting a registration request, and the tribunal's ability to determine its own jurisdiction is preserved in any event.[35] Further, it appears that the Secretary-General has exercised the right to refuse registration in only a handful of instances.[36]

Institutional discretion can also impact the initiation of Additional Facility arbitrations. Registration requirements differ slightly for an Additional Facility proceeding, and there is a further pre-initiation requirement that is assessed by the Secretary-General. For an Additional Facility arbitration, an agreement purporting to provide for arbitration under the Additional Facility must be approved by the Secretary-General.[37] Such approval can be sought at any time prior to the initiation of a dispute under the agreement. The Additional Facility Arbitration Rules further require that when a request for registration of a dispute is submitted, the Secretary-General must be satisfied that the requirements set out in Article 3 of the Additional Facility Arbitration Rules have been met.[38] One of these is the date on which the aforementioned agreement was approved; other elements are jurisdictional. Notably, the screening requirement does not stipulate an assessment of whether or not the claim is 'manifestly outside the jurisdiction of the Centre' and instead uses a formulation that arguably grants the Secretary-General more discretion in screening a request for registration (before registering, 'the

---

[33] Albeit that Regulation 23 of the ICSID Administrative and Financial Regulations mandates the creation and maintenance of a register that is to be made available to the public for inspection and includes details of (inter alia) the 'institution' of individual proceedings.

[34] See, e.g., Puig and Brown, 'The Secretary-General's Power to Refuse to Register a Request for Arbitration, 178, making an inference based on a journal article written by an ICSID Secretariat member that '[t]his practice suggests that despite not having a formal process, the Centre considers in good faith arguments aimed at preventing registration, but ultimately makes an independent assessment of jurisdiction for the purpose of registration.' See also 180–181 discussing the inferable meaning of 'manifestly' as equivalent to 'beyond reasonable doubt', but also canvassing other possible meanings.

[35] ICSID Convention, Article 41.

[36] Martina Polasek, 'The Threshold for Registration of a Request for Arbitration under the ICSID Convention' (2011) 5(2) *Dispute Resolution International* 177, 178.

[37] Additional Facility Rules, Article 4.

[38] See Arbitration (Additional Facility) Rules, Article 4, Schedule C.

Secretary-General shall have satisfied himself that the request conforms in form and substance to the provisions of Article 3 of these Rules'[39]).

4.3.3.2   Constitution of the Tribunal

The ICSID has a role to play in appointing arbitrators if the parties are unable to agree, or if an ad hoc committee is formed to consider annulment of an ICSID award.[40] Regarding the former, Article 38 of the ICSID Convention provides that the Chair of ICSID's Administrative Council (the President of the World Bank Group) will appoint any arbitrators that the parties have not been able to appoint within 90 days from the panel of arbitrators maintained by ICSID.[41] In practice, a default appointment by the Chair does not take place until a ballot process has been completed.[42] In the ballot process, the Secretariat circulates a list of candidate arbitrators to the parties. The parties indicate whether any of the balloted names are acceptable, and if there is convergence, they are deemed to have agreed to appoint the arbitrator that they both find acceptable.[43] As noted, if the Chair appoints, it must be from the panel of arbitrators. No criteria govern how the Chair should go about appointing an arbitrator from the panel, save that the parties must be consulted 'as far as possible',[44] and the arbitrators appointed must not have the nationality of either disputing party. Regarding formation of an ad hoc committee, here again, the Chair must appoint from the ICSID panel of arbitrators, must not appoint a national of either party or a person with the same nationality as the original tribunal members.[45]

---

[39] Puig and Brown, 'The Secretary-General's Power to Refuse to Register a Request for Arbitration, 188; Lucy Reed, Jan Paulsson and Nigel Blackaby, *Guide to ICSID Arbitration* (Kluwer Law International 2010), p. 128.

[40] The ICSID Secretary-General also acts as an appointing authority when designated to do so, but as that is a function designated under treaty or arbitration agreement, that function will not be addressed in detail here (see, e.g., Trans-Pacific Partnership, Articles 9.19 and 9.22, available at http://dfat.gov.au/trade/agreements/tpp/Pages/trans-pacific-partnership-agreement-tpp.aspx (last accessed 26 February 2018)).

[41] ICSID Member States are able to designate up to four arbitrators to the panel, and the Chair of the Administrative Council may designate ten arbitrators to the panel (ICSID Convention, Article 12).

[42] See 'Selection and Appointment of Tribunal Members – ICSID Convention Arbitration' available at https://icsid.worldbank.org/en/Pages/process/Selection-and-Appointment-of-Tribunal-Members-Convention-Arbitration.aspx (last accessed 26 February 2018).

[43] Reed et al., Guide to ICSID Arbitration, p. 132.

[44] ICSID Convention, Article 38.

[45] The Chair is also prohibited (axiomatically) from appointing one of the original tribunal members to the ad hoc committee (ICSID Convention, Article 53).

There is little information available about how the ICSID ballot process or appointments are carried out, and both processes are lightly regulated. With respect to appointments by the Chair, it is arguable that the fact that appointments must be from the panel of arbitrators counterbalances the lack of transparency. However, limitations in the composition of the panel may militate against this.[46] Additionally, a review of Chair appointees reveals that certain panel members have received far more appointments in original proceedings and to ad hoc committees than others.[47]

4.3.3.3   Determination Phase

Members of the ICSID Secretariat play a role in the determination phase of cases, and as with the PCA, this role is quite lightly regulated in a formal sense. The ICSID Administrative and Financial Regulations specifically envisage appointment of Secretariat members as secretaries to ICSID tribunals.[48] The relevant regulation also includes a list of functions that a tribunal secretary may perform, which is largely administrative but concludes with the open-ended 'other functions with respect to the proceeding at the request of the President of the Commission, Tribunal or Committee, or at the direction of the Secretary-General'.[49] Regulation 12 of the Administrative and Financial Regulations makes it clear that Secretariat staff are under the direction of the Secretary-General. In the same way that PCA cases may have a 'tribunal assistant' as well as an institutionally appointed secretary, ICSID arbitral tribunals often also have assistants as well as an ICSID secretary. The role of the assistant in an ICSID case is unregulated.

---

[46] Not all states have exercised their right to appoint members to the panel, for example, and the Chair's designation of ten panel members has lacked diversity (Chiara Giorgetti, 'Who Decides Who Decides in International Investment Arbitration?' (2013) 35(2) *The University of Pennsylvania Journal of International Law* 431, 446, 448, 483).

[47] Professor Karl-Heinz Bockstiegel, for example, has been appointed 10 times, and Professor Piero Bernardini 12 times. By contrast, Professor Andreas Buscher has been appointed 7 times, and there are a large number of panel members who have been appointed only once to ad hoc committees (see the UN Conference on Trade and Development's 'Investment Policy Hub,' available at http://investmentpolicyhub.unctad.org/ISDS). Of course a complete statistical analysis would need to take into account a range of factors, such as time served on the panel, but it does appear that certain panellists are more often repeat appointees than others. See also Sergio Puig, 'Social Capital in the Arbitration Market' (2014) 25(2) *European Journal of International Law* 387, 404, noting that former ICJ President Gilbert Guillaume has been appointed by the Chair 10 times.

[48] ICSID Administrative and Financial Regulations, Regulation 25.

[49] ICSID Administrative and Financial Regulations, Regulation 25.

4.4   Commercial Arbitration Institutions

Several arbitral institutions are dealt with together in this section. They are grouped together because of their commonality, but they are of course different in some respects, and those differences are addressed below where relevant. It is also worth noting that they are a selective group, and that there are many other commercial arbitration institutions that would be covered were this a comprehensive discussion rather than an overview. The institutions discussed are: the London Court of International Arbitration (LCIA); the International Chamber of Commerce's International Court of Arbitration (ICC); the Hong Kong International Arbitration Centre; and the Arbitral Institute of the Stockholm Chamber of Commerce (SCC) (referred to together as the 'commercial arbitration institutions').

4.4.1   Work of the Commercial Arbitration Institutions

Broadly speaking, these institutions administer a range of commercial arbitrations, as well as providing appointments and mediation or other alternative dispute resolution services.[50] The commercial arbitration institutions may also administer investor-State disputes, albeit typically to a lesser extent than the PCA or ICSID, with the exception of the SCC, which has a more significant caseload of investment disputes.[51]

4.4.2   Who are the Unseen Actors?

Each of the commercial arbitration institutions maintains a secretariat that supports the administration of cases (amongst other activities). They also each have a body (variously termed a court, committee or board)[52] that takes decisions that can impact upon cases.

---

[50] By way of example, in terms of volume, during a 24-month period over 2015–2016, 643 disputes were referred to the LCIA (see www.lcia.org/News/lcia-facts-and-figures-2016-a-robust-caseload.aspx (last accessed 26 February 2018)).

[51] See http://sccinstitute.com/dispute-resolution/investment-disputes/ (last accessed 26 February 2018).

[52] The LCIA and ICC have a court, the SCC has a board, and the HKIAC has a committee.

4.4.3 What Is the Role of the Unseen Actors and How Are the Institutions Regulated?

4.4.3.1 Initiation of a Claim

The commercial arbitration institutions have varying degrees of influence over the initiation of a claim. Although all of these commercial arbitration institutions enshrine the right for an arbitral tribunal to determine its own jurisdiction, some have reserved the right to refuse to initiate cases, or to make prima facie determinations on jurisdiction. The rules of the SCC, for example (SCC Rules[53]), provide that the Board of the SCC can dismiss a case if the SCC 'manifestly lacks jurisdiction over the dispute' or if an advance on costs is not paid. Pursuant to Article 4.7 of its rules (HKIAC Rules),[54] the HKIAC is able to refuse to initiate an arbitration if a claimant does not remedy a defect that HKIAC identifies in a notice of arbitration, and pursuant to Article 19.4, '[i]f a question arises as to the existence, validity or scope of the arbitration agreement(s) or to the competence of HKIAC to administer an arbitration before the constitution of the arbitral tribunal, HKIAC may decide whether and to what extent the arbitration shall proceed'. Similarly, under Article 6(3) of the ICC Rules,[55] the Secretary General of the ICC may refer a case to the ICC Court for a prima facie jurisdictional ruling. There is also evidence that even where there are no express provisions in the relevant rules, a commercial arbitration institution will refuse to register a case if there is a clear defect.[56]

4.4.3.2 Constitution of the Tribunal

Appointment of arbitrators is an area where commercial arbitration institutions can have significant impact on an arbitration. In some instances, before appointment occurs, an institution may also have the responsibility for determining how many arbitrators will constitute the tribunal, if the parties have not specified this. Article 6.1 of the HKIAC

---

[53] SCC Arbitration Rules 2017, available at http://sccinstitute.com/media/169838/arbitration_rules_eng_17_web.pdf (last accessed 26 February 2018).
[54] The HKIAC Administered Arbitration Rules 2013, available at http://hkiac.org/arbitration/rules-practice-notes/administered-arbitration-rules (last accessed 26 February 2018).
[55] ICC Arbitration Rules 2017 (ICC Rules), available at https://iccwbo.org/dispute-resolution-services/arbitration/rules-of-arbitration/.
[56] Remy Gerbay, *The Functions of Arbitral Institutions* (Kluwer Law International, 2016) 70, citing Adrian Winstanley, 'Review of the London Court of International Arbitration' in Horacio A. Grigera Naón and Paul E. Mason (eds.), *International Commercial Arbitration Practice: 21st Century Perspectives* (LexisNexis, 2010).

Rules entrusts the HKIAC with this task, and the SCC Rules have a similar provision. The ICC also retains some discretion in this regard where the parties have not come to an agreement.[57]

When it comes to appointing arbitrators, the rules of each of the commercial arbitration institutions bestow some degree of responsibility on the institution for this when the parties have failed to make the appointments themselves. Each institution uses its court, committee or board as the case may be to fulfil the appointment function. Those bodies are typically composed of experienced arbitration practitioners. Two of the commercial arbitration institutions (LCIA and HKIAC) maintain lists of suitable candidates for appointment.[58] The SCC does not, and the ICC seeks recommendations from 'national committees' (although it can also appoint arbitrators directly). The LCIA retains the most power over the appointment of arbitrators, and its rules make clear that whilst parties may *nominate* arbitrators, it is the LCIA Court that *appoints*. As such, the LCIA could override the parties' nominations if the nominees did not meet the requisite standards of impartiality and independence. By contrast, HKIAC, ICC and SCC appoint arbitrators when the parties have failed to do so.

All of the commercial arbitration institutions are regulated to some degree in their role of appointing arbitrators. The LCIA Court cannot appoint a presiding or sole arbitrator that has the same nationality as the parties.[59] Article 5.9 of the LCIA Arbitration Rules 2014 (LCIA Rules)[60] provides that

> The LCIA Court shall appoint arbitrators with due regard for any particular method or criteria of selection agreed in writing by the parties. The LCIA Court shall also take into account the transaction(s) at issue, the nature and circumstances of the dispute, its monetary amount or value, the location and languages of the parties, the number of parties and all other factors which it may consider relevant in the circumstances.

The SCC follows the same rule regarding nationality of the presiding or sole arbitrator as the LCIA, and the SCC Rules provide that the Board

---

[57] ICC Rules, Article 12(1).
[58] HKIAC maintains two lists and mandates minimum criteria for inclusion on both; the LCIA maintains a database of arbitrators but may appoint arbitrators not in the database (see 'LCIA Notes for Parties', section 8, available at www.lcia.org//adr-services/lcia-notes-for-parties.aspx#8. APPOINTMENT OF ARBITRATORS (last accessed 26 February 2018)).
[59] LCIA Rules, Article 7.1.
[60] Available at www.lcia.org/Dispute_Resolution_Services/lcia-arbitration-rules-2014.aspx (last accessed 26 February 2018).

must consider 'the nature and circumstances of the dispute, the applicable law, the seat and language of the arbitration and the nationality of the parties'.[61] Additionally, the SCC maintains a policy document that provides further detail on the issues that the SCC Board will take into account in appointing arbitrators.[62]

The ICC and HKIAC both follow the nationality rule described above. The ICC Rules also prescribe certain matters that must be taken into account by the ICC Court in appointing an arbitrator, whereas the HKIAC Rules are less prescriptive in this regard. The ICC additionally has published a 'Note to National Committees and Groups of the ICC on the Proposal of Arbitrators' that sets out the ICC's expectations of national committees that are called upon to provide nominations for appointment.[63] To promote transparency, as of 1 January 2016, the ICC publishes the following information: (i) the names of the arbitrators, (ii) their nationality, (iii) their role within a tribunal, (iv) the method of their appointment, and (v) whether the arbitration is pending or closed.[64]

4.4.3.3   Determination Phase

The secretariats of the commercial arbitration institutions assist with day-to-day case management and administration and, in some cases, offer services that may extend beyond the purely administrative. The ICC Secretariat, for example, also assists tribunals by providing template documents and supervising a sealed offer process. Additionally, the ICC scrutinises awards,[65] a three-stage process in which a secretariat member will first review the award, followed by the Secretary General, and the Deputy Secretary General or the Managing Counsel, before the award is submitted to the ICC Court. The ICC's scrutiny process is unique, and

---

[61] SCC Rules, Article 17(7).
[62] 'SCC Policy – Appointment of Arbitrators', available at www.sccinstitute.com/media/ 220131/scc-policy-appointment-of-arbitrators-2017.pdf (last accessed 26 February 2018).
[63] Available at https://iccwbo.org/dispute-resolution-services/arbitration/practice-notes-forms-checklists/ (last accessed 26 February 2018).
[64] Published information available at https://iccwbo.org/dispute-resolution-services/ arbitration/icc-arbitral-tribunals/ (last accessed 26 February 2018).
[65] See Article 33 of the ICC Rules ('[b]efore signing any award, the arbitral tribunal shall submit it in draft form to the Court. The Court may lay down modifications as to the form of the award and, without affecting the arbitral tribunal's liberty of decision, may also draw its attention to points of substance. No award shall be rendered by the arbitral tribunal until it has been approved by the Court as to its form.').

can and frequently does result in amendments to awards in both form and substance.[66]

The commercial arbitration institutions' board, committee or court, as the case may be, can impact the determination phase in other ways. All of these bodies have roles to play in making decisions that impact proceedings, specifically with respect to challenges to arbitrators and other matters such as consolidation of proceedings, costs of the arbitration and expedited proceedings. The amount of regulation and transparency around those decisions varies. Regarding the ICC, for example, two commentators have highlighted the 'unseen' nature of the ICC Court, noting:

> most of the decisions incumbent upon the arbitral institution under the ICC Rules are to be taken by the Court itself, as distinguished from its administrative staff. Parties and arbitrators in ICC cases, however, may only be dimly aware of this because they will not normally have any direct contact with the Court during the course of an ICC arbitration.[67]

However, as the discussion below (which focuses on challenges for the sake of brevity) shows, the ICC Rules are relatively explicit on the framework for ICC Court decisions (that is, there is regulatory certainty), and there is potential for, or a movement towards, transparency. The same is true for other institutions, as also discussed below.

The HKIAC's Proceedings Committee is mandated to determine challenges to arbitrators and all other matters under the HKIAC Rules that do not relate to appointments. The HKIAC rules provide a limited decision-making framework for the determination of challenge decisions by specifying grounds for challenge,[68] but this is supplemented by a practice note that clarifies challenge proceedings for parties. Similarly, the ICC Court determines challenges, and although the ICC Rules do not specify grounds in the way that the HKIAC Rules do, guidance issued by the ICC provides that the Court may, upon a party's request, communicate

---

[66] Herman Verbist, Erik Schäfer and Christophe Imhoos, *ICC Arbitration in Practice*, 2nd edn (Kluwer Law International, 2015), p. 182; Yves Derains and Eric A. Schwartz, *Guide to the ICC Rules of Arbitration*, 2nd edn (Kluwer Law International, 2005), pp. 313–314 (noting that in 2004 nearly two-thirds of all awards scrutinised were returned with comments).

[67] Derains and Schwartz, *Guide to the ICC Rules of Arbitration*, p.13.

[68] HKIAC Rules, Article 11.5 ('justifiable doubts as to the arbitrator's impartiality or independence, or if the arbitrator does not possess qualifications agreed by the parties, or if the arbitrator becomes de jure or de facto unable to perform his or her functions or for other reasons fails to act without undue delay').

reasons for a challenge decision to the parties (albeit that the Court may refuse the request).[69] The SCC Board determines challenges, and grounds for challenge are specified in the SCC Rules ('circumstances exist that give rise to justifiable doubts as to the arbitrator's impartiality or independence or if the arbitrator does not possess the qualifications agreed by the parties').[70] The LCIA Court determines challenges on specified grounds, and significantly from the perspective of transparency, has been publishing anonymised challenge decisions since 2010.[71]

Perhaps one of the most important, or at least the most topical, unseen actors in recent times are tribunal secretaries. The commercial arbitration institutions have been the vanguard in regulating the activities of tribunal secretaries.[72] These unseen actors have been controversial for some time, with commentators voicing concerns for several years that they may be 'fourth arbitrators'[73] and inappropriately doing work that a tribunal should be doing itself. Tribunal secretaries may or may not be part of the commercial arbitration institution that is administering an arbitration, but the institutions have taken on the role of regulating them regardless, through their rules or through the issuance of guidance, and in the case of HKIAC, through training. In this approach, the commercial arbitration institutions differ from ICSID and the PCA. This may be explicable by the different nature of these institutions. ICSID and the PCA are established under multilateral treaties, for example, which would tend to make policy and rule changes more difficult to achieve.

---

[69] Cf. Karel Daele, *Challenge and Disqualification of Arbitrators in International Arbitration* (Kluwer Law International, 2012), p. 200, noting that the lack of publication of ICC challenge decisions gives rise to criticism that there is insufficient transparency.

[70] SCC Rules, Article 19(1).

[71] The LCIA's challenge database is available at www.lcia.org/challenge-decision-database.aspx (last accessed 26 February 2018).

[72] UNCITRAL has also contributed, issuing a statement on the use of tribunal secretaries in its 'Notes on Organizing Arbitral Proceedings' in 1996 (these notes have been subsequently updated, most recently in 2016 (available at www.uncitral.org/pdf/english/texts/arbitration/arb-notes/arb-notes-e.pdf (last accessed 10 August 2018). The International Council for Commercial Arbitration has also made a significant contribution through the work of its Young ICCA group, which produced the 'Young ICCA Guide on Arbitral Secretaries' in 2014 (available at www.arbitration-icca.org/media/3/14235574857310/aa_arbitral_sec_guide_composite_10_feb_2015.pdf (last accessed 26 February 2018)).

[73] See, e.g., Michael Polkinghorne and Charles Rosenberg, 'The Role of the Tribunal Secretary in International Arbitration: A Call for a Uniform Standard' (2014) 8 *Dispute Resolution International* 2; Constantine Partasides, 'The Fourth Arbitrator? The Role of Secretaries to Tribunals in International Arbitration' (2002) 18 *Arbitration International* 2.

All of the commercial arbitration institutions require that tribunal secretaries maintain standards of impartiality and independence, and that
they are adequately supervised and directed by the arbitral tribunal. They
adopt various formulations for payment of tribunal secretaries. The discussion below focuses on the most controversial aspect of these unseen
actors: defining the scope of their duties.

The ICC first issued guidance on the use of secretaries in 1995, and
that guidance was updated in a 'Note on the Appointment, Duties
and Remuneration of Administrative Secretaries' in 2012.[74] The ICC's
guidance has now been further updated and included in the ICC's 'Note
to Parties and Arbitral Tribunals on the Conduct of the Arbitration'.[75] The
ICC's guidance prohibits delegation of any decision-making duties to a
tribunal secretary, and enumerates the administrative tasks that a secretary can undertake, as well as 'conducting legal or similar research' and
'proofreading and checking citations, dates and cross-references in procedural orders and awards as well as correcting typographical, grammatical
or calculation errors'.

Until 2017, the LCIA had minimal guidance on the use of tribunal
secretaries. This changed with amendments to the LCIA Notes for
Arbitrators,[76] which clarified several aspects of the use of tribunal secretaries in LCIA arbitrations. As with the ICC guidance, there is an absolute
prohibition on the delegation of decision-making functions. There is also
a heavy emphasis on consent of the parties. The LCIA guidance takes a
flexible approach to the types of task a tribunal secretary can carry out,
recognising that this might include quite substantive work such as preparing draft awards, so long as the parties have been informed of the tasks
that the secretary may carry out.

The HKIAC promulgated guidelines on the use of tribunal secretaries
in 2014.[77] The guidelines stress that decision-making functions cannot
be delegated, and provide a relatively expansive list of potential duties

[74] Polkinghorne and Rosenberg, 'The Role of the Tribunal Secretary in International
Arbitration: A Call for a Uniform Standard', 111.
[75] Available at https://iccwbo.org/publication/note-parties-arbitral-tribunals-conduct-
arbitration (last accessed 26 February 2018).
[76] See 'LCIA Implements Changes to Tribunal Secretary Processes' (26 October 2017),
available at www.lcia.org//News/lcia-implements-changes-to-tribunal-secretary-
processes.aspx (last accessed 26 February 2018).
[77] 'Guidelines on the Use of a Secretary to the Arbitral Tribunal', available at www.hkiac.org/
sites/default/files/ck_filebrowser/PDF/arbitration/6ai_HKIAC_Guidelines_on_Use_of_
Secretary_to_Arbitral_Tribunal.pdf (last accessed 26 February 2018).

that includes tasks such as drafting 'non-substantive' parts of awards and other decisions or orders. Unlike the ICC and LCIA, which contemplate that a tribunal secretary *will not* be drawn from their secretariats, the HKIAC makes members of its secretariat available to act as secretaries. Additionally, the HKIAC runs a pioneering training programme for aspiring tribunal secretaries that involves assessment. Those who successfully complete the course have their names published and form a pool of candidates for arbitrators to draw upon. The HKIAC's approach aligns with the Queen Mary/White & Case 2015 International Arbitration Survey results, in which 72 per cent of respondents said they believed that arbitral institutions should offer the services of tribunal secretaries.[78]

Revisions to the SCC Rules in 2017 included provisions on the appointment of tribunal secretaries (an 'Administrative Secretary' in the terminology of the SCC Rules). These provisions replaced limited guidance that was issued in 2014 in the SCC's 'Arbitrator's Guidelines'.[79] The 2014 guidance did not address the proper role of the secretary. The 2017 Rules do address the role of the secretary, but are still minimalistic compared with the approaches outlined above, specifying only that '[t]he Arbitral Tribunal shall consult the parties regarding the tasks of the administrative secretary' and the standard prohibition on delegating decision-making.[80]

4.5   Conclusions

This chapter has focused on how international arbitral institutions, such as the PCA, the ICSID, the LCIA, the HKIAC, the SCC and the ICC's International Court of Arbitration, regulate the behaviour of unseen actors, or provide transparency with regard to their actions. No argument has been made as to whether enhanced regulation or transparency is a panacea for legitimacy, but it is recognised that it is at least a possibility.

---

[78] '2015 International Arbitration Survey: Improvements and Innovations in International Arbitration,' available at www.whitecase.com/sites/whitecase/files/files/download/publications/qmul-international-arbitration-survey-2015_0.pdf (last accessed 26 February 2018).

[79] Available at http://sccinstitute.com/media/45948/scc_guidelines_english.pdf (last accessed 26 February 2018).

[80] SCC Rules, Article 24(2).

The World Trade Organization

DANIEL ARI BAKER AND GABRIELLE MARCEAU[1]

5.1 Introduction

Lawyers are essential players in the multilateral trading system.[2] In this chapter, we focus on one particular type of lawyer whose presence in the system has become increasingly prominent over the last sixty years – lawyers working in and for the Secretariats of the General Agreement on Tariffs and Trade (GATT) and the World Trade Organization (WTO). Secretariat lawyers, as we call them in this chapter, are active at all levels and across a wide range of activities bearing on the smooth and efficient operation of the international trading system. Although, as we explain in more detail below, they have no decision-making authority, they nevertheless play an important role in helping to ensure the successful functioning of the complex legal architecture established in the WTO Agreement. Their place in the system is therefore worthy of close consideration.

Although the story of the 'legalisation' of international trade relations since the establishment of the WTO in 1994 is well known, there is still a significant lack of understanding about the role of Secretariat lawyers in

---

[1] The views expressed in this chapter are personal, and neither represent nor bind the WTO, its Members, or the WTO or Appellate Body Secretariats. Thanks to Maria J. Pereyra and Kerry Allbeury for comments on an earlier draft.

[2] This chapter was written in late 2017 and early 2018, and describes the role of the WTO Secretariat in dispute settlement and other legal activities up until that time. Subsequent developments at the WTO, including with respect to the dispute settlement system, have shed light on concerns that some Members have with the current functioning of the system. Members are currently engaged in discussions about possible reforms and improvements to the dispute settlement system. The precise role and functions of the Secretariat in dispute settlement and other activities may be expected to evolve in the light of any decisions taken by the Members as a result of these discussions. Such possibility is, however, still speculative and the time this book goes to print, and is therefore beyond the scope of our discussion in this chapter.

the multilateral trading system today, especially outside the international trade law community. In this contribution, we aim to describe the work of Secretariat lawyers, and to show how their work fits into and supports the broader operation of the WTO. Additionally, we aim to shed some light on how lawyers came to occupy the position they now hold. For it was not always so: particularly in the early years of the GATT, lawyers were looked on with suspicion and sometimes outright disdain; and although they have always had a presence in the administrative apparatus of international trade, their emergence from 'behind the scenes' into the limelight coincides with the evolution of the multilateral trading system from an ad hoc arrangement into a sophisticated regulatory system administered by an international organization. Thus, one argument we make in this chapter is that if lawyers were 'hidden' in the early years of the GATT, this is certainly not true of lawyers in the WTO Secretariat.

The remainder of this chapter is divided in two parts. First, we provide a historical overview of the development of the role of lawyers in the trading system. We suggest that this history embodies a movement from 'hiddenness' to publicity and prominence. Second, we detail the work of Secretariat lawyers in the WTO today. Our goal is not only to describe the work of Secretariat lawyers for readers who may be less familiar with the WTO system, but also to suggest that Secretariat lawyers, while certainly actors in the WTO, are not unseen.

5.2 Lawyers in the GATT: Out of the Darkness and into the Light

5.2.1 *The Beginning of the GATT and the First Lawyers*

Our tour of GATT history starts with the wartime negotiations on post-war economic reconstruction.[3] Ambivalence concerning the role of law and lawyers was already evident at that time. Many of the original negotiators were 'statesmen and diplomats' who preferred to see the project of building a multilateral trading system as essentially political and economic, rather than legal. Indeed, during UK–US negotiations on future economic institutions,[4] the eminent economist and UK negotiator John Maynard Keynes remarked, '[i]sn't our scheme intended to

---

[3] This section is based on G. Marceau, A. Porges and D. A. Baker, 'Introduction and Overview' in G. Marceau (ed.), *A History of Law and Lawyers in the GATT/WTO* (Cambridge University Press, 2015), p. 1.

[4] D.A. Irwin, P.C. Mavroidis and A.O. Sykes, *The Genesis of the GATT* (Cambridge University Press, 2009), pp. 65 et seq.

get things done, whereas yours [the United States'] will merely provide a living for a large number of lawyers?'[5]

As GATT was never intended to be an international organisation, it had almost no institutional provisions. A very small number of persons were sent to the GATT 'on loan' from the Interim Commission for the International Trade Organization (ICITO), thereby creating the nucleus of what would become the GATT Secretariat.[6] Lawyers always had a presence in this Secretariat. The first two leaders of the Secretariat, Eric Wyndham White and his successor Olivier Long, were both lawyers by training. Wyndham White had only a handful of staff working directly under him, including a legal adviser, Alan Renouf, who was seconded from the United Nations in 1948.[7] Renouf was an Australian who had been closely involved in the establishment of the United Nations. He worked as a member of the preparatory commission and as Australia's delegate before taking up the post of Legal Adviser.

At this early stage, lawyers were not involved in the settlement of disputes, at least not as lawyers, even though the first steps towards third-party adjudication of trade disputes began almost from the inception of the GATT, with disputes referred to the chairperson of the contracting parties for a ruling. These requests for a ruling were dealt with at the session (periodic gatherings of the GATT membership) at which they were raised. By the time the third case was submitted to the chairperson of the contracting parties for a ruling in 1949, the proceedings included a more extensive discussion between the disputants and other contracting parties. However, there was no formalised role for lawyers or legal advice, and disputes were ultimately resolved by vote for or against the claim.

Other Secretariat activities also involved the application of law. Meetings needed to be organised and run, credentials needed to be checked, the GATT was amended and decisions were drafted. All of these activities had important legal aspects. It is likely, although we have no documentation to definitively establish this, that persons with some legal background or experience would have been involved in these tasks. There was, of course, no dedicated legal office in these early years. Thus, if as is likely, persons

---

[5] R. Skidelsky, *John Maynard Keynes: Fighting for Britain, 1937–1946* (Macmillan, 2000), p. 416.

[6] The Secretariat of the GATT was legally the ICITO Secretariat from 1948 until 1 January 1995 with the entry into force of the WTO Secretariat.

[7] Interim Commission for the International Trade Organization, Executive Committee, 'Report of the Executive Committee of the ICITO on the Work of the Secretariat' (ICITO/EC.2/5, 13 July 1948), p. 1.

with legal training were involved in these activities, they were involved discreetly, taking a back seat to political and diplomatic negotiation.

5.2.2   Wyndham White and the First Panels for Resolving Disputes

At the seventh session of the contracting parties (1952), and in response to growing dissatisfaction with the working party approach to resolving disputes (which involved representatives from several contracting parties, including the disputing parties, trying to resolve disputes diplomatically),[8] a 'Panel on Complaints' was established for the first time. The panel was a kind of quasi-standing body, whose six members and chair were empowered to hear all complaints arising during the session. Though not expressed in terms of the rule of law, the purpose of this panel was clearly to strengthen the objectivity, impartiality and rules-based nature of the dispute settlement process (while still maintaining the overall flexibility and informality of diplomatic settlement). The move to ad hoc panels was a significant step towards legalisation in the GATT. It was, however, still too early for the GATT to establish a division for legal affairs or hire anyone with the title of legal officer. Nonetheless, the Secretariat was involved in assisting the drafting of panel reports and advising panels on issues of fact, law and precedent.[9]

The Secretariat also continued its non-dispute-related legal work. The creation of the European Economic Community (EEC) in the late 1950s, and the uncertainty over whether the Treaty of Rome arrangements were GATT-consistent, gave rise to important legal questions and required careful consideration of the legal implications of this new entity for the multilateral trading system. The GATT Basic Instruments and Selected Documents (BISD), an annual compilation of important GATT documents prepared by the Secretariat, suggests the type of legal work the Secretariat performed during this period: for instance, drafting working procedures for meetings of GATT bodies;[10] preparing accession protocols;[11] the publication of the Analytical Index,

---

[8] General Agreement on Tariffs and Trade, 'Dispute Settlement in International Economic Agreements: Factual Study by the Secretariat' (MTN/SG/W/8, 6 April 1976), p. 3.

[9] Y. Xu and P. Weller, *The Governance of World Trade: International Civil Servants and the GATT/WTO* (Edward Elgar, 2004), p. 206.

[10] See e.g. General Agreement on Tariffs and Trade, 'Amendment to the Rules of Procedure for Sessions of the Contracting Parties', BISD 2S/7.

[11] See e.g. General Agreement on Tariffs and Trade, 'Protocol of Terms of Accession of Japan to the General Agreement on Tariffs and Trade', BISD 4S/7.

depositary services for amendments to the GATT; stewardship of the legal record of tariff concessions and tariff schedules in negotiating rounds or tariff renegotiations; and the compilation and monitoring of all modifications and amendments to the GATT provisions. By definition, these tasks required some legal expertise. And yet, it remained the case that lawyers were not so called in the Secretariat. There was no legal division, and lawyers, when hired, were hired in other capacities, even if they were often called upon to complete tasks involving the use of legal skills. Thus, while an increasing portion of GATT Secretariat work was legal or at least law-related, lawyers as such had no prominence on the scene, and carried out their work in the background.

5.2.3   The First 'Legal Officer' Positions

The 1960–1961 report to the contracting parties by a special group established to examine proposals relating to the organisation of the GATT proposed the creation of the position of a legal officer to assist the Executive Office.[12] In response to this report, and perhaps in light of the increasing complexity of GATT obligations, Wyndham White in 1961 hired a US lawyer, Noel Torres.[13] Torres' work was not in dispute settlement but embraced a wider range of legal work. It included checking accreditations, dealing with waivers and accessions and included some archival work. Additionally, Torres was involved in all sorts of legal research. Among other projects, he spent time researching the status of Berlin in international law and considering the territorial application of the GATT in that context.

In 1966, the organisation determined that it needed to recruit a junior officer in the Conference Secretariat Division to undertake legal research. In fact, there had always been an employee in the Secretariat to do 'housekeeping legal matters', including research as well as performing archival functions and looking after ratifications. But this post had never before been described as requiring 'legal' work (despite the obviously legal nature of many of the tasks required). In 1966 the GATT advertised for an 'assistant economic affairs officer'. The words

---

[12] General Agreement on Tariffs and Trade, 'Proposals on GATT Organization' (L/1216, 31 May 1960), p. 4.

[13] Torres' exact title was 'Economic Affairs Officer (Legal): General Agreement on Tariffs and Trade, Allocation of Staff' (Administrative Memorandum 158/GATT Office Circular 106, 10 April 1961) (copy on file with authors).

'legal officer' still did not appear, reflecting the continued suspicion and, in some cases, hostility still faced by lawyers and legalism. Nevertheless, the job description for the position of assistant economic affairs officer makes it quite plain that the candidate was intended to undertake at least some legal work.

5.2.4   Reconciling Pragmatism and the Rule of Law

Olivier Long became Director-General of the GATT in 1969.[14] Long had a pragmatic approach to the role and power of law in the multilateral trading system. He recognised the importance of rules, but, also emphasised the limitations of formal legality in a system that, to use a phrase he himself favoured, was situated 'precisely in [a] permanent association of law and interests'.[15] Long considered that the multilateral trading system was founded, functioned and evolved on the basis of legal rules, but acknowledged that political pressures affected the character and the operation of the GATT. In his opinion, this was to some extent inevitable 'in any attempt to regulate within a legal framework something as dynamic and fluctuating as world trade'.[16]

There were other people with legal backgrounds in the Secretariat at the time, including Åke Lindén, later to become Director of the GATT Office of Legal Affairs in 1983, but they too were never given the title of 'lawyer', although they were often involved in a range of legal tasks, including, on some occasions, arbitrating trade disputes between contracting parties.

Change was in the air, however, as the 1970s drew to a close. A number of important developments in the decade's final years crystallised a burgeoning recognition of the need for legal expertise. In the first place, the 1970s witnessed the increasing involvement of Secretariat staff in the work of dispute settlement panels. Generally, a single staff member from the Secretariat division with expertise in the subject of the dispute would assist a panel of three members. During the 1970s, some thirteen panel reports and three working party reports were circulated and adopted by the Council of Representatives. Inevitably, this increase in disputes put pressure on the Secretariat staff servicing the panels or working parties. The more disputes there were, the more Secretariat staff were required to assist

---

[14] He served in this capacity until 1980.
[15] O. Long, *Law and Its Limitations in the GATT Multilateral Trading System* (Martinus Nijhoff Publishers, 1985), p. 8.
[16] Ibid., p. 7.

panels. Moreover, the increasing complexity of trade disputes made it more and more difficult for non-lawyers to provide quality legal advice to panels. While the Secretariat was fully able to provide advice to panels on technical trade topics, the contracting parties were increasingly less satisfied with the manner in which panels handled difficult, technical, and cross-cutting legal issues. Delegations criticised the legal consistency and quality of a number of reports written in this period – including the tax legislation cases.[17] The GATT membership (and in particular the United States) became increasingly resistant and even opposed to decisions obviously based on politics rather than law or that included mistakes in legal interpretation. Amy Porges even writes that 'LAD [Legal Affairs Division] was born from failure: specially, a series of failed panel decisions in 1976–81'.[18]

5.2.5   The First Legal Office

In June 1980, Director-General Dunkel reorganised the Secretariat[19] in light of its new functions in servicing the new codes and their committees.[20] The creation of a specialised legal office became unavoidable in the aftermath of the 1981 *Spain – Soyabean Oil* panel.[21] The report was widely considered to be wrong about the law, and there was no consensus for its adoption in the GATT Council. This incident represented a tipping point. It led to a palpable shift in attitude, and convinced even the anti-legalists among delegations of the importance of lawyers employed and acting as lawyers within the Secretariat.

---

[17] GATT Panel Report, *United States Tax Legislation (US – DISC)*, L/4422, adopted 7 December 1981, BISD 23S, p. 98 (see also L/5271, BISD 28S, p. 114); GATT Panel Report, *Income Tax Practices Maintained by The Netherlands (Netherlands – Income Tax)*, L/4425, adopted 7 December 1981, BISD 23S, p. 137 (see also L/5271, BISD 28S, p. 114); GATT Panel Report, *Income Tax Practices Maintained by Belgium (Belgium – Income Tax)*, L/4424, adopted 7 December 1981, BISD 23S, p. 127 (see also L/5271, BISD 28S, p. 114); GATT Panel Report, *Income Tax Practices Maintained by France (France – Income Tax)*, L/4423 adopted 7 December 1981, BISD 23S, p. 114 (see also L/5271, BISD 28S, p. 114.

[18] See A. Porges, 'Legal Affairs Division and Law in the GATT and the Uruguay Round' in G. Marceau (ed.), *A History of Law and Lawyers in the GATT/WTO* (Cambridge University Press, 2015), p. 225.

[19] General Agreement on Tariffs and Trade, 'Changes in the Organizational Structure of the Secretariat' (GATT Office Circular No. 245, 3 June 1980) (copy on file with authors).

[20] These changes came into effect on 1 January 1981: personal email to Gabrielle Marceau from Jan-Eirik Sorensen, 8 May 2014.

[21] GATT Panel Report, *Spain – Measures Concerning Domestic Sale of Soyabean Oil – Recourse to Article XXIII:2 by the United States (Spain – Soyabean Oil)*, L/5142, 17 June 1981, unadopted.

In response to all of these issues, Director-General Dunkel decided to establish an Office of Legal Affairs on 1 January 1981 for a two-year trial period. Dunkel appointed the well-respected Assistant Director-General Hielke van Tuinen to direct the Office. Van Tuinen was a legally trained Dutch diplomat who had never practised law, but his GATT experience prepared him well to handle this task. Van Tuinen was transferred to the Conference Division in 1969, where he handled some distinctly legal matters. He checked accreditations, organised and ran GATT meetings, was responsible for anything dealing with signatures, including accessions and legal instruments, and organised and supervised all voting, including on waivers and accessions. Van Tuinen was also centrally involved in preparing the entry into force of Part IV of the GATT.

When Dunkel created the Office of Legal Affairs, he only changed van Tuinen's title and transferred his assistant Geraldine Murphy from Conference Affairs, providing him with no other staff. Van Tuinen was never referred to as the Head of the Office of Legal Affairs and moreover was never requested to do legal work per se, but simply dealt with legal issues as they arose. He never advised panels, although he did provide advice to individual contracting parties on occasion. The formal creation of a 'Legal Affairs Office' in early 1981 was the first signal that an important shift towards a strengthened rule of law was occurring in the organisation and in the multilateral trading system. Dunkel wanted to start small and gauge the reaction to having an official Legal Office within the Secretariat.

The Office of Legal Affairs reported directly to the Director-General. As an 'office',[22] it did not have a priori responsibility or expertise in any one particular issue, but was available for legal advice on general and cross-cutting issues. Panels continued to be serviced primarily by staff from the division with expertise on the subject matter of the dispute. On occasion, panels were assisted by staff from more than one division.

The early years of the Legal Office were not easy. The simple act of establishing a Legal Office did not engender an immediate change in anti-legalist attitudes. It may be that, while lawyers and legal advice were recognised as essential, the need for a specialised legal office, as opposed to simply having lawyers within the Secretariat's different operational divisions, was not universally acknowledged. At any rate, while the contracting parties acquiesced to the idea of a GATT Secretariat legal

---

[22] This would correspond in today's WTO Secretariat to a 'Section'. In 1983, the Office of Legal Affairs was briefly attached to the Session and Council Affairs Division.

office, they were still not ready in the early 1980s to see a lawyer appointed head of the legal division. After heading the Office of Legal Affairs for two years, van Tuinen became Head of the Department of Conference Affairs and Administration in 1983, retiring at the end of May that year. Dunkel appointed Åke Lindén as the new director of the Office of Legal Affairs, who had experience in law practice but had spent his career as a diplomat and in the Secretariat. Lindén's track record in trade policy and as director of the Tariff Division, and his even temperament in addition to his legal credentials, made him the ideal man for the job.

The gradually growing role of the Office of Legal Affairs in the GATT's day-to-day operations, and its increased assertiveness regarding involvement in dispute settlement panels, led to friction with other divisions in the Secretariat. Ernst-Ulrich Petersmann was hired in 1981 to work as a legal assistant to the Conference Affairs Division (headed by Stuart Robinson) and was transferred in 1983 to the Office of Legal Affairs. Frieder Roessler, who had arrived at the GATT in 1973,[23] was also transferred to the Office of Legal Affairs from the Technical and Other Barriers to Trade Division in the same year.[24] Both have recalled some hostility towards the Office and towards their own value as specialist legal staff. Petersmann has recalled being told by colleagues upon his arrival at the Conference Affairs Division that the GATT should never have a Legal Office and that a legal officer should never participate in GATT dispute settlement proceedings lest such participation led to undue legalisation of pragmatic GATT negotiations. He was advised to carry out his legal duties following the example of a 'U boat … with low visibility', and to focus as much as possible on 'practical work'.

5.2.6   *The Growing Importance of the Legal 'Office': Towards a Formal Legal Affairs 'Division'*

Thus, even as the Legal Office became an accepted part of the Secretariat landscape, its existence did not mean that other Secretariat divisions immediately recognised the utility of specialist legal advice. External

---

[23] Roessler joined the GATT Secretariat as an Economic Affairs Officer on 29 October 1973.
[24] General Agreement on Tariffs and Trade, 'Staff Movements – Professional and Higher Categories' (Administrative Memorandum No. 597, 18 April 1983) (copy on file with authors); General Agreement on Tariffs and Trade, 'Staff Movements – Professional and Higher Categories' (Administrative Memorandum No. 611, 17 January 1984) (copy on file with authors).

forces intervened again, however, in the form of a declaration on dispute settlement adopted at the GATT Ministerial Meeting of November 1982.[25] The declaration's ten paragraphs addressed various issues affecting the panel process, and expressed 'a rather strong political commitment to support effective dispute settlement'.[26] One of its paragraphs stated that the Secretariat 'has the responsibility of assisting the panel, especially on the legal, historical and procedural aspects of the matters dealt with'.[27] While the 1979 Tokyo Round Understanding had recognised that panels 'may seek advice or assistance from the secretariat in its capacity as guardian of the General Agreement, especially on historical or procedural aspects',[28] the 1982 declaration recognised explicitly for the first time that the Secretariat had a duty to assist panels, and that the Secretariat's assistance would include legal advice.

From 1984 onwards, Roessler and Petersmann began to participate in more and more GATT panel proceedings. Moreover, the Office of Legal Affairs quickly assumed responsibility for an increasing number of non-dispute-related legal tasks. Most of these involved preparing documents and books on legal topics, including revised editions of the Analytical Index and a treaty register, called the 'GATT – Status of Legal Instruments', which recorded the status and acceptances of past GATT amendments, protocols, GATT-related agreements and the codes. The Office also handled various institutional and house-keeping legal matters, including the GATT's depositary functions and advising on accessions in conjunction with the Development Division. Thus, by the end of the 1980s, the work of the Legal Affairs Office was spread across a wide range of areas.

In 1989, Roessler became director of the Office of Legal Affairs, which was renamed and raised in status to become the Legal Affairs Division (LAD). This decision by the Secretariat management made LAD formally equal with the other operational divisions, and expanded LAD's mandate to explicitly include '[m]atters concerning settlement of disputes'.[29] At around this time, a separate division – called the Rules Division – was

---

[25] Ministerial Declaration, section on 'Dispute Settlement Procedures', BISD 28S/13 (29 November 1982).

[26] R. E. Hudec, *Enforcing International Trade Law* (Salem, MA: Butterworth Legal Publishers, 1993), p. 166.

[27] Ministerial Declaration, 'Dispute Settlement Procedures', para. (iv).

[28] 1979 Understanding, Annex, para. 6(iv).

[29] General Agreement on Tariffs and Trade, 'Analytical Directory' (internal document, July 1989) (copy on file with authors), 3. The Division's mandate is also stated to include 'Preparation of Analytical Index. Matters Relating to the Status of China'.

also established to assist in negotiations on trade remedies and to advise dispute settlement panels hearing disputes concerning anti-dumping, subsidies and safeguards.[30]

Thus, by the time the Uruguay Round was completed and the WTO was established, lawyers had become involved in a range of areas, from dispute settlement to negotiations and treaty drafting. From unseen actors unable to call themselves lawyers, Secretariat lawyers had become accepted as necessary technocrats and advisers. Their relevance was further cemented in the WTO, with the adoption of new, highly complex legal agreements and the establishment of a formal, quasi-judicial dispute settlement system. The role of lawyers in the WTO is explored in the next section of this chapter.

5.3   Lawyers in the WTO Secretariat

If in the GATT era legal advisers tended to take a 'back seat to diplomats', as Valerie Hughes, former Director of the World Trade Organization's Legal Affairs Division has suggested,[31] the establishment in 1995 of the WTO marked a profound shift in the role, if not always the perception, of lawyers in the day-to-day functioning of the multilateral trading system. From their obscure offices, lawyers were catapulted into the limelight; over the last twenty years they have become increasingly prominent in both the operation of the WTO system and its diffusion and representation to the wider community beyond the walls of the Centre William Rappard, the WTO's home on the banks of Lake Geneva. In foreign and trade offices around the world, in law faculties and law firms, one finds individuals who have worked, in one capacity or another, as legal officers to the Organization. And inside the WTO, too, the number of lawyers employed on both short- and fixed-term contracts has increased significantly, especially in the second decade of the WTO's existence. Indeed, when Gabrielle Marceau, one of the co-authors of this chapter, began working with the WTO LAD in 1994, she was one of only four lawyers. Today, there are more than seventy lawyers practising as such in the WTO, spread across four separate legal divisions. This number does

[30]   See G. Marceau and D. A. Baker, 'A Short History of the Rules Division' in G. Marceau (ed.), *A History of Law and Lawyers in the GATT/WTO* (Cambridge University Press, 2015).
[31]   V. Hughes, 'The Role of Legal Advisers in the World Trade Organization' in A. Zidar and J. Gauci (eds.), *Legal Advisers in International Law* (Brill, 2017), p. 237.

not include the significant number of persons with legal qualifications working in non-legal divisions of the WTO Secretariat.

The four legal divisions mentioned above are: the Legal Counsel to the Administration; LAD; the Rules Division; and the Appellate Body Secretariat. Administratively and financially the Appellate Body is independent of the WTO Secretariat, but it is housed in the same building and its staff engages in much the same kind of work as staff in LAD and the Rules Division. We therefore consider it together with those divisions in this chapter. Although discussion of the work of these four divisions forms the core of the rest of this chapter, we will also mention the legal work carried out by lawyers in other non-legal divisions across the Secretariat.

The activities that constitute the quotidian work of legal staff in the WTO can be divided into five broad areas: first, dispute settlement; second, technical and committee-related work; third, institutional legal matters; fourth, general international law matters; and finally, training and outreach. We will examine each of these areas in the remainder of this chapter. Our goal is to describe the day-to-day work of lawyers in the WTO and to suggest that, far from being invisible, Secretariat lawyers are both involved and seen to be involved in a wide range of work, though always of course within the boundaries established by the WTO agreements.

5.3.1   Dispute Settlement

Perhaps the major role of Secretariat lawyers, and certainly the role for which they are most well known in the international legal community, is in the field of dispute settlement. Secretariat lawyers are closely involved in all stages of the dispute settlement process, and provide important services to WTO adjudicators, disputing parties and the WTO membership more generally.

Although, as will be clear from what follows, Secretariat lawyers are closely involved in the dispute settlement process, it must be clear from the outset that they have no adjudicative role. Decisions are made by the relevant adjudicators (panels in case of first instance proceedings, and the Appellate Body on appeal). Secretariat lawyers do, however, work closely with WTO adjudicators, providing them with legal, administrative and secretarial support.

The legal basis for Secretariat involvement in dispute settlement proceedings is Article 27 of the Understanding on Rules and Procedures Governing the Settlement of Disputes (hereafter 'DSU'), which is the treaty that established and regulates the dispute settlement process. According to Article 27.1:

> The Secretariat shall have the responsibility of assisting panels, especially on the legal, historical and procedural aspects of the matters dealt with, and of providing secretarial and technical support.

Pursuant to this authorisation, lawyers, and in particular LAD, the Rules Division and the Appellate Body Secretariat, are involved with all stages of the dispute settlement process.

LAD and the Rules Division work with dispute settlement panels.[32] Panels are the 'first instance' of WTO dispute settlement. They are ad hoc bodies of three experts constituted for the specific and limited purpose of objectively assessing a dispute[33], and making factual and legal findings concerning its resolution. The Rules Division primarily assists panels working on 'trade remedies' cases – that is, cases involving issues under the Anti-Dumping Agreement, the Subsidies Agreement, the Safeguards Agreement and the Agreement on Trade-Related Investment Measures. LAD assists panels working on cases under the remaining WTO agreements. The reasons for the existence of two distinct divisions assisting panel work are historical rather than strategic,[34] and some commentators[35] have called for the two divisions to be merged. Members, so far, however, have seen no need to merge the Divisions. Indeed, it is reasonable to suppose that the division of work in this way has allowed for specialisation and the development of technical expertise.

Lawyers in LAD and the Rules Division begin working as soon as a panel is established by the Dispute Settlement Body (DSB): they work closely with the disputing parties to assist them in selecting the members of their panel. Although the disputing WTO Members have the right to choose the three persons that will comprise the panel, in practice this happens only occasionally due to lack of agreement between the

---

[32] These divisions also work with arbitrators in certain circumstances, such as the setting of the permissible amount of retaliation. Although the role of Secretariat lawyers assisting arbitrators is similar to that of lawyers assisting panels, for reasons of space we are unable to deal specifically with arbitrations in this chapter.

[33] Article 11 of the DSU.

[34] See G. Marceau and D. A. Baker, 'A Short History of the Rules Division' in G. Marceau (ed.), *A History of Law and Lawyers in the GATT/WTO* (Cambridge University Press, 2015), especially at p. 113.

[35] P. J. Kuijper, 'From Seattle to Doha' in G. Marceau (ed.), *A History of Law and Lawyers in the GATT/WTO* (Cambridge University Press, 2015), p. 387.

disputing parties. The usual procedure is that lawyers from the relevant legal division propose qualified candidates based on the disputing Members' requirements and the particulars of the dispute. The disputing Members are not obliged to accept the Secretariat's proposals, but if they cannot agree on composition the Director-General of the WTO will decide the composition following a request by one of the parties, more often than not the complainant, usually on the basis of the Secretariat's recommendations.

Once a panel is composed, a team of lawyers from the relevant divisions (usually one senior lawyer and one or two junior lawyers, depending on the complexity of the case) is assigned to assist the panel. Because panellists are appointed ad hoc and often have full-time jobs in government or the private sector, it is important to ensure that their functions are supported by a Secretariat team. Lawyers from the relevant legal division are often joined by lawyers or technical experts from other divisions whose work relates to the subject matter of the dispute. Thus, the team assisting a panel hearing a dispute concerning a sanitary measure will often be joined by a staff member from the Agriculture and Commodities Division, while the team assisting a panel hearing a dispute on tariff treatment may be assisted by a staff member from the Market Access Division.

The Secretariat team's first task is to prepare a timetable and working procedures for the case. Once approved by the panel members, these drafts are sent to the parties for their feedback. An 'organisational meeting' is then arranged, at which the parties are given the opportunity to make oral comments on the proposed documents to the chairperson of the panel, who is present either in person or via video-conferencing technology.

On instructions from the panel, the Secretariat team then revises the timetable and working procedures in the light of any comments from the disputing parties. These documents are then adopted by the panel and becoming binding, subject to any revisions the panel may make after consulting with the parties.

Next, the disputing parties exchange written submissions. These are addressed to the panel, and panels are expected to read them carefully. The Secretariat team also reads the parties' written submissions, and then prepares an 'Issues Paper' for the panel, which is essentially a brief summarising the arguments, identifying and explaining the relevant legal principles, and setting out different approaches to the dispute that the panel could take. The Issues Paper is exploratory and advisory, and is meant to inform but certainly not bind the members of the panel. If requested by the panel, the Secretariat team may also work with the panel to draft questions to be sent to the parties for further argumentation or information.

The Secretariat team will then prepare for the panel's meeting with the disputing parties; most regular disputes have two meetings with the parties a few months apart. This process involves a number of administrative steps, including making travel arrangements for the panellists and organising interpretation (if necessary). The panel ordinarily spends the first day of the meeting week in closed session with the Secretariat team. During this meeting, the Secretariat team will provide an up-to-date briefing to the panellists, and the panellists are able to ask any questions or discuss any topics that may be relevant, including those raised in the Issues Paper. The panel will also decide which questions, if any, will be asked to the parties during the meeting.

The Secretariat team is present at the panel's meeting with the parties, but it usually takes the role of observer, with the Chair of the panel playing the key role in managing the proceedings. The Secretariat team will take comprehensive notes for the panel's record, and will also assist the panel if any legal issues arise during the hearing, for instance, concerning procedure or delegation composition.

Following the meetings with the parties and after deliberation, the panel informs the Secretariat team on how it intends to find on the issues before it and the reasoning behind those findings, At this stage, the Secretariat team may still be requested by the panel to carry out further research on particular legal or factual issues. The Secretariat team also supports the panel in drafting all or parts of the panel's decision pursuant to the panel's instructions.[36] It is important to emphasise that the Secretariat team's role in drafting the report is technical only, and the Secretariat team does not decide legal or factual issues (although panels may take into account the Issues Paper and other Secretariat research in arriving at their conclusions). The panel meets internally to discuss its draft decision (report) and finalise it. Once complete, the panel report is issued to the disputing parties, and will be adopted by the DSB, and thereby made legally binding, unless appealed by one or both disputing parties.

The work of the Appellate Body Secretariat has traditionally been very similar to that of LAD and the Rules Division, with certain differences stemming from the nature of appeal proceedings. For instance, appeals

---

[36] V. Hughes, 'The Role of Legal Advisers in the World Trade Organization' in A. Zidar and J. Gauci (eds.), *Legal Advisers in International Law* (Brill, 2017), p. 251.

have only one hearing, rather than the two usually held in panel proceedings. Additionally, in appeals proceedings all Appellate Body Members, and not only the three assigned to hear the dispute, will read the parties' submissions and engage in deliberations, though the ultimate decisions fall to be made solely by the three assigned to the case. But the role of Secretariat lawyers is essentially the same in the Appellate Body Secretariat as it is in LAD and the Rules Division: lawyers assist in making the necessary administrative arrangements, assist the adjudicators to understand the legal and factual questions at issue, and, after receiving instructions, supports the Division in drafting its report.[37]

In their dispute settlement work, Secretariat lawyers are constantly in contact both with panellists and with disputing parties. Their role, far from being hidden, is well known and transparent to WTO adjudicators, disputing parties, and the WTO Membership more broadly. At the same time, it must be emphasised that all Secretariat lawyers are subject to the same rules of conduct as are the adjudicators themselves.[38] This means that, although their role is well known, they are under an ongoing duty of confidentiality with respect to the submissions of the parties, the evidence on the record, and the deliberations of the panel or Appellate Body. This ensures that disputing parties' due process rights are protected over the course of a proceeding and beyond.

5.3.2   Technical and Committee-Related Work

Although dispute settlement is the primary job of most Secretariat lawyers working in legal divisions, very significant legal work goes on in other forums as well, most notably in the numerous committees established to oversee and administer the implementation of the WTO agreements. These committees undertake various activities and serve a range of purposes, from increasing transparency and providing a forum for the clarification and sometimes resolution of issues concerning particular trade-related measures or actions to the ongoing formal and informal discussions on amending and improving current treaty texts. Legally trained staff are frequently called upon to provide technical and

---

[37] D. Steger, 'The Founding of the Appellate Body' in G. Marceau (ed.), *A History of Law and Lawyers in the GATT/WTO* (Cambridge University Press, 2015), p. 447.
[38] The rules of conduct are contained in document WT/DS/RC/1 (11 December 1996).

substantive support to these committees in a range of ways and in a range of different contexts.

Most of the WTO committees are serviced by technical, non-legal divisions whose staff are experts in the subject(s) for which the committees have responsibility. Thus, the Market Access Division assists the Council for Trade in Goods, the Committee on Market Access, the Committee of Participants to the Information Technology Agreement, the Committee on Customs Valuation and Pre-Shipment Inspection, the Committee on Import Licensing Procedures and the Committee on Rules of Origin. Similarly, the Agriculture and Commodities Division is charged with servicing the Committee on Agriculture.[39] These divisions are sometimes distinguished from the more conventional 'legal offices' identified above, but in fact they often provide legal or quasi-legal services, such as preparing summaries of past cases on issues of interest to the committee. Moreover, a significant number of staff in these divisions have legal training, and many practised law prior to joining the Secretariat. This ensures that, when called upon to do so, they are able to advise committees taking into account the complex context of rules and practices within which the committees operate. Although the staff of these divisions do not participate substantively in committee meetings, their work contributes to the smooth functioning of the committees and the implementation of their work. Though they themselves may be somewhat 'hidden', often seated in committee meetings behind the chair-person, their facilitative work supports the successful operation of the committee system.

Of the Secretariat's four legal offices, only the Rules Division is routinely involved in committee work, although LAD is sometimes called upon to provide legal advice to the DSB. Thus, while LAD and the Appellate Body Secretariat are not formally responsible for assisting any committee,[40] the Rules Division is mandated to monitor and assist committees with responsibility in the areas of anti-dumping, subsidies and countervailing duties, safeguards, trade-related investment measures, state trading and civil aircraft. Such assistance ranges from the secretarial (for example, the

[39] See World Trade Organization, 'Divisions', www.wto.org/english/thewto_e/secre_e/div_e.htm (accessed 14 December 2017).
[40] Note, however, that as discussed below, LAD is responsible for assisting the so-called 'Special Session' of the DSB, which is a negotiating group working on revisions to the DSU. Moreover, although not responsible for servicing the DSB itself, LAD is responsible for processing DSB-related documentation, such as requests for the establishment of a panel.

preparation and publication of minutes of committee meetings) to the substantive (for example, preparing background papers about legal or factual issues on the committee's request).

Although not formally responsible for servicing any committees, LAD lawyers are sometimes asked to provide legal advice to committees, usually on the potential legal consequences of particular drafting proposals. Lawyers, usually from LAD, sometimes also assist in negotiation efforts among Members. For example, lawyers from LAD advise the Special Session of the DSB, which is an ongoing negotiating group comprising all WTO Members seeking to reform and improve the DSU. Although in this capacity LAD lawyers do not make substantive proposals for reform, they assist in the organization and facilitation of the negotiations, and may also assist the chairperson to present potential elements of convergence in the various issues under negotiation. They also work with the chairperson to produce annual reports of the negotiations' progress. These reports are made available to the public. The involvement of Secretariat lawyers thus contributes to the transparency of the ongoing negotiations.

5.3.3   Institutional Legal Matters

Like all large and complex organisations, whether public or private, the WTO deals daily with a range of institutional legal issues. Some, like employment relations, pension matters and procurement, are common to many if not all organisations, and the WTO's international status does not significantly affect their general commercial nature. Others, such as the privileges and immunities attaching to the WTO, its premises and its staff under the Headquarters Agreement between the WTO and Switzerland, are unique to the WTO's status as an intergovernmental organisation, and raise questions whose solutions demand knowledge not only of contract and employment law but also international administrative law, international organisations law and public international law. Prior to 2009, these kinds of legal issue were dealt with mainly by LAD staff, though apparently there was little work in this area before the late 1990s.[41] In that year, however, the new office of Counsel to the

---

[41] Y. Renouf, 'Legal Counsel to the Administration: A Legal Adviser Who Should Not Look Like One' in G. Marceau (ed.), *A History of Law and Lawyers in the GATT/WTO* (Cambridge University Press, 2015), p. 335.

Administration was established. This permanent office is now vested with responsibility for all legal matters not arising under one of the WTO covered agreements (and therefore not related to the multilateral trading system per se).

The establishment of the office of Counsel to the Administration should not suggest that legal staff in LAD and other divisions no longer play any role in the kinds of institutional matter that are dealt with by the Legal Counsel. To the contrary, legal staff throughout the WTO, and in LAD in particular, continue to play an important role, although in a somewhat less structured way. They may, for example, be called upon to contribute legal advice on particular issues, particularly those with public international law dimensions. Moreover, legally trained staff members from across the Organization are frequently represented on the WTO Staff Council, which, inter alia, assists and represents staff members in administrative and disciplinary proceedings, as well as on the Joint Appeals Board, which hears first instance complaints from staff members concerning employment matters and issues formal though non-binding opinions on the legal merits. Additionally, legally trained staff members often assist in procurement and pension-related activities, bringing their knowledge and skills to the administration and resolution of often complex contract and entitlements issues.

5.3.4   General International Law Matters

Although, as the preceding sections have suggested, the work of lawyers in the WTO Secretariat mostly relates to the substantive international trade law contained in the WTO-covered agreements, many lawyers also have occasion to work on public international law issues.

To some extent, public international law issues are inherent in the dispute settlement work that constitutes that primary activity of Secretariat lawyers. The Appellate Body famously recognised in its very first report that WTO law should not be read in 'clinical isolation' from the wider corpus of public international law[42], and it has become a vital part of general public international law.[43] Thus, lawyers advising panels and

---

[42] Appellate Body Report, *United States – Standards for Reformulated and Conventional Gasoline*, WT/DS2/AB/R, adopted 20 May 1996, DSR 1996:I, p. 3, at 16.

[43] J. Pauwelyn, 'Forward: The Panther Is a Cat! But Is it a Leopard or a Lion?' in G. Cook (ed.), *A Digest of WTO Jurisprudence on Public International Law Concepts and Principles* (Cambridge University Press, 2015), p. xiii.

the Appellate Body in specific disputes often have occasion to advise on public international law concepts such as attribution, sovereignty and due process. Moreover, and crucially, Article 3.2 of the DSU provides that the WTO-covered agreements must be interpreted 'in accordance with customary rules of public international law'. The Appellate Body has clarified that such rules include those codified in Articles 31 and 32 on the Vienna Convention on the Law of Treaties,[44] as well as others such as the principle of effective interpretation.[45] Lawyers advising panels and the Appellate Body are therefore constantly called upon to advise on the interpretation and application of the laws of treaty interpretation. This is especially significant at the panel level, since many panellists are not international lawyers and may thus be unfamiliar with the technicalities of treaty interpretation.

Lawyers in the WTO also engage with general international law outside the context of dispute settlement. One area where they do so is in the context of assisting the Director-General to exercise his function under Article XIV.3 of the Marrakesh Agreement Establishing the World Trade Organization. As Valerie Hughes has explained, this involves reviewing instruments of accession to the WTO, or instruments of acceptance of a protocol of amendment, to ensure that the instrument is in proper form, correctly expresses consent to be bound, and is signed by an individual with the necessary official credentials.[46] Lawyers are also often involved in checking credentials prior to important events, such as the biennial Ministerial Meetings. In this capacity, they are frequently in contact with delegations in Geneva as well as Member capitals.

5.3.5 Training and Outreach

Finally, Secretariat lawyers are often involved in training and outreach activities. Article 27 of the DSU charges the Secretariat with conducting 'special training courses for interested Members concerning these

[44] Appellate Body Report, *United States – Countervailing Duties on Certain Corrosion-Resistant Carbon Steel Flat Products from Germany*, WT/DS213/AB/R and Corr.1, adopted 19 December 2002, DSR 2002:IX, p. 3779, paras. 61–62.
[45] Appellate Body Report, *United States – Continued Existence and Application of Zeroing Methodology*, WT/DS350/AB/R, adopted 19 February 2009, DSR 2009:III, p. 1291, para. 268.
[46] Hughes, 'The Role of Legal Advisers in the World Trade Organization', p. 252.

dispute settlement procedures and practices so as to enable Members' experts to be better informed in this regard', and lawyers from LAD, the Rules Division, the Appellate Body Secretariat, and other non-legal divisions often provide training courses in Geneva and in the territory of requesting Member States. These activities enable trade officials in Member States to gain greater understanding of the dispute settlement system, and also encourage the development of professional relationships, including with Secretariat lawyers. These training courses therefore bolster not only knowledge of the dispute settlement system, but also transparency of the role and work of lawyers employed in the Secretariat.

5.4   Conclusion

In this chapter, we have argued that Secretariat lawyers have become increasingly relevant players in the multilateral trading system over the course of the history of the GATT and WTO. Although for many years lawyers were somewhat 'hidden' in the GATT Secretariat, carrying out legal work discreetly and often without even assuming the title of lawyer, since the creation of the WTO in 1995 lawyers have contributed to promoting the efficient and effective operation of the trading system. Today, lawyers are involved in a wide range of activities, including dispute settlement, committee-related work, in-house legal matters, and training and outreach.

Lawyers are, especially in their dispute-settlement-related work, subject to strict rules of confidentiality designed to protect the due process rights of disputing parties. But even if they are bound to confidentiality about the details of specific activities, the presence of Secretariat lawyers across the WTO Secretariat is well known by Members. Thus, although their work is purely technical in nature, and always in service to the decisions of the Membership, Secretariat lawyers contribute skills that help facilitate the functioning of the WTO.

The involvement of Secretariat lawyers in the WTO's work, and in particular in the dispute settlement system, has contributed to the legitimacy of the WTO's adjudicatory system. Together with more prominent actors, including, most importantly, the Members themselves, Secretariat lawyers have worked to promote the rule of law in international trade relations. Moreover, the increasing transparency of their work has brought legal work out of the shadows. Members and the public are thus better able to understand the working of the dispute settlement system and the role of Secretariat lawyers within it. This allows for meaningful Membership oversight while cultivating respect for the independence and expertise of the Secretariat, who of course remain committed to serving the interests of the Organization and its Members.

6

The International Criminal Court

PHILIPP AMBACH*

6.1 Introduction

Legitimacy is a key component for any court around the world. For national courts it is embedded in national constitutions and the domestic legal framework vesting these courts with their functions. For international courts, the issue of legitimacy is more complex as their constituting authority will be itself of a consent-based and often political nature. These courts' legitimacy towards the affected communities, victims, accused persons and anybody else affected by the judicial processes is not as evident as through, say, a constitution or any other laws with direct effect on the individual. Such legitimacy has to be established; through national laws implementing international agreements, but also through the respective courts' performance, thus generating legitimacy through societal support in addition to relevant laws. The International Criminal Court ('ICC')[1] is a prime example of an institution benefiting from different layers of legitimacy afforded by its different constituencies.

In order to provide some context, the ICC and its main features will be briefly introduced. The ICC was established to try individuals accused of committing the most serious crimes of concern to the international community, and to affirm that those crimes must never go unpunished.[2] The ICC is a permanent, independent international organisation, established through the Rome Statute[3] as its founding treaty in 1998, with currently 122 States Parties. It commenced operations in July 2002.

---

* The views expressed in this chapter are the author's alone and cannot be attributed to the aforementioned institution.
[1] General information on the ICC (also 'Court') is available at: www.icc-cpi.int.
[2] See Preamble of the Rome Statute, para. 4, at: www.icc-cpi.int/resource-library/Documents/RS-Eng.pdf.
[3] Ibid.

It does not belong to the United Nations,[4] other than its predecessors, the International Criminal Tribunal for the former Yugoslavia ('ICTY') and the International Criminal Tribunal for Rwanda ('ICTR').[5] The latter, having been established in 1993 and 1994, respectively, by the United Nations Security Council ('UNSC'), were only of a temporary (or ad hoc) nature and, while independent in their operations, represented UNSC measures to maintain international peace and security.[6] As a key novel feature of the ICC within the ambit of international criminal courts and tribunals, victims have access and are allowed to participate in the proceedings. They also have a right to claim reparations in case of a conviction of the accused.[7] This particular feature will be examined in more detail below, following a more general brief assessment of the ICC from an institutional perspective.

The ICC has four organs, namely the Presidency, Chambers (with its Pre-Trial, Trial and Appeals Divisions), the Office of the Prosecutor (OTP), and the Registry.[8] While being an integral part of the proceedings before the Court, the Defence is not incorporated in the ICC structure as a separate organ.[9] The ICC has jurisdiction over the crimes of genocide; crimes against humanity; war crimes; and the crime of aggression[10],

---

[4] The ICC, however, entertains a Relationship Agreement with the United Nations, detailing a number of areas of cooperation, privileges and immunities. See Article 2 of the Rome Statute and for the Agreement see: www.icc-cpi.int/pages/item.aspx?name=icc-un-rel-agr.

[5] For the ICTY: UN S/RES/827 (1993) of 25 May 1993; for the ICTR: UN S/RES/955 (1994) of 8 November 1994. These Tribunals have since been succeeded by the UN International Residual Mechanism for Criminal Tribunals ('MICT'), created through S/RES/1966 (2010) of 22 December 2010, which carries out a number of follow-up functions of the Tribunals. During the initial years of the MICT's existence, it operated in parallel with the ICTR and the ICTY, and today continues to operate after the Tribunals' closure. The ICTR closed on 31 December 2015 with the ICTY following on 31 December 2017. See: www.irmct.org/en.

[6] Refer, for instance, to UNSC Resolution 827 (1993) for the ICTY; see: www.icty.org/en/about/tribunal/establishment.

[7] Pursuant to Articles 68(3) and 75 of the Rome Statute, respectively.

[8] Article 34 of the Rome Statute.

[9] Yet, if and where a defendant cannot afford to pay for his/her own defence, the ICC provides adequate funds. Similarly, victim participation through legal representatives before the court is paid through the ICC budget. Since 2016, the interests of counsel in general before the ICC are represented through the International Criminal Court Bar Association (ICCBA). In contrast, at the Special Tribunal for Lebanon, the Defence is incorporated into that (hybrid) internationalised tribunal's structure as one of its four main organs, see www.stl-tsl.org/en/about-the-stl/structure-of-the-stl/defence-2/defence-office-69.

[10] Jurisdiction was activated by the Assembly of States Parties at its 2017 session, see ICC-ASP/16/Res. 5, Activation of the Jurisdiction of the Court Over the Crime of Aggression, 14 December 2017. Jurisdiction over the crime commenced on 17 July 2018 for those

committed by individuals.[11] An Assembly of States Parties acts as the governing body of the ICC, with various legislative and general oversight functions.[12]

The ICC conducts criminal investigations and trials against the world's most heinous perpetrators of international crimes. The press and other actors regularly report of important political or military leaders arrested and/or standing trial in the ICC courtrooms in The Hague, The Netherlands. The visible parts of the ICC are therefore the accused, the actors in the courtroom, the judges, and often even the building that houses the ICC premises. Yet, the biggest actor in terms of staff, operations and budget is the Registry. It consumes more than 60 per cent of the ICC budget, and employs more than half of the staff.[13] More than 20 different sections operate in three major divisions.[14] Most of the Registry support services are rendered to the judicial chambers and the OTP at Headquarters in The Hague, and many other services are provided in the various field presences – the ICC has six field offices at the time of writing.[15] The Registry represents the 'machine room' for the criminal procedure and all related processes, including all courtroom services and beyond, notably the protection of witnesses and the facilitation of victim participation in the proceedings and reparations.

The legitimacy of the Registry derives from the legitimacy of the ICC as a whole. Different from many other international institutions, the ICC requires legitimacy not only from its founders and funders (the Assembly of States Parties), but also from the affected population, and more broadly still from the international community as a whole. The present chapter will

---

States Parties that have accepted the amendments (see ICC-ASP/16/Res. 5, para. 2). See Dapo Akande, 'The International Criminal Court Gets Jurisdiction Over the Crime of Aggression', ejil *Talk!*, 15 December 2017, at: www.ejiltalk.org/the-international-criminal-court-gets-jurisdiction-over-the-crime-of-aggression/.

[11] See Articles 5–8*bis*, 25(1) of the Rome Statute.

[12] Article 112 of the Rome Statute.

[13] See, for the latest budget resolution of the ICC, ICC-ASP/16/Res.1, Resolution of the Assembly of States Parties on the Proposed Programme Budget for 2018, the Working Capital Fund for 2018, the Scale of Assessment for the Apportionment of Expenses of the International Criminal Court, Financing Appropriations for 2018 and the Contingency Fund, 14 December 2017, para. 1.

[14] See Proposed Programme Budget for 2018 of the International Criminal Court, ICC-ASP/16/10, 11 September 2017, available at: https://asp.icc-cpi.int/iccdocs/asp_docs/ASP16/ICC-ASP-16-10-ENG.pdf; see also Proposed Programme Budget for 2019 of the International Criminal Court, ICC-ASP/17/10, 25 July 2018.

[15] Proposed Programme Budget for 2018, 11 September 2017, pp. 119 et seq.

briefly assess, at the example of the Registry function to enable victims of ICC crimes to participate in the proceedings and claim reparations, how such legitimacy from 'above' and 'below' embeds the ICC in a pyramidal legitimacy structure.

6.2 The Registry of the ICC

6.2.1 General Functions

The Registry is responsible for the non-judicial aspects of the administration and servicing of the Court, pursuant to Article 43(1) of the Rome Statute. The Registry's responsibilities extend further than those of registries of national courts; for instance, it is responsible for the protection and support of witnesses and victims, support to the defence, assistance to victims appearing before the judges in court, the ICC detention centre housing suspects and accused before the ICC,[16] public information, security (both physical and IT) and also administrative services such as procurement, budget, finance, recruitment and other personnel services. The Registry also supports the parties' operations in field offices in a number of countries where the ICC conducts its operations. For instance, the Registry is responsible for public outreach in situation countries, for the protection of witnesses and victims and for the security of staff travelling on mission. At present, there are six different ICC field offices with a total of 11 different situations under investigation.[17]

The Registry supports administratively the judges and parties and participants to the proceedings. Certain sections of the Registry directly service proceedings before the ICC. For example:

- activities of the Victims Participation and Reparations Section are exclusively devoted to victims and their participation in the proceedings; this includes potential reparations in case of a conviction of an accused in the criminal proceedings before the chambers;[18]
- the Counsel Support Section assists legal counsel and also provides funds for legal aid;

---

[16] Housed within Dutch national prison facilities in The Hague.

[17] See: www.icc-cpi.int/pages/situations.aspx; see regarding the ICC field offices Proposed Programme Budget for 2018, 11 September 2017, pp. 119 et seq.

[18] See Articles 68(3) and 75 of the Rome Statute; rules 85 et seq. of the Rules of Procedure and Evidence.

- two independent offices, the Office of Public Counsel for the Defence (OPCD) and the Office of Public Counsel for Victims (OPCV), which are available to represent defendants or victims respectively, or to assist their representatives, are also located within the Registry.[19]

Other sections, such as language services, court management, security, human resources and information technology, serve all organs of the ICC. It is fundamental for the Registry to remain neutral in the provision of services[20], as it supports different actors with diverse, if not to a certain extent opposing, roles. The Registry supports counsel for the defence, just as it supports counsel for victims, the OTP and the Judiciary.[21]

While responsible for the *non*-judicial aspects of the administration and servicing of the proceedings, the Registry is also vested with a quasi-judicial role in certain areas such as detention, legal aid, witness protection and victim participation.[22] This multifaceted role has created a great number of links and connections between the Registry, the OTP and the Chambers. Questions of witness protection or the screening of victims applying to participate in the proceedings are but two examples. Similar to the situation at the ICTY and the ICTR, as well as other international(ised) tribunals, the task of the protection of witnesses is entrusted to the Registry.[23] However, the OTP also has a large number of contact points with victims and potential witnesses in particular during its investigations[24] and is even subject to a statutory obligation pursuant to Article 68(1) of the Rome Statute to take appropriate measures to protect the safety of victims and witnesses during the investigation and prosecution of statutory crimes. In the case of *The Prosecutor v. Germain Katanga and Mathieu Ngudjolo Chui*, the Appeals Chamber decided on the distribution of roles and responsibilities between

---

[19] See Regulations 77 and 81 of the Regulations of the Court, ICC-BD/01-01-04.

[20] ICC-ASP/16/10, para. 406.

[21] See, generally, *Behind the Scenes – The Registry of the International Criminal Court*, www.icc-cpi.int/iccdocs/PIDS/docs/behindTheSce.pdf.

[22] See for the latter Article 68(3) of the Rome Statute; Rules 16–19 of the Rules.

[23] At ICTY, the Victims and Witnesses Section (VWS) of the Registry supported and protected all witnesses, whether they were called by the Prosecution, Defence or Chambers. The VWS acted as an independent and neutral body, providing logistical, psychological and protective measures; see Rule 75 of the ICTY Rules of Procedure and Evidence, as well as Article 22 of the ICTY Statute. The ICTR had a similar regime, see Rules 34, 75 of the of the ICTR Rules of Procedure and Evidence (version of 13 May 2015). This has been continued in the MICT, see Rule 32 ('Witness Support and Protection Unit'), as amended on 16 April 2018, MICT/I/Amend.3, of the MICT's Rules of Procedure and Evidence, available at: www.irmct.org/sites/default/files/documents/180409-mict-rules-evidence-1-rev.3_en.pdf. Similarly, at the Special Tribunal for Lebanon, the Victims and Witnesses Unit is an independent and neutral body within the Registry, see Article 12(4) of the STL Statute (S/RES/1757 (2007)).

[24] See, e.g., Articles 53(1)(c) and (2)(c), 54(1) and (3)(f), and 68(1) of the Rome Statute.

the two organs, also defining the Prosecutor's role with regard to the preventive relocation of witnesses.[25] The Chamber highlighted the particular need for cooperation between the organs in this field.[26]

As regards the participation of victims in court proceedings, Chambers have decided already early in the life of the ICC that the Victims Participation and Reparations Section of the Registry ('VPRS') is to carry out an assessment of all victims applying to participate in the proceedings as regards the validity of their claims and submit such pre-assessment to the designated Chamber for validation.[27] A similar procedure applies for the Registry regarding the reparations regime at the ICC.[28] These roles create a strong responsibility of the institution towards a completely different set of stakeholders, namely those individually affected by crimes presented before the ICC. The ICC's legitimacy needs to be affirmed by this group, too, since redress to victims and affected communities is one of the main objectives of the ICC from a restorative and reparative justice viewpoint. The ICC's Trust Fund for Victims (TFV), established under article 79 of the Rome Statute, has an important role in this, since it is designed to facilitate Court-ordered reparations and to provide assistance to victims in ICC situations. The ICC Registry and the TFV cooperate closely.

The need to receive support from States Parties to the Rome Statute remains critical for the ICC, be it for the execution of arrest warrants or the

---

[25] ICC *The Prosecutor v. German Katanga*, Appeals Chamber, *Judgment on the appeal of the Prosecutor against the 'Decision on Evidentiary Scope of the Confirmation Hearing, Preventive Relocation and Disclosure under Article 67(2) of the Statute and Rule 77 of the Rules' of Pre-Trial Chamber I* of 26 November 2008, ICC-01/04-01/07-776, paras. 98 et seq.

[26] Ibid., para. 101.

[27] I.e., whether they were indeed victims of the crimes as outlined in the OTP document containing the charges, and indeed affected by the alleged criminal conduct in a manner sufficiently linking them to the proceedings, pursuant to Rule 85 of the ICC Rules of Procedure and Evidence. See *The Prosecutor v. Thomas Lubanga Dyilo*, Trial Chamber I, Decision on victims' participation, ICC-01/04-01/06-1119, 22 January 2008; see for a more recent decision *The Prosecutor v. Al Hassan Ag Abdoul Aziz Ag Mohamed Ag Mahmoud* (Situation in the Republic of Mali), Pre-Trial Chamber I, Decision Establishing the Principles Applicable to Victims' Applications for Participation, ICC-01/12-01/18-37-tENG, 24 May 2018; *The Prosecutor v. Alfred Yekatom and Patrice-Edouard Ngaïssona* (Situation in the Central African Republic II), Pre-Trial Chamber II, Decision Establishing the Principles Applicable to Victims' Applications for Participation, ICC-01/14-01/18-141, 5 March 2019.

[28] See, e.g., *The Prosecutor v. Thomas Lubanga Dyilo*, Trial Chamber II, *Order relating to the request of the Office of Public Counsel for Victims of 16 September 2016*, ICC-01/04-01/06-3252, 10 November 2016; *The Prosecutor v. Thomas Lubanga Dyilo*, Trial Chamber II, *Order for the Transmission of the Application Files of Victims who may be Eligible for Reparations to The Defence Team of Thomas Lubanga Dyilo*, ICC-01/04-01/06-3275-tENG, 22 February 2017; ICC, *The Prosecutor v. Ahmad Al Faqi Al Mahdi*, Trial Chamber VIII, *Reparations Phase Calendar*, ICC-01/12-01/15–172, 29 September 2016.

tracing and freezing of assets of suspected or accused persons.[29] The Registry
is tasked with encouraging and facilitating the necessary cooperation, be that
with State actors, international or regional organisations. However, much of
the technical case-related assistance and cooperation is also dealt with by the
OTP and relevant State authorities directly. The Registry, as a neutral service provider to *all* actors involved, provides services as required. Lastly, the
financial investigation of an accused's assets and proceeds also sits with the
Registry.[30] All these functions that involve external actors have a strong component that defines the institution's legitimacy: the more external support is
provided, the stronger an institution would appear to be; in turn, an institution with a low legitimacy level is likely to receive little external support and
cooperation.

6.2.2   Normative Legitimacy

Normative legitimacy represents, as is the case for any judicial institution, the highest layer of legitimacy. In the case of the ICC Registry,
it is attached to the legitimacy of the ICC itself, founded through an
international treaty, the Rome Statute. Articles 34 and 43 specify the
Registry's normative legitimacy. First, the Registry represents one of
the four main 'organs' of the ICC;[31] second, the Registry is responsible for the non-judicial aspects of the administration and servicing
of the Court, thus underlining the neutral role of the Registry particularly vis-à-vis the OTP and the Defence.[32] Third, the Registrar is the

---

[29] For States Parties, the Rome Statute stipulates a list of cooperation obligations in Part 9 of
the Statute ('International Cooperation and Judicial Assistance'); the ICC can, however,
also seek non-State Parties' – voluntary – assistance (see, for instance, Article 93(10)(c) of
the Rome Statute).

[30] ICC-ASP/16/10, paras. 641 et seq.

[31] Article 34 of the Rome Statute.

[32] Article 43(1) of the Rome Statute; the Prosecutor's independence is enshrined in Article
42(1) and repeated in Article 43(1), thus clarifying the fact that the Registry's functions
need to be cognisant of the 'functions and powers of the Prosecutor'. In practice, the OTP
also has a limited administrative structure within the office in order to safeguard the
Prosecutor's 'authority over the management and administration of the Office, including
the staff, facilities and other resources thereof'. See Article 42(2), second sentence. For a
more detailed analysis of the ICC's organs' competences towards each other see Philipp
Ambach and Klaus U. Rackwitz, 'A Model of International Judicial Administration? The
Evolution of Managerial Practices at the International Criminal Court' (2014) 76 *Law and
Contemporary Problems* 119.

principal administrative officer, operating under the President's general authority.[33] He/she is elected by the judges of the ICC. Article 43(3) of the Rome Statute further stipulates that the Registrar is a person of high moral character and highly competent. Both the statutory requirement of qualification and the election through the ICC judges provide authority and, more importantly, legitimacy to the Registrar as the principal representative of the Registry. It follows that by virtue of the statutory provisions, the legitimacy of the Registry sits at the normative highpoint of the ICC, its Statute, alongside the other organs of the ICC.[34]

6.2.3 *The ICC Registry – Distinct from the UN Ad Hoc Tribunals*

The ICC Registry, like any other institution of comparable size and structure, has relied heavily since its inception on managerial practices, over and above its written institutional and administrative framework. These practices and standards, some of them previously developed in different institutions, have evolved over the past fifteen years of the ICC's existence and have served to complete its administrative and operational framework. The latter has also developed in response to the growing demands of administrative regulation, in particular through Presidential Directives, Administrative Instructions and Information Circulars.[35] Many of these administrative texts took some inspiration from comparable regulations, procedures and so-called 'Practice Directions' of the UN ad hoc Tribunals.[36] Practices, be that in conjunction with governing administrative norms or in the absence of any formal codification, remain a major driver of the ICC's

---

[33] Article 43(1) of the Rome Statute; the Assembly of States Parties also provides management oversight to the Registrar regarding the administration of the ICC, Article 112(2)(b) of the Rome Statute.

[34] Article 112(2) of the Rome Statute ascribes a set of functions to the Assembly of States Parties that serves to guarantee some (financial and governance) control; as such, in subjecting the Registrar to the Assembly's management oversight, it lends further normative legitimacy to the Registrar.

[35] See ICC Vademecum of Administrative Issuances, available at: www.icc-cpi.int/resource-library/Pages/vademecum.aspx.

[36] See for the ICTY at: www.icty.org/en/documents/practice-directions; see for the MICT at: www.unmict.org/en/basic-documents/practice-directions.

managerial dynamics.[37] Similar observations can also be made for the ICC's Chambers[38] and the OTP.[39]

The ICC's administrative structure follows a normative pyramidal pattern: the Court's principal legal sources, the Rome Statute, the Elements of Crimes and its Rules of Procedure and Evidence,[40] have been issued by the States Parties. They contain limited administrative guidance and instead mandate the organs of the ICC to issue secondary legal texts governing the institutional administrative structure. For example, Article 44, paragraph 3 of the Rome Statute tasks the Registrar to draft Staff Regulations, containing the fundamental conditions of service and the basic rights and obligations of the staff of the ICC. The adoption of, and amendments to, the Regulations of the Court falls into the judges' competence pursuant to Article 52, paragraph 1 of the Rome Statute.[41] Other essential texts governing important areas of the institution's management fall within the remit of competence of the ICC's constitutive body, the Assembly of States Parties.[42] The Court's Financial Regulations and Rules[43] as well as its Independent Oversight Mechanism[44] are just two examples of this.

As mentioned previously, the Registry of the ICC was greatly inspired by its famous predecessors in the sphere of the recently (re-)born idea of international criminal justice, the ICTY and the ICTR. Yet, unlike these

---

[37] Ambach and Rackwitz, 'A Model of International Judicial Administration?'.

[38] See, for instance, the ICC 'Chambers Practice Manual', containing a number of major practices commonly agreed by the plenary of judges to be observed during the procedural phases of cases before the ICC; available, in its version of February 2016, at www.icc-cpi.int/iccdocs/other/Chambers_practice_manual--FEBRUARY_2016.pdf. For an overview over the ICC Chambers' advances in consolidating its practices in the recent past see Philipp Ambach, 'The 'Lessons Learnt' Process at the International Criminal Court – A Suitable Vehicle for Procedural Improvements?' (2016) 12 *Zeitschrift für Internationale Strafrechtsdogmatik* 854.

[39] See the various policy papers developed by the OTP at: www.icc-cpi.int/about/otp/Pages/otp-policies.aspx.

[40] See Article 21(1)(a) of the Rome Statute.

[41] Adopted by the judges of the Court on 26 May 2004; version currently in force: ICC-BD/01-03-11;

[42] See Article 112(2) of the Rome Statute.

[43] Financial Regulations and Rules ('FRR'), ICC-ASP/1/3 and Corr.1 of September 2002 and last amended by ICC-ASP/10. Article 113 of the Rome Statute stipulates that the FRR are to be 'adopted by the Assembly of States Parties'.

[44] See Article 112(4) of the Rome Statute; for the latest on the matter see Resolution ICC-ASP/12/Res.6 (2013) with the Operational mandate of the Independent Oversight Mechanism in its Annex. See also generally at: www.icc-cpi.int/iom.

ad hoc Tribunals established by the United Nations, the ICC is based on an international treaty, the Rome Statute. The ICC is thus not a UN organ, let alone, as the UN ad hoc Tribunals, a measure of the Security Council pursuant to Chapter VII.[45] From the treaty-based nature of the ICC as well as its relative independence from the UN system flows the liberty to provide the ICC with an administrative framework that does *not* mirror existing UN agencies, sub-organs or otherwise related bodies; on the other hand, with liberty comes responsibility – and with a multilateral founding treaty comes diversity of opinions, interests, administrative cultures and philosophies. The Rome Statute has been described as a 'unique compromise'[46] between the many different legal traditions which sought to influence the Rome Statute one way or another.[47] A similar assessment can be made of the ICC's institutional and administrative structure; while certain elements of the UN such as the United Nations Common System on Salaries and Entitlements have been adopted or incorporated into the Court's framework, the ICC has gone in new ways as regards its structure of administrative issuances and thus diverted in a number of aspects from one of its natural points of reference.

One of the major differences of the ICC compared to the UN ad hoc Tribunals ICTY and ICTR is the position of the Registrar vis-à-vis the Presidency. In the regulatory framework of the UN ad hoc Tribunals, the Registrar was appointed by the Secretary-General,[48] while the Prosecutor was appointed by the Security Council.[49] The judges were elected by the General Assembly.[50] While the appointment of the Registrar had to

---

[45] See for ICTY: UN Doc. S/RES/808 (1993) of 22 February 1993; for ICTR: UN Doc. S/RES/955 (1994) of 8 November 1994.

[46] Claus Kress, 'The Procedural Law of the International Criminal Court in Outline: Anatomy of a Unique Compromise' (2003) 1(3) *Journal of International Criminal Justice* 603.

[47] Also in terms of criminal procedure, a steady tension between those states favouring the inquisitorial approach in criminal legal doctrine and other states defending the adversarial approach continued to render negotiations leading to the adoption of the Rome Statute utterly complicated. See Article 42, para. 6 in Otto Triffterer and Kai Ambos (eds.), *Commentary on the Rome Statute of the International Criminal Court – Observers' Notes, Article by Article*, 3rd edn (Hart, 2016); Gerhard Werle and Florian Jessberger, *Principles of International Criminal Law*, 3rd edn (Oxford University Press, 2014), para. 366.

[48] Article 17(3) of the ICTY Statute; Article 16(3) of the ICTR Statute. This system is followed by the MICT, Article 15(3) of the MICT Statute.

[49] Article 16(4) of the ICTY Statute; Article 15(4) of the ICTR Statute. This system is followed by the MICT, Article 14(4) of the MICT Statute.

[50] Both permanent and *ad litem* judges were elected from a list submitted by the Security Council, Articles 13*bis*, 13*ter* of the ICTY Statute; Articles 12*bis*, 12*ter* of the ICTR Statute. This system is followed by Article 10 of the MICT Statute.

follow the Secretary-General's 'consultation with the President of the International Tribunal', the final prerogative rested with the Secretary-General. All three organs of the ad hoc Tribunals[51] thus had in common that their principals were elected or appointed by an external authority. Further, while the Tribunals' statutes determined the Registry's role as 'responsible for the administration and servicing of the International Tribunal',[52] nowhere did they establish an explicit *hierarchy* between the organs. Merely the Tribunals' Rules of Procedure and Evidence, adopted by the judges themselves, provided that the President supervised the activities of the Registry and that the Registrar operates '[u]nder the authority of the President'.[53] This is in contrast to the ICC, where it is the highest normative authority explicitly establishing the President's authority over the Registrar, Article 43(2) of the Rome Statute.[54] It can thus be argued that at the ad hoc Tribunals, the Registrar ultimately remained accountable to an outside actor.

The latter has not necessarily turned out as an advantage for the ICC. Since the beginning of its operations, a lack of clarity was often deplored as to how the exercise of the President's authority over the Registrar worked out in practice. In 2010, after lengthy negotiations amongst the principals of the Court, a report was issued describing the relevant aspects of the ICC corporate governance framework in an effort to increase clarity on the responsibilities of its organs.[55] The report and the annexed 'Corporate Governance Statement' delineate the roles and responsibilities of the different Organs of the ICC, and in particular address all areas of the Registry's activities with an inter-organ relevance, adding clarity to the distinction between the ICC's administrative and judicial functions.[56] No such document was ever issued for the UN ad hoc Tribunals – or any other international(ised) tribunal thereafter. More recently, the ICC's

---

[51] Pursuant to Article 11 of the ICTY Statute (Article 10 of the ICTR Statute) the Tribunals consisted of the Chambers, the Prosecutor and the Registry.

[52] Article 17(1) of the ICTY Statute; Article 16(1) of the ICTR Statute. See also Article 11(c) of the ICTY Statute (Article 10(c) of the ICTR Statute).

[53] Rule 19(A) of the Rules of Procedure and Evidence of both ad hoc-Tribunals. Rule 31(A) of the MICT Rules of Procedure and Evidence stipulates that the Registrar operates '[u]nder the authority of the President'.

[54] It bears noting that the sole authority to amend the Rome Statute is the Assembly of States Parties; Articles 121, 122 of the Rome Statute.

[55] *Report of the Court on Measures To Increase Clarity on the Responsibilities of the Different Organs*, ICC-ASP/9/34, of 3 December 2010, previously issued as ICC-ASP/9/CBF.1/12 ('Governance Report').

[56] Governance Report, paras. 27–30.

complex governance structure has been managed rather well; the ICC's reporting on its own performance indicators since 2014 bares testimony to this in providing a transparent picture of its internal processes and proceedings.[57]

6.2.4 Legitimacy Through Credibility

The next key question in terms of internal governance is how an institution's normative legitimacy permeates the Registry. How does that legitimacy translate into the plethora of different Registry functions and services in the execution of its mandates? The Registry has a pyramidal hierarchical structure: it divides, at the highest levels, into three divisions: i) the Division of Judicial Services; ii) the Common Administrative Services Division; and iii) the Division of External Operations. Each of these divisions divides into a multitude of different sections, making up for more than 20 different sections and offices altogether. Most of the latter further divide into different units. All these different actors have distinct task lists that go towards a comprehensive network of Registry functions servicing the actors of the criminal process from the initiation of an investigation to the implementation of reparation orders once a conviction has become final. All Registry functions therefore respond ultimately to those that finally judge the quality and effectiveness of all Registry services: clients, both internal to the ICC and outside the institution.

One key component to the institution's legitimacy both internally and external ly is its credibility. Senior management needs to be credible to its staff to instil mission spirit and motivation, with a view to ultimately providing high-level services throughout. The ICC needs to be credible in its output in order to generate support from States Parties, civil society, affected communities and the international community as a whole. Regarding its internal credibility, key elements of a well-run Registry are first and foremost transparency, an effective flow of information and a clearly communicated strategy. In order to maximise its impact on the aforementioned principles, in 2013 the ICC Registry embarked on an organisational review of working methods, procedures and its structural

---

[57] See the latest 'Third Court's Report on the Development of Performance Indicators for the International Criminal Court', of 15 November 2017, at: www.icc-cpi.int/itemsDocuments/171115-Third-Report-performance-indicators-ENG.pdf. The first and second reports (2015 and 2016) are also available on the ICC homepage. It is as yet unclear whether the ICC will continue this exercise in 2019 and/or thereafter, after not issuing an update report on performance indicators in 2018.

layout. The aim was to design a Registry that renders its services more effectively and comprehensively within stable budgetary confines.[58] The process ended in 2015, after a structural overhaul of the Registry and a comprehensive assessment of all workflows, standard operating procedures and reporting structures.[59] As with any large organisation, change management has presented a major challenge to the Registry's senior managers, who needed to encourage staff to accept and embrace the new realities. However, years after the Registry reorganisation, its benefits became more visible and the credibility of senior management is reciprocated by the trust of the staff, which in essence increased the institution's inner legitimacy.

To the external world the ICC speaks not only through its public court proceedings, which are live-streamed and well documented on the ICC's homepage. It also provides news clips, tweets, background information and a comprehensive jurisprudence database on its homepage. In addition, extensive reporting to the Assembly of States Parties at the yearly Assembly meetings provides additional relevant documentation regarding the ICC's internal procedures, governance, audit compliance, budgetary discipline, risk management and institutional strategy.[60] The ICC performance indicator exercise regarding its judicial proceedings, governance, security and victims' access to justice is another important reporting tool adding to the credibility of the institution as a whole and therefore its legitimacy – not only in budgetary terms but also from a (reparative/restorative) justice perspective.

---

[58] See generally on the entire exercise *Comprehensive Report on the Reorganisation of the Registry of the International Criminal Court*, August 2016, available at: www.icc-cpi.int/itemsDocuments/ICC-Registry-CR.pdf.

[59] See ibid. and *Report on the Review of the Organizational Structure of the Registry Outcomes of Phase 4 of the ReVision Project Decisions on the Structure of the Registry*, ICC-ASP/14/18, 4 May 2015; *Report of the Registry on the Outcome of the ReVision Process*, ICC-ASP/14/19, 15 June 2015.

[60] See only the extensive list of ICC 'Court Reports' for each Assembly of States Parties session at: https://asp.icc-cpi.int/en_menus/asp/sessions/documentation/16th-session/Pages/default.aspx. The amount of reporting by the ICC to its States Parties is unprecedented and surpasses by a margin the reporting of any other international(ised) court or tribunal in past and present. The benefit of this is an increasing wealth of data on an array of aspects of an international criminal court that will assist in designing lean and mean future international(ised) justice mechanisms that will stand in a relationship of complementarity with the ICC (see Article 17 of the Rome Statute). The downside is the amount of time and resources that need to be devoted, on the ICC's part, to preparing and providing the requested reports.

6.2.5   The ICC's Pyramidal Legitimacy – Using the Example of the Victims Participation and Reparations Section of the Registry

The legitimacy of the ICC Registry is not only pyramidal regarding its internal hierarchy and legitimacy, but also externally the Registry serves a broad spectrum of clients that in turn provide legitimacy to the institution as a whole by way of a 'mandate support foundation'. Victims and affected communities of mass atrocity crimes within the ICC's mandate provide an illustrative example of this in that they instil legitimacy upwards *into* the institution. A number of Registry offices provide specific services for affected communities, ranging from public information and outreach, to victim protection services, to enabling victims to participate in court proceedings and to request reparations. Victims and affected communities thus provide the reason for the relevant Registry offices' existence, and they also determine those offices' required output and performance. The following pyramidal legitimacy model can therefore be established:

The higher up in the ICC's governance structure, the clearer its legitimacy is derived from a single high authority (i.e. the applicable law, its founding treaty, and the Assembly of States Parties as governing body), but this legitimacy becomes increasingly polynomial at the many different servicing Registry offices. In turn, the further one moves down in the legitimacy pyramid of the institutional framework towards Registry support structures, the more concrete and tangible the bottom-up legitimacy becomes. Such bottom-up legitimacy is provided by the support for the ICC through external clients such as victim communities, the affected population, the international community, and finally States (particularly through relevant international cooperation with and judicial assistance to the Court[61]). The bottom-up legitimacy is thus not normative but in most relevant part societal through support from civil society and the international community. The latter may even be expressed through relevant resolutions of UN bodies such as the General Assembly or the Security Council, pledging support for the ICC or even referring a situation to it under Article 13(b) of the Rome Statute.

---

[61] See Part 9 of the Rome Statute, commencing at Article 86. It has to be said though that such cooperation is a State's legal obligation ('States Parties shall … cooperate fully with the Court'; Art. 86 of the Rome Statute), and therefore also part of the normative top-down legitimacy thread through the ICC's founding document. Yet, experience has shown that societal legitimacy may be a strong influencer in how rigorously cooperation requests are being followed up by those States to be approached.

A key indicator for the ICC's societal legitimacy is its impact on victim communities. Victims' opinions on the ICC, their access to the Court and their assessment of how effective its victim participation and reparations features are constitute essential values to measure. This has been often underlined by civil society.[62] Only if both legitimacy threads – normative and societal – are properly understood and well connected can an institution prosper. This is particularly so for the ICC with its humanitarian mandate, and for the Registry as the institution's operational enabler for affected communities and victims on the ground.

A practical example of the meeting of both vertical threads of legitimacy is represented in the Registry's Victims Participation and Reparations Section ('VPRS'). Mandated to assist victims in the field in connecting to the judicial proceedings at the ICC in The Hague and ensure victims' subsequent access to the ICC throughout the proceedings including reparations, the Section's highest normative legitimacy is stipulated in Article 68(3) of the Rome Statute. While this provision only very generally describes victim participation in the proceedings, the Rules of Procedure and Evidence of the ICC contain a number of more detailed provisions on how to define victims and how they can participate in the proceedings and claim reparations.[63] The VPRS is structurally situated in the Division of Judicial Services; its case-related reporting and other mandates are both normatively framed and guided by decisions and orders of the judges. At the same time, the Section is an important catalyst of direct legitimacy from various clients of the ICC: first, the most directly affected client group is the one of victim applicants in the proceedings, victims already recognised by the Chambers as participants in the proceedings, and finally

---

[62] See, e.g. the *Second Court's Report on the Development of Performance Indicators for the International Criminal Court,* 11 November 2016, paras. 78, 93, 100, available at: www.icc-cpi.int/itemsDocuments/ICC-Second-Court_report-on-indicators.pdf; see also Redress, *Victims' Rights Working Group,* available at: www.vrwg.org/; Redress, *Independent Panel of Experts Report on Victim Participation at the International Criminal Court* 2013, available at: https://redress.org/publication/independent-panel-of-experts-report-on-victim-participation-at-the-international-criminal-court/; FIDH, *Enhancing Victims' Rights Before the* ICC 2013, available at: www.fidh.org/IMG/pdf/fidh_victimsrights_621a_nov2013_ld.pdf; Coalition for the International Criminal Court, *Impact on Victims and Affected Communitie*s, available at: http://iccnow.org/index.php?mod=impactonvictims; P. Ambach, 'Reparation Proceedings at the International Criminal Court – a Means to Repair or Recipe for Disappointment?' in U. Sieber, V. Mitsilegas, C. Mylonopoulos, E. Billis and N. Knust (eds.), *Alternative Systems of Crime Control. National, Transnational, and International Dimensions* (Duncker and Humblot GmbH, 2018), pp. 109 *et seq.*

[63] See Rules 85 et seq. of the ICC Rules of Procedure and Evidence.

victims that have applied for reparations. To date, approximately 14,000 individuals fall into this category.[64] As a second group providing relevant legitimacy elements, civil society regularly assesses the ICC's strategy and processes regarding victims. Civil society reports on select topics provide relevant indicators of performance and improvement needs.[65] The VPRS has a role to play in translating this external input into internal initiatives to improve services and processes, and to test new initiatives with its external stakeholders for feedback. These multiple client-related mandates provide the VPRS with a very broad base of societal legitimacy from outside, and a clear line of operational/normative legitimacy from the ICC institutional framework internally.

6.3   Conclusion

The ICC Registry provides an illustrative example of the backbone of an international organisation that, while largely unseen in its operations, plays a major role in the legitimacy of the institution as a whole. In the case of the ICC, a pyramidal legitimacy structure can be observed, with a singular normative legitimising document (the Rome Statute) and a single governing body (the Assembly of States Parties) at the top of the structure and a broad and varied legitimising support base, carrying the institution with its mandate to fight impunity for the worst crimes and to provide redress to victims of these crimes.

Particularly where the unseen actor is a big administration with a plurality of sections and units, a powerful internal legitimising factor is a register of (key) performance indicators, measuring the different major sections' output and thus providing a transparent yardstick of the effectiveness of the institution's output and governance structure. Yet, the most essential factor remains the powerful link between the normative and societal legitimacy establishing the vertical axis between both ends of the legitimacy pyramid. The key to this is highly skilled and motivated staff, and a powerful common vision.

---

[64] Judge Silvia Fernández de Gurmendi, President of the International Criminal Court, Remarks at the 48th Pacific Islands Forum, 6 September 2017, Apia, Samoa, p. 4, available at: www .icc-cpi.int/itemsDocuments/ICC_President_remarks_to_Pacific_Islands_Forum_ Leaders.pdf.

[65] See, e.g., Human Rights Watch, 'Who Will Stand for Us? – Victims' Legal Representation at the ICC in the Ongwen Case and Beyond', 29 August 2017, available at: www.hrw .org/report/2017/08/29/who-will-stand-us/victims-legal-representation-icc-ongwen-case-and-beyond.

The European Court of Human Rights

LEDI BIANKU AND PETER KEMPEES

7.1   Introduction

There are a few still serving in the Registry of the European Court of Human Rights (the Court) who began their careers writing drafts for the Court's judgments in longhand.[1] At that time, the judges outnumbered the Registry lawyers. Those were the Court's pioneering days: the judgments it delivered then established precedent that is studied, and followed, by its successor institution to the present day. Then, the European Commission of Human Rights (the Commission) received all applications in contentious cases and decided which were fit to be referred to the Court.[2] As a consequence of the comparatively higher number of cases introduced before the Commission, the Commission's Secretariat was necessarily an organisation on a larger scale: at its maximum, it numbered perhaps several dozen members. Its working methods were correspondingly less artisanal than those of the old Court.

As the caseload of the Commission and the Court increased, resulting from the expansion of the Council of Europe's membership so as to include States from Central and Eastern Europe that had shaken off the yoke of dictatorship, the decision was taken to replace the two institutions – Commission and Court – by a single one, the new Court, and merge the secretariat of the Commission and the registry of the Court into a single Registry. The Court in its present form came into existence on 1 November 1998.[3] Today the Court comprises 47 judges, served by a Registry numbering approximately

---

[1] The second author is one of them.

[2] Articles 25–32 of the European Convention on Human Rights (text of 1950). Hereafter 'Article' refers to Articles of the European Convention on Human Rights – 'the Convention' – unless otherwise specified.

[3] Date of the entry into force of Protocol No. 11 to the European Convention on Human Rights, ETS 155.

650 members at any given time, some two-thirds of whom are lawyers. The present relationship between the Court's judges and the Registry is shaped by two main factors. The first is the sheer size of the Court's caseload, which is a function of the number of applications introduced and the Court's efficacy in dealing with them. The second is the variety of judicial formations created to deal with it, which is a feature of the system. To these we now turn.

7.2   Caseload

On 31 December 2016,[4] there were 79,750 applications pending before the Court. These varied from the relatively straightforward, suitable for standardised treatment, to the extremely complex – the latter including inter-State cases and cases arising from international armed conflicts.[5] Over half of the pending applications concerned only five of the 47 Contracting States – Ukraine, Turkey, Hungary, Romania and Russia, in that order.

By 31 December 2018 the number of pending applications had decreased slightly to 56,350.[6] The number of applications communicated to respondent Governments in 2018 was 7,644. The number of applications decided by a decision or a judgment in 2018 was 42,761, of which 2,738 were decided by judgment delivered; the number declared inadmissible or struck out was 40,023. By the end of the year 9,750 applications remained pending at the pre-judicial stage – that is, yet to be considered by a formation of the Court. The number of applications decided was 909.80 for each one of the Court's 47 judges. If one considers only the applications pending at year's end 2018, there were nearly 1,200 per judge.

7.3   Organisation of the Court and its Registry

7.3.1   The Court

The Court sits in single-judge formations, in committees of three judges, in Chambers of seven judges and in Grand Chambers of seventeen judges.[7] The Court as a whole is headed by the President. The President's tasks include directing the work and administration of the Court and

---

[4] Annual Report of the Court for 2016.
[5] *Chiragov and Others v. Armenia* [GC], no. 13216/05; *Sargsyan v. Azerbaijan* [GC], no. 40167/06; *Georgia v. Russia (I)* [GC], no. 13255/07.
[6] Annual Report of the Court for 2018.
[7] Article 26 § 1.

representing the Court to the outside world. For this reason, the President is exempted from ordinary casework in Chambers unless he or she is the national judge in a particular case.[8]

The basic organisational unit of the Court is the section. There are five, counting either nine or ten judges (47 being, of course, indivisible by 5 or for that matter any integer), and each with its own Section President and Vice-President. They are set up for three years.[9] Within the sections the Chambers and the Committees are composed. Their composition is fixed for a definite period: three years in the case of a Chamber–corresponding to the life span of its parent section – and one year in the case of a Committee.[10] This helps to ensure, as far as possible, that case-law developments are not peculiar to particular sections.

7.3.2   The Registry

The official in charge of the Registry is the Registrar of the Court, who is responsible for the organisation and activities of the Registry under the authority of the President of the Court.[11] The Registrar and one or more Deputy Registrars – in practice, there is only one Deputy Registrar – are elected by the Court's judges.[12] The other members of the Registry are appointed by the Registrar under the authority of the President of the Court.[13] The Court's expenditure is borne by the Council of Europe.[14] Of the Registry's 650-odd members, some two-thirds are lawyers and administrative staff involved in case-processing. The remainder include research lawyers, administrative staff charged with duties other than case-processing, personnel managers, archivists, information technology experts, librarians and other support staff such as one expects to find assisting any major court. The Court's language department is small, especially in comparison with that of the European Court of Justice: it numbers some 30 linguists, whose duties include not only translation but also ensuring that the use of the Court's two official languages – English and French – in official documents is of an adequate standard.

---

[8]   Article 26 § 4 and Rule 9 of the Rules of Court. Hereafter 'Rule' refers to a Rule contained in the Rules of Court unless otherwise specified.
[9]   Rule 25 § 1.
[10]   Rule 27 § 2.
[11]   Rule 17 § 1.
[12]   Article 25(e).
[13]   Rule 18 § 3.
[14]   Article 50.

The Registry members charged with day-to-day case-processing are organised in Section Registries, one attached to each of the five Sections. The remainder are organised in other departments necessary to provide the legal and administrative services required by the Court.[15] Each Section Registry is headed by its own Section Registrar and Deputy Registrar.[16] The bulk of the case-processing work – which includes assisting the judges in the work of the Chambers, the committees and the single-judge formations – is done within the Section Registries. The Section Registries are further divided into Divisions, which are composed largely according to State Party to the Convention, the aim being to group together lawyers and administrative staff with complementary legal and linguistic skills.

A separate administrative entity, the Filtering Section, assists the Section Registries in managing the flow of incoming new applications. It includes teams of case-processing lawyers ('filtering teams') dealing specifically with applications directed against four high case-count countries (Russia, Ukraine, Turkey and Romania), plus administrative support staff. It also comprises a specialist unit set up for the processing of requests for interim measures (the Rule 39 Unit, named after Rule 39 of the Rules of Court – see under 'Interim Measures' below). Like the Section Registries, it is headed by a Registrar. The Grand Chamber has its own Registry, which is not mentioned separately in the Rules of Court: like the Filtering Section, it is one of the 'other departments' that provide legal and administrative services. It is comprised of a small number of senior lawyers and administrative assistants. Its role is essentially a supervisory and coordinating one, the actual casework being done by lawyers and administrative assistants within the Sections. A further such 'other department' is the Directorate of the Jurisconsult. The Jurisconsult is a very senior Registry member whose task it is to assist the Court in ensuring the quality and consistency of its case law.[17] The Directorate of the Jurisconsult includes the Research and Library Division and the Case-Law Information and Publications Division.

7.4   Involvement of the Registry in the Court's Work

7.4.1   *Filtering*

It is not appropriate to use expressions such as 'standard cases'. Individual applications[18] are lodged by human beings, each of them an individual;

---

[15] Rule 18 § 1.
[16] Rule 18 § 2.
[17] Rule 18B.
[18] Article 34.

each case is therefore individual also and deserves to be considered on its own merits. Nevertheless, not all cases merit the same attention. Some can be declared inadmissible, or struck out of the list of cases, without further examination; others, though well-founded, follow established precedent without raising novel legal issues. The smaller formations of the Court – the single-judge formations and the committees – deal with cases of these two categories. Incoming applications are 'filtered', as the expression is – identified by Registry case-processing lawyers as suitable for decision by a single-judge formation or by a committee, or as requiring examination by a Chamber if they are not. Some applications may be disposed of administratively at this stage, without judicial involvement; so may certain requests for interim measures.

7.4.2   Decisions and Judgments

7.4.2.1   Single-Judge Formations

A single-judge formation – one judge deciding alone – may declare an individual application inadmissible or strike it out of the list 'where such a decision can be taken without further examination'.[19] Some 33,200 applications met this fate in 2016.[20] The Rules of Court provide that '[w]here the material submitted by the applicant is on its own sufficient to disclose that the application is inadmissible or should be struck out of the list, the application shall be considered by a single-judge formation unless there is some special reason to the contrary'.[21] Single-judge formations are assisted by (non-judicial) 'rapporteurs' – Registry lawyers functioning under the authority of the President of the Court.[22] The Section Registrars and Deputy Registrars are non-judicial rapporteurs *qualitate qua*. Others are chosen from among the most experienced case lawyers and appointed by the President of the Court.[23]

Typically, the cases presented to single-judge formations are those: in which the domestic remedies have not been exhausted or the time limit of six months from the final domestic decision has not been respected;[24] in which no complaint under the Convention can be detected; or in which

---

[19] Article 27 § 1.
[20] Annual Report of the Court for 2018, p. 161.
[21] Rule 49 § 1.
[22] Article 24 § 2.
[23] Rule 18B.
[24] Article 35 § 1.

any complaint made under the Convention would be incapable of leading to a finding of a violation. If a case is identified as belonging to this category, a case lawyer (usually the one who made the identification in the first place) will prepare a brief note setting out the facts as presented by the applicant (and as apparent from the documents submitted), the applicant's complaints and the reasons for which the application is inadmissible. This note must be approved by the non-judicial rapporteur before being forwarded to the single-judge formation for decision. Either the non-judicial rapporteur or the single-judge formation may seek further information from the case lawyer or examine the case file. Either may decide that the case merits more than superficial examination, whether by a committee or by a Chamber. In any event, responsibility for the actual decision to declare the application inadmissible or strike it out is taken by a judge of the Court, not by a member of the Registry.

The judge sitting as a single-judge formation may not examine any application against the High Contracting Party in respect of which he or she has been elected.[25] This means that if – as is usually the case – that judge is not conversant with the language or the legal system of the High Contracting Party against which the application is directed, a relationship of trust and cooperation has to exist between him or her and the Registry lawyers who prepare the cases for decision.

7.4.2.2 Committees and Chambers

If for whatever reason an application is not declared inadmissible by a single-judge formation, its further fate depends on the decision of a Judge Rapporteur appointed by the Section President. Unless the President of the Section directs that the case be considered by a Chamber or a Committee, the Judge Rapporteur decides whether the application is to be considered by a Committee or by a Chamber; if there has been no prior involvement of a single-judge formation, the Rapporteur may decide that the application should be relegated to the single-judge formation after all.[26]

Committees of three judges may declare an application inadmissible or strike it out by a unanimous vote where such decision can be taken without further examination, or alternatively declare it admissible and at the same time give judgment on the merits (and, if appropriate, award just satisfaction) if the substantive legal problem under the

---

[25] Article 26 § 3.
[26] Rule 49 §§ 2 and 3.

Convention (or its Protocols) is already the subject of 'well-established case-law of the Court'.[27] If the Judge Rapporteur decides that the case is not one to be considered by a committee, or if the committee is not unanimous, its admissibility and merits are considered by a Chamber.[28] Whether an application is decided by a committee or by a Chamber, there is no involvement of a non-judicial rapporteur. Instead, it is the Judge Rapporteur who takes responsibility for presenting the case to the formation.

In practice, a case-processing lawyer will – perhaps after taking specific instructions from the Judge Rapporteur – prepare the necessary drafts. The work of insufficiently experienced case lawyers will be supervised by more experienced colleagues. In every case, drafts are subject to quality check by a Section Registrar and Deputy Registrar before being submitted to the Judge Rapporteur, who may give whatever instructions he or she thinks fit. In Chamber cases, the judge elected in respect of the High Contracting Party concerned is required to participate.[29] There is no such requirement in Committee cases. This means that the members of the Committee may be called to consider a case on the basis of the preparation provided for them by the Registry.

7.4.2.3   Grand Chamber

Cases may end up before the Grand Chamber either when a Chamber relinquishes jurisdiction in favour of it or when the Grand Chamber panel accepts a request for referral.[30] In either case, the Grand Chamber's internal working procedure is the same. The President of the Grand Chamber (normally the President of the Court[31]) designates a Judge Rapporteur (or in inter-State cases, one or more Judges Rapporteur).[32] The drafting lawyer in Grand Chamber cases is chosen from among the more experienced Registry lawyers and therefore need not be a lawyer familiar with the language and legal system of the respondent State; if such is the case, he or she will work in tandem with a colleague who is and who knows the file well. Notes and drafts of judgments are prepared, in accordance with the prior instructions of the Judge Rapporteur, by the drafting lawyers working under the close supervision of a member of the

---

[27]   Article 28 § 1.
[28]   Article 29 § 1.
[29]   Article 26 § 4.
[30]   Articles 30 and 43 respectively.
[31]   Rules 9 § 2 and 24 § 2(a).
[32]   Rule 50.

Grand Chamber Registry – a lawyer of great experience (one of those who began their Registry careers drafting in handwriting) – before they are presented to the Judge Rapporteur for his or her approval.

The practice is that draft Grand Chamber judgments are first presented by the Judge Rapporteur to a drafting committee selected from among judges representing the view of the majority in the Grand Chamber; the drafting committee's draft is discussed in detail by the Grand Chamber and put to the vote. In Grand Chamber cases as in Chamber cases, the judge elected in respect of the High Contracting Party must take part.[33] The other judges of the Grand Chamber, including the Judge Rapporteur, thus enjoy the benefits of that judge's knowledge and understanding, without which they might well be excessively dependent on a single Registry lawyer who alone had a grasp of the domestic legal system and language.

7.4.3   Administrative Disposal

In 2018, 19,550 applications were disposed of administratively, without judicial involvement of any description.[34]

7.4.3.1   Application forms

Rule 47 of the Rules of Court provides, in essence, that an application under Article 34 of the Convention shall be made on the application form provided by the Registry, which must be completed and must be accompanied by the documentary evidence. The purpose is to ensure that the Court is provided with all the information needed in order for there to be a meaningful examination of whether the admissibility criteria are fulfilled. At the same time the Court is entitled to establish what constitutes a valid application: it may therefore require the applicant to provide all the essential information in an official document which is the basis of the application and which is sent to the respondent Government if the case is communicated. Applicants are warned in no uncertain terms of the consequences of any shortcomings in this regard:

> If you decide to apply to the Court, please ensure that your application complies with Rule 47 of the Rules of Court, which sets out the information and documents that must be provided.

---

[33] Rules 9 § 2 and 24 § 2(a).
[34] Annual Report of the Court for 2018.

> Failure to provide any of the information or documents required by Rule
> 47 §§ 1 and 2 will result in the complaints not being examined by the
> Court. It is imperative that all fields in the application form are filled in.[35]

The application form is available online, with an explanatory notice that gives detailed guidance.[36] Applications received at the Registry are subjected to detailed scrutiny by a filtering lawyer or an experienced administrative assistant. Frequent errors include submitting a scanned or photocopied form without an original signature (a scanned signature is not accepted); overrunning the maximum number of pages permitted for setting out the applicant's complaints; and if the applicant is not a natural person (as in the case of a company or an NGO with legal personality), omitting to submit proof that the person signing on the applicant body's behalf is authorised to do so – in the form, for example, of an extract from the commercial register. The Registry informs the applicant that the application, as submitted, does not interrupt the running of the six-month time limit prescribed by Article 35 § 1 of the Convention; it is then up to the applicant to re-submit the application in due time if that is still possible.

7.4.3.2   Interim Measures

Rule 39 of the Rules of Court provides for the possibility of indicating – in effect, ordering[37] – interim measures to be taken aimed at freezing the situation until the Court can finally dispose of the case before it by a decision or a judgment. The Court may do so at the request of a party (usually an applicant) or of its own motion. Interim measures are applied only rarely: the most typical cases are those in which there are fears of a threat to life (situation falling under Article 2 of the Convention) or ill-treatment prohibited by Article 3 of the Convention (prohibition of torture and inhuman or degrading treatment).[38] In practice these are almost exclusively extradition or expulsion cases. In practice, there are no contentious proceedings before a decision of this nature is taken – there simply is not enough time. A decision is taken by a duty judge, the Vice-President of a Section appointed by the President

---

[35] See the Court's website, www.echr.coe.int/, under 'Applicants'.
[36] Practice direction 'Institution of proceedings', issued by the President of the Court. See www.echr.coe.int/, under 'Applicants'.
[37] *Mamatkulov and Askarov v. Turkey* [GC], nos. 46827/99 and 46951/99, ECHR 2005-I
[38] Information on the Court's interim measures, including statistics, is available on the Court's website, www.echr.coe.int/, under 'Applicants'.

of the Court,[39] on the basis of the evidence submitted by the applicant. The duty judge is assisted by a specialised team of Registry lawyers with relevant knowledge and experience (the Rule 39 Unit set up within the Filtering Section).

The Court receives many hundreds of requests for interim measures from applicants each year: there were 1,540 in 2018 alone. Many do not fall within the limited scope of application of Rule 39 as it has developed over the years: for example, requests to order release from detention or stay the execution of a fine or prison sentence. A filtering lawyer who receives a request for an interim measure that he or she suspects is out of scope informs the Registry specialists. With their permission, he or she may send a written reply informing the applicant accordingly; the letter is reviewed and signed by a senior Registry colleague. The duty judge is not involved.[40] It is then left up to the applicant whether he or she wishes to maintain the application, in which case it should be made to meet the requirements of Rule 47 if it does not do so already.

7.4.4   The Jurisconsult

Until the entry into force of Protocol No. 14 to the Convention in 2010 the Court's judges, though appointed for a set period, could be re-elected for further terms. Since then, they are elected for a single period of nine years without the possibility of re-election.[41] Judges whose terms of office come to an end leave the Court for ever, taking with them their wealth of knowledge and experience. A recent creation within the Court's Registry is the function of Jurisconsult. This is a high-ranking Registry member whose task is to 'provide opinions and information, in particular to the judicial formations and the members of the Court' with a view to 'ensuring the quality and consistency of [the Court's] case-law'.[42] Subject to no predetermined term of office, the Jurisconsult embodies the Court's institutional memory. He is assisted by a Deputy.

7.4.4.1   The Directorate of the Jurisconsult

As mentioned, the Jurisconsult is in charge of the Research and Library Division and the Case-law Information Division, which together

---

[39] Rule 39 § 4.
[40] See the General Presentation on interim measures, available on the Court's website.
[41] Article 23 § 1.
[42] Rule 18B.

constitute the Directorate of the Jurisconsult. The Research and Library Division carries out legal research at the request of the Judge Rapporteur in Grand Chamber and (occasionally) Chamber cases. Such research may concern questions of domestic and international law but also the Court's prior case law. The Case-law Information and Publication Division, as its name suggests, disseminates the Court's case law both within and outside the Court and its Registry. Its media include the searchable database HUDOC, which is available to the public free of charge; the Case-law Information Notes, which can be found on the Court's website; and the official Reports of Judgments and Decisions, which may be purchased in paper form from a private publisher but which are also available online.[43]

7.4.4.2   Case-Law Conflict Prevention

The Jurisconsult's duties include reviewing the drafts of judgments and decisions intended to be placed before the five Sections for decision in order to ensure that the approaches followed by the Sections are consistent with existing case law of the Court and with each other. The Jurisconsult brings any discrepancies to the attention of the Sections before they meet to discuss the cases. The Chambers seized of the cases concerned remain free to take any decision they deem necessary in response. The Jurisconsult is assisted by a Deputy and by a team of experienced lawyers drawn from the Research and Library Division and the Case-law Information Division and also from case-processing divisions. Members of this team attend the meetings of the Sections and clarify the Jurisconsult's observations if so requested by the Section President.

7.5   Working Parties

Working parties exist within the Court for a variety of purposes. Their remit, in brief, is to make proposals to improve the Court's functioning in the widest sense. Examples are the Standing Committee on the Rules of Court and the Committee on Working Methods. They are composed of judges assisted by experienced Registry members; the Registry members may be lawyers but, depending on the particular expertise required, may also be drawn from other categories such as administrative support. Working parties make proposals which are considered by the plenary Court.[44]

---

[43] See the Court's website, www.echr.coe.int/, under 'Case-law'. The publisher is Wolf Legal Publishers, Oisterwijk, Netherlands.
[44] Rule 20.

7.6   Conclusion

The days are long gone when the judges of the European Court of Human Rights and the Members of the European Commission of Human Rights, the institutions created by the Convention of 1950, could consider every single case placed before them in detail. The Convention of 1950 did not mention either the Secretariat of the Commission or the Registry of the Court. In the years since the entry into force of the Convention,[45] the situation has evolved to a point where the successor body to the two original institutions, the Court of 1998, is forced to rely to a considerable extent on its support structure simply to function in its intended role. From this perspective, Article 24 § 1 of the Convention – 'The Court shall have a Registry, the functions and organisation of which shall be laid down in the rules of the Court' – merely recognises an existing reality.

It is important to remember that the Court is not in the first place intended to offer a legal remedy to applicants. Its task is '[t]o ensure the observance of the engagements undertaken by the High Contracting Parties in the Convention and the Protocols thereto'.[46] In those formations where the Court's supervisory task is exercised to greatest effect – the Grand Chamber and the Chambers – the involvement of the judges is therefore greatest, and the role of the Registry correspondingly more supportive. On the level of dispensing individual justice, the Registry does much to shield the Court's judges from the day-to-day drudgery of casework. The administrative disposal of applications for failure to comply with formal requirements is to be seen in this light. Such delegation of the duty to ensure compliance with formal requirements, together with the attendant authority, is not unique to this Court: the European Patent Office, for example, makes very similar use of 'formalities officers'.[47]

Where formal requirements are met, however, the admissibility and merits of applications are in all cases decided by the Court, whatever the judicial formation. Indeed, all decisions that are binding on Contracting Parties – including the indication of provisional measures – are given

---

[45] The Convention entered into force on 3 September 1953. The Commission and Court were established in 1955 and 1959 respectively.

[46] Article 19.

[47] Convention on the Grant of European Patents (European Patent Convention), Article 19; Implementing Regulations to the Convention on the Grant of European Patents, Rules 41, 57 and 58; European Patent Office, Guidelines for Examination, Part A, Chapter III, section 16.1.

by at least one duly elected judge. In simple terms, the Registry is indispensable to the Court. The success of the Convention system depends on public confidence in the independence and impartiality of the Court, and therefore on the perception that a relationship of trust exists between the Court and its Registry – which in turn depends in no small measure on the Registry's professionalism.

The Court of Justice of the European Union

CAROLINE HEEREN[1]

8.1 Overview of the Court of Justice of the European Union and Its Jurisdictions

The Court of Justice of the European Union (CJEU) is one of the institutions of the European Union (EU).[2] It constitutes the judicial authority of the EU and as such has the mission to ensure that the law is observed in the interpretation and application of the Treaties governing the EU.[3] It consists of two jurisdictions: the Court of Justice and the General Court.[4]

8.1.1 Legal Framework

The Treaty on the European Union (TEU), the Treaty on the Functioning of the European Union (TFEU)[5] and the Treaty establishing the European

---

[1] The views and opinions expressed in this article are those of the author.

[2] Article 13 of the Treaty on European Union (TEU) (Treaty on European Union, Maastricht, 7 October 1992, in force on 1 November 1993 Consolidated Version: 59 OJ 2016, C202/13).

[3] Article 19 TEU.

[4] In 2015, in view of the increase in litigation and the excessive length of proceedings in cases being dealt with in the General Court, the legislature of the European Union (EU) decided to gradually increase the number of judges at the General Court (Regulation 2015/2422 of the European Parliament and of the Council of 16 December 2015 amending Protocol No. 3 on the Statute of the Court of Justice of the European Union (OJ 2015 L341, p. 14) and to transfer to it the jurisdiction of the Civil Service Tribunal (CST). The latter was dissolved on 1 September 2016 (Regulation (EU, Euratom) 2016/1192 of the European Parliament and of the Council of 6 July 2016 on the transfer to the General Court (OJ 2016 L200, p.137)), and all cases pending before it were transferred to the General Court. Since that date, the General Court exercises again jurisdiction over staff cases, as it did between 1989 and 2005. Over the period of its existence, the CST welcomed a total of 14 judges from 14 different Member States and a Registrar of German nationality, and delivered 1,549 judgments.

[5] Treaty on the Functioning of the European Union, Lisbon, 13 December 2007, in force 1 December 2009, 59 OJ 2016, C202/47 (consolidated).

Atomic Energy Community[6] provide the legal basis for the judicial system of the EU. They describe the nature of the EU jurisdictions, the number of judges in each legal instance, the various legal remedies available to Member States, institutions and private parties, as well as other fundamental characteristics of the EU judicial proceedings. The Statute of the Court of Justice of the European Union, attached as protocol No 3 to the TFEU[7] (the Statute of the CJEU), is the framework legislation which is directly applicable to the structure and the functioning of the CJEU.

This framework is further implemented through the Rules of Procedure of the Court of Justice[8] and the General Court.[9] Article 253(5) TFEU provides that the Court of Justice shall establish its rules and that those rules require the approval of the Council. Article 254(5) TFEU provides that the General Court shall establish its rules in agreement with the Court of Justice, and that those Rules require the approval of the Council. On the basis of their Rules of Procedure, the Court of Justice and the General Court further autonomously, i.e. without involving the Council or any other institution, adopted implementing rules of a more practical nature, the "Practice directions to parties concerning cases brought before the Court,"[10] on the one hand, and the "Practice rules for the implementation of the Rules of Procedure of the General Court" (Practice Rules),[11] on the other.

All abovementioned texts are published in the *Official Journal of the EU* before entering into force. As such it is clear that all provisions governing the organization, functioning and mission of the Registry, derive from the Treaties, the ultimate source ruling the EU.

---

[6] Treaty establishing the European Atomic Energy Community (EAEC), Rome, 25 March 1957, in force 1 January 1958, OJ 2016 C 203/1 (consolidated).

[7] Article 281 TFEU provides that the Statute of the Court of Justice of the European Union must be laid down in a separate Protocol, annexed to the Treaties.

[8] Rules of Procedure of the Court of Justice of 25 September 2012 (OJ 2012 L265) as modified on 18 June 2013 (OJ 2013 L173, p. 65) and 19 July 2016 (OJ 2016 L217, p. 69).

[9] Rules of Procedure of the General Court of 24 March 2015 (OJ 2015 L105, p. 1), as modified on 13 July 2016 (OJ 2016 L217, p. 71), (OJ 2016 L217, p. 72) and (OJ 2016 L217, p. 73).

[10] OJ 2014 L31, p. 1, to be found at: curia.europa.eu.

[11] The consolidated version of the Practice Rules for the Implementation of the Rules of Procedure of the General Court adopted by the General Court (Practice Rules) on 20 May 2015 (OJ 2015 L152, p. 1), the corrigendum (OJ 2016 L196, p. 56) and the amendments adopted on 13 July 2016 (OJ 2016 L217, p. 78), can be found at: curia.europa.eu.

8.1.2   Judges and Advocates General

The Court of Justice is composed of 28 judges[12] and 11 advocates general.[13] The advocates general assist the Court. They are responsible for presenting, with complete impartiality and independence, an "opinion" in the cases assigned to them[14]. At the time of publication, the General Court is composed of 46 judges[15]. No advocates general sit in the General Court. However, should the General Court, sitting in plenum,[16] decide that the legal difficulty or the factual complexity of a case requires the assistance of an advocate general, one of its members will be called upon to perform this task[17].

All judges and advocates general are chosen from persons whose independence is beyond doubt and who possess the qualifications required for appointment to the highest judicial offices in their respective countries or who are jurisconsults of recognized competence.[18] They are appointed by

---

[12] Article 19 TEU provides that the Court of Justice shall consist of one judge from each Member State.

[13] Article 252 TFEU provides that the Court of Justice shall be assisted by eight advocates general and that should the Court of Justice so request, the Council, acting unanimously, may increase that number. This happened through Council Decision of 25 June 2013 increasing the number of advocates general of the Court of Justice of the European Union (OJ 2013 L 179, p. 92).

[14] Article 252 TFEU.

[15] Article 19(2) TEU provides that the General Court shall include at least one judge per Member State. Article 254 TFEU provides that the number of judges of the General Court shall be determined by the Statute of the Court of Justice. Article 48 of the Statute of the CJEU states that the General Court shall consist of (a) 40 judges as from 25 December 2015, (b) 47 judges as from 1 September 2016; and (c) two judges per Member State as from 1 September 2019.

The order of the Member States to present a second judge was drawn by lot, excluding those Member States that had a judge appointed at the CST, as those would automatically be "absorbed" by the General Court in September 2016. This gave the following result: Member States to have a second judge appointed by 15 December 2015: the Czech Republic, Sweden, Spain, Hungary, Poland, Cyprus, Lithuania, Greece, Latvia, Luxembourg, the Slovak Republic and Malta; Member States with a Judge at the CST, to be integrated in the General Court on 1 September 2016: Bulgaria, Portugal, Belgium, Denmark, Ireland, Italy and the Netherlands; and, finally, Member States to have two judges at the General Court as from 1 September 2019: Estonia, Austria, Romania, Finland, Croatia, Germany, Slovenia, France and, subject to Brexit, the United Kingdom. In reality, those deadlines have not always been respected, due to long national selection proceedings or negative advice from the panel provided for in Article 255 TFEU.

[16] Article 30 Rules of Procedure of the General Court (RP GC).

[17] Article 254(1) TFEU; Article 49(1) of the Statute of the CJEU; Articles 3(3), 30 and 31 RP GC.

[18] Articles 253 and 254 TFEU.

common accord of the governments of the Member States for six years, after a panel, set up pursuant to Article 255 TFEU, has given an opinion on the candidate's suitability to perform the duties of a judge or an advocate general.[19] The panel's opinions, whether favorable or unfavorable, have always been followed by the governments of the Member States, which means that it has a de facto veto right[20]. Retiring judges and advocates general may be reappointed.[21] Before taking up their duties, all judges and advocates general[22] must, before the Court of Justice sitting in open court, take an oath to perform their duties impartially and conscientiously and to preserve the confidentiality of the deliberations of the Court.[23]

8.1.3 Jurisdiction

The Court of Justice has jurisdiction over references for preliminary rulings,[24] actions for failure to fulfill obligations, whether brought by the Commission[25] or another Member State,[26] actions for annulment and failure to act brought by a Member State against the European Parliament

---

[19] The panel was established by the Treaty of Lisbon. The panel comprises seven persons chosen from among former members of the Court of Justice and the General Court, members of national supreme courts and lawyers of recognized competence, one of whom shall be proposed by the European Parliament. The first panel started working in March 2010 (Council Decision 2010/124/EU of 25 February 2010 relating to the operating rules of the panel provided for in Article 255 TFEU (OJ 2010 L50, p. 18) and Council Decision 2010/125/EU of 25 February 2010 appointing the members of the panel provided for in Article 255 TFEU (OJ 2010 L50, p. 20) and examined during its four-year term 67 candidatures for the offices of judge or advocate general. In total, 7 of the 67 opinions delivered were unfavorable. The second panel (Council Decision 2014/76/EU of 11 February 2014 appointing the members of the panel provided for in Article 255 TFEU (OJ 2014 L41, p. 18) and Council Decision 2016/296 (EU, Euratom) of 29 February 2016 appointing a member of the panel provided for in Article 255 TFEU (OJ 2016 L55, p. 14) started work on March 1, 2014 and examined until the end of its term 80 candidatures, 7 of which received an unfavorable opinion. The third panel (Council Decision (EU, Euratom) 2017:2262 of 4 December 2017 appointing the members of the panel provided for in Article 255 TFEU (OJ 2017 L324, p. 50), took up its functions on March 1, 2018.

[20] For more information on the activities of and the criteria applied by the panels, see the five "Activity reports of the panel provided for by Article 255 TFEU," available at: curia.europa. eu.

[21] Article 19(2) TEU.

[22] Article 8 of the Statute of the CJEU provides that the provisions of Articles 2 to 7 shall apply to the advocates general.

[23] Article 2 of the Statute of the CJEU.

[24] Article 267 TFEU.

[25] Article 258 TFEU.

[26] Article 259 TFEU.

and/or the Council (apart from Council measures in respect of State aid, dumping and implementing powers) or brought by one European institution against another[27] as well as over appeals on points of law brought against judgments and orders of the General Court.[28]

The General Court has jurisdiction to hear and determine:[29] (i) actions brought by natural or legal persons against acts of the institutions, bodies, offices or agencies of the European Union and against regulatory acts or against a failure to act on the part of those institutions, bodies, offices or agencies;[30] (ii) actions brought by the Member States against the Commission;[31] (iii) actions brought by the Member States against the Council relating to acts adopted in the field of State aid, trade protection measures (dumping) and acts by which it exercises implementing powers;[32] (iv) actions seeking compensation for damage caused by the institutions or the bodies, offices or agencies of the European Union or their staff;[33] (v) actions based on contracts made by the European Union which expressly give jurisdiction to the General Court;[34] (vi) actions relating to intellectual property brought against the European Union Intellectual Property Office and against the Community Plant Variety Office;[35] (vi) disputes between the institutions of the European Union and their staff.[36]

8.1.4   Organization

The Court may sit as a full court, in a Grand Chamber of 15 judges or in Chambers of three or five judges.[37] The General Court may sit in a Grand Chamber of 15 judges,[38] in Chambers of three or five judges[39] or as a single

---

[27] Articles 263 and 265 TFEU *juncto* Article 51 of the Statute of the CJEU.
[28] Article 56 of the Statute of the CJEU.
[29] Article 256 TFEU.
[30] Articles 263 and 265 TFEU.
[31] Ibid.
[32] Article 51 of the Statute of the CJEU.
[33] Article 268 TFEU.
[34] Article 272 TFEU.
[35] Article 72 of Regulation (EU) 2017/1001 of the European Parliament and of the Council of 14 June 2017 on the European Union trade mark (OJ 2017, L154, p. 1). Article 61 of Council Regulation (EC) No 6/2002 of 12 December 2001 on Community designs (OJ 2002, L3, p. 1). Article 73 of Council Regulation (EC) No 2100/94 of 27 July 1994 on Community plant variety rights (OJ 1994, L227, p. 1).
[36] Article 270 TFEU.
[37] Article 251 TFEU; Article 16 of the Statute of the CJEU.
[38] Article 50 Statute of the CJEU; Articles 15 and 23 RP GC.
[39] Article 50 Statute of the CJEU; Articles 14(1)(2) and 24 RP GC.

judge.[40] All decisions relating to the organization of the Court of Justice and the General Court are published in the *Official Journal of the EU*. The Court of Justice appoints its Registrar.[41] The Registrar is not only the head of the Registry of the Court of Justice,[42] but also manages the departments of the Court of Justice[43] under the authority of the President of the Court. The General Court also appoints its Registrar.[44] The Registrar is the head of the Registry of the General Court, which is the sole service of the jurisdiction. The legal framework, composition and mission of the Registry are further described below.

8.2   The Registry of the General Court

8.2.1   Legal Framework Governing the Registry

As previously explained, the organization, functioning and mission of the Registry are ultimately ruled by the Treaties. Article 254(4) TFEU states that the General Court shall appoint its Registrar. Article 10 of the Statute of the CJEU[45] adds that the Registrar shall take an oath before the General Court to perform his/her duties impartially and conscientiously and to preserve the secrecy of the deliberations of the Court. The Rules of Procedure of the General Court describe in detail how the Registrar is appointed,[46] as well as what his duties and responsibilities

---

[40] Article 50 Statute of the CJEU; Articles 14(3) and 29 RP GC.
[41] Article 253(5) TFEU; Article 18 ff. of the Rules of Procedure of the Court of Justice concerning the Registry.
[42] The Registry of the Court of Justice is, just like the Registry of the General Court, responsible for maintaining the case files for pending cases and for keeping the register in which all the procedural documents are entered. It receives, keeps and serves the applications, pleadings and other procedural documents sent to the Court by the lawyers and agents for the parties. It is responsible for all correspondence relating to the progress of proceedings before the Court.
[43] The departments are divided into three main groups: the administrative support services in the Directorate-General for Administration; the language services in the Multilingualism Directorate-General; and the information services in the Information Directorate-General. The Research and Documentation Directorate and the Protocol and Visits Directorate are under the direct control of the Registrar of the Court. Those departments support the work of both courts.
[44] Article 254(4) TFEU.
[45] Which, in accordance with Article 47 of that Statute applies *mutatis mutandis* to the Registrar of the General Court.
[46] When the post of Registrar is vacant, an advertisement is published in the *Official Journal of the European Union* (Article 32(2) RP GC). The Registrar is appointed for a renewable term of six years. The General Court may decide to renew the term of office of the

are.[47] The mission of the Registry, its composition and its working methods are further, in a precise way, described in the Rules of Procedure of the General Court[48] and the Practice rules for their implementation, or result from other sources, such as decisions taken by the General Court sitting in plenum, or by the Presidents of Chambers, sitting in chambers.

8.2.2 Composition of the Registry

The Registry of the General Court is headed by the Registrar.[49] On December 31, 2018, the Registry comprised 72 budgetary posts, one of them occupied by the Deputy Registrar,[50] one by a Head of Unit, 14 by administrators, all serving as acting Registrars,[51] one of which has specifically been appointed to assist the Registrar in his administrative functions, and the others by assistants. Administrators of the Registry are required to have a law degree. It is important to highlight that all officials and other servants are responsible to the Registrar of the General Court under the authority of the President of the General Court.[52]

8.2.3 Mission of the Registry – Judicial Assistance

It is the Registry's mission to offer all assistance needed to allow the judges to fully accomplish, in an efficient way and within a reasonable time, their judicial work. All the activities of the Registry are thus conditioned by the need to assist the jurisdiction in the decision-making process and to ensure that this can be terminated without delay. Within this context, the Registry must ensure three essential activities of a judicial nature:[53] (a) ensuring the communication between representatives of the parties and the judges; (b) keeping records and ensuring that proceedings run

---

incumbent Registrar without publishing an advertisement in the *Official Journal* (Article 32(4) RP GC). The candidate needs to obtain votes of more than half the Judges composing the General Court to be elected. The election takes place by secret ballot (Article 9(3) RP GC).

[47] Articles 32 and 35 RP GC. Point 1 ff. Practice Rules.

[48] Articles 32 to 39 RP GC.

[49] Since its creation in 1989, the General Court has had two registrars: Mr. Hans Jung (1989–2005) and Mr. Emmanuel Coulon (since 2005). The current mandate of the Registrar expires in 2023.

[50] Article 33 RP GC.

[51] Article 34 RP GC.

[52] Article 39 RP GC.

[53] Article 35 RP GC.

smoothly; and (c) providing assistance to the judges and their staff. These activities will be further elaborated below.

Moreover, the Registrar is, under the authority of the President, responsible for the administration of the General Court, its financial management and its accounts, thereby assisted by the departments of the CJEU.[54] In the context of this activity, the Registrar is vested with particular responsibilities. This element of the mission of the Registry is not, however, addressed in this article.

8.2.3.1   Communication Between Representatives of the Parties and the Judges

Contrary to what is the rule in certain Member States, a direct exchange of procedural documents between representatives of parties, whereby a copy is sent to the court, is not allowed. Within the framework of proceedings before the General Court, all procedural documents are to be sent to the Registry, which, after entering them in the register, transmits them to the judges, on the one hand, and serves them on the representatives of the other parties, on the other hand.[55]

Procedural documents can be lodged either in paper form, where appropriate, after transmission of a copy of the original of the document by telefax, or by electronic means, by e-Curia.[56] Procedural documents are internally communicated to the judges in an electronic way, as an attachment to what is called a transmission slip (*fiche de transmission*). Whereas the communication with the parties' representatives, be it orally or in writing, must always be conducted in the language of the case, contacts between the Registry and the judges, oral or written, occur in French, as it is the language of the deliberations of the CJEU.

8.2.3.2   Keeping Records and Ensuring that Proceedings Run Smoothly

The Registry is responsible for keeping the records of the General Court, in which all procedural documents are entered in the order in which they are lodged.[57] It is equally responsible for the archiving of all files. The

---

[54] Article 35 RP GC; Article 1 Practice Rules.
[55] Article 35(1) RP GC.
[56] Articles 72(1), 73(3) and 74 RP GC. Decision of the General Court of 14 September 2011 on the lodging of procedural documents by means of e-Curia (OJ 2011, C289, p. 9). E-Curia is an application of the CJEU allowing the exchange of procedural documents with the Registry by exclusively electronic means.
[57] Article 36(1) RP GC.

Registry is also responsible for ensuring that proceedings run smoothly, by offering support of different kinds, at any time dictated by the mission, to allow the judges to fully accomplish, in an efficient way, their judicial work within a reasonable time limit.

As such: the Registry ensures the management of the e-Curia application; processes applications for legal aid;[58] and, where appropriate, pays the sums due and/or demands recovery of the debt. The same goes for Registry charges that are recoverable and other sums due to the Tribunal treasury. The Registry is tasked with the translation of everything said or written in the course of the proceedings, at the request of a judge or a party, into the language of the case or, where necessary, into another language as provided for in Article 45(1) of the Rules of Procedure.[59] Where, for the purpose of the efficient conduct of the proceedings, a translation into another language of the EU is necessary, the Registry also arranges for such translation to be made. The Registrar is furthermore in charge of the publications of the General Court and of the dissemination on the Internet of documents concerning the General Court.[60] Finally, the Registry is responsible for the proper management of the procedural files, a duty linked to the provision of legal assistance to the judges and their staff.

8.2.3.3   Assistance to the Judges and Their Staff

General
Throughout the proceedings, the Registry offers truly (pro)active assistance to the judges in relation to procedural matters. Owing to the specific jurisdiction of the General Court, its procedure is quite detailed and somewhat burdensome. Contrary to the Court of Justice, actions before the General Court can be lodged by private parties, thus entailing

---

[58] Article 146 RP GC.
[59] Article 47 RP GC; Point 38 Practice Rules. The CJEU is a multilingual institution: each of the 24 official languages of the EU can be the language of a case. The CJEU is required to observe the principle of multilingualism in full, because of the need to communicate with the parties in the language of the proceedings and to ensure that its case law is disseminated throughout the Member States.
    As a consequence, the Court of Justice has large interpretation and translation departments (with around 70 and 911 staff members, respectively). In order to ensure that judicial terms are correctly translated and take into account the Member States' specific legal systems, translators at the CJEU are required to have a law degree. They are called lawyer-linguists. The judges and advocates general, however, have, for the purpose of their deliberations, opted to communicate and work in one single language, i.e. French.
[60] Article 35 RP GC; Points 52 to 56 Practice Rules.

representation issues and anonymity requests. Moreover, the General Court deals with more fact-finding cases, meaning that questions regarding the lodging of new evidence are often raised. Many cases involve the intervention of interested parties and, consequently, confidentiality issues. In short, actions before the General Court give rise to a number of complex procedural matters and whereas the judges and their staff are naturally occupied by the merits of the case, the Registry is there to assist them on such procedural questions.

In this context, procedural documents are not merely transmitted to the judges, but, in order to assist them in the decision-making on a procedural issue, the transmission will, where appropriate, be accompanied by a proposal or a set of options from which the judge decides, a summary of decisions taken so far on similar issues or the applicable case law. What follows is an overview of the different steps of the proceedings before the General Court and a description of the procedural guidance offered by the Registry in relation to each of these steps.

Introduction of a Case

Examination of the application – Upon receipt, any application initiating proceedings is examined by an administrator of the Registry in order to determine whether procedural requirements are complied with. Some procedural requirements are considered to be essential and non-compliance with them might lead the action to be declared manifestly inadmissible without the application even being notified to the defendant.[61] The procedural requirements are: (i) the case must fall within the jurisdiction of the General Court;[62] (ii) the applicant must be represented in line with the conditions of Article 51 of the Rules of Procedure of the General Court and Article 19 of the Statute of the CJEU as interpreted by case law;[63] (iii) the application must be received within

---

[61] Article 126 RP GC.

[62] As described in Article 256 TFEU.

[63] Article 19 of the Statute of the CJEU, applicable to proceedings before the General Court pursuant to its Article 53, provides that parties other than the Member States or States which are parties to the EEA and the EU institutions or the EFTA Surveillance Authority must be represented by a lawyer. Only a lawyer authorized to practice before a court of a Member State or of another State of the EEA may represent or assist a party before the Court. University teachers who are nationals of a Member State whose law accords them a right of audience have the same rights. Moreover, Article 19 uses the term "represented," meaning that a party is not authorized to act itself but must use the services of a third person which is sufficiently distant from the legal person it represents.

the time limit for bringing an action; (iv) the application must be correctly signed.[64]

If a failure to comply with one of these requirements is identified by the Registry, this will be communicated to the President of the General Court and confirmation sought as to whether the application should be served on the defendant or not. Where non-compliance with an essential procedural requirement is confirmed by the President,[65] the action will be rejected by reasoned order, drafted in certain circumstances by the Registry. Other procedural requirements are considered to be of a less essential nature and non-compliance with them only leads to a delayed service of the procedural document concerned, as the party having lodged it will be given a period of time to make good any formal irregularity.[66]

Assignment of cases – Upon receipt of an application initiating proceedings, the administrator prepares a so-called slip for assignment (*fiche d'attribution*) and sends it to the President of the General Court. This slip contains not only a description of the subject-matter of the case, but also, where appropriate, an enumeration of connected cases, in order to allow the President of the General Court to have as much information as possible when assigning cases to the Chambers. The assignment of cases by the President of the General Court is done following strict rules. Cases that are not considered to be manifestly inadmissible are assigned to the Chambers in turn, in accordance with the date on which they are registered at the Registry, following four separate routes:[67] one for cases concerning the application of competition rules applicable to undertakings, the rules on State aid and the rules on trade protection measures; one for cases concerning intellectual property rights; one for civil service cases; and one for all other cases.

---

[64] Where the application is lodged in paper form, where appropriate after transmission of a copy of the original of that document by telefax in accordance with Article 73(3) RP GC, it must bear the handwritten signature of the party's agent or lawyer (Article 73 RP GC). Where the application is lodged by electronic means, the representative's user identification and password, used to effect the lodging, constitutes the signature of the document concerned (Article 74 RP GC and Article 3 of the Decision of the General Court of 14 September 2011 on the lodging and service of procedural documents by means of e-Curia).

[65] Article 2(b) of RP GC provides that "President" unless otherwise specified, means, in cases assigned to Chambers, the President of the Chamber to which the case is assigned.

[66] Articles 77(2), 78(6), 81(2) RP GC; Points 104 ff. Practice Rules.

[67] Articles 25 and 26 RP GC and Decision on the criteria for the assignment of cases to Chambers (OJ 2016 C296, p. 2).

The President of the General Court may derogate from these only to take account of a connection between cases, for the identification of which he is assisted by the Registry, or with a view to ensuring an even spread of the workload. The President of the Chamber to whom the case has been assigned following the abovementioned rule, proposes to the President the designation of a judge to act as reporting judge ("Judge-Rapporteur").[68] The President of the General Court decides on the proposal.

Publication of the notice in the Official Journal of the EU – The administrator responsible for the case prepares, in accordance with Article 79 of the Rules of Procedure of the General Court, and on the basis of the summary submitted by the applicant(s) in accordance with Point 130 of the Practice Rules, a notice indicating, amongst others, the forms of order sought by the applicant(s) and a summary of the pleas in law and of the main supporting arguments. The publication of this notice in the *Official Journal of the EU* is an important step in the proceedings, as it constitutes the starting point for the time limit of six weeks prescribed by Article 143(1) of the Rules of Procedure of the General Court for the submission of an application to intervene.

Written Phase of the Proceedings

Follow-up and management of time limits – The Registry checks whether procedural documents are lodged within the time limit prescribed. Time limits are generally prescribed by the Treaties, the Statute of the CJEU or the Rules of Procedure of the General Court, or set by the President or the Registrar. Article 61(2) of the Rules of Procedure of the General Court provides that the President may delegate to the Registrar the power of signature for the purposes of setting certain time limits which, pursuant to these Rules, it falls to the President to prescribe or extend.[69] In practice, every President of Chamber, when taking up his or her functions, is invited by the Registrar to sign such delegation of power of signature. This allows the Registry to ensure the smooth and harmonious running of all proceedings. Time limits will be set by the Registry according to strict rules. Moreover, under certain circumstances, upon request of one of the parties, time limits can be extended by the Registry without the prior authorization of the President of Chamber.

[68] Article 26(2) RP GC.
[69] See also Point 64 Practice Rules.

Draft orders prepared by the Registry – In accordance with the Rules of Procedure of the General Court, certain procedural questions are decided upon by order. As part of the procedural guidance provided, and in order to avoid unnecessary translation work, a limited number of these orders are under certain circumstances prepared by the Registry[70]. These orders are prepared on the basis of templates approved by the General Court. Their final adoption lies with the composition of the Chamber deciding on the case.

After the Written Part: Participation in the Meeting of the Chamber (*Conférence*)

When the written part of the procedure is closed, the President fixes a date on which the Judge-Rapporteur is to present a preliminary report to the General Court.[71] In practice, the report is presented to the Chamber during a meeting of the Chamber (the *conférence*). Present at such meeting are not only the judges of the composition of the Chamber deciding on the case, but also an administrator of the Registry in his capacity as acting Registrar. He or she has the task of assisting the judges, drawing up the minutes of the meeting[72] and ensuring that procedural questions raised are decided upon while respecting the applicable rules. The Chamber decides what action to take on the proposals of the Judge-Rapporteur and, where appropriate, whether to open the oral part of the procedure. The minutes of the meeting are signed by the President of the Chamber. The Registry is in charge of the execution of the decisions taken.

---

[70] The following orders are, under specific conditions, concerned: orders rejecting actions manifestly bound to fail before the application being served (Article 126 RP GC), orders refusing legal aid (Article 148 RP GC), orders joining cases with confidentiality issues (68 RP GC), orders reserving the decision on the plea of inadmissibility (Article 130(7) RP GC), orders on discontinuance (Article 125 RP GC), orders accepting an uncontested request for leave to intervene (Article 144(5) RP GC), orders concerning actions devoid of purpose in cases concerning intellectual property rights, orders reopening the oral part of the procedure (Article 113 RP GC), and rectification of orders and judgments (Article 164 RP GC).

[71] Article 87, §1 RP GC. The preliminary report contains an analysis of the relevant issues of fact and of law raised by the action, proposals as to whether measures of organization of procedure or measures of inquiry should be undertaken, whether there should be an oral part of the procedure and whether the case should be referred to the Grand Chamber or to a Chamber sitting with a different number of judges, or whether the case should be delegated to a single judge.

[72] Article 43 RP GC.

Oral Part of the Proceedings

The procedure before the General Court includes, in the oral part, a hearing arranged either of the General Court's own motion or at the request of a main party.[73] The hearing is presided over by the President of the Chamber, who is responsible for the proper conduct of the hearing and declares the oral part of the procedure closed at the end of it.[74] The Registry ensures the management of the different hearing rooms and checks the availability of any interpreters required. Just before the hearing starts, the parties' representatives are invited to an informal meeting with the judge, where they are asked whether they have observations on the report for the hearing and where the organization of the hearing is discussed. The acting Registrar is always present at this informal meeting in order to reply, if necessary, to any question related to a procedural matter. Furthermore, the acting Registrar draws up the minutes of the hearing, in the respective language of each case. The minutes are signed by the acting Registrar and by the President of the Chamber[75] before being notified to the parties.

Delivery and Notification of Judgments and Orders

The parties are informed of the date of delivery of the judgment in their case.[76] The judgment is delivered in open court, in the presence of an administrator of the Registry, in his capacity as acting Registrar. The original version is signed by the President, by the judges who took part in the deliberations and by the acting Registrar present at the hearing during which the judgment was delivered. A copy of the judgment is served on the parties.[77] Orders are not delivered in open court. Their original version is signed by the President and the Registrar before a copy of the order is served on the parties.[78]

Other Duties

Still within the framework of its mission to provide procedural guidance to the judges, the Registry is in charge of the calendar of the General Court and its distribution. Furthermore, the Registry provides on a regular basis statistics on the judicial activity, the activity of the Registry and

---

[73] Article 106 RP GC.
[74] Articles 110 and 111 RP GC.
[75] Article 114 RP GC; Point 211 Practice Rules.
[76] Article 116 RP GC.
[77] Article 119 RP GC.
[78] Article 120 RP GC.

the publication of the decisions of the General Court. It ensures their distribution amongst the judges and the staff of the General Court.

8.3 Conclusion

The mission of the Registry of the General Court consists in essence of offering the jurisdiction all the support needed in order to allow the judges to fully and efficiently accomplish their judicial work within a reasonable period of time. This mission is explicitly foreseen in the legal texts governing the judicial structure of the EU, i.e. the Treaties (TEU, TFEU), the Statute of the CJEU, the Rules of Procedure of the General Court and the Practice Rules. These texts are adopted in line with well-defined procedures and published in the *Official Journal of the EU*. The Registrar is elected following a precise procedure and nominations are published. The Registrar's staff is responsible to him under the authority of the President of the General Court.

The scope of the actions undertaken by the Registry is conditioned by the mission provided in the legal texts. Through its role as intermediary between the parties and the judges, its keeping of records and its offering of necessary technical and administrative support and procedural guidance to the judges, the Registry is an indispensable part of the judicial apparatus. The direct impact of its activities on the decision-making process remains limited, however. True, the sooner it processes incoming procedural documents and decisions taken by the judges, the more rapidly proceedings advance. However, at a substantive level, its procedural guidance is limited to the drafting of documents and the formulating of proposals, which remain just that: drafts and proposals. At any time, the ultimate decision lies with the judges.

PART II

Nomination and Appointment

.

9

Gatekeeper Secretariats

KATHLEEN CLAUSSEN*

9.1 Introduction

It was not until the late twentieth century that the term 'gatekeeper' came into metaphorical use.[1] Prior to that time, the narrative of 'gatekeeping' over the ages reflects a stagnant storyline about watchpersons in charge of physical gates 'usually to identify, count, supervise, etc., the traffic or flow through' them.[2] As access to that which was gated became more limited, and the stakes behind having access grew, the role of the gatekeeper developed into a substantial power. That power could be wielded only by those so specially entrusted. With this evolution in meaning, the word 'gatekeeper' now implies a degree of privilege or authority. No longer do the gatekeepers merely supervise or count entry – now they control it.

Precisely this shift has occurred in international dispute settlement bodies with respect to the gatekeeping role of their administrative institutions. That is, the administrative units that provide support to adjudicators in the resolution of international disputes often referred to as 'secretariats' or 'registries' do far more than just identify, count, and supervise traffic through those dispute resolution bodies. Secretariats have an influence on shaping international dispute settlement and its legitimacy.

Across international courts and tribunals, there are many types of institutional design. As the name 'registry' suggests, these staff are responsible for the registration of cases and at least administrative duties such

* My thanks to PluriCourts and Freya Baetens for the invitation to be a part of this project, to the participants in the Unseen Actors workshop in The Hague and in the European Society of International Law workshop on the Judicialization of International Law in Oslo, to Arim J. Kim for research assistance, and to the several practitioners and secretariat staff who provided useful feedback based on their experiences.

[1] K. Lewin, 'Frontiers in Group Dynamics,' (1947) 1 *Human Relations* 5, 145.
[2] Random House Unabridged Dictionary of American English.

as maintaining records, overseeing or performing secretarial tasks, and transacting business on behalf of the institution as a whole. In the case of public dispute settlement bodies, the focus of this study, States charge secretariats with a wide range of roles. Two questions present themselves: one is whether States have appropriately delineated their delegations. Do secretariats have appropriate mandates to effectively achieve the goals States set for them? The second question is whether secretariats are operating within those mandates.[3] Examining secretariat mandates also illuminates legitimacy concerns. In particular, the accountability mechanisms for the secretariat, the secretariat's financial independence, and the range of activities and innovation supported by the secretariat are relevant considerations with respect to the legitimacy of the institution.

This chapter and the study from which it is drawn begin an overdue descriptive and analytical discussion about secretariat practices and their systemic implications. It studies why and how secretariats have come into this gatekeeping function, maps their values, and analyzes the normative implications. As secretariat practices are rarely publicly available, this chapter reports on views and experiences drawn from in-person interviews and correspondence with international adjudicators, attorneys appearing before international courts and tribunals, and secretariat staff.

The issues addressed in this chapter are particularly critical as States design new secretariats.[4] The parties involved in those negotiations are likely to consider options from among the designs of existing secretariats as well as alternatives. As we consider the influence of secretariats, we uncover some lessons for the future construction of these institutions.

The chapter proceeds by giving an overview of the size and shape of the secretariat landscape. Second, it describes the roles States have delegated to secretariats and offers a taxonomy for thinking about secretariat design. Third, it analyzes work undertaken by secretariats that arguably exceeds some of those mandates and that has made secretariats gatekeepers.

---

[3] This chapter does not take up concerns about the role of the arbitral secretary, which is a distinct position sometimes within the secretariat but sometimes with no relationship to the secretariat, despite the similarity in name.

[4] Binyamin Applebaum, 'U.S. Begins Negotiations on Trade Pact with Harsh Words,' *The New York Times*, August 17, 2017, p. B3; European Commission, The Multilateral Investment Court Project, http://trade.ec.europa.eu/doclib/press/index.cfm?id=1608 (last updated 20 March 2018).

Finally, the chapter concludes with reflections on the implications of this evolution for the legitimacy of international adjudication.

9.2   Secretariats and Their Accountability Structures

The word 'gatekeeping' tells us very little without its dependent preposition 'to.' To say that a person or institution is a 'gatekeeper' begs the question 'to what' does the gatekeeper manage access and entry? It may also prompt the queries: 'for whom?' or 'on whose behalf?' The latter questions address the origins of the gatekeeper's authority. Typically, gatekeepers receive their mandate from a higher authority. In exercising this delegation, gatekeepers have the power to issue decisions with the force of that authority. As a result, a gatekeeper is necessarily subject to questions of accountability and of legitimacy.

This section examines the relationship between States and the secretariats to which they delegate. It sets out the activities and structures of secretariats over time before proposing a taxonomy to better understand the secretariat design models in use today and then compares their operations to their original mandates as located in their founding legal instruments.

9.2.1   Secretariat-building and Landscape

The development of service providers for international dispute settlement has a varied history. In contrast to today, with an extensive menu of international dispute settlement designs from which to choose, the concept had a slow start. At the end of the nineteenth century, arbitral agreements had become a centerpiece of inter-State relations, but each was self-contained.[5] That is, the arbitral arrangement, and any arbitration

---

[5] For example, the 1794 Jay Treaty, which launched a 'modern movement' for a standing arbitral body, provided that three temporary joint commissions would handle three types of disputes coming out of the war between Great Britain and the United States. The Jay Treaty did not provide for a secretariat. Jay Treaty, November 19, 1794, 52 CTS 243. See also C. Copeland, 'The Use of Arbitration to Settle Territorial Disputes' (1999) 67 *Fordham Law Review* 3073. Before that time, commissions 'appeared occasionally in connection with England's colonial problems during the seventeenth and eighteenth century.' Ibid. For example, the Treaty of Westminster of 1654 referred claims concerning the East Indies and the Americas to a commission. But this and other international agreements of that period failed to arrive at decisions to be implemented. The Alabama Claims Commission also served a major role in managing a maritime controversy between the United States and the United Kingdom related to the US Civil War. For a useful discussion of the

that might occur under it, was confined to the system of its own bilateral or multilateral agreement. There was no common institution to facilitate the process of administering disputes.

An important impetus to spur the later proliferation of international courts was the Lake Mohonk Conference convened in 1895 to explore and eventually to promote international arbitration and the possible founding of a permanent international court.[6] Four years later, a group of 26 states convened in The Hague to address the rampant arms race among the major powers. They concluded the 1899 Convention for the Pacific Settlement of International Disputes, which established the Permanent Court of Arbitration (PCA), and was further elaborated through an additional 1907 Convention.[7] The two Hague Conventions provided for an International Bureau that would serve as the PCA's secretariat, headed by a Secretary-General who would also act as Registrar of the Court.[8] All staffing and other decisions relevant to the Bureau were to be made by an Administrative Council (the PCA's assembly of parties), although control of the Bureau staff and the drafting of the Court's budget was left to the PCA Secretary-General.[9] The original vision of the founders was that a small group of six staff would facilitate the PCA's work.[10]

Following the world wars and the short experiment of the Permanent Court of International Justice, a rapid development began of permanent dispute settlement bodies, most of which remain operational today.[11] Karen Alter has chronicled what she counts as 24 permanent courts issuing thousands of decisions, of which 91 percent have been issued

---

Alabama Claims Commission's contribution, see C. Brower II, 'The Functions and Limits of Arbitration and Judicial Settlement Under Private and Public International Law' (2008) 18 *Duke Journal of Comparative and International Law* 259. Arbitration was not limited to these nations, however. The United States, for one, had arbitrations and entered into arbitration agreements with over a dozen European and Latin American States at that time.

[6] Predecessors to the conference were discussions and proposals regarding international standing body ideas that were introduced in the US Senate and UK House of Commons.

[7] Convention for the Pacific Settlement of International Disputes, The Hague, 29 July 1899, in force 4 September 1900, 32 Stat. 1779; Convention on the Pacific Settlement of International Disputes of 1907, The Hague, 18 October 1907, in force 26 January 1910, 1 Bevans 577, 36 Stat. 2199, Treaty Series 536, p. 577.

[8] Rules Concerning the Organization and Internal Working of the International Bureau of the Permanent Court of Arbitration (1900), Art. I.

[9] Ibid.

[10] Ibid., Art. II.

[11] Left out from this discussion is any treatment of the criminal court registries, which add a number of layers of complexity not dealt with among the civil courts and tribunals.

since the fall of the Berlin Wall.[12] Just as the courts vary in their principal function and other characteristics, the secretariats of these courts take a variety of shapes and sizes, and maintain varying degrees of transparency about those details.[13] Most institutions typically maintain some sort of headquarters in which to house their secretariat staff.[14]

Table 9.1 sets out a selection of secretariat information, although certainly each court operates differently, straining any comparison. Given the space constraints of the chapter, the list is a necessarily imperfect sampling. In recent years, the proliferation of private arbitral bodies to administer commercial and investor-State disputes has also transformed the landscape and the debate on public-private international lawmaking.

9.2.2 Secretariat Mandates

Secretariats serve in a variety of capacities in managing international disputes. In some instances, secretariats work so closely with their court or tribunal that they have been called 'extension[s] of the tribunals themselves.'[15] As the treaty instruments that govern the work of these international courts and tribunals show, the principal role of registries and secretariats is to support the management and administration of disputes occurring under the auspices of that institution; however, just as there is no one-size-fits-all secretariat structure, likewise there is no archetypal secretariat mandate. Support can mean many things and indeed each institution studied here frames the idea of support slightly differently. This section examines selected secretariats' enumerated powers, the instruments in which they are found, and their limits.

To better understand secretariats' accountability structures, one might consider them in a taxonomy. This proposed structural and functional taxonomy assumes States design secretariats to play the roles delegated to them as agents rather than trustees, but it does not exclude that other

[12] K. Alter, *The New Terrain of International Law: Courts, Politics, Rights* (Princeton University Press, 2013), p. 4.

[13] By one count, in 2013, there were approximately 2,228 staff members across all international civil and criminal courts. S. Cartier and C. Hoss, 'The Role of Registries and Legal Secretariats in International Judicial Institutions', in C. Romano, K. Alter and Y. Shany (eds.), *The Oxford Handbook of International Adjudication* (Oxford University Press, 2014).

[14] Since around 2008, some institutions have experimented with regional outposts. The franchising of international dispute settlement is a direct result of the increased competition.

[15] N. Grossman, 'Legitimacy and International Adjudicative Bodies' (2009) 41 *George Washington International Law Review* 107, 141.

Table 9.1 *Selected secretariat information*

Institution name	Date of creation	Approximate staff size	Approximate size of court docket (in current year unless otherwise noted)
Permanent Court of Arbitration (PCA)[a]	1899	40	129 arbitrations
International Court of Justice (ICJ)[b]	1945	120	18 disputes
European Court of Human Rights (ECHR)[c]	1959	Hundreds	80,000 applications
International Centre for Settlement of Investment Disputes (ICSID)[d]	1966	65	235 arbitrations
Inter-American Court of Human Rights (IACtHR)[e]	1979	2 officials plus support staff	16 contentious cases
East African Community Court of Justice (ECOWAS Court of Justice)[f]	1991	>30	30 cases
World Trade Organization (WTO)[g]	1994	80 in divisions managing disputes	70 disputes
International Tribunal for the Law of the Sea (ITLOS)[h]	1996	34	1 dispute
East African Court of Justice (EACJ)[i]	2001	25	80 decisions issued since 2014 and additional cases pending
African Court of Human and Peoples' Rights (ACtHPR)[j]	2004	2 officials plus support staff	Several dozen applications

[a] https://pca-cpa.org/en/cases/.
[b] www.icj-cij.org/en/registry.

Table 9.1 (*cont.*)

c European Court of Human Rights, Information Documents, http://echr.coe
.int/Pages/home.aspx?p=court&c=#newComponent_1346149514608_pointer;
European Court of Human Rights, How the Court Works, http://echr.coe.int/
Pages/home.aspx?p=court/howitworks&c=#newComponent_1346157759256_
pointer; European Court of Human Rights, Statistics, http://echr.coe.int/Pages/
home.aspx?p=reports&c=.

d Convention on the Settlement of Investment Disputes between States and
Nationals of Other States, 18 March 1965, 575 UNTS 159; ICSID Secretariat,
ICSID Annual Report 2017, p. 7.

e Inter-American Court of Human Rights, Annual Report 2016, p. 41.

f www.courtecowas.org/site2012/index.php?option=com_content&view=article&i
d=157&Itemid=27.

g www.wto.org/english/thewto_e/secre_e/intro_e.htm.

h 1996 was the year in which the first judges were elected to the Tribunal.
International Tribunal for the Law of the Sea, History, www.itlos.org/the-tribunal/
history/; International Tribunal for the Law of the Sea, The Registry, www.itlos
.org/en/the-registry/.

i East African Court of Justice, Establishment, http://eacj.org/?page_id=1; East
African Court of Justice, Staff, http://eacj.org/?page_id=1024; East African Court
of Justice, Recent Decisions, http://eacj.org/?page_id=2298.

j www.african-court.org/en/index.php/about-us/court-in-brief (accessed December
2018). See now www.echr.coe.int/Documents/Stats_art_39_01_ENG.pdf.

factors, such as politics, may interfere.[16] First, one might consider the
model employed by the WTO. In that model, states maintain a heavy hand
in the work of the institution, approving outcomes issued by adjudicators
and commenting on interpretations of the underlying international
agreements. This model may be called the 'State-centric' or, as others have
used to describe the WTO, 'member-driven'[17] model.

Second is the model exemplified by the PCA and to some degree by the
ICJ and by ICSID in light of their relationships with the United Nations

---

[16] As noted, the taxonomy reflects the varying relationships between the secretariat and
the States that are members or founders of the institution. They of course vary along
other dimensions as well. Reflected above is also a notable spectrum of size. Importantly,
secretariats could also be grouped and analyzed according to their sources of income.
Some institutions are funded exclusively by State contributions whereas others benefit from fees associated with their dispute management services, each of which creates
different incentives for secretariat staff.

[17] See, e.g., G. Shaffer, 'The Role of the WTO Director-General and Secretariat' (on file with
the author).

and World Bank, respectively. In this model, States are quite removed from both dispute settlement and other decision-making of the secretariat. Still, States meet to approve matters such as the budget of the institution or the election of the Secretary-General. This model may be labeled the 'partly removed' or 'arm's length' model.

A third model is a 'hybrid secretariat' model found in certain free trade agreements. It involves the creation of a secretariat or multiple secretariats for disputes arising under that agreement only. Under the North American Free Trade Agreement (NAFTA), for example, each of the three parties to the agreement maintains its own secretariat office to handle secretariat matters, i.e., rosters, cases, etc. The administration of disputes under that agreement is managed by these offices working together. Those offices are part of their home governments, but expected to act independently and impartially. The NAFTA side agreements on labor and environment also call for the creation of a separate standing secretariat for labor matters and another for environmental matters. Those secretariats are instrumental in managing potential disputes. Each has a reviewing function over complaints brought by third parties toward the NAFTA parties. Where the requisite criteria are present, those investigations may escalate into State-to-State dispute settlement.

Finally, a fourth 'ad hoc model' requires the respondent State to be responsible for facilitating the logistics of the dispute and for creating a temporary secretariat. A number of trade agreements use this model such as the Central America–Dominican Republic–United States free trade agreement (CAFTA-DR) as well as the European Union–Canada Comprehensive Economic Trade Agreement (CETA).

The models take as their foundation the observed practices and practical operation of the institutions. The taxonomy draws attention especially to the ongoing and quotidian engagements between the institutions and the States that created them. Some of these types of engagement have evolved over time just as some of the original mandates delegated by those States to the secretariats may have done.

The 1899 Hague Convention describes the PCA's 'International Bureau' as the 'record office' to serve as a 'channel of communications', to 'maintain custody of the archives' and to 'conduct administrative business' on behalf of the Court.[18] Authority over the rules of procedure, the 'necessary regulations to decide all questions of administration', as well as the 'entire

---

[18] PCA 1899 Convention, Article 22.

control over the appointment, suspension, or dismissal of the officials and employees of the Bureau' was left to the Administrative Council.[19] Articles 30 through 57 cover the procedure for the Court and none of these mentions a role for the Bureau. The 1907 Convention charges the Bureau with serving as the 'registry' to the Court's cases and indicates that it will have 'charge of the archives.'[20] Article 46 of the 1907 Convention requires the Bureau to communicate the *compromis* from one party to others if needed and to 'make arrangements' for any meetings of the parties or tribunal at the outset of the proceedings. Article 63 of the 1907 Convention also provides for the Bureau to serve as an intermediary in the exchange of pleadings.

The record of the proceedings from the Conventions suggests that some delegations had more expansive ideas as to the role of the Bureau or the potential contribution it could make to the furtherance of peace. For example, the Russian delegation proposed that the Bureau be empowered to advise the States of the Administrative Council on requests for arbitration and to take decisions in respect of such requests.[21] The French delegation likewise felt the Bureau could contribute to uniformity, procedural developments, jurisprudence, and that it could initiate proceedings.[22] Neither of these suggestions received the necessary traction, however. A minority of countries was opposed to the creation of any permanent dispute settlement institution, but 'reluctantly agreed to [the final choice of] institution, provided it would be passive and weak. The Bureau, it was thought, could only be a modest secretariat.'[23] The PCA website today advertises a collection of services beyond those discussed above.[24]

In contrast to these enumerated powers in the PCA founding instruments, the ICJ Statute makes only a small reference to the role of its Registrar: 'The Court shall appoint its Registrar and may provide for

---

[19] Ibid., Article 28.

[20] PCA 1907 Convention, Article 43.

[21] S. Rosenne, *The Hague Peace Conferences of 1899 and 1907 and International Arbitration: Reports and Documents* (TMC Asser Press, 2001), p. 50.

[22] Ibid.

[23] H. Jonkman, 'The Role of the Permanent Court of Arbitration in International Dispute Resolution: Addresses on 6 and 27 July 1999, at the Hague Academy of International Law, Peace Palace, The Hague, on the Occasion of the Centennial Celebration of the Permanent Court of Arbitration' in *Collected Courses of the Hague Academy of International Law*, vol. 279, (Brill/Nijhoff, 1999), p. 22.

[24] Permanent Court of Arbitration, http://pca-cpa.org.

the appointment of such other officers as may be necessary.'[25] The ICJ
Handbook, prepared by the ICJ Registry, states:

> Since the ICJ is both a court of justice and an international organ, the
> Registry's tasks include both helping in the administration of justice – with
> sovereign States as litigants – and acting as an international secretariat. Its
> activities are thus on the one hand of a judicial and diplomatic nature.[26]

Some former secretariat members and others have written at length about
the actual workings of the ICJ secretariat and their contributions to the
development of international law.[27]

The ITLOS Tribunal developed its Rules in which it provides that the
Registry is to:

> (a) be the regular channel of communications to and from the
> Tribunal ...; (b) keep, under the supervision of the President of the
> Tribunal, and in such form as may be laid down by the Tribunal, a List
> of cases, ... (c) keep copies of declarations and notices of revocation
> or withdrawal ...; (d) keep copies of agreements conferring jurisdic-
> tion on the Tribunal; ... (h) be present ... at meetings of the Tribunal,
> and of the chambers, and be responsible for preparing records of such
> meetings; ... (j) sign all judgments, advisory opinions and orders of
> the Tribunal ... [among several other administrative tasks].[28]

The WTO Secretariat's responsibilities are more robust than those of
other institutions as it is responsible for much more than assisting with
the settlement of disputes, but it has not always been that way. Prior to
the creation of the WTO, the General Agreement on Tariffs & Trade
member governments 'borrowed' a secretariat from the unsuccessful
negotiations to create the International Trade Organization (ITO). The
Interim Commission for the ITO had no substantive function after the
ITO was abandoned but it continued to provide a legal basis for a GATT
Secretariat. That secretariat likely played a substantial role in scripting the
early GATT plenary meetings that issued the first GATT legal rulings.
Robert Hudec notes that the GATT secretariat evolved to be responsive

---

[25] Statute of the International Court of Justice, www.icj-cij.org/en/statute, Article 21(2).
[26] International Court of Justice, Handbook of the Court, pp. 29–30.
[27] See, e.g., Philippe Couvreur, 'The Registrar of the International Court of Justice: Status
and Functions', in C. Jiménez Piernas (ed.), *The European Practice in International Law
and European Community Law: A Spanish Perspective* (Martinus Nijhoff Publishers,
2007); Hugh Thirlway, 'The Drafting of ICJ Decisions: Some Personal Recollections and
Observations' (2006) 5(1) *Chinese Journal of International Law* 15.
[28] International Tribunal for the Law of the Sea, Rules of the Tribunal, Article 36.

to the GATT Contracting Parties' legalization of disputes, hiring more lawyers to advise panels, for example.[29]

Today, the WTO Secretariat facilitates ongoing negotiations, provides technical assistance, and oversees the corpus of committees and working groups that make up the WTO apparatus. With respect to dispute settlement, the Dispute Settlement Understanding states that: 'The Secretariat shall have the responsibility of assisting panels, especially on the legal, historical and procedural aspects of the matters dealt with, and of providing secretarial and technical support.'[30]

The ICSID Convention describes how the ICSID Secretariat will consist of a Secretary-General, Deputy Secretary-General, and staff. The Convention charges the Secretary-General with overseeing the Secretariat and further states that the Secretary-General 'shall perform the function of registrar and shall have the power to authenticate arbitral awards rendered pursuant to this Convention, and to certify copies thereof.'[31] The ICSID Administrative and Financial Regulations provide that, for each proceeding, a secretary from among the secretariat staff shall 'keep summary minutes of hearings' and 'perform other functions with respect to the proceeding at the request of the President of the … Tribunal … or at the direction of the Secretary-General.'[32]

At the IACtHR, the founding instruments provide that '[t]he Secretariat of the Court shall function under the immediate authority of the Secretary, in accordance with the administrative standards of the OAS General Secretariat, in all matters that are not incompatible with the independence of the Court.'[33] The Rules of Procedure of the Court, approved by the Inter-American Commission on Human Rights (a standing body of seven individuals serving in a personal capacity, further provide:

> The functions of the Secretary shall be to: a. serve notice of the judgments, advisory opinions, orders, and other rulings of the Court; b. keep the minutes of the sessions of the Court; c. attend the meetings of the Court

---

[29] R. Hudec, 'The Role of the GATT Secretariat in the Evolution of the WTO Dispute Settlement Procedure' in J. N. Bhagwati, and M. Hirsch (eds.), *The Uruguay Round and Beyond: Essays in Honor of Arthur Dunkel* (University of Michigan Press, 1998), pp. 101–120.

[30] Understanding on Rules and Procedures Governing the Settlement of Disputes, Annex 2 of the Agreement Establishing the World Trade Organization, Article 27.

[31] ICSID Convention, Article 11.

[32] ICSID Financial and Administrative Regulations, Article 25.

[33] Statute of the InterAmerican Court, adopted by the General Assembly of the OAS, October 1979 (Resolution No. 448), Article 14.

held at its seat or elsewhere; d. process the correspondence of the Court; e. certify the authenticity of documents; f. direct the administration of the Court, pursuant to the instructions of the Presidency; g. prepare drafts of the work schedules, rules and regulations, and budgets of the Court; h. plan, direct, and coordinate the work of the staff of the Court; i. carry out the tasks assigned to him or her by the Court or the Presidency; j. perform any other duties provided for in the Statute or in these Rules.[34]

The ECOWAS Court issued the following practice direction for its secretariat: 'The Chief Registrar shall be responsible, under the authority of the President, for the acceptance, transmission and custody of documents and for effecting service as provided for by these Rules... The Chief Registrar shall assist the Court, the President and the Judges in all their official functions.'[35]

The ECtHR Rules drafted by the Court set out that the registrar:

> shall assist the Court in the performance of its functions and shall be responsible for the organisation and activities of the Registry under the authority of the President of the Court ... [;] shall have the custody of the archives of the Court and shall be the channel for all communications and notifications made by, or addressed to, the Court in connection with the cases brought or to be brought before it ...[;] shall, subject to the duty of discretion attaching to this office, reply to requests for information concerning the work of the Court, in particular to enquiries from the press.[36]

The ECtHR also employs secretariat staff to serve in two unique roles. The first is the role of jurisconsult: 'For the purposes of ensuring the quality and consistency of its case-law, the Court shall be assisted by a *Jurisconsult* [who] shall provide opinions and information, in particular to the judicial formations and the members of the Court.'[37] Second, under certain circumstances, the Court is to be assisted by 'non-judicial rapporteurs.'[38]

The ACtHPR Rules of Court, adopted by the Court, include a lengthy list of tasks for the secretariat, enumerating 17 in total. These include serving as the channel of communications for the proceedings, coordinating logistics of disputes and of the institution, and answering press inquiries, among other administrative tasks.[39] The secretariat is not empowered to address legal or procedural matters.

---

[34] IACtHR Rules of Procedure, Article 10.
[35] ECOWAS Practice Directions, Article 14.
[36] ECtHR Rules, Rule 17.
[37] Ibid., Rule 18-b-3.
[38] Ibid., Rule 18-a.
[39] ACtHPR, Rules of Court, Rule 25.

The EACJ Rules of Procedure list three tasks for the secretariat or, as the Rules state, 'Powers of the Registry.' These 'powers' are 'to be responsible for the acceptance and custody of documents and for effecting service'; 'to have custody of the seal of the Court and shall be responsible for the records and the publications of the Court'; and 'to be responsible for all administrative work and in particular for the accounts and financial administration in accordance with the financial procedures of the Community.'[40] In a separate rule, the Registrar is empowered to refuse to accept documents that do not comply with the rules.[41]

In addition to these standing bodies, bilateral and regional trade agreements often specify rules for a secretariat either in the agreement or in an annex or protocol. For example, the NAFTA establishes a secretariat to provide 'administrative assistance' to arbitral panels.[42] The CAFTA-DR provides in case of dispute that the responding party will maintain an ad hoc 'responsible office' to assist with the management of the dispute.[43] The CAFTA-DR Model Rules state that the responsible office 'shall provide administrative assistance to the [dispute settlement] panel; … organize and coordinate the logistics …; [and] maintain permanently a copy of the complete record.'[44] The CETA, like the CAFTA-DR, does not create a secretariat, but rather provides for the responding party to serve as coordinator of logistics.[45]

Despite these rather mundane although somewhat diverse enumerations, any examination of the impact of international courts and tribunals would be incomplete without taking into account the influence of secretariats in their gatekeeping capacities and areas in which they have expanded upon their enumerated powers to enhance their respective roles.

9.3   Secretariats as Gatekeepers

With the mandates and design described above, secretariats find themselves in a difficult place. On the one hand, some constituents demand

---

[40] EACJ Rules, Rule 5.
[41] Ibid., Rule 9.
[42] NAFTA, Article 2002.
[43] Central America–Dominican Republic–United States Free Trade Agreement, 5 August 2004.
[44] CAFTA-DR Model Rules of Procedure, Rule 95.
[45] European Union–Canada Comprehensive Economic Trade Agreement, provisionally in force as of 21 September 2017, Annex 29-A: Rules of Procedure for Arbitration, para. 2.

more from them than the mandates above suggest; on the other hand, the dangers of employing expansive case management techniques, or mandate-creep, could endanger their legitimacy.

Apart from their administrative and dispute-settlement support functions, secretariats play substantial, often overlooked, roles in at least four respects. First, secretariats regularly decide whether certain adjudicators will adjudicate a particular case. Second, secretariats are called upon to screen cases for administration. Third, secretariats have substantial influence in the procedural elements of the proceedings they administer. Finally, secretariats have an important role in facilitating public access to cases.

9.3.1   Screening

As one US judge has put it, the institution must 'begin managing the life of a case the moment it arrives.'[46] Secretariats make administrative decisions on admissibility, evaluating whether a litigant met the technical or formulaic prerequisites set by the institution, and assign cases to judges. For example, in the 1930s, the PCA Secretary-General took the decision to accept for administration a case that arguably fell outside the mandate of the Court under the Conventions. Only after admitting the case did the Secretary-General 'inform' the Administrative Council.[47] The 1934 Report of the Administrative Council states:

> The Bureau concluded that it could accept their request, considering that if it is true that, generally speaking, international arbitration should be understood as a jurisdiction between two or more States, the drafting of [Article 47] does not imply that special boards of arbitration, as to which a broader interpretation ends to appear, are so conditioned.

Later, relying on the precedent set in the prior case, the Administrative Council in 1960 authorized the administration of disputes between States or State entities on the one hand, and private parties or corporations on the other.

Some institutional rules give authority to secretariats to conduct a prima facie examination of the documentation submitted by the party

---

[46] J.C. Wallace, 'Improving the Appellate Process Worldwide Through Maximizing Judicial Resources' (2005) 38 *Vanderbilt Journal of Transnational Law* 187, 192.

[47] Note of the Secretary-General Concerning the Functioning of the Permanent Arbitration Court of March 3, 1960. See also the PCA Annual Report of 1934 in which it states that 'the *Bureau* concluded that it could accept [the parties'] request' (emphasis added).

making the request for arbitration.[48] Other institutions do not empower the secretariat in that way and provide clear steps for registering a request regardless of its jurisdictional merit.[49]

In cases in which the secretariat is empowered to screen a litigation request, the intensity of screening is not dependent on written standards and secretariats have considerable non-reviewable discretion in this respect. Complex jurisdictional issues are not necessarily deferred to adjudicators and secretariats serve as screening gatekeepers on the basis of their own criteria. For example, the screening process may require questions of treaty interpretation. The ICSID secretariat has faced such questions on multiple occasions. In 1985, the ICSID secretariat refused to register a case on the basis that the alleged dispute related to a mere commercial sale and thus could not be considered as arising out of an investment despite the fact that there was no definition of investment in the convention or case law.[50] In 1999, the secretariat again refused registration of a request for arbitration arising out of a supply contract for the sale of goods, stating that it was 'manifestly outside the jurisdiction of the centre as not involving investments.'[51] In *Tokios Tokeles v. Ukraine*, the ICSID secretariat concluded the application did not meet the requirements of the ICSID Convention for nationality reasons.[52] Likewise, in *Biwater Gauff v. Tanzania*, the secretariat found no offer to arbitrate in the national legislation and refused to register the case on the basis of the national legislation.[53]

9.3.2   Player Selection and Deselection

Secretariats are also 'gatekeepers' in that – unlike judges – they regulate admission to international lawmaking in their selection of adjudicators or

---

[48] For example, the ICSID Convention, Article 36(3) ('The Secretary-General shall register the request unless he finds, on the basis of the information contained in the request, that the dispute is manifestly outside the jurisdiction of the Centre.'). Some rules are formulated in the negative whereas others are affirmative; that is, some require a finding on the part of the secretariat, while other cases proceed in the absence of a finding.

[49] For example, Chapter 20, Article 20.6.2 of the CAFTA-DR provides that an arbitral panel is 'established upon delivery of the request.' That is, upon delivery of the claimant's quest for arbitration, a panel is considered established, even though it is not yet constituted.

[50] ICSID, *Annual Report* (1985), p. 6.

[51] I. Shihata and A. Parra, 'The Experience of the International Centre for Settlement of Investment Disputes' (1999) 14 *ICSID Review* 308.

[52] ICSID Case No. ARB/02/18.

[53] *Biwater Gauff (Tanzania) Ltd. v. United Republic of Tanzania*, ICSID Case No. ARB/05/22.

proposal of adjudicators, and in their decision-making on ethical challenges to adjudicators. In many instances, particularly in international investment arbitration and also in trade law, secretariats are called upon to propose or select one or more adjudicators for a dispute. In some instances, the parties or the instrument governing the arbitration will call for an 'appointing authority' to appoint an adjudicator or decide a challenge and there again, the secretariat will support the appointing authority in doing so.

Even though secretariats make far fewer appointments than litigants, the number is not insignificant. ICSID has noted that it makes about 25 percent of appointments, either through its Secretary-General or through the Chair of the Administrative Council of the World Bank.[54] Since World War II, and especially with the advent of the 2010 UNCITRAL Arbitration Rules, the PCA Secretary-General has increasingly been called upon to appoint arbitrators in circumstances in which one or more of the parties is unable to select an arbitrator, a role that under prior State practice would typically be left to a third State.[55]

The single-bite-at-the-apple approach to dispute settlement makes getting the 'best' chairperson or the 'right' party-appointed arbitrator a critical element in determining the outcome of the dispute.[56] For this reason, arbitrators with long track records are preferred and the barrier to entry into the community is nearly insurmountable.[57] Fear of an unfavorable outcome and of the unknown on the part of those selecting the arbitrators constrains the pool, but it also constrains secretariats. Moreover, practitioners have noted how there is a symbiotic relationship between popular arbitrators and secretariats.[58] In those practitioners' view, secretariats will repeatedly appoint arbitrators who are willing to adopt the secretariats' strongly suggested approach or view (and reject others who are unwilling). Those same arbitrators will bring secretariats cases when they are next appointed.

The WTO secretariat assists parties in composing panels by proposing nominations for potential panelists to hear the dispute.[59] This selection

[54] *Comments of the ICSID Secretary-General*, ICCA Congress (2014).

[55] Rosenne, The Hague Peace Conferences of 1899 and 1907, xxi; see Jackson H. Ralston, *International Arbitral Law and Procedure* (Ginn & Co., 1910) (discussing how the role of 'umpire' was to be left to the chief magistrate of a neutral State).

[56] K. Claussen, 'Keeping Up Appearances: the Diversity Dilemma' (2015) 4 *Transnational Dispute Management*.

[57] Ibid.

[58] *Comments of the ICSID Secretary-General*.

[59] DSU, Article 8.6.

process resembles what is known in investment arbitration as a 'list process': the secretariat provides the parties with a list of possible candidates to strike out or accept. While parties have respected the list process for more than 20 years, the formula behind the creation of the lists remains unclear. This process differs from the more transparent, but historically more problematic exercise of selecting arbitrators for disputes arising under free trade agreements. Under many US trade agreements, there is no secretariat with the power to constitute tribunals in the absence of party agreement or action, giving the parties the opportunity to block panel composition. In this sense, a secretariat-driven process, even if opaque, seems preferable.

Some commentators have been critical of secretariats' adjudicator selection function.[60] Jan Paulsson has spoken about secretariats' disproportionate influence in controlling the players in the field, noting their inability to

> convince disputants that their selection process is untainted by undue influence …. [T]he organizations that call themselves arbitral institutions need to look at themselves and ask why it is that they are so exposed to suspicions of poor selection of arbitrators and maybe even worse: cronyism and other forms of corruption.[61]

The relationship between the appointing authority and the secretariat remains underexplored. Some counsel have noted surprise when learning that a secretariat heavily influenced the appointing authority in respect of an appointment or challenged decision.[62] Without any clear rules or guidance from States or parties, some secretariats appear to have adopted the view that they should work closely with the appointing authority in the same way they work closely with the tribunal. On at least one occasion, a secretariat was believed to have influenced the outcome of a case as a result of the influence of its staff in the appointing authority's sustaining an arbitrator challenge; some counsel believe this occurs frequently at both public and private institutions.[63] Other counsel consider assisting the appointing authority part of the secretariat's mandate.[64]

---

[60] See, e.g., T. Cole, 'Authority and Contemporary International Arbitration' (2010) 70 *Louisiana Law Review* 801, 855.

[61] J. Paulsson, 'Moral Hazard in International Dispute Resolution' (2011) 2 *Transnational Dispute Management*, 20.

[62] Comments among communications from 42 counsel, secretariat staff, and arbitrators (September 2017–January 2018) (interview notes on file with the author).

[63] Ibid.

[64] Ibid.

This section reflects mixed views on the part of scholars and practitioners as to the appropriate role of secretariats in player selection and deselection. What is clear is that the mandates are largely incomplete in this respect. Party expectations, diversity among the international bench, and the legitimacy of these processes may benefit from greater transparency in this area.

9.3.3   Procedure 'Plus'

Although descriptions of such instances do not often appear in the record of a proceeding, secretariats move forward dispute resolution processes by prompting adjudicators to take action when necessary, manage files, and facilitate or issue payments, organize hearings and evidence, and coordinate and arrange site visits and experts, among other activities. In addition, some secretariats engage in procedural decision-making, particularly at the early stages of a dispute. They also provide substantial research for procedural and substantive decisions taken by the tribunal. Together, these activities may be considered 'procedure plus' – secretariats exert considerable control over procedure and also indirectly over substance.

In addition to the screening exercise described above, some secretariats have codified rules for their management of disputes. Often these rules are adopted by the States party to the institution, but not always. The PCA secretariat has undertaken drafting with committees of experts of new rules for the institution. The rules have then been approved and adopted by the PCA Administrative Council. More unusually, in 2012, after the Council's adoption of new PCA rules, the PCA secretariat issued an 'Explanatory Note of the International Bureau of the Permanent Court of Arbitration ('PCA') Regarding Time Periods Under the PCA Arbitration Rules 2012 ('2012 PCA Rules')':[65]

> Where the 2012 PCA Rules empower the PCA International Bureau to extend default time periods provided in the Rules (see Articles 4(1), 8(2) (b), 9(3) and 43(4) of the 2012 PCA Rules) and the International Bureau receives a request to extend a time period that it considers justified, the

---

[65] Explanatory Note of the International Bureau of the Permanent Court of Arbitration ('PCA') Regarding Time Periods Under the PCA Arbitration Rules 2012 ('2012 PCA Rules'), available at: https://pca-cpa.org/wp-content/uploads/sites/175/2016/01/Explanatory-Note-of-the-International-Bureau-of-the-PCA-Regarding-Time-Periods-Under-the-PCA-Arbitration-Rules-2012.pdf.

time periods set forth in the 1990s PCA Rules will serve as a guideline for the extensions that the International Bureau may decide to grant.

Other secretariats have likewise issued 'practice directions' for parties with guidance on the rules and other procedures. Secretariats then apply the rules they create, ensuring that the parties' communications or pleadings conform with requirements and guiding litigants accordingly.

In addition, secretariats influence substantive outcomes in their role providing legal research. Some practitioners have noted that secretariat staff have a tendency to draw from cases that the secretariat previously administered.[66] That research and those contributions facilitate the development of a common law style engagement with prior case law. As seen above, many of the institutional founding instruments do not speak to a role for the registry or secretariat in doctrinal research or articulation.

These management and research responsibilities give the secretariat substantial control, often off the record and out of reach of any review. In the early days of the WTO Appellate Body, for example, 'by working together, the Appellate Body members and Secretariat ... [were] anticipating issues and preparing research papers ... before appeals were filed.'[67] The secretariat staff 'was always included in the members' deliberations and meetings, together with the lawyers working on the particular cases.'[68] Secretariat members were called upon to provide 'legal analyses and views on the merits of the issues appealed.'[69] Thus, the secretariat has been heavily engaged in the merits of Appellate Body disputes.[70]

Similar activity was strongly criticized by one arbitrator in an ICSID case. Recall that the ICSID founding instruments are nearly silent on the tasks of the secretariat, but where they do provide guidance they do not make reference to legal drafting or any type of legal or procedural assistance. Jan Dalhuisen in his separate opinion in the *Vivendi v. Argentina* Second Annulment Proceedings heavily decried the secretariat's engagement in the proceedings, stating that the 'the role of the ICSID Secretariat

---

[66] *Comments of the ICSID Secretary-General.*
[67] D. Steger, 'The Founding of the Appellate Body' (2017) *Ottawa Faculty of Law Working Paper No. 2017–33.*
[68] Ibid.
[69] Ibid.
[70] In one instance, a member of secretariat staff was dismissed for overstepping the secretariat's mandate. E. Preeg, 'Uruguay Round Negotiations and the Creation of the WTO' in *The Oxford Handbook on the World Trade Organization* (Oxford University Press, 2012), p. 139.

in this matter ... has led to multiple complications and has delayed the final decision by many months.'[71] Dalhuisen elaborated:

> It is clear that the Secretariat wants to obtain for itself a greater role in the conduct of ICSID cases and in the process also wants to involve itself in the drafting of the decisions ... I believe this in general to be outside the Secretariat's remit and undesirable ... it is clear that the Secretariat has no original powers in the dispute resolution and decision taking process.[72]

In respect of substantive matters, Professor Dalhuisen catalogued the ways in which he believed the secretariat also interfered with the substance of the resulting decision. Today, nearly all major secretariats contribute fundamental research to forward the decisions that the courts and dispute settlement bodies issue. In this research role, secretariats are twice delegated – both by States in their institutional creation and also by the judges and arbitrators themselves. The evolution of new technologies to enable research, more advanced lawyering, the push for increased transparency in the case law, etc., have each contributed to the same effect. Each of these influences is augmented by the secretariats drawing from them. Through the reinvocation of past case law, secretariats contribute to both the expansion and constraint of judicial argumentation. Suffice it to say that in answering these gatekeeper-like questions among many others, institutions influence the future of the regime. In Professor Dalhuisen's view, at least on the occasion of the *Vivendi* award, the ICSID secretariat overstepped its mandate in engaging in this activity.[73]

Stories of secretariats imposing their own interpretations of treaties or rules in a way that affects the proceedings are not uncommon in arbitration circles though they are not often written, with the exception of Professor Dalhuisen's noteworthy critique. For example, it is well known that some secretariats have asked tribunals to adopt practices or interpretations of the rules that would enhance the secretariat's reputation.[74] In other instances, secretariats have been known to encourage or counsel arbitrators or appointing authorities to reach a certain outcome not just on legal grounds but also with an eye to the instrumental benefits

---

[71] *Compañía de Aguas del Aconquija S.A. and Vivendi Universal S.A. v. Argentine Republic*, ICSID Case No. ARB/97/3 (formerly *Compañía de Aguas del Aconquija, S.A. and Compagnie Générale des Eaux v. Argentine Republic*), award of August 20, 2007, separate opinion of J.H. Dalhuisen, para. 1.

[72] Ibid., paras. 2–3.

[73] Ibid., paras. 16–21.

[74] *Comments of the ICSID Secretary-General.*

and publicity that such an outcome could grant, or simply because that was the secretariat's interpretation of the relevant legal instrument or even simply the secretariat's preference.[75] When the adjudicator's decision, consistent with the secretariat's insistence, may later be highly criticized, any error is ascribed to the decision-maker while the secretariat remains the unseen source of the perceived difficulty. As one former secretariat staff member put it: 'The [secretariat staff] feel like owners of the process in a way that constrains decisionmaking on the part of the actual, legal decisionmaker.'[76] These types of critique of secretariats rarely reach the public domain given the incentives for arbitrators to maintain good relationships with the secretariats that may appoint them.

On other occasions, although rare, States have publically criticized secretariats for expanding or exceeding their mandates. In the course of a dispute between the United States and Guatemala, the United States sought the assistance of the ICSID Secretary-General to review redacted evidence for presentation to the tribunal in the dispute, even though ICSID was not administering the dispute. Guatemala strongly criticized the ICSID secretariat for undertaking the task at the US request, claiming that such a task was beyond the scope of authority of the ICSID staff.[77]

9.3.4   Transparency and Public Access

Some secretariats have undertaken initiatives to enhance the transparency of their institution's work by encouraging tribunals under their administration to make the proceedings known to the public. Among private bodies, as well, these efforts are growing substantially in recognition of a renewed interest in transparency among both private practitioners and States and in light of the competition among those bodies.[78] Many public secretariats have taken steps to facilitate or enhance website access to decisions and submissions in the cases they are administering.[79] This type of discretion allows secretariats to effect directly and indirectly the prospects for legal change as well as the deployment of information to lawyers and the public.

---

[75] Ibid.
[76] Ibid.
[77] Rebuttal Submission of Guatemala, *Obligations Arising under the CAFTA-DR: United States v. Guatemala*, 27 April 2015, para. 6.
[78] *Comments of the ICSID Secretary-General.*
[79] See, e.g., www.pcacases.com.

Moreover, secretariats convene international conferences that promote legal development and exchange of information among international lawyers. Many secretariat staff regularly speak about the work of their respective institutions in ways that enhance the public's understanding of international dispute settlement and the legitimacy of the system. The WTO *Report of the Consultative Board on The Future of the WTO* describes how the Director-General of the WTO, who heads the WTO secretariat, has served as an 'international spokesperson and marketing executive' as well as a 'spiritual leader.'[80] In most instances today, secretariat staff are contributing intellectual input to the public and political debate on international disputes.

9.4 Legitimacy Lessons

While some commentators have been critical of secretariats' expansive functions, many of the contributions made by secretariats may be seen as positive developments both to the legitimacy of the international dispute resolution system and the success of the dispute management process. Secretariats help build confidence among the participants which can in turn enhance their legitimacy. Their institutional resources and memories are useful for the smooth operation of the proceedings, especially where the underlying instruments fail to anticipate gaps in dispute management.

Although scholars have surveyed well questions of legitimacy of international judiciaries,[81] none has studied in full the contributions or detractions of the international court secretariats in that context nor has the literature review analyzed what makes a secretariat itself legitimate. Commentators and public officials have shared different views on the roles secretariats *should* fill, apart from whatever their mandate may state. Hans Jonkman has commented that secretariats should be 'known,' 'trusted,' 'independent,' and 'impartial.'[82] They should offer a good set of

---

[80] WTO, *Report of the Consultative Board on The Future of the WTO*, p. 74.
[81] See, e.g., H. Cohen, A. Follesdal, N. Grossman and G. Ulfstein, 'Legitimacy and International Courts – A Framework' in N. Grossman, H. Cohen, A. Follesdal and G. Ulfstein (eds.), *Legitimacy and International Courts* (Cambridge: Cambridge University Press, 2018), pp. 1–40; Shai Dothan, 'How International Courts Enhance Their Legitimacy' (2013) 14(2) *Theoretical Inquiries in Law* 455.
[82] H. Jonkman, 'Remarks on New Activities of the Permanent Court of Arbitration' in ASIL (eds.) *Contemporary International Law Issues: Opportunities at a Time of Momentous Change: Proceedings of the Second Joint Conference Held in the Hague, The Netherlands, July 22–24, 1993* (Brill, 1993), pp. 165–166.

procedural rules, offer a good location for adjudication, be well organized and not costly, and, as a further benefit, they should carry political or economic weight.[83] Petros Mavroidis speaking of the WTO secretariat has written that the term 'secretariat' 'denotes the will of the … framers to reduce the international officials appointed to clerk-like functions only.'[84] Still others argue that, in the WTO context, '[t]he perception that the Secretariat does and should not have any views of its own is outdated. It is a fiction that does not correspond to reality.'[85]

Some scholars have advocated that secretariats ought to do still more to meet the needs of the international community. In David Caron's view, for one, within the marketplace of dispute resolution bodies, public entities' motivation should be to look for where the market fails to offer services suggested by community objectives within its purview.[86]

As shown above, secretariats are powerful in part because of their special gatekeeping status. Like all bureaucracies, they make rules[87] – rules about access and jurisdiction as well as about procedure and evidence. They seek to build policy preferences and to appear apolitical while they serve constituencies with diverse preferences. However, secretariats are not without limitations. They may be subject to institutional capture, politicization, or may simply lack the ability to accurately gauge larger extra-institutional factors. They may privilege some values over others based on their own self-interest.[88] They may seek to promote their institution to ensure the continuation of their positions. Secretariats also compete with one another.[89] Each case can provide substantial financial

---

[83] Ibid.

[84] P. Mavroidis, *The Regulation of International Trade: GATT* (The MIT Press, 2016), p. 70.

[85] T. Cottier, *The Challenge of WTO Law: Collected Essays* (Cameron May, 2007), p. 210. See also WTO, *Report by the Consultative Board to the Former Director-General Supachai Panitchpakdi*, Ch. IX.

[86] D. Caron, 'Remarks on New Activities of the Permanent Court of Arbitration' in *Contemporary International Law Issues: Opportunities at a Time of Momentous Change: Proceedings of the Second Joint Conference Held in the Hague, The Netherlands, July 22–24, 1993* (Brill, 1993), pp. 166–169.

[87] M. Barnett and M. Finnemore, 'The Politics, Power, and Pathologies of International Organizations' (1999) 53 *International Organization* 699.

[88] David Caron raised the concern about capture several years ago. See D. Caron, 'Towards A Political Theory of International Courts and Tribunals' (2006) 24 *Berkeley Journal of International Law* 401, 416–417.

[89] See, e.g., J. Katz Cogan, 'Competition and Control in International Courts' (2008) 48 *Virginia Journal of International Law* 411, 416 (arguing that competition among international courts has grown).

support for a secretariat and thus may force it to act strategically when possible. The commercialization of dispute settlement institutions is largely understudied in part due to a lack of transparency on the part of the institutions.

One result of this behavior is that secretariats may be inclined toward 'secretariat mandate creep' – the aggrandizement of the secretariat's role not sanctioned by parties or States. Because the work of secretariats is less visible and usually unreviewable, secretariats have considerable authority, while litigants have fewer procedural safeguards to protect them from abuse of that authority. Thus, to the extent one considers State consent as a or *the* source of legitimacy for courts and for secretariats, mandate creep would prove problematic. By this thin measure, the institution's legitimacy would be threatened by secretariats making decisions that are not easily viewed as part of the general or specific consent or delegation that States have given and made.

In short, the impact of secretariats' gatekeeping role on the legitimacy of the international dispute settlement system is difficult to discern given that greater secretariat involvement has been viewed positively by some and negatively by others on both legal and functional grounds. In Professor Dalhuisen's words: 'it is urgent that the Secretariat ... separates itself entirely and meticulously from the substance of the proceedings, appreciates that in legal matters wording is substance, organizes itself accordingly, and seeks financial support for this limited role only.'[90] The alternate view is that the confidentiality of the secretariat protects it in its work in which it must be trusted by both sides. A lack of consensus on the secretariat's role may explain how and why secretariats have engaged in expansive activity.

In the twenty-first century internet-based environment, secretariats are increasingly seen. The use of internet-based tabloids and international arbitration and reporting services has exacerbated the hype surrounding secretariats. Secretariats may be cautious about the optics of their heavy-handedness, but they remain heavily engaged in dispute management behind the scenes. In other words, as described above, secretariats are seen actors, but with unseen roles.

Secretariats' increased role, both the seen and unseen elements, may nevertheless be a basis for States to ask more questions and consider increasing levels of accountability. States may wish to assess whether

---

[90] Dalhuisen, *Vivendi*, para. 23.

granting such gatekeeper authority to tribunal and court secretariats makes sense or serves to achieve their goals. Discussions about the power that secretariats as gatekeepers wield raise significant questions about whether secretariats can or will deploy such powers in ways that enhance rather than undermine the international public good and the values that States seek to reflect in international dispute resolution. Finding a balance between oversight and allowing a secretariat a right to manage the cases before it, between deference and flexibility, between conflicts of interest and intensification of work may require revisiting the mandate and job description given to secretariats.

9.5   Conclusion

Whether the role of the secretariat ought to be that of gatekeeper or not is a question for States. This chapter only begins to draw attention to the trends among secretariats in recent years and acknowledges the potential for further growth. Much more could and should be said to explain secretariat practices taking into account differences in institutional priorities and dockets. As challenging as it may be to gather information about secretariats, normative questions that are central to the design questions that States face require elaboration.

Given the outsized role secretariats play while remaining largely unseen, and insofar as they contribute to establishing standards for sovereign behavior, their contributions should not go unnoticed. By taking account of these underestimated institutional actors as they work with busy repeat actors, the perceived legitimacy crises may become clearer, and we may focus instead on realizing solutions.

10

Appointing Authorities

Self-Appointment, Party Appointment and Non-Appointment

PETER TZENG[1]

10.1 Introduction

At first glance, paragraph 14 of the arbitral tribunal's order on provisional measures in *Enrica Lexie (Italy v. India)* appears quite mundane.[2] It states in relevant part that 'on 30 September 2015, the President of [the International Tribunal for the Law of the Sea ('ITLOS')] appointed ... H.E. Judge Vladimir Golitsyn as arbitrator and President of the Arbitral Tribunal'.[3] It becomes much more interesting, however, when one realizes that on 30 September 2015, the President of ITLOS was none other than Judge Golitsyn himself.

A similar phenomenon occurred in another high-profile arbitration: Coastal State Rights (*Ukraine v. Russia*).[4] On 23 December 2016, the Ministry of Foreign Affairs of Ukraine revealed that Judge Boualem Bouguetaia would be a member of the tribunal, 'express[ing] its gratitude to the Vice-President of [ITLOS] for rapid formation of the tribunal'.[5] The

---

[1] The views expressed in this chapter are solely those of the author. The chapter is based on a blog post by the author published on *EJIL: Talk!*. See Peter Tzeng, 'Self-Appointment in International Arbitration', *EJIL: Talk!* (7 June 2017), www.ejiltalk.org/self-appointment-in-international-arbitration/.

[2] See *The "Enrica Lexie" Incident (Italy v. India)*, PCA Case No. 2015–28, Request for the Prescription of Provisional Measures, Order (29 April 2016), para. 14.

[3] Ibid.

[4] See *Dispute Concerning Coastal State Rights in the Black Sea, Sea of Azov, and Kerch Strait (Ukraine v. Russia)*, PCA Case No. 2017-06. This arbitration should not be confused with other cases that Ukraine has filed against Russia before the International Court of Justice, the European Court of Human Rights, and the World Trade Organization.

[5] Ministry of Foreign Affairs of Ukraine, Press Release, 'The hearing of the case Ukraine v. Russian Federation under UNCLOS will start at the beginning of 2017' (23 December 2016), http://mfa.gov.ua/en/press-center/news/53422-na-pochatku-2017-roku-.

Ministry failed to note, however, that on 23 December 2016 the Vice-President of ITLOS was none other than Judge Bouguetaia himself.

In short, Judges Golitsyn and Bouguetaia appointed themselves as arbitrators to their respective tribunals. They were able to do so because the applicable procedural rules designated them as the appointing authority for their respective arbitrations. Although these instances of self-appointment may be surprising news to some, what is even more surprising is that the two self-appointments have largely escaped the attention of commentators. This lapse is perhaps due to the fact that appointing authorities are rarely the subject of academic discourse.[6]

The lack of attention given to appointing authorities is unjustified. Appointing authorities wield tremendous power in international arbitration. Not only may they appoint arbitrators, but they may also replace arbitrators, decide on challenges to arbitrators, and play other roles in arbitral proceedings. In order for the system of international arbitration to function properly, it is critical that appointing authorities execute their functions impartially and professionally. Improper conduct on the part of appointing authorities risks undermining the legitimacy of international arbitration as an institution.

Although a comprehensive study on the conduct of appointing authorities would be desirable, the scope of this chapter is not so broad. Rather, this chapter focuses on the conduct of appointing authorities only in the context of public international arbitrations (including both inter-State and investor-State arbitrations), and only in the context of three specific phenomena: self-appointment (where the appointing authority appoints him or herself to the tribunal); party appointment (where one or both parties appoint the appointing authority to the tribunal); and non-appointment (where the appointing authority refuses to appoint an arbitrator).

These three phenomena are not purely hypothetical. As mentioned above, the appointing authority appointed himself to the tribunal in *Enrica Lexie* and Coastal State Rights.[7] One or both parties appointed the appointing authority to the tribunal in *Eritrea/Yemen*, *Guyana v. Suriname*,

---

[6] Only a few commentators have examined appointing authorities in recent years. See e.g. Peter Tzeng, 'Self-Appointment in International Arbitration', *EJIL: Talk!* (7 June 2017), www.ejiltalk.org/self-appointment-in-international-arbitration/; Jianjun Gao, 'Appointment of Arbitrators by the President of the ITLOS pursuant to Article 3 of Annex VII to the LOS Convention: Some Tentative Observations' (2017) 16 *Chinese Journal of International Law* 723; David Gaukrodger, OECD Consultation Paper, *Appointing Authorities and the Selection of Arbitrations in Investor-State Dispute Settlement: An Overview* (March 2018).

[7] See below Section 10.3.2.

and *Croatia/Slovenia*.[8] And the appointing authority refused to appoint an arbitrator in a series of investor-State arbitrations arising under the Investment Agreement of the Organisation of the Islamic Conference.[9] In the wake of these relatively recent events, this chapter undertakes an analysis of the propriety of self-appointment, party appointment, and non-appointment.

The chapter is organized as follows. Section 10.2 provides background on the powers of appointing authorities. The subsequent three sections then examine, respectively, the three phenomena in question: self-appointment (Section 10.3); party appointment (Section 10.4); and non-appointment (Section 10.5). Section 10.6 then concludes the chapter.

10.2   Appointing Authorities

In international arbitration, the appointing authority is the individual or institution that has the power to appoint an arbitrator under certain circumstances.[10] As mentioned above, the appointing authority may have more than just an appointing power; it can also have the power to replace arbitrators, decide on challenges, and play other roles in the arbitral proceedings.

Appointing authorities derive their powers primarily from the jurisdictional instrument(s) and the applicable procedural rules. It would be impossible to examine the powers of appointing authorities in all public international arbitrations, as in many cases the rules applicable to the appointing authority are *sui generis*.[11] This chapter thus focuses on the powers of appointing authorities under four regimes that were designed

---

[8] See below Section 10.4.2.

[9] See below Section 10.5.2.

[10] Some instruments expressly call the appointing authority the 'appointing authority'. See e.g. UNCITRAL Arbitration Rules (2013), art. 6. Other instruments simply grant the appointing authority appointing powers without giving the authority a specific name. See e.g. United Nations Convention on the Law of the Sea, Montego Bay, 10 December 1982, in force 16 November 1994, 1833 UNTS 3 (UNCLOS), annex VII, art. 3(e).

[11] For example, in the two arbitrations instituted by Timor-Leste against Australia under the Timor Sea Treaty, the rules were laid out in an annex to the Timor Sea Treaty. See Timor Sea Treaty Between the Government of East Timor and the Government of Australia, Dili, 20 May 2002, in force 2 April 2003, 2258 UNTS 3, annex B. As another example, in *Indus Waters Kishenganga (Pakistan v. India)*, the rules were laid out in an annexure to the Indus Waters Treaty. See The Indus Waters Treaty Between the Government of India, the Government of Pakistan, and the International Bank for Reconstruction and Development, Karachi, 19 September 1960, in force 12 January 1961, 419 UNTS 126, annexure G.

for and/or most often deal with public international arbitrations: the Permanent Court of Arbitration ('PCA') Arbitration Rules 2012 (Section 10.2.1); Annex VII of the United Nations Convention on the Law of the Sea ('UNCLOS') (Section 10.2.2); the International Centre for Settlement of Investment Disputes ('ICSID') Convention (Section 10.2.3); and the United Nations Commission on International Trade Law ('UNCITRAL') Arbitration Rules (Section 10.2.4).

10.2.1   PCA Arbitration Rules 2012

The PCA Arbitration Rules 2012 are the PCA's newest set of procedural rules.[12] They are a useful starting point for the study of appointing authorities in public international arbitration because they were specifically designed for disputes involving at least one State, State-controlled entity, or intergovernmental organization.[13]

Under the PCA Arbitration Rules 2012, the appointing authority, who is by default the PCA Secretary-General,[14] has four powers. First, the appointing authority has an appointing power. The authority may appoint an arbitrator if one party fails to appoint an arbitrator,[15] or if the parties or party-appointed arbitrators fail to agree on the appointment of an arbitrator.[16] In addition, the PCA Arbitration Rules 2012 provide that '[i]n the event of any failure to constitute the arbitral tribunal under these Rules, the appointing authority shall, at the request of any party, constitute the arbitral tribunal'.[17] Although the PCA maintains a list of 'Members' who are selected as potential appointees to arbitral tribunals, the appointing authority is free to appoint persons who are not Members of the PCA.[18]

Second, the appointing authority has a replacing power. If an arbitrator has to be replaced during the course of the arbitral proceedings, a substitute arbitrator is appointed or chosen pursuant to the procedure that was applicable to the appointment or choice of the arbitrator being replaced.[19]

---

[12] Permanent Court of Arbitration, 'PCA Arbitration Rules' (effective 17 December 2012), https://pca-cpa.org/en/services/arbitration-services/pca-arbitration-rules-2012/(accessed 17 August 2018).
[13] PCA Arbitration Rules, Introduction.
[14] Ibid., art. 6(1).
[15] Ibid., art. 9(2).
[16] Ibid., arts. 8(1), 9(3).
[17] Ibid., art. 10(3).
[18] Ibid., art. 10(4).
[19] Ibid., art. 14(1).

So if the original appointing procedure involved the appointing authority, then the replacing procedure also involves the appointing authority. It should also be noted that in 'exceptional circumstances', a party may be deprived of its right to appoint a substitute arbitrator and the appointing authority may appoint the arbitrator in its place.[20]

Third, the appointing authority has a disqualifying power. If a party challenges an arbitrator and not all parties agree to the challenge or the challenged arbitrator does not withdraw, then the party making the challenge may elect to pursue it, in which case the appointing authority decides on the challenge.[21]

Fourth and finally, the appointing authority has a costs-reviewing power. This power consists of two elements. First, the appointing authority may, upon the referral of a party, review and make necessary adjustments to the tribunal's proposal on how it will determine its fees and expenses.[22] Second, the appointing authority has the power to review and make necessary adjustments to the tribunal's determination of its costs.[23]

In summary, under the PCA Arbitration Rules 2012, the appointing authority has not only an appointing power, but also a replacing power, a disqualifying power, and a costs-reviewing power.

10.2.2 Annex VII of UNCLOS

In 1982, the UN General Assembly adopted UNCLOS, Part XV of which establishes a compulsory dispute settlement mechanism for any dispute concerning the interpretation or application of the Convention, with a range of exceptions. Article 287 of UNCLOS establishes the default mechanism for the settlement of such disputes to be arbitrated under Annex VII of UNCLOS.[24] As of August 2018, there have been 14 publicly known disputes submitted to arbitration under Annex VII ('Annex VII arbitrations').[25] For these arbitrations, the rules applicable to the appointing authority may be found in Annex VII of UNCLOS, as well as any ad hoc rules of procedure adopted by the tribunals. Among the 14

---

[20] Ibid., art. 14(2).
[21] Ibid., art. 13(4).
[22] Ibid., art. 41(2).
[23] Ibid., art. 41(3).
[24] UNCLOS, art. 287(3) and (5).
[25] This number does not include cases submitted to arbitration under Annex VII but later transferred to ITLOS.

publicly known Annex VII arbitrations, at least 12 of them adopted ad hoc rules of procedure.[26]

Under Annex VII of UNCLOS, the appointing authority, unless the parties agree otherwise, is the ITLOS President or, if the President is unable to act or is a national of one of the parties to the dispute, the next most senior member of ITLOS.[27] For simplicity, this section assumes that the appointing authority is always the ITLOS President.

Annex VII of UNCLOS grants the ITLOS President two powers. First, the ITLOS President has an appointing power. Annex VII tribunals by default consist of five arbitrators.[28] The applicant appoints one arbitrator,[29] the respondent appoints a second arbitrator,[30] and the parties appoint the remaining three arbitrators by agreement.[31] The appointing authority may appoint an arbitrator, however, if the respondent party fails to appoint an arbitrator,[32] or if the parties fail to agree on any of the remaining three arbitrators.[33] This appointing power is subject to certain limits. First, the ITLOS President may only make appointments from a list of arbitrators maintained by the Secretary-General of the United Nations.[34] Second, the ITLOS President must make the appointment 'in consultation with the parties'.[35] And third, the arbitrators appointed by the ITLOS President must 'be of different nationalities and may not be in the service of, ordinarily resident in the territory of, or nationals of, any of the parties to the dispute'.[36]

In addition to the appointing power, the ITLOS President also has a replacing power. Article 3(f) of Annex VII succinctly states: 'Any vacancy shall be filled in the manner prescribed for the initial appointment'.[37]

---

[26] The *Southern Bluefin Tuna (New Zealand v. Japan; Australia v. Japan)* award on jurisdiction and admissibility and the *Land Reclamation (Malaysia v. Singapore)* award on agreed terms do not mention that the tribunals adopted any institutional or ad hoc rules of procedure. See *Southern Bluefin Tuna (New Zealand v. Japan; Australia v. Japan)*, Award on Jurisdiction and Admissibility (4 August 2000), 23 RIAA 1; *Land Reclamation (Malaysia v. Singapore)*, PCA Case No. 2004–05, Award on Agreed Terms (1 September 2005).

[27] UNCLOS, Annex VII, art. 3(e).

[28] Ibid., Annex VII, art. 3(a).

[29] Ibid., Annex VII, art. 3(b).

[30] Ibid., Annex VII, art. 3(c).

[31] Ibid., Annex VII, art. 3(d).

[32] Ibid., Annex VII, art. 3(c) and (e).

[33] Ibid., Annex VII, art. 3(d) and (e).

[34] Ibid., Annex VII, arts. 2, 3(e).

[35] Ibid., Annex VII, art. 3(e).

[36] Ibid.

[37] Ibid., Annex VII, art. 3(f).

The ITLOS President's disqualifying power is less clear. On this question, Annex VII of UNCLOS is silent. Instead, one must look to the ad hoc rules of procedure adopted by the tribunals. In the first UNCLOS Annex VII arbitration, *Southern Bluefin Tuna (New Zealand v. Japan; Australia v. Japan)*, the award on jurisdiction and admissibility did not mention that the tribunal adopted any institutional or ad hoc rules of procedure.[38] In the second arbitration, *MOX Plant (Ireland v. United Kingdom)*, the tribunal adopted ad hoc rules of procedure, according to which if an arbitrator is challenged and does not withdraw, the other members of the tribunal decide on the challenge.[39] The rules did not, however, contain any provision on what happens if the other members of the tribunal are evenly divided. In the third arbitration, *Land Reclamation (Malaysia v. Singapore)*, there was no indication that the tribunal adopted any rules of procedure.[40] In the next three arbitrations, *Barbados v. Trinidad and Tobago*, *Guyana v. Suriname*, and *Bangladesh v. India*, the tribunals adopted ad hoc rules of procedure, but they did not contain any provisions on challenges whatsoever.[41]

An interesting event occurred in the seventh arbitration, *Chagos Marine Protected Area (Mauritius v. United Kingdom)*. In that case, Mauritius challenged one of the arbitrators before the tribunal adopted its ad hoc rules of procedure. In response, the tribunal proposed that the decision on the challenge would be made by a majority vote of the four other arbitrators, with the president of the tribunal having a casting vote in the absence of a majority,[42] and the two parties agreed to this proposal.[43] After deciding the challenge, the tribunal then adopted its ad hoc rules of procedure, which, like the *MOX Plant* ad hoc rules of procedure, provided that if an arbitrator is challenged and does not withdraw, the other

---

[38] See *Southern Bluefin Tuna (New Zealand v. Japan; Australia v. Japan)*, Award on Jurisdiction and Admissibility (4 August 2000), 23 RIAA 1.

[39] *MOX Plant (Ireland v. United Kingdom)*, PCA Case No. 2002-01, Rules of Procedure (25 October 2001), art. 6(2).

[40] See *Land Reclamation (Malaysia v. Singapore)*, PCA Case No. 2004–05, Award on Agreed Terms (1 September 2005).

[41] See *Barbados v. Trinidad and Tobago*, PCA Case No. 2004-02, Rules of Procedure (23 August 2004); *Guyana v. Suriname*, PCA Case No. 2004-04, Rules of Procedure (24 February 2004); *Bay of Bengal Maritime Boundary Arbitration between Bangladesh and India (Bangladesh v. India)*, PCA Case No. 2010–16, Rules of Procedure (26 May 2010).

[42] *Chagos Marine Protected Area (Mauritius v. United Kingdom)*, PCA Case No. 2011-03, Reasoned Decision on Challenge (30 November 2011), para. 13.

[43] Ibid., para. 14.

members of the tribunal decide on the challenge, without making clear what happens if the other members of the tribunal are evenly divided.[44] In the next three arbitrations, *ARA Libertad (Argentina v. Ghana), South China Sea (Philippines v. China),* and *Atlanto-Scandian Herring (Denmark in respect of the Faroe Islands v. European Union),* the tribunals adopted ad hoc rules of procedure that granted the ITLOS President the power to decide on challenges.[45] Nevertheless, in the eleventh arbitration, *Arctic Sunrise (Netherlands v. Russia),* the ad hoc rules of procedure reflected those of *MOX Plant* and *Chagos Marine Protected Area* whereby the other members of the tribunal are the ones who decide on a challenge.[46] And this time, the rules of procedure further specified that in the case of no majority, the president or presiding member of the tribunal has a casting vote.[47] Still, this procedure does not appear to contemplate the possibility that the president or presiding member of the tribunal could be the one who is challenged, as it would be awkward to have the president or presiding member render a casting vote when he or she does not have a vote in the first place, and especially since he or she is the one being challenged.

In the twelfth arbitration, *Duzgit Integrity (Malta v. São Tomé and Príncipe),* the tribunal adopted ad hoc rules of procedure,[48] but they are not publicly available. In the two most recent arbitrations, *Enrica Lexie* and *Coastal State Rights,* the tribunals adopted ad hoc rules of procedure, but for some reason they do not contain any provisions on challenges.[49] One may suspect that the absence of provisions on challenges may be related to the fact that the appointing authority appointed himself to the arbitral tribunal in these two cases, but this is pure speculation.

---

[44] *Chagos Marine Protected Area (Mauritius v. United Kingdom),* PCA Case No. 2011-03, Rules of Procedure (29 March 2012), art. 6(3).

[45] *ARA Libertad (Argentina v. Ghana),* PCA Case No. 2013-11, Rules of Procedure (31 July 2013), art. 7(4); *South China Sea (Philippines v. China),* PCA Case No. 2013–19, Rules of Procedure (27 August 2013), art. 8(5); *Atlanto-Scandian Herring (Denmark in respect of the Faroe Islands v. European Union),* PCA Case No. 2013–30, Rules of Procedure (15 March 2014), art. 6(4).

[46] *Arctic Sunrise (Netherlands v. Russia),* PCA Case No. 2014-02, Rules of Procedure (17 March 2014), art. 8(5).

[47] Ibid.

[48] The *Duzgit Integrity* award cites the Rules of Procedure on multiple occasions. See *Duzgit Integrity (Malta v. São Tomé and Príncipe),* PCA Case No. 2014-07, Award (5 September 2016), paras. 13, 24, 31, 213, 336, 339.

[49] See The *"Enrica Lexie" Incident (Italy v. India),* PCA Case No. 2015–28, Rules of Procedure (19 January 2016); *Dispute Concerning Coastal State Rights in the Black Sea, Sea of Azov, and Kerch Strait (Ukraine v. Russia),* PCA Case No. 2017-06, Rules of Procedure (18 May 2017).

In summary, in Annex VII arbitrations, the ITLOS President has an appointing power and a replacing power, and sometimes also a disqualifying power, depending on the ad hoc rules of procedure adopted by the tribunal.

10.2.3   ICSID Convention

As of December 2017, there have been 855 publicly known arbitrations instituted by investors against States under international investment agreements ('IIAs').[50] Among the 855 publicly known arbitrations, 467 arbitrations have been instituted under the ICSID Convention ('ICSID arbitrations') and 262 under the UNCITRAL Arbitration Rules ('UNCITRAL arbitrations').[51] As ICSID arbitrations and UNCITRAL arbitrations are by far the most popular types of investor-State arbitrations, this section focuses on the former, and the next section focuses on the latter.[52]

For ICSID arbitrations, the rules applicable to appointing authorities may be found in the ICSID Convention, the ICSID Arbitration Rules, and the IIA in question. As it would be impractical to examine the complete diversity of provisions in IIAs, this section examines only the ICSID Convention and the ICSID Rules. Under the ICSID Convention, the appointing authority is the Chair of the Administrative Council,[53] an office assumed *ex officio* by the President of the World Bank.[54]

The ICSID Convention and the ICSID Arbitration Rules grant the Chair four powers. First, the Chair has an appointing power. If the tribunal is not constituted within a certain period of time, the Chair, at the request of either party and after consulting both parties as far as possible, appoints the arbitrator or arbitrators not yet appointed.[55] There are

---

[50] UNCTAD, 'Investment Dispute Settlement Navigator', http://investmentpolicyhub.unctad .org/ISDS (accessed 17 August 2018).

[51] UNCTAD, 'Investment Dispute Settlement Navigator: Arbitral rules and administering institution', http://investmentpolicyhub.unctad.org/ISDS/FilterByRulesAndInstitution (accessed 17 August 2018).

[52] For a more comprehensive discussion of appointing authorities in investor-State dispute settlement, see Gaukrodger, *Appointing Authorities and the Selection of Arbitrations in Investor-State Dispute Settlement*.

[53] Convention on the Settlement of Investment Disputes between States and Nationals of Other States, Washington, 18 March 1965, in force 14 October 1966, 575 UNTS 159 (ICSID Convention), art. 38.

[54] Ibid., art. 5.

[55] Ibid., art. 38; International Centre for Settlement of Investment Disputes, Rules of Procedure for Arbitration Proceedings (10 April 2006) (ICSID Arbitration Rules), rule 4.

two important limits, however, on the Chair's appointing power. First, arbitrators appointed by the Chair may not be nationals of the Contracting State party to the dispute or of the Contracting State whose national is a party to the dispute.[56] Second, arbitrators appointed by the Chair must be from the Panel of Arbitrators,[57] a list of potential arbitrators maintained by the ICSID Secretariat.[58]

Second, the Chair has a replacing power. If an arbitrator is disqualified, dies, becomes incapacitated, or resigns, the vacancy is filled by the same method by which his or her appointment was made,[59] which, as described above, can be an appointment by the Chair. In addition, if a party-appointed arbitrator resigns without the consent of the tribunal, the Chair appoints his or her replacement from the Panel of Arbitrators.[60] Furthermore, if there is any vacancy and no replacement is made and accepted within a certain period of time, then, at the request of either party, the Chair may appoint the replacement from the Panel of Arbitrators.[61]

Third, the Chair has a disqualifying power. If there is a proposal to disqualify an arbitrator, ordinarily the other members of the arbitral tribunal decide on the disqualification.[62] Nevertheless, if the other members are equally divided on the question, or if there is a proposal to disqualify a sole arbitrator or a majority of the arbitrators, then the Chair decides on the disqualification.[63]

Fourth, the Chair has an appointing power with respect to the annulment body. If either party requests annulment of the award, the Chair appoints from the Panel of Arbitrators an ad hoc Committee of three persons, which has the authority to annul the award or any part thereof.[64]

In summary, the Chair of the Administrative Council has an appointing power and a replacing power in ICSID arbitrations, just like the PCA Secretary-General and the ITLOS President in, respectively, arbitrations under the PCA Arbitration Rules and Annex VII of UNCLOS. The Chair's disqualifying power is quite limited: it only comes into play if the other

---

[56] ICSID Convention, art. 38.
[57] Ibid., art. 40(1).
[58] Ibid., arts. 3, 12–16.
[59] Ibid., art. 56(1); ICSID Arbitration Rules, rule 11(1).
[60] ICSID Convention, art. 56(3); ICSID Arbitration Rules, rule 11(2)(a).
[61] ICSID Arbitration Rules, rule 11(2)(b).
[62] ICSID Convention, art. 58; ICSID Arbitration Rules, rule 9(4).
[63] ICSID Convention, art. 58; ICSID Arbitration Rules, rules 9(4)–(5).
[64] ICSID Convention, art. 52(3); ICSID Arbitration Rules, rule 52(1).

members of the tribunal are equally divided on the question, or if there is a proposal to disqualify a sole arbitrator or a majority of the arbitrators. Nevertheless, the Chair has an additional power to appoint the members of ad hoc annulment committees.

10.2.4   UNCITRAL Arbitration Rules

As mentioned above, 262 of the 855 publicly known investor-State arbitrations have been instituted under the UNCITRAL Arbitration Rules, of which there are three versions: the 1976 version, the 2010 version, and the 2013 version. In addition, some inter-State arbitrations have been instituted under the UNCITRAL Arbitration Rules.[65]

The three versions of the UNCITRAL Arbitration Rules have very similar provisions governing the appointing authority. Under all three versions, the appointing authority is not a fixed person or institution. Instead, the parties may agree on the appointing authority.[66] Indeed, in many IIAs, the contracting States provide for the ICJ President to be the appointing authority, particularly in inter-State dispute settlement. In fact, the UNCITRAL model arbitration clause for contracts notes that parties should consider specifying the appointing authority in the contract.[67] If, however, the parties have not agreed on the choice of an appointing authority within a certain period of time, any party may request the PCA Secretary-General to designate the appointing authority.[68]

All three versions of the UNCITRAL Arbitration Rules grant the appointing authority five powers. The first four powers – the appointing power,[69] the replacing power,[70] the disqualifying power,[71] and the costs-reviewing power[72] – are very similar to the four powers under the PCA

---

[65] See eg *Ecuador v. United States* (Award) PCA Case No. 2012–5 (29 September 2012).

[66] UNCITRAL Arbitration Rules (2013), art. 6(1); UNCITRAL Arbitration Rules (2010), art. 6(1); UNCITRAL Arbitration Rules (1976), arts. 6(1)(b), 7(2).

[67] UNCITRAL Arbitration Rules (2013), annex; UNCITRAL Arbitration Rules (2010), annex; UNCITRAL Arbitration Rules (1976), art. 1.

[68] UNCITRAL Arbitration Rules (2013), art. 6(2); UNCITRAL Arbitration Rules (2010), art. 6(2); UNCITRAL Arbitration Rules (1976), arts. 6(2), 7(2)(b).

[69] UNCITRAL Arbitration Rules (2013), arts. 7–10; UNCITRAL Arbitration Rules (2010), arts. 7–10; UNCITRAL Arbitration Rules (1976), arts. 6–8.

[70] UNCITRAL Arbitration Rules (2013), art. 14; UNCITRAL Arbitration Rules (2010), art. 14; UNCITRAL Arbitration Rules (1976), art. 13.

[71] UNCITRAL Arbitration Rules (2013), art. 13(4); UNCITRAL Arbitration Rules (2010), art. 13(4); UNCITRAL Arbitration Rules (1976), art. 12.

[72] UNCITRAL Arbitration Rules (2013), art. 41; UNCITRAL Arbitration Rules (2010), art. 41; UNCITRAL Arbitration Rules (1976), art. 39.

Arbitration Rules 2012, as discussed above in Section 10.2.1. The fifth power is unique: the appointing authority has a consultative power for deposits; that is, under certain circumstances the arbitral tribunal may fix the amounts of deposits only after consultation with the appointing authority.[73]

10.3 Self-Appointment

It is not common for an appointing authority to appoint him or herself to the tribunal as an arbitrator. Nevertheless, as mentioned above in Section 10.1, it has occurred in two UNCLOS Annex VII arbitrations: *Enrica Lexie* and Coastal State Rights. This phenomenon thus deserves further scrutiny.

As a preliminary matter, it should be noted that none of the instruments examined above – the PCA Arbitration Rules 2012, Annex VII of UNCLOS, the ad hoc rules of procedure of Annex VII tribunals, the ICSID Convention, the ICSID Arbitration Rules, or the UNCITRAL Arbitration Rules – expressly prohibits self-appointment. The ICSID Convention and Annex VII of UNCLOS require that the appointee be from a specific list of individuals, but in both cases, there is nothing preventing the appointing authority from being on the list.

Despite the lack of an express prohibition, self-appointment raises a series of concerns. Section 10.3.1 elaborates on three of them: conflicts of interest (Section 10.3.1.1); influence over fellow arbitrators (Section 10.3.1.2); and contravention of the parties' intentions (Section 10.3.1.3). Section 10.3.2 then further discusses the phenomenon in the context of the two cases of self-appointment.

10.3.1 Concerns

10.3.1.1 Conflicts of Interest

The first concern is that there may be conflicts of interest.[74] Such a conflict would be most apparent if the appointing authority is called upon to

---

[73] UNCITRAL Arbitration Rules (2013), art. 41; UNCITRAL Arbitration Rules (2010), art. 43(3); UNCITRAL Arbitration Rules (1976), art. 41(3).

[74] For an examination of conflicts of interest in investor-State arbitration in general, see IBA Guidelines on Conflicts of Interest in International Arbitration (2014); Maria Nicole Cleis, *The Independence and Impartiality of ICSID Arbitrators: Current Case Law, Alternative Approaches, and Improvement Suggestions* (2017); James D. Fry and Juan Ignacio Stampalija, 'Forged Independence and Impartiality: Conflicts of Interest of International Arbitrators in Investment Disputes' (2014) 30 *Arbitration International* 189.

decide on a challenge to him or herself. As noted above in Section 10.2, the PCA Arbitration Rules 2012, the UNCITRAL Arbitration Rules, and three UNCLOS Annex VII tribunals' ad hoc rules of procedure grant the appointing authority the power to decide on challenges, without containing any special provision for cases where the appointing authority, as a member of the tribunal, is the arbitrator being challenged. Moreover, even though the ICSID Convention and the ICSID Arbitration Rules provide that the other members of the tribunal ordinarily decide on challenges,[75] under certain circumstances, the appointing authority is the one deciding.[76] In light of this power to decide on challenges, if an appointing authority appoints him or herself to a tribunal and is subsequently challenged, he or she could potentially be called on to decide on the challenge. This creates a clear conflict of interest. Under the principle of *nemo iudex in causa sua* ('no one should be a judge in his or her own cause'), the appointing authority should not have the power to decide on a challenge to him or herself.

Even outside this particular scenario, conflicts of interest could arise whenever the appointing authority is asked to appoint another arbitrator, replace an arbitrator (including him or herself), and/or decide on a challenge to an arbitrator (including him or herself). The reason is that the appointing authority, as an arbitrator in the case, likely has a position concerning how he or she believes the case should turn out. As a result, he or she might make the appointment, replacement, or decision on the challenge in a manner that is influenced by his or her position. For example, he or she may be inclined to appoint an individual who has views aligned with his or her own, or to disqualify an arbitrator whose views are not so aligned.

In ICSID arbitrations, another conflict of interest would arise whenever the appointing authority appoints an ad hoc annulment committee to decide on the annulment of the award. The conflict of interest is clear: the appointing authority, so as to save face, would be inclined to appoint individuals who are not likely to annul the award.

10.3.1.2   Influence Over Fellow Arbitrators

The second concern is that the appointing authority may have inappropriate influence over a fellow arbitrator by virtue of his or her role as

---

[75] ICSID Convention, art. 58; ICSID Arbitration Rules, rule 9(4).
[76] ICSID Convention, art. 58; ICSID Arbitration Rules, rule 9(4)–(5).

appointing authority. Once again, this could be the case if the appointing authority is called upon to appoint a fellow arbitrator, replace a fellow arbitrator, and/or decide on a challenge to a fellow arbitrator. The influence could function *ex-post* or *ex-ante*. As an example of *ex-post* influence, an arbitrator might be inclined to vote in line with the vote of the appointing authority if the appointing authority appointed him or her or rejected a challenge to him or her. As an example of *ex-ante* influence, an arbitrator might have the same inclinations concerning a vote on an interim decision in anticipation of the fact that the appointing authority would be the one deciding on a prospective challenge to him or her.

10.3.1.3. Contravention of the Parties' Intentions

The third concern is that the appointing authority's self-appointment may contravene the intentions of the parties. As the argument goes, the very fact that the parties only agreed, directly or indirectly, on the appointing authority and not on the arbitrators reveals that they did not intend the appointing authority to serve as an arbitrator. In addition, the parties are likely not have intended for the two aforementioned concerns to arise.

On the other hand, one can argue that the parties' agreement on the appointing authority demonstrates that they consider the appointing authority to be an impartial figure, making him or her an appropriate arbitrator. Furthermore, had the parties not intended the appointing authority to serve as an arbitrator, they could have expressly stipulated so in the underlying treaty.

10.3.2. Cases and Discussion

As mentioned above, the appointing authority in the two most recent Annex VII arbitrations appointed himself to the arbitral tribunal. In *Enrica Lexie*, then-President Golitsyn appointed himself as the presiding member of the tribunal. And in Coastal State Rights, then-Vice-President Bouguetaia, a Russian national acting as appointing authority, appointed himself as a member of the tribunal. The author of the present chapter examined all recent inter-State arbitrations and investor-State arbitrations, but did not find any other case where the appointing authority appointed him or herself.

As for conflicts of interest, certain aspects of *Enrica Lexie* and Coastal State Rights mitigate this concern. In particular, as mentioned above in Section 10.2.2, the ad hoc rules of procedure adopted by the two tribunals do not grant the appointing authority the power to decide on challenges to arbitrators. Indeed, perhaps the tribunals purposely deviated from the *ARA Libertad, South China Sea,* and *Atlanto-Scandian Herring* precedents of naming the appointing authority as the decision-maker for challenges because they were conscious of the possibility that the appointing authority, as an arbitrator, could be challenged, leading to the undesirable situation where he is called upon to decide on a challenge to himself.

Nevertheless, conflicts of interest could still arise. First, since the *Enrica Lexie* and Coastal State Rights ad hoc rules of procedure do not specify any challenge procedure, if a party were to challenge an arbitrator in either case, the tribunal would have to establish an ad hoc procedure for deciding on the challenge, as the Annex VII tribunal did in *Chagos Marine Protected Area.*[77] In theory, this procedure could potentially grant the appointing authority the power to decide on the challenge, though one would think, or at least hope, that the tribunal would not adopt such a procedure. Second, conflicts of interest could also arise if the appointing authority is asked to replace an arbitrator on the tribunals. In such a circumstance, one may be concerned that the appointing authority may appoint an arbitrator who is more aligned with his own views.

As for the concern of influence, it is certainly possible that the other arbitrators on the two tribunals are influenced by the appointing authority's presence on the tribunal. In particular, the potential for *ex-post* influence is present because in both arbitrations the appointing authority appointed not only himself, but two other arbitrators on the tribunal under Article 3(e) of Annex VII. At the time of writing this chapter, the proceedings in *Enrica Lexie* and Coastal State Rights are still ongoing, but when the awards are rendered, it will be interesting to see how the appointing authority's vote compares with the vote of the arbitrators whom the appointing authority appointed.

As for the parties' intentions, it may be helpful to give a fuller account of the procedure behind the constitution of Annex VII tribunals. All 14 Annex VII arbitrations can be neatly divided into two categories:[78] cases where the parties jointly appointed all the non-single-party-appointed arbitrators under Article 3(d) of Annex VII ('Article 3(d) cases');[79] and

---

[77] *Chagos Marine Protected Area (Mauritius v. United Kingdom)*, PCA Case No. 2011-03, Reasoned Decision on Challenge (30 November 2011), para. 13.

[78] In theory, it could be the case that some of the non-single-party-appointed arbitrators are appointed jointly by the parties, whereas others are appointed by the ITLOS President, but this has never happened.

[79] These five cases are *Southern Bluefin Tuna, MOX Plant, Barbados v. Trinidad and Tobago, Guyana v. Suriname,* and *Atlanto-Scandian Herring.*

cases where the parties did not jointly appoint the non-single-party-appointed arbitrators, such that the ITLOS President (or Vice-President) made the appointments under Article 3(e) of Annex VII ('Article 3(e) cases').[80] It should be recalled, however, that for Article 3(e) cases, the ITLOS President (or Vice-President) must make the appointment(s) 'in consultation with the parties'.[81] As a matter of practice, what this means is that if the parties cannot agree on the appointment of any of the non-single-party-appointed arbitrators, then the ITLOS President (or Vice-President) convenes a meeting with the two parties. During this meeting, again as a matter of practice, the parties, with the help of the ITLOS President (or Vice-President), tend to come to an agreement on the non-single-party-appointed arbitrators. As a result, when the ITLOS President (or Vice-President) appoints himself to the tribunal, it would not be surprising if the parties had actually agreed on the appointment.

With regard to *Enrica Lexie*, it is not known whether Italy and India explicitly agreed to Judge Golitsyn's self-appointment. And with regard to Coastal State Rights, it is similarly unclear whether Ukraine and Russia actually agreed to Judge Bouguetaia's self-appointment. Nevertheless, even if the parties agreed to these self-appointments, it should be remembered that the decision to appoint Judge Golitsyn came out of a meeting with Judge Golitsyn and the decision to appoint Judge Bouguetaia came out of a meeting with Judge Bouguetaia. One thus cannot help but speculate as to whether Judges Golitsyn and Bouguetaia were the ones who proposed the idea that they serve as arbitrator on their respective tribunals. At the very least, it seems quite unlikely that the proposal came purely from the parties, given that they had originally failed to jointly appoint the three non-single-party-appointed arbitrators. In any case, since there has been no complaint from either of the parties in either of the cases that the appointing authority appointed himself, one can reasonably argue that even if the parties did not expressly consent to Judge Golitsyn's or Judge Bouguetaia's self-appointment, they have impliedly given such consent.

Although one can discuss the three aforementioned concerns in greater detail, in the opinion of the present author, there is a greater overarching concern. Today, there are many more investor-State arbitrations occurring than inter-State arbitrations. Why, then, has this phenomenon

---

[80] These nine cases are *Land Reclamation, Bangladesh v. India, Chagos Marine Protected Area, ARA Libertad, South China Sea, Arctic Sunrise, Duzgit Integrity, Enrica Lexie*, and Coastal State Rights.

[81] UNCLOS, Annex VII, art. 3(e).

of self-appointment occurred only in inter-State arbitrations? One can speculate as to the answer to this question. But here is one possibility: there is no compulsory control mechanism in inter-State arbitration. That is, an unsatisfied State cannot apply to annul the arbitral award without the consent of the other State to the annulment proceeding. As a result, perhaps Judge Golitsyn in *Enrica Lexie* and Judge Bouguetaia in *Coastal State Rights* felt more emboldened to appoint themselves to their respective tribunals, knowing that there would be no compulsory mechanism of recourse for any complaint in this regard. To further support this thesis, one could perform a study of international commercial arbitrations – which are subject to a compulsory control mechanism – and examine whether appointing authorities have ever appointed themselves. If the answer is, as it is with investor-State arbitration, that the appointing authority has never appointed him or herself, then we perhaps need to start thinking about whether the time has come for a compulsory control mechanism for inter-State arbitration.[82]

10.4 Party Appointment

As with self-appointment, party appointment (where one or both parties appoint the appointing authority as arbitrator to the tribunal) is not a common phenomenon. Nevertheless, as mentioned above in Section 10.1, it has occurred in three recent inter-State arbitrations: *Eritrea/Yemen*, *Guyana v. Suriname*, and *Croatia/Slovenia*. This section first elaborates on the concerns raised by party appointment (Section 10.4.1), and then discusses the phenomenon in the context of the three cases (Section 10.4.2).

10.4.1 Concerns

The three concerns mentioned above for self-appointment may also apply to party appointment. The conflict of interest concern still arises because, regardless of who appointed the appointing authority, he or she could still be called upon to appoint another arbitrator, to replace an arbitrator (including him or herself), to decide on a challenge to an arbitrator (including him or herself), and, in the context of ICSID arbitrations,

---

[82] See Peter Tzeng, 'The Annulment of Interstate Arbitral Awards', *Kluwer Arbitration Blog* (1 July 2017), http://arbitrationblog.kluwerarbitration.com/2017/07/01/the-annulment-of-interstate-arbitral-awards/.

to appoint an ad hoc annulment committee. The concern of influence remains for the same reasons. And the concern of parties' intentions could arise if only one party appointed the appointing authority to the tribunal. By contrast, if both parties jointly appointed the appointing authority to the tribunal, this concern would no longer be present.

Although an appointing authority who is appointed by one or both parties to the tribunal may appear to be completely innocent, one must remember that when the appointing authority is appointed, he or she has the option to decline the appointment. Indeed, an appointing authority who is appointed as an arbitrator to the tribunal should consider the three concerns mentioned above, and if they are significant, the appointing authority should probably decline such an appointment.

10.4.2   Cases and Discussion

As already mentioned, one or both parties have appointed the appointing authority to an arbitral tribunal at least three times in inter-State arbitrations. First, in *Eritrea/Yemen*, Eritrea appointed Judge Stephen Schwebel as one of its two party-appointed arbitrators.[83] Not too long after, Judge Schwebel was elected President of the ICJ, and thus became the appointing authority under Article 1(5) of the arbitration agreement.[84] In this particular case, the aforementioned concerns did not arise. Judge Schwebel was never asked to appoint another arbitrator, to replace an arbitrator (though he could have been called on to replace the president of the tribunal in certain circumstances under Article 3(2)(b) of the arbitration agreement[85]), or to decide on a challenge to an arbitrator. In fact, the applicable procedural rules, enshrined in the arbitration agreement, did not provide for a challenge procedure. Moreover, even if there were valid concerns regarding Judge Schwebel's appointment, one could not chastise him for not declining the appointment because he had been appointed as arbitrator before he was elected ICJ President.

Second, in *Guyana v. Suriname*, the parties agreed to appoint Judge Dolliver Nelson as president of the UNCLOS Annex VII tribunal.[86] At the time, Judge Nelson was serving as the President of ITLOS, so he was

---

[83] *Eritrea/Yemen*, PCA Case No. 1996-04, Award on Territorial Sovereignty and Scope of the Dispute (9 October 1998), para. 4.

[84] Ibid., Annex 1, art. 1(5).

[85] Ibid., Annex 1, art. 3(2)(b).

[86] *Guyana v. Suriname*, PCA Case No. 2004-04, Award (17 September 2007), para. 4.

thus also the Annex VII tribunal's appointing authority under Article 3 of Annex VII. Once again, the concerns raised above were not significant in this case. Judge Nelson was never asked to appoint another arbitrator, to replace an arbitrator, or to decide on a challenge to an arbitrator. In fact, Article 6 of the tribunal's ad hoc rules of procedure provided, possibly contrary to Article 3(f) of Annex VII, that Judge Nelson would not have the power to replace an arbitrator on his own in the case of death or withdrawal of the arbitrator.[87] And the ad hoc rules of procedure did not mention a challenge procedure.

Third, in *Croatia/Slovenia*, after Slovenia's party-appointed arbitrator resigned from the tribunal, Slovenia appointed Judge Ronny Abraham to replace him.[88] At the time, Judge Abraham was serving as President of the ICJ, and Article 2(1) of the arbitration agreement designated the President of the ICJ as the appointing authority.[89] Conflicts of interest could have arisen in this case. Since the PCA Optional Rules for Arbitration Disputes between Two States were the applicable procedural rules by virtue of Article 6(2) of the arbitration agreement,[90] Judge Abraham could possibly have been asked to decide on a challenge to his fellow arbitrators and even himself.[91] Furthermore, under Article 2 of the arbitration agreement, Judge Abraham could have been called upon to appoint a replacement of some of his colleagues on the tribunal.[92] Nevertheless, these concerns ultimately did not arise because Judge Abraham – for reasons not entirely clear – resigned from the tribunal a few days after his appointment.[93]

---

[87] *Guyana v. Suriname*, PCA Case No. 2004-04, Rules of Procedure (24 February 2004), art. 6.

[88] *Croatia/Slovenia*, PCA Case No. 2012-04, Partial Award (30 June 2016), para. 42.

[89] Arbitration Agreement between the Government of the Republic of Slovenia and the Government of the Republic of Croatia, Stockholm, 4 November 2009, in force 29 November 2010, art. 2(1).

[90] Ibid., art. 6(2).

[91] See Permanent Court of Arbitration, Permanent Court of Arbitration Optional Rules for Arbitrating Disputes between Two States (effective 20 October 1992), art. 12. It is not completely clear that Judge Abraham would have been the one deciding on a potential challenge, as the arbitration agreement did not expressly designate him as an 'appointing authority' for the purposes of Article 12 of the PCA Optional Rules for Arbitrating Disputes between Two States.

[92] See Arbitration Agreement between the Government of the Republic of Slovenia and the Government of the Republic of Croatia, Stockholm, 4 November 2009, in force 29 November 2010, art. 2.

[93] The Partial Award suggests that Judge Abraham resigned on or before 31 July 2015. See *Croatia/Slovenia*, PCA Case No. 2012-04, Partial Award (30 June 2016), paras. 45–46. The

In conclusion, in the three cases where one or both parties appointed the appointing authority to the tribunal, none of the aforementioned concerns actually arose.

10.5   Non-Appointment

The third phenomenon worthy of examination in light of recent cases is non-appointment – where an appointing authority is called upon to appoint an arbitrator but does not do so. As with the previous two sections, this section first examines the concerns raised by non-appointment (Section 10.5.1), and then discusses them in the context of real cases (Section 10.5.2).

10.5.1   Concerns

The concerns with non-appointment are of a fundamentally different nature than the concerns with self-appointment and party appointment. At first, one may be eager to chastise non-appointment: it interrupts the efficient operation of arbitral proceedings, and can even halt the proceedings altogether. At the same time, however, one can make a strong argument that appointing authorities are, at least in the majority of cases, not legally bound to appoint an arbitrator when a party requests it to do so. There are three reasons for this.

First, the language of the relevant provisions sometimes does not impose a clear obligation. For example, the PCA Arbitration Rules 2012 state that, in arbitrations where three arbitrators are to be appointed, if the second party does not appoint an arbitrator within a certain period of time, 'the first party may *request* the appointing authority to appoint the second arbitrator'.[94] The sentence does not specify that the appointing authority must actually make the appointment. By contrast, if the two party-appointed arbitrators do not agree on the third and presiding arbitrator, then the PCA Arbitration Rules 2012 provide that 'the remaining arbitrators and/or the presiding arbitrator *shall* be appointed by the appointing authority',[95] which more clearly signals an obligation. Similarly, Annex VII of UNCLOS provides that if the parties are unable

---

Final Award states that Judge Abraham notified the tribunal of his registration on 3 August 2015. *Croatia/Slovenia*, PCA Case No. 2012-04, Final Award (29 June 2017), para. 186.

[94]   PCA Arbitration Rules 2012, art. 9(2) (emphasis added).

[95]   Ibid., art. 9(3) (emphasis added).

to reach agreement on the appointment of one or more of the members of the tribunal to be appointed by agreement, then, by default, the ITLOS President '*shall* make the necessary appointments'.[96] At least one commentator has thus opined that 'the President of the ITLOS is not entitled to decline the role as an appointment authority where the requirements have been met'.[97] If one examines all procedural rules concerning the appointing power of appointing authorities, one will find that sometimes a permissive formulation is used, and other times a mandatory formulation is used.

Second, even if the language imposes a clear obligation, the appointing authority can be considered a 'third party' not subject to the treaty in question without its consent. Article 34 of the Vienna Convention on the Law of Treaties provides the general rule that '[a] treaty does not create either obligations or rights for a third State without its consent'.[98] Article 35 then provides: 'An obligation arises for a third State from a provision of a treaty if the parties to the treaty intend the provision to be the means of establishing the obligation and the third State expressly accepts that obligation in writing'.[99]

Articles 34 and 35 apply only to third States, but the same logic can be applied to other third parties such as appointing authorities.[100] As the logic goes, it would be unreasonable to allow two States to, by bilateral treaty, impose an obligation on the appointing authority without its consent. This is perhaps why the ICJ recommends: 'States proposing to insert [a provision granting the ICJ President appointing powers] in a treaty should consult the President as to his or her willingness to accept such a task'.[101] This principle of consent, however, may be less clear in circumstances where the institution of the appointing authority is established by or is the author of the very same instrument that imposes

---

[96] UNCLOS, Annex VII, art. 3(e) (emphasis added).

[97] Gao, 'Appointment of Arbitrators by the President of the ITLOS', para. 3.

[98] Vienna Convention on the Law of Treaties (VCLT), Vienna, 22 May 1969, in force 27 January 1980, 1155 UNTS 331 (VCLT), art. 34. For a detailed discussion of Article 34, see Eric David, 'Article 34' in Olivier Corten and Pierre Klein (eds.), *The Vienna Conventions on the Law of Treaties* 887 (2011).

[99] VCLT, art. 35. For a detailed discussion of Article 35, see Caroline Laly-Chevalier, 'Article 35' in Olivier Corten and Pierre Klein (eds.), *The Vienna Conventions on the Law of Treaties* 902 (2011).

[100] See Peter Tzeng, 'Non-State Actors as Respondents before International Judicial Bodies' (2018) 24 *ILSA Journal of International & Comparative Law* 397, 402–403.

[101] International Court of Justice, *CIJ Annuaire – ICJ Yearbook 2015–2016* (No 70) 68.

on it an obligation to make an appointment. For example, one can argue that Annex VII of UNCLOS may properly impose an obligation on the ITLOS President to appoint arbitrators in certain circumstances because UNCLOS is the very instrument that established ITLOS to begin with.[102] As another example, one can argue that the PCA Arbitration Rules 2012 may properly impose an obligation on the PCA Secretary-General to appoint arbitrators in certain circumstances because it is the PCA itself that developed the arbitration rules.

Third, even if the language imposes a clear obligation on the appointing authority and even if the latter somehow consents to the obligation, one can question whether the appointing authority – as a non-State actor – is even capable of holding such an obligation.[103] But this is a question that goes well beyond the scope of this chapter.

In summary, in cases of non-appointment, one may argue that the appointing authority is inappropriately interrupting the arbitral proceeding, but one must also realize that appointing authorities may not necessarily be legally bound to make appointments when asked to do so.

10.5.2 Cases and Discussion

As mentioned above in Section 10.1, the appointing authority refused to appoint an arbitrator in a series of investor-State arbitrations arising under the Investment Agreement of the Organisation of the Islamic Conference ('OIC Agreement').[104] Article 17(2)(b) of the Agreement provides that in the case of the arbitration mechanism being activated, the claimant appoints one arbitrator, the respondent appoints a second arbitrator, and the two party-appointed arbitrators then choose 'an umpire who shall

---

[102] As one commentator argues, 'requesting the President of the ITLOS to appoint members for the Annex VII arbitral tribunal does not depend on 'his or her willingness to accept such a task', since the design itself constitutes one inherent part of the dispute settlement mechanism of the LOS Convention'. Gao, 'Appointment of Arbitrators by the President of the ITLOS', para. 3.

[103] On the question of whether non-State actors can hold international obligations, see James Summers and Alex Gough (eds.), *Non-State Actors and International Obligations: Creation, Evolution and Enforcement* (2018); Anne Peters, *Beyond Human Rights: The Legal Status of the Individual in International Law* (2016), pp. 60–114; Kate Parlett, *The Individual in the International Legal System* (2011).

[104] Agreement on Promotion, Protection and Guarantee of Investments Among Member States of the Organisation of the Islamic Conference, Baghdad, 5 June 1981, in force 23 September 1986.

have a casting vote in case of equality of votes'.[105] The provision's last sentence then reads:

> If the second party does not appoint an arbitrator, or if the two arbitrators do not agree on the appointment of an Umpire within the prescribed time, either party may request the Secretary General to complete the composition of the Arbitration Tribunal.[106]

Notably, this provision is one of those that, by its text, only authorizes either party to *request* the OIC Secretary General to make the requisite appointments; it does not expressly *require* the OIC Secretary General to make such an appointment.

In 2014, it was reported that a Saudi investor had attempted to institute three investor-State arbitrations against Egypt under the OIC Agreement, but Egypt had responded by denying that the OIC Agreement obliges it to arbitrate disputes with investors.[107] The claimants subsequently requested that the OIC Secretary General make the necessary appointments, but he refused to do so, effectively leading to a dead-end for the arbitrations.[108]

These cases, however, contrast with a more recent case brought under the OIC Agreement. In 2016, a claimant incorporated in the United Arab Emirates similarly instituted arbitration proceedings against Libya under the OIC Agreement, and once again Libya and subsequently the OIC Secretary General refused to make the necessary appointments.[109] In March 2017, however, the PCA Secretary-General decided that, in the absence of an appointment by the OIC Secretary General, he had competence under the 1976 UNCITRAL Arbitration Rules to designate an appointing authority, and proceeded to do so, allowing the arbitration

---

[105] Ibid., art. 17(2)(b).

[106] Ibid.

[107] Luke Eric Peterson, 'Viability of Investor-State Arbitration Under Inter-Islamic Investment Treaty Now Lies in Hands of Secretariat, Following Petitions to OIC', *Investment Arbitration Reporter* (31 July 2014); IAReporter, 'Egypt Arbitration Round-Up: Updates on U.S. and German Investor Claims at ICSID, and on Three Ad-Hoc Claims Under OIC Agreement', *Investment Arbitration Reporter* (5 November 2014).

[108] Jarrod Hepburn and Luke Eric Peterson, 'Investigation: As New Cases Emerge Under Islamic Investment Treaty, Initial Viability of Claims Seems to Hinge on Willingness of Respondents to Appoint Arbitrators', *Investment Arbitration Reporter* (2 March 2017).

[109] Luke Eric Peterson, 'After Organisation for Islamic Cooperation Fails to Nominate an Arbitrator to Sit in Investor-State Case, PCA Breaks Stalemate by Designating an Appointing Authority', *Investment Arbitration Reporter* (31 March 2017).

to continue.[110] Indeed, Article 7(2) of the 1976 UNCITRAL Arbitration Rules – not unlike Article 6(4) of the 2010 and 2013 UNCITRAL Arbitration Rules – provides:

> If within thirty days after the receipt of a party's notification of the appointment of an arbitrator the other party has not notified the first party of the arbitrator he has appointed:
>
> (a) The first party may request the appointing authority previously designated by the parties to appoint the second arbitrator; or
>
> (b) If no such authority has been previously designated by the parties, or *if the appointing authority previously designated refuses to act* or fails to appoint the arbitrator within thirty days after receipt of a party's request therefor, the first party may request the Secretary-General of the Permanent Court of Arbitration at The Hague to designate the appointing authority. The first party may then request the appointing authority so designated to appoint the second arbitrator.[111]

Although the PCA Secretary-General faithfully applied Article 7(2) of the 1976 UNCITRAL Arbitration Rules, this decision was nonetheless controversial because the OIC Agreement does not expressly incorporate those rules. Rather, the claimant had invoked a most-favoured-nation clause in Article 8(1) of the OIC Agreement to bring in Article 7(2) of the 1976 UNCITRAL Arbitration Rules. Regardless of whether one considers that the PCA Secretary-General appropriately designated an appointing authority, the reality is that the arbitration is proceeding. A similar chain of events has reportedly occurred in another investor-State arbitration brought under the OIC Agreement against Oman.[112] Since these are investor-State arbitrations and not inter-State arbitrations, Libya and Oman could potentially apply to annul the final award on the ground of improper constitution of the tribunal.

10.6 Conclusion

In conclusion, it cannot be denied that appointing authorities wield tremendous power in international arbitration. Depending on the applicable rules, they can have an appointing power, a replacing power, a

---

[110] Ibid.

[111] UNCITRAL Arbitration Rules (1976), art. 7(2) (emphasis added).

[112] Luke Eric Peterson, 'An Update on Investor Arbitration Claims under the Organization for Islamic Cooperation Investment Treaty', *Investment Arbitration Reporter* (15 August 2018).

disqualifying power, a costs-reviewing power, and even a consultative power for deposits. Moreover, there is no legal provision preventing them from appointing themselves or accepting an appointment as an arbitrator on the tribunal over which they serve as appointing authority, even though doing so raises concerns regarding conflicts of interest, influence over fellow arbitrators, and contravention of parties' intentions. Furthermore, it appears that appointing authorities may even have the power to stop arbitrations altogether by refusing to appoint arbitrators.

These concerns are not merely theoretical. There are now a handful of precedents of self-appointment, party appointment, and non-appointment. As a result, the international arbitration community needs to pay attention to these phenomena and be aware of the consequences to which they lead. In order to defend the legitimacy of international arbitration as a whole, one must develop rules that can appropriately govern this sort of conduct.

The bottom line is that more attention needs to be paid to appointing authorities. The rules applicable to them appear not to contemplate self-appointment, party appointment, and non-appointment. In inter-State arbitrations, there is no compulsory control mechanism to review their conduct. And scholars also seem to overlook their significance. It is therefore the hope of the author that this chapter helps direct greater attention towards regulating the conduct of appointing authorities.

11

Before The Law

Assessing the Process and Impact of Judicial Screening Bodies

BRIAN MCGARRY AND JOSEF OSTŘANSKÝ

11.1   Introduction

> Before the Law stands a doorkeeper. To this doorkeeper there comes a man from
> the country and prays for admittance to the Law. But the doorkeeper says that he
> cannot grant admittance at the moment. The man thinks it over and then asks
> if he will be allowed in later. 'It is possible,' says the doorkeeper, 'but not at the
> moment.'[1]

So begins the central parable in Kafka's *The Trial*: a standoff between a
man seeking the Law, and a doorkeeper serving an unclear function. The
latter's ambiguity is an appropriate prelude to an examination of the role
of screening bodies within the judicial appointment processes of international courts. Such advisory bodies have been conceptualized as a way of
infusing objectivity into the appointment process, and ensuring appropriate legal expertise on the bench, thereby improving perceptions of the
legitimacy of international courts. Yet the question of whether and how
these bodies satisfy concerns over legitimacy in international dispute
settlement[2] – and indeed, whether they should serve this purpose – is
a question that is highly relevant to the establishment of future international courts.

The present contribution surveys and analyses advisory expert panels
for the appointment of international judges, a type of body which has thus

---

[1] F. Kafka, *The Complete Stories* (Schocken, 1971), p. 22.
[2] See generally A. von Bogdandy and I. Venzke, *In Whose Name: A Public Law Theory of
International Adjudication* (Oxford University Press, 2014); N. Hayashi and C.M. Bailliet,
The Legitimacy of International Criminal Tribunals (Cambridge University Press, 2017);
R. Howse, H. Ruiz-Fabri, G. Ulfstein, and M. Zang (eds.), *The Legitimacy of International
Trade Tribunals* (Cambridge University Press, 2018); G.A. Caldeira and J.L. Gibson, 'The

far been discussed tangentially rather than comprehensively.[3] The chapter proceeds in three further parts. Section 11.2 provides a general overview of international judicial appointments and sets the three discussed advisory panels within that context. At the same time, it sketches out official rationales for the establishment of these panels and looks for common threads in those rationales, such as the notions of legitimacy, professionalism, competence, expertise, independence, accountability, and transparency.

Section 11.3 surveys the modalities of three advisory panels selected for their depth of practice and the specificity of their founding instruments: the Council of Europe's Advisory Panel of Experts on Candidates for Judges to the European Court of Human Rights ('CoE panel'); the EU's Article 255 Panel for the nominations of Judges to the Court of Justice and the General Court and Advocates General ('Article 255 panel'); and the International Criminal Court's Advisory Committee on nominations of judges ('ICC committee'). It compares their relevant legal characteristics, their institutional design, and the modalities of their activities.

In Section 11.4, we evaluate whether the data provided in Section 11.3 may serve as a ground for some generalized conclusions despite the fact that the three advisory panels operate in distinct institutional environments. This section aims to answer the question as to whether these bodies are apt to address the challenges of judicial legitimacy for which they were established. Finding that their modalities may be systematized for general application, it considers what broader lessons may be learned for other existing and future international courts regarding the selection of judges. This leads to some concluding observations on the illustrative application of screening body modalities to the appointment processes of a prospective international investment court.

This chapter does not address courts to which judges are entirely appointed by independent non-State selection bodies, such as the

---

Legitimacy of the Court of Justice in the European Union: Models of Institutional Support' (1995) 89 *American Political Science Review* 356; special issue of (2013) 14(2) *Theoretical Inquiries in Law* on 'International Courts and the Quest for Legitimacy'.

[3] For accounts of some of the existing screening bodies discussed individually as well as comparatively, see T. Dumbrovský, B. Petkova and M. van der Sluis, 'Judicial Appointments: The Article 255 TFEU Advisory Panel and Selection Procedures in the Member States' (2014) 51(2) *Common Market Law Review* 455; M. Bobek (ed.), *Selecting Europe's Judges* (Oxford University Press, 2015); R. Mackenzie, K. Malleson, P. Martin, and P. Sands, *Selecting International Judges* (Oxford University Press, 2010), pp. 148–152.

Caribbean Court of Justice,[4] nor does it discuss special selection committees for the internal administrative courts of international organisations, such as the UN Dispute Tribunal and the UN Appeals Tribunal.[5] Equally, we do not consider various screening and advisory mechanisms which operate in tribunals where parties choose their adjudicators for a particular dispute. Lastly, the screening mechanism of the World Trade Organization (WTO) Appellate Body is excluded as well, as this body uses the existing institutional structure of the WTO (not a separate advisory panel), and serves to consult with Member States as to which candidates would be politically acceptable and 'broadly representative' of the WTO membership (rather than functioning as an expert body).[6]

11.2   A Brief Overview of International Judicial Appointments

Designs of selection procedures tend to reflect the characteristics of particular international courts. Hence it is not surprising that the ways in which international adjudicators are appointed or selected to their respective courts and tribunals vary widely. The present section briefly overviews the aspects of the relevant international courts that have a bearing on the analysis of advisory panels. These are chiefly the composition of the court (i.e., as truly representative or partially representative) and the processes of nominations and appointments.

11.2.1   Composition of the Courts

Apart from dispute settlement systems where adjudicators are appointed by the parties for a particular dispute, there are essentially two types of court composition. Some of these courts are what may be termed truly representative, while others are partially representative.

[4] Agreement Establishing the Caribbean Court of Justice (St. Michael, 14 February 2001).
[5] See UN General Assembly, Administration of Justice at the United Nations, A/RES/62/228, 6 Feb. 2008, paras. 39–45; UN General Assembly, Appointment of the full-time and half-time judges of the United Nations Dispute Tribunal, Memorandum by the Secretary-General, A/63/700, 3 Feb. 2009; Mackenzie et al., Selecting International Judges, pp. 147–152.
[6] See Preparatory Committee for the World Trade Organization, Establishment of the Appellate Body, WTO PC/IPL/13, 8 December 1994, para. 13; Dispute Settlement Body, Minutes of the Meeting, WTO WT/DSB/M/1, 28 February 1995.

11.2.1.1   Truly Representative Courts

A truly representative court composition presupposes that each Contracting Party has its (or one of its) candidate(s) sitting on the bench[7] – in other words, there are as many judges as Contracting Parties. This practice is common in the European regional courts, such as the European Court of Human Rights (ECtHR) and the Court of Justice of the European Union (CJEU), the latter of which consists of the EU's Court of Justice and General Court. Tellingly, we do not find examples of such a court or tribunal on a global level.

A clear benefit of such a system is that it avoids politicking for the seat that usually accompanies the partially representative compositions discussed below. It also allows more focus on the most appropriate procedure to select the most qualified candidates at the national level. However, it presupposes that every Member State is able to propose well-qualified candidates.[8] Courts operating in the one-country-one-judge model may still require other criteria of representativeness to be considered (such as gender).[9] On the other hand, the issue of representation of different legal systems or geographic regions does not arise.

11.2.1.2   Partially Representative Courts

The Rhodes Resolution of the *Institut de droit international* observes in its first article that States should ensure adequate geographical representation on international courts.[10] This suggests that the default framework for international courts is still a number of adjudicators lower than the number of Contracting Parties. This is clearly the case for four permanent international courts: the International Court of Justice (ICJ), the ICC, the International Tribunal for the Law of the Sea (ITLOS), and the WTO

---

[7] On norms of independence and impartiality, see International Law Association, The Burgh House Principles on the Independence of the International Judiciary, 1 July 2005, www.ucl.ac.uk/laws/cict/docs/burgh_final_21204.pdf; Institut de droit international, La situation du juge international, 6/RES/FR, 9 Sep. 2011, Art. 3(3).

[8] Concerning the EctHR, see further D. Kosař, 'Selecting Strasbourg Judges: A Critique', in Bobek (ed.), *Selecting Europe's Judges*, p. 157.

[9] As to gender, see Committee on the Election of Judges to the European Court of Human Rights, AS/Cdh/Inf (2016) 01 rev 4, 22 June 2016, para. 8; CoE, Parliamentary Assembly Res. 1366 (2004), Art. 2; Parliamentary Assembly Res. 1426 (2005); *Advisory Opinion (provided to the Committee of Ministers) on certain legal questions concerning the lists of candidates submitted with a view to the election of judges to the European Court of Human Rights*, Grand Chamber, 12 February 2008.

[10] Institut de droit international, La situation du juge international, Art. 1(1).

Appellate Body. Each of these courts includes on its bench a number of judges significantly lower than the number of Contracting Parties. This framework is present also in some regional courts that do not operate with the one-country-one-judge model.[11] In partially representative courts, the selection procedure at the international level has increased importance, as it implies the heightened interest of the Contracting Parties in seeing their candidate on the bench. Consequently, political considerations gain force.

11.2.2 Selection Process: Nomination, Screening, Appointment

Most commonly, the judicial selection procedure consists of the phases of nomination and appointment. One can immediately notice that the dynamics of these two phases are influenced by the character of the bench, as discussed above. Clearly, in the court where each Member State has its 'own' judge, the appointing body, whichever that is, exerts less control over the selection than the nominating State.[12] In other words, the appointing body's control over the quality of the ultimate appointment is more or less dependent upon the quality of the candidates the nominating State puts forward.

Nominations may take one of two forms. Indirect nominations are evident in the typical practice of ICJ candidates being nominated through the National Groups of the Permanent Court of Arbitration.[13] Direct discretionary nominations by governments are evident in the nominations of judges of the ICC prior to 2012,[14] or at the EU's Court of Justice and

---

[11] See, e.g., Protocol to the African Charter on Human and Peoples' Rights on the Establishment of an African Court of Human and Peoples' Rights (Ouagadougou, 9 June 1988), Art. 14(2).

[12] See further CoE, Committee of Ministers, Guidelines of the Committee of Ministers on the selection of candidates for the post of judge at the European Court of Human Rights, CM(2012)40-final, 28 March 2012; CoE, Parliamentary Assembly, Nomination of candidates and election of judges to the European Court of Human Rights, Report no. 11767, 1 December 2008; ICC Judicial Nomination – Model curriculum vitae, https://asp.icc-cpi.int/iccdocs/asp_docs/Elections/EJ2017/ICC-ASP-EJ2017-LES-CV-ENG.pdf; Council of the EU, Fourth Activity Report of the Panel provided for in Article 255 of the Treaty on the Functioning of the European Union, Annex 6: Curriculum vitae template, 10 February 2017.

[13] Convention for the Pacific Settlement of International Disputes (The Hague, 18 October 1907), Art. 44; Statute of the International Court of Justice (San Francisco, 26 June 1945), Art. 4(1).

[14] See further M. Bohlander, 'Article 36' in O. Triffterer and K. Ambos (eds.), *Commentary to the Rome Statute of the International Criminal Court*, 3rd edn (Beck/Hart, 2016), pp. 1216, 1223.

General Court prior to the Lisbon Treaty.[15] Within these two modes, international vetting of candidates may be achieved through advisory panels established for that purpose, or through other control mechanisms at the international level. The former is the subject of this chapter, whereas the latter includes the WTO Appellate Body Selection Committee.[16]

11.2.3   Rationales for Judicial Screening Bodies

Calls for more professional, independent, qualified, and competent judges at international courts have been made frequently over recent decades.[17] These calls are directly linked to the perceptions of legitimacy of international courts. The more judges are viewed as independent, competent, and professional, the argument goes, the greater the legitimacy of the court. This legitimacy may relate to judicial selection – a question of input legitimacy – or be viewed through the perspective of output legitimacy (i.e., the court's judicial activity).[18]

One may also distinguish between the sources of legitimacy. In particular, democratic sources of legitimacy may be contrasted with expert, or technocratic, legitimacy. While the former is linked to the selection process which gives voice to as many constituencies of international courts as possible and acknowledges the essentially political character

---

[15] J.-M. Sauvé, 'Selecting the European Union's Judges: The Practice of the Article 255 Panel' in Bobek (ed.), *Selecting Europe's Judges*, p. 78. One can also mention open candidacies whereby interested individuals put forward their own nominations. This is the practice of the Carribean Court of Justice. See above, note 4.

[16] See above note 6.

[17] See generally MacKenzie et al., *Selecting International Judges*, pp. 172–175. In the ICC context, see M. Bohlander, *International Criminal Justice: A Critical Analysis of Institutions and Procedures* (London, 2007), pp. 325–390; M. Bohlander, 'Pride and Prejudice or Sense and Sensibility? A Pragmatic Proposal for the Recruitment of Judges at the ICC and other International Criminal Courts' (2009) 12 *New Criminal Law Review* 529; International Crisis Group, International Criminal Tribunal for Rwanda: Delayed Justice, 7 June 2001, www.crisisgroup.org/africa/central-africa/rwanda/international-criminal-tribunal-rwanda-delayed-justice; B. Schiff, *Building the International Criminal Court* (Cambridge University Press, 2008), p. 107; W. Schabas, *The International Criminal Court: A Commentary on the Rome Statute* (Oxford University Press, 2010), p. 530. For the European Regional Courts see Kosař, 'Selecting Strasbourg Judges'; K. Lemmens, '(S)electing Judges for Strasbourg: A (Dis)appointing Process?', in Bobek (ed.), *Selecting Europe's Judges*, p. 95.

[18] On various notions of legitimacy, see e.g. J.H.H. Weiler, 'In the Face of Crisis: Input Legitimacy, Output Legitimacy, and the Political Messianism of European Integration' (2012) 34 *Journal of European Integration* 825.

of the selection process, the latter is derived from the expertise, competence, knowledge, skills, and reputation of the candidates, and is generally infused through peer-review by other experts in order to 'depoliticize' the process.[19] Although these two sources often overlap, it is evident that the establishment of advisory panels for the appointment of judges seeks to boost expert legitimacy in particular.[20]

On the one hand, this addition may be welcomed, as the selection of international judges has been traditionally a domain of unelected executives, not necessarily experts in international law.[21] The executives may be led by the goal of appointing a judge who may be inclined to vote in the State's favour, or whom the executive otherwise views as falling within its political agenda.[22] On the other hand, the introduction of advisory panels may raise a host of further concerns. These include who chooses the experts, what qualities these experts should possess, and whether this institutional innovation further removes the international judge from sources of democratic legitimacy. Some of these concerns may no doubt be easily put to rest through an appropriate institutional design, whereas others pertain to more fundamental questions.

The relative success or failure of judicial screening bodies hinges upon a number of modalities that, when examined comparatively, reveal dramatically different approaches by international organizations. In the context of the CJEU, ECtHR, and ICC, these variant approaches in some instances appear to reflect different institutional constituencies, but in other instances simply reflect divergent approaches to innovating

---

[19] For more on the notions of democratic and technocratic legitimacy see R.D. Kelemen, 'Selection, Appointment, and Legitimacy: A Political Perspective', in Bobek (ed.), *Selecting Europe's Judges*, p. 245; M. Bobek, 'Prologue: The Changing Nature of Selection Procedures to the European Courts', in Bobek (ed.), *Selecting Europe's Judges*, pp. 17–23; M. Bobek, 'Epilogue: Searching for the European Hercules', in Bobek (ed.), *Selecting Europe's Judges*, pp. 298–303.

[20] See further D. Kosař, 'The Least Accountable Branch' (2013) 11 *International Journal of Constitutional Law* 234; N. Garoupa and T. Ginsburg, 'Guarding the Guardians: Judicial Councils and Judicial Independence' (2009) 57 *American Journal of Comparative Law* 103.

[21] A. Torres Pérez, 'Can Judicial Selection Secure Judicial Independence?: Constraining State Governments in Selecting International Judges', in Bobek (ed.), *Selecting Europe's Judges*, p. 181.

[22] See E. Voeten, 'The Politics of International Judicial Appointments' (2009) 9 *Chicago Journal of International Law* 387; E. Voeten, 'The Politics of International Judicial Appointments: Evidence from the European Court of Human Rights' (2007) 61 *International Organization* 669.

practices towards common objectives, such as screening out highly politicized candidates who lack independence.[23]

11.3   Modalities of Screening Bodies

Judicial screening bodies have developed from different institutional
origins, but in some instances have shared tortuous paths. For example,
the establishment of a judicial selection panel for what is now known as
the CJEU was first considered in 2000, but did not enter into operation
until 2010 (with the Treaty of Lisbon).[24] Similarly, whilst the Rome Statute
envisaged the establishment of the ICC's judicial screening body, it was
not formally established until 2013.[25]

A fundamental distinction that may be drawn from among these institutional origins – and which may inform the design of a judicial screening
body – is the jurisdictional scope of the courts these bodies serve. A considerable difference regarding the ICC and, on the other hand, the
ECtHR and CJEU, is that the ICC is a global institution with potentially
universal reach.

The following discussion addresses four key modalities of these
screening bodies: their composition; the evaluation criteria that they
apply; their operative procedures; and the binding character of their
decisions.

11.3.1   Composition of Screening Bodies

The institutions under consideration are notable not only in the manner
in which these screening bodies function and interact with the judicial appointment process, but also in the manner in which the bodies

---

[23] In the Art. 255 panel context, see Kelemen, 'Selection, Appointment, and Legitimacy',
pp. 253–254.
[24] See H. de Waele, 'Not Quite the Bed that Procrustes Built: Dissecting the System for
Selecting Judges at the Court of Justice of the European Union', in Bobek (ed.), *Selecting
Europe's Judges*, note 3, pp. 24, 26. See further European Commission, Report by the
Working Party on the Future of the European Communities' Court System, January
2000, p. 56.
[25] ICC Statute (Rome, 17 July 1998), Art. 36(4)(c). See also ICC, Assembly of States Parties,
Report of the Advisory Committee on Nominations of Judges on the Work of its First
Meeting, ICC-ASP/12/23, 31 May 2013; ICC, Assembly of States Parties, Designation of the
Members of the Advisory Committee on Nominations, ICC-ASP/11/18, 9 November 2012.
See further P. Mahoney, 'The International Judiciary – Independence and Accountability'
(2008) 7 *The Law and Practice of International Courts and Tribunals* 313, 329.

are themselves composed. For example, the CoE panel consists of seven members, which are selected among members of the highest national courts, former judges of international courts (including the ECtHR), and other lawyers of recognized competence, all of whom serve in their personal capacity. The composition of the panel is geographically and gender balanced.[26] The members of the panel are appointed by the Committee of Ministers (by a simple majority) following consultations with the President of the ECtHR. The members serve terms of three years, renewable once. The Secretary General of the CoE provides the secretariat to the panel.

The Article 255 panel is also composed of seven experts, who are appointed by the Council on the initiative of the President of the Court of Justice; the EU Parliament proposes one member.[27] Beyond this last requirement regarding a lone parliamentary appointment, the specific methods used in appointing the members of the Article 255 panel are veiled in relative secrecy.[28] In general, they are chosen from among former members of the Court of Justice and the General Court, members of national supreme courts, and lawyers of recognized competence.[29] Governments have thus far opted to follow the proposals of the president of the Court of Justice regarding the composition of the Article 255 panel.[30] Article 255 panel members are appointed for four years and may be reappointed once.

The ICC Committee, on the other hand, is composed of nine members who are nationals of States Parties, designated by the Assembly of States Parties ('ASP') by consensus on the recommendation of the Bureau of the Assembly (also made by consensus). The membership of the Committee must reflect the principal legal systems of the world and equitable geographical and gender-based representation, taking into account the

---

[26] CoE, Committee of Ministers, 'Resolution on the Establishment of an Advisory Panel of Experts on Candidates for Election as Judge to the European Court of Human Rights', CM/Res (2010) 26, 10 November 2010, Art. 2.

[27] Council of the EU, Decision of 25 February 2010 relating to the operating rules of the panel provided for in Article 255 of the Treaty on the Functioning of the European Union, 2010/124/EU; Council of the EU, Decision of 25 February 2010 appointing the members of the panel provided for in Article 255 of the Treaty on the Functioning of the European Union, 2010/125/EU. See further A. von Bogdandy and C. Krenn, 'On the Democratic Legitimacy of Europe's Judges: A Principled and Comparative Reconstruction of the Selection Procedures', in Bobek (ed.), *Selecting Europe's Judges*, pp. 162, 174.

[28] See further Dumbrovský et al., 'Judicial Appointments', 460.

[29] Treaty on the Functioning of the European Union (Lisbon, 13 December 2007), Art. 255.

[30] Ibid.

regional diversity of States Parties to the Rome Statute. Members of the Committee should be drawn from eminent interested and willing persons of a high moral character, who have established competence and experience in criminal or international law.[31]

11.3.2   Evaluation Criteria Applied

The three judicial screening bodies under consideration apply somewhat different sets of criteria to the candidates they review. The Article 255 panel's criteria for evaluating judicial candidates are deemed to flow from the interpretation of the TFEU,[32] and include: legal expertise concerning the conditions and mechanisms of the application of EU law; professional experience at the appropriate level (of at least twenty years for the Court of Justice, and at least twelve years for the General Court); the ability to perform the duties of judge; independence and impartiality; language skills; the ability to work in a team-based international environment; and views on the nature, role, and scope of the office of judge or advocate-general.[33] The inclusion of this last criterion implies that the panel should evaluate candidates' professional convictions.[34] Notably, the Article 255 panel has stated that linguistic skills are not decisive, whereas manifest lack of any of the other criteria may itself provide grounds for a negative review.[35] The Article 255 panel has stressed that its mandate does not include consideration of the overall composition of the Court, including issues of social representativeness, gender balance, or any need to balance professional backgrounds or obtain specific legal expertise.[36] Despite the individual opinions of the Article 255 panel not being public, the panel's

---

[31] See further Bohlander, 'Article 36', p. 1223.

[32] See Council of the EU, First Activity Report of the Panel provided for in Article 255 of the Treaty on the Functioning of the European Union, 6509/11, COUR 3 JUR 57, 11 February 2011, p. 4. The elaboration of the broadly worded criteria in Articles 253 and 254 by the Article 255 Panel has been subject to some criticism as to arbitrariness. See, e.g., Dumbrovský et al., 'Judicial Appointments'; A. Alemanno 'How Transparent is Transparent Enough?: Balancing Access to Information Against Privacy in European Judicial Selections', in Bobek (ed.), *Selecting Europe's Judges*, p. 202; Bobek, 'Epilogue', p. 279.

[33] See Council of the EU, First Activity Report, pp. 6–9.

[34] Ibid., p. 10.

[35] See de Waele, 'Not Quite the Bed that Procrustes Built', p. 38.

[36] See Council of the EU, Third Activity Report of the Panel provided for in Article 255 of the Treaty on the Functioning of the European Union, SN 1118/2014, 13 December 2013, p. 11; Lord Mance, 'The Composition of the European Court of Justice', speech delivered

Activity Reports reveal that the criteria derived from its interpretation of the TFEU are in fact more onerous than those mentioned in Article 253.[37]

In terms of resources to which these criteria are applied when reviewing candidates for a first term of office, the Article 255 panel has examined: the reasons behind the nominating government's proposal; the candidate's statement regarding the reasons for his or her candidature; the bibliography of the candidate's publications; the text of recent publications authored by the candidate; information on the national procedure resulting in the candidate's nomination; and other publicly available works authored by the candidate.[38] Consideration of the national selection process underlying the nomination involves 'in particular whether there is a national merit-based selection procedure and, if so, how it is organized'.[39] The Article 255 panel has made use of this information because judicial independence, 'which is indispensable, is undoubtedly difficult to assess solely on the basis of candidates' dossiers as submitted by Member States' governments and hearings conducted by the panel where appropriate'.[40] The panel has established slightly modified procedures for judges applying for a renewal of the office.[41]

The Article 255 panel has issued negative reviews of candidates on the basis of insufficient high-level professional experience, the 'complete absence of any professional experience relevant to EU law', and the inadequacy of legal abilities.[42] Whereas the Article 255 panel has also in some instances issued a negative review on the basis of close familial connection between the candidate and the president of the nominating government,

---

to the UK Association for European Law, 19 October 2011, www.supremecourt.uk/docs/speech_111019.pdf, pp. 14–17.

[37] See further Council of the EU, Third Activity Report, pp. 17–21 (considering as 'exhaustive' Article 253's requirements of 'persons whose independence is beyond doubt and who possess the qualifications required for appointment to the highest judicial offices in their respective countries or who are jurisconsults of recognised competence', yet elaborating four pages of detailed criteria from this brief provision). See also M. Bobek, 'The Court of Justice of the European Union' in D. Chalmers and A. Amull (eds.), *The Oxford Handbook of European Union Law* (Oxford University Press, 2015), p. 164.

[38] See de Waele, 'Not Quite the Bed that Procrustes Built', p. 36.

[39] Council of the EU, First Activity Report, pp. 6–7.

[40] Council of the EU, Second Activity Report of the Panel provided for by Article 255 of the Treaty on the Functioning of the European Union, 5091/13, COUR 2 JUR 5, 26 December 2012, p. 13.

[41] These candidates are not generally interviewed and are solely assessed on the basis of written materials. To date, no applicant for a renewal has received an unfavourable decision. Council of the EU, Third Activity Report, p. 12.

[42] Council of the EU, Second Activity Report, p. 13.

similar reviews by the CoE panel on this basis have been disregarded, resulting in the nominating government managing to secure election of the candidate.[43]

The CoE panel has opted to add to the criteria listed in Article 21.1 of the ECHR and the ethics criteria dictated in 2008 by the Plenary of the Court by borrowing from criteria stipulated in the Article 255 panel's annual reports.[44] It has elaborated upon the ECHR's requirement for judges to possess 'the qualifications required for appointment to high judicial office', suggesting that the use of 'high' (rather than 'highest', which is distinguished in the EU treaties)[45] implies 'judges who have held office in national supreme or constitutional courts', but noting in the same breath that '(e)ven in the case of candidates holding office in a highest national Court, the Panel's view is that such persons should not, for that reason alone, be automatically considered qualified to be candidates for election to the Court'.[46] Echoing the link between age and professional experience supported by the Article 255 panel,[47] the CoE panel has further elaborated that the Court 'assumes that its members already have, on election, all the fully developed judicial qualities that come from long experience. It would appear unlikely to find such qualities in a candidate of a relatively young age'.[48]

The ICC committee reviews candidates according to either List A or List B criteria. List A requires that candidates have established competence in criminal law and procedure, and the necessary experience, whether as judge, prosecutor, advocate, or in other similar capacity, in criminal proceedings. List B requires that candidates have established competence in relevant areas of international law such as international humanitarian law and the law of human rights, and extensive experience in a professional legal capacity which is of relevance to the judicial work of the Court.[49] Article 36(5) of the Rome Statute requires that at least nine

---

[43] See Torres Pérez, 'Can Judicial Selection Secure Judicial Independence?' pp. 181, 194–195.

[44] See further Steering Committee for Human Rights, Draft Report on the Review of the Functioning of the Advisory Panel of Experts on Candidates for Election as Judge to the European Court of Human Rights, Written Contribution from the Advisory Panel, GT-GDR-E (2013), 19 September 2013, p. 3.

[45] Cf. TFEU, Arts. 253, 254.

[46] Steering Committee for Human Rights, Draft Report.

[47] See Council of the EU, First Activity Report.

[48] Steering Committee for Human Rights, Draft Report.

[49] See ICC, Assembly of States Parties, Procedure for the Nomination and Election of Judges of the International Criminal Court, ICC-ASP/3/Res.6, 10 September 2004, para. 27(c). See further Mackenzie et al., Selecting International Judges, p. 20.

List A judges and five List B judges be elected in the first elections of the ICC and that this proportion be maintained, in order to ensure sufficient numbers of adequately qualified judges for the trial and pre-trial divisions.[50]

In addition, the ICC requires at least three judges from the Africa group, Latin America and the Caribbean group, and Western Europe and Other States group, and two judges each from Eastern Europe and Asia, as well as at least six judges of each gender.[51] The inclusion of criteria for judges concerning gender balance and legal expertise in violence against women and children is an unprecedented success in the design of international courts.[52]

11.3.3   Operative Procedures

Given the political compromises entailed in the establishment and design of these screening bodies, the operative procedures adopted for each body may not intuitively reflect its *raison d'être*. Considering that the main purpose of the CoE panel is to advise the parties whether their candidates for election as judges of the ECtHR meet the criteria stipulated in Article 21 ECHR,[53] it may seem striking that the panel's assessments are limited to documents without hearing the candidates. Currently, judges of the ECtHR are selected in a three-step process. In the first step, a list of three candidates with their curriculum vitae is submitted by the parties,[54] and subsequently posted to the CoE's website.[55] The CoE recommends public calls for submissions to ensure fair and transparent selection, although there are still remaining country variations.[56] Along these lines,

---

[50]   Ibid., pp. 20–21.

[51]   See ICC, Assembly of States Parties, Resolution ICC-ASP/3/Res.6, paras. 20(b)–(c).

[52]   See P. Spees, 'Women's Advocacy in the Creation of the International Criminal Court: Changing the Landscapes of Justice and Power' (2003) 28(4) *Signs* 1233.

[53]   CoE, Committee of Ministers, 'Resolution on the Establishment of an Advisory Panel of Experts'.

[54]   Convention for the Protection of Human Rights and Fundamental Freedoms (Rome, 4 Nov. 1950), Art. 22.

[55]   See Torres Pérez, 'Can Judicial Selection Secure Judicial Independence?' p. 196.

[56]   CoE, Committee of Ministers, Guidelines of the Committee of Ministers on the Selection of Candidates for the Post of Judge at the European Court of Human Rights, CM(2012)40-final, 29 March 2012; CoE, Parliamentary Assembly, Nomination of Candidates and Election of Judges to the European Court of Human Rights, Report no. 11767, 1 December 2008. See also CoE, Parliamentary Assembly, Effective Implementation of the European Convention on Human Rights: The Interlaken process, Resolution 1726, 29 April 2010,

the Parliamentary Assembly of the Council of Europe ('PACE') has further required that governments describe the manner in which specific candidates have been selected.[57]

Before the elections, in the second step, candidates are interviewed and scrutinized *in camera* by a special committee of parliamentarians with legal experience (the Committee for the Election of Judges to the European Court of Human Rights),[58] currently consisting of twenty-two members. If the Committee considers that the candidates are unsatisfactory, it contacts the nominating State or States to obtain further information. It may do so because there is 'no real choice' between the candidates, an absence of a 'fair, transparent and consistent national selection procedure', or that the list has failed to meet gender requirements.[59]

If the Committee considers the candidates to be suitable, it ranks them by order of merit. It considers the candidates not only as individuals, but also with an eye towards a harmonious composition of the Court. In the third step, the PACE elects the judges by a majority of votes in a secret ballot.[60] As such, the CoE panel interacts with the States Parties that propose nominees and with the PACE, which elects them. The PACE is trusted to assess candidates' qualities after a process involving the CoE panel's review and the Committee's subsequent recommendation to the PACE identifying the most qualified candidates.[61]

As to the EU model, the Council of the EU has since the Lisbon Treaty jointly appointed judges and advocates general for the Court only after consultation with the Article 255 panel.[62] Despite the fact that this

---

para. 7. For a praised national selection model see the UK model, in A. Lang, A New UK Judge for the European Court of Human Rights, House of Commons Briefing Paper no. 7589, 7 June 2016. See further A. Coomber, 'Judicial Independence: Law and Practice of Appointments to the European Court of Human Rights' (2003) 5 *European Human Rights Law Review* 486, 492.

[57] CoE, Parliamentary Assembly, Nomination of Candidates and Election of Judges to the European Court of Human Rights, Resolution 1646, 27 January 2009, para. 2.

[58] CoE, Parliamentary Assembly, Procedure for Electing Judges to the European Court of Human Rights, AS/Cdh/Inf (2016) 01 rev 4, 22 June 2016.

[59] See Mackenzie et al., *Selecting International Judges*, p. 156.

[60] ECHR, Art. 22. See further J. Limbach, P. Cruz Villalón, R. Errera, Lord Lester of Herne Hill, T. Morschtschakowa, Lord Justice Sedley and A. Zoll, 'Judicial Independence: Law and Practice of Appointments to the European Court of Human Rights' (May 2003) *Interights*, www.corteidh.or.cr/tablas/32795.pdf.

[61] See further *Advisory Opinion on certain legal questions concerning the lists of candidates submitted with a view to the election of judges*, 12 February 2008, para. 43.

[62] TFEU, Art. 255.

mechanism was established as a response to criticism of the lack of transparency and accountability in the selection of the CJEU judges,[63] the panel's deliberations take place *in camera*. Decisions as to candidate suitability are communicated to the Member States. The Presidency of the Council may request the panel to elaborate on the decision. Barring this, however, the decision remains confidential, and has been construed as a 'third party document' under general EU transparency rules, whereupon the Council is bound to refuse access to a document where disclosure would undermine the privacy and integrity of individuals' personal data.[64] No information about EU judicial candidates' profiles is published prior to appointment.[65]

The practice at the Court of Justice is to nominate only one candidate per Member State. The Article 255 panel has recourse to not only information provided by nominating governments (from whom it may request further information on candidates), but also other sources of information through an independent fact-finding mandate.[66] The most important feature of the Article 255 panel's consideration is the interview, which is conducted confidentially over the course of one hour.[67] These interviews consist of a short presentation by the candidate, followed by questions posed in English or French by the members of the panel on aspects of the candidacy and the candidate's follow-up responses.[68] Candidates for renewal are considered only on paper during a meeting of the panel.[69]

Looking to the ICC, the Rome Statute had envisaged the establishment of the ICC committee as an alternative to the ICJ appointment system,[70] in order to assist States in electing judges by providing more information regarding candidates.[71] To that end, parties to the Rome Statute can pursue

---

[63] Dumbrovský et al., 'Judicial Appointments', p. 455.

[64] See European Parliament, Regulation Regarding Public Access to European Parliament, Council and Commission Documents, Resolution 1049/2001, OJ L145/43, 30 May 2001. See further *European Commission v. The Bavarian Lager Co. Ltd.*, Case C-28/08 P, ECR I-6055, 29 June 2010.

[65] See Council of the EU, Decision 25 February 2010, above note 27, Annex, Arts. 5, 7–8.

[66] See further Alemanno, 'How Transparent is Transparent Enough?' p. 207.

[67] See further de Waele, 'Not Quite the Bed that Procrustes Built', pp. 36–37.

[68] See Council of the EU, First Activity Report, p. 4.

[69] See Lord Mance, 'The Composition of the European Court of Justice'.

[70] See S. Rosenne, *The Law and Practice of the International Court: 1920–2005* (Martinus Nijhoff, 2006), p. 366, n. 30.

[71] See further T. Ingadottir, 'Nomination and Election of Judges' in T. Ingadottir (ed.), *The International Criminal Court: Recommendations on Policy and Practice – Financing, Victims, Judges, and Immunities* (Transnational, 2003), pp. 173–176.

one of two options in response to a resolution of the ASP requesting judicial nominations. These can be nominated either according to the process for nominations to the highest judicial offices of the state, or by the procedure set out specifically for ICC nominations.[72] The Rome Statute does not require States to declare which procedure is adopted.[73]

Each Member State may nominate one candidate and communicate this selection to the ASP.[74] Nominations must be accompanied by a statement that describes how the candidate meets the criteria specified in Article 36(3) of the Rome Statute.[75] This statement, along with the candidate's curriculum vitae, is posted on the ICC website.[76] There is no formal channel through which the statement can be questioned or tested, and it has not appeared that the requirement to provide such a statement has any significant impact on the nomination process.[77] As to the election process, while candidates are elected by secret ballot requiring a two-thirds majority of present parties,[78] virtually nothing else is publicly known regarding these internal processes at the ASP.[79]

11.3.4   Binding Character of Decisions

One of the most salient considerations when evaluating the function and efficacy of these screening bodies is the binding or recommendatory character (be it de facto or de jure) attributed to their opinions. Experts involved in reforms to the ECtHR within the Steering Committee for Human Rights have proposed that the Parliamentary Assembly grant a greater degree of 'due consideration' to the CoE panel's findings, but there appears to be no general intention to make the panel's findings binding.[80]

Looking to the CJEU, the opinion of the Article 255 panel is effectively mandatory. The panel's opinions are given on one candidate only, and the

---

[72] Rome Statute, Art. 36(4)(a)(i)–(ii).
[73] See Mackenzie et al., *Selecting International Judges*, p. 67.
[74] Assembly of States Parties Resolution 6, para. 5.
[75] Ibid., para 6.
[76] Ibid., para 8.
[77] See Mackenzie et al., *Selecting International Judges*, p. 85.
[78] Assembly of States Parties Resolution 6, paras. 15–16.
[79] See Mackenzie et al., *Selecting International Judges*, p. 100.
[80] See Lemmens, '(S)electing Judges for Strasbourg', p. 107. See further Steering Committee for Human Rights, Draft Report, p. 14; Steering Committee for Human Rights, Report on the Review of the Functioning of the Advisory Panel of Experts on Candidates for Election as Judge to the European Court of Human Rights, CDDH(2013)R79 Addendum I, 29 November 2013, p. 14.

unanimity among the Member States required for that candidate to be elected means that a negative assessment by the Article 255 panel implies a de facto veto power.[81]

As a matter of law and practice, there is no question that the ICC committee's function is merely advisory. This reflects a compromise advanced by Egypt and France,[82] following negotiations between some delegations that had sought a more dispositive screening mechanism,[83] and many which greeted such proposals 'with suspicion and reservations'.[84]

11.4   Design Flaws, Institutional Contexts, and Lessons to be Learned?

The present section assesses what lessons one may draw from the institutional modalities and practice of the three screening bodies surveyed in Section 11.2. In particular, it assesses approaches to the composition of screening bodies, the impact of screening bodies on the judicial selection process, and the importance of transparency in the operation of screening bodies. This section considers the different sources of legitimacy discussed in Section 11.1 (i.e., democratic versus expert legitimacy), and queries in this context the significance of a court's regional or global character.

11.4.1   Composition of Screening Bodies

As noted above, the establishment of advisory panels responds mostly to calls for greater competence, qualification, and professionalism. If advisory panels are to carry out their function effectively, their composition is indeed crucial. Requirements and qualifications for being a member of one of the three studied panels overlap significantly; in fact, they overlap also with the criteria for the judges themselves. Nevertheless, some of the criteria reflect certain specificities which merit emphasis. Following this analysis, the present section addresses the appointment mechanisms utilized in the composition of these bodies.

---

[81] See further de Waele, 'Not Quite the Bed that Procrustes Built', p. 44.

[82] See Mackenzie et al., *Selecting International Judges*, p. 21.

[83] See M.H. Arsanjani, 'The Rome Statute of the International Criminal Court' (1999) 93(1) *American Journal of International Law* 22, 37–38.

[84] M.R. Rwelamira, 'Composition and Administration of the Court', in R.S. Lee (ed.), *The International Criminal Court: The Making of the Rome Statute – Issues, Negotiations, Results* (Kluwer, 1999), pp. 153, 163–164.

11.4.1.1   Qualifications for Members of Screening Bodies

The ICC committee members' qualifications reflect the specialized jurisdiction of the Court, with emphasis on competence and experience in
criminal or international law.[85] Primary candidates for the Article 255
panel, on the other hand, are 'former members of the Court of Justice and
the General Court'.[86] This is significant as it may contribute to continuity
on the bench. The actual composition of the Article 255 panel, marked
by a majority presence of senior national judges, may help to legitimizing a process which has been seen as too political and government-
driven.[87] At the same time, this factor may impact on the perception of the
candidates and lead towards replication of similar profiles on the bench.
Some authors have even referred to risks of ossification.[88] In addition, in
terms of the actual composition, criticism should be levelled as to the
gender imbalance of the membership, as only one out of the seven current
members of the Panel is female.[89] Even greater gender imbalance is found
on the ICC committee, where only one out of nine members is female.[90]
The CoE panel's composition is similarly oriented towards the presence
of senior and former judges;[91] however, it fares better in terms of gender
balance, as three out of seven members are female.[92]

11.4.1.2   Mechanisms Utilized in the Composition of
Screening Bodies

As opposed to the selection of judges, which is by and large left to the
political bodies of a given institution, such as PACE, the Council, or the
ASP, the selection of screening body members involves important input
from other actors, despite the fact that the ultimate decision is in the
hands of the same political organs. Therefore, the CoE panel is appointed
by the Committee of Ministers, but only after consultations with the
President of the ECtHR. The role of the Court's President is even more
prominent in the appointment of Article 255 panel members. Although
the Council appoints these members, it does so on the initiative of the

---

[85] ICC, Assembly of States Parties, Report of the Bureau Working Group on the Advisory
        Committee on Nominations, ICC-ASP/14/42, 16 November 2015, Annex, A(2).
[86] TFEU, Art. 255.
[87] Bobek, 'The Court of Justice of the European Union', p. 165.
[88] Dumbrovský et al., 'Judicial Appointments', p. 483.
[89] de Waele, 'Not Quite the Bed that Procrustes Built', p. 29.
[90] ICC, Report of the Bureau Working Group, 16 November 2015, para. 21.
[91] Committee of Ministers, Resolution, above note 26, para. 2.
[92] Secretariat of the Advisory Panel, www.coe.int/en/web/dlapil/advisory-panel.

President of the Court of Justice; only one out of seven members is proposed by the EU Parliament.[93] This evidently gives great powers to the President of the Court. The designation of the ICC committee members, on the other hand, does not operate with involvement of the Court or its organs. Still, the committee's members are designated by the ASP, on the recommendation of the Bureau of the Assembly,[94] the latter feature not being present in the selection of ICC judges. This aspect aligns with the idea of screening bodies as boosting the expert legitimacy of the courts in which they operate.

If a similar mechanism is to be put in place for existing or future international courts, much will depend on the institutional environment of the court in question. Setting up an advisory panel undoubtedly changes and influences the distribution of power and authority among relevant actors and institutions, as some of the power and authority is assumed by the advisory panel itself as well as by the actors involved in the selection of its members. This should be borne in mind when assessing the impact of such panels' operation on the legitimacy of a given court or tribunal.

An often-voiced concern in the appointment of international judges is politicization. This term is often employed loosely to contrast the political, represented by the involvement of the State (or democratic processes more generally), with the legal, represented by recourse to third-party dispute settlement or expertise.[95] Unless one is willing to accept the dubious proposition that the use of expertise is an inherently apolitical act, involvement of an expert body needs to be considered carefully, particularly as to those who exert control over that body and its composition. Some have observed that fully 'depoliticized judges' (i.e., without democratic or political input in their selection) may lose democratic legitimacy in the eyes of their constituencies, and that procedures claimed to be purely expert-based are hardly free of any political choices.[96] In short, the more one resorts to third-party expertise, the more the legitimacy of the process turns on technocratic or managerial, rather than democratic grounds.[97] This consideration may play a role especially when one

---

[93] Council Decisions of 25 February 2010 (2010/125/EU) and (2010/124/EU).

[94] Terms of Reference for the Establishment of an Advisory Committee on Nominations of Judges of the International Criminal Court, para. 1.

[95] See, e.g., M. Paparinskis, 'The Limits of Depoliticisation in Contemporary Investor-State Arbitration' (2010) 3 *Selected Proceedings of the European Society of International Law*, p. 271.

[96] Kelemen, 'Selection, Appointment, and Legitimacy', p. 256.

[97] See von Bogdandy and Krenn, 'On the Democratic Legitimacy of Europe's Judges', p. 162.

assesses the appropriate sources of legitimacy for a court with universal or global jurisdiction, as the case may be.

11.4.2   Comparative Impact

In terms of effects on judicial appointment, the CoE panel seems to be the least potent among the mechanisms discussed above. This can to a large extent be attributed to its institutional parameters. The selection of judges to the ECtHR is undoubtedly controlled by political bodies (i.e., the PACE and its sub-organs). It is actually the PACE Committee, not the CoE panel, which interviews and scrutinizes the list of candidates and has the power to request a fresh list if it deems the candidates unsuitable. On some occasions, States have not waited for the CoE panel's opinion before submitting their lists, whilst on other occasions the PACE Committee has rejected a list which had been approved by the CoE panel. Perhaps most alarmingly, there have been situations where a candidate whom the CoE panel deemed unsuitable for the position of an ECtHR judge was eventually elected by the PACE.[98] The deficiencies in the design of the procedure have caused some to assert that the Advisory Panel's wings were clipped at its birth.[99] However, the actual institutional practice of the selection of Strasbourg judges follows neither the letter nor the spirit of the procedures. Although the above-mentioned excesses have become less common, they still occur.[100] In this sense, the CoE Advisory Panel appears to be a tiger without teeth.

The situation for the Article 255 panel is quite different. This panel seems to enjoy a fairly high level of deference, despite its opinions not being formally binding. Interestingly, prior to the establishment of the panel the Council had not officially rejected a Member State's nominee to the CJEU.[101] Since the introduction of the Article 255 panel, however, a few candidates (those who received unfavourable opinions by the panel)

[98] See Steering Committee for Human Rights, Ministers' Deputies Exchange of Views with Mr. Luzius Wildhaber, Chairman of the Advisory Panel of Experts on Candidates for Election as Judge to the European Court of Human Rights, DH-GDR (2013)005, 5 February 2013, p. 2.
[99] See Bobek, 'Epilogue', p. 284.
[100] See Council of the EU, Second Activity Report, paras. 48–54.
[101] See Bobek, 'The Court of Justice of the European Union', p. 164; for criticism, see A. Arnull, *The European Union and Its Court of Justice*, 2nd edn (Oxford University Press, 2006), pp. 23–24.

have not been ultimately appointed.[102] This suggests great authority in the panel's recommendations; some authors even speak of the panel giving de facto required assent to the appointment.[103]

Nevertheless, before one rushes to conclude that the CoE panel is useless and the Article 255 panel is a success story, one must consider further institutional dynamics which may affect the relative effectiveness of the two European screening bodies. The PACE reviews three candidates proposed by a Member State, as opposed to one in the case of the Article 255 panel. This gives the political organs inherently greater opportunities of choice.[104] Taking into account the practice of majoritarian elections in the ECtHR since the establishment of the Advisory Panel, it seems that this institutional setting has led to a dilution of responsibility, with political considerations having the upper hand in the election procedure. The institutional setting of the Article 255 panel makes it more difficult to disregard the opinion of the panel. As the advisory opinion of the Article 255 panel is coupled with unanimity in the selection of a judge, it is hard to 'overrule a formally "non-binding" opinion of the panel'.[105]

The practice of the ICC committee has a shorter history in which to assess its impact. Assessment of the committee's impact is aided by the publicity of its opinions. At the same time, review of the elections that have taken place since the committee was established allows for only qualified conclusions, due to the nature of the ICC election process. As the ICC is a partially representative court in our terminology, there is necessarily a lower number of seats on the bench than States Parties. This sets apart the dynamic of the judges' selection at the ICC from its European counterparts. In such a process, the influence of political bargaining is to an extent inevitable. This is in spite of the fact that the drafters of the Rome Statute took pains to avoid some pitfalls commonly associated with the selection of ICJ judges.[106] In such an institutional environment, it is difficult to draw conclusions as to the exact extent to which a positive or negative opinion by the committee has played a role.

One vivid sign of the committee's effectiveness occurred in its 2014 review of candidates, in which it expressed reservations regarding five

[102] See Council of the EU, Third Activity Report; Second Activity Report.
[103] See Sauvé, 'Selecting the European Union's Judges', p. 83.
[104] See Lord Mance, 'The Composition of the European Court of Justice', p. 24.
[105] See Bobek, 'The Court of Justice of the European Union', p. 164.
[106] Mackenzie et al., Selecting International Judges, pp. 144–152.

of the seventeen nominated candidates.[107] The fact that none of these five candidates was elected may suggest a degree of effectiveness in the review system.[108] In its most recent review (as of December 2017) of candidates, the committee expressed language-related reservations concerning two of twelve candidates.[109] Of these twelve candidates, nine were presented as List A candidates and three as List B candidates.[110] All candidates were rated as either 'formally qualified' or 'particularly well qualified'. This methodology had not appeared in prior reports. While all List A candidates receiving a 'particularly well qualified' rating were elected in rounds earlier than those rated as 'formally qualified', the List B candidates rated as 'particularly well qualified' were rejected in favour of the only candidate rated as 'formally qualified'.[111] One could hypothesize that the qualifications for List A judges lend themselves to a lower degree of political considerations being at play in the selection process than the qualifications of List B judges.[112] If this were the case, it would show that the potential impact of a screening body interacts in important ways with more or less specified qualifications of judges.

Taken together, if a screening body similar to those studied here were to be considered for an international court with a potentially universal coverage and partially representative bench – for example, a multilateral investment court or an international environmental court – the ICC committee perhaps provides the closest analogy to that setting. It cannot be excluded that similar excesses to those documented in the ECtHR selection process occur also at the ICC.[113] Nevertheless, in combination with the ICC's partially representative character, the lobbying and bargaining power of the nominating government is significantly diluted. Although the committee's impact is limited, there are reasons for optimism because, in statistical terms, none of the candidates for whom the committee raised its collective eyebrows has ever made it to the bench.

---

[107] ICC, Assembly of States Parties, Report of the Advisory Committee on Nominations of Judges on the Work of its Third Meeting, Annex I, ICC-ASP/13/22, 29 September 2014.

[108] But see the 2014 ICC election results, https://asp.icc-cpi.int/en_menus/asp/elections/judges/2014/Nominations/Pages/2014-JE-results.aspx (in which a candidate for whom the committee had expressed reservations progressed to the 22nd round of balloting).

[109] ICC, Assembly of States Parties, Report of the Advisory Committee on Nominations of Judges on the Work of its Sixth Meeting, ICC-ASP/16/7, 10 October 2017.

[110] Ibid.

[111] See ibid., pp. 6–12; cf. the results of the 2017 ICC election, https://asp.icc-cpi.int/en_menus/asp/elections/Pages/Results-elections-jusdges-2017.aspx.

[112] For the specifications of the qualifications see above note 49.

[113] See above note 98.

11.4.3   Transparency

In the context of the two European panels, concerns about transparency have often been raised. Both screening bodies provide their opinions only to the relevant organs (the Council of the EU and the PACE) or to the nominating government, without making them public. Both bodies publish activity reports, which provide relevant statistics and summarize the working procedures and activities of the panel for a given period.[114] As far as the CoE panel is concerned, it has been stated that it 'has shrouded itself in secrecy',[115] which seems to be vigorously guarded. Still, the CoE panel also releases general activity reports, which alleviate this criticism to some extent.[116]

Despite the publication of the activity reports, scholars and activists are particularly critical of the secrecy of the Article 255 panel's reports and of the reasons provided therefor, particularly given the fact that the panel was ostensibly established in order to promote transparency, openness, and democracy in the selection of EU judges.[117] Yet it seems at least counter-intuitive to aim to increase legitimacy, transparency, and openness in the selection of EU judges by adding to the process a new body with significant authority, the work of which is largely removed from public scrutiny.

The practice of the ICC committee confirms that the debate about transparency of screening bodies in Europe ought not to be taken as a universal benchmark. The committee publishes its reports on all the reviewed candidates, and it seems that none of the concerns voiced by the Council of the EU regarding the Article 255 panel's transparency has materialised in the ICC context. The dearth of potentially qualified judges may be less of an issue in a global court with a potentially universal reach, in comparison to regional courts operating on the basis of a one-country-one-judge model. Indeed, if the ICC committee's opinion were not publicized, it would be close to impossible to assess its effectiveness in any manner. It is one thing to discount the impact of political negotiations on the election procedure at the ASP in order to isolate the impact of the

---

[114] See, e.g., Council of the EU, Second Activity Report; Third Activity Report.
[115] Bobek, 'Epilogue', p. 284.
[116] See, e.g., Council of the EU. Second Activity Report.
[117] Alemanno, 'How Transparent is Transparent Enough?'; Request for Information by Ellen Derbishire, on behalf of Access Info Europe, Confirmatory Application to the General Secretariat of the Council, Ref. No. 16/0414-mjB/dm, 24 May 2016.

committee's negative opinion. It is quite another to be left in the dark as to whether the committee has actually given a negative opinion in the first place. As transparency has close links with perceptions of legitimacy, the ICC committee may be considered a standard-bearer in this respect.

11.5   Conclusion

From the foregoing, we can surmise that if the judicial screening body is not quite the ghostly doorkeeper of Kafka's prose, it is nevertheless a malleable concept, with modalities that have been tailored – with argu-ably mixed results – to the three courts under discussion. Given this flex-ibility, it is worth gauging the potential application of such modalities to the establishment of screening bodies for new international courts. The reform of investor-State arbitration under the jurisdiction of a new judicial institution – a prospect which UNCITRAL began formally considering in November 2017[118] – provides a timely illustration of how a screening body might be adapted to the distinct dynamics of international investment disputes. Ultimately, however, the value of this mechanism would hinge upon whether it furthers a principal objective of shifting to an investment court model: improving perceptions of systemic legitimacy.

If the screening body models discussed above were to be adapted to the needs of an international investment court, an important modality would be the screening body's composition. Shifting focus from the composi-tion of the bench to the composition of an effective screening body could prove helpful during the negotiation of the prospective court's statute. For example, the qualifications required for appointment to the CoE panel could be reformulated so as to ensure an equitable balance of experience and knowledge relating to the interests of both governments and private enterprises.

A related point concerns the specific evaluation criteria to be applied by a screening body serving an international investment court. The ICC committee's use of criteria which ensures cultural diversity and an equi-table balance of experience and knowledge on the bench could be adapted to the present context, in particular to ensure competence in not only public international law, but also international business law. This approach

---

[118] UNCITRAL Working Group III (Investor-State Dispute Settlement Reform), 34th session (Vienna, 27 November–1 December 2017), Note by the Secretariat, A/CN.9/WG.III/WP.142, 18 September 2017.

may prove far less onerous than, for example, the direct appointment of some judges by representatives of the international investment community – presuming there exist any agreed-upon 'representatives' of this community.

Given the general conception of screening bodies as reducing the latitude of stakeholders in appointing judges, it may be argued that such technocratic mechanisms are not well suited to a court established in response to an outcry for greater democratic influence in investor-State dispute settlement. For this reason, the incorporation of a screening body whose evaluations of judicial nominees are de facto binding on member States would seem to be a difficult prospect.

Yet other modalities may be adapted to better preserve public interests and perceptions of the legitimacy of these 'unseen actors' and the judicial institutions which they serve. In particular, the promotion of transparency in the screening process may prove well suited to meeting the legitimacy aims of a prospective investment court. Moreover, this approach may be seen to buttress the effectiveness of nevertheless non-binding evaluations. Finally, the presence of a judicial screening body with the authority to deliver clear guidance as to judicial appointments may provide adequate political 'cover' to vote against a candidate, whereas power imbalances among States parties might otherwise restrict the free and informed voting of less influential parties.

The sensitivities associated with the reform of investor-State dispute settlement thus appear to confirm the adaptability of judicial screening bodies beyond the established contexts of international criminal law, human rights, and regional integration. As such, their envisaged function as a legitimizing force within those frameworks – and in particular, the modalities through which they have pursued this objective – merit the careful study of negotiators and stakeholders in the establishment of new international courts.

PART III

Case Management and Deference to the Bench

The Essence of Adjudication

Legitimacy of Case Managers in International Arbitration

CHRISTINE SIM

12.1 Introduction

Case managers in international arbitration include those working in dispute resolution institutions such as the Permanent Court of Arbitration (PCA),[1] the International Chamber of Commerce's International Court of Arbitration (ICC),[2] and the London Court of International Arbitration (LCIA):[3] the officers of such institutions, tribunal secretaries, tribunal assistants and arbitrators' assistants. These 'unseen' arbitral institutions and assistants form the foundations of efficient and effective dispute resolution,[4] but their legitimacy has attracted significant controversy lately.[5]

12.1.1 'Unseen' Case Managers and Decision-Making

Questioning the roles of these 'unseen' case managers should not be perceived as another sign of the legitimacy crisis facing international

---

[1] Website available at https://pca-cpa.org/en/home/, accessed 8 August 2017.

[2] Website available at https://iccwbo.org/dispute-resolution-services/arbitration/, accessed 8 August 2017.

[3] Website available at www.lcia.org/LCIA/introduction.aspx, accessed 8 August 2017.

[4] P. Tercier, 'The Role of the Secretary to the Arbitral Tribunal', in L.W. Newman and R.D. Hill (eds.), *The Leading Arbitrators' Guide to International Arbitration*, 2nd edn (Juris, 2014), pp. 531–554; C. Partasides, 'The Fourth Arbitrator? The Role of Secretaries to Tribunals in International Arbitration' (2002) 18 (2) *Arbitration International* 147–163.

[5] A. Ross, 'Was the Tribunal's Assistant the Fourth Yukos Arbitrator?' *Global Arbitration Review*, 27 January 2015; M. Altenkirch and B. Schmeil, 'The Substantial Involvement of Arbitral Secretaries', *Global Arbitration News*, 17 September 2015; D. Galagan 'The Challenge of the Yukos Award: An Award Written by Someone Else – A Violation of the Tribunal's Mandate?' *Kluwer Arbitration Blog*, 27 February 2015; K. Singh and S. Chandran, 'Tribunal Secretaries: A Tale of Dependence and Independence' *Kluwer Arbitration Blog*, 11 December 2016.

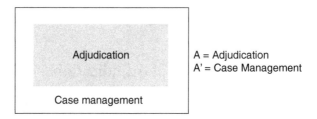

Figure 12.1 Adjudication and case management

arbitration.[6] Seeking best practices in case management and closely examining its legitimacy is a sign of a maturing system of dispute resolution. Arbitral institutions are leading efforts to set out the proper limits of case management. According to the London Court of International Arbitration (LCIA), the duties of the tribunal secretary should not 'constitute any delegation of the Arbitral Tribunal's authority'.[7] The ICC mandates that the:

> [A]dministrative secretary must not assume the functions of an arbitrator, notably by becoming involved in the decision-making process of the tribunal or expressing opinions with respect to the issues in dispute.

But what constitutes a 'decision-making process'? To distinguish permissible from impermissible tasks for case managers, there must first be a coherent understanding of the functions of international arbitrators.[8] Case management tasks could be described as ancillary, peripheral or merely as support. The legitimate perimeters of case management are best defined as complementary to adjudication. Figure 12.1 illustrates the complementary relationship between case management and decision-making.

---

[6] S. Franck, 'The Legitimacy Crisis in Investment Treaty Arbitration' (2005) 73(4) *Fordham Law Review* 10; Z. Douglas, 'The Secretary to the Arbitral Tribunal', in B. Berger and M.E. Schneider (eds.), *Inside the Black Box: How Arbitral Tribunals Operate and Reach their Decisions*, ASA Special Series No. 42 (JurisNet, 2015), p. 88: 'Such a challenge would be very damaging – and I am talking of the perfect storm – to the reputation of international arbitration. We have had challenges on this basis in the past. There have been cases before the French and German courts. There was a famous case in the Iran-US Claims Tribunal where there was an internal challenge relating to the role of a secretary but we have not had this perfect storm.'

[7] LCIA Notes for Arbitrators, 29 June 2015, para. 69.

[8] International Chamber of Commerce (ICC) Arbitration Rules (1 March 2017), Rule 15(2): 'An arbitrator shall also be replaced on the Court's own initiative when it decides that the arbitrator is prevented de jure or de facto from fulfilling the arbitrator's functions, or that the arbitrator is not fulfilling those functions in accordance with the Rules or within

In the following discussion, examples of case management tasks are indispensable, but they are only illustrative, and cannot be taken as definitive conclusions on which are permissible or impermissible tasks for case managers. The focus is on three key theoretical issues.

12.1.2   Three Key Questions

Three questions are central to the legitimacy of 'unseen actors' in international arbitration. First, what is arbitration?[9] Second, how does an arbitrator decide? Third, what are the institutional bounds of decision-making? The following sections of this chapter will explore these questions.

12.2   Social Ordering

Fuller defined adjudication as: '[A] device which gives formal and institutional expression to the influence of reasoned argument in human affairs'.[10]

Similarly, international arbitration is a form of international social ordering. Most importantly, arbitration procedures entrust arbitrators with the duty to apply reasoned argument to disorderly human affairs – a dispute. The ICC Rules require the arbitrator to 'establish the facts of the case'[11] and to make a reasoned[12] and enforceable award.[13] The LCIA Rules require the arbitrator to impose a form of social order by deciding the parties' dispute[14] and producing a written reasoned award.[15]

---

the prescribed time limits.' Available at https://iccwbo.org/dispute-resolution-services/arbitration/rules-of-arbitration/, accessed 8 August 2017.

[9]   K. Winston (ed.) *The Principles of Social Order, Selected Essays of Lon L. Fuller* (Duke University Press, 1981).

[10]   L. Fuller, 'The Forms and Limits of Adjudication' (1978) 92 *Harvard Law Review* 353, 393–398; S. Besson, 'Legal Philosophical Issues of International Adjudication', in C.P.R. Romano, K. Alter and Y. Shany (eds.) *The Oxford Handbook of International Adjudication* (Oxford University Press, 2014), p. 419.

[11]   ICC Arbitration Rules 2017, Rule 25(1).

[12]   ICC Arbitration Rules 2017, Rule 32.

[13]   G.J. Horvath, 'The Duty of the Tribunal to Render an Enforceable Award' (2001) 18 *Journal of International Arbitration* 135, 136; W.W. Park, 'Arbitration in Autumn' (2011) 2 *Journal of International Dispute Settlement* 287, 292; M. Hunter and A. Philip, 'The Duties of an Arbitrator', in L.W. Newman and R.D. Hill (eds.), *Leading Arbitrator's Guide to International Arbitration*, 3rd edn (Juris, 2014) 485; ICC Arbitration Rules 2017, Rule 35.

[14]   LCIA Arbitration Rules 2014, Rules 22.3, 26.5.

[15]   LCIA Arbitration Rules 2014, Rule 26.2.

12.2.1   Foundations of Arbitration

What is the source of an arbitrator's powers? Dispute resolvers generally – including judges, arbitrators and mediators – face this common theoretical debate. Speaking about a mediator, Fuller raised the question 'whether his power rests on a tacit contract with the affected parties, or derives from some charismatic qualities possessed by the mediator himself, or should be attributed to some role or office assigned to him by tradition or higher authority.'[16] Similar questions are being asked about the mandate and authority of an arbitrator.[17]

For court judges, even if their jurisdiction depends on the selection of their court by a forum selection clause, a large part of their legitimacy is derived directly from the state. Arbitral tribunals lack such legitimacy derived from a State's constitution.[18]

According to the contractual theory, the basis of arbitration lies in the consent of the parties.[19] Arbitration is a private form of justice where arbitrators charge for their services.[20] The terms of appointment[21] usually contains the arbitrator's obligations including confidentiality, independence and impartiality, the duty to decide on the parties' submissions, remuneration, rights to resign or terminate, and a governing law.[22] As participation implies a tacit agreement to abide by the result, a person

---

[16] L. Fuller, 'Mediation – Its Forms and Functions' (1970–71) 44 *Southern California Law Review* 305, 314.

[17] Tercier, 'The Role of the Secretary', 538.

[18] R. Michaels, 'Roles and Role Perceptions of International Arbitrators', in W. Mattli and T. Dietz (eds.), *International Arbitration and Global Governance: Contending Theories and Evidence*, pp. 48–73, 67; W. Kidane, *The Culture of Arbitration* (Oxford University Press, 2017), 117–118; M. Mustill, 'Arbitration: History and Background' (1989) 6 *Journal of International Arbitration* 43, 56.

[19] A. Redfern, M. Hunter, N. Blackaby and C. Partasides, *Law and Practice of International Commercial Arbitration* (Sweet & Maxwell, 2004), pp. 239–244; P. Fouchard, 'Relationships between the Arbitrator and the Parties and the Arbitral Institution' (December 1995) *ICC International Court of Arbitration Bulletin* 12, 22–23.

[20] E. Gaillard, 'Sociology of International Arbitration', in D.D. Caron, S.W. Schill, A.C. Smutny and E.E. Triantafilou (eds.), *Practising Virtue: Inside International Arbitration* (Oxford University Press, 2015), p. 4.

[21] B.M. Cremades, 'The Use and Abuse of Due Process in International Arbitration', 16 November 2016, CIArb Lecture, 11, available at www.ciarb.org/media/1376/may-2017.pdf, accessed 19 March 2019.

[22] M. Feit and C. Terrapon Chassot, 'The Swiss Federal Supreme Court Provides Guidance on the Proper Use of Arbitral Secretaries and Arbitrator Consultants under the Swiss lex arbitri: Case Note on DFC 4A_709/2014 dated 21 May 2015' (2015) 4 *ASA Bulletin* 879, 913.

who voluntarily submits a dispute to arbitration is bound by the result and impliedly undertakes to carry out the award.[23]

If seen as a mere private service provider,[24] the arbitrator could arguably delegate his duties to a case manager as long as the arbitrator fulfils his contracted terms of appointment and provides the agreed services to the parties.[25] In *Vivendi v. Argentina* annulment proceedings, one arbitrator suggested that it would be wiser for each member of the ad hoc annulment committee to appoint his own assistant, 'subject to their full control and direction', rather than allow the ICSID Secretariat to assist in drafting.[26] If party autonomy is the overriding principle, the solution for improving the legitimacy of case management could be more transparency.

Furthermore, as a provider of ad hoc services, attempts to codify and hold arbitrators accountable to a universal set of rules developed on the basis of opinions of a majority of respondents to a survey would thus not be appropriate.[27] The role of an arbitrator and case manager are strictly private matters. The Dutch building industry, for instance, has an established practice where the secretary examines the reasoning of the decision, asks the arbitrators questions to establish their motivation and drafts the award.[28]

---

[23] ICC Arbitration Rules 2017, Rule 35(6); *Squire v. Grevell*, 87 Eng. Rep. 797, 6 Mod. 34 (1703); *Purslow v. Bailey*, 92 Eng. Rep. 190, 2 Ld. Raym. 1039 (1705), cited in P.S. Atiyah, 'Book Review: The Principles of Social Order, Selected Essays of Lon L. Fuller' (1983) 32(2) *Duke Law Journal* 669, 674.

[24] Y. Dezalay and B. Garth, 'Merchants of Law as Moral Entrepreneurs: Constructing International Justice from the Competition for Transnational Business Disputes' (1995) *Law and Society Review* 29.

[25] Arbitration Institute of the Stockholm Chamber of Commerce (SCC), 'Arbitrator's Guidelines', 2 June 2014, available at https://sccinstitute.com/media/171486/guidelines-january-2017.pdf, accessed 19 March 2019. The SCC's 2017 Arbitrator's Guidelines have since set out a more interventionist approach, requiring the tribunal to first submit a proposal for the appointment of the secretary to the SCC Secretariat with the proposed secretary's curriculum vitae and signed statement of availability, available at www .sccinstitute.com/media/171486/guidelines-january-2017.pdf, accessed 30 November 2017; Nederlands Arbitrage Instituut (NAI) Arbitration Rules (2010), Article 59(2); NAI, 'Secretary', available at www.nai-nl.org/en/info.asp?id=339, accessed 6 May 2017.

[26] *Compañía de Aguas del Aconquija SA & Vivendi Universal SA v. Argentine Republic*, ICSID Case No ARB/97/3 (Annulment Proceeding), Additional Opinion of Professor J.H. Dalhuisen under Art. 48(4) of the ICSID Convention, 30 July 2010, para. 6.

[27] Cf. M. Polkinghorne and C.B. Rosenberg 'The Role of the Tribunal Secretary in International Arbitration: A Call for a Uniform Standard' 5 March 2015, International Bar Association, *Dispute Resolution International*, available at www.ibanet.org/Article/NewDetail.aspx?Art icleUid=987D1CFC3BC248D3959EE18D7935F542, accessed 6 May 2017.

[28] Raad van Arbitrage voor de Bouw in A. Meier, 'Assistance to the Tribunal: An Overview', in B. Berger and M.E. Schneider (eds.), *Inside the Black Box: How Arbitral Tribunals Operate and Reach their Decisions*, ASA Special Series No. 42 (Juris 2013), p. 81.

Alternatively, if the arbitrator's competence is derived from state sovereignty, the arbitrator is a 'quasi judge' and thus a public actor.[29] In relation to investment arbitrations,[30] the push for greater transparency due to their potential to affect the public, suggests that arbitrators deciding investment treaty disputes should face a higher threshold for delegation of duties than arbitrators deciding purely private commercial disputes.

Finally, it has been proposed that instead of a two-dimensional public/ private divide – through a convergence of national legal orders recognising the arbitration process and award without review on the merits – the international community has created a distinct legal order.[31] In this distinct legal order, trends in procedural matters that are observable, widespread practices may constitute transnational legal rules.[32] Examples of transnational norms which have evolved in international arbitration include guidelines on permissible and impermissible arbitrators' conflicts of interests in the green, orange and red lists[33] and obligations to disclose evidence.[34] Proponents of international arbitration as an autonomous legal order offer the third theory that the arbitrator's power to delegate duties to a case manager depends on the evolving norms of that autonomous legal order.[35]

12.2.2   Society of Arbitration

Arbitration fulfils sociological needs of the international business and governance community.[36] Fuller's view that law has authority only if it is based on

---

[29] Michaels, 'Roles and Role Perceptions of International Arbitrators', p. 59.
[30] UNCITRAL Transparency Rules, Mauritius Convention.
[31] E. Gaillard, *Legal Theory of International Arbitration* (Martinus Nijhoff, 2010), p. 59; cf. J. Paulsson, 'Arbitration in Three Dimensions' LSE Law, Society and Economy Working Papers 2/2010, 33.
[32] Gaillard, *Legal Theory*, pp.105–107; M. Renner, 'Private Justice, Public Policy: The Constitutionalization of International Commercial Arbitration', in W. Mattli and T. Dietz (eds.), *International Arbitration and Global Governance: Contending Theories and Evidence* (Oxford Scholarship Online, 2014); cf. W. Kidane, *The Culture of International Arbitration*(Oxford University Press, 2017), pp. 123–124; O. Glossner, 'From New York (1958) to Geneva (1961) – A Veteran's Diary', in *Enforcing Arbitration Awards Under the New York Convention: Experience and Prospects* (UN, 1999), pp. 5–9, 6.
[33] IBA Guidelines on Conflicts of Interest in International Arbitration (22 May 2004).
[34] IBA Rules on the Taking of Evidence in International Commercial Arbitration (1 June 1999).
[35] J. Paulsson, 'Awards Set Aside at the Place of Arbitration', in *Enforcing Arbitration Awards under the New York Convention: Experience and Prospects* (UN, 1999), pp. 24–26, 25–26.
[36] W. Kidane, *The Culture of International Arbitration* (Oxford University Press, 2017), p. 116: 'International arbitration is a "system" or a "framework" whose advantages are limited to bridging the gap between courts of different nations. It is a gap filler – nothing

general societal acceptance[37] is even more valid in a system based on consent rather than authority. As Jan Paulsson accurately described: '[a] legal order is therefore not the product of a set of positive laws, but rather the inevitable result of the formation of a social group.[38] Delineating the society of international arbitration is far more difficult than identifying the parameters of a domestic jurisdiction. The arbitrator 'ceases to be part of a national state and instead becomes integrated in a "global adjudication system" … he adopts a transnational role within a transnational system.'[39] Yet there are markers identifying this imagined community.[40] Practitioners have urged the 'international arbitration community' to promulgate guidelines on the role of the tribunal secretary.[41]

Empirically, it is easier to identify a society of international arbitrators, referred to as the 'cartel', 'club' or 'mafia'.[42] Nomenclature of professionalism has been used in international arbitration as a marker of this society.[43] There is an increasingly identifiable specialised social group of lawyers, service providers and expert witnesses emerging, who share a 'common understanding of what arbitration is and how it works'.[44] Apart from practitioners, regular participants in the society of arbitration include nongovernmental organisations, inter-governmental organisations such as the United Nations Commission on International Trade Law (UNCITRAL) and the United Nations Conference on Trade and Development (UNCTAD),[45]

---

else – but market forces of its own have supplied and grown theories and promotional justifications that have become true because of repetition.'

[37] Fuller, 'Mediation – Its Forms and Functions', 338; L. Fuller, 'Human Interaction and the Law' (1969) 14 *American Journal of Jurisprudence* 13, 24.

[38] J. Paulsson, 'Arbitration in Three Dimensions', LSE Law, Society and Economy Working Papers 2/2010, 20; see also Santi Romano, *L'ordinamento giurdico* (*The Legal Order*) (1918), cited in J. Paulsson, 'Arbitration in Three Dimensions', 16.

[39] C.N. Brower, C.H. Brower II and J.K. Sharpe, 'The Coming Crisis in the Global Adjudication System' (2003) 19(4) *Arbitration International* 415–440.

[40] B. Anderson, *Imagined Communities* (Verso, 1983).

[41] Polkinghorne and Rosenberg, 'The Role of the Tribunal Secretary', 1.

[42] S. Puig, 'Social Capital in the Arbitration Market' (2014) 25(2) *EJIL* 387–424; Michaels, 'Roles and Role Perceptions of International Arbitrators', p. 54; Y. Dezalay and B. Garth, *Dealing in Virtue* (University of Chicago Press, 1999), p. 50; W. Kidane, *The Culture of International Arbitration* (Oxford University Press, 2017), pp. 110–112.

[43] C.A. Rogers, 'The Vocation of International Arbitrators' (2005) 20 *American University International Law Review* 957, 976–977.

[44] Gaillard, 'Sociology', pp. 5–6; '2016 Analysis: Who's Who Legal–Commercial Arbitration' (Law Business Research, London, October 2015), available at http://whoswholegal.com/news/analysis/article/32630/arbitration-2016-analysis/, accessed 18 July 2017.

[45] Gaillard, 'Sociology', p. 8; E. De Brabandere, 'NGOs and the "Public Interest": The Legality and Rationale of Amicus Curiae Interventions in International Economic and Investment

and international organisations such as the International Council for Commercial Arbitration (ICCA) and the International Bar Association (IBA).[46] Generally, these organisations contribute to collective values.[47]

If international arbitration is indeed a sociological construct, the legitimacy of using 'unseen' case managers would depend on how the 'arbitration society' views these unseen actors. Arguably, insofar as the society of international arbitration approves of a practice, it becomes a permissibly delegable task. For instance, 97 per cent of respondents in a 2012 survey agreed that a secretary may handle organisational and administrative tasks on behalf of the tribunal.[48]

12.2.3   Arbitration as Dialogue

Due to its lack of 'unidirectional authority', international arbitration may be seen as 'an interactional process'.[49] International law, which shares a similar absence of hierarchy of norms, has certainly been seen as such an interactional dialogue.[50] If international arbitration is created via dialogue, the legitimacy of 'unseen' case managers would be best resolved through such dialogue.

It is directly applicable to international arbitration that 'the constraints and powers that make up a social order are in interaction with one another; each serves in part to determine the meaning and efficacy of the other'.[51] One arbitral institution declaring or one state legislating, for instance, that

Disputes' (2011–2012) 12 *Chicago Journal of International Law* 85; P. Eberhardt and C. Olivet, *Profiting from Injustice* (Corporate Europe Observatory and the Transnational Institute, 2012); C. Olivet and P. Eberhardt, *Profiting from Crisis* (The Transnational Institute and the Corporate Europe Observatory, 2014).

[46] IBA Guidelines on Conflicts of Interest in International Arbitration 2014, available at www.ibanet.org/Document/Default.aspx?DocumentUid=e2fe5e72-eb14-4bba-b10d-d33dafee8918, accessed 31 August 2017; IBA Rules on the Taking of Evidence in International Arbitration 2010, available at www.ibanet.org/Document/Default .aspx?DocumentUid=68336C49-4106-46BF-A1C6-A8F0880444DC, accessed 31 August 2017.

[47] Gaillard, 'Sociology', p. 8.

[48] Queen Mary University of London, White & Case, '2012 International Arbitration Survey: Improvements and Innovations in International Arbitration', 12, available at www .arbitration.qmul.ac.uk/research/2012/, accessed 19 March 2019.

[49] L. Fuller, *The Morality of Law* (Yale University Press, 1969), p. 223.

[50] H.H. Koh 'Why Do Nations Obey International Law? Review Essay' (1997) *Faculty Scholarship Series, Paper* 2101, 2648; C. Chinkin and R. Sadurska, 'Anatomy of International Dispute Resolution' (1991) 7(1) *Journal of Dispute Resolution* 39, 46–47.

[51] L. Fuller, 'The Case Against Freedom', in K. Winston (ed.), *The Principles of Social Order Selected Essays of Lon L. Fuller* (Hart Publishing, 2001), 322.mb.

case managers should be prohibited from drafting awards, would have no authoritative effect on other arbitral institutions or states, but would merely open a dialogue. Even if the issuing arbitral institution or state is a leading international arbitration location, its position on permissible case management practices would have at best a persuasive effect on the others.

Some see international arbitration as so diverse and practical that it cannot be reined into one coherent theory. Veijo Heiskanen argues that international arbitration is not even academically relevant, because it is a practical dispute resolution method composed of differences in applicable laws, conflicts of laws and differences between the parties.[52] Some others agree that adjudication, like all human activity, cannot be entirely articulated or explained by explicit rules, and that a 'practical reasoning' approach to adjudication is better.[53]

When considering how to impose case management standards, it is important to keep in mind that 'for a given social context one form of law may be more appropriate than another, and that the attempt to force a form of law upon a social environment uncongenial to it may miscarry with damaging results'.[54] This is confirmed by Pierre Tercier's cautionary statements that the role of tribunal secretaries have to be tailored to each arbitration depending on the arbitrators and expectations of the parties.[55] Ideally, the definitions of case management in each arbitration should be negotiated, defined and tailored to its particular social context.

12.3   Reasoning and Legitimacy

How does an arbitrator decide? Adjudication represents an institutional commitment to rationality and principle.[56] The arbitrator's duty to reason, to

---

[52] V. Heiskanen, 'Book Review: Emmanuel Gaillard. Aspects philosophiques du droit de l'arbitrage international' (2009) 20 *European Journal of International Law* 919–964.

[53] B. Leiter, 'Heidegger and the Theory of Adjudication' (1996) 106(2) *The Yale Law Journal* 253–282; G. Souri, 'Heidegger and the Essence of Adjudication' (2011), available at http://works.bepress.com/george_souri/2/, accessed 5 May 2017.

[54] Fuller, 'Human Interaction and the Law', 27.

[55] Tercier, 'The Role of the Secretary', 554: 'The solution lies in counsel and arbitrators learning how to better manage each other's expectations. Arbitrators need to be clear on how they intend to manage the proceedings and how they intend to be assisted by their own team, and counsel need to speak out about their own expectations of what the arbitrators should be doing personally. This needs to be done at an early stage, ideally even before an appointment is formalized and at the latest at the case management conference.'

[56] H.H.L. Cheng, 'Beyond Forms, Functions and Limits: The Interactionism of Lon L. Fuller and Its Implications for Alternative Dispute Resolution' (July 2013) 26(2) *Canadian Journal of Law and Jurisprudence* 257–292, 277.

apply the law chosen by the parties and to make those reasons transparent in an award are linked to the perceived legitimacy of the arbitration process. If the arbitrator is seen not to have fulfilled these duties, the legitimacy of the award suffers. This section discusses the arbitrator's duty to reason, the method of reasoning employed by a tribunal and the legitimacy or soft power wielded by arbitrators.

12.3.1 Duty to Reason

The legitimacy of 'unseen' tribunal secretaries depends in part on the content of the arbitrator's duty to reason. The LCIA recommends that tribunal secretaries should confine their activities to such matters as organising papers for the tribunal, highlighting relevant legal authorities, maintaining factual chronologies, reserving hearing rooms and sending correspondence on behalf of the tribunal.[57] The 2014 Young ICCA Guide on Arbitral Secretaries provides that with appropriate direction and supervision by the tribunal, the secretary's role may go beyond the purely administrative and may include handling and organising correspondence, submissions and evidence on behalf of the tribunal, researching questions of law, researching discrete questions relating to factual evidence and witness testimony and drafting appropriate parts of the award.[58] To interrogate *why* these tasks are permissible, we have to define the core duty of the arbitrator.

The arbitrator has the 'duty to decide'.[59] This means that, above all, an international arbitrator's mandate is to apply reasoning. Arbitrators' 'personal decision-making function' may be described as taking account of the rival submissions of the parties and bringing their own personal and

---

[57] LCIA Note to Arbitrators, para. 71.
[58] 2014 Young ICCA Guide on Arbitral Secretaries; see also Hong Kong International Arbitration Centre (HKIAC), 'Guidelines on the Use of a Secretary to the Arbitral Tribunal': unless the parties agree or the tribunal directs otherwise, the tribunal secretary may also: (i) conduct legal research; (ii) collect case law or published commentaries on legal issues defined by the tribunal; (iii) research discrete questions relating to factual evidence and witness testimony; (iv) draft memoranda summarising the parties' submissions and evidence; (v) attend the tribunal's deliberations; and (vi) prepare drafts of nonsubstantive parts of the tribunal's orders, decisions and awards (such as procedural histories and chronologies of events).
[59] American Arbitration Association, Code of Ethics for Arbitrators in Commercial Disputes, 1 March 2004, para. V(C); HKIAC 2014 Guidelines states that the 'decision-making functions' of a tribunal cannot be delegated to a tribunal secretary: para. 3.2; in 1996 UNCITRAL published its 'Notes on Organizing Arbitral Proceedings'; see para. 27.

independent judgment to bear on the decision in question.[60] Therefore, distinguishing between the nonsubstantive and substantive portions of the decision is often recommended.[61] The case manager risks influencing the arbitrator's evaluation if he or she drafts the reasoning in the substantive portions.[62]

Parties expect the arbitrator to apply their minds to the issues in hand, and engage their knowledge, understanding and expertise to come to their conclusions.[63] International arbitrators have both the duty and power to apply reason. The arbitrator cannot simply decide with a 'gut feeling' or exercise 'rough justice'.[64] Neither can the arbitrator decide arbitrarily, in private, or irrationally split the difference.[65]

Fuller explains that rationality is more important in adjudication than in contract or voting.[66] This is because of the mode of participation involved in the process. In contract, there is generally no formal assurance that a party will be given an opportunity to make reasoned argument nor that the other contracting party will listen to reasoned arguments in striking a bargain.[67] Voting is the expression of preferences of voters, which are ultimately emotional, inarticulate and not subject to rational defence.[68] Adjudication consists in the opportunity to present proofs and arguments. Since the purpose of this participation in adjudication is the presentation of reasoned argument, the whole proceeding would become a farce if the decision that emerges is not tethered to rationality.[69]

The arbitrator's duty to apply his or her mind personally to the dispute is linked to the *intuitu personae* nature of his or her appointment. In practice, it may be good advice that a secretary should not be tasked with anything that involves 'expressing a view on the substantive merits of an

---

[60] *P v. Q* 2017 EWHC 194 (Comm), Judgment of the English High Court of Justice, 9 February 2017, para. 65.

[61] HKIAC 2014 'Guidelines on the Use of a Secretary to the Arbitral Tribunal', para. 3.4.

[62] Polkinghorne and Rosenberg, 'The Role of the Tribunal Secretary', 3.

[63] A. Beaumont, 'Reasons and Reasons for Reasons Revisited: Has the Domestic Arbitral Award Moved Away from the Fundamental Basis Behind the Reasoned Award, and Is It Now Time for Realignment?' (2016) 32 *Arbitration International* 523–534, 525.

[64] M. Infantino, 'International Arbitral Awards' Reasons: Surveying the State-of-the-Art in Commercial and Investment International Dispute Settlements' (2014) 5 *Journal of International Dispute Settlement* 175, 187.

[65] T. Bingham, 'Reasons and Reasons for Reasons: Differences between a Court Judgment and an Arbitration Award' (1988) 4 *Arbitration International* 141, 142.

[66] Fuller, 'The Forms and Limits of Adjudication', 367.

[67] Ibid., 366.

[68] Ibid., 367.

[69] Ibid., 365–367.

application or issue'.[70] It is not sufficient to simply draw up a list of permissible and impermissible tasks. Even when highlighting relevant legal authorities and maintaining factual chronologies,[71] the secretary should be cautious about usurping the arbitrator's mandate to reason.

Understanding the arbitrator's duty to apply his mind explains why in any event, he can still discharge his or her decision-making duty *after* receiving a secretary's views. The English Court in *P v. Q* decided:

> There is nothing offensive per se to performance of that function in receiving the views of others, provided the adjudicator makes his own mind up by the exercise of independent judgment. A judge may be assisted by the views of a judicial assistant or law clerk, but that does not prevent him or her from reaching an independent judgment in accordance with the judicial function.[72]

Discharging the duty to reason turns on the arbitrator's exercise of 'reasonable diligence'. Reasoning cannot be 'lazy', 'uninformed' nor based on unquestioned 'initial impulses'.[73] It also cannot be the product of bias, self-interest, insufficient reflection or excess haste.[74] Grounds for challenge of the arbitrator based on competence imply that their duty to reason is held to a standard of intellectual diligence. The 2012 ICC Note under the ICC Rules illustrates this standard of diligence: a tribunal may request the secretary to prepare written notes or memoranda, but it has a duty 'personally to review the file'[75] and 'draft any decision'.[76]

12.3.2   Method of Reasoning

How an arbitrator decides is intimately connected with the nature of decision-making. Significant controversy exists whether the tribunal secretary or

---

[70] *P v. Q* 2017 EWHC 194 (Comm), Judgment of the English High Court of Justice, 9 February 2017, para. 68.

[71] LCIA Note to Arbitrators, para. 71.

[72] *P v. Q*, paras. 65–70.

[73] A.S. Rau, 'On Integrity in Private Judging' (1998) 14(2) *Arbitration International* 146, 187; W. Godwin, 'Arbitration and Reasons: The North Range Decision' (2002) 5(4) *International Arbitration Law Review*, 109–112, 112; P. Gillies and N. Selvadurai, 'Reasoned Awards: How Extensive Must the Reasoning Be?' (2008) 74 *Arbitration* 125–132, 126; Infantino, 'International Arbitral Awards' Reasons', 182.

[74] F. Schauer, 'Giving Reasons' (1995) 47 *Stanford Law Review* 633, 657.

[75] 2012 ICC 'Note on the Appointment, Duties and Remuneration of Administrative Secretaries', reproduced in International Chamber of Commerce, 'Part II-5', *Soft Law in International Arbitration* (JurisNet, 2014), 237.

[76] 2016 ICC Note to Parties and Arbitral Tribunals on the Conduct of the Arbitration under the ICC Rules of Arbitration, September 2016, para. 87.

institution's secretariat should draft parts of the procedural order or award.[77] This question is about usurping the arbitrator's method of reasoning.

For some, the case manager 'drafting part or all of the decisions and reasoning would appear wholly inappropriate' because they believe that how the key facts and relevant arguments should be presented in the final decision or award is connected to the arbitrators' function to 'select and decide'.[78] Some believe that the 'act of writing is the ultimate safeguard of intellectual control over the decision-making process'.[79]

Room for the arbitrator's discretion in decision-making arises from the tension between identifying the legal principle and applying it to the facts. As Richard Posner describes, 'a legal question might be at once determinate and indeterminate: determinate because a clear rule covers it, indeterminate because the judge is not obligated to follow the rule'.[80] This is reflected in the consistent responses to the 2012 and 2015 Queen Mary University of London–White & Case Surveys where only 47–55 per cent agreed that tribunal secretaries may conduct legal research and only 10–13 per cent agreed that tribunal secretaries may prepare drafts of substantive parts of the award, compared to 72–75 per cent who agreed that tribunal secretaries may prepare procedural orders and non-substantive parts of the award.[81]

In domestic law, theoretical discussions about the way judges should decide are more developed. Still, the method of reasoning that adjudicators should use to decide disputes is subject to intense debate. First, as argued by H.L.A. Hart, there may be a 'master rule' of recognition that an

---

[77] C. Spalton, 'Are Tribunal Secretaries Writing Awards?' (9 November 2012) *Global Arbitration Review*, available at https://globalarbitrationreview.com/article/1031741/are-tribunal-secretaries-writing-awards, accessed 19 March 2019; A. Ross, 'What Goes on in Arbitrator Deliberations?' (29 May 2013) *Global Arbitration Review*, available at http://globalarbitrationreview.com/news/article/31618/, accessed 19 March 2019.

[78] *Compañía de Aguas del Aconquija SA & Vivendi Universal SA v. Argentine Republic*, ICSID Case No ARB/97/3 (Annulment Proceeding), Additional Opinion of Professor J.H. Dalhuisen under Art. 48(4) of the ICSID Convention, 30 July 2010, paras. 4, 7.

[79] Douglas, 'The Secretary to the Arbitral Tribunal', p. 89; 2013 ICCA Survey cited in ICCA Guide on Arbitral Secretaries, 14, 62; Queen Mary University of London, White & Case, '2012 International Arbitration Survey: Improvements and Innovations in International Arbitration', 12, available at www.arbitration.qmul.ac.uk/research/2012/, accessed 19 March 2019.

[80] R.A. Posner, *The Problems of Jurisprudence* (Harvard University Press, 2001), p. 47.

[81] Queen Mary University of London, White & Case, '2012 International Arbitration Survey: Improvements and Innovations in International Arbitration', 12; Queen Mary University of London, White & Case, '2015 International Arbitration Survey: Improvements and Innovations in International Arbitration', 43, available at www.arbitration.qmul.ac.uk/research/2015/, accessed 19 March 2019.

adjudicator would use to identify 'a conclusive affirmative indication that it is a rule of the group to be supported by the social pressure it exerts'.[82]

Second, as an alternative, Ronald Dworkin sought to identify a rule of interpretation 'by trying to find the best justification they can find, in principles of political morality'.[83] Similarly, it may be impossible to identify a common theory of international arbitration anchoring arbitrators' method of reasoning.

Third, others prefer a practical approach to judicial reasoning which resonates with international arbitration. Posner proposed that:

> The amount of legislating that a judge does depends on the breadth of his 'zone of reasonableness' – the area which he has discretion to decide a case either way without disgracing himself. The zone varies from judiciary to judiciary and from judge to judge... The breadth of the zone varies with the field of law. It is narrower in fields of ideological consensus... for example, contract law.[84]

The 'zone of reasonableness' is suited to the development of international arbitration. Although comprised of parallel, independent tribunals, each with no authority over another, arbitration has developed a strikingly stable set of transnational principles and best practices. Transnational arbitral legal principles include separability, competence-competence, and due process.[85] Procedural innovations such as the Redfern Schedule are also common practice.[86] Straying outside this 'zone of reasonableness'

---

[82] H.L.A. Hart, *The Concept of Law* (Oxford University Press, 1994), p. 107.

[83] R. Dworkin, 'Law as Interpretation' (1982) 60 *Texas Law Review* 527–550, 528.

[84] R.A. Posner, *How Judges Think* (Harvard University Press, 2008), p. 87.

[85] See E. Gaillard, *Legal Theory*, pp. 52–66; c.f. T. Schultz, 'The Concept of Law in Transnational Arbitral Legal Orders and Some of Its Consequences' (2011) 2(1) *Journal of International Dispute Settlement* 59, 76–81; J. Karton, *The Culture of International Arbitration and the Evolution of Contract Law* (Oxford University Press, 2013), p. 46; J. Karton, 'International Arbitration Culture and Global Governance', in W. Mattli and T. Dietz (eds.), *International Arbitration and Global Governance: Contending Theories and Evidence* (Oxford University Press, 2014), pp. 103–104.

[86] P. Tan and S. Seow, 'An Overview of Procedural Innovations in International Commercial Arbitration', *Singapore Law Gazette*, October 2014, available at www.internationalarbitrationasia.com/articles/singapore/international-commercial-arbitration, accessed 19 March 2019; IBA Guidelines on Conflicts of Interest in International Arbitration 2014, available at www.ibanet.org/Document/Default.aspx?DocumentUid=e2fe5e72-eb14-4bba-b10d-d33dafee8918, accessed 31 August 2017; S. Luttrell, 'Bias Challenges in Investor–State Arbitration: Lessons from International Commercial Arbitration', in C. Brown and K. Miles (eds.), *Evolution in Investment Treaty Law and Arbitration* (Cambridge University Press, 2011), p. 451.

in international arbitration raises the risk that an arbitrator will not be appointed again in this self-regulating market.

Fuller referred to a 'community of interest from which adjudication can draw intellectual sustenance'.[87] Some argue that it is already possible to identify such a community of interest, or even a transnational legal order:

> Quite clearly we can speak of a transnational community of international arbitration practitioners. International arbitration fulfils all criteria traditionally listed for an epistemic community. We find a shared set of normative and principled beliefs in the superiority of private over state based adjudication. We find agreement on a central set of problems, in particular autonomy from the state on the one hand, the need for due process principles on the other. We find shared notions of validity – in principle – on the doctrinal treatment of problems, regardless of the applicable national law. And we find a common policy enterprise: to make international arbitration more and more autonomous.[88]

If we speak of investment treaty arbitration, which commonly requires the arbitrators to apply international law,[89] the process of interpreting international law has a more public nature, with expectations of coherence and consistency.[90] An arbitrator's reasoning adds to the process of interaction, interpretation and internalisation of norms to create Hart's 'secondary rules' or 'rules of recognition' for the international legal order.[91]

In tribunals of three or more arbitrators, the method of reasoning involves a crucial additional step – the deliberations.[92] Deliberations can take any imaginable shape. For instance, deliberations may be structured

---

[87] Fuller, 'Form and Limits', 378.

[88] Michaels, 'Roles and Role Perceptions of International Arbitrators', pp. 52–53; see also Gaillard, 'Sociology', pp. 2–3; K. Lynch, *The Forces of Economic Globalization* (Kluwer Law International, 2003), pp. 99–100; T. Schultz, 'Secondary Rules of Recognition and Relative Legality in Transnational Regimes' (September 2011) *American Journal of Jurisprudence* 56, 59, 88; Karton, 'The Culture of Arbitration and the Evolution of Contract Law, 21–24; cf. R. Banakar, 'Reflexive Legitimacy in International Arbitration', in V. Gessner and A. Cem Budak (eds.), *Emerging Legal Certainty: Empirical Studies on the Globalization of Law* (Ashgate, 1998), p. 391; P.M. Haas, 'Introduction: Epistemic Communities and International Policy Coordination' (Winter 1992) 46(1) *International Organization* 1, 3; Michaels, 'Roles and Role Perceptions of International Arbitrators', p. 53.

[89] ICSID Convention, Article 42(1).

[90] Koh, 'Why Do Nations Obey International Law?', 2659.

[91] Hart, *The Concept of Law*, p. 214.

[92] D.W Rivkin, 'Form of Deliberations', in B. Berger and M.E. Schneider (eds.), *Inside the Black Box: How Arbitral Tribunals Operate and Reach Their Decisions* (Juris 2014), pp. 21–26; B. F. Meyer, 'Structuring a Bargaining Process', in Berger and Schneider (eds.), *Inside the Black Box*, pp. 59–66.

around social interactions,[93] discussions in advance of a hearing on how to handle the issues,[94] an exchange of written views[95] or more technical steps, such as using 'decision trees' to establish their interpretation of the law before applying it to the facts.[96] Often, they involve arbitrators attempting to persuade each other of their views and delicate bargaining processes between the arbitrators.[97] The tribunal's method of reasoning may involve one arbitrator threatening the others with the drafting of a dissenting opinion.[98] These balances are regarded as so delicate that we recognise the secrecy of deliberations.[99]

Understood in this way, the case manager's participation in deliberations is controversial because the deliberations are the most significant part of the tribunal's decision-making. The HKIAC Guidelines permits the secretary to '*attend* the tribunal's deliberations'.[100] A secretary's attendance at deliberations serves a valuable note-taking function, recognised in the ICSID Financial and Administrative Regulations.[101] The 2013 ICCA Survey reported that 72.5 per cent of respondents believed that the secretary may attend deliberations, but only 16.5 per cent accepted that the secretary may participate in deliberations.[102]

The distinction between assistance and participation lies in defining the tribunal's method of reasoning. In *Sonatrach v. Statoil*, the English Courts found that the tribunal secretary had prepared notes for the

---

[93] See, for example, the 'Reed retreat' in Tan and Seow, 'An Overview of Procedural Innovations in International Commercial Arbitration'.

[94] Rivkin, 'Form of Deliberations', p. 22.

[95] Ibid., 23.

[96] Meyer, 'Structuring a Bargaining Process', pp. 60–61.

[97] Ibid., 62–66.

[98] Ibid., 64.

[99] M.J. Goldstein, 'Living (or not) with the Partisan Arbitrator: Are There Limits to Deliberations Secrecy?' (2016) 32 *Arbitration International* 589–600, 594–595; see also the denial of an application for disclosure of communications between tribunal members and the tribunal secretary in *P v. Q* 2017 EWHC 194 (Comm), Judgment of the English High Court of Justice, 9 February 2017, paras. 11, 26, 67.

[100] HKIAC 'Guidelines on the Use of a Secretary to the Arbitral Tribunal', 1 June 2014, para. 3.4(e) (emphasis added).

[101] ICSID Arbitration Rules, Article 15(2); ICSID Financial and Administrative Regulations, Article 25(c), (d); Tercier, 'The Role of the Secretary', 547; 'Guidelines for Use of Clerks and Tribunal Secretaries in Arbitrations', JAMS International, available at www.jamsinternational.com/wp-content/uploads/JAMS-International-Clerks-Secretaries-in-Arbitrations.pdf.

[102] 2013 ICCA Survey in 2014 ICCA Guide on Arbitral Secretaries, 78, question 26.

tribunal which were used in the deliberations, but this did not constitute her participation in the decision.[103]

12.3.3 Legitimacy

Arbitrators may be perceived as 'legal dignitaries'.[104] Yves Dezalay and Brian Garth describe how the leading international arbitrators of the older generations came to play these roles rather incidentally – their prestige stems from their positions as 'grand old men', and the nature of their authority was charisma.[105] Similarly, Ottoarndt Glossner described the role of the arbitrator as a 'noble task':

> To be an arbitrator is to exercise an honourable function. It is no profession… [The arbitrator need] not be a lawyer. He can be just as well a technical expert, an engineer, but he must be a person of knowledge and high moral standards… It is only natural that the parties listen more intensely to somebody who speaks to them from a higher elevation of experience, knowledge, reputation'[106]

Apart from feats of intellectual gymnastics, the arbitrator also asserts a great amount of soft power throughout the process. The HKIAC's 2014 Guidelines refer not only to 'decision-making functions', but also hint at other 'essential duties of the tribunal'.[107]

At the stage of rendering an award on the merits, an arbitrator's soft power is no less significant. The reputations of eminent international arbitrators are associated with correctness of the award.[108] Within international tribunals consisting of three or more arbitrators, adjudication goes beyond merely reasoning individually, but includes asserting soft power in a social context – debating the issues with co-arbitrators.[109]

---

[103] *Sonatrach v. Statoil* 2014 EWHC 875 (Comm) (2 April 2014), paras. 46–50.

[104] Max Weber, *On Law in Economy and Society* (Harvard University Press, 1954), pp. 784–808, cited in Michaels, 'Roles and Role Perceptions of International Arbitrators', p. 59.

[105] Y. Dezalay and B. Garth, *Dealing in Virtue* (University of Chicago Press, 1999), pp. 34–37.

[106] O. Glossner, 'Sociological Aspects of International Commercial Arbitration' (1982) 10 *International Business Lawyer* 311–314; Michaels, 'Roles and Role Perceptions of International Arbitrators', p. 59.

[107] HKIAC 'Guidelines on the Use of a Secretary to the Arbitral Tribunal', 1 June 2014, para. 3.2.

[108] *Sanum Investments Ltd v. Government of the Lao People's Democratic Republic* 2016 SGCA 57, Singapore Court of Appeal Judgment of 29 September 2016, para. 16.

[109] Rivkin, 'Form of Deliberations', p. 21; L. Reed, 'The 2013 Hong Kong International Arbitration Centre Kaplan Lecture: Arbitral Decision-Making: Art, Science or Sport?' (2013) 30 *Journal of International Arbitration* 85, 96.

The role of the arbitrator is not entirely juridical. Credibility, personal integrity and an authoritative understanding of commercial and technical issues could be just as important as legal competence.[110] The importance of the arbitrator's ethical reputation became evident in the *Croatia/Slovenia* arbitration, for example, in which the lack of credibility of the Slovenian-appointed arbitrator, conducting secret telephone calls with Slovenian government officials, has contributed to Croatia's declaration that it is not bound by the arbitral award.[111]

Given the moral authority of an arbitrator, there are some functions that will be impossible for a case manager to usurp. Consider the practice that the Registrar of the PCA signs awards alongside the arbitrators.[112] While an arbitrator's personal legitimacy is often at no risk of being confused with the case manager's, an established institution such as the PCA could wield substantial moral influence of its own.

12.4   Institutional Actor

What are the institutional limits of international arbitration? Ultimately, Fuller argues that 'the essence of adjudication lies not in the manner in which the affected party participates in the decision but in the office of judge'.[113]

12.4.1   Institutional Powers and Limits

Parties may specify the legitimate role of the tribunal secretary in their agreement, arbitral rules or in a procedural order. Some arbitrators are

---

[110] Michaels, 'Roles and Role Perceptions of International Arbitrators', p. 59; K.S. Carlston, 'Psychological and Sociological Aspects of the Judicial and Arbitration Processes', in P. Sanders (ed.), *Liber Amicorum for Martin Domke*, 44, 47–49; C.A. Rogers, 'Fit and Function in Legal Ethics: Developing a Code of Conduct for International Arbitration', (2002) 23 *Michigan Journal of International Law* 341–424, 350–353.

[111] S. Menon, 'Adjudicator, Advocate, or Something in Between? Coming to Terms with the Role of the Party-appointed Arbitrator' (2017) 34(2/1) *Journal of International Arbitration* 347–371; *Arbitration between the Republic of Croatia and the Republic of Slovenia*, Final Award (29 June 2017), available at https://pcacases.com/web/view/3, accessed 6 July 2017; S. Milekic, 'Croatia Set To Ignore Ruling on Piran Gulf' (29 June 2017), available at www.balkaninsight.com/en/article/stalemate-in-croatia-slovenia-sea-dispute-amid-court-decision-06-28-2017, accessed 6 July 2017.

[112] See, for instance, *South China Sea Arbitration (Philippines v. China)*, PCA Case No. 2013-19, Award of 12 July 2016, 479.

[113] Fuller, 'Forms and Limits', 365.

given the powers to decide a dispute *ex aequo et bono*, or even to deny the parties a hearing. If the parties agree to the appointment of a secretary without qualification, it could be interpreted as not placing any limits on the tasks and functions which the secretary might perform.[114]

States have both the legitimacy and the ability to influence arbitration directly within the limits of their territory. Most arbitrations are seated in a State.[115] The function of case managers under the arbitration legislation of the seat may be limited by mandatory laws. States may also specify the requirements which must be satisfied before the State will recognise awards, which can include specifying which tasks are impermissible for case managers. In investor-State arbitration, States have the direct ability to impose limits on the roles of case managers within their investment treaties.

Even outside the confines of a State-seated arbitration, in an ICSID arbitration, international arbitration principles expressed by State organs may gain extra-territorial reach.[116] For instance, Gaillard argues that when the French court pronounced in *Putrabali* that an international award is a 'decision of international justice', the court expressed its characterisation of what is arbitration to a broader audience than the parties themselves, and similarly, when the UK House of Lords recognised the severability of the arbitration agreement in *Fiona Trust*, it set forth an international standard of competence-competence.[117] These institutional limits expressed by States delineate the legitimacy of 'unseen actors'.

12.4.2   Interactive Institutions

Arbitral institutions participate in defining the essence of adjudication. As Fuller elaborated: 'Our institutions are a part of the pattern of our lives. The task of perfecting them furnishes an outlet for the most vigorous of moral impulses.'[118] Arbitral institutions draft rules, conduct consultations on the

---

[114] *P v. Q* 2017 EWHC 194 (Comm), Judgment of the English High Court of Justice, 9 February 2017, para. 50.

[115] With the exception of ICSID arbitrations.

[116] Gaillard, 'Sociology', p. 7.

[117] Gaillard, 'Sociology', pp. 7–8; See for example the elaboration of principles in domestic court cases such as *Fiona Trust and Holding Corporation and Others v. Yuri Privalov and Others* 2007 EWCA Civ 2, and *PT Putrabali Adyamulia v. Rena Holding*, 2007(3) *Revue de l'arbitrage*, 507.

[118] L. Fuller, 'Means and Ends', in K. Winston (ed.), *The Principles of Social Order: Selected Essays of Lon L. Fuller* (Hart, 2001), p. 75.

procedures, compete to introduce new procedural mechanisms, appoint arbitrators, administer the cases and even perform a sociological function by organising conferences on arbitration.[119]

By engaging the arbitral institution to administer their dispute, the parties implicitly agree to carve out certain decision-making powers from the scope of the arbitrators' duties. For instance, the LCIA informs arbitrators that the 'LCIA Secretariat will deal with *all matters required of it under the LCIA Rules*' besides providing procedural timetable reminders, arranging hearing venues and transcripts.[120] The ICC Court makes decisions on the consolidation of proceedings before the tribunal.[121]

Arbitral institutions may issue rules or soft law instruments such as institutional practice guidelines.[122] The ICSID Secretariat currently provides assistance to the parties and the tribunal in the form of a case team,[123] and holds public consultations on improvements.[124]

Certainly, compared to court registries, arbitral institutions are 'not an inert mirror reflecting current mores but an *active* participant in the enterprise of articulating the implications of shared purposes'.[125] In particular, the LCIA recommends that after the tribunal has secured the parties' agreement to the appointment of a tribunal secretary, the LCIA should obtain a statement of independence from the secretary.[126]

Arbitral institutions even participate in the normative dialogue on why we should use case managers. Parties and arbitrators are advised to 'be alive to the rules and guidance on the role of tribunal secretaries'.[127] The

[119] Gaillard, 'Sociology', pp. 12–13.
[120] LCIA Note to Arbitrators, para. 70 (emphasis added).
[121] ICC Arbitration Rules 2017, Article 10; G.B. Born, *International Commercial Arbitration*, 2nd edn (Kluwer Law International, 2014), pp. 2565–2567.
[122] LCIA Arbitration Rules 2012, Article 14(5).
[123] ICSID Case Administration Services available at https://icsid.worldbank.org/en/Pages/Services/Case-Administration.aspx, accessed 11 March 2019; E. Obadia and F. Nitschke, 'Institutional Arbitration and the Role of the Secretariat', in C. Giorgetti (ed.), *Litigating International Investment Disputes: A Practitioner's Guide* (Brill, 2014), pp. 80–144.
[124] ICSID Secretariat, 'ICSID Rules Amendment Process' (7 October 2016), available at https://icsid.worldbank.org/en/documents/about/icsid%20rules%20amendment%20process-eng.pdf, accessed 11 March 2019; ICSID Secretariat, 'List of Topics for Potential ICSID Rule Amendment' (February 2017), available at https://icsid.worldbank.org/en/Documents/about/List%20of%20Topics%20for%20Potential%20ICSID%20Rule%20Amendment-ENG.pdf, accessed 11 March 2019.
[125] Fuller, 'Forms and Limits', 378.
[126] LCIA's Note to Arbitrators, para. 73.
[127] P. Hirst, 'When Does a Tribunal Secretary Overstep the Mark?', *Kluwer Arbitration Blog*, 18 April 2017, http://kluwerarbitrationblog.com/2017/04/18/when-does-a-tribunal-secretary-overstep-the-mark/, accessed 11 March 2019.

LCIA's Note to Arbitrators justifies activities of the tribunal secretary 'on the basis that the secretary's work will save the Arbitral Tribunal time'.[128] The 2014 Young ICCA Guide on Arbitral Secretaries also favours a cost-benefit justification: 'this is a risk outweighed by the benefits inherent in the use of arbitral secretaries'.[129] An investor-State or inter-State arbitration with potentially significant public interests at stake may adopt a different philosophical approach in evaluating the use of arbitral secretaries.

12.5   Conclusion

Although it is impossible to define 'true adjudication' because it is something that 'never fully exists', it is only with the aid of a theoretical model that 'we can pass intelligent judgment on the accomplishments of adjudication as it actually is'.[130] By engaging with legal theory, the legitimacy of 'unseen' case managers in international arbitration could be improved in two ways.

Externally, much livelier public debate – over what is arbitration, what are the tribunal's duties, and how we are shaping these definitions – would generate understanding and greater acceptance. Internally, from within the system of international arbitration, case managers with a deep understanding of the nature and role of international adjudication would, in practice, be less likely to stray into the impermissible realms of decision-making. Such a theoretical endeavour could in time contribute to ostensible practical effects, by improving the overall standards and legitimacy of these 'unseen' actors.

---

[128] LCIA's Note to Arbitrators, para. 72.
[129] International Council for Commercial Arbitration, '2014 Young ICCA Guide on Arbitral Secretaries', *The ICCA Reports No. 1*, available at https://pca-cpa.org/wp-content/uploads/sites/175/2016/01/ICCA-Reports-No.-1_Young-ICCA-Guide-on-Arbitral-Secretaries.pdf, accessed 8 August 2017, 6, Article 1(5).
[130] Fuller, 'Forms and Limits', 357.

13

Procedural Reforms at The Court of Arbitration of The International Chamber of Commerce: How to Ensure that Party Autonomy Will Continue Serving as a Legitimization Tool

GIACOMO MARCHISIO*

13.1 Introduction

Since the 1990s, the rise of arbitral institutions has brought about a complex institutional framework for the adjudication of international disputes. In an effort – some may say, a displaced one – to imitate the sophistication of public courts and tribunals, the adjudicative powers granted to the arbitrators and the administrative powers assigned to the arbitral institutions have become more variegated and diversified. The growth of these powers increasingly puts in question the role of party autonomy in international arbitration, which has long served as a key tool of legitimization. This chapter addresses the tensions between party autonomy and the some of the case management powers of arbitral institutions, which are often presented as administrative in nature, by looking at the International Court of Arbitration of the International Chamber of Commerce (ICC) and the 2017 ICC Rules of Arbitration.[1]

Before delving into the characteristics of the International Court of Arbitration, this chapter deals with the preliminary matter of determining whether the notion of international arbitration can be subsumed under the concept of international adjudication. Here, Romano, Alter, and Shany's highly influential account of international adjudication[2] provides

---

* I wish to thank Benjamin Jarvis for his help in the preparation of this chapter.

[1] ICC International Court of Arbitration, 2017 Arbitration Rules and 2014 Mediation Rules (Paris: ICC, May 2018), available at https://iccwbo.org/publication/arbitration-rules-and-mediation-rules/ (last accessed 6 November 2018).

[2] Cesare P.R. Romano, Karen J. Alter and Yuval Shany, 'Mapping International Adjudicative Bodies, the Issues, and Players' in C.P.R. Romano, K.J. Alter and Y. Shany (eds.), *The Oxford Handbook of International Adjudication* (Oxford University Press, 2013), p. 4.

an instructive definition of international adjudicative institutions by which an analysis can proceed. According to them, international adjudicative institutions are:

1. international governmental organizations, or bodies and procedures of international governmental organizations that;
2. hear cases where one of the parties is or could be a State or an international organization, and that;
3. are composed of independent adjudicators who;
4. decide the question(s) brought before them on the basis of international law;
5. following pre-determined rules of procedure and;
6. issue binding decisions.

It is fairly uncontroversial to state that international arbitration satisfies the above definition – beyond the first criterion of governmental character. However, whether the governmental nature of the institution should play such a defining role is not entirely clear, and the authors use these criteria non-exhaustively in view of narrowing down the number and type of potentially relevant international adjudicative bodies. Therefore, inasmuch as international arbitral institutions are called to intervene in public international disputes (e.g. investment arbitration) by resorting to an adversarial adjudicative procedure, they deserve to be analysed and scrutinized as international adjudicative institutions. Further recent research demonstrates that the institutions administering arbitrations increasingly resemble permanent adjudicative bodies playing a material function in the resolution of international disputes.[3] Thus, it is not only possible but compelling to investigate the role and legitimacy of these important actors.

13.2 The 'Traditional' Functions of the Court of Arbitration of the ICC

The Court of Arbitration of the ICC has traditionally performed two functions in disputes under its auspices: the scrutiny of the quality of its arbitrators' awards, and the handling of preliminary jurisdictional objections. Let us treat each of these in turn.

---

[3] Rémy Gerbay, *The Function of Arbitral Institutions* (Kluwer Law, 2016).

13.2.1   *The Scrutiny of Arbitral Awards*

The role of the Court has traditionally been understood as purely administrative.[4] It does not resolve disputes, but merely appoints or confirms the arbitrators and approves the award.[5] The extent of the latter power, however, has been subjected to vigorous debate.[6]

Motivated by pragmatic considerations that focused on maximizing the enforceability of ICC awards, the scrutiny of arbitral awards is often presented as a hallmark of ICC arbitration – a distinctive feature which guarantees the high quality of ICC awards.[7] The Court of Arbitration can review form and suggest changes to the substance of the award.[8]

---

[4] See e.g. Art. 1(2), 2017 ICC Rules: The Court does not itself resolve disputes. It administers the resolution of disputes by arbitral tribunals, in accordance with the Rules of Arbitration of the ICC (the 'Rules'). The Court is the only body authorized to administer arbitrations under the Rules, including the scrutiny and approval of awards rendered in accordance with the Rules. It draws up its own internal rules, which are set forth in Appendix II (the 'Internal Rules').

[5] It should be noted that other institutions, such as the Singapore International Arbitration Center (SIAC), carry out a similar scrutiny. See Gary Born, *International Commercial Arbitration*, 2nd edn (Kluwer, 2014), p. 2154.

[6] Emmanuel Gaillard and John Savage, *Fouchard, Gaillard & Goldman on International Commercial Arbitration* (Kluwer Law, 1999), p. 750 ('The ICC International Court of Arbitration thus has the power to review the form of the award, and to draw the attention of the arbitrators to substantive issues which it considers to be problematic. This distinction between form and substance is sometimes delicate. Contrary to the view put forward by some authors, the scrutiny by the International Court of Arbitration of the form of the award does not extend to ensuring compliance with the entire arbitral procedure'). For a critique, see generally: Antoine Kassis, *Réflexions sur le règlement d'arbitrage de la chambre de commerce internationale – les déviations de l'arbitrage institutionnel* (Librairie générale de droit et de jurisprudence (LGDJ), 1988).

[7] L. William Craig, W.W. Park, and J. Paulsson, *International Chamber of Commerce Arbitration* (ICC Publishing, 1990), p. 252 ('the institution has an interest in ensuring that an award bearing the ICC cachet have an international currency, and be entitled to execution in the largest possible number of States … [I]t is important that there be a central authority having experience with recognition and enforcement practices throughout the world'). The current version of the ICC Rules (updated in 2017) reads as follows:

Article 34 – Scrutiny of the Award by the Court
Before signing any award, the arbitral tribunal shall submit it in draft form to the Court. The Court may lay down modifications as to the form of the award and, without affecting the arbitral tribunal's liberty of decision, may also draw its attention to points of substance. No award shall be rendered by the arbitral tribunal until it has been approved by the Court as to its form.

[8] Gerbay, The Function of Arbitral Institutions, p. 100. As noted by the same author, in 2012, only 2 per cent of the awards did not undergo any changes as to the form or suggestions as to the substance.

One should not underestimate the importance of the former function. As Derains and Schwartz note:[9]

> [d]efects of form ... typically include typographical or computational errors, the absence of elements that may be required to be included in the Award under the law of the place of the arbitration, the absence of reasons or the Award's failure to respect the Arbitral Tribunal's mandate, i.e., where it is *infra* or *ultra petita*.

The provision has two important effects. First, it imposes a prerequisite for the issuing of the final award. Second, it grants a degree of review, which in some cases approaches what – in the context of domestic litigation – is a type which falls under the purview of an appellate court. Challenges against a lower court's decision based on the fact that the judgment exceeds the claims or counterclaims filed by the parties (*ultra petita*), fall squarely within the role of an appellate court.

13.2.2 Jurisdictional Objections Prior to the Appointment of the Arbitrators

Another traditional function exercised by the Court of Arbitration is the preliminary screening of jurisdictional objections. Until the 1998 version of the Rules, whenever the respondent objected to the existence, validity, or scope of the arbitration agreement prior to the beginning of the arbitration, the Court was required to make a decision as to whether the arbitration ought to continue. In doing so, the Court had to be satisfied of the prima facie existence of the arbitration agreement.[10]

Under the current version of the Rules, the role of the Court has changed. The default is now that the Secretariat itself will decide such jurisdictional objections, referring to the Court only the most delicate cases. In practice, however, the application of this mechanism proves rather obscure:[11]

---

[9] Y. Derains and E.A. Schwartz, *Guide to the ICC Rules of Arbitration* (ICC Publishing, 2005), p. 313 (emphasis added).

[10] See Art. 6(2), 1998 ICC Rules: 'If the Respondent does not file an Answer, as provided by Article 5, or if any party raises one or more pleas concerning the existence, validity or scope of the arbitration agreement, the Court may decide, without prejudice to the admissibility or merits of the plea or pleas, that the arbitration shall proceed if it is prima facie satisfied that an arbitration agreement under the Rules may exist.'

[11] See Jason Fry, S. Greenberg and F. Mazza, *The Secretariat's Guide to ICC Arbitration* (ICC Publishing, 2012), paras. 3–207.

> Where all claims are brought pursuant to a single contract that appears to
> be signed by all parties and contains an arbitration agreement clearly refer-
> ring disputes to ICC arbitration, the case will be referred directly to the
> arbitral tribunal … Any other situation will prompt a review of the case by
> the Secretary General. To assist the Secretary General in this task, the team
> assigned to the case will prepare a brief written report on the case. Upon
> completing such review, the Secretary General may then decide, where
> appropriate, to submit the case to the Court for a decision pursuant to
> Article 6(4).

A classic example of a pathological clause which would not satisfy the
prima facie test spelled out in Article 6(4) is an arbitration agreement
where the parties have agreed upon a dispute resolution mechanism other
than arbitration, or an institution other than the ICC. The 2012 reform,
meant to streamline arbitrations, added an additional layer of complexity,
making it difficult to understand which considerations will be accounted
for by the Secretariat in its decision on the preliminary jurisdictional
objection in the absence of an explicit criterion.

Aside from these decision-making areas delegated to the Court, there are
two new instances where the Court of Arbitration has been granted important powers: the emergency arbitration provisions and the new 2017 expedited procedure. Given that the emergency arbitration does not apply to
investment cases[12] and has been extensively scrutinized by several authors,[13]
this chapter will focus exclusively on the new expedited procedure.

13.3   The New Functions of the Court of Arbitration of the ICC under the 2017 ICC Expedited Procedure Rules

The 2017 ICC Rules imagine a new role for the Court of Arbitration in the
context of the newly introduced expedited procedure. This is evident in

---

[12] Cf. Art. 29(5) of the 2017 ICC Rules ('the Emergency Arbitrator Rules set forth in
Appendix V … shall apply only to parties that are either signatories of the arbitration
agreement under the Rules that is relied upon for the application or successors to such
signatories.'). See also: Koh Swee Yen, 'The Use of Emergency Arbitrators in Investment
Treaty Arbitration' (2016) 31(3) *ICSID Review* 534, 535 (noting, however, that two other
international institutions, namely, the Stockholm Chamber of Commerce and the SIAC,
do allow the use of emergency arbitration in investment disputes).

[13] See, among others, Nathalie Voser and Christopher Boog, *ICC Emergency Arbitration
Proceedings* (ICC Publishing, 2011); Christian Aschauer, 'The Use of ICC Emergency
Arbitrator to Protect the Arbitral Proceedings' (2012) 23(2) *ICC Bull* 5; Eliseo Castineira,
'The Emergency Arbitrator in the 2012 ICC Rules of Arbitration' (2012) 4 *Cahiers arb*
67; Baruch Baigel, 'The Emergency Arbitrator Procedure under the 2012 ICC Rules: A
Juridical Analysis' (2014) 31(1) *Journal of International Arbitration* 1.

the prescribed structure generally, as well as the powers allocated to the Court explicitly. To illustrate this point, this section will first address the general requirements triggering the application of the expedited procedure, turning then to the powers granted to the Court of Arbitration and the challenges that may lie ahead.

13.3.1   General Observations and Overall Philosophy

In a nutshell, the expedited procedure will apply to proceedings where the amount in dispute does not exceed US\$2 million[14] or where the parties have agreed upon this particular procedure.[15] Where its application is triggered exclusively by the monetary value of the claims, this determination will be based on the amounts stated in the request for arbitration (Article 4(3)(d)) and respondent's answer (Article 5(5)(b)).[16]

The underlying goal behind the 2017 ICC Expedited Procedure Rules was to predefine a cost-effective procedure with a level of complexity proportional to the value of a dispute. Many readers will be familiar with such a move, as several jurisdictions have already attempted to improve access to justice by passing legislation that introduces simpler and less expensive types of proceedings in civil litigation.[17] And indeed, these reforms were inspired by the so-called principle of proportionality, according to which the procedural means invested in a dispute should be proportional to the value of the dispute itself.[18]

13.3.2   The Powers of the Court of Arbitration under the Expedited Procedure

The constituent elements of ICC's expedited procedure are split between Article 30 of the ICC Rules and the new Appendix VI. For the purposes of

---

[14] Article 30(2)(a), 2017 ICC Rules.

[15] Article 30(2)(b), 2017 ICC Rules.

[16] The latter amount can be affected by a respondent's decision to file a counterclaim. This can entail some difficulties: while a respondent is expected to file any counterclaims with its answer, circumstances may not allow it to do so, and the counterclaim could happen to be filed at a later date. Similarly, difficulties can arise when a claimant merely seeks declaratory relief.

[17] See e.g., for a UK perspective, Rupert Jackson, Review of Civil Litigation Costs – Final Report (London, December 2009), 31 (the principle of proportionality, which was implemented with the Woolf Reforms, is formulated as follows: 'Procedures and cost should be proportionate to the nature of the issues involved').

[18] For a discussion, see Adrian Zuckerman, *On Civil Procedure* (Sweet & Maxwell, 2013), pp. 12–17.

the present discussion, it is worth noting that the Court of Arbitration has the final say on the procedure's application, as it may determine 'upon the request of a party before the constitution of the arbitral tribunal or on its own motion … that it is inappropriate in the circumstances to apply the Expedited Procedure Provisions'.[19] Symmetrically, the Court may, after the tribunal has been constituted, determine that the expedited procedure no longer applies.[20] This latter situation raises a delicate question regarding the fate of the constituted tribunal. In such a case, the general rule will be to preserve the appointed tribunal, unless the ICC Court considers that it is appropriate to replace or reconstitute it.[21]

Another key aspect of the new expedited procedure is the referral to a sole arbitrator, who will either be appointed by the Court of Arbitration or nominated by the parties, depending on the terms of their arbitration clause (and on whether or not the parties were able to agree upon the same individual).[22] Other key features are the absence of terms of reference[23] – which means that new claims will be barred, in principle, after the constitution of the arbitral tribunal, unless the tribunal determines otherwise[24] – and the accelerated schedule for the case management conference, which will take place 'no later than 15 days after the date on which the file was transmitted to the arbitral tribunal'.[25] However, the Court may extend this time limit 'pursuant to a reasoned request from the arbitral tribunal or on its own initiative if it decides it is necessary to do so'. Finally, a shorter time limit applies to the rendering of the award, which is six months from the date of the case management conference. However, the ICC Court maintains a discretionary power allowing it to extend such term.[26]

Although there might be a risk of exaggerating the practical consequences of the new powers granted to the Court of Arbitration – especially given that they were brought about by recent reforms – this chapter will briefly focus on one specific power: the ruling on objections to the applicability of the expedited procedure prior to the constitution of the arbitral tribunal. These are problematic because they not only expand the range of possible decisions

---

[19] Article 30(3)(c), 2017 ICC Rules.
[20] Article 1(4), Appendix VI, 2017 ICC Rules.
[21] Ibid.
[22] Article 2(1) and 2(2), Appendix VI, 2017 ICC Rules.
[23] Article 3(1), Appendix VI, 2017 ICC Rules.
[24] Article 3(2), Appendix VI, 2017 ICC Rules.
[25] Article 3(3), Appendix VI, 2017 ICC Rules.
[26] Article 4, Appendix VI, 2017 ICC Rules.

that the Court of Arbitration can render without providing guidelines regarding the grounds relied on to rule in these instances, but also because they increase certain discretionary powers which may have a bearing on party autonomy. One cause of concern is Article 30(1) of the 2017 ICC Rules, which states that the Expedited Procedure Provisions shall take precedence over any contrary terms of the arbitration agreement. In other words, if an ICC arbitration clause negotiated by parties after the entry into force of the 2017 ICC Rules provides that all disputes must be resolved by a tribunal composed of three arbitrators, then this provision can be disregarded by the Court of Arbitration if the value of the dispute triggers the application of the expedited procedure. The principle is reiterated in Article 2(1) of Appendix VI, which states that '[t]he Court may, notwithstanding any contrary provision of the arbitration agreement, appoint a sole arbitrator'.

Let us imagine that an arbitration agreement contains a reference to a three-member tribunal, and the ICC Court decides that the arbitration should proceed under the Expedited Procedure Rules. What is the consequence of this decision on the award rendered by the sole arbitrator? Could the losing party resist enforcement under the 1958 New York Convention by arguing that the composition of the arbitral authority or the arbitral procedure was not in accordance with the agreement of the parties?[27]

As noted by one authoritative commentator, 'this ground has only infrequently provided the basis for denying recognition to an award'.[28] There have been instances, however, where it proved to be successful.[29] In *AQZ v. ARA*,[30] a 2015 Singapore case, a similar argument was rejected.

---

[27] See Art. V(1)(d) of the Convention on the Recognition and Enforcement of Foreign Arbitral Awards, New York, 10 June 1958, in force 7 June 1959, 330 UNTS 38 (the 'New York Convention'): 'Recognition and enforcement of the award may be refused, at the request of the party against whom it is invoked, only if that party furnishes to the competent authority where the recognition and enforcement is sought, proof that: [...]

    (d) The composition of the arbitral authority or the arbitral procedure was not in accordance with the agreement of the parties, or, failing such agreement, was not in accordance with the law of the country where the arbitration took place.'

[28] Born, International Commercial Arbitration, p. 3572.

[29] US No. 520, *Encyclopaedia Universalis S.A. (Luxembourg) v. Encyclopaedia Britannica, Inc.* (US), United States Court of Appeals, Second Circuit, Docket No. 04-0288-cv, 31 March 2005, (2005) 30 Y.B. Comm. Arb. 1136, p. 1140. See generally: Sigvard Jarvin, 'Irregularity in the Composition of the Arbitral Tribunal and the Procedure' in Emmanuel Gaillard and Domenico Di Pietro (eds.), *Enforcement of Arbitration Agreements and International Arbitral Awards – The New York Convention in Practice* (Cameron May, 2008), p. 729.

[30] [2015] SGHC 49.

The reasoning upheld by the High Court was that Article V(1)(d) of the New York Convention refers to 'the agreement of the parties' and, in institutional arbitration, the content of the parties' agreement is largely determined by the chosen institution's rules.[31] The parties had originally entered into a contract in December 2009 and agreed on a three-member tribunal. The disputes that arose under the contract were eventually arbitrated under the 2010 version of the SIAC Rules, which had introduced a new default expedited procedure for claims under a certain value. Given the amounts of the claims filed in the arbitral proceedings, the case was dealt with by a sole arbitrator under the expedited procedure. The court held that the decision to apply the 2010 version of the rules was sensible, for 'there is a presumption that reference to rules of a particular tribunal in an arbitration clause refers to such rules as are applicable at the date of commencement of arbitration and not at the date of contract, provided that the rules contain mainly procedural provisions'.[32] The fact that the arbitration clause contained a reference to a three-member tribunal, moreover, was held not to be problematic. Similar facts, however, led a Chinese court to annul the award rendered by a sole arbitrator appointed under SIAC's expedited procedure, as the arbitration agreement provided for a three-member tribunal.[33] This meant, according to the court, that the parties' terms had to prevail over SIAC's arbitration rules, which, in any event, granted the President of the institution discretion to accommodate the parties' will to appoint three arbitrators.

This being acknowledged, the question then is to what extent courts can imply terms into an otherwise perfectly clear and exhaustive arbitration agreement. From a civilian perspective, one could raise the principle that implying terms is not permissible unless the contract is lacking in clarity. Moreover, the decision to opt for a sole arbitrator could be seen as a violation of party autonomy when the parties have agreed upon a panel of arbitrators – especially if one considers that the choice of a panel is often motivated by the occasionally (misguided) desire to increase the impartiality and quality of the final award.

These observations underscore the fact that the Court of Arbitration enjoys an important discretionary power within the new expedited procedure mechanism. This decision to allocate such a power to the Court is

---

[31] Charles Jarrosson, 'Le statut juridique de l'arbitrage administré' (2016) 2 Rev Arb 445, 453.

[32] AQZ v. ARA, para. 125.

[33] China No. 15, Noble Resources International Pte. Ltd. v. Shanghai Xintai International Trade Co. Ltd., 11 August 2017 (2017) 42 Y. B. Comm. Arb. 367, 369.

clearly motivated by the pragmatic concern that objections to the applicability of the expedited rules ought to be decided prior to the tribunal's constitution. However, these changes also fundamentally challenge the Court of Arbitration's traditional role as an ancillary entity detached from the resolution of the dispute into question. Most importantly, they challenge the role of party autonomy as a key tool of legitimization.

The general trend extending the powers of the Court of Arbitration – already visible in the 2012 edition of the Rules and the emergency arbitration proceedings – was therefore confirmed in 2017 with the new expedited procedure. This will entail a more important role for this actor going forward, often to the detriment of the capacity of arbitrators themselves. The managerial and more intrusive powers of the Court are likely to place additional limits on the case management powers of arbitral tribunals. These new powers could also limit the will of the parties as set out in their arbitration agreements, fundamentally changing how we understand this type of adjudicatory process.

It must be asked, then, how much room is there for party autonomy in institutional arbitration? This is a fundamental question which might determine the legitimacy of ICC arbitration going forward.

13.4 How to Ensure that Party Autonomy Will Continue Serving as a Legitimization Tool

Generally speaking, it is fairly easy to distinguish between administrative and adjudicative functions within international arbitral institutions. The former are usually understood as a specific type of case management meant to support the functions of the arbitrators, while the latter characterize the fulfillment of the arbitrators' dispute resolution role, as entrusted to them by the parties. Both powers, moreover, do not question the importance of party autonomy in international arbitration – the arbitrators and the institutions operate within the boundaries set by party autonomy and public policy. The issues raised above do not lie in the way in which party autonomy and the administrative powers of the institutions interact, an inevitable occurrence, but rather in the way in which a conflict between them can be brought to the attention of the competent State court.

Some decisions, like costs and arbitrator's fees, clearly do not have a significant impact on the parties' ability to seek justice. But the same cannot be said in instances where a decision disregards the party autonomy. The main issue, in this instance, is the lack of further recourse after such a decision. This is an area that can raise several concerns for the legitimacy of arbitral institutions.

State courts do not control administrative decisions. Their jurisdiction is limited to the arbitral awards rendered by the arbitrators because international instruments such as the New York Convention[34] do not provide for the review of unilaterally qualified administrative decisions rendered by the competent bodies of arbitral institutions. As Gerbay points out, this becomes problematic when the said decisions have a material impact on the outcome of the case or the parties' ability to seek justice.[35] There is now also an asymmetry in the standards imposed on arbitrators because arbitral institutions operate within a framework of *laissez-faire* where, in theory, due process and the protection of party autonomy are not a compulsory requirement.

Perhaps the time has therefore come to re-examine the mechanisms used for reviewing private justice to ensure they can meet the needs of today's users. While the notion of the arbitral award is under increased pressure to expand and include a greater variety of elements (e.g. decisions on arbitral jurisdiction, provisional measures, and emergency orders – to name a few),[36] decisions rendered by arbitral institutions themselves are entirely neglected by applicable international instruments. This brings into focus the limitations of State courts' abilities to supervise international arbitration in an effective and useful manner. Taken to the extreme, this trend could risk damaging the legitimacy of the institution as a whole.

The most obvious way to tackle this problem would be to replace the existing enforcement mechanisms by amending, for example, the New York Convention. To what extent, however, is this a viable solution? The Convention is a victim of its own success – ratified by over 150 countries, the effort required to recreate such a large consensus around a new uniform instrument would be enormous. Let us not forget that one of the main motors of the negotiation and enactment of the Convention was the ICC itself.[37] It is unlikely in the present context, that

---

[34] See Art. I(2) of the New York Convention ('The term "arbitral awards" shall include not only awards made by arbitrators appointed for each case but also those made by permanent arbitral bodies to which the parties have submitted').

[35] Gerbay, *The Function of Arbitral Institutions*, p. 188 ff.

[36] Giacomo Marchisio, *The Notion of Award in International Commercial Arbitration* (Kluwer, 2016), p. 179 ff.

[37] See F. Grisel, E. Jolivet and E. Silva Romero, 'Aux origines de l'arbitrage commercial contemporain: l'émergence de l'arbitrage CCI (1920–1958)' (2016) 2 *Rev Arb* 403, 472 ff.

the ICC – or any other large arbitral institution for that matter – will be interested in modifying a legal framework which provides them with a great deal of autonomy, excluding administrative decisions from review by state courts. Ultimately then, the viability of this strategy will depend in large part on the degree of satisfaction of international arbitration's users going forward.

14

Will an Investment Court Be a Better Fact-Finder?

The Case of Expert Evidence

MATTHEW W. SWINEHART*

Recent efforts to reform investor-State dispute settlement with an 'investment court' – like their many predecessors over the years – aim to enhance the role of institutions and institutional actors in the resolution of investment disputes.[1] The reformers' objective is to enhance the legitimacy of both the decision-makers and the legal interpretation process.[2] But they ignore a third and similarly fundamental aspect of legitimacy, the legitimacy of the fact-finding process.[3] To fill that gap, this chapter begins to answer the question: how would a transition to a more institutionalized

---

* The views expressed here are the author's own and not necessarily the views of the Department of the Treasury or the US government. The author thanks Freya Baetens, David Biggs, Andrea Bjorklund, Christopher Bradley, Susan Franck, Jared Hubbard, Meg Kinnear, Hannes Lenk, William Park, Bruno Simma, and the participants of the October 2017 conference on the Legitimacy of Unseen Actors in International Adjudication in The Hague.

[1] See, e.g., European Commission, 'Investment Provisions in the EU-Canada Free Trade Agreement' (February 2016), at p. 1 (promising a 'more … institutionalised system'). Thomas Walde traced the idea of an appellate mechanism for investor-State disputes back to at least 1991. See David A. Gantz, 'An Appellate Mechanism for Review of Arbitral Decision in Investor-State Disputes: Prospects and Challenges' (2006) 39 *Vanderbilt Journal of Transnational Law* 39, 40; J.E. Alvarez, 'To Court or Not to Court?' (2017), www.iilj .org/working-papers/to-court-or-not-to-court/ (describing the general scope of the debate regarding investor-State arbitration reforms).

[2] See, e.g., European Commission, 'Investment in TTIP and Beyond – The Path for Reform Enhancing the Right to Regulate and Moving from Current Ad Hoc Arbitration Towards an Investment Court' (5 May 2015), pp. 6–9.

[3] See José E. Alvarez, 'What Are International Judges For? The Main Functions of International Adjudication,' in C.P.R. Romano, K.J. Alter and Y. Shany (eds.), *The Oxford Handbook of International Adjudication* (Oxford University Press, 2014), p. 166 ('Finding facts is as essential as identifying the law.'); see also Scott Brewer, 'Scientific Expert Testimony and Intellectual Due Process' (1997) 107 *Yale Law Journal* 1535, 1672 ('[E]pistemic nonarbitrariness in the process of "finding" scientifically discerned facts is a necessary condition of the practical legitimacy of a decision that relies on that factfinding.').

investment court system affect fact-finding quality? As an initial step, the focus here is on the case of expert evidence, a critically influential source of facts in modern international dispute settlement, and one that depends in large part on often unseen actors, including expert witnesses and other specialized advisors, as well as on unseen actions of institutions and institutional actors.[4]

This chapter looks to three arguments that could support a view that enhancing the influence of institutions and institutional actors over fact-finding improves quality. In the end none of these arguments is persuasive. If proponents of investment dispute reform are serious about enhancing legitimacy, then they should look to other reforms, rather than elements of an investment court, to improve fact-finding quality.

14.1   Identifying 'Better' Fact-Finders: The Objective of Quality

The EU is at the forefront of the investment court movement, having concluded in recent years a number of agreements contemplating investment court mechanisms.[5] One example is the Comprehensive Economic and Trade Agreement (CETA) with Canada. Under that agreement, the parties are to establish a standing first-instance tribunal and a standing appellate tribunal authorized to review awards for errors of law and manifest errors of fact.[6] Each tribunal is to be composed of 'members' who will hear disputes as part of randomly selected 'divisions' of three. The EU and Canada will select fifteen members for the first instance tribunal, each with five- or six-year terms, renewable once. CETA does not establish the number or tenure of appellate tribunal members, nor does it establish an

---

[4] See, e.g., Matthew W. Swinehart, 'Reliability of Expert Evidence in International Disputes' (2017) 38 *Michigan Journal of International Law* 287, 290–302 (tracing the history of expert evidence in international disputes from 1794 to 2016); Kate Miles, 'Climate Change: Trading, Investing and the Interaction of Law, Science and Technology', in B. Mercurio and Kuei-Jung Ni (eds.), *Science and Technology in International Economic Law: Balancing Competing Interests* (Routledge, 2014), p. 155; C.E. Foster, *Science and the Precautionary Principle in International Courts and Tribunals: Expert Evidence, Burden of Proof and Finality* (Cambridge University Press, 2011), p. 77.

[5] These include agreements with Canada, Mexico, Singapore, and Vietnam. See, e.g., European Commission, 'Key Features of the EU-Mexico Trade Agreement,' http://trade.ec .europa.eu/doclib/press/index.cfm?id=1831.

[6] See, e.g., Comprehensive Economic and Trade Agreement (CETA), 30 October 2016, provisionally in force 21 September 2017, Arts. 8.27 ('Constitution of the Tribunal') and 8.28 ('Appellate Tribunal').

administrative apparatus for the appellate tribunal mechanism, leaving open for future decision the details of administration.[7] The CETA Joint Committee, composed of representatives of the two parties, is to 'adopt a decision' on 'administrative and organizational matters regarding the functioning of the Appellate Tribunal,' including 'administrative support,' 'procedures for the initiation and conduct of appeals,' and 'any other elements it determines to be necessary for the effective functioning of the Appellate Tribunal.'[8]

Both parties have cast these reform efforts, in part, as an attempt to expand the influence that institutions and institutional actors exercise over dispute resolution,[9] with an overarching objective to enhance 'legitimacy'[10] and provide 'fair and transparent dispute settlement,' 'while ensuring a high level of protection for investments,' and preserving 'the right of governments to regulate in the public interest.'[11] This emphasis on fairness, legitimacy, and transparency echoes the consensus view that the primary function of an international dispute settlement system is to provide information about the facts and the law (and in the cases of international commercial and investment arbitration, to render an enforceable monetary award), and to do so in an unbiased manner.[12] An element that

---

[7] See CETA, Art. 8.28.

[8] CETA, Art. 8.28(7).

[9] See, e.g., Global Affairs Canada, 'Chapter Summaries,' www.international.gc.ca/trade-commerce/trade-agreements-accords-commerciaux/agr-acc/ceta-aecg/chapter_summary-resume_chapitre.aspx?lang=eng#a8; European Commission, Investment Provisions in the EU-Canada Free Trade Agreement (CETA) (February 2016), p. 1.

[10] See, e.g., European Commission, 'Investment Provisions in the EU-Canada Free Trade Agreement' (highlighting a concern for 'fairness'); European Commission, 'Investment in TTIP and Beyond' (highlighting a concern for 'legitimacy').

[11] See Joint Interpretative Instrument on the Comprehensive Economic and Trade Agreement (CETA) Between Canada and the European Union and its Member States (27 October 2016), para. 6(a).

[12] Scholars who hold this view have largely focused on state-to-state dispute settlement. See, e.g., Andrew T. Guzman, 'International Tribunals: A Rational Choice Analysis' (2008) 157 *University of Pennsylvania Law Review* 171, 187 (noting consensus); Eric A. Posner and John C. Yoo, 'Judicial Independence in International Tribunals' (2005) 93 *California Law Review* 1, 17; Laurence R. Helfer and Anne-Marie Slaughter, 'Why States Create International Tribunals: A Response to Posner and Yoo' (2005) 93 *California Law Review* 899, 931–936. The information function observed in state-to-state disputes may of course coexist with additional functions in other systems, such as the function of compensation commissions or investment tribunals to provide compensation or other monetary award to injured parties. See David D. Caron, 'International Claims and Compensation Bodies,' in Romano et al., *The Oxford Handbook on International Adjudication*, p. 281; Gary Born, 'A New Generation of International Adjudication' (2012) 61 *Duke Law Journal* 776, 779. And remedies that allow for monetary damages and trade retaliation arguably do not

increases fairness, legitimacy, and transparency – and the perception of adjudicator-provided information as accurate and reliable – will increase the quality of a system's decisions and the information they provide.[13] The ability to produce 'higher quality decisions … that are more likely to reach accurate conclusions with respect to the facts and the law', then, is a key component of what makes a decision-maker 'better'.[14]

But because users of a dispute settlement system may value finality and efficiency in addition to quality,[15] system designers (and disputing parties that are able to select among systems for the adjudication of particular disputes) must 'carefully weigh the benefits and costs' of elements that are intended to increase quality.[16] At least some designers of dispute settlement systems will take both quality and efficiency into account. From their perspective, then, a 'better' decision-maker is one that contributes toward achieving an optimal balance between quality and efficiency.[17] A better fact-finder, in turn, is more likely to achieve that balance when it comes to the production and evaluation of evidence.

14.2   Possible Effects of CETA's Investment Court on Fact-Finding Quality

Although the EU and Canada have not specifically marketed CETA's investment court as a means of improving the quality of fact-finding, commentators have over the years put forward a variety of arguments as to why enhancing the influence that institutions and institutional actors exercise over decision-making could have positive effects on a system's production and evaluation of evidence. The most prevalent argument

---

change the incentives to comply with international decisions. See W. Mark C. Weidemaier, 'Toward a Theory of Precedent in Arbitration' (2010) 51 *William and Mary Law Review* 1895, 1913.

[13] See Guzman, 'International Tribunals: A Rational Choice Analysis', 205, 207.

[14] See Susan D. Franck, A. van Aaken, J. Freda, C. Guthrie and J.L. Rachlinski, 'Inside the Arbitrator's Mind' (2017) 66 *Emory Law Journal* 1115, 1128 (arguing that 'integrity and quality' is 'central to arbitration's legitimacy as a form of dispute settlement' and noting that uncertainty about that quality has 'created apprehension and debate' in the public discourse).

[15] See David D. Caron, 'Reputation and Reality in the ICSID Annulment Process: Understanding the Distinction between Annulment and Appeal' (1992) 7 *ICSID Foreign Investment Law Journal* 21, 49.

[16] See Franck et al., 'Inside the Arbitrator's Mind', 1171.

[17] See William W. Park, 'Arbitrators and Accuracy' (2010) 1 *Journal of International Dispute Settlement* 25, 27.

is that institutionalization of dispute settlement improves fact-finding quality by increasing the independence of the adjudicators from disputing parties. Another argument focuses on the apparent ability of court systems, especially those with appellate review, to enhance the consistency and predictability of fact-finding. And a third argument conceives of standing courts as institutions capable of increasing the specialized expertise of its decision-makers in the course of adjudicating disputes over time.

The following analysis begins to do the work necessary to examine questions of legitimacy in the context of fact-finding at an investment court.[18] The analysis concludes that an investment court is likely to have marginal effects on fact-finding quality, possibly negative on net, while increasing the cost and length of dispute resolution.

14.2.1 Will an Investment Court Improve Fact-Finding Quality by Increasing Independence in the Consideration of Expert Evidence?

By far the most common argument made in support of enhancing the influence of institutions and institutional actors over dispute settlement is that it will increase adjudicator independence from the parties to a dispute and as a result positively influence the quality and efficacy of a decision-maker.[19] The EU and Canada have themselves emphasized that establishing an investment court will enhance decision-maker independence.[20] According to this argument, independence frees decision-makers to decide cases based on their own views of the facts and the law, rather than the views of the disputing parties (or the States that have established the court or institution).[21]

---

[18] Others are beginning to note the lack of evidence that an investment court will have positive effects on decision-making, including when it comes to fact-finding. As José Alvarez has argued, '[i]nternational courts, including the European ones that presumably the EU has in mind as models, have not always issued the well-reasoned decisions that rule of law proponents want nor engaged in the credible fact-finding that is crucial to many [investor-state dispute settlement] disputes.' Alvarez, 'To Court or Not to Court.'

[19] See, e.g., Elizabeth Warren, 'The Trans-Pacific Partnership Clause Everyone Should Oppose,' *Washington Post* (25 February 2015) (arguing that there is a lack of arbitrator independence in investment arbitration).

[20] See, e.g., Joint Interpretative Instrument on CETA, para. 6.

[21] See, e.g., Guzman, 'International Tribunals: A Rational Choice Analysis,' 208–213; Helfer and Slaughter, 'Why States Create International Tribunals,' 901–909; Benedict Kingsbury, 'Neo-Madisonian Global Constitutionalism: Thomas M. Franck's Democratic

The issue of independence and whether it increases decision-making quality is a matter of extensive debate, and others have put forward a variety of metrics for assessing independence. In one analysis of state-to-state disputes, Eric Posner and John Yoo identified five core attributes of independence, roughly defined as: (1) the possibility that a State could be bound to a ruling without its consent in a particular dispute; (2) the possibility that no national of the State parties is on the panel that hears the dispute; (3) the ability of third parties to participate in the proceeding; (4) a permanent body of judges; and (5) judicial tenure that extends beyond a given dispute.[22] Other commentators, including Andrew Guzman, have argued that additional factors, such as an adequately funded administrative apparatus[23] and non-renewable judicial terms[24] may also increase a tribunal's independence.

According to these metrics, the ICJ, ITLOS, and the WTO are relatively independent; traditional commercial and investment arbitration and ad hoc State-to-State arbitration are relatively dependent; and the Iran-US Claims Tribunal is somewhere in between. As for CETA, it would introduce at least two new independence-granting elements – a standing body of judges and judicial terms that extend beyond a given dispute – to existing investment arbitration mechanisms (as well as a third – an administrative apparatus – as compared to ad hoc investment arbitration). This means that CETA scores higher than existing investment arbitration systems on these measures of independence, in line or even slightly above the WTO, ICJ, and ITLOS.

14.2.1.1   The Influence of Independence on Fact-Finding Sources and Methods

Proponents of decision-maker independence point to a number of positive effects on fact-finding quality. Independence, they say, allows an adjudicator to 'play an active role in the collection of factual evidence,'[25] conduct evidence gathering and evaluation 'without reliance on the parties,'[26]

Cosmopolitan Prospectus for Managing Diversity and World Order in the Twenty-First Century' (2003) 35 *New York University Journal of International Law and Policy* 291, 296.
[22] See Posner and Yoo, 'Judicial Independence in International Tribunals,' 52.
[23] Guzman, 'International Tribunals: A Rational Choice Analysis,' 207–209.
[24] See Jeffrey L. Dunoff and Mark A. Pollack, 'The Judicial Trilemma' (2017) 111 *American Journal of International Law* 225, 259.
[25] G.M. White, *The Use of Experts by International Tribunals* (Syracuse University Press, 1965), p. 4.
[26] See, e.g., Guzman, 'International Tribunals: A Rational Choice Analysis,' 208–209 and note 114.

'accept views beyond those of the litigants,'[27] and ultimately 'discover the truth independently of the information and evidence brought by the parties.'[28] These are at base arguments that independence influences, for the better, a decision-maker's choice of sources and methods in fact-finding. According to these arguments, independent decision-makers are, in a word, more "self-reliant" in the production and evaluation of evidence.

According to these proponents, relatively dependent decision-makers, by contrast, are reluctant to appear uninterested in the presentations of the disputing parties, which, in the case of expert evidence, usually involves testimony from party-appointed experts. When parties present testimony of experts they have engaged, the adjudicators must referee a 'battle of the experts' and choose between a set of competing views and outcomes.[29] The system employs the adversarial process – including the ability of counsel to cross-examine experts of the other party – as the primary means to explore and challenge the reliability of expert evidence.[30]

It does appear that the practices of international courts and tribunals roughly sort according to their relative independence, with more independent systems tending toward self-reliance in evidence gathering and evaluation. In relatively dependent systems, such as investment and commercial arbitration, as well as at the Iran-US Claims Tribunal, parties are primarily responsible for supplying expert evidence, especially through party-appointed experts.[31] In relatively independent systems, by contrast, adjudicators are known for relying on other sources of expert evidence. Observers and even members of the ICJ have repeatedly noted the Court's reluctance to engage with party-produced expert evidence of any sort[32] or to appoint expert assistance of its own in a manner that affords the disputing parties an opportunity to test any evidence that is produced.[33] The ICJ is known instead for a tendency to rely on documentary evidence rather than oral testimony[34] and for 'attaching considerable

[27] See Alvarez, 'The Main Functions of International Adjudication,' pp. 165–166.
[28] White, *The Use of Experts by International Tribunals*, p. 4.
[29] See Swinehart, 'Reliability of Expert Evidence in International Disputes,' 303–304.
[30] See ibid.
[31] See Born, 'A New Generation of International Adjudication,' 874–875; C.N. Brower and J.D. Brueschke, *The Iran-United States Claims Tribunal* (Springer International, 1998), pp. 199–200, 202.
[32] *Pulp Mills on the River Uruguay (Argentina v. Uruguay)*, ICJ Reports (2010) 108 (Al-Khasawneh, A. and Simma, B., dissenting), paras. 3–13.
[33] Anna Riddell, 'Evidence, Fact-Finding, and Experts,' in Romano et al., The Oxford Handbook on International Adjudication, p. 849 at p. 857.
[34] J.R. Crook, 'Fact-Finding in the Fog: Determining the Facts of Upheaval and Wars in Inter-State Disputes,' in C.A. Rogers and R.P. Alford (eds.), *The Future of Investment Arbitration* (Oxford University Press, 2009), pp. 315–320.

probative value to reports compiled and communicated by [United Nations] agencies' and other international organizations,[35] including the World Health Organization.[36] There is also evidence that systems with a standing judicial body and an administrative apparatus rely on input from an institution's own in-house team of administrative or research staff, or informal input from third-party experts. The ICJ is perhaps the most well-known example of an institution whose adjudicators apparently engage in this practice,[37] but ITLOS also appears to rely routinely on these 'unseen experts,'[38] although it has also relied on tribunal-appointed expert witnesses who formally participate in the proceedings.[39] The input of unseen experts is generally not included within the formal evidentiary record of the dispute settlement proceeding nor subject to testing or comment by the parties.[40]

When it comes to independence in fact-finding, the WTO is a special case. Although highly independent overall, the WTO is more dependent at the panel stage because, unlike the WTO Appellate Body, panels are not standing bodies and do not have adjudicators with terms beyond a single dispute. Empirical studies have observed that this may mean that the parties to a dispute exercise significant control over the appointment of panelists.[41] This relative dependence at the panel stage, embedded

[35] Anna Riddell and Brendan Plant, *Evidence Before the International Court of Justice* (British Institute of International and Comparative Law, 2009), p. 237.

[36] See, e.g., *Legality of the Use by a State of Nuclear Weapons in Armed Conflict* (Advisory Opinion), ICJ Reports (1996) 66, p. 78.

[37] See Giorgio Gaja, 'Assessing Expert Evidence in the ICJ' (2017) 15 *The Law and Practice of International Courts and Tribunals* 409, 413 ('The Court has often attempted to acquire scientific or technical knowledge by informally consulting experts.'); *Pulp Mills* (Dissent), para. 14; Durward V. Sandifer, *Evidence Before International Tribunals* (University Press of Virginia, 1975), pp. 162–163 (noting in 1975 that the Court's registrar participated in the production of evidence only 'to a very limited extent').

[38] G.Y.J. Gros, 'Unseen Actors as Unseen Experts: Ghosts in International Adjudication,' Chapter 18 of the present book.

[39] See, e.g., *Case Concerning Land Reclamation by Singapore in and Around the Straits of Johor (Malaysia v. Singapore)*, Provisional Measures, Case No 12, Order of 8 October 2003, p. 27.

[40] Gaja, 'Assessing Expert Evidence in the ICJ,' 413.

[41] See generally Ryan Brutger and Julia C. Morse, 'Balancing Law and Politics: Judicial Incentives in WTO Dispute Settlement,' (2015) 10 *The Review of International Organizations* 179; see also Born, 'A New Generation of International Adjudication,' 872–873 (classifying WTO panels as relatively dependent because parties exercise significant control over panel appointments). But see Joost Pauwelyn, 'The Rule of Law Without the Rule of Lawyers: Why Investment Arbitrators are from Mars, Trade Adjudicators from Venus,' (2015) 109 *The American Journal of International Law* 761, 784–787 (arguing that WTO panels are 'more "neutrally" appointed' than ICSID arbitrators).

within the context of a larger, highly independent institution, could provide some explanation of the WTO's hybrid approach to fact-finding.

Commentators have observed that the WTO, unlike the ICJ, has traditionally engaged in substantial fact-finding, relying heavily on party-presented evidence.[42] For instance, despite a lack of procedural rules that provide for the examination of witnesses at panel hearings, parties to a WTO dispute (and third-party participants) often present specialized evidence through members of their delegations, including lawyers, economists, and scientists.[43] These delegates function as party-appointed experts in some ways, although they are not subject to cross-examination by other parties.[44] At the same time, the WTO – much like the relatively independent ICJ and ITLOS – is also known for consulting with staff of the WTO Secretariat who possess specialized knowledge and training, without the input of the disputing parties.[45] The Secretariat's Economic Research and Statistics Division, for example, routinely provides support to panels on economic questions.[46]

Taking these examples together with the caveat of the WTO as a special case, it appears, then, that independence of decision-makers is a predictor of self-reliance. This can produce some positive effects on fact-finding quality to a degree if self-reliance means that an adjudicator's focus is on the facts of the case rather than the preferred outcomes of the disputing parties and the potential implications of those preferences on the adjudicator.[47] An adjudicator's active participation can provide structure to the fact-finding process and streamline the production of evidence.[48] Without guidance from the adjudicator, the parties may produce significant amounts of irrelevant information, for example, leading to an inefficient fact-finding process.[49] And a degree of active participation and substantive engagement with specialized evidence is necessary given the

[42] See, e.g., Born, 'A New Generation of International Adjudication,' 874–875.
[43] See Swinehart, 'Reliability of Expert Evidence in International Disputes,' 298–299.
[44] See Joost Pauwelyn, 'Expert Advice in WTO Dispute Settlement,' in G.A. Bermann and P.C. Mavroidis (eds.), *Trade and Human Health and Safety* (Cambridge University Press, 2006), p. 235.
[45] Gros, 'Unseen Actors as Unseen Experts,' Chapter 18 of the present book.
[46] See C.P. Bown, 'The WTO Secretariat and the Role of Economics in DSU Panels and Arbitrations,' https://ssrn.com/abstract=1274732, p. 36.
[47] See Guzman, 'International Tribunals: A Rational Choice Analysis,' 209.
[48] M.T. Grando, *Evidence, Proof, and Fact-Finding in WTO Dispute Settlement* (Oxford University Press, 2009), pp. 306–307.
[49] Ibid.

challenges associated with party-presentation of evidence[50] and the complexity of the questions presented.[51] When it comes to party-appointed expert witnesses, for example, the experts take oaths to present evidence in an independent and impartial manner and are bound to uphold the ethical standards of their fields, but the parties remain able to select experts who they know will provide testimony that generally supports their positions.[52]

Self-reliance also presents a number of potential concerns, particularly when it may decrease opportunities for meaningful evaluation of party-presented evidence or party participation in the evaluation of other evidence.[53] Independent and self-reliant decision-makers are more likely to pursue their own objectives – such as the achievement of particular public policies, attendance to the interests of non-disputing States or interest groups, or the enhancement of the dispute settlement system's authority and prestige[54] – to the detriment of fact-finding quality. Dependent decision-makers at the same time, with a focus on the adversarial process and the fact presentations of the parties, are thought to engage in more 'substantial fact-finding, including … the evaluation of expert evidence.'[55] A lack of self-reliance, then, may have positive effects on the quality of fact-finding, especially when a comprehensive evidentiary record is necessary to answer difficult questions.[56]

It is also true that, although an adjudicator's appointment of its own expert may avoid a battle between competing party-appointed experts, that appointment process usually involves a debate between the parties that is just as contentious and fraught.[57] An adjudicator's appointment of an expert witness also heightens concerns of outsourcing decision-making

[50] *See* ibid., p. 16.
[51] Sergey Ripinsky and Kevin Williams, *Damages in International Investment Law* (British Institute of International and Comparative Law, 2008), pp. 190–191.
[52] Swinehart, 'Reliability of Expert Evidence in International Disputes,' 304–306.
[53] See Grando, *Evidence, Proof, and Fact-Finding in WTO Dispute Settlement*, pp. 307–308.
[54] See, e.g., Lawrence Baum, 'What Judges Want: Judges' Goals and Judicial Behavior,' (1994) 47 *Political Research Quarterly* 749, 752.
[55] Born, 'A New Generation of International Adjudication,' 873–876; see also Rosalyn Higgins, 'The Desirability of Third-Party Adjudication: Conventional Wisdom or Continuing Truth,' in J.E.S. Fawcett and R. Higgins (eds.), *International Organizations: Law in Movement* (Oxford University Press, 1974), pp. 42–46.
[56] See S.S. Diamond, 'Psychological Aspects of Dispute Resolution: Issues for International Arbitration,' in A.J. van den Berg (ed.), *International Commercial Arbitration: Important Contemporary Questions* (Kluwer Law International, 2003), pp. 340–341; see also Grando, *Evidence, Proof, and Fact-Finding in WTO Dispute Settlement*, p. 15.
[57] I. Marboe, *Calculation of Compensation and Damages in International Investment Law* (Oxford University Press, 2009), p. 182.

authority to the expert,[58] while a tendency of self-reliant decision-makers to seek out and rely on the views of international organizations may present a similar dynamic.[59]

There are perils, too, when a system relies too much on an adjudicator's own research into complex subjects or relies on specialized input from institutional staff. Because few if any lawyers are equipped to assess and weigh complex scientific, economic, or other technical evidence,[60] they are likely to make errors when they attempt to do their own research.[61] Self-study and reliance on unseen experts may also diminish or prevent any opportunity for the parties to subject expert evidence to critical and transparent assessment, raising a concern that the adjudicator has relied on 'intuition or supposition.'[62] Party participation facilitates the development and exchange of information,[63] and even proponents of independent courts have argued that such participation is critical to ensuring quality in fact-finding.[64] Institutions such as the ICJ that have relied on the work of staff generally do not make that work available to the parties or the public, and do not disclose in their decisions if or how they relied on that work, affording no opportunity for the parties to participate in the selection of 'experts,' challenge their conclusions, or introduce rebuttal evidence.[65]

14.2.1.2   Other Influences on Fact-Finding Sources and Methods

This analysis suggests that elements that enhance the institutional nature of dispute settlement and as a result increase independence may have subtle effects – some positive, others negative – on an adjudicator's

---

[58] Riddell, 'Evidence, Fact-Finding, and Experts,' p. 857.

[59] See generally Nancy Morawetz, 'Convenient Facts: Nken v. Holder, the Solicitor General, and the Presentation of Internal Government Facts' (2013) 88 *New York University Law Review* 1600 (observing a 'special standing" in the US Supreme Court for the solicitor general's office and other government actors).

[60] *Pulp Mills*, Dissent, para. 4.

[61] See Ryan Gabrielson, 'It's a Fact: Supreme Court Errors Aren't Hard to Find,' *ProPublica* (17 October 2017) (arguing that, in *Maryland v. King*, 133 S. Ct. 1958 (US Supreme Court, 2013) Justice Anthony Kennedy 'inaccurately defin[ed] scientific terms' and 'overstated the reliability of DNA analysis' after his own review of a textbook and that, in *Shelby County v. Holder*, 133 S. Ct. 2612 (US Supreme Court, 2013), Chief Justice John Roberts included a table of inaccurate voting registration data in his majority opinion).

[62] See Franck et al., 'Inside the Arbitrator's Mind,' 1171.

[63] Grando, *Evidence, Proof, and Fact-Finding in WTO Dispute Settlement*, p. 14.

[64] See Laurence R. Helfer and Anne-Marie Slaughter, 'Toward a Theory of Effective Supranational Adjudication' (1997) 107 *Yale Law Journal* 273, 304 and note 122.

[65] Gros, 'Unseen Actors as Unseen Experts,' Chapter 18 of the present book.

method of fact-finding. At the same time, CETA will carry forward many traditional dispute settlement practices that will continue to exert their own influence over the methods – and quality – of fact-finding. One practice that will continue largely unchanged under CETA is reliance on a basic framework of procedural and evidentiary rules. Although the founding documents of nearly all systems vest adjudicators with broad authority to control the production of evidence and to evaluate it in any way they see fit, evidentiary rules impose some meaningful constraints on fact-finding. Those rules establish an array of fundamental parameters, including time periods for decision, allowances for party and third-party submissions, grounds for early dismissal, available means of evidence gathering and presentation, and requirements for the content of awards.[66]

The feature of primary significance to this chapter's analysis is that the rules of most systems – including those of CETA – contemplate witness testimony and cross-examination at hearings, and that those systems in fact follow those rules and provide opportunities for oral testimony.[67] The WTO is a notable exception, with rules that provide for highly structured fact-finding, including procedures similar in some respects to civil law practices that channel factual development primarily through party-submission of written evidence, rather than oral testimony. As a result, the practical function of oral hearings in the WTO is 'mainly to provide an opportunity to clarify issues and focus the discussion on the questions which the panel believes are the most important.'[68] Both in the WTO and elsewhere, then, it is the influence of evidentiary and procedural rules, and not the institutional character of a decision-maker, that is the predictor of whether oral testimony is available.

WTO rules specific to expert evidence also seem to influence panel fact-finding methods. Although WTO panels are known for appointing experts more often than other decision-makers,[69] the WTO has appointed experts in only a small minority of cases, and usually in cases involving scientific issues under the Sanitary and Phytosanitary Measures (SPS)

[66] See G.B. Born, *International Commercial Arbitration: Commentary and Materials*, 2nd ed. (Wolters Kluwer, 2001), pp.1–2.

[67] See Born, 'A New Generation of International Adjudication,' 874–875; CETA, Art. 8.23 (providing for submission of claims under rules that contemplate oral testimony at a hearing).

[68] Grando, *Evidence, Proof, and Fact-Finding in WTO Dispute Settlement*, pp. 246–247.

[69] Ibid., pp. 298–299.

Agreement,[70] which by its own terms expresses a preference for consultation with panel-appointed experts.[71] The use of these experts, then, may again reflect the influence of evidentiary and procedural rules rather than the effects of an enhanced role for institutions and institutional actors.

Organic factors – not embodied in a system's design as expressed in treaty or rule – may also influence the production and evaluation of expert evidence. Dispute settlement systems operate against a background of accepted procedural and evidentiary norms that reflect the accumulated expectations of state and non-state participants in international dispute settlement, such as those embodied in general principles of international law or based on influences from civil law and common law traditions. These norms reinforce the flexibility of adjudicators that is established in most procedural rules. The pull of norms that privilege flexibility over other priorities may provide an alternative or additional explanation for evidentiary practices such as the WTO's practice to hear expert testimony in the form of party delegates, despite the lack of an express authorization permitting party-appointed experts in WTO rules.[72] It may also explain why adjudicators in systems without detailed evidentiary rules have nonetheless appointed their own experts.[73]

Lastly, evidentiary and procedural rules may produce their own independence-enhancing effects that compete with the influences of institutional character. Some rules grant adjudicators specific authorities in fact-finding or set out specific expectations for an adjudicator's fact-finding methods, including relatively common provisions that specify that an adjudicator may consider particular sources of evidence.[74]

---

[70] See Gros, 'Unseen Actors as Unseen Experts,' Chapter 18 of the present book (counting 15 panels that appointed experts out of 225 adopted panel reports, 'almost exclusively in SPS cases').

[71] Agreement on the Application of Sanitary and Phytosanitary Measures, 33 ILM 15 (1994), Art. 11.2 ('In a dispute under this Agreement involving scientific or technical issues, a panel should seek advice from experts chosen by the panel.').

[72] Pauwelyn, 'Expert Advice in WTO Dispute Settlement,' p. 235.

[73] See, e.g., *Guyana v. Suriname*, Award, PCA Case Repository 2004-04 (2007), para. 47 (noting that the tribunal had appointed its own expert, although the pre-existing rules of procedure under Annex VII of the United Nations Convention on the Law of the Sea state only that a tribunal may follow its own rules of procedure).

[74] See, e.g., *Philip Morris v. Uruguay*, Request to File a Written Submission (Amicus Curiae Brief) by the World Health Organization and the WHO Framework Convention on Tobacco Control Secretariat (28 January 2015), para. 1 (citing Article 37 of the ICSID Arbitration Rules, which expressly vests a tribunal with the authority to accept and consider non-disputing party submissions).

These rules both allow designers of systems to constrain adjudicators in advance[75] and grant adjudicators additional independence from the disputing parties' attempts to use their own preferred procedures.[76]

In sum, the new independence-granting elements of CETA will at best have only subtle effects on fact-finding quality while competing with other, potentially more significant influences.

14.2.2   Will an Investment Court Improve Fact-Finding Quality by Increasing Consistency and Predictability?

A second possible argument to be made about the benefits of enhancing the role of institutions and institutional actors is that the approach will, primarily through the introduction of substantive appellate review, enhance the consistency and predictability of fact-finding.[77] This is a corollary to broader arguments made in support of the increased institutionalization of investment disputes. The EU and Canada intend CETA's appellate tribunal, for example, to correct legal errors and instill greater 'consistency' in case law.[78] The corollary examined here seeks to apply this same logic to fact-finding.

14.2.2.1   Consistency and Predictability in Legal Interpretation

To understand how investment court elements might affect the consistency and predictability of fact-finding, it is important to first review theories of consistency in the interpretation of legal rules. Consistency and predictability in legal interpretation is a function of three basic elements: the degree to which rules are incorporated into legal texts, the ability of a system to interpret those rules in a manner that future

---

[75] See Helfer and Slaughter, 'Why States Create International Tribunals,' 994–996.

[76] See Paulsson, Introduction, 3.

[77] See, e.g., Riddell, 'Evidence, Fact-Finding, and Experts,' pp. 849–850.

[78] Joint Interpretative Instrument, para. 6(g). Other proposals for appellate review in investment arbitration also center on objectives related to consistency and predictability of legal interpretation. See, e.g., Irene J. Ten Cate, 'International Arbitration and the Ends of Appellate Review' (2012) 44 *New York University Journal of International Law and Policy* 1109, 1111–1112. This chapter does not address whether the existing system in fact lacks consistency or predictability to any material degree. See J.E. Alvarez, 'Implications for the Future of International Investment Law,' in K.P. Sauvant (ed.), *Appeals Mechanism in International Investment Disputes* (Oxford University Press, 2008), p. 33 ('Creating a supertribunal of investment judges may be a solution in search of a problem – if the lack of consistent results proves not as serious in reality as in prediction.').

decision-makers will follow, and the availability and scope of an appellate review mechanism to reconcile competing interpretations.

The first element – the existence of written rules – is a feature of all international dispute settlement systems in that they all adjudicate disputes arising out of legal texts that set out, with varying degrees of specificity, substantive legal obligations.[79] A legal text serves as a fixed reference point for decision-makers, who must justify their interpretations of the plain text, ensuring some degree of consistency and predictability.[80] The more specific the legal text, the more difficult it becomes to justify deviations from prior interpretations.[81]

The second element of consistency and predictability – rule formation – is theoretically present in only a subset of dispute settlement systems. All courts and tribunals, domestic and international, serve at least one of two essential dispute resolution functions – the job of determining whether a party to a particular dispute has violated a legal rule.[82] But not all systems serve a second function, the creation of rules in the course of one dispute that indicate the likely outcome of similar disputes in the future.[83] It is this second dispute resolution function, rule formulation, that is a driver of consistency and predictability.[84] Rule formulation in common law jurisdictions occurs through a system of precedent, which binds judges to rules set out in previous decisions.[85] Civil law systems technically lack binding precedent but serve this function to a degree because they generally attribute precedential authority to a line of consistent precedents that has crystalized over time.[86]

International law mechanisms do not, classically speaking at least, participate in rule formation because their decisional law is not considered precedential.[87] Nothing in the CETA text indicates that its investment

---

[79] See Helfer and Slaughter, 'Why States Create International Tribunals,' 945–946.

[80] Ibid.

[81] Ibid.

[82] See William M. Landes and Richard A. Posner, 'Adjudication as a Private Good' (1979) 8 *Journal of Legal Studies* 235, 236.

[83] Ibid.

[84] See Park, 'Arbitrators and Accuracy,' 49 n. 122; Landes and Posner, 'Adjudication as a Private Good,' 236.

[85] Landes and Posner, 'Adjudication as a Private Good,' 236.

[86] See generally Vincy Fon and Francesco Parisi, 'Judicial Precedents in Civil Law Systems: A Dynamic Analysis' (2006) 26 *International Review of Law and Economics* 519.

[87] See Park, 'Arbitrators and Accuracy,' 49.

court system will deviate from this usual approach and formally treat first instance or appellate decisions as binding precedent for purposes of future disputes. CETA instead provides only that tribunals must interpret its provisions 'in accordance with the Vienna Convention on the Law of Treaties.'[88]

And yet, to achieve CETA's objective of consistency and predictability in legal interpretation, the appellate tribunal would need to follow its own decisional law and in some form 'bind' first instance tribunals, and first instance tribunals might also need to consider their own decisions (that are not appealed) as binding in some way, too.[89] Of course it is widely understood that, even without express rules establishing a system of precedent, a de facto system of 'soft' precedent can take hold, as observed in many current systems.[90] That phenomenon may lead to informal adherence to previously settled doctrine within a single system[91] or informal recourse to persuasive authority of other systems in a manner that promotes interpretive consistency.[92] Perhaps it is this informal soft law system that the EU and Canada silently intend as the mechanism for rule formation in CETA's dispute settlement system.

In systems where decisional law has either formal or informal precedential authority, the third element of consistency and predictability – substantive appellate review – may further deepen rule formation through the substantive evaluation of the legal, and to a more limited degree factual, correctness of the original decision, direct modification of any errors, and the ability to reconcile competing

---

[88] CETA, Art. 8.38(1).

[89] The WTO Appellate Body is viewed by some as exercising its interpretive function, see World Trade Organization, Dispute Settlement Understanding, Art. 3.2, so that the WTO has developed into a hierarchical system in which Appellate Body reports are in some senses precedent that panels follow. See Stephen S. Kho, Alan Yanovich, Brendan Casey, and Johann Strauss, 'The EU TTIP Investment Court Proposal and the WTO Dispute Settlement System: Comparing Apples and Oranges?' (2017) 32 *ICSID Review* 326, 330.

[90] See Harlan Grant Cohen, 'Lawyers and Precedent,' (2013) 45 *Vanderbilt Journal of Transnational Law* 1025, 1027–1028 (noting precedent's 'apparent authority' in international investment arbitration, international trade, international criminal law, and international human rights).

[91] See, e.g., Michael Wood, 'Choosing between Arbitration and a Permanent Court: Lessons from Inter-State Cases' (2017) 32 *ICSID Review* 1, 10; P. Juillard, 'Variation in the Substantive Provisions and Interpretation of International Investment Agreements,' in K.P. Sauvant (ed.), *Appellate Mechanisms in International Investment Disputes* (Oxford University Press, 2008), p. 101.

[92] See Juillard, 'Variation in the Substantive Provisions and Interpretation of International Investment Agreements,' p. 93.

interpretations.[93] The CETA appellate mechanism will have the authority to 'uphold, modify[,] or reverse' the first instance award based on 'errors in the application or interpretation of applicable law.'[94] This is distinct from the practice of extraordinary review or annulment in existing investment arbitration systems, which allows only for an assessment of the procedural legitimacy of the original proceeding and binary validation or invalidation.[95]

Appellate review contributes to rule creation in legal interpretation in at least two ways. First, an appellate mechanism allows the reviewer to modify the legal reasoning of first instance decisions and to standardize underlying legal rules. And second, the standing nature of an appellate body might further contribute to the creation of soft law precedent in that a standing body may show more deference to its own decisional law than it does to decisions from other systems,[96] and might enhance incentives, beyond the usual duty to state the reasons for a decision, to produce rules rather than to resolve each dispute on narrow grounds.[97]

14.2.2.2   Consistency and Predictability in Fact-Finding

The features of an investment court that may promote consistency and predictability in legal interpretation, however, are unlikely to have similar effects on fact-finding for at least three reasons. The first reason is that international agreements and institutional frameworks do not prescribe evidentiary rules in meaningful detail,[98] suggesting that the drafters were not particularly concerned with ensuring that adjudicators within a system use common approaches to fact-finding. That lack of detail affords adjudicators greater flexibility and limits the constraining influence of textual rules.[99]

---

[93] Caron, 'Reputation and Reality,' 23.
[94] CETA, Art. 8.28(2).
[95] See Caron, 'Reputation and Reality,' 23, 34 ('The ICSID annulment process, like the prototypical annulment process, provides a quite limited remedy.'); see also ICSID Rules of Procedure for Arbitration Proceedings (10 April 2006), Rule 50.
[96] See Wood, 'Choosing Between Arbitration and a Permanent Court,' 9; Christoph Schreuer, 'Preliminary Rulings in Investment Arbitration,' in K.P. Sauvant (ed.), *Appeals Mechanism in International Investment Disputes* (Oxford University Press, 2008), p. 209.
[97] See Landes and Posner, 'Adjudication as a Private Good,' 238–239.
[98] International Bar Association, 'Commentary on the Revised Text of the 2010 IBA Rules on the Taking of Evidence in International Arbitration' (2010), pp. 1–4.
[99] Helfer and Slaughter, 'Why States Create International Tribunals,' 945–946.

The second reason that an investment court is unlikely to enhance the consistency and predictability of fact-finding is that evidentiary practices are relatively resistant to rule formation. Fact-finders do create their own norms, which give participants in a system a general sense of what to expect in future disputes. But they do not purport to follow rigid evidentiary processes, and instead favor general, adaptive approaches that can respond to the specific circumstances of a dispute and achieve an optimal balance between efficiency and accuracy.[100] These adjudicator-made norms may reflect a well-developed consensus within an institution or otherwise among adjudicators to avoid a highly prescriptive approach to fact-finding, consistent with the drafting intent of system designers. Because the norms are general and informal, they are easier to change from dispute to dispute, more susceptible to differences in views among adjudicators, and more likely to lead to processes for the production and evaluation of evidence that participants are unable to predict in advance.[101]

The third reason that an investment court is unlikely to enhance the consistency and predictability of fact-finding is that appellate review is much more limited with respect to factual questions as compared to the review of legal ones. The CETA appellate tribunal will be able to consider allegedly 'manifest errors' in the fact-finding of a first instance tribunal, including with respect to expert evidence.[102] But the restricted character of that review indicates that the investment court's architects, as with the designers of the WTO and designers of domestic appellate mechanisms, did not believe that appellate bodies are better placed to engage in fact-finding than first instance tribunals.[103]

Even those who see the value of substantive appellate review are skeptical that it has the potential to improve factual accuracy[104] and they stop

---

[100] See Alvarez, 'The Main Functions of International Adjudication,' p. 167 (referring to 'the "common rules of international procedure" on which some international courts and tribunals rely').

[101] See Helfer and Slaughter, 'Why States Create International Tribunals,' 945–946.

[102] CETA, Art. 8.28(2).

[103] Factual questions are not within the jurisdiction of the WTO Appellate Body, although the Appellate Body considers that '[w]hether or not a panel has made an objective assessment of the facts before it … is a legal question which, if properly raised on appeal, would fall within the scope of appellate review.' Appellate Body Report, *European Communities – Measures Concerning Meat and Meat Products*, WT/DS26/AB/R, WT/DS48/AB/R, adopted 16 January 1998, para. 132.

[104] See, e.g., Caron, 'Reputation and Reality,' 54 ('[T]here is little reason to believe that the review panel's decision would be more accurate.')

short of suggesting that those mechanisms should have any substantial opportunity to second-guess findings of fact.[105] This position is an acknowledgment of an appellate mechanism's limited ability to assess many sources of evidence, including witness testimony and other evidence originally presented at first instance hearings.

Most systems, including at the domestic level, do not allow appellate mechanisms to duplicate the fact-finding function of first instance adjudicators, as there is no reason to think that complete repetition of the fact-finding process by different people will produce better results the second time over.[106] The WTO Appellate Body, for example, cannot conduct its own fact-finding, although that it may be able to opine on the propriety of fact-finding procedures in the course of identifying serious errors of fact.[107] But even then it is unable to promote model fact-finding procedures, resolve any remaining factual questions, or conduct additional evidence gathering.[108]

These constraints – including the general nature of rules governing fact-finding, the obstacles to developing even soft-law precedent, and the highly circumscribed scope of review on fact questions – limit the ability of an appellate mechanism to serve either an error correction function or a rule creation function.[109] Even if the introduction of substantive appellate review into a system will improve the consistency and predictability of legal interpretation, there is little support for a claim that an investment court will measurably affect the consistency and predictability of evidence production and evaluation.

---

[105] Doak Bishop, 'The Case for an Appellate Panel and its Scope of Review,' in F. Ortino, A. Sheppard and H. Warner (eds.), *Investment Treaty Law: Current Issues Volume 1* (British Institute of International and Comparative Law, 2006), p. 20.

[106] See Bart Legum, 'Options to Establish an Appellate Mechanism for Investment Disputes,' in K.P. Sauvant (ed.), *Appellate Mechanisms in Investment Disputes* (Oxford University Press, 2008), p. 237 ('[A] certain level of inconsistency is inevitable in any system of administration of justice. Reasonable judges and juries can reasonably reach different results based on the same facts. And advocacy – how a case is argued and presented – really does make a difference.'); Paulsson, 'Avoiding Unintended Consequences,' p. 247 ('[S]uch things [like incongruent findings of fact] happen when a story is told in different ways on different occasions to different people.')

[107] WTO Dispute Settlement Understanding, Art. 17.6 ('An appeal shall be limited to issues of law covered in the panel report and legal interpretations developed by the panel.').

[108] Ibid.

[109] See Legum, 'Options to Establish an Appellate Mechanism,' p. 237; Kho et al., 'EU TTIP Investment Court Proposal,' 345.

14.2.3   Will an Investment Court Improve Fact-Finding Quality by Increasing Subject-Matter Expertise?

A third argument in favor of enhancing the influence of institutions and institutional actors is that the elements of a traditional court – including a standing judicial body, an administrative apparatus, and judicial tenures that extend beyond a single dispute – increase the quality of a tribunal's fact-finding by increasing subject-matter expertise of decision-makers.[110] Decision-makers with specialized expertise in handling a complex, routinely encountered subject are, in turn, better able to understand the objectives and methods of that area of specialization.[111]

There is some logic to the argument that an investment court could afford decision-makers and institution staff the opportunity to develop specialized knowledge on issues that frequently arise on the court's docket, at least in some circumstances.[112] Reliance on a combination of a decision-maker's own review of documentary evidence and input from an institution's research or administrative staff may over time result in improved decisions on complex topics such as damages calculations, aided by the accretion of knowledge and expertise.[113] Adjudicators and their staff might develop this expertise as a simple consequence of performing their duties, or they may do it strategically to attract new cases to the system.[114]

Despite the intuitive appeal of the argument, however, designers of dispute settlement mechanisms cannot depend on the organic development of institutional expertise to increase the quality of fact-finding. For one, participation in dispute settlement is unlikely, in and of itself, to provide the type of systematic training that is necessary to obtain meaningful expertise in most specialized areas.[115] This is especially true given

---

[110] See, e.g., Helfer and Slaughter, 'Why States Create International Tribunals,' 948–949.

[111] See Brewer, 'Scientific Expert Testimony and Intellectual Due Process,' 1539.

[112] See Posner and Yoo, 'Judicial Independence in International Tribunals,' 25.

[113] See Brewer, 'Scientific Expert Testimony and Intellectual Due Process,' 1680 ('Perhaps some judges, by virtue of background or repeat "on the bench" experience with scientific evidence, will become sufficiently epistemically competent to render decisions about scientific expert testimony that are epistemically legitimate and that meets the demands of intellectual due process.')

[114] See Helfer and Slaughter, 'Why States Create International Tribunals,' 948–949.

[115] See Brewer, 'Scientific Expert Testimony and Intellectual Due Process,' 1680 (arguing that judges are unlikely to develop meaningful specialized knowledge unless they are 'routinely and systematically trained in scientific theories and methods').

that most institutions are unlikely to adjudicate disputes at a frequency sufficient to enable decision-makers to develop expertise over the course of a judicial tenure period, even one that may extend to ten or twelve years, as in CETA.[116] And relying on experience obtained while acting as a decision-maker in a system means that, even in ideal circumstances, disputes early in a decision-maker's tenure cannot benefit from that experience. A system will realize any benefits only after an initial learning period.

Reliance on an adjudicator's own capacity to understand complex and specialized subject matter may, in any event, decrease the transparency and analytical rigor of the facti-finding process. As discussed above, this is of particular concern when decision-makers rely on their own review of documents or on unseen experts to the exclusion of other sources of evidence.

Finally, to the extent that the development and exercise of institutional expertise is desirable, individual arbitrators participating in existing investor-State dispute settlement systems already have opportunities to develop subject-matter expertise in subjects that frequently arise in investment disputes, such as the calculation of damages methodologies.[117] If it is possible, then, to gain expertise through repeated exposure to complex subjects in the course of dispute settlement, presumably at least some arbitrators are already operating as subject-matter experts.[118]

14.3   Conclusion

This chapter has asked a question of the investment court proposals that they do not ask of themselves but that is of considerable importance to the legitimacy of international dispute resolution: Will an investment court be a better fact-finder? The focus here has been on how to improve the quality of fact-finding with respect to expert evidence, a critically influential source of facts that relies heavily on expert witnesses and other, often unseen actors.

---

[116] Cf. Guzman, 'International Tribunals,' 206 (presenting a similar argument with respect to the possibility of improved reputation over judicial tenure periods).

[117] See Georgios Dimitropoulos, 'Constructing the Independence of International Investment Arbitrators: Past, Present, and Future' (2016) 36 *Northwestern Journal of International Law and Business* 371, 375–376; Franck et al., 'Inside the Arbitrator's Mind,' 1119.

[118] See Franck et al., 'Inside the Arbitrator's Mind,' 1119.

A conceptual analysis indicates that enhancing the role of institutions and institutional actors through the creation of an investment court will not meaningfully improve fact-finding quality. The changes reflected in CETA may instead increase fact-finding quality to a limited degree in certain ways, while detracting from that quality in others. It may also increase costs and impose delays, further casting doubt on an argument that an investment court will be a better fact-finder. Proponents of an investment court, in other words, do not yet have a convincing case that any improvements that a court may bring will not be subject to countervailing downsides when it comes to its critical role as a fact-finder. Further analysis is necessary to identify alternatives to elements of an investment court that would improve fact-finding quality without negative effects on efficiency and finality.

15

Unseen and Unsung

Language Services at the International Criminal Court and Their Impact on Institutional Legitimacy

LEIGH SWIGART

15.1   Introduction

In June 2017, a witness testified in the case of *The Prosecutor v. Dominic Ongwen*[1] at the International Criminal Court (ICC or the Court) in The Hague. Ongwen stands accused[2] of directing attacks by members of the Lord's Resistance Army in May 2004 against civilians in an internally displaced persons' camp in northern Uganda. The alleged war crimes and crimes against humanity committed by those under Ongwen's command include murder, enslavement, inhumane acts of inflicting serious bodily injury and suffering, cruel treatment of civilians, sexual and gender-based violence, and pillaging.[3]

The witness testifying that day was a victim of the attacks. She recounted how her newborn child was thrown into the bush by the attackers, and how she was subsequently pursued and brutally beaten as she searched for her baby. As a protected witness, her face was purposely distorted so that she was unrecognizable to the public. But her background was nonetheless clear – her experiences were that of a young woman from a rural area, her dress was traditional, and she testified in Acholi.

How does such a witness find herself in The Hague, addressing international judges, prosecutors, and defence lawyers in a modern courtroom that is outfitted with the latest technology? Who takes her initial witness statement? Helps her arrange her travel to Europe once she has been

---

[1] *The Prosecutor v. Domnic Ongwen*, Case No. ICC-02/04-01/15.
[2] Ibid., Decision on the confirmation of charges against Dominic Ongwen (23 March 2016), available at www.icc-cpi.int/CourtRecords/CR2016_02331.PDF.
[3] Ibid., Alleged crimes (non-exhaustive list), available at www.icc-cpi.int/uganda/ongwen/pages/alleged-crimes.aspx.

selected to testify? Who orients her to the courtroom procedures, the microphones she will speak into, and the images that will flash before her on a screen? And very importantly, who interprets her critical testimony about what she experienced from Acholi into the working languages of the Court[4], conveying the tone of her speech along with her inevitable hesitation and emotion, so that it can become part of the official trial record?

Every international court must accommodate in some way the multilingualism found both across its geographic jurisdiction and within its own professional ranks. This task may not be particularly daunting if the court has official or working languages that are widely spoken and for which there exists a large cadre of trained translators and interpreters. For institutions that must accommodate speakers of rarer languages, however, the challenges are considerably greater. Indeed, the difficulties associated with using such languages throughout the various phases of an international criminal process may raise fundamental questions about accuracy, fairness, and budgetary allocation.

This chapter is based on the author's ongoing ethnographic study of how the ICC is responding to a broad range of multilingual challenges, particularly those related to African languages. These difficulties arise from a variety of factors, including the absence of trained language professionals for many of the target languages, the lack of existing lexical items to denote international legal concepts, the languages' frequent lack of a written tradition, and low rates of literacy in victim communities.

As of the publication of this volume, the ICC is using well over thirty languages from the African continent in its investigations, trials, interactions with victims, and outreach activities.[5] Despite the centrality of these languages to various ICC situations and cases[6], African language

---

[4] The working languages of the Court are English and French. The official languages of the Court, in which judgments and other decisions resolving fundamental issues are to be published, are Arabic, Chinese, English, French, Russian, and Spanish. See Article 50, 'Official and working languages', Rome Statute of the International Criminal Court (last amended 2010), adopted on 17 July 1998 by the United Nations Diplomatic Conference of Plenipotentiaries on the Establishment of an International Criminal Court, entered into force on 1 July 2002, ISBN No. 92-9227-227-6.

[5] 'LSS Field and Operational Interpretation and Situation Languages' (n.d.), Language Services Section (internal ICC document).

[6] These terms carry particular meanings at the ICC: '[t]he jurisprudence of the Court distinguishes between "situations", which are generally defined in terms of temporal, territorial and in some cases personal parameters, and "cases", which comprise specific incidents within a given "situation" during which one or more crimes within the jurisdiction of the Court may have been committed'. See 'Policy Paper on Case Selection and

experts, along with the structures created to support their work, operate largely in the shadows. Furthermore, the innovative strategies developed by ICC language services staff around recruitment and training of African language interpreters, development of legal lexicons, and other vital activities are rarely acknowledged publicly. Despite the obvious multilingual nature of all ICC situations and cases, the constant use of interpretation and translation (even between its working languages), and the visible presence of interpreters in the courtroom, the Court's language services remain strangely unseen and unsung.

The next section of the chapter describes a wide range of language activities that take place at the ICC, largely behind the scenes. The following section lays out the ways in which these services and their outputs may be misunderstood by the very people whose work depends on them – leading to frustration, delays, and less than optimal working conditions – and then offers suggestions about some ways to correct this situation.

15.2   Working Behind the Scenes: Unseen Activities of Language Services Staff

What I'm proud to say is that I know we have given a voice to the voiceless. And I think that's worth something.

ICC interpreter[7]

Many daily activities central to the work of the ICC are mediated or facilitated by language specialists. Simultaneous interpreters may be the most obvious members of this group, visible in their booths when one attends a trial hearing in an ICC courtroom and audible if one listens to testimony through a headset. The wide range of written information available to the public in both working languages of the Court, English and French, is testament to the existence of translators as well. The complex procedures and knowledge that make the work of interpreters, translators, and other language experts possible and successful are not widely understood,

---

Prioritisation', ICC Office of the Prosecutor (15 September 2016), available at www.icc-cpi .int/itemsDocuments/20160915_OTP-Policy_Case-Selection_Eng.pdf. The crimes falling under the jurisdiction of the ICC 'shall be limited to the most serious crimes of concern to the international community as a whole', namely genocide, crimes against humanity, war crimes, and the crime of aggression. See Article 5, 'Crimes within the jurisdiction of the Court', Rome Statute of the International Criminal Court.

[7]   Author interview RL-9, 5 June 2017.

however, even among those who routinely use their services. This lack of awareness may be particularly acute in relation to ICC 'situation languages' – those relevant to conflicts and crimes under investigation or prosecution – when they have few speakers in a given location, are non-standardized and largely oral, and for which few or no accredited interpreters exist. In linguistic circles, these are called 'languages of lesser diffusion' (LLDs).[8]

The following descriptions are based on interviews conducted with ICC language staff, which represent a subset of interviews about language issues conducted to date with persons working across the Court. The aim of this section is to present the range of activities carried out by language professionals, many of which are invisible even to other ICC employees, as well as the significant and rather unique challenges that they face.

15.2.1   Language Services Section: An Overview

The central provider of language-related services at the ICC is the Language Services Section (LSS or the Section), housed in the Registry. Other Registry entities depend on LSS for the majority of their language needs, including the Victims and Witnesses Section, Office of Public Counsel for Victims, Office of Public Counsel for Defence, Counsel Support Services, Victims Participation and Reparations Section, Public Information and Outreach Section, and Human Resources. LSS also provides services to the ICC Presidency and Chambers. The Office of the Prosecutor (OTP) has its own Language Services Unit (LSU) to ensure independence of investigations and prosecutions, although LSS and LSU collaborate on some activities.[9] As of May 2019, LSS had a full-time staff of fifty-five persons, which included professionals taken on to respond to particular needs and cases on a temporary but full-time basis.[10] In addition, at any given moment, LSS has additional staff working on short-term contracts as the need arises.[11] A number of staff members worked at other international criminal tribunals before joining the ICC, and thus

---

[8] Heidi Salaets, Katalin Balogh and Dominique Van Schoor, 'Languages of Lesser Diffusion (LLDs): The Rationale Behind the Research Project and Definitions', in Katalin Balogh, Heidi Salaerts and Dominique Van Schoor (eds.), *TraiLLD: Training in Languages of Lesser Diffusion* (Lannoo Campus Publishers, 2016).

[9] 'Behind the Scenes: The Registry of the International Criminal Court' (2010), available at www.icc-cpi.int/iccdocs/PIDS/docs/behindTheSce.pdf.

[10] Author interview RL-1, 29 May 2017; personal conversation with same interviewee for update, 4 May 2019.

[11] Ibid.

brought with them the lessons learned about providing language services at those institutions.

Unlike the international criminal tribunals that preceded it, the ICC faces a fundamental challenge that has direct and serious ramifications for the work of LSS: with its broad jurisdictional reach, the Court cannot predict with any certainty the locations of the crimes it might be called upon to investigate and pursue, nor the languages in which accused persons, witnesses, and victims may wish to communicate.[12] This means that language staff must be poised to provide services in a timely manner for languages that may have only recently appeared on their radar screens.

The central activities of LSS – terminology development, translation, and interpretation – and the ways in which LSS staff members satisfy the language needs of the Court are presented in the remainder of this section.

15.2.2   Terminology

An essential but perhaps little-known aspect of the Court's language work revolves around the development of terminology, which supports both translation and interpretation activities. As described by one staff member involved in this work, terminology is a different branch of translation that goes more into pure linguistics, exploring the origins of a word and the various meanings it has in different contexts.[13] Even in relation to English and French, the job of verifying and codifying 'equivalents' is complex and challenging. Each position described by Human Resources, for example, needs to have a title that conveys the same meaning in French and English. But does *unité* mean the same thing as 'division' or alternatively 'unit'? When translations are made of job postings, these details need to be precise and clear.

At the ICC, terminologists have painstakingly gone through the official ICC documents – the Rome Statute, Rules of Procedure and Evidence, Elements of Crimes, and so on – to extract all the terms and then enter them into a terminology database which serves as a resource for both translators and interpreters. Terminology bulletins on various subjects have also been published and distributed across the Court. When it comes to LLDs, the Section has devised a strategy for codifying non-existent legal and judicial terms in languages that play a starring role in

---

[12] Leigh Swigart, 'Linguistic and Cultural Diversity in International Criminal Justice: Toward Bridging the Divide' (2016) 48(2) *University of the Pacific Law Review*, p.197.
[13] Interview with RL-13, 8 June 2017.

certain situations and cases, such as Acholi (Uganda) – the Court's first situation language to emerge – Sango (Central African Republic), Lingala (Republic of the Congo, hereafter DRC), Swahili-Congolese variant (DRC), Standard Swahili (Kenya), and Dyula (Côte d'Ivoire). LSS often establishes 'expert panels', made up of individuals with a deep knowledge of the target languages (usually older speakers),[14] along with linguists and professional terminologists. Together, they decide on which lexical items or explanatory phrases should be chosen to express relevant ICC terms.[15] For LLDs that play more of a supporting role in a case, the use of scarce resources to put together expert panels and create databases is usually not justified.[16]

A very helpful product created by LSS is a terminology bulletin on legal phrases used in the ICC courtroom, translated from English and French into Lingala, Sango, Arabic, and both Congolese and standard variants of Swahili. This 'courtroom phraseology' features dozens of pre-dictable phrases used at the pre-trial and trial stages of ICC proceedings, setting a standard for their interpretation.[17] More recently, a glossary has been devised for terms that are key to the mandate of the ICC so that field interpreters, in particular, can be consistent when they explain and define them to witnesses, victims, and members of affected communities. Importantly, the definition of one key term cannot contain another key term, the idea being to strip definitions down to their basic semantic components.[18] This glossary contains more than 400 entries for concepts such as 'counsel', 'crime', 'defence', 'dignity', 'jurisdiction', 'mutilation', 'obstruction of justice', 'prosecutor', 'protection', 'rape', 'reparations', 'victim', and 'witness'. However, given the early activity of OTP staff in situation countries and their necessary use of field interpreters, the development of

[14] Interview with Alexandra Tomić (2015), *Ad Hoc Tribunals Oral History Project*, International Center for Ethics, Justice and Public Life, Robert D. Farber University Archives & Special Collections Department, Brandeis University, available at www.brandeis.edu/ethics/internationaljustice/oral-history/interviews/tomi%C4%87.html.
[15] Author interview RL-1, 29 May 2017; author interview RL-11, 6 June 2017; author interview RL-7, 2 June 2017.
[16] Author interview RL-6, 1 June 2017.
[17] 'Terminology Bulletin no. 11' (2012), Section de Traduction et d'Interprétation de la Cour (internal ICC document). See also Leigh Swigart, 'African Languages in International Criminal Justice: The International Criminal Tribunal and Beyond', in Charles Chernor Jalloh and Alhagi B.M. Marong (eds.), *Promoting Accountability under International Law for Gross Human Rights Violations in Africa: Essays in Honour of Prosecutor Hassan Bubacar Jallow* (Brill Nijhoff, 2015).
[18] Author interview RL-14, 26 June 2017.

terminology and establishment of definitions cannot remain vested solely in the Registry's LSS. Instead, it is an evolving process with both practical and conceptual input provided over time and from across the Court.

It is not only LLDs, however, that may lack a particular term to express legal and judicial notions. The ICC is an institution with a hybrid legal system; it has borrowed concepts and practices from both common law and civil law traditions – and their respective adversarial and inquisitorial procedural systems – and added in original ones as well. A number of terms used in the founding documents of the Court have been coined specifically for ICC purposes; they are what scholar Ludmila Stern calls 'pre-emptively minted ... meaning-based neologisms'.[19] An example is the legal notion of 'complementarity', unique to the ICC, *complémentarité* in French.[20] Other terms used at the ICC may have a clear denotation in one working language but not the other, so that staff must 'learn the lingo' upon joining the Court. An interpreter observed, '[t]here are usage issues at ICC, for sure. Everywhere else, "disclosure" is *communication des pièces*. At the ICC, it is *divulgation*'.[21] Furthermore, language experts at the Court are required to use these terms, no matter how much they deviate from mainstream usage or, more importantly, from the terms used in other international criminal tribunals. Terminological work happens very much under the radar at the ICC. This invisibility notwithstanding, its significance for successful translation and interpretation cannot be overestimated.

15.2.3   Translation

The process of rendering the words of a text written in one language into those of another is a critical part of LSS's work and one without which the

[19] Ludmila Stern, 'Courtroom Interpreting', in Kirsten Malmkjaer and Kevin Windle (eds.), *The Oxford Handbook of Translation Studies* (Oxford University Press, 2011), p. 337.
[20] 'The [Rome] Statute recognizes that States have the first responsibility and right to prosecute international crimes. The ICC may only exercise jurisdiction where national legal systems fail to do so, including where they purport to act but in reality are unwilling or unable to genuinely carry out proceedings. The principle of complementarity is based both on respect for the primary jurisdiction of States and on considerations of efficiency and effectiveness, since States will generally have the best access to evidence and witnesses and the resources to carry out proceedings.' See 'Informal Expert Paper: Complementarity in Practice', ICC Office of the Prosecutor (2003), p. 3, available at www.icc-cpi.int/NR/rdonlyres/20BB4494-70F9-4698-8E30-907F631453ED/281984/complementarity.pdf.
[21] Author interview RL-7, 2 June 2017.

ICC could not function. Translation of ICC official and administrative documents – for example, from the Presidency, Public Information and Outreach Section, Human Resources, Information Technology, and the Legal Office – is part of the translators' workload. And as the majority of such documents is originally produced in English, there are many more translators working from that language into French than the other way around. It is translation related to the core mandate of the Court, however – all judicial decisions, interlocutory appeals, judgments, and so on – that comes first for translators, and it is also the work they view with the most passion.[22]

Translating an ICC judgment, generally 400–700 pages in length, from its original language into the other working language may take six to eight months from start to finish, including the important revision and proofreading phases. A draft may be ready within the first two months after work begins. Translation of any major document, 100+ pages, has a project manager – 'un chef d'orchestre'[23] – who supervises the division of the text into parts so that it can be translated by a team. The work is staggered, so that revisers can start before the translators have finished, and proofreaders can take over after the revisers have completed their task. Making mistakes in a judgment is serious, said a translator,[24] and the aim is to minimize corrigenda to judgments after their publication.

Legal translation would appear to be an art form, much like literary translation. But the artistry does not take the form of a beautiful turn of phrase; instead it resides in the skilful translation of text that must be precise, readable, and engaging. Furthermore, if language in the original text is not clear, it is not the job of the translator to clarify it: '[t]he function of the legal translator is to match the degree of fuzziness, because that is where the judicial debate happens. That's where the judicial conversation happens. And if you smooth the translations, if you remedy the defects in the original, you are de facto intervening in the judicial discussion'.[25]

It is also essential that the legal terms used in translations of judgments match those used in the Rome Statute. But the disparity between some of the legal terminology used at the ICC and that, for example, used at the International Criminal Tribunal for the former Yugoslavia (ICTY) and International Criminal Tribunal for Rwanda (ICTR), can lead to

---

[22] Author interview RL-2, 29 May 2017.
[23] Ibid.
[24] Ibid.
[25] Ibid.

confusion when ICC judgments cite jurisprudence from those tribunals. Translation strategies need to be devised to make clear that, despite different terminology, the legal concepts are the same. Sometimes an original English source word may have to be included in the French translation for purposes of clarification.

Another experienced translator noted that certain legal officers believe that translators do not need to understand the legal argumentation in a judgment; they just need to translate it. That view reveals a misunderstanding of the translation process, whereby the original text is 'deverbalized' into its essential meaning and then 'reverbalized' in the target language. Indeed, requests for clarification by translators may lead legal assistants to sit down with judges to revisit the original text of a judgment and figure out why translators are unable to make sense of it. Sometimes it turns out that the translator has uncovered an inconsistency or a real conceptual problem.

Translation at the ICC is not confined to English and French, of course. LSS has a unit devoted to situation language translation as well. The types of ICC materials translated into situation languages may include arrest warrants, service of sentence agreements, and documents pertaining to investigations and state cooperation. The Rome Statute and other foundational documents of the Court have also been translated into selected situation languages. Translation into certain African languages may be limited, depending on how commonly they are used for written communication in the situation country or the level of literacy found there. The unit may also be called upon to produce translations into 'languages of judicial cooperation', for example when a new country joins the Assembly of States Parties and requests ICC documents in its national language. Such an undertaking may raise, of course, new terminological challenges.[26]

Everyone at the Court is aware of the high bar set by Article 67(1) of the Rome Statute for the linguistic rights of accused persons: 'a) To be informed promptly and in detail of the nature, cause and content of the charge, in a language which the accused fully understands and speaks', and 'f) To have, free of any cost, the assistance of a competent interpreter and such translations as are necessary to meet the requirements of fairness, if any of the proceedings of or documents presented to the Court are not in a language which the accused fully understands and

---

[26] Author interview RL-10, 5 June 2017.

speaks'.[27] If an accused person is not proficient in English or French but able to read an African language, then an arrest warrant and a document containing the charges will be translated accordingly. Dominic Ongwen, for example, was presented with an Acholi translation of all seventy charges against him[28], and later with a translation of the Pre-Trial Chamber's decision on the confirmation of charges in his case,[29] all produced by LSS.[30] The early terminology work done on Acholi was critical for this endeavour. Nonetheless, the use of Acholi interpretation since the Ongwen trial began in late 2016 has indicated to language experts that some of the terminology developed 'in the abstract' needs to be revised for optimal clarity in a trial proceeding. To this end, a second expert panel on Acholi was subsequently convened.[31]

A more innovative strategy was devised for Abdallah Banda Abakaer Nourain.[32] An accused person from the Darfur region of Sudan, Banda's native language is Zaghawa, an LLD for which no written conventions exist. In order to satisfy Article 67(1) of the Rome Statute, the Court needed to inform Banda of the charges against him and allow him to review the evidence against him as disclosed by the OTP, but it had to be done aurally. The solution was for interpreters to do recorded 'sight translation' of the relevant documents into Zaghawa. The interpreters were then trained by LSS to use an audio editing suite so they could digitally mark the long audio translation with the paragraph and page divisions found on the written version. The document containing the charges alone was 140 pages long and it took six months to complete this audio translation process.[33]

[27] Article 67, 'Rights of the Accused', Rome Statute of the International Criminal Court. See also the ICC Case Matrix Network, available at www.casematrixnetwork.org/cmn-knowledge-hub/icc-commentary-clicc/commentary-rome-statute/commentary-rome-statute-part-6/.
[28] *Prosecutor v. Domnic Ongwen*, Alleged crimes (non-exhaustive list), above note 3.
[29] Decision on the confirmation of charges against Dominic Ongwen, above note 2. This was apparently a partial translation, however. See Defence Request for Findings on Fair Trial Violations and Remedy, Pursuant to Articles 67 and 64 of the Rome Statute, in the Case of the Prosecutor v. Dominic Ongwen, ICC-02/04-01/15, 8 January 2018, available at www.icc-cpi.int/CourtRecords/CR2018_00099.PDF. This request was followed by a number of other submissions around the translation issue, a trial chamber decision, a request by the defence to appeal the decision, and so on.
[30] Author interview PL-1, 6 June 2017.
[31] Personal communication with LSS staff member, 24 October 2017.
[32] *The Prosecutor v. Abdallah Banda Abakaer Nourain*, ICC-02/05-03/09. See www.icc-cpi.int/darfur/banda.
[33] Author interview RL-9, 5 June 2017.

More recently, the OTP's opening of an investigation into crimes allegedly committed in the Republic of Georgia[34] has brought with it new challenges for language services staff, as well as new opportunities for collaboration within LSS itself. Several units worked together to put together a Georgian expert panel to develop three training modules: (1) a module for field interpretation into Georgian that covered core glossary terms applying to all ICC situations, as well as terms specific to the Georgian situation; (2) a module on the transliteration of the Georgian script into the Roman script, which involved standardizing several competing transliteration systems; and (3) a module on translating the Rome Statute into Georgian.[35]

A look at the Georgian situation also illustrates the difficulty facing LSS as it seeks to prepare for new languages in which it may soon be asked to provide services. It prefers to be involved 'upstream' – early in the life of a situation – so it has some control over how the initial translations are done in order to ensure maximum terminological consistency from the start. To this end, it works closely with the LSU of the OTP, whose staff are usually first in the field. At the same time, some circumspection is necessary since a preliminary examination, the earliest prosecution phase, may never develop into a full-fledged investigation and LSS does not wish to develop language resources and expertise that may never be used. Only when Chambers have authorized opening an investigation through a judicial decision may LSS take concrete actions in relation to a situation. In preparation for this decisive moment, LSS's best line of action is to make discreet inquiries with relevant international organizations and academic institutions to identify language experts and determine which language resources may already exist.[36]

15.2.4 Interpretation

The conversion of oral messages in one language into oral messages in a second language is vital for the functioning of diverse units and sections across the Court. The Interpretation Unit in LSS handles all requests for interpretation, both judicial and non-judicial, which may include meetings and seminars at the Court and visits by various delegations. Judicial work always takes precedence, however.

---

[34] Situation in Georgia, ICC-01/15. See www.icc-cpi.int/georgia.
[35] Author interview RL-10, 5 June 2017.
[36] Ibid.

The Court Management Section communicates directly with prosecution and defence teams about their interpretation needs, which depend in turn on the language skills of the witnesses who will be called to testify. French and English interpretation are always provided in the courtroom. As of November 2017, there were fourteen full-time interpreters employed by LSS, with freelancers being taken on when demand surpasses supply. All interpreters, even if they work only occasionally for the Court, need to have security clearance. Not all freelancers, however, have the skill or temperament for courtroom interpretation, which is particularly stressful and demanding.[37] The Interpretation Unit also responds to the interpretation needs of the Victims and Witnesses Section, which takes care of all persons who participate in hearings. Some of these are expert witnesses who are used to testifying in Court and may not find the process daunting.[38] 'Crime-based' witnesses, usually victims, may require much more preparation, familiarization with the courtroom set-up, and assistance – often in a language other than English or French – when they arrive at the Court to testify.[39]

Interpretation requests may also come from Counsel Support Services if defence teams require interpretation outside the courtroom, for example at the ICC detention centre. Sometimes an interpreter may be asked to assist a medical professional in consulting with an accused person or witness.[40] One interpreter described assisting with IT training at the detention centre for staff learning a new detainee monitoring system.[41] Basically, interpreters are deployed wherever they are requested, be it for counselling sessions with the Court's psychological services, for the Office of Public Counsel for Victims, for the Office of Public Counsel for Defence, for the Victims Participation and Reparations Section, or anywhere else. Although the Rome Statute enshrines translation and interpretation rights only for accused persons, the Court generally extends these rights to witnesses and victims as well.[42]

---

[37] Author interview RL-12, 7 June 2017; personal communication with same interviewee for update, 6 May 2019.

[38] Although Richard Ashby Wilson has noted of trials at the ICTY, 'Expert historians and social scientists, no matter how high their standing in their chosen field of academic or scholarly inquiry, often struggled in the transition to the courtroom, with its adversarial process and uniquely legal ways of knowing'. See Richard Ashby Wilson, *Writing History in International Criminal Trials* (Cambridge University Press, 2011), p. 113.

[39] Author interview RV-2, 7 June 2017.

[40] Author interview RL-3, 30 May 2017.

[41] Ibid.

[42] Author interview RL-12, 7 June 2017; author interview RV-2, 7 June 2017; author interview RL-6, 1 June 2017.

In the subsections below, the activities associated with interpretation occurring both outside and inside the courtroom are detailed.

15.2.4.1   Field Interpretation

This category of interpretation refers to all non-courtroom work, whether it be in a situation country or at the seat of the Court (where it is sometimes called operational interpretation). This interpretation is done in the consecutive mode, that is, interpreters listen to a short stretch of speech and then deliver their interpretation after the speaker has finished.[43] ICC field interpreters are normally independent freelance workers engaged by the Court to provide high-quality linguistic services on a short-term basis and as required. In some cases, staff members of language services may be deployed as field interpreters.[44]

Field and Operational Interpretation of the LSS is responsible for sourcing, recruiting, training, and deploying interpreters for all non-judicial tasks. This undertaking is time-consuming and multifaceted, rendered even more challenging by the unpredictability of which languages will become relevant to ICC activities. The OTP's LSU works closely with LSS on all activities related to sourcing, recruiting, and training field interpreters, an unusual arrangement given the strict independence normally maintained by the OTP vis-à-vis the other organs of the Court. This arrangement is justified by the cost- and labour-saving advantages of joint accreditation in this area.

Once a group of field interpreters is ready to deploy, LSS and LSU will 'split the roster'. Although the two entities recruit and train interpreters together, 'from the moment that an interpreter is deployed by the OTP, in principle this interpreter will stay with the OTP, will go on OTP missions and will support investigators with their work'.[45] LSS field interpreters, especially if they have been deployed to defence, will not work with the OTP. Normally, there is little overlap between field and courtroom interpretation. But the boundaries may be crossed by situation language experts in particular, if they are needed to interpret in the detention centre, help assess the security needs or vulnerability of witnesses, go on

---

[43] *Guidelines for Court Staff Using the Services of Field Interpreters* (Version 2, June 2012), International Criminal Court (internal draft document).

[44] *Guidelines for Field Interpreters Working with the International Criminal Court* (Version 2, June 2012), International Criminal Court (internal draft document).

[45] Author interview PL-1, 6 June 2017.

training missions with LSS and LSU, or even join field missions with legal representatives for victims.

Given the broad range of contexts in which field interpretation is used, LSS and LSU have felt the need to draft guidelines for both field interpreters and those who use their services.[46] These guidelines cover issues such as what may and may not be asked of an interpreter; the professional standards of impartiality, confidentiality, and accuracy that are expected of interpreters; the mechanics of this service; and optimal working conditions, including the timing of breaks and length of working hours. The field interpreter guidelines[47] also encourage freelancers to create their own glossaries of useful terms and vocabulary that they encounter during the course of their work, and to share terminology and knowledge with the Court to assist with the creation of resource documents in their languages.

15.2.4.2   Courtroom Interpretation

International criminal justice and simultaneous interpretation were born of the same historical moment – after World War II when the Nuremberg Trials prosecuted alleged perpetrators of mass crimes and undertook to hold expeditious proceedings in four languages.[48] Ever since, simultaneous interpretation has been the preferred mode for international criminal proceedings, whether at the ICTY, ICTR, Special Court for Sierra Leone, Extraordinary Chambers in the Courts of Cambodia, or the Special Tribunal for Lebanon.

It is especially important that interpreters convey to listeners not only the message but also the demeanour of the speaker as reflected through speech: '[a]ccording to codes of ethics, interpretation must be complete and contain no addition, omissions, or distortions of meaning (misinterpretations). In court, this applies not only to content but to style and manner, especially important in witness testimony.'[49] An ICC interpreter stressed the importance of using the proper linguistic 'register', a term which refers to the variety of language used for a particular purpose or social setting, its level of formality or informality, and so on.[50]

---

[46] Above notes 43 and 44.
[47] Above note 44.
[48] Andrew M. Constable, 'Effective Communication in Multilingual Judicial Proceedings', in E. King, R. Letschert, S. Garkawe and E. Pobjie (eds.), *Victim Advocacy Before the International Criminal Court* (Springer Law, forthcoming).
[49] Stern, above note 19, p. 334.
[50] See the *Cambridge Dictionary*, available at dictionary.cambridge.org/grammar/british-grammar/types-of-english-formal-informal-etc/register.

The ICC provides simultaneous interpretation for every court hearing in French and English and produces transcripts in the two working languages. Many speakers in the courtroom also communicate in those two languages, be they counsel for the prosecution and defence, accused persons (although they rarely testify), or witnesses; indeed, many hail from anglophone or francophone countries, in Europe, Africa, or elsewhere. Judges are also required to be proficient in one of the court's working languages.

A large pool of simultaneous interpreters working between French and English already exists. They ordinarily work in one direction: into their primary 'Language A' from a secondary 'Language B'. Thus, a 'French interpreter' or 'French booth interpreter' listens to English and interprets it with just a short time lag into French. Some courtroom interpreters at the ICC worked previously in European institutions and bring with them a long experience in so-called 'conference interpreting'. Others have already worked in the context of international criminal justice and thus are used not only to specialized courtroom requirements but also various legal notions and terminology. Whatever their background, they still need training in order to understand how it all works at the ICC, which includes becoming comfortable with the complex technology of the interpretation booth and understanding the specificities of particular situations and cases.

The real challenge facing LSS is that no simultaneous interpreters exist for many situation languages, some of which are key to specific trials: Acholi for Ugandan-related proceedings, Sango for the Central African Republic, Zaghawa for Sudan, and so on. The ICC must consequently train them in-house, often using their own staff as trainers, and within a short time-frame – usually six to eight months. The point of the training is to create courtroom interpreters and not conference interpreters. The trainees need to start with consecutive interpretation, which teaches them to analyse the message, something that will need to be done very quickly in simultaneous work.

Unlike English or French booth interpreters, situation language interpreters usually work bi-directionally – between English and Acholi, for example, or between French and Sango. One ICC interpreter has skills that allow him to interpret from Kinyarwanda, Lingala, and Swahili into French, and from English into the three African languages.[51] Sometimes

---

[51] Author interview RL-11, 6 June 2017.

interpretation will be required in a language more peripheral to a case, for example for the testimony of a single witness in Kilendu (DRC). In these circumstances, a consecutive interpreter will be deployed after receiving short training on how to work in a courtroom.

How does the ICC approach the task of training a simultaneous interpreter in an LLD, especially if there are few or no other speakers of the target language around to assist in the process? Several ICC courtroom interpreters from the English and French booths have undertaken a specialized course at the University of Geneva to become in-house trainers of LLD simultaneous interpreters. The techniques developed have recently been described in a publication focused on the training of legal interpreters in LLDs in the European Union.[52]

15.2.5   Unsung Professionals

The work of language services staff is highly complex, requiring not only long and painstaking training but also intense concentration, flexibility, resilience, and dedication. But how different is this from the work carried out by other parts of the Court? The activities of investigators, security personnel, outreach staff, legal professionals across the organs of the Court, and, of course, judges – to name just some obvious roles – all demand special skills that the layperson can hardly begin to imagine.

It could be argued, however, that language professionals occupy a unique and critical niche in that it is *their* work that underpins the functioning of all other activities at the Court. In an institution with two working languages and several dozen situation languages, the work and expertise of LSS play a *sine qua non* role. A courtroom interpreter said: 'Without the interpretation, there wouldn't be a single trial here; nothing would function, nothing would work.'[53] A translator reflected on the status of the Section at the Court: '[t]here is a general recognition of what we do, but there is perhaps less awareness of what we do and how we do it. I would make a difference between recognition and awareness.'[54]

To return to the Acholi-speaking witness described in the opening to this chapter, it should be clear that 'giving her a voice' is the result of lengthy, well planned, and carefully orchestrated efforts on the part of multiple categories of language experts. Terminologists developed the necessary

---

[52] Balogh et al., TraiLLD: Training in Languages of Lesser Diffusion, above note 8.
[53] Author interview RL-9, 5 June 2017.
[54] Author interview RL-10, 5 June 2017.

legal lexicon in Acholi. Field interpreters assisted OTP investigators on the ground in Uganda as they took initial witness statements. Translators prepared documents so the accused could read the charges against him in Acholi and thereby receive his fair trial rights. Field interpreters assisted the Victims and Witnesses Section in bringing the witness to The Hague and preparing her to testify. And finally, courtroom interpreters rendered her testimony understandable to the Court, and the larger world, in both English and French.

15.3   The Risks of Invisibility

They only notice interpretation when it's not there.

ICC field interpretation supervisor[55]

All LSS staff take an oath to be neutral and accurate in their activities, to guard the confidentiality of the texts and testimony they work with, and more generally to exercise their profession ethically. But another professional stance shared by language experts at the ICC does not seem to be articulated explicitly: the absolute humility with which they play a supporting role to the rest of the Court. 'We try to meet every request,' said an interpretation supervisor, 'because in the end, we are service providers.'[56] Another top LSS staff member noted, '[w]e are not there to be brilliant for the sake of being brilliant; we are there to provide language services to court officials.'[57] A translator described the care she takes to preserve the integrity of judgments she renders into French, even when the original is unclear or problematic: '[w]hat standing do I have to intervene in the judicial debate? I do not have any standing.'[58] Another remarked, '[t]he best day for an interpreter is when no one knows you've been in the room.'[59] This humble attitude appears to be very much wrapped up in an awareness of the Court's essential mandate. 'From a professional and ethical perspective, it's not about me,' stated an interpreter. 'I'm here to provide a service. And the ultimate goal is justice for the victims, that justice be done.'[60] Invisibility, in

---

[55]   Author interview RL-6, 1 June 2017.
[56]   Author interview RL-12, 7 June 2017.
[57]   Interview with Alexandra Tomić (2015), *Ad Hoc Tribunals Oral History Project*, above note 14.
[58]   Author interview RL-2, 29 May 2017.
[59]   Author interview RL-7, 2 June 2017.
[60]   Ibid.

other words, would seem to be an ethic in and of itself among ICC language service professionals.

But remaining below the radar screen also creates certain risks for the success of the entire language enterprise. Indeed, there appears to be an essential tension in the work of language experts at the ICC, whereby their preference to remain behind the scenes collides against the need for better understanding by those who utilize their services. Some level of discretion is required to protect the identities of language staff, for example that of field interpreters who might be vulnerable to backlash should it become known in their home country that they work for the ICC, especially if there is ongoing conflict.[61] This particular circumstance notwithstanding, increased visibility of how language experts work and a better understanding of the necessary constraints they face could optimize the performance of LSS staff and, by extension, of the Court overall.

15.3.1   Misunderstandings about Language Services and Processes

The whole process of interpretation remains mysterious to many, especially when an institution does not have a sufficiently developed 'interpretation culture'. One ICC courtroom interpreter with prior experience in European institutions was shocked when staff at the ICC Court Management System, in the early days, proposed reversing the direction of interpretation from Language A towards Language B, in other words 'flipping' the normal direction used by professional conference interpreters.[62] Some LSS staff members express dismay at the ICC policy that places field interpreters on either a Registry or OTP roster, which guarantees that they will work for either defence or prosecution but never both. This reveals a basic misunderstanding by the Court, they suggested, of an interpreter's professional commitment to confidentiality and neutrality.[63] It also creates less flexibility in deploying interpreters across the Court where they are needed most at any given moment.

A recurring concern for LSS staff is the phenomenon of 'overlapping speakers' on courtroom interpretation channels. This occurs when a sufficient pause – five seconds is the rule – has not been observed between the end of one utterance in the courtroom and the beginning of the next.

---

[61] Author interview RL-1, 29 May 2017.
[62] Author interview RL-3, 30 May 2017.
[63] Author interview RL-9, 5 June 2017.

Without this critical pause, the interpreted message, which necessarily lags behind what is happening on the floor, is still occupying the interpretation channel and thus blocks the beginning of the next utterance. Yet a strategy for making this essential message sink in has not yet been found.[64] A related challenge has to do with rapid speech on the floor, which may also cause interpreters to lag behind in their production. Unlike a conference interpreter, a courtroom interpreter cannot simply remove pauses and hesitations in order to 'catch up'. These features are part of a speaker's demeanour and need to be assessed by judges, and thus cannot be eliminated for the sake of expediency.

A complaint voiced about legal counsel in particular is that they do not consistently provide interpreters in advance with a written version of the more formal and prepared statements that they intend to present in the courtroom, such as opening and closing statements. Prepared speeches, particularly if they are read verbatim and thus do not have the pauses of spontaneous speech, are extremely 'dense' and challenging to interpret.[65] Complex legal language and argumentation only contribute to the density. The inevitable consequence is that the official hearing transcripts – the written version of interpreted speech – may have gaps and errors. When parties express discontent with inaudible parts of the transcript, interpreters will undertake transcript revisions, usually by comparing the English and French transcripts and filling in gaps in one or the other.[66] This is a frustrating process as it is time-consuming and occurs on top of regular interpretation schedules (although it is sometimes taken on when trials are in recess). Parties may also request that interpreters review transcripts if they believe there are inaccuracies – ironic, given that some of the alleged problems may have resulted from their own lack of collaboration.

If some users of language services exhibit fundamental misunderstandings around the process of courtroom interpretation and their own responsibilities to the process, they often seem equally ill informed about its written product – the transcript that serves as the official record of everything said during a trial hearing and which will be consulted in the writing of judgments and appeals. Multilingual members of both prosecution and defence teams scrutinize the transcripts – produced in real time by court transcribers – as they scroll before them on the

---

[64] Author interview RL-1, 29 May 2017.
[65] Constable, 'Effective Communication in Multilingual Judicial Proceedings', above note 48.
[66] Author interview RL-3, 30 May 2017.

omnipresent screens in the ICC's technologically advanced courtrooms. As they listen to testimony in its original form or through their chosen language channel, they reflexively look for what they think the interpreted form should be. If a witness testifies in French, for example, counsel or legal assistants search the English language transcript for key words they heard in the original testimony, expecting to see their English equivalents. If they are absent, misinterpretation is often assumed to be the reason.

Language experts at the LSS believe that this almost obsessive following of the transcript stems from a basic misconception about what interpretation is. As already described, interpreters aim to communicate not the surface but the deep meaning of an utterance. The English and French transcripts will thus not be 'mirror images' of one another. Some of this confusion is almost certainly increased by the 'irregular' use of hearing transcripts at the ICC. Interpretation is intended to facilitate communication in the moment, to be heard but not recorded for all time. But transcripts at the ICC serve as the official written record and thus constitute evidence, despite not being the product of a careful and methodical translation process. Several ICC interpreters explained that whereas a translator is expected to produce 1500 words per day, an interpreter does about 150 words per minute – the speed of normal human speech – and thus produces the same output over ten minutes.[67] A translator can read the whole original text before beginning the translation process and has eight hours to do reference work and produce the finished document, which is then gone over by a reviser. An ICC interpreter 'does work in reference to nothing, on the fly.'[68]

Finally, actors in the courtroom often forget that the recruiting and training of situation language interpreters is a long and complex process. Counsel may not give enough advance notice of their need for an interpreter of a certain language, expecting that one can be provided from one week to the next. Judges have been known to react in such situations with criticism, attributing the long delay needed to produce the requested interpreter to inefficiencies at the LSS.

15.3.2   Improving Languages Services Through Greater Visibility

What can language experts do to counter the misunderstandings held by their 'clients' about the services they routinely use and without which

---

[67] Author interview RL-9, 5 June 2017.
[68] Ibid.

their work at the ICC would be impossible? Can increased visibility of the full range of activities performed by LSS and better knowledge of how language staff actually accomplish them lead to more cooperation among language service providers and users? LSS already makes an effort to explain to the various units and sections they serve across the Court the constraints under which they operate. The Section also stresses the importance of making requests for their services in a timely manner. But there appears to be a tendency to take language services for granted, assuming LSS staff will be ready and prepared to respond whenever a client needs them.

It has been a particular challenge to have judges and parties understand the complex process whereby courtroom interpreters are trained in situation languages, and particularly in LLDs. The Section has begun sharing a short video prepared by the European Commission that documents the six-month-long process of training English–Mongolian simultaneous interpreters for a conference scheduled to last only three days.[69] Some judges and counsel seem to get the message about the difficulties of producing a courtroom interpreter for situation languages after learning of the European Commission experience. Ideally, they also recognize that the long LSS training process produces interpreters who will be engaged over the length of a trial, so the preparatory effort and expense are well worth it.

At the start of each ICC trial, LSS also convenes a meeting with the judges and parties so that fundamental aspects of the Section's work can be explained. The responsibilities of interpretation users are clearly laid out: requests for situation language interpreters who are not permanent ICC staff need to be scheduled far in advance and not changed at the last minute; there should be strict observance of the 'five-second rule'; speech should be neither too fast nor too slow; and more. Judges are also asked to be active in creating an 'interpreter-friendly' courtroom. Some trials achieve these conditions while others do not, whether this results from the presiding judge's inattention to language details, the behaviour of counsel, or other aspects of a particular trial.[70] And as a trial progresses, certain responsibilities tend to be forgotten or ignored. One ICC interpreter, Andrew Constable, has gone on record in a publication to articulate recommendations for counsel participating in multilingual judicial proceedings.[71]

---

[69] See www.youtube.com/watch?v=2WrAvwuat8c.
[70] Author interview RL-12, 7 June 2017.
[71] Constable, 'Effective Communication in Multilingual Judicial Proceedings', above note 48.

As to creating better conditions for ICC translation, these seem to revolve mainly around providing translators with sections of the important judicial texts they need to work on, in a progressive manner, so that deadlines can be met and official versions of judgments and other important decisions, when made available to the public, can be in the best and most accurate form possible. Ideally, translators will have the opportunity to consult with those drafting the judgments.

What more can LSS do to improve the all-important 'user input' to their work? It would perhaps be useful for the Section to create an internal courtroom interpretation user guide, much like the one currently in draft form for users of field interpretation, so that judges and parties can remind themselves of their responsibilities over the full length of a trial instead of having them fade into invisibility. A set of recommendations for those who regularly use translation might also prove helpful. More generally, LSS may need to lessen its attachment to the 'ethics of invisibility' in order to raise its profile within the ICC itself. Some at LSS admit that they need to do more 'internal outreach' to users of their services in order to communicate these vital messages effectively.[72] Such openness might move the ICC towards an institutional attitude shift vis-à-vis language services and those who provide them, and an increased recognition of their essential role in an institution characterized by multilingualism at every level. Such a shift would ideally include a rethinking of the view that language services represent 'an expense to be minimized'.[73]

15.4   From More Visible Language Services to Increased Legitimacy

It is important to consider the question of acceptance in situation countries.

ICC Judge Christine Van den Wyngaert[74]

The goals established by international courts internally may be out of sync with those that external audiences expect them to reach. Such 'goal divergence' would seem to be especially wide for the ICC:

---

[72] Author interview RL-6, 1 June 2017.
[73] Author interview RL-10, 5 June 2017.
[74] 'The Authority of International Courts and Tribunals: Challenges and Prospects', report of the Brandeis Institute for International Judges 2016, p. 23, available at www.brandeis.edu/ethics/pdfs/internationaljustice/biij/BIIJ2016.pdf.

> Its most important goals from the inside are ending impunity by increasing accountability of state officials for international crimes, deterrence or prevention of these crimes, ensuring international peace and security, enhancing international cooperation in the prosecution of international crimes, and guaranteeing lasting respect for and the enforcement of international justice. However, the common goals projected on the ICC from the outside may be quite different, coming from states parties, accused persons, victims' groups, and various NGOs.[75]

The most disgruntled ICC states parties are found in Africa, where a common narrative about the Court, seemingly generated by the powers-that-be, includes accusations of neocolonial attitudes and unfair targeting of crimes committed on the continent. This caveat notwithstanding, it clearly behoves the Court to do some 'repair work' vis-à-vis the African continent. ICC officials and judges hailing from Africa may find themselves in an awkward position, representing an institution that is the object of such scorn and rejection by African leaders, some of whom have personally been accused of crimes by the Court itself, such as Omar al-Bashir of Sudan and Uhuru Kenyatta of Kenya. Judge Sanji Monageng, a recently retired ICC judge from Botswana who also served as First Vice-President of the Court from 2012 to 2015, reflected on the dilemma of African nationals at the ICC: '[w]e are part of this institution and the problems come from our continent. You just wish you could go to bed, wake up and find this relationship normalized'.[76]

The ICC has clearly gone to extraordinary lengths to accommodate the language needs of accused persons and crime-based witnesses from Africa, especially those who speak LLDs. In the process, LSS has created new expertise around these languages, expanded their lexicons to include legal terminology, and more generally heightened the profile of the languages themselves. One LSS staff member has even taken as his personal mission the certification of simultaneous interpreters of African languages by the premier professional association for conference interpreters, l'Association Internationale des Interprètes de Conférence (more commonly known by its acronym AIIC). Through his efforts, interpreters working in Swahili,

---

[75] Ibid., pp. 22–23. For more about the disparity between global and local conceptions of the ICC's aims and accomplishments, see Margaret M. deGuzman, 'The Global-Local Dilemma and the ICC's Legitimacy', in Harlan Grant Cohen, Andreas Follesdal, Nienke Grossman and Geir Ulfstein (eds.), *Legitimacy and International Courts* (Cambridge University Press, 2018).

[76] Leigh Swigart, 'Bringing Soft Power to a Life's Work: the Professional Trajectory of Judge Sanji Mmasenono Monageng', *AFLA Quarterly*, Special Edition 2018 Commemorating the 20th Anniversary of the Rome Statute of the International Criminal Court, p. 55.

Lingala, and Acholi have now been recognized.[77] Most of this critical work by LSS staff members remains entirely hidden, however. The list of situation languages that LSS has worked with is absent from the Court's website; the innovative strategies adopted to facilitate communication by LLD speakers is shared mostly with others in this specialized field; and only when an interested researcher comes along to investigate does the full array of impressive language activities come to light.

Yet this success in 'giving a voice to the voiceless'[78] is not a negligible achievement and it deserves to be more widely recognized, and perhaps even actively publicized. When interacting with African audiences – be they government officials, members of the local press, victims who seek to participate in a proceeding, or NGOs working with affected communities – the Court should highlight the important work of LSS and its ability to facilitate communication in a diverse range of languages. The activities of LSS belie the negative narrative generated by certain parties in Africa, demonstrating not a neocolonial attitude but instead an appreciation of the expressive potential and creativity of languages that have rarely played a part on the world stage.[79] Understanding the Court's commitment to facilitating communication in these languages could well enhance its acceptance by situation countries, described by Judge Van den Wyngaert as so important for the authority of the ICC.[80]

Looking back to the internal goals of the Court, it is clear that bringing about accountability for perpetrators of crimes, deterring future crimes, ensuring international peace and security, and all the rest also depend to a large extent on good communication – among staff from diverse units of the ICC, in the courtroom, and in the messages that the Court sends out to victims and affected communities. The more the ICC can do to support the work of LSS – including the provision of a sufficient operating budget – and to ensure that all who use its services understand their responsibilities vis-à-vis translation and interpretation, the better the language-related outputs of the Court will be. Such outputs will include trials that are not subject to undue delay because of poor planning by parties around language services, as well as judgments and other official

---

[77] Author interview RL-9, 5 June 2017.

[78] Ibid.

[79] Indeed, the ICC has outstripped most African countries in this area, as they have not yet developed a consistent or professionalized approach to using local languages in their own courtrooms, as discussed at the 2017 Language and Development Conference (www .britishcouncil.com.sn/en/programmes/language-development-conference-2017).

[80] See 'The Authority of International Courts and Tribunals: Challenges and Prospects', above note 74.

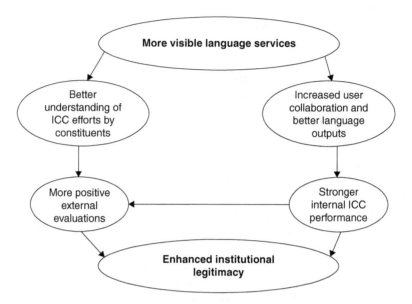

Figure 15.1 How language services' visibility can lead to enhanced ICC legitimacy

documents that are made available to the public in both French and English in a timely manner.

The internal and external pathways connecting more visible and better-understood language services with increased ICC legitimacy are represented schematically in Figure 15.1.

This chapter ends with a question: what can other international courts learn from the experiences of the ICC? Although language challenges play out in a particularly acute manner at the Court, the role of language services is fundamental to all judicial institutions whose jurisdictions extend across linguistic borders, whether they deal with criminal matters, human rights claims, or interstate disputes. These courts would thus be well advised to step back and reflect on the need to support multilingual communication at all levels of their institutions, and acknowledge the inevitable challenges raised by translation and interpretation, even when interactions occur between European languages with large pools of trained experts. International courts can reach their full potential only if they recognize how the languages in which they work mediate meaning, not only during proceedings that shape international law but also in the activities designed to share the resultant jurisprudence. Realising this potential should, in turn, reinforce the legitimacy of these institutions in the eyes of diverse and multilingual constituencies.

Rights and Expertise

Assessing the Managerial Approach of the Court of Justice of the European Union to Conflict Adjudication

MARIE-CATHERINE PETERSMANN*

16.1 Introduction

This chapter explores the role played by scientific experts in the decision-making process of the Court of Justice of the European Union (CJEU) when EU environmental laws collide with fundamental rights and freedoms protected under the European Union Charter on Fundamental Rights (EUCFR).[1] The study assesses the recourse of parties to scientific expertise in their argumentation, and the implications thereof for the legitimacy of the dispute resolution process. The analysis shows how the CJEU has developed a managerial approach to conflict adjudication, where reliance on scientific expertise is central. In this interpretative process, scientific experts grant justificatory power to specific arguments when complex and technical normative aspirations collide. As 'unseen' actors, scientific experts act as a key exogenous source of authority for the CJEU to determine optimal outcomes.

The chapter questions how judges assess adversarial and selective production of expert evidence and, most importantly, what this tells us about the adjudicative praxis of the CJEU and its legitimacy when deciding conflicts between normatively charged legal regimes. Such questions have been widely debated in international legal settings and with regard to specific dispute settlement bodies.[2] This chapter applies these queries to the

---

* I would like to thank Caroline Foster, Joanne Scott and Dimitri Van den Meerssche for their insightful feedback on an earlier draft.

[1] Charter of Fundamental Rights of the European Union [2012] OJ C 326 (3 October 1983).

[2] See e.g. the conference on 'The Expert in the International Adjudicative Process' (Symposium at the Max Planck Institute in Luxembourg, 27–28 April 2017), www.mpi.lu/news-and-events/2017/april/27-28/the-expert-in-the-international-adjudicative-process/, last accessed 20 December 2017. On the *roles* of experts in the adjudicative process of the ICJ, ITLOS and the WTO, see e.g. C.E. Foster, *Science and the Precautionary Principle*

CJEU in specific cases of conflicts between EU environmental regulations and fundamental rights. While the role, the risks and the legitimacy of expertise in determining the appropriateness of EU environmental laws in light of scientific uncertainty and risk regulations have been extensively commented upon in legal literature,[3] this chapter is interested in the way scientific experts grant legitimacy and authority to environmental regulations over competing concerns of fundamental rights at the adjudicative level. Three areas of tension are scrutinized: conflicts between climate change and economic freedoms; conflicts between animal welfare and indigenous peoples' rights; and conflicts between animal welfare and religious freedoms.[4]

The case law analysis reveals how the CJEU has developed an expert-based managerial approach to conflict adjudication. The argument unfolds in three parts. First, the recourse to expertise is traced back to the growing fragmentation, complexity and indeterminacy of international and EU law. Second, the impact of scientific justification on the decision-making process of the CJEU is examined through the *Arcelor,* the *Inuit* and the *Liga van Moskeeën* cases. The case law analysis demonstrates how, in a fragmented and complex legal order, recourse to scientific expertise is anchored in a broader managerial reasoning through which the CJEU settles the dispute. Finally, the chapter concludes by reflecting on three main issues of legitimacy that an expert-based managerial approach to conflict adjudication raises. First, it questions the legitimacy of scientific evidence and argumentation in light of the indeterminacy critique. Second, it further reflects on the politics that lie behind scientific expertise and the normative, cultural and social realities in which it is embedded. Finally, it highlights a gap in the legal protection of fundamental rights that results from scientific expertise in court. Overall, the chapter underlines the merit of an expert-based managerial approach to conflict adjudication in a legal order defined by growing fragmentation into specialized, complex and technical fields of legal regulation, but warns of the limits and risks that scientific expertise can pose to the protection of fundamental rights and freedoms.

---

in *International Courts and Tribunals: Expert Evidence, Burden of Proof and Finality* (Cambridge University Press, 2011).

[3] See e.g. M. Weimer and A. de Ruijter (eds.), *Regulating Risks in the European Union: The Co-production of Expert and Executive Power* (Hart Publishing, 2017).

[4] Seen through the prism of environmental ethics and nature conservation, animal welfare concerns are here understood as forming part of environmental protection laws. On the specificities of 'animal welfare law', see D. Cao and S. White (eds.), *Animal Law and Welfare – International Perspectives* (Springer, 2016).

16.2 Fragmentation, Complexity and Indeterminacy of International and EU Law

Experts have become essential in law-making processes today. An expert can be defined as a 'person who has, or is deemed or claimed to have, extensive skill or knowledge in a particular field and who is part of a wider group consisting of persons holding similar expertise'.[5] There is a collective and social dimension to the production of expertise, since '[t]he group operates on the basis of a common knowledge base and shared values, and uses accepted methods to present its findings'.[6] This exemplifies what Sacks coined a 'membership category', which is not only a category used by persons in a society to classify people and activities, but an expression that claimants to the category use in reference to themselves and their activities.[7] Expertise, as such, represents a specific field of knowledge, often known only to experts.[8]

Applied to the legal realm, experts can have different roles. In international and EU law, the role of experts is most visible at the legislative level, where policy- and law-makers rely on technical expertise to delineate the regulation of certain measures and propose appropriate actions to be taken. Yet, the role experts play at the legislative level heavily impacts upon the adjudicative practice. In order to interpret laws that draw on technical expertise, adjudicators become dependent upon the expert knowledge that determined the legislation in the first place. Schematically, the role of experts can be conceived as a spiral of influence, where the greater the degree of complexity of the object of legislation, the greater the influence of experts on the design of such legislation will be, and the more

---

[5] M. Ambrus, K. Arts, E. Hey and H. Raulus, 'The Role of "Experts" in International and European Decision-Making Processes: Setting the Scene', in M. Ambrus, K. Arts, E. Hey and H. Raulus (eds.), *The Role of 'Experts' in International and European Decision-Making Processes: Advisors, Decision Makers or Irrelevant Actors?* (Cambridge University Press, 2014), pp. 1–17, p. 12.

[6] Ibid.

[7] Lynch argues that 'science' or 'expertise' is more than a label; it is a term of praise and a mark of privilege often used self-referentially. M. Lynch, 'Circumscribing Expertise: Membership Categories in Courtroom Testimonies', in S. Jasanoff (ed.), *States of Knowledge: The Co-production of Science and the Social Order* (Routledge, 2004), p. 164.

[8] Kennedy describes this 'expert knowledge' as a set of shared 'intellectual history'; shared 'issues about which they disagree'; shared 'vocabulary of arguments'; shared 'outcomes', 'policies', 'doctrines', 'theories, methods and political commitments'; as well as 'style and consciousness'. D.W. Kennedy, 'Challenging Expert Rule: The Politics of Global Governance' (2005) 27 *Sydney Law Review* 5, 14–16.

dependent adjudicators become on scientific experts' knowledge when interpreting the technical legislation at stake.

The increasing recourse to experts in international law coincides, thus, with the growing complexity of the international legal order. This complexity is itself embedded in the growing fragmentation of international law and the emergence of ever-more specialized, functionally delineated, regulatory legal regimes. Both international environmental law and human rights law act as prime examples of such specialized rule-complexes. Each legal regime produces an increasing number of laws and policies that cover ever-more substantive and procedural matters. As a mirror of the international sphere, the EU legal order is scattered into specialized fields of legal and policy regulation. Aside from the growing fragmentation of international and EU law, the protection of transnational public goods requires a form of collective action that must be organized and managed at a supranational level. Both the protection of the environment and the proliferation of human rights laws[9] are examples of this cooperative configuration of the international legal order.[10] In these processes, the position of states and their sovereignty becomes 'increasingly ambiguous'.[11] By requiring the cooperation of various actors at different levels to effectively implement transnational collective actions to protect global public goods, specialized legal regimes tend to result in complex and technical rules and procedures. They often escape the traditional confines of positive law, as demonstrated by the emergence of a vast body of regulatory 'soft law' instruments and policies in the fields of both environmental and human rights law.[12] Functionally delineated legal regimes that aim to resolve collective action problems are inherently outcome-oriented, each favouring the *telos* that lies at the core of its *raison d'être*.[13] To determine

---

[9] On human rights and environmental protection as global public or common goods, see F. Lenzerini and A.F. Vrdoljak (eds.), *International Law for Common Goods: Normative Perspectives on Human Rights, Culture and Nature* (Hart Publishing, 2014).

[10] On the passage from a 'law of co-existence' to a 'law of cooperation', where states become interdependent in regulating common goods, see W. Friedmann, *The Changing Structure of International Law* (Columbia University Press, 1964).

[11] C. Tomuschat, 'International Law: Ensuring the Survival of Mankind on the Eve of a New Century: General Course on Public International Law', *Collected Courses of The Hague Academy of International Law*, vol. 281 (Brill, Nijhoff, 1999), p. 95.

[12] See Chapters 5 (The Environment and Natural Resources) and 7 (Human Rights) in D. Shelton (ed.), *Commitment and Compliance: The Role of Non-Binding Norms in the International Legal System* (Oxford University Press, 2000).

[13] At the judicial level, specialized courts will also tend to be 'structurally biased' towards the *telos* of the legal regime they belong to, or their 'mission' or 'special mandate'. Koskenniemi

functionally coherent and effective outcomes, specialized regimes draw heavily on optimization through expertise. This process has resulted in an increasing demand for technical and scientifically grounded rules that seek to 'manage global problems efficiently'.[14]

The regime of international environmental law provides a straightforward example of the expert-based design and adjudication of technical environmental regulations. The intricate entanglement of environmental law with scientific knowledge makes it a complex legal regime, where laws cannot be articulated only through rules and principles but must be complemented with empirical analyses and scientific experiments that carry out risk assessments and provide for technical laws of risk management.[15] As textual objects, environmental laws are often a mix of words, numbers, statistics, figures and graphs, setting out complex rules and compliance mechanisms, with annexes listing substances or methods that comply with risk assessments, which in turn must be regularly updated on the basis of the most recent scientific knowledge available. The interdisciplinary interactions underlying environmental laws render legal experts increasingly dependent on the input of scientific experts.[16]

Under EU law, Article 191(3) of the Treaty on the Functioning of the European Union (TFEU) explicitly provides that in preparing its policy on the environment, the EU legislator must take account of all 'available scientific and technical data'.[17] This requirement recalls the principle of 'best available techniques not entailing excessive costs' (BATNEEC) that was used to stipulate suitable measurement and assessment techniques of air pollution.[18] The concept of 'best available technique' or 'technology' (BAT) has, since, widely spread across EU environmental laws and has become

sees judicial institutions as 'mechanised producers of outcomes that are internally validated by their embedded hierarchies of preference – their structural biases'. See M. Koskenniemi, 'Hegemonic Regimes', in M.A. Young (ed.), *Regime Interaction in International Law: Facing Fragmentation* (Cambridge University Press, 2012), pp. 305–324, p. 317.

[14] M. Koskenniemi, 'The Fate of Public International Law: Between Techniques and Politics' (2007) 70 *Modern Law Review* 1–30, p. 14.

[15] P. Gardoni, C. Murphy and A. Rowell (eds.), *Risk Analysis of Natural Hazards: Interdisciplinary Challenges and Integrated Solutions* (Springer, 2016).

[16] For Werner, environmental laws are 'legal norms [that] can often only be applied on the basis of scientific expert knowledge'. W. Werner, 'The Politics of Expertise: Applying Paradoxes of Scientific Expertise to International Law', in M. Ambrus et al. The Role of 'Experts', pp. 44–62, p. 55.

[17] Consolidated version of the Treaty on the Functioning of the European Union [2008] OJ C115/13.

[18] Council Directive 84/360/EEC of 28 June 1984 on the combating of air pollution from industrial plants, Article 8 (no longer in force since 29 October 2007).

a determining factor in environmental decision-making. The dependence of environmental laws on scientific and technical assessments distributes authority to a specific type of actor. With an eye to optimization, precaution, efficiency and reduction of regulatory burdens, scientific experts are key to determining the standards of 'best' 'available' 'techniques/technology', three terms whose meaning can vary greatly according to societal evolution, scientific developments and technological innovations.

Thus, in designing environmental laws, scientific experts are granted a central role. When such laws collide with competing norms, applicants must prove the alleged violation of their rights by the environmental legislation. In doing so, parties to a case tend to argue on the basis of scientific and technical data. To substantiate their claims, they resort to scientific expert evidence that the court then needs to review.

Let us now turn to three case studies to explore the dynamics of judicial assessment of expert evidence when EU environmental laws and human rights collide.

16.3   Scientific Expertise as Justification: The Rise of Managerial Adjudication

In this section, the *Arcelor,* the *Inuit* and the *Liga van Moskeeën* cases are analysed to assess the role played by experts in the adjudication of conflicts between EU environmental laws and fundamental rights and freedoms of the applicants. In line with the traditional rule on the burden of proof, a party making an allegation must prove that assertion. When an EU environmental legislation impedes on fundamental rights, the applicant will have to prove the alleged right infringement by the environmental regulation and argue on the basis of scientific expert evidence to grant authoritative weight to its arguments.[19] Reference to *ex curia* scientific experts by the parties compels the court to interpret scientific questions and draw a line between scientific facts and law. The analysis demonstrates how this process gives birth to a specific form of managerial adjudication, where the court avoids assessing the scientific merits of the arguments invoked by the parties and determines efficient outcomes on the basis of criteria of objectivity, optimization, reduction of administrative burdens and overall effective functioning of the system.

---

[19] On the allocation of the burden of proof in light of expert evidence and scientific complexity and uncertainty, see Foster, Science and the Precautionary Principle in International Courts and Tribunals, Ch 5.

16.3.1   Conflicts Between Climate Change and Economic Freedoms: The Arcelor Case

In 2003, the EU established a scheme for greenhouse gas emission allowance trading (Emission Trading System (ETS) Directive) to enable the EU and its Member States to meet the commitments to reduce greenhouse gas (GHG) emissions as established under the Kyoto Protocol to the UN Framework Convention on Climate Change.[20] In the *Arcelor* case, the CJEU had to determine whether the EU legislator breached the principle of equal treatment with respect to the steel sector by applying an unjustifiable different treatment to comparable situations when excluding the plastics and aluminium sectors from the Directive.[21]

When assessing whether the ETS Directive breached Arcelor's right to equal treatment, the CJEU first recalled that '[a] difference in treatment is justified if it is based on an objective and reasonable criterion, that is, if the difference relates to a legally permitted aim pursued by the legislation in question, and it is proportionate to the aim pursued by the treatment'.[22] Criteria of objectivity and reasonableness were thus central to the arguments of the parties. To demonstrate that the ETS Directive was based on objective criteria, the EU legislator held that '[o]ne of the objective criteria that were decisive for determining the scope of the Directive' was the level of direct CO_2 emissions per sector.[23] In establishing these levels, the EU legislator relied on a scientific report entitled 'Economic Evaluation of Sectoral Emission Reduction Objectives for Climate Change: Top-down Analysis of [GHG] Reduction Possibilities in the EU (final Report, March 2001)', which was prepared by Pantelis Capros, a Professor of Energy Economics and Operation Research at the Department of Electrical and Computer Engineering of the National Technical University of Athens; Nick Kouvaritakis, an energy lawyer; and Leonidas Mantzos, an energy engineer.[24] Except for their names, no information was disclosed in the

---

[20] 'The EU Emissions Trading System (EU ETS)', www.ec.europa.eu/clima/policies/ets/index_en.htm, last accessed 20 December 2017.

[21] Case C-127/07 *Société Arcelor Atlantique et Lorraine and Others v. Premier ministre, Ministre de l'Écologie et du Développement durable and Ministre de l'Économie, des Finances et de l'Industrie* [2008] ECR I-09895.

[22] Ibid., para. 47.

[23] Ibid., para 5.2.

[24] The 120 pages report commissioned by DG Environment is available at http://ec.europa.eu/environment/enveco/climate_change/pdf/top_down_analysis.pdf, last accessed 20 December 2017.

case regarding these experts' skills, the context of their research or who commissioned it. In addition to these findings,[25] the EU legislator also invoked concerns of administrative complexity and feasibility,[26] as well as the wide discretion it enjoys in designing the legislation at stake.[27]

Yet, to enjoy broad discretion, the political, economic and social choices that the EU legislator is called on to undertake must be based on objective criteria appropriate to the aim pursued,[28] and take account of all the facts and technical and scientific data available at the time of adoption, in line with Article 191(3) of the TFEU. To contest the objectivity and the appropriate account of the scientific and technical data put forward by the EU legislator, the applicant invoked statistics supplied by the European Pollutant Emission Register (EPER) that contradicted the scientific data of the EU legislator on three grounds.[29] First, Arcelor argued that the EPER's statistics for 2001 demonstrate that 'the chemical sector emits a much greater amount of CO_2 than that mentioned by the Parliament, the Council and the Commission'.[30] Here, Arcelor clearly attempted to create doubt by questioning the veracity of the scientific data put forward by the EU legislator. Second, it argued that the inclusion in the scope of the Directive of 'chemical undertakings emitting quantities of CO_2 above a certain threshold would not have created administrative problems, since nearly 59% of total CO_2 emissions of the chemical sector came from only 96 installations'.[31] In so doing, Arcelor questioned the administrative feasibility invoked by the EU legislator to justify the scope of the scheme. Finally, Arcelor challenged the objective justification of the scope of the Directive by holding that '[t]he report referred to by the institutions ... itself shows that [the aluminium] sector emits 16.2 million tonnes of CO_2 while the pulp and paper sector, which is included in the scope of Directive 2003/87, emits only 10.6 million tonnes of CO2'.[32] Thereby, Arcelor pointed to the selective and therefore incomplete and non-objective reference to scientific data by the EU legislator.

---

[25] The report concluded that CO_2 emissions in 1990 were 174.8 million tonnes for the steel sector, 26.2 million tonnes for the chemical sector and 16.2 million tonnes for the non-ferrous metal sector. Ibid., para. 52.

[26] Ibid., para. 53.

[27] Ibid., para. 54.

[28] Ibid., paras. 57–58.

[29] *Arcelor*, para. 55. The EPER has since been replaced by the European Pollutant Release and Transfer Register (E-PRTR).

[30] *Arcelor*, para. 55.

[31] Ibid.

[32] Ibid., para. 56.

In reviewing these allegations, the CJEU started by recognizing the 'novelty' and 'complexity' of the scheme and justified the 'step-by-step approach' adopted by the EU legislator in light of the administrative disturbances that the involvement of too great a number of participants would cause.[33] Yet, this could not dispense with necessity that the EU legislator base its choices on objective criteria. Considering the competing findings of the scientific reports invoked by the parties, the CJEU had the difficult task of assessing the objectivity of the technical and scientific information submitted to it. In doing so, the court sided with the EU legislator and rebutted the arguments of the applicant. First, regarding the scientific findings advanced by Arcelor, the CJEU observed that the EPER mentions 'facilities' while the ETS Directive refers to 'installations' and that, therefore, 'the data produced by the applicants in the main proceedings in support of their abovementioned argument *do not enable the Court to verify the assertion* that a small number of installations in the chemical sector were responsible for a large part of the total CO_2 emissions of the sector'.[34] Second, regarding the administrative feasibility of the scheme, the CJEU noted that the chemical sector 'has an especially large number of installations, of the order of 34 000', and that, consequently, the inclusion of that sector in the scope of the ETS Directive would 'have made the management of the allowance trading scheme more difficult and increased the administrative burden, so that the *possibility* that the functioning of the scheme would have been disturbed at the time of its implementation as a result of that inclusion *cannot be excluded*'.[35] The exclusion of the aluminium sector was justified by the court in reference to the scientific report invoked by the EU legislator.[36] On these grounds, the CJEU concluded that the EU legislator adhered to the requisite legal standard that it makes use of objective criteria in determining the scope of the Directive and did not infringe the principle of equal treatment.

The *Arcelor* case clearly demonstrates how science is subject to disagreement, and most importantly, how the CJEU opts for an outcome in a context of factual indeterminacy. Indeed, the court explicitly acknowledges that the arguments of the applicant on the first point, 'cannot be verified', and on the second point, 'cannot be excluded'. The interpretation evidently points to a context of scientific indeterminacy. To justify its decision in

---

[33] Ibid., paras. 60–61.
[34] Ibid., para. 68 (emphasis added).
[35] Ibid., para. 65 (emphases added).
[36] Ibid., para. 70.

this context of factual/scientific indeterminacy, the court focused on the 'novelty', 'complexity', 'step-by-step approach' and 'administrative feasibility' of the ETS Directive in light of its necessary and legitimate aim of protecting the environment by reducing GHG emissions.[37] Hence, while the scientific data on which the parties rely cannot be epistemologically assessed by the court, the arguments of the EU legislator are granted the presumption of legality in view of criteria of complexity, apparent accuracy and administrative efficiency.

A managerial approach to conflict adjudication is discernible in the court's reasoning. The CJEU justifies the ETS Directive on the basis of its administrative efficiency;[38] the effective functioning of the scheme;[39] and its capacity to reduce GHG emissions in a cost-effective and economically efficient manner.[40] The emphasis put on the step-by-step approach that requires to proceed in light of the experience gained further epitomizes these priorities.[41] The ETS Directive, in sum, is justified on grounds of the appropriate management of administrative burdens and proper handling of complex issues for the legitimate objective of reducing GHG emissions. These expert-based managerial concerns are further invoked to justify what ought to be done in the general interest. The applicant's interests, in other words, are integrated in the understanding of the 'common good' that results from the experts' studies and is legally translated into the Directive.[42] The optimal outcome, determined on scientific grounds and embodying all the interests involved, thereby portrays the judicial decision as being 'in the common good'.[43]

---

[37] Ibid., paras. 60–64.

[38] 'Administrative feasibility', the court recalls, 'is also a legitimate criterion for assessing the appropriateness of legislative action'. Ibid., para. 53. Overall, administrative complexity, feasibility, problems and burden were referred to six times in the case at paras. 53, 55, 65, 66, 71.

[39] Ibid., referred to four times in the case at paras. 34, 37, 60, 65.

[40] Ibid., referred to six times in the case at paras. 31, 32, 33, 35, 40, 43; and emphasized by A.G. Maduro at paras. 5, 43, 48, 49, 52, 56. On the identification of managerialism through a 'vocabulary of law and economics', see M. Koskenniemi, 'The Fate of Public International Law', p. 12.

[41] Referred to six times in the *Arcelor* case at paras. 57, 61, 63, 69, 71, 72; and emphasized by A.G. Maduro at paras. 44–47.

[42] 'When exercising its discretion, the Community legislature must, in addition to the principal objective of protecting the environment, fully take into account all the interests involved'. Ibid., para. 59.

[43] On the hegemonic nature of courts in determining this 'common good', see M. Koskenniemi, 'Hegemonic Regimes', p. 306.

The optimal outcome dictated by the managerial approach, thus, counters the scientific indeterminacy in which the dispute is anchored. The resulting impediments to the economic interests of the applicant are, here, legitimately justified in light of the general interest in environmental protection. The (moral) justification of such an approach is, however, more difficult to sustain when the competing interests concern subsistence rights of indigenous peoples.

16.3.2   Conflicts Between Animal Welfare and Indigenous Peoples' Rights: The Inuit Case

In response to citizens' concerns on animal welfare, in 2009 the EU adopted a Regulation forbidding the trade of seal products on the EU market, with the exception of seal products originating 'from hunts traditionally conducted by Inuit and other indigenous communities [that] contribute to their subsistence'.[44] In the *Inuit* case, the CJEU had to assess the legality of the Regulation on trade in seal products in light, inter alia, of the Inuit's right to property and right to adequate living conditions.[45] The Inuit fought against the total ban on seal products in the EU market as provided for in the Regulation despite the existence of the Inuit exemption. They contested not only the effectiveness of this exception in terms of the administrative and practical burdens for such remote communities, but further claimed that even with the indigenous exception, their incomes would be heavily reduced. Since their earnings depend entirely on the selling of seal products, they argued their very subsistence was put at risk as the demand for seal products would inevitably collapse as a result of the EU seal ban. Instead of a general ban with an Inuit exemption, they insisted, the EU legislator should instead adopt strict labelling requirements or quotas.[46]

In assessing the Inuit's argument that a labelling measure would be less restrictive and more effective in achieving the objectives of the Regulation, the CJEU referred to arguments put forward by the European Food Safety Authority (EFSA), which published on behalf of the Scientific

---

[44] Council Regulation (EC) 1007/2009 on Trade in Seal Products [2009] OJ L 286, Article 3(1).

[45] Case T-526/10 *Inuit Tapiriit Kanatami and Others v. Commission* [2013] ECR 00000; confirmed on appeal in Case C-398/13 P *Inuit Tapiriit Kanatami and Others v. Commission* [2015] EU:C:2015:535.

[46] D. Cambou, 'The Impact of the Ban on Seal Products on the Rights of Indigenous Peoples: A European Issue' (2013) 5 *Yearbook of Polar Law*, 389–415.

Panel on Animal Health and Welfare (AHAW) and at the request of the Commission, a scientific report on that matter.[47] AHAW's 162-page report contained graphs, tables, figures, statistics, pictures, information on the biology of various species of seals, descriptions of seal hunting practices in all regions of the world and evaluations of their killing methods.[48] Once again, no information concerning the experts who drafted the scientific opinion was disclosed. The twenty authors are all either veterinarians or biologists and almost all university professors of animal hygiene, ethology, animal welfare, veterinary medicine, epidemiology, anatomy, wildlife virology, virus discovery, psychology, biomedical sciences or epizootiology. On the basis of their scientific findings, on which the Regulation is based, the CJEU concluded that '[a]lthough it *might* be possible to kill and skin seals in such a way as to avoid unnecessary pain, distress, fear or other forms of suffering', given the conditions in which seal hunting occurs, 'consistent verification and control of hunters' compliance with animal welfare requirements is *not feasible in practice* or, at least, is *very difficult to achieve in an effective way*, as concluded by [EFSA] on 6 December 2007'.[49] Moreover, on the basis of this scientific report, the CJEU specified that:

> [i]t is also clear that other forms of harmonised rules, such as labelling requirements, would not achieve the same result [and that a]dditionally, requiring manufacturers, distributors or retailers to label products that derive wholly or partially from seals would impose a significant burden on those economic operators, and would also be disproportionately costly in cases where seal products represent only a minor part of the product concerned[, whereas c]onversely, the measures contained in this Regulation will be *easier to comply with*, whilst also reassuring consumers.[50]

In light of the above, the CJEU justified the total ban on seal products in the EU market with a general exception for Inuit products. This reaffirms the decisive, yet almost invisible, role played by scientific experts in providing the arguments on the basis of which decisions by the CJEU are taken. Furthermore, the legal reasoning of the CJEU is clearly oriented towards an optimal outcome articulated through a managerial vocabulary

---

[47] Scientific Opinion of the Panel on Animal Health and Welfare (AHAW) of the European Food Safety Authority on 'Animal welfare aspects of the killing and skinning of seals' (2007) 610 *The EFSA Journal* 1, www.efsa.europa.eu/en/efsajournal/pub/610, last accessed 20 December 2017.

[48] Ibid.

[49] *Inuit* case (n 46), para. 95 (emphases added).

[50] Ibid. (emphasis added).

that promises to achieve results in an effective way without imposing significant burdens on the parties concerned. While the possibility of killing seals in a traditional way without imposing unnecessary suffering is not rejected, the verification of steps that such a method would impose is advised against in light of its 'feasibility in practice', 'overall effectivity' and difficult 'compliance' requirements.[51]

In contrast to the EU legislator, the Inuit did not refer to scientific data supported by qualified experts. Instead, the court reckoned that 'the applicants confine themselves to referring to specific paragraphs of the application [which] describe only the way of life of Inuit communities, the seal hunting they practise and the difficulties of the life and survival of the people'.[52] Yet for the CJEU, '[s]uch considerations, which are very general in nature and not substantiated, do not demonstrate that the Inuit communities have suffered harm which is disproportionate compared with the objective pursued by the basic regulation'.[53] Without entering into the details of the case, it suffices to emphasize that in reviewing the alleged breach of fundamental rights of the Inuit, the court found that their rights and interests had been sufficiently taken into account. It concluded that it is precisely in light of 'the particular situation of Inuit communities' that the EU legislator 'took the view that an exemption for products which result from hunts traditionally conducted by them for the purposes of subsistence should be authorised'.[54] This conclusion does not respond to the Inuit's allegation that this exemption is an 'empty box'.[55] Yet, in the absence of any convincing evidence put forward by the Inuit to substantiate their claims, the court rejected these concerns as unfounded.[56]

The *Inuit* case points, thus, to an imbalance in terms of authoritative argumentation between the scientific expertise invoked by the EU legislator and the traditional knowledge evoked by the applicants, which was qualified as unsubstantiated by the court. The technical nature of the Regulation privileges a certain type of justificatory discourse, which favours specific authoritative expertise and scientific skills that indigenous traditional knowledge might not be able to counter.[57] This disparity risks

---

[51] Ibid.
[52] Ibid., para. 98.
[53] Ibid.
[54] Ibid., para. 115.
[55] Ibid., para. 108.
[56] Ibid., para. 117.
[57] The documentary *Angry Inuk* (2016) offers powerful insights on this issue: www.unikkaat .com/projects/angry-inuk/, last accessed 20 December 2017.

creating a gap in legal protection of fundamental rights and freedoms of applicants that do not possess the material and immaterial means to support their claims with scientific and technical expertise. Hence, when emphasis is placed on scientific evidence, fundamental rights and freedoms risk being interpreted away.[58] Let us now turn to a third example to demonstrate similar dynamics.

16.3.3   Conflicts Between Animal Welfare and Religious Freedoms: The Liga Van Moskeeën Case

In 2009, the EU adopted a Regulation on the protection of animals at the time of killing to lay down common rules in the EU.[59] The general rule laid down by the Regulation provides that '[a]nimals shall only be killed after stunning' and that '[t]he loss of consciousness and sensibility shall be maintained until the death of the animal'.[60] Yet, Article 1(3)(a) (iii) of the Regulation excludes from its scope the slaughter of animals during 'cultural [...] events' and Article 4(4) provides that '[i]n the case of animals subject to particular methods of slaughter prescribed by religious rites, the requirements of [the general rule] shall not apply provided that the slaughter takes place in a slaughterhouse'.[61] Since 1998, the Belgian Federal Minister had approved temporary slaughterhouses each year which, together with approved slaughterhouses, catered for ritual slaughtering during the Muslim Feast of Sacrifice. In 2014, the Flemish Regional Minister announced that from 2015 onwards it would no longer issue approvals for temporary slaughterhouses at which ritual slaughtering could be practised during the Feast of Sacrifice, as such slaughterhouses did not satisfy the requirements of the Regulation. A circular was sent to Flemish municipalities informing them that all animal slaughtering without stunning, even if performed within the context of the Feast of Sacrifice, must be carried out solely in approved slaughterhouses that satisfy the requirements of the Regulation. Following this decision, various Muslim associations and umbrella organizations of mosques brought proceedings against the Flemish Region before the Belgian Court of First Instance (CFI).

---

[58] I am grateful to Joanne Scott for this observation.
[59] Council Regulation (EC) No 1099/2009 on the Protection of Animals at the Time of Killing [2009] OJ L 303.
[60] Ibid., Article 4(1).
[61] Ibid., Articles 1(3)(a)(iii) and 4(4).

The CFI introduced a request for preliminary ruling before the CJEU asking it to review the validity of Article 4(4) of the Regulation, which in its view indirectly placed a restriction on Muslims' freedom of religion. In *Liga van Moskeeën*, the CJEU assessed the validity of the Regulation in light of the freedom of religion protected by Article 10 of the EUCFR.[62] The CFI argued that, to comply with the technical requirements on the construction, layout and equipment of establishments laid down by the Regulation, practising Muslims were obliged to carry out ritual slaughter during the Feast of Sacrifice in approved slaughterhouses. Yet, since approved slaughterhouses are not sufficient in number to satisfy the increase in demand for halal meat recorded during the Feast of Sacrifice, these requirements prevented many practising Muslims from complying with their religious duty to slaughter or have an animal slaughtered on the first day of the Feast of Sacrifice in accordance with the prescriptions of the ritual.[63] The CFI also argued that these requirements were neither relevant nor proportionate to the legitimate objective of protecting animal welfare, first because until 2014, approved temporary slaughterhouses succeeded in ensuring that animal suffering was reduced to a sufficient extent and complied with public health requirements, and second, the conversion of these temporary slaughterhouses into establishments that comply with the technical requirements would require high investment that would be disproportionate to the temporary nature of the ritual slaughter carried out there.[64]

In assessing whether the Regulation restricts the right to freedom of religion, the CJEU recalled that Article 4(4) 'gives expression to the positive commitment of the EU legislature to allow the ritual slaughter of animals without prior stunning in order to ensure effective observance of the freedom of religion, in particular of practising Muslims during the Feast of Sacrifice'.[65] As such, by laying down the obligation to carry out ritual slaughter in an approved slaughterhouse, Article 4(4) 'simply aims to organise and manage, from a technical point of view, the freedom to carry out slaughter without prior stunning for religious purposes'.[66] The

---

[62] Case C-426/16 *Liga van Moskeeën en Islamitische Organisaties Provincie Antwerpen VZW and Others v. Vlaams Gewest* [2018] ECLI:EU:C:2018:335. I thank Geert Van Calster for having brought this case to my attention.
[63] Ibid., para. 23.
[64] Ibid., para. 24.
[65] Ibid., para. 56.
[66] Ibid., para. 58.

technical framework relating to the construction, layout and equipment laid down aimed, in other words, to reconcile the main objective of animal welfare pursued by the Regulation with the specific methods of slaughter prescribed by religious rites. The court judged, therefore, that the Regulation did not, in itself, give rise to any restriction on the right to freedom of religion of practising Muslims during the Feast of Sacrifice. Regarding the disproportionality of the expense that the establishment of new approved slaughterhouses would require in relation to the added value for animal welfare, the court observed that the fact that existing approved slaughterhouses in the Flemish Region do not have sufficient slaughter capacity to satisfy the increase in demand for ritual slaughter during the Feast of Sacrifice was a purely domestic issue which could not affect the validity of Article 4(4) of that Regulation.[67] On these grounds, it concluded that the doubts expressed by the CFI as to a possible infringement of the freedom of religion were unfounded.[68]

The *Liga van Moskeeën* case points again to the risks that an expert-based managerial approach to conflict adjudication can cause with regard to the fundamental rights of the applicants. The decisive arguments that led to the ban of temporary slaughterhouses during the Feast of Sacrifice in the Flemish Region were conclusions drawn from the final report of an audit carried out by the European Commission in Belgium in 2014 to assess the monitoring and supervision of animal welfare during slaughter.[69] This report stated that the 'killing of animals without stunning for religious rites outside a slaughterhouse does not comply with the Regulation'.[70] The report, which triggered the Flemish Regional Minister's decision to no longer issue approvals for temporary slaughterhouses, was mentioned by Advocate General (AG) Wahl in his Opinion and referred to by the CJEU in its judgement.[71] Yet, except for this report, the CJEU failed to refer to any other scientific expert evidence put forward by AG Wahl that questioned the proportionality of the technical requirements of the Regulation.

In his Opinion, AG Wahl argued that it is 'difficult to conclude that, even if it creates a limitation of religious freedom, the obligation ... to

---

[67] Ibid., paras. 70–78.
[68] Ibid., para. 80.
[69] Ibid., para. 19.
[70] Final report of an audit carried out in Belgium from 24 November to 3 December 2014 to evaluate the animal welfare controls in place at slaughter and during related operations (DG SANTE, 2014–7059 – RM, 30 July 2015).
[71] Opinion of A.G. Wahl, footnote 12; *Liga van Moskeeën* case, para. 19.

use a slaughterhouse approved in accordance with [the Regulation] is necessary and proportionate to the pursuit of a legitimate objective'.[72] He started by considering slaughtering of animals without stunning as 'undeniably likely to cause the animal greater pain and suffering'.[73] In support of his statement, he referred to an EU report that concluded that 'it is scientifically proven that stunning animals in order to render them unconscious when they are killed is an effective method of reducing animal suffering'.[74] Yet he continued, '[t]here is nothing to rule out the possibility that slaughtering without stunning, carried out in proper circumstances, will be less painful for the animal than slaughtering the animal after stunning it in circumstances in which, for obvious reasons of profitability, and given the widespread industrialisation of the production of food of animal origin, the stress and suffering experienced by the animal when it is killed are exacerbated'.[75] For these reasons, he admitted that '[he is] not convinced', and emphasized that 'a good number of studies and inquiries say as much', that the 'use of approved slaughterhouses is always an effective bulwark against animal suffering such that it could by itself justify a limitation of religious freedom'.[76] On this point, he insisted again that '[a]ssociations for the protection of animals regularly refer to the deplorable conditions in which slaughtering is carried out even in approved slaughterhouses'.[77]

What comes to light when comparing the judgment of the CJEU with the Opinion of AG Wahl is a disagreement regarding the best way to manage the legitimate objective of animal welfare in light of the freedom of religion. Both sides of the managerial debate are equally supported by scientific reports carrying authoritative weight that come to varying

---

[72] Ibid., para. 100.
[73] Ibid., para. 102. Wahl warned that this 'should not lead to the conclusion that religious communities that recommend slaughtering animals without stunning them have no regard for animal welfare and are following archaic practices that are barbarous and out of step with the principles of a modern democratic society' and deplored that 'behind the specific question of ritual slaughtering the spectre of stigmatisation very swiftly appears'.
[74] Report on Good and Adverse Practices – Animal Welfare Concerns in relation to Slaughter Practices from the Viewpoint of Veterinary Sciences, EU project on Encouraging Dialogue on issues of Religious Slaughter (DIALREL), www.dialrel.eu/dialrel-results/veterinary-concerns.html, last accessed 7 June 2018.
[75] Opinion of A.G. Wahl, para. 107.
[76] Ibid., para 109.
[77] Ibid., footnote 43, quoting a Report from the French Assemblée Nationale warning about the 'temptation among certain players to use the issues raised by ritual slaughtering to obfuscate the often very serious difficulties ... encountered by traditional slaughtering in terms of animal welfare'.

conclusions. All parties agree that there is a general interest in preventing 'savage' slaughtering from being carried out in dubious conditions. Yet they disagree on the best way to manage animal welfare. While the EU legislator opts for management through technical equipment in approved slaughterhouses; AG Wahl suggests that in light of the peak in demand for slaughtering during the three days' celebration of the Feast of the Sacrifice, the use of temporary slaughter plants that meet precise health standards without, however, corresponding to the definition of approved slaughterhouses might be a better solution to manage animal welfare concerns.[78] The CJEU however, referred neither to these arguments, nor to the scientific reports mentioned by AG Wahl in his Opinion. This illuminates not only the court's selective reference to scientific expert evidence, but also the contested managerial approaches to conflict adjudication which it has to face. These considerations bring us to the third and final part of this chapter, which questions the legitimacy of the court's managerial mode of conflict adjudication.

16.4   Assessing the Legitimacy of an Expert-Based Managerial Adjudication

A close reading of the *Arcelor,* the *Inuit* and the *Liga van Moskeeën* cases sheds light on fundamental yet largely overlooked dynamics in the adjudication of conflicts between, on the one hand, complex, technical and scientifically grounded environmental regulations, and on the other hand, the fundamental rights and freedoms of the applicants. The cases evidence how scientific experts play a determining role in the argumentative framework. Parties to a case must demonstrate that the contested legislation was based on objective criteria appropriate to the aim pursued and that all the scientific and technological data available at the time of the adoption was duly considered. These requirements lead parties to draw on scientific expertise to grant authoritative weight to their arguments. Yet the increasing reliance on scientific evidence in legislative and judicial decision-making processes confront us with important questions of legitimacy.

[78] Wahl argued that '[t]he creation of [temporary] plants could, by lightening the burden on approved slaughterhouses, ultimately help slaughtering to be carried out under the best conditions for the animal, in particular in so far as concerns the stress it suffers' and that 'the structural requirements relating ... to cutting plants and the refrigerated storage of meat, may ... prove superfluous ... inasmuch as the plants in question will be used only once a year and the meat from them will, in principle, be given directly to the final consumer'. Ibid., paras. 114–119 and 124–128.

To start with, the case law analysis echoes the critique of the indeterminacy of science. While 'Science' has carried through time a connotation of neutrality, impartiality, truth, objectivity and universality, it is now commonly accepted that scientific findings are socially constructed, and therefore prone to disagreement. 'Even scientific knowledge,' Jasanoff holds, 'built up over centuries as the one domain of human experience that is independent of personal and cultural biases, is now widely, if still controversially, acknowledged to be a social achievement'. Jasanoff defines science as 'a form of organized work, a site of politics, a marketplace of ideas, an exercise in meaning-making, and an instrument of power'. 'Scientific claims,' she warns, 'remain uncertain, controversial, interest-ridden, and historically and culturally situated'.[79] These concerns equally hold when applied to the realm (or role) of science in law[80] and adjudication.[81] The indeterminacy of scientific expertise was evidenced in all three cases, where parties referred to distinct and sometimes contradictory scientific findings. Both sides of the scientific debate were backed by authoritative experts that grant validity and authority to the claims put forward by the parties. When scientific findings are contested, we have seen, disputing parties tend to focus on the contingencies in each other's account of 'objective facts'. The indeterminacy of scientific evidence is amplified when opposing parties call on expertise to delegitimize a legislative decision.[82] The relative uncertainty of scientific findings due to the perpetual evolution of research and innovation is uncontested. But scientific uncertainty can also be artificially created, and most importantly, can be artificially maintained by specific actors capable of extracting certain benefits from a grey area.[83] Adjudicators should, therefore, undertake a more stringent procedural and substantive review when so-called 'corporate science' arguments are invoked.[84]

---

[79] S. Jasanoff, 'Heaven and Earth: The Politics of Environmental Images', in S. Jasanoff and M. Martello (eds.), *Earthly Politics: Local and Global in Environmental Governance* (MIT, 2004), pp. 32, 35 and 36.

[80] See e.g. J. Ellis, 'Scientific Expertise and Transnational Standards: Authority, Legitimacy, Validity' (2017) 8 *Transnational Legal Theory* 2.

[81] See e.g. J. D'Aspremont and M.M. Mbengue, 'Strategies of Engagement with Scientific Fact-finding in International Adjudication' (2014) 5 *Journal of International Dispute Settlement* 240.

[82] As clearly illustrated in the *Arcelor* case, para. 55.

[83] See e.g. D. Michaels, 'Manufactured Uncertainty: Contested Science and the Protection of the Public's Health and Environment', in R.N. Proctor and L. Schiebinger (eds.), *Agnotology: The Making and Unmaking of Ignorance* (Stanford University Press, 2008).

[84] S. Jasanoff, 'What Judges Should Know about the Sociology of Science', in S. Jasanoff (ed.), *Science and Public Reason* (Routledge, 2012), pp. 186–187.

The indeterminacy of scientific arguments leads to a second concern relating to the legitimacy of the judicial decision-making process analysed above. When adjudicators give credit to one body of expertise and disregard another in a context of scientific indeterminacy, the judicial outcome inevitably represents a normative or political preference. In a landmark article in which Bodansky assessed the role of expertise in granting legitimacy to environmental laws, he recognized that 'science can provide us with useful information about feasibility and effectiveness', but that ultimately, 'the choice among [various possible response measures] is a question of policy, not science'.[85] If assessing environmental harm is a scientific task, he reckoned, determining what to do in response to this harm and choosing between different options or rational choices requires value judgements about what levels of environmental risks and legal stringency are acceptable.[86] The case law analysis showed that alternative regulatory frameworks that would have infringed the competing norms to a lesser extent were possible and equally supported by scientific experts. Thus, when weighing the environmental and human rights interests at stake, the court seemingly opts for an optimal outcome that favours one normative objective over another. This practice points to the essence of managerial adjudication, where optimal outcomes are predetermined by the court, which 'then goes for the reasoning'.[87] From this perspective, the scientific expertise that is used in the 'justificatory scaffolding' constructed to legitimize the optimal outcome arguably plays an instrumental role. This observation echoes Werner's theory on 'the politics of scientific expert knowledge', or 'the way in which truth claims are used to pursue political aims'.[88] When the court legitimizes what it portrays as an optimal outcome in light of the scientific evidence to which the EU legislator refers, and when this evidence is contested by adversarial scientific evidence put forward by the applicant, the court

---

[85] D. Bodansky, 'The Legitimacy of International Governance: A Coming Challenge for International Environmental Law?' (1999) 93 *American Journal of International Law* 596, 621.

[86] Ibid., 600, 621.

[87] When presenting my case law analysis at the workshop on 'The Environment in Court: Contemporary Issues and Challenges' (EUI, May 2018), Prof. Lüdwig Krämer (who worked for more than thirty years at DG Environment) believed that the 'court always looks first at the result to be reached in a conflict and then goes for the reasoning'.

[88] Seen through this prism, the ultimate goal behind the reliance on expertise is 'not to find the "truth" as such, but rather to establish a factual basis that makes it possible to take action and justify choices'. Werner, 'The Politics of Expertise', pp. 48–49.

seemingly pursues a political/normative goal disguised as an objective and scientifically grounded 'truth claim'.

This points to the crux of the theme addressed in this book, namely the legitimacy of 'unseen' actors in international adjudication. When the court follows the scientific arguments or the expert knowledge advanced by one party, due attention should be paid to the identity – or the collective and social dimension of expertise referred to in Section 16.2 – of the expert and epistemic community it draws on as well as the interests it represents. As pointed out by Koskenniemi, it is the normative or political objective defended by each party that will determine who qualifies as an expert in a case.[89] Seeking the authoritative claim of experts' knowledge implies cherry-picking between various epistemic communities and referring to the one most likely to further ones' interests. In other words, a party to a dispute will select the expertise it refers to depending on which point of law it must prove, and which outcome it desires to achieve.[90] The selection of expertise by the parties pursues, in sum, a normative objective and is the result of a political process.

Besides the politics of expertise, to ensure greater legitimacy to the judicial decision-making process, equal awareness should be paid to the culture in which the scientific expertise is embedded. The *Inuit* case evidenced how 'modern' scientific expertise on the killing methods of seals referred to by the EU institutions was contested in light of a different cultural understanding of the practice and its spiritual significance for the applicants. Similar dynamics were observed in the *Liga van Moskeeën* case. Against this backdrop, Klabbers warns that '[e]xpert knowledge may owe much to time and place [and] … not be universally valid, but may be influenced by the culture in which it is embedded'.[91] Recent work on scientific and social co-production of knowledge calls for a greater awareness paid to the intertwinement of scientific and social/cultural practices.[92] When political/legal choices are made and justified in an idiom of scientific expertise, specific social and cultural representations are mobilized

---

[89] M. Koskenniemi, 'Hegemonic Regimes', p. 324.

[90] The *Arcelor* case evidenced how the EU legislator referred to the final report on GHG emission reduction while Arcelor referred to the EPER's statistics. *Arcelor* case, paras. 52 and 55.

[91] He concludes that, if this is the case, 'the truth-claim of the expert knowledge is compromised'. J. Klabbers, 'The Virtues of Expertise', in M. Ambrus et al., *The Role of 'Experts'*, pp. 82–101, p. 83.

[92] At the forefront, Jasanoff claims that scientific knowledge 'both embeds and is imbedded in social practices, identities, norms, conventions, discourses, instruments and institutions – in short, in all the building blocks of what we term the social'. S. Jasanoff, States of Knowledge, p. 3.

against others. Once again, the virtues of expertise are hereby questioned and raise important legitimacy concerns regarding the judicial decision-making process.

This brings us to a final, and related, problem of legitimacy induced from the case law analysis, which relates to the risk that scientific expertise poses in terms of the gaps in legal protection of fundamental rights. In the cases analysed above, the CJEU decided in favour of strict environmental protection regulations despite the uncertainty of the scientific arguments advanced by the parties, and the existence of alternative (less stringent) regulatory frameworks. The invocation of expertise to legitimize the polit-ical objective and normative goal behind the legislation (the aim of which was, in the first case, to reduce GHG emissions, and in the last cases, to respond to animal welfare concerns) are 'easily' justifiable when the com-peting concerns are economic interests of private corporations (such as Arcelor). Yet, the scientific rationale and managerial approach to dispute settlement might prove more difficult to 'rationalize' when the competing interests involve the right to (cultural) subsistence of Inuit peoples whose way of life depends on the selling of seal products; or when the practice of religious rites of the Muslim community in Flanders depends on the avail-ability of slaughterhouses capable of responding to the increased demand for slaughter during the Feast of the Sacrifice. Fundamentally, in the two latter cases, the applicants did not question the legitimacy of animal welfare concerns but argued instead that those concerns were already accounted for in their practice and formed an integral part of their beliefs.[93] These observations point to a gap in terms of the protection of fundamental rights that an expert-based managerial adjudication can create. Arguments which do not fit a 'modern/scientific' mould but draw on different 'traditional/cultural' belief systems and discourses are more difficult to back with sci-entific expertise, thereby creating an imbalance in terms of argumentative power/authority between the parties. It is thus important to underline that in certain cases, the voices of those claiming human rights protection can be silenced by a scientific expert-based managerialism of the court. The gap in legal protection that can result from scientific expertise in court can have largely unseen implications for human rights.

[93] While the Inuit argued that seal hunting forms an intrinsic part of their traditional culture and did not contravene the threshold of pain endured by animals through 'modern' killing methods, the various Muslim associations, and AG Wahl, recalled that 'it is precisely on account of respect for animals and the importance which is attached to their welfare that the act of killing them is ritualised in Jewish and Muslim traditions'. Opinion of A.G. Wahl, footnote 42.

16.5   Conclusion

The CJEU's expert-based managerial approach to conflict adjudication has emerged to adapt to an ever-more fragmented, technical and scientifically grounded EU legal order. This expert-based managerial adjudication can be conceived as a creative solution concerned with effectively solving trade-offs between norms pertaining to distinct functional legal regimes, here environmental and human rights law. It also comes, however, with certain risks since at its core it entails a struggle for competing interests translated into a new language of validity.[94] In this argumentative framework, scientific experts play a decisive role in providing the evidence on the basis of which decisions are taken. Yet little information on the experts and the epistemic communities they are part of is disclosed. As 'unseen' actors, scientific experts contribute in 'secretly' shaping EU law.[95] Induced from an analysis of the *Arcelor,* the *Inuit* and the *Liga van Moskeeën* cases, this chapter has evidenced three main legitimacy concerns posed by an expert-based managerial approach to conflict adjudication. First, in light of the *scientific indeterminacy* critique, the legitimacy of judicial outcomes is challenged when the court relies on scientific expert evidence that it is unable to adequately review. Second, a managerial approach to conflict adjudication runs the risk of providing a veil behind which the *politics of expertise* are hidden. Finally, expert-based managerialism presumes a specific concept of law that privileges scientific evidence and optimization-driven analyses as ultimate sources of determinacy. This expert-based managerialism risks obstructing the protection of fundamental rights that do not fit a scientific argumentative framework, thereby creating a *gap in legal protection.* The chapter concludes by acknowledging the merit but also warning about the limits of scientific expert evidence when adjudicating conflicts between EU environmental laws and fundamental rights and reminds us of the responsibility of the court in handling scientific expertise in a cautious manner.

---

[94] For Kennedy, ' "economic, technical and scientific vocabularies seemed to bring certainty and solidity (i.e. universal validity) to the regime-world that techniques of interpretation lacked", since recurring interpretative controversies undermined effective strategy'. D. Kennedy, *A Critique of Adjudication (fin de siècle)* (Harvard University Press, 1997), cited in M. Koskenniemi, 'Hegemonic Regimes', p. 312.

[95] To echo D. Bethlehem, 'The Secret Life of International Law' (2012) 1 *Cambridge Journal of International and Comparative Law* 23.

PART IV

Confidentiality and Transparency

17

The Politics of Invisibility

Why Are International Judicial Bureaucrats Obscured from View?

TOMMASO SOAVE*

17.1 Introduction

For decades, people from all over the world have been speculating about Area 51. The thick veil of secrecy surrounding the Nevada military base has, over time, given rise to all sorts of conspiracy theories. For some, the United States government would be using the site to conduct studies on captured extraterrestrials; according to others, the area would host laboratories for the development of teleportation and time-travelling technologies. Meanwhile, every year thousands of tourists travel State Route 375 – aptly renamed 'Extraterrestrial Highway' – and go take a peek at the base's surroundings. From sci-fi novels to Hollywood blockbusters, from cartoons to videogames, everyone talks about Area 51. That is, everyone except the United States government. Up until 2013, national authorities never officially acknowledged the site's existence. Area 51 did not appear on official geological survey maps; the Air Force kept denying that there ever was a facility by that name; and any reference to it was redacted from official documents. The almost comical mismatch between, on the one hand, the government's cover-up efforts and, on the other hand, the fame that the base had meanwhile acquired was well captured in an article by the *Los Angeles Times*, which referred to Area 51 as 'the most famous military institution in the world that doesn't officially exist'.[1]

---

* Research for this chapter was conducted in the framework of a broader research project titled 'The Other Side of Judging: Social Practices and the Construction of International Judicial Fields' and funded by the Swiss National Science Foundation. The views expressed are personal.
[1] *Los Angeles Times, The Road to Area 51*, www.latimes.com/entertainment/la-mag-april 052009-backstory-story.html (last accessed 13 July 2017).

Something similar is happening, albeit at a more modest level, with the institutional bureaucracies tasked with assisting international courts and tribunals in the conduct of their daily operations. Those bureaucracies constitute the backbone of the international judiciary and, like all 'background forces' in global governance, have a crucial impact on the perceived legitimacy of 'foreground deliberation'.[2] A recent survey estimates that permanent international dispute settlement bodies, such as the International Court of Justice (ICJ), the International Tribunal on the Law of the Sea (ITLOS), the World Trade Organization (WTO) Appellate Body, the European and Inter-American Courts of Human Rights (ECtHR and IACtHR, respectively), and the Court of Justice of the European Union (CJEU) rely on the assistance of over 2,200 individuals, including some 430 legal experts.[3] These support personnel, organized in registries or secretariats depending on the system concerned, are usually recruited through public competitions and not through political appointment by member states. In a similar fashion, ad hoc adjudicatory mechanisms, such as investor-State arbitral tribunals, routinely appoint legal secretaries to help manage and expedite disputes. While there is no uniform or standardized procedure for their appointment, secretaries are often selected among young professionals or academics having pre-existing affiliations with at least one arbitrator – usually the tribunal's president. Tribunals usually seek the parties' consent before appointing secretaries.[4] However, on occasion, arbitrators also hire legal assistants in a private capacity, without disclosing to the litigants their contribution.[5]

Thanks to recent scholarly efforts, we now know that these staff servicing international adjudicators (hereinafter referred to as 'international

---

[2] D.W. Kennedy, 'Challenging Expert Rule: The Politics of Global Governance' (2005) 27 *Sydney Law Review* 1, at 3.

[3] S. Cartier and C. Hoss, 'The Role of Registries and Legal Secretariats in International Judicial Institutions', in C.P.R. Romano, K.J. Alter and Y. Shany (eds.), *The Oxford Handbook of International Adjudication* (Oxford University Press, 2014), p. 712, at p. 713.

[4] See e.g. Model Letter from Arbitral Tribunal to Parties on the Appointment of an Arbitral Secretary or Assistant, in G. Kaufmann-Kohler and A. Rigozzi, *International Arbitration: Law and Practice in Switzerland*, 3rd edn (Oxford University Press, 2015), p. 312.

[5] See e.g. Z. Douglas, 'The Secretary to the Arbitral Tribunal', in B. Berger and M.E. Schneider (eds.), *Inside the Black Box: How Arbitral Tribunals Operate and Reach Their Decisions* (Juris Publishing, 2013), p. 87 (stating that arbitrators often receive CVs from students and junior professionals offering to serve as their assistants).

judicial bureaucrats') play a key role in the judicial process.[6] Besides ensuring the smooth administration of proceedings and handling the correspondence between the bench and the parties, international judicial bureaucrats also carry out a variety of tasks related to the judicial function proper. For instance, they provide 'legal … support to the [c]ourt in the exercise of its judicial functions'; prepare 'files and analytical notes for the [j]udges'[7]; participate in deliberations; and, in some systems, draft portions of the final decisions under the judges' oversight.[8] In addition, they embody 'the institutional memory'[9] of their courts of allegiance, thereby ensuring the consistency of judgments with prior jurisprudence. Indeed, their terms of employment often outlast those of the judges they serve, thus making them the only long-term institution in the respective adjudicatory bodies. These functions are instrumental to the success of the international judicial process. Thanks to the work of international judicial bureaucrats, adjudicators are relieved of the burdens of going through every page of the parties' submissions, memorizing the entirety of existing case law, or worrying about certain turns of the sentence in their written judgments. As a result, adjudicators are, in principle, free to focus their attention on the deliberation of cases.

Hence, it is safe to say that while international judicial bureaucrats do not themselves decide cases, they *do* constitute part and parcel of the professional community whose social interactions and expert knowledge incessantly shape the interpretation of international law. Thus, one might

---

[6] D. Caron, 'Towards a Political Theory of International Courts and Tribunals' (2007) 24 *Berkeley Journal of International Law* 401, at 416.

[7] ECtHR website, *How It Works*, www.echr.coe.int/Pages/home.aspx?p=court/howitworks (last accessed 25 March 2017). See also Cartier and Hoss, 'The Role of Registries and Legal Secretariats', pp. 718–720.

[8] See e.g. Cartier and Hoss, 'The Role of Registries and Legal Secretariats', pp. 720–721; H. Thirlway, 'The Drafting of ICJ Decisions: Some Personal Recollections and Observations' (2006) 5 *Chinese Journal of International Law* 15, at 16–20; L. Garlicki, 'Judicial Deliberations: The Strasbourg Perspective', in N. Huls, M. Adams and J. Bomhoff (eds.), *The Legitimacy of Highest Courts' Rulings* (Asser Press, 2009), p. 389, at 392; V. Hughes, 'Working in WTO Dispute Settlement: Pride Without Prejudice', in G. Marceau (ed.), *A History of Law and Lawyers in the GATT/WTO: The Development of the Rule of Law in Multilateral Trading System* (Cambridge University Press, 2015), p. 259, at p. 262; Brussels Legal website, *Interview with Margarita Peristeraki, Référendaire at the Court of First Instance in Luxembourg*, www.brusselslegal.com/article/display/2924/Margarita_ Peristeraki_Rfrendaire_at_the_Court_of_First_Instance_in_Luxembourg (last accessed 25 March 2017).

[9] Cartier and Hoss, 'The Role of Registries and Legal Secretariats', p. 722.

expect overt and thorough discussions about their identities, functions, and relevance. However, to this day, such expectations remain largely frustrated. Despite their importance for the legitimacy of the dispute settlement process, the role of international judicial bureaucrats, their daily tasks and duties, their professional and personal relationships with the adjudicators, and their impact on the merits of decisions remain glaringly absent from official discourse, public debate and scholarly analysis. To paraphrase the *Los Angeles Times*, this invisible army of legal professionals constitutes the most pervasive player in the game of international adjudication that 'doesn't officially exist'.

The silence surrounding international judicial bureaucracies has a twofold dimension. On the one hand, courts and tribunals are quite reticent to reveal their internal decision-making processes and impose strict confidentiality duties on their employees. This reluctance can be understood as an effort to preserve the secrecy of deliberations, whose breach would impair a court or tribunal's ability to render its judgments in conformity with the appropriate procedures and may even call into question its impartiality vis-à-vis the litigating parties. Also, a principal-agent dynamic such as that between judges and their assistants entail a certain degree of discretion, lest one undermines the mutual trust implicit in such a relationship. On the other hand, commentators and scholars remain almost entirely oblivious to the expert communities in which adjudicators are embedded,[10] and still conceive of judges as Herculean 'loner[s]' who 'converse[] with no one' and 'ha[ve] no encounters'.[11] This attitude is quite striking, given that academics are not subject to any particular confidentiality duties.

This chapter, which forms part of a broader research project on legal communities, does not seek to pierce the veil of silence that surrounds international judicial bureaucracies. Instead, it takes silence *as an object of interest in itself* and attempts to shed light on its socio-political determinants. Some may be disappointed at this apparent lack of analytical ambition. Yet, the way in which a profession describes its own operations is often revealing of its self-perception as an agent in society, its tacit rules and ingrained assumptions, its ambitions and idiosyncrasies. The spoken

---

[10] A. Vauchez, 'Communities of International Litigators', in Romano et al. (eds.), *The Oxford Handbook of International Adjudication*, p. 655, at p. 656.

[11] F.I. Michelman, 'The Supreme Court 1985 Term' (1986) 100 *Harvard Law Review* 4, at 76. See also J. Habermas, *Between Facts and Norms: Contributions to a Discourse Theory of Law and Democracy* (MIT Press, 1996), p. 224.

and the unspoken in the international judicial community reflect the ever-evolving power relations between its participants, give prominence to certain actors while relegating others to marginality, and delineate the horizon of discursive possibilities within the field.[12]

The argument proceeds as follows. Section 17.2 analyses the ways in which international judicial bureaucrats have been obscured in international law discourse, from the reticence of courts and tribunals to reveal their inner workings to the passive acquiescence of legal scholars. The claim is that such marginalization is not the haphazard result of miscommunication and inattention, but rather requires the methodical obstinacy of collective denial. Section 17.3 seeks to explain why the international legal community conspires to maintain silence as to the role and impact of judicial bureaucrats. In so doing, it assesses some arguments commonly offered in this respect, before providing this author's own views. Finally, conclusive Section 17.4 examines the few attempts being made to open up the system to more overt discussions of the topic, as well as the reactions that such attempts may prompt.

To be clear, this chapter does not advocate a jettisoning of confidentiality altogether. A certain degree of discretion in judicial proceedings is crucial to ensure the independence of international courts and tribunals. Under no circumstance, for instance, should an international judicial bureaucrat breach the secrecy of deliberations or disclose sensitive details about a specific dispute. Yet, it is one thing to respect these intuitive rules of thumb and another to deny agency to an entire class of actors in the field of international dispute settlement. As it will be argued, this staunch refusal to acknowledge the obvious may, in the long run, undermine the legitimacy of the international judicial process as a central node of global governance.

17.2 The Sound of Silence and the Three Wise Monkeys

From one military base to another. During World War II, a poster placed at the entrance of the premises of the Manhattan Project depicted the traditional Japanese simian trio – the three wise monkeys who speak no evil, see no evil and hear no evil – to invite the participants in the nuclear

---

[12] See P. Bourdieu, 'The Force of Law: Toward a Sociology of the Juridical Field' (1987) 38 *Hastings Law Journal* 805, 827; J. Crawford and M. Koskenniemi, 'Introduction', in J. Crawford and M. Koskenniemi (eds.), *The Cambridge Companion to International Law* (Cambridge University Press, 2012), p. 1, at p. 4.

development programme to the utmost discretion. The caption under-neath the picture read: 'What you see here, what you do here, what you hear here, when you leave here, let it stay here'. Depictions of this kind, so often associated with classified activities, perfectly capture the essence of collective silence, the social phenomenon whereby 'a group of people tacitly agree to outwardly ignore something of which they are all person-ally aware'.[13] What distinguishes collective silence from a mere secret is the cooperation between its participants – a collaborative endeavour that 'presupposes discretion on the part of the non-producer of the informa-tion as well as inattention on the part of its non-consumers'.[14] The three wise monkeys cannot be separated: the first monkey's refusal to speak would be meaningless if the other two did not equally refuse to see and to hear.

The routine activities of international judicial bureaucrats, as well as their potential impact on judicial outcomes, are subject to collective silence on the part of the legal profession – a sort of mutual denial aimed at obscuring their role from public view. Not convinced? Then try to ask an international adjudicator whether she ever receives assistance in conducting the relevant legal research, deciding the issues arising in a dis-pute, and/or drafting her judgments. At best, she will provide a generic response praising the 'terrific' support provided by the legal experts affili-ated to her judicial institution,[15] without providing any meaningful details. At worst, she will ask you to leave the room, outraged by your impudence. Knocking at the door of a registry or secretariat would hardly yield better results: those who try are usually met with poker-faced detachment and precooked answers.

Such a dismissive attitude would probably bewilder a domestic lawyer desiring to learn something about international adjudication. In many domestic legal traditions, the functions and prerogatives of court assistants have long been discussed and examined by both academics and the general media, to the point that few would consider the topic taboo. For instance, it is well known that United States Supreme Court Justices rely heavily on the assistance of clerks, who, among other things, conduct

---

[13] E. Zerubavel, *The Elephant in the Room: Silence and Denial in Everyday Life* (Oxford University Press, 2006), p. 2.

[14] Ibid., p. 48.

[15] See e.g. the statement of an anonymous ECtHR judge in D. Terris, C.P.R. Romano and L. Swighart, *The International Judge: An Introduction to the Men and Women Who Decide the World's Cases* (Oxford University Press, 2007), p. 82.

legal research, summarize the parties' briefs, make recommendations, edit, cite-check or draft portions of opinions.[16] America's most prominent lawyers proudly list their Supreme Court clerkships near the top of their CVs, and many recent judicial appointments have been made among the ranks of former clerks. To be sure, the suspicion that clerks act as the judges' 'ghostwriters', without being subject to 'the usual security or loyalty checks', occasionally caused some controversy.[17] Yet, these forms of contestation and the reactions thereto tend to take place in the open, from scholarly pieces[18] to newspaper articles,[19] without necessarily giving way to censorship as to clerks' existence and activities. Other national legal discourses, albeit perhaps less overt about judicial bureaucracies, nonetheless feature specialized discussions of the topic. For instance, Bruno Latour provided a detailed description of the routine operations of the myriad actors helping the French *Conseil d'État* resolve its cases.[20] By contrast, in vain would our naïve domestic lawyer look for similar references to the registries, secretariats and clerks servicing international adjudicators. With some rare exceptions, which will be discussed in a moment, all he would find is a resounding, deafening silence.

---

[16] See e.g. R. Stern, E. Gressman and S. Shapiro, *Supreme Court Practice*, 6th edn (Bureau of National Affairs, 1986), pp. 257–258, 573; S.J. Kenney, 'Beyond Principals and Agents: Seeing Courts as Organizations by Comparing Référendaires at the European Court of Justice and Law Clerks at the US Supreme Court' (2000) 33 *Comparative Political Studies* 593, at 603; S.J. Kenney, 'Puppeteers or Agents? What Lazarus's Closed Chambers Adds to Our Understanding of Law Clerks at the US Supreme Court' (2001) 25 *Law and Social Inquiry* 185, at 193–211.

[17] C.A. Newland, 'Personal Assistants to Supreme Court Justices: The Law Clerks' (1961) 40 *Oregon Law Review* 299, at 311.

[18] In addition to the few pieces already cited, see e.g. J.B. Oakley and R.S. Thompson, *Law Clerks and the Judicial Process: Perceptions of the Qualities and Function of Law Clerks in American Courts* (University of California Press, 1980); J.D. Mahoney, 'Law Clerks: For Better or for Worse?' (1988) 54 *Brooklyn Law Review* 321; E.P. Lazarus, *Closed Chambers: The First Eyewitness Account of the Epic Struggles Inside the Supreme Court* (Times Books, 1998); T.C. Peppers, *Courtiers of the Marble Palace: The Rise and Influence of the Supreme Court Law Clerk* (Stanford University Press, 2006); R.C. Black, C.L. Boyd and A.-C. Bryan, 'Revisiting the Influence of Law Clerks on the US Supreme Court's Agenda-Setting Process' (2014–2015) 98 *Marquee Law Review* 75.

[19] See e.g. 'The Bright Young Men Behind the Bench', *US News and World Report*, 12 July 1957, pp. 45–48; W.H. Rehnquist, 'Who Writes Decisions of the Supreme Court?', *US News and World Report*, 13 December 1957, pp. 74–75; A. Liptak, 'A Sign of the Court's Polarization: Choice of Clerks', *New York Times*, 6 September 2010, www.nytimes.com/2010/09/07/us/politics/07clerks.html (last accessed 18 March 2019).

[20] B. Latour, *The Making of Law: An Ethnography of the Conseil d'État*, trans. M. Brilman and A. Pottage (Polity Press, 2009).

Who, then, are the participants in this peculiar from of collective denial? Who are the three wise monkeys who do not speak, hear and see international judicial bureaucrats?

17.2.1   The Closed-Door Policy of International Courts and Tribunals

The part of the mute primate – the 'non-producer of information'[21] – will be played by international judicial institutions themselves, which maintain strict confidentiality with respect to their inner workings. All phases of the resolution of an international dispute, from the instruction of the case to the drafting of the final decision, are classified, and none of the inputs provided by the adjudicators' assistants is supposed to be disclosed to the public.[22] The prohibition to speak publicly about what happens behind closed doors applies to adjudicators and bureaucrats alike, and is strictly enforced through a series of interlocking and overlapping measures. Upon recruitment, registry and secretariat lawyers are required to sign confidentiality agreements prohibiting them from ever discussing the conduct of specific proceedings and the content of deliberations. So far, nothing strange. As indicated above, a modicum of discretion concerning specific cases is the hallmark of an independent and impartial court. More generally, governance systems need to balance transparency with the need to ensure that decision-makers are in a position to air their opinions freely, without being subject to undue pressures while the governance output – the statute, the policy report, the judgment – is still in the making.[23] Very few would argue, for example, that transparency commands a full disclosure of a single adjudicator's views in the initial stages of the proceedings or her opinions as expressed in the deliberations room. After all, the crystallization of judicial positions is a slow, tentative and hesitant journey that requires dialogue, contestation and continuous testing of one's instincts. If any differences are to emerge, they ought to do so at the end of the process, e.g. through concurring and/or dissenting opinions.

---

[21] Zerubavel, The Elephant in the Room, p. 48.

[22] As a partial exception, the procedure of the CJEU requires that the opinions of advocates-general be published as part of the official record.

[23] See e.g. G. Guillaume, 'Some Thoughts on the Independence of International Judges vis-à-vis States' (2003) 2 *The Law and Practice of International Courts and Tribunals* 163, at 165.

However, the confidentiality duties imposed on international judicial bureaucrats go well beyond the secrecy of deliberations in specific disputes, and extend to their *general* assignments, i.e. the concrete steps they are expected to undertake every time a new case is filed. So, for instance, an ICJ clerk would be frowned upon were she to admit to contributing to her judge's Note.[24] An ECtHR Registry lawyer must seek her supervisor's approval before mentioning that she routinely prepares draft judgments in advance of deliberations.[25] And so forth. Assistants to investor-State arbitral tribunals are in a particularly delicate situation. Usually, the tribunal seeks the parties' consent to appoint an official secretary to assist it in the conduct of the proceedings. This is usually done through a letter to the litigants indicating the reasons for which such assistance is needed and what functions the designated person would fulfil. Typical tasks include 'the review of submissions and evidence', the 'preparation of summaries and/or memoranda', 'research on specific factual or legal issues', the preparation of the 'initial drafts of procedural orders and awards' and 'support ... during hearings and deliberations'.[26] When the parties authorize the appointment, the secretary is under an obligation not to disclose her work to anyone extraneous to the arbitration. When the parties do *not* consent to the appointment, the conditions get even trickier. The unrecognized assistant will often keep working for one or more tribunal members, but completely off the radar: no mention that she is involved in an arbitration whatsoever; no reference to her assignments to friends and colleagues – nothing at all.

Failure to comply with confidentiality rules may have serious repercussions on an international judicial bureaucrat's career prospects. In certain systems it could constitute a grave violation of staff regulations, subject to severe disciplinary action. But there are additional, subtler

---

[24] The Note is a document, prepared in advance of deliberations, in which each ICJ judge must express her 'views on the case' and indicate, among other things, 'whether any questions which have been called to notice should be eliminated from further consideration', the 'precise questions which should be answered by the Court', her 'tentative opinion as to the answers' to be given to such questions and the 'reasons therefor', and her 'tentative conclusion as to the correct disposal of the case'. (Article 4 of the Resolution Concerning the Internal Judicial Practice of the Court (12 April 1976))

[25] See Garlicki, 'Judicial Deliberations: The Strasbourg Perspective'.

[26] Kaufmann-Kohler and Rigozzi, International Arbitration: Law and Practice in Switzerland, p. 312.

ways in which judicial institutions ensure discretion on the part of their employees. These include a general duty to secure authorization before delivering lectures, submitting publications or speaking to journalists. Sometimes, supervisors even take pains to redact their supervisees' CVs to ensure that the relevant job descriptions do not to raise any eyebrows. As a result, the field of international adjudication is increasingly populated by professionals whose main qualifications are, say, having 'clerked with ICJ Judge Smith', having 'assisted the ECtHR in the preparation of positions and arguments towards the deliberation of pending disputes', and the like. To be sure, these may well be significant selling points for prospective recruiters. However, the situation is bleaker for unrecognized assistants to arbitral tribunals, who may find themselves unable to justify long 'gaps' in their résumés. Over time, their invisible condition can grow quite uncomfortable, as the inability to 'convey the full extent of [one's] experience' may foreclose future employment opportunities.[27]

Through the combined operation of these techniques, international judicial bureaucrats are made aware of their invisibility. As the temptation to speak up is always and invariably an attempt at relevance,[28] it is as though the international judicial machinery sought to distinguish between more and less significant actors among its workforce. Not only does the first monkey not speak: it also imparts an injunction to silence on others, a no-comment posture whereby 'there [is] nothing to say …, nothing to see, and nothing to know'.[29] Over time, the addressees of the injunction internalize the culture of the unspoken, begin to appreciate its virtues, and eventually become its unwitting champions. Breaking the silence is not just a potential breach of one's contractual duties: it is also perceived as an unsavoury, inelegant, and – heaven forbid! – *unprofessional* act. Those who deviate from the rules are not only at risk of swift punishment, they are also marginalized by their own peers as violators of trust. For example, when Hugh Thirlway, a former senior legal secretary at the ICJ, published an article disclosing his pervasive role in shaping the text and content of judgments,[30] some people in The Hague may have applauded his attempt at raising public awareness of the World Court's

---

27 Douglas, 'The Secretary to the Arbitral Tribunal', p. 87.
28 Zerubavel, The Elephant in the Room, p. 33.
29 M. Foucault, *The History of Sexuality* trans. R. Hurley (Pantheon Books, 1978), p. 4.
30 Thirlway, 'The Drafting of ICJ Decisions'.

internal dynamics, while some others may have perceived his efforts as an unwarranted attack on the system.[31]

17.2.2 The Obstinate Inattention of Scholars and Commentators

So, to the blind and the deaf monkeys. If international courts and tribunals act as the non-producers of information, international law scholars play along as its non-consumers.[32] To date, only a handful of published works have dared to engage in general discussions of the role and impact of international judicial bureaucrats. In addition to Thirlway's article referred to above, it is worth mentioning two book chapters in the 2014 *Oxford Handbook of International Adjudication*. The first, written by Stéphanie Cartier and Cristina Hoss,[33] sketches an outline of the main functions of legal assistants to the various international courts and tribunals and describes their modes of appointment. The second, authored by Antoine Vauchez,[34] focuses on the co-dependence between judges and their legal communities of reference, of which registry and secretariat lawyers constitute a relevant subgroup. These pieces helpfully draw the reader's attention to the invisible army of international judicial bureaucrats, but hardly constitute an exhaustive discussion of the topic. Some additional references can be found in a 2007 article by David Caron,[35] which, however, does little more than highlighting the functions played by institutional bureaucracies in advising their respective judges. Beyond these works, references to this class of unseen actors in international adjudication are few and far between.[36]

The only partial exception to this dearth of literature relates to the secretaries and assistants to arbitral tribunals, which has attracted some attention over the last few years.[37] Such an interest arose from a

---

[31] Professor Thirlway himself wished that the article be seen as a 'slight' and 'discreet' disclosure of the Court's deliberation and drafting processes. H. Thirlway, 'The International Court of Justice: Cruising Ahead at 70' (2016) 29 *Leiden Journal of International Law* 1103, footnote 12.

[32] Zerubavel, The Elephant in the Room, p. 48.

[33] Cartier and Hoss, 'The Role of Registries and Legal Secretariats'.

[34] Vauchez, 'Communities of International Litigators'.

[35] Caron, 'Towards a Political Theory of International Courts and Tribunals'.

[36] See e.g. L. Garlicki, 'Judicial Deliberations: The Strasbourg Perspective', pp. 391–392; J. Pauwelyn, 'The Rule of Law Without the Rule of Lawyers? Why Investment Arbitrators Are from Mars, Trade Adjudicators from Venus' (2015) 109 *American Journal of International Law* 761, at 795–798.

[37] See e.g. C. Partasides, 'The Fourth Arbitrator? The Role of Secretaries to Tribunals in International Arbitration' (2002) 18 *Arbitration International* 147; E. Onyema, 'The

few incidents that allegedly tarnished the reputation of investor-State dispute settlement. On occasion, the litigants before arbitral tribunals have questioned the extent to which arbitrators may legitimately rely on assistants in carrying out their duties. The first such case saw a top arbitrator being forced to resign from a tribunal after one of his clerks had posted views on legal issues related to the case in an online blog.[38] The second, not yet resolved, relates to the mammoth dispute in *Yukos*, which saw Russia condemned to pay over USD50 billion to the claimants.[39] In its writ for annulment of the award before The Hague District Court, Russia alleged that, unbeknownst to the parties, the arbitrators had delegated substantive responsibilities to the tribunal's assistant (an associate with the tribunal president's law firm), thereby breaching their mandate to perform their duties personally.[40] While these occurrences made enough noise to arouse some curiosity, they remained mostly confined to specialized circles and failed to open the door to a comprehensive analysis of the relationship between international adjudicators and their assistants.

Role of the International Arbitral Tribunal Secretary' (2005) 9 *Vindobona Journal of International Commercial Law and Arbitration* 99; C.J. Restemayer, 'Secretaries Always Get a Bad Rep: Identifying the Controversy Surrounding Administrative Secretaries, Current Guidelines, and Recommendations' (2012) 4 *Yearbook on Arbitration and Mediation* 328; P. Tercier, 'The Role of the Secretary to the Arbitral Tribunal', in L.W. Newman and R.D. Hill (eds.), *The Leading Arbitrators' Guide to International Arbitration*, 3rd edn (Juris Publishing, 2014), p. 531; M. Polkinghorne and C.B. Rosenberg, 'The Role of the Tribunal Secretary in International Arbitration: A Call for a Uniform Standard' (2014) 8 *Dispute Resolution International* 107; T. Timlin, 'The Swiss Supreme Court on the Use of Secretaries and Consultants in the Arbitral Process' (2016) 8 *Yearbook on Arbitration and Mediation* 268.

[38] See e.g. L. Markert, 'Challenging Arbitrators in Investment Arbitration: The Challenging Search for Relevant Standards and Ethical Guidelines' (2010) 3 *Contemporary Asia Arbitration Journal* 237, at 265 and fn 127 thereto.

[39] *Hulley Enterprises Limited (Cyprus), Yukos Universal Limited (Isle of Man) and Veteran Petroleum Limited (Cyprus) v. Russian Federation*, PCA Cases Nos. AA 226, AA 227 and AA 228, Final Award (18 July 2014).

[40] See Pleading Notes of Professor A.J. Van Den Berg before the Hague District Court (9 February 2016), available at http://res.cloudinary.com/lbresearch/image/upload/v1455205591/rf_pleading_notes_9_february_2016_final_edited_111116_1546.pdf (last accessed 27 July 2017), paras. 94–114; Russia's defence on appeal before the Hague Court of Appeal (28 November 2017), available at: www.yukoscase.com/wp-content/uploads/2017/12/Defence-on-Appeal-unofficial-UK-translation-Final-1.pdf (last accessed 18 March 2019), paras. 966–1065. For discussion, see e.g. R. Howse, 'The Fourth Man: An Intriguing Sub-Plot in the Yukos Arbitration', *International Economic Law and Policy Blog* (29 March 2017), http://worldtradelaw.typepad.com/ielpblog/2017/03/the-fourth-man-an-intriguing-sub-plot-in-the-yukos-arbitration-.html (last accessed 27 July 2017).

This systematic, obstinate inattention on the part of scholars may be superficially dismissed as a mere failure to notice, as a casual analytical omission. After all, we lawyers like to talk about law, not social structures. We are trained to dissect the minutiae of any given judicial decision, to connect findings with precedents, to criticize possible inconsistencies. But we are not expected to have the 'sociological imagination'[41] that would enable us to see power dynamics, influence networks and institutionalized rationalities. Or, perhaps, the fact that international judicial bureaucrats operate mostly off the radar makes them epistemically 'unmarked'[42] – so mundane that no one could possibly consider them as an interesting research object. Yet, such a dismissal would be disingenuous. That international adjudicators are embedded in institutional structures tasked with assisting them in all sorts of ways is, quite simply, too important a fact for us to overlook. It is part of those 'highly conspicuous matters' we deliberately *choose* not to see.[43]

17.2.3   An Open Secret?

If you are not yet convinced that the three wise monkeys operate in concert, consider one last element. As mentioned above, the participants in collective silence are typically aware of the truth they are outwardly ignoring. They have all seen with their own eyes that the emperor is naked, and yet no one dares break the silence. Our object of inquiry is no exception. The existence and role of international judicial bureaucrats, while zealously kept secret from the public, are no mystery to some insiders to the legal community – at least those who, having served as judges or assistants, have since joined national governments, private law firms or academia.

Anyone close to the field of international adjudication can testify to this. When a court or tribunal renders a new judgment, the counsel of the losing party will invariably blame judicial bureaucrats in private discussions with the client. 'I do not know what is wrong with [name of the bureaucrat]. Normally she writes much better than this mumbo-jumbo!' When a distinguished international litigation expert intervenes at an academic conference, she may adjust her speech, and even turn it

---

[41] C.W. Mills, *The Sociological Imagination* (Oxford University Press, 1959), pp. 5–11.
[42] See W. Brekhus, 'A Sociology of the Unmarked: Redirecting Our Focus' (1998) 16 *Sociological Theory* 34.
[43] Zerubavel, The Elephant in the Room, p. 9.

into a 'coded pleading', if she spots an adjudicator's assistant sitting in the audience. This author once witnessed two prominent scholars, who had both worked as officers for the same international court, criticizing certain judgments in order to covertly attack each other's legal views. These examples do not necessarily suggest that judicial outcomes rest solely in the hands of international judicial bureaucrats: however blurred the line might be at times,[44] there remains a difference between providing advice and calling the shots. They do suggest, however, that the existence and role of bureaucracies in the international judicial process are a *secret de Polichinelle*.

Of course, the fact that some 'insiders' to the community are aware of the phenomenon does not prevent them from feigning ignorance, especially when interacting with 'outsiders'. During hearings or public speeches, they will strictly respect the boundaries of their assigned roles and carefully avoid any express statements that would reveal their inside knowledge. At most, they will wink and nod at each other as if to say: 'I know you helped out drafting this: well done!' (or: 'Go back to law school!'). Some may find this double standard quite amusing. Others will retort that 'there are few aspects of the practice of international [dispute settlement] that better deserve the unwelcome moniker of "hypocrisy"'.[45] Certainly, on occasion, the obstinacy of silence borders on the surreal. Consider, for instance, the already mentioned writ for annulment in the *Yukos* arbitration. In support of its contention that the tribunal delegated too much of its decisional authority to the assistant, Russia's counsel produced the expert testimony of a top forensic linguist, who attested, 'with over 95% percent certainty', that the assistant 'wrote approximately 70% of the [award's] three most important chapters'.[46] Ironically, Russia's counsel is himself part of the super-arbitrator elite. As such, even without hiring a presumably costly expert, he should be well aware of the drafting tasks often assigned to tribunal assistants.

17.3   Why So Shy? The Socio-Political Determinants of Silence

Having outlined the essential features of the collective silence surrounding international judicial bureaucrats, it is worth asking: *cui bono*? What are

---

[44] See Thirlway, 'The Drafting of ICJ Decisions', p. 21.
[45] C. Partasides, 'Secretaries to Arbitral Tribunals', in B. Hanotiau and A. Mourre (eds.), *Players' Interaction in International Arbitration* (Kluwer Law International, 2015), p. 84.
[46] Howse, 'The Fourth Man'.

the reasons behind their invisibility in international legal discourse? This section addresses two sets of arguments commonly put forward by practitioners and scholars alike, namely: (1) concerns about the perceived legitimacy of international adjudication; and (2) accusations of bad faith on the part of judicial bureaucracies themselves. Ultimately, neither account seems able to fully capture the complexity of the problem or shed light on its deep roots. Therefore, this section concludes by providing an alternative narrative, based on the professional reflexes and the self-constructed image of the international judicial community.

17.3.1 Delegation of Judicial Authority and the Legitimacy of International Dispute Settlement

The first set of arguments relates to the legitimacy of international adjudication as an increasingly central node of global governance. Over the last two decades, the world has witnessed the explosion of international and mixed dispute settlement mechanisms, administering an ever-growing body of rules on an ever-widening array of subject matters. Many saluted the judicialization of international relations as the dawn of a new era – the victory of the international rule of law over the cynicism and self-interest of state politics. However, given their relatively young age, most international courts and tribunals remain in a fragile institutional position, certainly more so than their domestic counterparts. Indeed, even the most powerful among them must rely to a great extent on 'the goodwill of their constituents for both support and compliance'.[47] The legitimacy of an international court – its 'right to rule'[48] – is a relational concept[49] that depends very much on whether the addressees of that court's decisions are willing and able to accept the legal authority of such decisions, even when they disagree with or are seriously prejudiced by them.[50] One way to ensure that states remain committed to international adjudication is

[47] J.L. Gibson, G.A. Caldeira and V.A. Baird, 'On the Legitimacy of National High Courts' (1998) 92 *American Political Science Review* 343, at 343.
[48] D. Bodansky, 'Legitimacy in International Law and International Relations', in J.L. Dunoff and M.A. Pollack (eds.), *Interdisciplinary Perspectives on International Law and International Relations: The State of the Art* (Cambridge University Press, 2013), p. 321 at p. 324.
[49] See e.g. I. Hurd, 'Legitimacy and Authority in International Politics' (1999) 53 *International Organization* 379, at 381.
[50] On this notion of legitimacy as 'diffuse support', see J.L. Gibson and G.A. Caldeira, 'The Legitimacy of Transnational Legal Institutions: Compliance, Support, and the European

to give them tools to exercise some measure of political oversight over the functioning of courts and tribunals. In particular, diplomats routinely engage in complex negotiations when it comes to the appointment of new judges.[51] Given the delicate nature of the selection process, emphasizing the routine activities of judicial assistants may convey the impression that adjudicators abdicate their responsibilities in favour of faceless bureaucrats with no direct investiture. In turn, this impression may diminish the legitimacy of courts and tribunals in the eyes of their constituent states, which may prove less inclined to comply with judicial decisions.

The problem is particularly acute in the field of investor-State dispute settlement, whose legitimacy has been suffering a severe backlash in recent years. As the parties' counsel invest considerable time and money setting up the strategy for the appointment of arbitrators, the members of the tribunal are contractually bound to discharge their mandate in person, without delegating their judicial functions to third parties. Failure to do so would amount to a breach of the principle of *intuitu personae*,[52] erode state support to the system and exacerbate the 'lack of trust towards arbitrators and their commitment to properly fulfill their duties.'[53] These preoccupations have led a number of arbitral institutions to adopt rules and recommendations on the use of secretaries. According to such guidelines, only the members of an arbitral tribunal are allowed to participate in deliberations, with no other person admitted unless the tribunal decides otherwise.[54] Secretaries are, at most, expected to perform mere organizational and administrative tasks.[55] Against this backdrop, it has been argued that revealing the involvement of judicial assistants in investor-State dispute settlement – especially when the parties are

---

Court of Justice' (1995) 39 *American Journal of Political Science* 459, at 460; Bodansky, 'Legitimacy in International Law and International Relations', pp. 326–327.

[51] See e.g. Anne-Marie Slaughter and Laurence R. Helfer, 'Why States Create International Tribunals: A Response to Professors Posner and Yoo' (2005) 93 *California Law Review* 899, at 946–949.

[52] See e.g. Tercier, 'The Role of the Secretary to the Arbitral Tribunal', p. 537; C.J. Moxley, Jr., 'Selecting the Ideal Arbitrator' (2005) 69 *Dispute Resolution Journal* 1, at 3–4; Polkinghorne and Rosenberg, 'The Role of the Tribunal Secretary in International Arbitration'; T. Carbonneau, *Cases and Materials on Arbitration Law and Practice*, 7th edn (Thomson/West 2015), p. 14; Timlin, 'The Swiss Supreme Court', 268, 272–274.

[53] Tercier, 'The Role of the Secretary to the Arbitral Tribunal', p. 554. See also Restemayer, 'Secretaries Always Get a Bad Rep', 337–338.

[54] See e.g. Article 15(2) of the ICSID Rules of Procedure for Arbitration Proceedings.

[55] See e.g. International Chamber of Commerce, *Note on the Appointment, Duties and Remuneration of Administrative Secretaries* (2012), available at https://iccwbo.org (last accessed 26 July 2017).

unaware of that involvement – may unleash a 'perfect storm' able to destroy the system altogether.[56]

Albeit compelling at first glance, the legitimacy narrative proves unconvincing on closer scrutiny. For one thing, its proponents show little confidence in the ability of international adjudicators to remain in charge of the process. In fact, issues arising from principal-agent relationships are common to most expertise-driven systems, from statutory legislation to economic policy-making, without for that reason spurring the same level of concern as those associated with international judicial bureaucrats. When a client seeks the services of a legal counsel, she does not expect the firm's managing partner to perform all the required tasks personally, or to write all the briefs without the help of subordinates.[57] Similarly, our representatives in parliament seldom write – and sometimes do not even read – the bills that affect our daily lives.[58] By comparison, most international adjudicators arguably retain greater control over their duties. Yet, curiously, we seem more inclined to accept that the lawmaker we elected delegates the drafting of statutes than to concede that an international judge relies on the help of assistants. At this point, someone may retort that adjudicators are in a unique position, which differs from that of all other decision-makers. But how so, exactly? When it comes to legitimacy, how can we distinguish the duty to impartially interpret and apply legal rules from, say, the duty to faithfully fulfil an electoral mandate? Actually, assertions about the exceptionalism of judges[59] often go hand in hand with claims about the determinate and objective nature of legal norms.[60] If international law has a preordained meaning, ready to be 'excavated' from the relevant legal sources,[61] why should anyone be concerned about the

---

[56] Douglas, 'The Secretary to the Arbitral Tribunal', p. 88.

[57] Tercier, 'The Role of the Secretary to the Arbitral Tribunal', p. 538.

[58] See e.g. S. Gailmard, 'Accountability and Principal-Agent Theory', in M. Bovens, R.E. Goodin and T. Schillemans (eds.), *The Oxford Handbook of Public Accountability* (Oxford University Press, 2014), p. 90, at pp. 95–101.

[59] See e.g. E. O'Connell, 'The Natural Superiority of Courts', in U. Fastenrath, R. Geiger, D. Erasmus-Kahn, A. Paulus, S. Von Schorlemer and Christoph Vedder (eds.), *From Bilateralism to Community Interest: Essays in Honour of Judge Bruno Simma* (Oxford University Press, 2011), p. 1040.

[60] See e.g. A. Orakhelashvili, *The Interpretation of Acts and Rules in Public International Law* (Oxford University Press, 2008), p. 286 (expressing confidence in an interpreter's ability to 'deduce the meaning exactly of what has been consented to and agreed' by the parties to a treaty).

[61] J. Klabbers, 'Virtuous Interpretation', in P. Merkouris, M. Fitzmaurice and O. Elias (eds.), *Treaty Interpretation and the Vienna Convention on the Law of Treaties: 30 Years On* (Martinus Nijhoff, 2010), p. 17, at p. 23. See also J. D'Aspremont, 'The Multidimensional

interpreter relying on assistance in carrying out the excavation exercise? The force of law will always prevail!

17.3.2   The Alleged Bad Faith of Judicial Bureaucracies: Invisibility as a Cloak for Power

The second common explanation turns, so to speak, the legitimacy narrative on its head. Instead of focusing on the perceived authority of international adjudicators vis-à-vis their constituencies, it points the finger at the alleged *mauvaise foi* of international bureaucracies themselves. In a nutshell, the story goes as follows. Far from being the impartial and benevolent 'guardians of the law',[62] international courts and tribunals are inescapably inclined to interpret and apply the relevant rules in accordance with their own ideological commitments and deeply ingrained worldviews. Judicial reasoning and legal technique constitute little more than rhetorical tools to confer a veneer of objectivity and authority to the discretional expression of policy preferences.[63] International judicial bureaucracies are very much part of this power struggle, and serve as the agents of structural bias in international dispute settlement. Working in the shadows like puppet masters, they set out the courts' agendas, guide their judges in the articulation of legal analysis, and keep jurisprudential departures from established case law in check. Seen from this angle, the invisibility of bureaucrats ceases to be a condemnation to irrelevance and, instead, becomes a convenient shield behind which they preserve the 'back-room discourse'[64] of judicial politics from public accountability and overt challenge.

The roots of this narrative can be traced back to the critical legal studies school. In his trenchant *Critique of Adjudication*, for instance, Duncan Kennedy targeted the false-consciousness of United States courts, which seek shelter from contestation by casting their political decisions as the

---

Process of Interpretation: Content-Determination and Law-Ascertainment Distinguished', in A. Bianchi, D. Peat and M. Windsor (eds.), *Interpretation in International Law* (Oxford University Press, 2015), p. 111, at pp. 116–122.

[62] Terris et al., *The International Judge*, p. xix. See also A. Føllesdal, 'To Guide and Guard International Judges' (2014) 46 *NYU Journal of International Law and Politics* 793, at 793–795.

[63] Latour, *The Making of Law*, p. 141 (criticizing Pierre Bourdieu's classic formulation of rationalization as conferring symbolic force to otherwise arbitrary decisions).

[64] D. Kennedy, *A Critique of Adjudication (Fin de Siècle)* (Harvard University Press, 1997), p. 369.

inevitable product of legal rationality and technical necessity. People running judicial institutions, writes Kennedy, 'operate in bad faith in the same way judges do'.[65] While they perceive their missions as technically defined, they 'constantly deploy their resources, they constantly work, just as judges do, to shape and reshape the necessity that they are supposed merely to submit to'.[66] In the same vein, many have observed that international bureaucracies, just like other classes of global experts, prefer to operate beneath the surface in order to perpetuate their 'hugely unrecognized influence' and exercise 'invisible governance'.[67] The continued relevance of international judicial bureaucrats rests precisely on their depiction as technical experts with no political clout. Any recognition of their discretion would expose them to controversy and therefore diminish their power.[68]

For all its apparent poignancy, this 'bad faith' inaccurately portrays the international judicial community as sharply divided into two camps: on the one hand, courts and tribunals concealing their shady secrets behind closed doors; on the other hand, the rest of the community – government officials, private counsel, civil society organizations, scholars, etc. – desperately trying to penetrate those secrets in the name of transparency and accountability. If collective silence were that one-sided, with one camp withholding information and the other seeking access to it, it would not be very collective at all. In fact, as discussed in the previous section, things do not work this way. At least some participants in the community, irrespective of their roles and functions, are aware of the existence and tasks of judicial bureaucrats and acquiesce to silence in a staunch display of mutual denial. The three monkeys always act in concert.

17.3.3   Disciplinary Reflexes, Professional Habitus and the Struggle for the Autonomy of the International Judicial Field

If legitimacy concerns and institutional *mauvaise foi* are not at stake, what drives our reluctance to recognize international judicial bureaucrats as relevant actors in the adjudication game? Probably the rituals, the *habitus*

---

[65] Ibid.
[66] Ibid.
[67] J. Trondal, T. Larsson, M. Marcussen and F. Veggeland, *Unpacking International Organizations: The Dynamics of Compound Bureaucracies* (Manchester University Press, 2010), pp. 97, 99. See also e.g. Kennedy, 'Challenging Expert Rule', 17.
[68] Kennedy, 'Challenging Expert Rule', 17.

TOMMASO SOAVE

and the self-image that the international legal profession has cultivated over the last century. Like any other community of practice, we, international lawyers, are 'informally as well as contextually bound by a shared interest in learning and applying a common practice', while also resorting to a common 'repertoire of communal resources, words, tools, ways of doing things, stories, symbols, and discourse'.[69] Some of the most pervasive foundational myths in our discipline derive from Anglo-Saxon legal traditions,[70] where judges enjoy great prestige and are elevated above and beyond the lowlier ranks of the legal profession. In our endless quest for a *raison d'être*, we have carefully constructed a fictional (or at least outdated) image of The Judge as a learned gentleman who, from the heights of wisdom, gracefully pens the decisions that we study at law school.[71] In a world of irrational politics, this high-minded vision confers an aura of sanctity, mystery and even beauty to our enterprise. Its careful preservation from more prosaic accounts serves to fuel the world's *amour impossible* with international adjudication. Revealing the inner workings of international courts and tribunals may shatter the magical image of the Herculean Judge and show the international judicial process for what it really is: a humble laboratory where very important decisions are taken collectively by very ordinary men and women, with no other instruments than texts and words.

At the same time, silence is key to the perpetuation of our profession's status vis-à-vis external interferences coming from competing social actors. The modern international judicial field revolves around a close-knit group of individuals who gained universal recognition only in recent times, after having long suffered the derision of their domestic colleagues.[72] The relative tightness of our community stems from the close connections, both formal and informal, that exist among its members. Besides sharing a common educational background, many international judicial professionals serve simultaneously in different capacities: international judges often have academic

---

E. Adler, *Communitarian International Relations: The Epistemic Foundations of International Relations* (Routledge, 2005), p. 15. See also H.G. Cohen, 'Finding International Law, Part II: Our Fragmenting Legal Community' (2012) 44 *NYU Journal of International Law and Politics* 1049.

See e.g. M. Koskenniemi, *The Gentle Civilizer of Nations: The Rise and Fall of International Law 1870–1960* (Cambridge University Press, 2004), pp. 353–412.

Douglas, 'The Secretary to the Arbitral Tribunal', p. 89.

J. D'Aspremont, 'The Professionalisation of International Law', in J. D'Aspremont, T. Gazzini, A. Nollkaemper and W. Werner (eds.), *International Law as a Profession* (Cambridge University Press, 2017), p. 19, at pp. 22–23.

pedigrees,[73] top arbitrators appear regularly as counsel before other tribunals; etc. The various actors also trade places frequently, and a revolving door exists between the bench, a registry or secretariat, government departments, multinational law firms, NGOs and research centres.[74] Not surprisingly, this exclusive club wishes to maintain its capital for at least some time to come. And the most effective way to secure relevance and prestige is to remain the only ones in the know, the sole initiates to the arcane mysteries of international dispute settlement. Hence, while the various participants in the field often clash with one another in an endless contest for internal authority, they all show a certain 'closeness of interests'[75] and class solidarity when it comes to the external relationships of the field with society at large.

The twofold structure of the field – internal struggle and external autonomy – helps explain why the international judicial community acquiesces to the injunction of silence imparted by judicial institutions concerning the role and impact of institutional bureaucracies. On the one hand, experienced counsel regularly appearing before international courts and tribunals 'have an enormous self-interest' in defending them and 'proclaiming their courtness'.[76] Their knowledge of the inner workings of international adjudication grants them a competitive advantage over new entrants in the litigation market. On the other hand, many academics devoted to the study of the international judicial system have direct or indirect stakes in the system itself. For instance, much of the writing on investment treaty arbitration 'is done by authors who themselves are involved in [it]'[77] as either adjudicators or counsel. Similarly, European Union law scholarship is dominated by 'authors working for institutions structurally geared towards the expansion and consolidation of a genuine European legal order'.[78] Similar

---

[73] According to some estimates, roughly 40 per cent of all international judges have significant academic credentials, and about one-third of investment arbitrators are former or current scholars. See Terris et al., *The International Judge*, p. 20; J.A. Fontoura Costa, 'Comparing WTO Panelists and ICSID Arbitrators: The Creation of International Legal Fields' (2011) 1 *Oñati Socio-Legal Series* 17.

[74] J. D'Aspremont et al., 'Introduction', in D'Aspremont et al. (eds.), *International Law as a Profession*, p. 1, at p. 8.

[75] Bourdieu, 'The Force of Law', 842.

[76] M. Shapiro and A. Stone Sweet, *On Law, Politics and Judicialization* (Oxford University Press, 2002), p. 175. See also Vauchez, 'Communities of International Litigators', p. 660.

[77] S. Schill, 'W(h)ither Fragmentation? On the Literature and Sociology of International Investment Law' (2011) 22 *European Journal of International Law* 875, at 894.

[78] H. Schepel and R. Wesseling, 'The Legal Community: Judges, Lawyers, Officials and Clerks in the Writing of Europe' (1997) 3 *European Law Journal* 165, at 171.

findings may apply to different degrees to human rights and trade law scholarship as well. The gravitation of scholars around specific judicial regimes is strengthened by a panoply of thematic fora, ranging from traditional academic conferences to dedicated internet spaces, such as the OGEMID[79] or the International Economic Law and Policy Blog,[80] where practitioners and academics, selected on an invitation basis, exchange opinions every day. Given this contiguity between the bench and the academe, any attempt to speak up could expose an author to the resentment of her colleagues on the court, and even undermine her continued membership of the club.

What really surprises is the resilience of silence even in those who, voluntarily or not, abandon the game. This might reflect the fear that breaching the trust of one professional community today may hamper one's career prospects with another community tomorrow. However, something else may be at work. Perhaps the enduring allegiance to the profession one has belonged to for a long time, which withstands the passage of time and sacrifices retrospective self-reflexivity at the altar of nostalgia. Or, perhaps, the need to believe that serving the international Rule of Law meant something nobler or more durable than the 'humble immanence'[81] of the judicial field.

17.4   Conclusions: Breaking the Silence?

This chapter sought to question the silence surrounding the role of judicial bureaucrats in international dispute settlement. As discussed, this peculiar form of collective denial cannot be fully explained by a desire to preserve the legitimacy of international courts and tribunals vis-à-vis their constituencies. Indeed, principal-agent relationships exist in many other areas of global governance without causing much anxiety. Nor can silence be understood purely as a deliberate strategy by judicial bureaucracies to perpetuate their invisible influence and shield themselves from overt contestation. In fact, numerous participants in the international law

---

[79] Transnational Dispute Management website, www.transnational-dispute-management.com/ (last accessed 28 March 2018). For a description of the social role of OGEMID, see S. Schill, 'W(h)ither Fragmentation?', 886–887.

[80] International Economic Law and Policy Blog, http://worldtradelaw.typepad.com/ielpblog/ (last accessed 28 March 2018).

[81] Latour, *The Making of Law*, p. 196.

community – including government officials, counsel and academics – are fully aware of the existence and role of those unseen actors, but acquiesce to the fiction that judges handle each and every aspect of proceedings. Ultimately, the reluctance to recognize international judicial bureaucrats as a player in the adjudication game appears to be just another way in which the international law profession describes its own operations and preserves its prestige and autonomy vis-à-vis competing social sectors.

There are admittedly good reasons to maintain some discretion as to the role and functions of international judicial bureaucrats. The secret of deliberations in specific disputes should never be breached, lest the perceived impartiality and independence of international courts and tribunals be tarnished forever. However, the deafening silence we are currently facing might also backfire, as it could fuel conspiracy theories as to what really happens inside international courts and tribunals. To recall, the United States government's cover-up efforts regarding Area 51 prompted all manner of speculation about aliens, time-travel and the like. Similarly, if no one ever speaks about international judicial bureaucracies, the suspicion may arise that these faceless agents fully control the dispute settlement process and decide cases in lieu of adjudicators. Of course, bureaucrats are neither irrelevant nor omnipotent. They are simply part of the 'multitude of … amanuenses'[82] who tirelessly grapples with the complexities of international disputes. This is why it could be a good idea for the international judicial community to acknowledge their existence and put rumours to rest.

While the culture of silence still exerts its pull, the situation is timidly changing. In recent years, the social, professional and institutional contexts in which international adjudicators operate have acquired prominence as an object of study. The organization of the conference that inspired the publication of this book is proof of a renewed interest in the invisible work of registries, secretariats and clerks. Faced with increasing pressure to reveal their internal dynamics, some international courts have begun to reveal some aspects of the working relationships between judges and their assistants.[83] Similarly, some top arbitrators have taken particular care to disclose the work of their secretaries.[84] Albeit still embryonic,

---

[82] B. Latour, note 20 above, p. 77.

[83] See e.g. G. Marceau (ed.), *A History of Law and Lawyers in the GATT/WTO: The Development of the Rule of Law in the Multilateral Trading System* (Cambridge University Press, 2015); Garlicki, 'Judicial Deliberations: The Strasbourg Perspective'.

[84] See e.g. G. Kaufmann-Kohler and A. Rigozzi, International Arbitration: Law and Practice in Switzerland, p. 312.

this overt recognition of the unseen and the unspoken would refocus our attention and help us overcome the many tensions silence carries with it. By finally recognizing the elephant in the room, we might stop 'gingerly skirt[ing] the perimeter' of taboo topics[85] and break free from the 'labyrinthine social maze of closed doors and ever-narrower passages'.[86] At the same time, the elephant would shrink in size and become less threatening, eventually turning into another social fact with which to grapple – and upon which to keep building a bright future for international adjudication.

[85] R. Wajnyb, *The Silence: How Tragedy Shapes Talk* (Allen and Unwin, 2001), p. 246.
[86] Zerubavel, The Elephant in the Room, p. 84.

18

Unseen Actors as Unseen Experts

Ghosts in International Adjudication

GUILLAUME GROS[1]

18.1 Introduction

As international disputes are increasing in technical complexity, experts gain considerable practical influence in the judicial process.[2] From a theoretical standpoint, questions concerning the role and status of the expert have recently begun to attract attention.[3] New light shed on the importance of these actors' roles has revealed some interesting yet unconventional practices. Indeed, along with the usual process of using ex-curia experts and expert witnesses to address a dispute's complexity, an additional method seems to be applied in international dispute settlement, even if not in an official fashion, by means of the use of 'in-house experts' or 'ghost experts'. Before the International Court of Justice (ICJ or the Court), the International Tribunal for the Law of the Sea (ITLOS) and the Dispute Settlement Body of the World Trade Organization (WTO), i.e. the adjudicative bodies covered in this chapter, the function of providing expertise is usually performed by members of the Secretariat or by individuals occasionally joining the Registry in an undefined capacity. These actors can be labelled 'unseen', because their presence, identity, and exact function remain unknown to the parties. Arguments put forward in favour of this practice are of a pragmatic nature, related to efficiency,

---

[1] The author gratefully acknowledges Dr. Jason Rudall for his kind review and advice.
[2] Experts are not new players at the international level: as early as 1891, the arbitral tribunal in the *Delagoa Bay Railroad* case organised the appointment of experts. For a historical perspective see G. White, *The Use of Experts by International Tribunals* (Syracuse University Press, 1965).
[3] Some scholars explained this relative lack of interest by arguing that international law focuses on the interpretations of the legal provisions, rather than the establishment of facts. See A. Riddell and B. Plant, *Evidence Before the International Court of Justice* (British Institute of International & Comparative Law, 2009), p. 310.

cost, and time. However, the intervention of outsiders influencing the evaluation of the facts without any oversight by the parties raises serious concerns in terms of due process. Transparency with regard to fact finding is becoming a pivotal element to the judicial decision-making process, especially in disputes involving technical or scientific questions. The absence of transparency directly impacts the legitimacy of this process, which is problematic with regard to the credibility of rulings settling disputes involving high factual complexity.

The following reflections represent the results of a project entitled 'Experts and International Courts and Tribunals' conducted at the University of Geneva and financed by the Swiss National Research Fund.[4] This research project, which investigated the legal texts but also the practice of international dispute settlement, draws on the opinions of experienced judicial actors (magistrates, councils, and experts), consulted through questionnaires and interviews. More than 60 testimonies were received and assessed by means of qualitative analysis.

This chapter will address the following question: is a Registry legitimate in performing an epistemological function of support,[5] in particular if it remains unseen by the parties? This enquiry into the legitimacy of unseen experts will be dealt with both in terms of legal validity and practical efficiency. A first step, in the next section, will consist of describing this unofficial practice and the potential peculiarities before the three fora considered, after which the third section will review the existing formal and practical justifications of this practice. The chapter will then consider the weaknesses of these legal justifications in Section 18.4 before turning to a critical assessment of the pragmatic legitimacy of ghost experts in Section 18.5.

18.2   Unseen Experts in Practice

Describing a judicial practice designed to be unseen is by definition a difficult endeavour. To evaluate the importance of ghost experts in practice, data from four different sources will be pulled together: statements from judicial actors publicly discussing unseen experts; results from the

---

[4] The research is led by Prof. Laurence Boisson de Chazournes and Prof. Makane Mbengue assisted by two researchers, Ms. Rukmini Das and the author. Swiss National Research Fund, Project n°10001A_156117
[5] See below Section 18.2.1.

interviews conducted by the author; judicial decisions; and, finally, scholarly articles. The analysis reveals the existence of two types of unseen
expert. Before the ICJ and ITLOS, the expertise provided by the outsiders
is totally invisible to the parties, while before the WTO Dispute Settlement
Body, the Secretariat's support is known to the parties in principle, but not
its exact modalities and content.

18.2.1   Invisible expertise

The first mention of what have come to be known as 'ghost experts'
was made by Sir Robert Jennings, a former President of the Court, in
a 1996 article: 'The Court has not infrequently employed cartographers,
hydrographers, geographers, linguists, and even specialised legal experts
to assist in the understanding of the issue in a case before it; and has not
on the whole felt any need to make this public knowledge or even to
apprise the parties.'[6] The diversity of specialists mentioned indicates that
this use of experts is not rare, as the expression 'not infrequently' suggests.
It is interesting to note the apparent absence of any reaction in international literature at the time of this 'revelation'.

Another direct 'testimony' with regard to unseen experts was provided
by the ICJ Registrar, Philippe Couvreur, a few years later and deserves to
be quoted verbatim as the most comprehensive description of the practice
by a Court official:

> experts may also be engaged by the Registry of the Court for purely internal
> purposes. These experts do not participate in the proceedings as such, do
> not appear at hearings, and do not produce an official report. Their status
> is equivalent to that of short-term Registry members or consultants. They
> are subject to the same technical competence requirements and the same
> duty of confidentiality as the latter. No mention of their intervention there-
> fore appears in the decision or in another public document. Their role is
> to assist the Court as such, its members individually, and the Registry for
> various technical purposes, such as, for example, studying cartographic
> material provided by the parties or mapping or realizing specific sketches.[7]

---

[6] R. Jennings, 'International Lawyers and the Progressive Development of International Law',
    in J. Makarczyk (ed.), *Theory of International Law at the Threshold of the 21st Century: Essays
    in Honour of Krzysztof Skubiszewski* (1996), p. 413.

[7] Translation by the author. P. Couvreur, « Le règlement juridictionnel », in Institut du Droit
    Economique de la Mer, *Le processus de délimitation maritime: Etude d'un cas fictif* (Colloque
    international de Monaco du 27 au 29 mars 2003), (2004), pp. 349, 384.

The described regime encompasses the appointments, status, and role of the expert. It is not exempt from ambiguities, which reveal its practical origin, i.e., not rooted in a direct application of the text. Couvreur reported that the ghost experts' status (even though, like Sir Robert Jennings, Couvreur did not use that term) was equivalent to that of temporary staff members; they were not retained as experts pursuant to Article 28.1 of the ICJ Rules of Court (1978).[8] This absence of a direct and clear inclusion of the unseen experts in the Registry would explain why Couvreur stated that ghost experts can simultaneously support the Court, judges individually, and the Registry, whose task is also to support the Court. Stating that these experts assist, among others, the Registry implies that they are external to it. The status of 'consultant' referred to by the Registrar does not seem to have any textual support. With regard to the function of this 'private' expert, it appears polymorphic. The 'expert' may be tasked with aiding the understanding, assessment, and weighing of evidential material or complex factual questions embedded in legal arguments.[9] Simultaneously, the expert can intervene after the deliberations to draw the factual consequences of legal determinations.[10] The legal character of the insights provided by ghost experts is problematic: can it take a written form as a report?[11] If so, does it have an evidential nature, albeit without the status? Or do the expert insights have a purely intellectual character, incapable of formal classification?[12] The function of the unseen expert is to provide assistance of an epistemological nature as the ghost expert helps the adjudicator to apprehend and understand specific knowledge outside the realm of law, in order to assess its value and validity. In particular cases where experts are required to perform tasks such as 'realizing specific sketches', the operations entail interpreting and processing complex knowledge, encompassed in the assistance function defined as epistemological. Former ICJ President Peter Tomka has described these actors as 'walking encyclopaedias'[13] delivering their 'expert knowledge' to

---

[8] See below Section 18.3.1.

[9] See G. Gaja, 'Assessing Expert Evidence in the ICJ' (2017) 15(3) *The Law & Practice of International Courts and Tribunals*, p. 413; *Application for Revision and Interpretation of the Judgment of 24 February 1982 in the Case concerning the Continental Shelf* (Tunisia/ Libyan Arab Jamahiriya) *(Tunisia v. Libyan Arab Jamahiriya)*, Judgment, I.C.J. Reports 1985, p. 228.

[10] This point was repeatedly confirmed in the responses to the questionnaire.

[11] L. Savadogo, 'Le recours des juridictions internationales à des experts' (2004) 50 *Annuaire français de droit international*, p. 235.

[12] G. Gaja, 'Assessing Expert Evidence in the ICJ', p. 418.

[13] International conference: 'A Bridge Over Troubled Waters: Dispute Resolution in the Law of International Watercourses and the Law of the Sea', Max Planck Institute, Luxembourg, 25–26 September 2017.

whomever may need it. Their 'essence' lies in their completely invisible nature rather than in their precise function, because parties are unaware of their intervention.

Finally, the use of ghost experts became the centre of attention in the aftermath of the *Pulp Mills* case,[14] fostering a lively debate on the fact-finding methods of the Court.[15] In their Joint Dissenting Opinion, Judges Al-Khasawneh and Simma took a clear stance against the practice, which they famously named 'experts fantômes'.[16] The two judges did not, however, personally attest to the existence of any such actor in the case at hand, but rather relied on the two aforementioned articles. However, ghost experts are certainly employed in ICJ procedures, as confirmed by Judge Giorgio Gaja: '[t]he Court has often attempted to acquire scientific or technical knowledge by informally consulting experts',[17] and recently by President Yusuf before the Sixth Committee of the General Assembly.[18]

The influence of unofficial experts is occasionally apparent in cases where the Court draws conclusions of a technical nature and arrives at solutions that were not advocated by either of the parties. Especially in delimitation cases, it is doubtful that judges would elaborate on highly technical solutions without some exterior expert insight.[19] In *Nicaragua v. Honduras*,[20] the Court decided to combine the two methods of delimitation put forward by the parties involving intricate technical models. The methodological creativity of the adjudicators in such highly complex scientific issues suggests the intervention of unseen technical support.[21]

---

[14] *Pulp Mills on the River Uruguay (Argentina v. Uruguay)*, Judgment of 20 April 2010, I.C.J. Reports 2010, p. 108.
[15] See G. Gros, 'The ICJ's Handling of Science in the Whaling in the Antarctic Case: A Whale of a Case?' (2015) 6 *Journal of International Dispute Settlement*, pp. 579–580.
[16] Joint dissenting opinion of Judges Al-Khasawneh and Simma, p. 104, § 14.
[17] G. Gaja, 'Assessing Expert Evidence in the ICJ', p. 413.
[18] Speech by H.E. Mr. Abdulqawi Ahmed Yusuf, President of the International Court of Justice, to the Sixth Committee of The General Assembly, Recourse to Court-appointed experts under Article 50 of the Statute, 26 October 2018.
[19] M. Pratt, 'The Role of the Technical Expert in Maritime Delimitation Cases', in R. Lagoni and D. Vignes (eds.), *Maritime Delimitation* (Martinus Nijhoff, 2006), p. 84.
[20] *Territorial and Maritime Dispute between Nicaragua and Honduras in the Caribbean Sea (Nicaragua v. Honduras)*, Judgment, I.C.J. Reports 2007, p. 659.
[21] See A. Riddell and B. Plant, *Evidence before the International Court of Justice*, p. 337; T. Daniel, 'Expert Evidence before the ICJ', Third bi-annual conference of ABLOS expert evidence before the ICJ, p. 4, available at: www.iho.int/mtg_docs/com_wg/ABLOS/ABLOS_Conf3/PAPER1-3.PDF; Pratt, 'The Role of the Technical Expert in Maritime Delimitation Cases', p. 82.

A similar conclusion can be drawn from the *Cameroon v. Nigeria*[22] and *Qatar v. Bahrain*[23] judgments on the basis of certain conclusions which had not been advocated by either of the parties.[24] The answers provided by the interviewees for the purpose of the present project, irrespective of their critical appraisal of the practice, demonstrate a general acknowledgment of the 'not infrequent' use of unseen experts by the Court, thus seemingly consolidating its non-incidental nature.

The situation before ITLOS is less clear-cut in the absence of widespread public acknowledgement by 'insiders'. Judge Chandrasekhara Rao revealed that in the *M/V 'SAIGA'* Case,[25] '[t]he secretary-general of the International Seabed Authority, a cartographer and the authorities in charge of the construction of the permanent premises have been invited on different occasions to be present at meetings of the Tribunal.'[26] The presence of unofficial expertise was also mentioned by respondents to the questionnaire, who referred to outsiders occasionally assisting the Registry in assessing the scientific evidence and redacting the decision.

18.2.2   Opaque Expertise

Before the ICJ and ITLOS, the in-house experts seem to be invisible. Their identity, function, and input remain out of view, as does their very existence. The situation is different in the WTO dispute settlement system, because the practice of in-house expertise is acknowledged (perhaps approved) by the parties. WTO disputes may be characterised as technical, given the factual economic considerations and tests involved. The appraisal of numerous legal issues requires dealing with highly complex econometrics and scientific issues.[27] Nevertheless, on the basis of more than 225 adopted panel reports, one can conclude that experts were

---

[22] *Land and Maritime Boundary between Cameroon and Nigeria (Cameroon v. Nigeria: Equatorial Guinea intervening)*, Judgment, ICJ Reports 2002, p. 30.

[23] *Maritime Delimitation and Territorial Questions between Qatar and Bahrain*, Merits, Judgment, ICJ Reports 2001, p. 40.

[24] T. Daniel, 'Expert Evidence before the ICJ', p. 5.

[25] *M/V 'SAIGA' Case (Saint Vincent and the Grenadines v. Guinea), Prompt Release*, Judgment of 4 December 1997, ITLOS Report 1997.

[26] 'ITLOS: The First Six Years', *Max Planck Yearbook of United Nations Law*, vol. 6, 2002, p. 183; P. Chandrasekhara Rao and P. Gautier, *The Rules of the International Tribunal for the Law of the Sea: A Commentary* (Brill, 2006).

[27] B. Mercurio and K.-J. Ni (eds.), *Science and Technology in International Economic Law Balancing Competing Interests*, (Routledge, 2014), particularly pp. 9–53.

appointed by panels in 15, almost exclusively Sanitary and Phytosanitary Measures (SPS)-related cases.[28] This difference of treatment between SPS cases (appointment of ex-curia experts) involving 'hard' (physical) sciences and those containing technical or economic questions can be explained by the role of the Secretariat. Confronted with complex evidence or arguments of an economic character, the panellists rely on specialists within the Secretariat divisions, especially the Economic Research and Statistics Division.[29] This practice is considered part of the normal procedural functioning of the dispute settlement system.[30] As Chad P. Bown stated: '[t]he WTO's DSU adjudication process inherently involves bringing about changes to Member nation's economic policies. Therefore, panellist and arbitrator's decisions and rulings should be informed by the best available economic analysis and support that the Secretariat can provide.'[31] The existence of specialists and their intervention is acknowledged by the parties, but their exact function, terms of reference, and intellectual production are not established in a transparent and adversarial fashion and not even communicated *post factum* to parties.

Several arguments have been developed to ascertain the legitimacy of ghost experts by explaining and justifying why scientific or technical specialists can be used by the adjudicator without full acknowledgement of the parties.

18.3   A Legitimate Practice? Possible Justifications

When it comes to supporting the legitimacy of members of the Registry or Secretariat acting as experts, the arguments are twofold: legal and practical. According to some authors, the practice of using unseen experts is supported by a sound legal basis, even though it is not described in rulings. The most common justification for the presence of unseen experts is of a pragmatic nature.

---

[28] C. Valles, 'Different Forms of Expert Involvement in WTO Dispute Settlement Proceedings' (2018) 9(3) *Journal of International Dispute Settlement*, p. 367.

[29] G.Z. Marceau, and J.K. Hawkins, 'Experts in WTO Dispute Settlement' (2012) 3(3) *Journal of International Dispute Settlement*, p. 504.

[30] Y. Fukunaga, 'Experts in WTO and Investment Litigation', in J.A. Huerta-Goldman, Antoine Romanetti and Franz X. Stirnimann (eds.), *WTO Litigation, Investment Arbitration, and Commercial Arbitration*, (Kluwer Law International, 2014), p. 165.

[31] C.P. Bown, 'The WTO Secretariat and the Role of Economics in DSU Panels and Arbitrations', 2008, p. 36, available at SSRN: https://ssrn.com/abstract=1274732 or https://dx.doi.org/10.2139/ssrn.1274732.

18.3.1   Legal Arguments

Two sets of legal arguments are used to justify the practice of ghost experts: their presence can be the result of their inclusion as temporary members of an assisting body (Registry or Secretariat) or of the Court exercising its investigative power. According to the practitioners interviewed, the most commonly used justification is inclusion in the Registry.

The advice provided by these internal experts as members of the Registry forms part of this institution's support to the Court in administering justice. Indeed, the *ratio essendi* and functions of the Registry could be concisely described as follows: 'The Registry is the permanent administrative organ of the ICJ ... the Registry's tasks include both helping in the administration of justice ... and acting as an international secretariat.'[32] Arguably, this includes providing timely insights to the Court on technical elements contained in evidence or assisting the judges with regard to the factual implications of the decision. The Court can enlarge this list of functions and entrust the Registrar with any task it sees as fitting in the particular circumstances.[33]

Beyond the functional explanation, the precise legal basis of the practice can be found in Article 28.1 of the ICJ Rules: 'The Registry shall comprise the Registrar, the Deputy-Registrar, and such other staff as the Registrar shall require for the efficient discharge of his functions.' As a consequence, along with over a hundred officials, the Registry consists of 'additional temporary staff engaged by the Registrar as and when the Court's work may so require: including interpreters, translators, typists ...',[34] as well as, according to Sir Robert Jennings,[35] geographers, hydrographers, or linguists. The expression 'temporary staff', absent from the Rules, is used in Article 4 of the 'Instructions for the Registry'.[36]

In addition, Article 62 of the Rules has been put forward as a valid way for the Court to informally use expert advice: 'The Court may at any time call upon the parties to produce such evidence or to give such

---

[32] *The International Court of Justice: Handbook*; UN Publications, 15 Sept. 2016, p. 29.
[33] Article 26.2 of the ICJ Rules.
[34] *ICJ Handbook*, p. 30.
[35] R. Jennings, 'International Lawyers' p. 413.
[36] Instructions for the Registry (as drawn up by the Registrar and approved by the Court on 20 March 2012) Article 4: 'The Registrar makes the necessary arrangements for the engagement of temporary staff.'

explanations as the Court may consider to be necessary for the elucidation of any aspect of the matters in issue, or may itself seek other information for this purpose.' Riddell and Plant remarked that neither the kind of information to be sought nor the related methods of investigation are defined in the provision[37] and therefore suggest that this leeway has been interpreted[38] as enabling judges to solicit the advice of experts without the knowledge of the parties.[39]

The respective provisions of the ICJ Rules and the ITLOS Rules concerning the Registrar are almost identical so the legal justifications of – and the criticism on – the use of unseen experts before the ICJ apply *mutatis mutandis* to ITLOS. Two other provisions contained in the 'Instruction for the Registry' at ITLOS seem to confirm the possibility for the Registrar, both functionally and statutorily, to include technicians or scientists in her or his staff. In other words, the texts seem to provide justifications for the inclusion of experts in terms of the role of the Registrar and the practical possibility of special appointment. More precisely, Article 2 states that '[t]he Registrar is responsible for the preparation of cases … and assists the Committee established by the Tribunal to prepare drafts of judgments' and Article 10 provides that '[t]he Registrar will make arrangements for the recruitment of temporary staff'.

A common argument in support of the legitimacy of the use of unseen experts in specific cases relates to the 'importance' of the information at stake. In other words, the validity of the practice would depend upon the significance of the investigated question for the resolution of the dispute. If the insight sought from experts is not 'likely to affect the decision', recourse to such experts without the knowledge of the parties is perfectly legitimate. In the words of Giorgio Gaja: '[s]hould experts simply be engaged by the Court for determining the precise geographic coordinates of certain points clearly identified by the Court or for drawing a chart comprising those points, *there seems to be little justification for querying the experts' role*'.[40] The argument relies on the possibility of conducting a valid form of triage between the types of insights provided by the invisible experts, whereby the practice is considered acceptable for some insights but not others. Even authors generally critical of the use of ghost experts identify a threshold of acceptability: 'information in the interest

---

[37] A. Riddell and B. Plant, *Evidence before the International Court of Justice*, p. 336.
[38] Relying on the T. Daniel's article, 'Expert Evidence before the ICJ', p. 4.
[39] A. Riddell and B. Plant, *Evidence before the International Court of Justice*, p. 336.
[40] G. Gaja, 'Assessing Expert Evidence in the ICJ', p. 414, emphasis added.

of a proper administration of justice, the Court's practice, as described by Sir Robert ... thus should be restricted to issues of minor importance'.[41] Also Judges Al-Khasawneh and Simma seem to go in that direction, explaining that '[w]hile such consultation of such invisible experts would be pardonable if the input they provide relates to the technical margin of case ...'[42]

Before the WTO, the textual pattern relevant for the question of unseen experts is similar to the one identified for the ICJ and ITLOS, relying on the conjunction of two factors: the function of the Secretariat being described in very broad terms as providing support to the adjudicators, and the capacity of the adjudicators to search for any information they consider suitable for the resolution of the case. Pursuant to Article 27.1 of the WTO Understanding on Rules and Procedures Governing the Settlement of Disputes (DSU), the Secretariat 'shall have the responsibility of assisting panels, especially on the legal, historical and procedural aspects of the matters dealt with, and of providing secretarial and technical support'. This provision has been interpreted as conferring onto the Secretariat not only the capacity to help the panel in assessing technical or scientific elements submitted by the parties,[43] but a more general function of participation in the decision-making process concerning economic analyses. In particular, the 'technical support' element is understood as referring to the task of assisting the panel in grappling with any aspect of a dispute that can be characterised as technical, i.e. encompassing scientific or complex economic issues. The term 'technical' receives a very extensive interpretation, describing any type of function and topic situated outside the law. In this sense, Chad P. Bown, who supports the role of the secretariat acting as an expert, mentions the 'technical economic support'[44] it provides. According to this debatable interpretation,[45] 'technical support' does not refer so much to the nature of the assistance as to its object. Referring to the nature of the assistance, the interpretation of the term 'technical' excludes the principal intellectual elements characterising expertise in a judicial context. This general role of assistance attributed to the Secretariat is to be understood in conjunction with the broad powers

[41] C. Tams, 'Article 50', in A. Zimmermann, C. Tomuschat, K. Oellers-Frahm and C.J. Tams (eds.), *The Statute of the International Court of Justice, a Commentary*, 2nd edn (Oxford University Press, 2012), p. 1298.
[42] Joint dissenting opinion, Judges Simma and Al-Khasawneh, *Pulp Mills* case, p. 104.
[43] G.Z. Marceau and J.K. Hawkins, 'Experts in WTO Dispute Settlement', p. 495.
[44] Bown, 'The WTO Secretariat and the Role of Economics', p. 36.
[45] See Section 18.4.1.

of the panels to find relevant information and epistemic support in a very inclusive fashion.[46] Pursuant to Article 13.1 of the DSU, panels are entitled to 'seek information and technical advice from any individual or body which it deems appropriate.' If the use of invisible experts is made possible by a certain interpretation of the texts, the main justifications of the practice are of a pragmatic nature.

18.3.2   Beyond Legal Possibility: Practical Advantages

For adjudicators, the advantages of relying on 'internal "expert fantômes" are evident'[47] at every stage of the expert process and substantiate the legitimacy of the mechanism. When using the opportunity of soliciting expert advice and choosing the individual(s) concerned, the process is considerably eased by the absence of a possible challenge or even mere comment by the parties. Identifying an expert is particularly difficult in certain specialised fields and could involve a fierce battle between the parties.[48] The same reflection applies to the definitions of the terms of reference. The direct personal interaction between the judges and the expert could indeed easily be understood as the most 'efficient means of clarifying matters',[49] precisely because it is not constrained by a predefined framework. In a nutshell, this practice could prove useful because normally the expert 'procedure … may be rather cumbersome'.[50] Unseen experts could result in saving considerable time and resources, serving the purpose of a good administration of justice. Another potential advantage is the complete liberty afforded to the judge in receiving, assessing, and integrating the unofficial expert advice into the decision.[51] It would be very difficult for the adjudicator to deviate from the conclusions reached by an expert which it has publicly appointed itself due to the epistemological and statutory legitimacy he or she enjoys. The expert is by definition more legitimate in its technical or scientific findings than the judge because of his or her specific knowledge and skills. This fear is commonly used as an argument to explain the reluctance of international judges to appoint experts.[52]

---

[46]   G.Z. Marceau and J.K. Hawkins, 'Experts in WTO Dispute Settlement', pp. 499–500.

[47]   C.J. Tams, 'Article 50', p. 1298.

[48]   See Y. Fukunaga, 'Experts in WTO and Investment Litigation', pp. 144–145.

[49]   C.J. Tams, 'Article 50', p. 1298.

[50]   Ibid.

[51]   A. Riddell and B. Plant, *Evidence before the International Court of Justice*, p. 334.

[52]   See G. Gros, 'The ICJ's Handling of Science in the Whaling in the Antarctic Case', pp. 589–590.

In the WTO context, economists within the Secretariat are deemed better suited to address the specificities of the technical disputes which require in-house institutional culture and an understanding of the complementary roles of legal and political elements.[53] Their experience and knowledge within this framework, along with their academic expertise, is considered of incomparable value in the context of technical economic disputes before a panel. Secretariat economists can be involved at an early stage in the process and can usefully influence the panellists in forming the conceptual or technical categories beneficial to a sound understanding of the case. Finally, the direct interaction with the panellists allows the experts to provide them with 'forecasting ability'[54] as to the effect of their decision.

This hypothesis was largely confirmed by the responses to the questionnaire. Interviewed actors almost systematically display a great deal of satisfaction about the work of the Secretariat, or Registry, function and production. The quality of the work provided is often praised as well as the skills of the Secretariat members, their expertise, competence, and dedication. This consideration of a pragmatic nature seems to frequently outweigh, if not completely overshadow, the possible concern about an insufficient transparency of the process. Especially in the WTO context, the partially visible presence of experts is seen as legitimate if not necessary to a sound functioning of the system of dispute settlement.[55] Some concerns, however, are voiced about this use of invisible experts and a critical analysis reveals the groundless character of some arguments presented to justify the practice.

18.4   Critical Assessment of the Unseen Expertise: A Legal Perspective

18.4.1   Absence of Legal Bases

In-house expertise is frequently justified by reference to the investigative capacities of the adjudicator and by the role of the Secretariat or Registry.[56]

---

[53] C.P. Bown, 'The WTO Secretariat and the Role of Economics', p. 14.
[54] Ibid., p. 12.
[55] Ibid., p. 14.
[56] The two set of arguments can be cumulative as well; the investigative power of the adjudicator will, in the case of the ICJ, be formally translated by appointment of an expert as a temporary member of the registry.

It is proposed that neither of these bases is convincing, as it leads to an untenable division between different types of expert insights.

18.4.1.1   Appointment by the Judge

For the ICJ, the extensive interpretation of Article 62 of the Rules leads to untenable consequences.[57] The capacity for the judges to seek any kind of insight, without specific procedural framework, would provide the Court with very strong inquisitorial powers. Allowing for the consultation of unseen experts would undermine every other existing provision governing the appointment of experts that requires the involvement of the parties. The provision, even interpreted in isolation from the other rules governing experts, by its use of the word 'information' can scarcely be regarded as encompassing expert evidence or expert opinion, but refers rather to archival[58] or publicly available knowledge.[59]

A similar reasoning can be put forward in the WTO context and the argument based on Article 13.1 of the DSU. Considering that panels can seek any type of expert opinion without the knowledge of the parties opens the door to possible inquisitorial justice, which is at odds with the spirit and function of the dispute settlement system designed by the Marrakech agreements.[60] The unconstrained use of experts would result in circumventing the rules regarding the appointment of experts by a panel. Over time a subsequent practice as to the appointment of experts and their presentation has developed,[61] reaching a balance between control of the panel and involvement of the parties. For example, since the *EC-Hormones* case,[62] panels decide which individuals to appoint based on the suggestions from the parties (and international organisations, if appropriate). The Appellate Body has specified that panellists enjoy a

---

[57] T. Daniel seemed to have mentioned the argument in his 2000 article precisely to exclude its potential application, 'Expert Evidence before the ICJ', p. 4.

[58] Ibid.

[59] A. Riddell and B. Plant, *Evidence before the International Court of Justice*, p. 181.

[60] C.A. Thomas, 'Of Facts and Phantoms: Economics, Epistemic Legitimacy, and WTO Dispute Settlement' (2011) 14(2) *Journal of International Economic Law*, p. 295; Ernst-Ulrich Petersmann, *The GATT/WTO Dispute Settlement System: International Law, International Organizations and Dispute Settlement*, (Martinus Nijhoff Publishers, 1997).

[61] See Y. Fukunaga, 'Experts in WTO and Investment Litigation', pp. 143–148; G.Z. Marceau and J.K. Hawkins, 'Experts in WTO Dispute Settlement', p. 493, and p. 502; J. Pauwelyn, 'The Use of Experts in WTO Dispute Settlement' (2002) 51(2) *The International and Comparative Law Quarterly*, p. 325.

[62] *EC – Measures Concerning Meat and Meat Products (Hormones) (EC – Hormones)*, WTO Appellate Body Report, February 1998, WT/DS26/AB/R, WT/DS48/AB/R 13.

discretionary power regarding the individual experts they wish to appoint, based on the parties' suggestions and in accordance with the due process requirement of the DSU.[63] In addition, considering expert insights, which may have an evidentiary nature, as 'information' is problematic. The conflation of information (freely accessible) with evidence may automatically lead the adjudicator to interfere in the discharge of the burden of proof by the parties.[64]

Before any of these adjudicative bodies, the assimilation of expert opinions with information results in the coexistence of two different types of *ex-curia* expert regimes. One regime is characterised by the sole discretion of the adjudicator, experts being employed outside any specific framework and without any involvement or even knowledge of the parties. The other, more 'formal', regime sets conditions with regard to the designation of the expert, the identification of the terms of reference, and the involvement of the parties.[65] No sound and consistent criteria can justify such a difference between applicable regimes and the resulting use of 'private expertise'. In other words, it is not legitimate for unseen actors to provide expert insights, because the adjudicator lacks the legal basis to demand this in the first place. The division of the factual questions according to their 'importance' seems inappropriate and will prove to be impracticable.[66] Similar conclusions can be drawn with regard to the argument of the inclusion of an expert as a member of a Registry or Secretariat.

18.4.1.2   Inclusion in the Assisting Body

The ICJ and the ITLOS Registries are both entrusted with a function that can be described as 'helping in the administration of justice',[67] and would be, according to some practitioners and academics,[68] subsequently competent to provide expert insights. It is submitted that the function of support or help cannot encompass assistance of an epistemological nature. A mission of support in this judicial context cannot be interpreted as the capacity to take an active and direct part in the administration of justice *per se*, by providing insights on the substance of a case (be it related to factual complexity). The

[63] AB 16 October 2008, US continued suspension pp. 433, 435, 436.
[64] Y. Fukunaga, 'Experts in WTO and Investment Litigation', p. 149.
[65] As provided for by Article 50 of the Statute of the Court, Article 82 of the Rules of the ITLOS or Article 13 of the WTO DSU.
[66] See Section 18.4.1.3.
[67] ICJ, 'The Registry' www.icj-cij.org/en/registry. ITLOS, 'The Registry', www.itlos.org/the-registry/.
[68] See also above Section 18.3.1.

unseen character of this help, provided behind the scenes, is obviously not likely to change this conclusion. *A contrario*, even if an expert, appointed by the judge or presented by a party, by its insights enables the adjudicator to take a stance on a factual issue, he or she is not 'helping' the administration of justice. In other words, an expert in a judicial context is not formally 'supporting' the judge. He or she is an integral part of the judicial process, as a counsel would be. The opposite stance would logically lead to the untenable conclusion that every other actor involved in a judicial procedure, counsel or witness, is potentially 'helping' or supporting the judge in the discharge of its function. Nobody would argue that the Registry can include unseen witnesses to support the bench in its fact-finding mission. The same reasoning should be applied to experts. Similar reasoning can be applied to Article 27.1 of the DSU dealing with the mission of the Secretariat. This article has been interpreted as enabling the Secretariat to provide epistemological assistance to the panellists, especially with economics-related matters.[69] This interpretation is debatable.

From a general perspective, an expert process, regardless of the form it takes, cannot be characterised as 'technical support' for a court or tribunal. The operation leading to expert insight in a judicial context is merely intellectual and relates to the interpretation of facts and the evidentiary process. Those facts can be of a technical nature as can the methods used to analyse them but the support provided to the adjudicator resulting from the expertise is by no means technical *per se*. In other words, epistemological support is distinct from technical support, because the term 'technical' in this context refers to the nature of the assistance, i.e. dealing with practical issues affecting the adjudicators but not directly related to the substance of the case. That being said, the wording of Article 27.1 is congruent with this idea of a distinction between expertise and technical support. Whereas the capacity of the Secretariat to assist with 'legal, historical and procedural' elements is 'framed in the context of "the matter dealt with", the word technical is [not] placed [in] any such context'.[70] By being unrelated to the substantive elements of a case, the technical assistance refers, most likely, to 'incidental administrative matters'.[71] Finally, this interpretation is confirmed by the position of 'technical' in

---

[69] See G.Z. Marceau and J.K. Hawkins, 'Experts in WTO Dispute Settlement', p. 499 and P. Bown 'The WTO secretariat and the Role of Economics', p. 4, *contra* C.A. Thomas 'Of Facts and Phantoms', p. 317.

[70] C.A. Thomas, 'Of Facts and Phantoms', p. 317.

[71] Ibid.

the provision, placed at the end of the sentence after 'secretarial', which renders it rather doubtful that the adjective describes a crucial function for the adjudicative process per se akin to the one performed by an expert.

This equation between the function of an expert and the function of a Secretariat, both providing epistemological 'support' to the judge, is untenable and has far-reaching consequences as it blurs categories and conceptual structures underlying the judicial process. The equation between functions is permitted by a conflation (even partial) of evidence, information, data, argumentation, advice, and facts. The conflation of assistance and evidentiary processes in particular could undermine the confidence of the parties in the legally rigorous character of the international adjudicative process, and its legitimacy. With regard to the lack of a distinction between the function of certain judicial actors, similar concerns were expressed in connection with the *Pulp Mills* case. In his separate opinion, Judge Greenwood criticised the practice of experts, addressing the Court in a counsel capacity. The judge expressed in very clear terms the damaging implications of such practice:

> The distinction between the evidence of a witness or expert and the advocacy of counsel is fundamental to the proper conduct of litigation before the Court. ... For a person who is going ... to offer his expert opinion on scientific data to address the Court as counsel is *to circumvent these provisions* of the Rules and ... *unacceptably to blur the distinction between evidence and advocacy*.[72]

The way in which the question of unseen experts is treated is telling with regard to the relative indeterminacy of both the expert and Registry regimes in international law. For example, the question of the nature and classification of the experts' insights (evidence, information, or data), despite having pivotal repercussions, has only just come to the fore in international law[73] and is not settled. From a broader perspective, the use of ghost experts seems to be permitted by the rather underdeveloped character of the rules concerning evidence in the international adjudicative process.[74] In any event, the legitimate functions of assistance to the

---

[72] Separate opinion of Judge Greenwood, *Pulp Mills* case, p. 231 § 27 (emphasis added).

[73] *The Expert in the International Adjudicative Process*, Symposium, Max Planck Institute, Luxembourg, 26 & 27 April 2017.

[74] See F. Romanin Jacur, 'Remarks on the Role of Ex Curia Scientific Experts in International Disputes', in N. Boschieno, T. Scovazzi, C. Pitea and C. Ragni (eds.), *International Courts and the Development of International Law. Essays in Honor of T. Treves* (Springer, 2013), p. 442.

judge performed by a Registry does not and should not encompass expertise. As things stand currently, the practice of a member of the Registry
or Secretariat to provide expert insights to the bench is not supported by
the law.

18.4.1.3   Division Between Experts' Insights

Another argument as to the legal validity of the unseen expert practice
relates to the importance and content of the insights provided. This 'division theory' is unsatisfactory and raises many questions. The first concern
relates to the doubtful possibility of identifying 'advice that is [not] likely
to affect the content of the decision'.[75] Indeed, it seems fair to wonder how
a technical point, whose determination is needed by the adjudicator, is not
susceptible to influencing the decision.[76] The possibility of distinguishing
between types of expert insight appears to rely on another debatable
assumption: the existence of technical or scientific issues whose determination is unanimous and not susceptible to divergence, as to the methods
used and/or results obtained. What test should be applied to differentiate
between the two types of situation? How to set the criteria to determine
what a 'very simple point' is? Judges should be deciding this question
without involving the parties. However, it seems paradoxical to rely on the
sole perception of the judge, who de facto is not competent to assess the
factual matter considered, to decide upon the significance of the elements
forming part of this factual matter. Even if such identification between
important and minor technical points was conceptually and practically
possible, its consequences remain problematical as it legitimises the violation of rules or principles on the basis of pragmatic arguments. It also
leads to the hardly acceptable conclusion that a violation of a principle
is acceptable if the violation originates in a point of minor importance.
The use of unseen experts would be, if not completely legitimate, at least
'pardonable'[77] when dealing with points of minor importance. It would,
however, undoubtedly be considered unacceptable for a judge to solicit
a party for the communication of a document or ask an expert of a party
for clarification, without notice to the opposite party, even if the information sought was not 'likely to affect the content of the decision'. In the

[75] G. Gaja, 'Assessing Expert Evidence in the ICJ', p. 414.
[76] G. Gaja remarks with regard to the difficulty: 'However, as observed in the text, the deter-
      mination of a base point is likely to affect the content of a decision on a maritime boundary
      and should not be left to 'invisible' experts.' Ibid., p. 413.
[77] Judges Al-Khasawneh and Simma, Joint dissenting opinion, p. 7.

case of in-house experts, if the unfairness is mitigated by the fact that both parties are treated equally, through their respective equal ignorance of the process, '[t]he issue of principle, however, remains'.[78]

18.4.2   A Practice Contra Legem?

Using experts without the knowledge of the parties appears to lack solid legal basis. Practices can validly be developed to accommodate a 'light' legal framework.[79] In the WTO context, for instance, flexibility is an important component of the dispute settlement system,[80] and practices play a significant role in the overall development of the institution.[81] In the case of the 'unseen expert', however, not only is the legal foundation fragile or inexistent, but the practice seems to directly infringe upon other rules and even fly in the face of due process requirements.

The use of unseen experts does not make up for a procedural void regarding experts or more generally the handling of complex facts: the legitimacy of a registrar acting as expert cannot be found in the deficiency of the legal framework surrounding fact-finding. Rules governing the use of experts exist before every adjudicative body covered in this chapter and the use of unseen experts has not been provided for. The presence of unseen experts constitutes a violation of those rules. The contradiction between the texts and the ghost experts' practice is highlighted by Tams in the context of the ICJ Statute: 'It is necessary ... briefly to consider whether the Court can seek expert advice through other means, without making an order under Art. 50. On the face of it, The Statute and Rules seem to exclude this possibility – after all, Art. 50 is the only provision empowering the Court to appoint experts.'[82] The same reflexion applies to ITLOS *vis-à-vis* Article 82 of its Rules. This argument concerning the appointment of experts can be extended to the situation of assessors, which the ICJ can appoint under Article 30(2) of the Statute.[83] From a

---

[78] Separate opinion of Judge Greenwood, §28.
[79] For a discussion of the efficiency of the practices, see Sir Arthur Watts, 'Enhancing the Effectiveness of Procedures of International Dispute Settlement', in J.A. Frowein and R. Wolfrum (eds.), *Max Planck Yearbook of United Nations Law*, vol. V (2001).
[80] P. Pescatore, *Handbook of GATT/WTO Dispute Settlement* (1991), p. 7.
[81] G.Z. Marceau and C. Marquet, 'Practice, Practices and Ways of Doing Things in the World Trade Organization (WTO) Law', in H. Ruiz-Fabri (ed.), *International Law and Litigation: A Look into Procedure* (Nomos & Hart Publishing, 2018).
[82] C. Tams, 'Article 50', p. 1298.
[83] Article 30(2) of the Statute '[t]he Rules of the Court may provide for assessors to sit with the Court or with any of its chambers, without the right to vote'.

functional point of view, assessors can be considered as experts: due to their expertise, they are appointed to sit with the Court in order to provide insights to the judges.[84] The function of an assessor appears to be similar to the role that the ghost expert seems to play and its innovative character in international law has been highlighted.[85] Several respondents to the questionnaire suggested assessors could be used as an alternative to using ghost experts. The presence of unseen experts, however, may be seen as a violation of the Article dealing with assessors. The infringement seems even clearer in the case of ITLOS. Following Article 289 UNCLOS,[86] a specific and detailed mechanism has been stipulated in the Rules of the Tribunal,[87] providing for the appointment of two assessors selected from pre-existing lists.[88] The system of assessors has, however, never been used in the Tribunal's[89] or the Court's histories. Judge Giorgio Gaja considers that adjudicators would be reluctant to sit with specialists and would rather consult them informally for fear of undue influence.[90]

In the context of the WTO, the use of experts may be seen as a violation of Article 13 of the DSU. The question is less about compliance with Article 18.1, which states that '[t]here shall be no ex parte communications with the panel or Appellate Body concerning matters under consideration by the panel or Appellate Body.' Thomas regrets that this prohibition

---

[84] See S. Rosenne, *Procedure in the International Court: A Commentary on the 1978 Rules of the International Court of Justice* (Martinus Nijhoff, 1983), p. 32. See also *Western Sahara (Advisory Opinion)* (Sep Op Petren), p. 113; A. Riddell and B. Plant, *Evidence before the International Court of Justice*, p. 335.

[85] S. Rosenne, *Fact-finding before the International Court of Justice*, p. 245.

[86] 'In any dispute involving scientific or technical matters, a court or tribunal exercising jurisdiction under this section may, at the request of a party or proprio motu, select in consultation with the parties no fewer than two scientific or technical experts chosen preferably from the relevant list prepared in accordance with Annex VIII, article 2, to sit with the court or tribunal but without the right to vote'.

[87] Particularly Subsection 4 of the Rules of the Tribunal.

[88] See L. Boisson de Chazournes and G. Gros, 'L'expert et le Tribunal international du droit de la mer', in G. Le Floch, *Les vingt ans du Tribunal international du droit de la mer*, (Pedone, 2018), p. 186.

[89] In the case of ITLOS, Treves explains that 'the reason lies in that the scientific or technical experts as envisaged in Article 289 are too close to being judges or arbitrators', T. Treves, 'Law and Science in the Interpretation of the Law of the Sea Convention' (2012) 3(3) *Journal of International Dispute Settlement*, p. 485.

[90] G. Gaja, 'Assessing Expert Evidence in the ICJ', p. 418; M. Bennouna, 'Experts Before the International Court of Justice: What for?' (2018) 9(3) *Journal of International Dispute Settlement*, p. 345; and C. Foster, *Science and the Precautionary Principle in International Courts and Tribunals: Experts' Evidence, Burden of Proof and Finality* (Cambridge University Press, 2011), p. 128.

would only be directed towards the experts of the parties.[91] By depriving the parties of the opportunity to respond or comment upon evidence or information potentially harmful to their case, the practice of using in-house expertise might constitute a violation of the principle *audi alteram partem* according to which both parties should be equally treated and heard on every aspect of the dispute. For this reason, Pauwelyn suggests 'to explicitly prohibit any ex parte communications between the panel and the panel-appointed experts. The disputing parties should get an opportunity to comment on all input provided by the experts, no matter how trivial it may seem.'[92] Before the ICJ and ITLOS, the situation is dealt with respectively by Articles 67.2[93] and 82.2 of their Rules, which encapsulate this necessity. These rules demand the communication of 'every report or record of an enquiry and every expert opinion'. Benzing comments in this respect that 'the practice of … so called "phantom experts" … is problematic in particular with regard to the right of the parties to comment on expert opinion (Art. 67, para. 2 of the Rules of the Court)'.[94]

18.5   Doubtful Pragmatic Justifications

The practice of ghost experts, potentially used *contra legem*, finds its rationale in pragmatic reasoning aimed at optimising efficiency in the judicial process. Commentators often balance the practical advantages of unseen experts with a strict adherence to a ('cumbersome') procedural framework to establish the legitimacy of unseen experts.[95] This could mean that ends would matter more than means, and in-house expertise would sometimes be the most 'efficient means of clarifying matters'.[96] A careful review of the case law indicates that this assumption is debatable. If the fact-finding methods of international courts and tribunals are discussed in legal literature,[97] their results should be as well. The adjudicative bodies

---

[91] C.A. Thomas, 'Of Facts and Phantoms', p. 310.
[92] Pauwelyn, 'The Use of Experts', p. 350.
[93] 'Every report or record of an enquiry and every expert opinion shall be communicated to the parties, which shall be given the opportunity of commenting upon it.'
[94] M. Benzing, 'Evidentiary Issues' in Zimmermann et al., *The Statute of the International Court of Justice, a Commentary*, pp. 1109, 1118.
[95] C.A. Tams, 'Article 50', p. 1298.
[96] Ibid.
[97] P. Sands, 'Water and International Law: Science and Evidence in International Litigation' (2010) 22 *Environmental Law & Management*, p. 161.

discussed above have faced criticism with regard to factual errors that affect several of their decisions in cases where unseen experts were used.

In two recent ICJ cases that are known to have involved ghost experts,[98] the decisions are seemingly affected by technical flaws. In the *Cameroon v. Nigeria* case, 'a number of serious technical errors and limitations' concerning coordinate issues may have affected the decision, as alleged by Schofield and Carleton.[99] Daniel reached similar conclusions, explaining that the delimited line cutting through both Nigerian and Equatorial Guinea offshore concessions resulted in a zone won by Nigeria where the oil reserves are evaluated at $30 billion.[100] As revealed by the same authors along with M. Pratt,[101] besides the extent of the consequences implied by the errors, the nature of these errors is worthy of interest.[102] Some mistakes in the decision are not related to a lack of available evidence but result from simple technical misconceptions.[103] Another example is the *Qatar v. Bahrain* case,[104] in which the Court has allegedly made an error with respect to a question of fact. Daniel, informed by an expert involved in this dispute resolution, comments that 'the maritime boundary line the Court drew succeeds in passing over dry land belonging to each of the parties'.[105] If the ghost experts have not directly caused these technical errors, their use at the very least did not prevent technical shortcomings of significant consequences. In addition, the lack of transparency directly affects the legitimacy of the decision-making process. Pratt considers in this respect that '[t]he Court has not always delivered a technically sound boundary. In such instances, the lack of transparency concerning the determination of the line leaves the Court open to criticism for being incompetent and even negligent.'[106]

---

[98] See Section 18.2.1.

[99] C.M. Carleton and C.H. Schofield, 'Technical Considerations in Law of the Sea Dispute Resolution', in A.G. Oude Elferink and D.R. Rothwell (eds.), *Oceans Management in the 21st Century* (Brill, 2004), p. 247.

[100] T. Daniel, 'Expert Evidence before the ICJ', p. 5.

[101] M. Pratt explained that 'Worryingly, when the ICJ defined the maritime boundary between Cameroon and Nigeria in 2002, it neglected to indicate the datum to which the coordinates of the turning point of the boundary should refer', M. Pratt, 'The Role of the Technical Expert in Maritime Delimitation Cases', p. 84.

[102] J.G. Devaney, *Fact-Finding Before the International Court of Justice* (Cambridge University Press, 2016), p. 87.

[103] C.M. Carleton and C.H. Schofield 'Technical Considerations', p. 251; Pratt 'The Role of Technical Expert in Maritime Delimitation Cases', p. 84.

[104] See T. Daniel, 'Expert Evidence before the ICJ', p. 5

[105] Ibid.

[106] M. Pratt, 'The Role of the Technical Expert in Maritime Delimitation Cases', p. 82.

Also in the WTO context, errors, inaccuracies, and methodological deficiencies have been identified in panel reports involving factual complexity in the economic field. While convenient, the use of in-house experts has had significant consequences for the technical bases of some panel recommendations. The use of the Secretariat for judicial expertise has resulted 'in inaccurate, opaque, and unconvincing judgements with uncertain implications',[107] stemming from an absence of thorough and transparent engagement with economic evidence.[108] On several occasions panels have been criticised by the Appellate Body for their fact-finding approach and their lack of visible or intelligible analysis of economic facts;[109] especially when resulting in insufficient substantiation for their decision with regard to findings on economic facts.[110] Those shortcomings originate in a lack of transparency within the decision-making process, fostered by the unseen nature of the 'expertise'. Arguably, the presence of unseen experts made the analysis of certain panels 'look arbitrary'.[111] Constrained by its mandate, namely to review questions of law,[112] the Appellate Body faces limitations in addressing the substance of 'economic mistakes' that potentially impair panel reports.[113] 'Economic flaws' per se present in the WTO adjudicative bodies' decisions have been analysed by teams of academics, bringing together legal and economic experts in the context of a research project by the American Law Institute.[114] This critical analysis conducted over 12 years identified numerous errors and analytical flaws, 'including some of a fundamental economic nature, across a wide variety of disputes.'[115]

---

[107] C.A. Thomas, 'Of Facts and Phantoms', p. 298.

[108] Ibid., 305–312.

[109] WTO Appellate Body Report, EC – Measures Concerning Meat and Meat Products (Hormones) (EC – Hormones), WT/DS26/AB/R, WT/DS48/AB/R 13, February 1998, WTO Appellate Body Report, US – Continued Dumping and Subsidy Offset Act of 2000 (US – Offset Act (Byrd Amendment)), WT/DS234/AB/R 27 January 2003); WTO Appellate Body Report, US – Subsidies on Upland Cotton – Recourse to Article 21.5 by Brazil (US – Upland Cotton 21.5), WT/DS267/AB/RW 20 June 2008. Hylke Vandenbussche, 'Upland Cotton Case: Prepared for the ALI Project on the Case Law of the WTO' (2008) 7 *World Trade Review* 211; Thomas, 'Of Facts and Phantoms', 305 ff.

[110] WTO Appellate Body Report, US – Continued Existence and Application of Zeroing Methodology (US – Continued Zeroing), WT/DS350/AB/R 19, February 2009.

[111] H. Vandenbussche, 'Upland Cotton Case', p. 216.

[112] Article 17.6, DSU.

[113] AB, EC – Hormones, paras. 132 and 292.

[114] 'World Trade Law: The World Trade Organization' WTO Case Law Analyses (2001–2013), American Law Institute.

[115] C.P. Bown, 'The WTO Secretariat and the Role of Economics', 8; as an example of the type of analysis conducted on the case cited in this article, see W.J. Davey and A. Sapir, 'United

The pursuit of flexibility and time-saving through the use of unseen experts has led on some occasions to errors and flaws connected to the nature of the expert process itself, i.e. the lack of debate and transparency in the findings process. The transparent and effective adversarial nature of the expert process improves the assessment of factual complexity from an epistemological standpoint. Procedural requirements do not conflict with efficiency in terms of scientific validity; on the contrary. In consideration of the issues at stake at the international level and the corresponding consequences of factual flaws, pragmatism would logically command a condemnation of the practice. It is important at least to thoroughly rethink the relevance of using ghost experts in modern international litigation. In 1939, Sandifer argued:

> [t]he vital interest of States, directly concerning the welfare of thousands of people, may be adversely affect by a decision based upon a misconception of the facts. The maintenance of friendly relations between the States involved may well depend upon the fairness and thoroughness of the proceedings through which a decision is reached.[116]

Due process requirements and the importance of reaching a factually accurate decision cannot be mitigated or form part of a balancing process with pragmatic considerations such as time-saving and cost efficiency.

18.6 Conclusion

A Registry or Secretariat lacks legitimacy in performing an epistemological function of support: there is no sound legal basis for the practice of unseen experts. The practice even appears to directly infringe several rules of procedure within the fora in which ghost experts are used. Given that the essence of the practice involves a circumvention of adversarial proceedings, this compromises the due process rights of the parties and good administration of justice. Considering the faulty outcomes of certain decisions, the practical efficiency of using unseen experts can reasonably be challenged.

Despite having been publicly acknowledged for years, the practice has not attracted overwhelming condemnation. Especially before the WTO

States – Subsidies on Upland Cotton Resource to Article 21.5 by Brazil' in Henrik Horn and Petros C. Mavroidis (eds.), *The WTO Case Law of 2008: Legal and Economic Analysis* (Cambridge University Press, 2010), p. 181.
[116] D.V. Sandifer, *Evidence Before International Tribunals* (University Press of Virginia, 1975), pp. 28–29.

Dispute Settlement Body, it still appears to be largely seen as legitimate, if not necessary. This discrepancy between an objective assessment of the practice and its actual use maybe be found in the specificities of the international adjudicative process. The legitimacy of a judicial decision in international law relies arguably on the identification of an acceptable solution for both parties and submitted to the paramount requirement of peace between States.

The recent and growing attention given to evidence and experts in international adjudication can be interpreted as a potential evolution of the expectations of international society towards the role of the judge in its fact-finding mission. There is a growing awareness that '[l]egitimacy issues are clearly intrinsically linked to the use of experts'.[117] Parties seem eager to have their case settled through an exact and precise definition of the facts. Transparency has become a crucial element of the decision-making process. External experts providing insights without knowledge of the parties preclude the judicial assessment from being transparent. This lack of transparency may affect the credibility of international rulings. An adversarial system which acknowledges scientific inputs and allows these to be refuted would help to fulfil the specificities of the international judicial function.

[117] G.Z. Marceau and H.K. Hawkins, 'Experts in WTO Dispute Settlement', p. 504.

Arbitral Institutions' Response to Perceived Legitimacy Deficits

Promoting Diversity, Transparency and Expedition in Investor-State Arbitration

KSENIA POLONSKAYA[1]

19.1 Introduction

Arbitral Institutions (AIs) facilitate the resolution of disputes between the parties.[2] In particular, they formulate procedural rules and exercise a residual power to appoint arbitrators when parties are incapable or unwilling to do so. These institutions review parties' challenges of the arbitrators who have been appointed, confirm arbitral appointments and ensure that parties make filings promptly. They can collect advanced fees and costs.[3] From a functional perspective, AIs provide vital support for the timely and cost-effective resolution of international disputes.

Besides commercial disputes between private parties, AIs also administer disputes between foreign investors and States.[4] This form of dispute resolution is widely known as investor-State arbitration, which allows foreign investors to challenge actions of States that allegedly breach International Investment Agreements (IIAs) by submitting a claim to an investor-State arbitration tribunal.[5] Over the past several years, investment disputes have given rise to strong resistance of certain governments, civil society groups and organizations against IIAs and investor-State

---

[1] I am grateful to Joshua Karton, Eric de Brabandere, Jean-Frédéric Morin and Moin Yahya for their suggestions and comments on earlier drafts.

[2] R. Gerbay, *The Functions of Arbitral Institutions* (Kluwer Law International, 2016).

[3] G. Born, *International Arbitration and Forum Selection Agreements: Drafting and Enforcing* (Kluwer Law International, 2006), p. 45.

[4] M. Dimsey, *The Resolution of International Investment Disputes: Challenges and Solutions* (Eleven International Publishing, 2008), p. 140.

[5] R. Dolzer and C. Schreuer, *Principles of International Investment Law* (Oxford University Press, 2012).

arbitration. This phenomenon is widely known under the label 'backlash'.[6] The underlying reason for such a backlash is a perception that IIAs and their dispute settlement system lack legitimacy.[7] Admittedly, the concept of legitimacy can have multiple meanings depending on the particular setting within which it is invoked.[8] This chapter adopts Weber's understanding of the term under which institutions are legitimate only if their users have trust in the authority that emanates from such institutions and believe that its exercise of such authority is just.[9] In the context of investor-State arbitration, tribunals not only settle disputes but also contribute 'to stabilizing and generating normative expectations in transborder social relations and therefore exercise transnational authority that demands justification in order to be considered as legitimate'.[10] Hence, a deficit of trust may generate non-compliance by participants in the system. In turn, non-compliance may eventually lead to the collapse of the regime.[11]

In particular, critics point out that arbitral panels lack diversity,[12] as most arbitrators are white men from developed States.[13] Other reasons

---

[6] M. Waibel, A. Kaushal, K.-H. Chung and C. Balchin (eds.), *The Backlash Against Investment Arbitration: Perceptions and Reality* (Kluwer Law International, 2010).

[7] Max Weber's sociological account of legitimacy as discussed in: W. Mommsen, *The Political and Social Theory of Max Weber: Collected Essays* (University of Chicago Press, 1992), p. 21. S. Schill, 'Conceptions of Legitimacy of International Arbitration' in D. Caron, S. Schill, A. Cohen Smutny and E. Triantafilou, *Practising Virtue: Inside International Arbitration* (Oxford University, Press 2015), p. 106. J. Alvarez, *The Public International Law Regime Governing International Investment* (Martinus Nijhoff Publishers, 2011), p. 75.

[8] For example, J. Brunnée and S. Toope, *Legitimacy and Legality in International Law: An Interactional Account* (Cambridge University Press, 2010), pp.53–55. S. Wheatley, *The Democratic Legitimacy of International Law* (Bloomsbury Publishing, 2010), pp. 6–10.

[9] For example, W. Mommsen, The Political and Social Theory of Max Weber, p. 21.

[10] S. Schill, 'Conceptions of Legitimacy', p. 110. F. Garcia, L. Ciko, A. Gaurav and K. Hough, 'Reforming the International Investment Regime: Lessons from International Trade Law' (2015) 18 *Journal of International Economic Law* 861, 876. Garcia characterizes the regime as 'an allocative social institution' that 'allocates social resources'. Garcia et al. explain that the treaties and the tribunals 'allocate rights, privileges, and burdens between investors and host states'.

[11] J. Maupin, 'Public and Private in International Investment Law: An Integrated Systems Approach' (2014) 54 *Virginia Journal of International Law* 1; S. Schill, 'Enhancing International Investment Law's Legitimacy: Conceptual and Methodological Foundations of a New Public Law Approach' (2011) 52 *Vanderbilt Journal of International Law* 57, 67.

[12] M. Scherer, 'Arbitral Institutions Under Scrutiny', http://kluwerarbitrationblog.com/2011/10/05/arbitral-institutions-under-scrutiny/?doing_wp_cron=1503279209.750910997 3907470703125 (arguing that the institutions had conveyed that the five most favourite nationalities for arbitrators are the Swiss, French, American, Dutch and German and less than 10 per cent of arbitrators appointed are women).

[13] Ibid.

why both the panels and the adjudicatory process allegedly lack legiti-macy include, but are not limited to, a lack of transparency, the excessive cost and length of the arbitral process and the inconsistency of arbitral decisions.[14] Due to these perceived legitimacy deficits, investor-State arbi-tration is seen by some as an unsuitable legal mechanism for resolving investment disputes, so several governments have terminated their IIAs while others have embarked upon a structural reform of their existing treaties.[15]

As the creators of the system, States have the most powerful options to conduct such reform, but other actors, such as AIs, could also meaningfully contribute to improving the system's perceived legitimacy. Interestingly, the respondents to the Queen Mary Survey (2018) indicated that AIs are seen 'to be the best placed' to determine the direction of the 'evolution in international arbitration', including ensuring greater diversity, trans-parency and expedition.[16] This chapter, accordingly, explores how AIs, as independent participants in the investment arbitration system, could respond to these perceived legitimacy deficits, in particular with regard to the recurring complaints that the system lacks diversity, transparency and expedition.

To achieve this goal, this chapter examines AIs through the lens of the political system, a theory developed by Dupont and Schultz, pursuant to which States, foreign investors, investment tribunals and AIs are viewed as participants in the investment regime.[17] As such, they make 'inputs', i.e. actions that instigate the reactions of other participants ('outputs') that eventually result in the decisions of the investment tribunals ('outcomes'). By virtue of inputs, outputs and outcomes, these actors shape the devel-opment of the investment regime. These outputs do not exist in a vacuum but within an environment; outputs interact with their environment and introduce changes to it. Hence, the political system is a 'mechanism that

---

[14] Ibid.
[15] L. Trakman, 'The ICSID Under Siege' (2012) 45 *Cornell International Law Journal* 603, 604–605; Comprehensive Economic and Trade Agreement between the European Union and the Government of Canada (2016) (CETA), http://trade.ec.europa.eu/doclib/docs/2014/september/tradoc_152806.pdf.
[16] White & Case and Queen Mary University of London, *International Arbitration Survey: The Evolution of International Arbitration* (2018), www.whitecase.com/sites/whitecase/files/files/download/publications/qmul-international-arbitration-survey-2018-18.pdf, pp. 3, 27–28.
[17] C. Dupont and T. Schultz, 'Towards a New Heuristic Model: Investment Arbitration as a Political System' (2016) 7 *Journal of International Dispute Settlement* 3, 7.

transforms certain types of input into certain types of output, thereby furthering certain goals by authoritatively allocating values'.[18] Dupont and Schultz do not provide a detailed explanation of the input of AIs. They only note that AIs can make an input by 'exercis[ing] their residual arbitrator appointment powers' and 'reform[ing] their procedural rules, within the limits of applicable treaties, if any'.[19]

This theoretical framework appears suitable for examining the role of AIs as independent participants in the investment regime. As such, AIs have a unique capacity to instigate positive change to address some of the persisting legitimacy concerns that generate the backlash in the system of investment arbitration, in particular, complaints that the system lacks diversity, transparency and expedition. This unique capacity could be explained by the position of AIs at the focal point of information flows;[20] they have 'intimate knowledge' of arbitral procedures, parties' preferences, their approaches and ongoing activities.[21] The ability of AIs to formulate and amend the arbitration rules de facto confers them with power to oversee the market of arbitration services. For example, AIs set the rules for disclosure and disqualification for arbitrators, can regulate the parties' conduct with regards to the selection of arbitrators and enforce timely submissions of documents.[22] Some AIs even perform a so-called 'quality control' over the substance of the final award.[23] For example, the International Chamber of Commerce's Court of International Arbitration can send an award back to the tribunal if the arbitrators did not provide sufficient reasoning or the award fails to meet formal requirements.[24] The

---

[18] Ibid., 5 and 19.

[19] Ibid., 29.

[20] C. Drahozal, 'Of Rabbits and Rhinoceri: A Survey of Empirical Research on International Commercial Arbitration' (2003) 20 *Journal of International Arbitration* 23, 25 (arguing that 'the most obvious source of data on international commercial arbitration is the institutions that administer arbitration proceedings… Because of the administrative services these institutions provide to parties, they have access to substantial amounts of information about the arbitral process').

[21] C. Rogers, 'The Vocation of the International Arbitrator' (2005) 20 *American University International Law Review* 973, 1011.

[22] Schill, 'Enhancing International Investment Law's Legitimacy', 111–112, 122.

[23] P. Habegger et al., (eds.), *Arbitral Institutions Under Scrutiny: ASA Special Series No. 40* (Juris Publishing, 2013), pp. 24–25. Note: 'quality control' is broadly defined and includes 'procedures that guide the participants of the arbitration processes through the proceedings, the requirements for the arbitrators to submit the statements of independence, requirements for the candidates to be listed as arbitrators, scrutiny of the formal and substantial elements of the final award'.

[24] Ibid.

availability of 'extra-legal' sanctions, such as blacklisting, also contributes to the ability of AIs to impose pressure on arbitrators.[25] AIs determine (or, at least, heavily influence) the timeline of the arbitration process, the availability of dispositive motions, fee structures, the scope of document production and the conflict checks.[26] By formulating and amending the institutional rules of procedure, practice guides, codes of conduct and submission templates, AIs may influence the conduct of parties and arbitrators within the investment regime by building the parameters within which the users make their decisions.

This chapter argues that AIs can respond to the perceived legitimacy deficits of investor-State arbitration through the creation of the 'architecture of choice', by establishing the 'default provisions' in arbitration rules. The term 'architecture of choice' is borrowed from the literature on libertarian paternalism and is better understood by providing an example.[27] As Thaler and Sustein explain, in the USA, universities sign up their employees for retirement plans as a default option.[28] For greater clarity, the default provision is 'an option that will [be] obtain[ed] if the chooser does nothing'.[29] The employees retain their right to withdraw from the university retirement plan, although they must send a written notice to the university's office to do so. The alternative would be that the universities would not sign up their faculty and staff for the retirement plan automatically but would require each single individual to opt in to the retirement plan. These two options are reflective of the choice architecture. This chapter proposes that AIs set up their own choice architecture by establishing certain default provisions in the arbitration rules that may address legitimacy issues relating to a lack of transparency, diversity and expedition.

This chapter proceeds in the following order. First, it examines the current state of affairs with regard to AI activities that aim to increase

---

[25] V. Gessner (ed.), *Contractual Certainty in International Trade: Empirical Studies and Theoretical Debates on Institutional Support for Global Economic Exchanges* (Bloomsbury Publishing, 2008), p. 122 (discusses blacklisting as an 'extra-legal sanction').

[26] B. Warwas, *The Liability of Arbitral Institutions: Legitimacy Challenges and Functional Responses* (Springer, 2016), pp. 322–324. M. McIlwrath and R. Schroeder, 'Transparency in International Arbitration: What Are Arbitrators and Institutions Afraid of?' in A. Rovine, (ed.), *Contemporary Issues in International Arbitration and Mediation: The Fordham Papers (2010)* (Martinus Nijhoff Publishers, 2011), pp. 348–352.

[27] R. Thaler and C. Sunstein, *Nudge: Improving Decisions About Health, Wealth, and Happiness* (Penguin, 2009), pp. 3–4.

[28] Ibid., pp. 106–108.

[29] Ibid., p. 85.

diversity, transparency and expedition. Second, it explains the concept of 'choice architecture' and its relation to the default provisions. Finally, specific initial proposals are put forward as to how AIs may employ the choice architecture framework in practice.

19.2 Current State of Affairs

AIs already have undertaken some steps to ensure greater diversity, transparency and expedition in investment arbitration. This section examines the current state of affairs and scrutinizes particular activities of AIs. Before continuing, it is worth highlighting why AIs should commit to increasing diversity, transparency and expedition in the regime. Most notably, AIs have to 'compete for market share ... [t]he major houses seek to structure the broader field in their own image; smaller ones work to develop regional, or niche, services that will enable them to survive and prosper'.[30] Such competition is an important factor in contextualizing the activities, values and preferences of AIs as independent participants in the investment regime.[31] Alec Stone Sweet and Florian Grisel explain that '[e]very major centre is continuously engaged in an assessment of their Rules with an eye to improving them ... consultations with users serve to identify recurrent problems and emergent needs'.[32] AIs monitor trends in the investment regime, including the activities of their competitors, to increase the quantity of cases on their dockets.[33] While AIs compete to increase their number of clients, they also hold a long-term interest in preserving the investment regime. The reason is a purely economic one: the investment regime is a revenue generator for AIs.[34]

---

[30] A. Sweet and F. Grisel, *The Evolution of International Arbitration: Judicialization, Governance, Legitimacy* (Oxford University Press, 2017), p. 45. See also D. Lehmkuhl, 'Resolving Transnational Disputes: Commercial Arbitration and Linkages Between Multiple Providers of Governance Services' in M. Koenig-Archibugi and M. Zurn (eds.), *Modes of Governance in the Global System* (Palgrave Macmillan, 2006), p. 112. (discussing proliferation of arbitration rules).

[31] J. Karton, *The Culture of International Arbitration and the Evolution of Contract Law* (Oxford University Press, 2013), p. 26.

[32] Sweet and Grisel, The Evolution of International Arbitration, p. 83.

[33] Y. Dezalay and B. Garth, *Dealing in Virtue: International Commercial Arbitration and the Construction of a Transnational Legal Order* (University of Chicago Press, 1996), p. 7. Warwas, note above 26, p. 186.

[34] Warwas, The Liability of Arbitral Institutions, pp. 29–30, 24, 101.

19.2.1   Diversity

AIs have made some advances in the area of arbitrators' diversity. In 2016, the Singapore International Arbitration Centre (SIAC) made 'a total of 167 individual appointments of arbitrators',[35] who were from 'Australia, Canada, China, France, Germany, Greece, Hong Kong, India, Ireland, Italy, Malaysia, New Zealand, the Philippines, Singapore, South Africa, South Korea, Switzerland, Taiwan, UK, USA and Vietnam'.[36] With regard to gender diversity, SIAC appointed 38 female arbitrators out of 167 (22.8 per cent); the parties appointed only 5 female arbitrators of the 145 arbitrators they nominated (3.4 per cent); and, the co-arbitrators nominated only one female arbitrator out of 29 (3.4 per cent). Overall 341 arbitrators were appointed in SIAC procedures and only 44 of them were female. The International Centre for Settlement of Investment Disputes (ICSID) reports that the pool of arbitrators in 2017 was 'increasingly diverse':[37] '14% of the new appointees were women' and '23% of the first time appointees were nationals of low or middle income economies'.[38] Reportedly, to ensure gender representation, the Centre employs the 'list procedure' when it exercises its residual right to conduct arbitral appointments.[39] According to this procedure, 'ICSID proposes a ballot with at least five candidates' including 'both emerging and established arbitrators … each ballot contains the name of at least one female arbitrator'.[40]

The London Court of International Arbitration (LCIA) appointed 40.6 per cent women out of 197 arbitrators.[41] The parties appointed only 4.1 per cent women out of 219 arbitrators and the co-arbitrators appointed 16.3 per cent women out of 80 arbitrators.[42] Interestingly, the LCIA reports that in 2016, the LCIA and the co-arbitrators appointed more female

[35]   SIAC Annual Report 2016, p.16, http://siac.org.sg/images/stories/articles/annual_report/SIAC_AR_2016_24pp_WEBversion.pdf.

[36]   Ibid.

[37]   Ibid.

[38]   ICSID 2017 Annual Report, p. 35, https://icsid.worldbank.org/en/Documents/icsiddocs/ICSID%20AR%20EN.pdf.

[39]   Valuing Women in International Adjudication, https://icsid.worldbank.org/en/Pages/resources/ICSID%20NewsLetter/2017-Issue2/Valuing-Women-in-International-Adjudication.aspx.

[40]   Ibid.

[41]   LCIA, Facts and Figures – 2016: A Robust Caseload, p. 12, www.lcia.org/lcia/reports.aspx.

[42]   Ibid.

arbitrators than in 2015, whereas 'the selection of female candidates by the parties ... saw [a] considerable decrease' as the parties nominated female arbitrators in only 6.9 per cent of cases.[43] The LCIA arbitrators were predominantly British (321), others came from Europe and the Commonwealth. Other nationalities included Nigerian, Singaporean, Egyptian, Russian and Latin American arbitrators.[44] This data permits us to draw two conclusions. First, AIs appoint female arbitrators more frequently than the parties or co-arbitrators do, so new rules are needed to 'nudge' parties and co-arbitrators into making more female appointments.

Second, the reports overwhelmingly focus on *gender* diversity without full appreciation of other elements of diversity, potentially excluding diverse experiences that depend on geographical, racial, disability and religious backgrounds as well as the intersection of such elements.[45] These backgrounds arguably inform and shape (potential) arbitrators' approaches to lawyering and decision-making.[46] The current discourse on diversity in investment arbitration needs to embrace the idea that diversity cannot be limited to gender.[47] The arbitral pool requires not only female adjudicators but individuals of distinctive (and overlapping) backgrounds in terms of geographical origin, religion, race and legal culture.[48] The investment regime cannot legitimately rely on arbitral services provided by a selected group of individuals with a virtually uniform background.[49] Such homogeneity of the arbitral pool reinforces the perception of arbitrators as a 'club' or 'mafia', encouraging mistrust in the existing system.[50]

---

[43] Ibid.

[44] Ibid., p. 11.

[45] E. Rackley, *Women, Judging and the Judiciary: From Difference to Diversity* (Routledge, 2013), p. 45. See also Andrea Bjorklund, https://www.ejiltalk.org/the-diversity-deficit-in-investment-arbitration/.

[46] Billiet explains that 'the proportion of women appointed as arbitrators across all cases amounts to only 4% (from 247 arbitrators appointed, 10 of them were women). What is even more fascinating is that of all these women Gabrielle Kaufmann-Kohler and Brigitte Stern made up for 75% of these appointments'. J. Billiet, *International Investment Arbitration: A Practical Handbook* (Maklu Publishers, 2016), p. 72.

[47] C. Sweetman (ed.), *Gender, Development, and Diversity* (Oxfam, 2004), p. 71 (showing that often other aspects of diversity *beyond* gender are ignored).

[48] Grisel and Sweet explain that 'Puig found that only 19 of the 419 arbitrators appointed to date were female and that 46 per cent of all appointees hailed from just five states (the United States, France, the United Kingdom, Canada, and Switzerland – in that order)'. Sweet and Grisel, *The Evolution of International Arbitration*, p. 72.

[49] Schill, 'Enhancing International Investment Law's Legitimacy', 120.

[50] M. Hirsh, *Invitation to the Sociology of International Law* (Oxford University Press, 2015), pp. 110–111.

Margaret Moses emphasizes that 'some institutions and a few individual members of the arbitration community have made efforts to broaden the pool. For example, the LCIA has signed a pledge of Equal Representation in Arbitration to promote gender diversity, and has invited members and friends to sign'.[51] The Pledge is a voluntary commitment of individual lawyers, organizations, law firms and institutions.[52] It acknowledges the underrepresentation of women in the arbitration field and aims to encourage users to 'include a fair representation of female candidates on rosters and lists of potential arbitrator appointees'.[53] Notably, the pledge has gained popularity in the field as the SIAC, SCC and ICC have all joined it, together with 1,967 signatories.[54] Since the pledge is a non-binding commitment, its signatories are not obliged to follow it; there are also no voluntary reporting requirements to monitor whether the signatories fulfil their promise. Nevertheless, AIs are making some progress on gender issues, even though the lack of diversity continues to persist.[55]

19.2.2   Transparency

In 2006, Catharine Rogers observed that 'AIs have led or promoted many of the major transparency innovations … collectively AIs have been adding precision and detail to attract more business parties to the system and to gain market share'.[56] AIs contributed 'added clarity and transparency' on the issue of arbitrator disclosures and disqualification decisions.[57] The input of AIs on transparency has not been limited to disclosures but has also related to third-party participation in investment disputes. This section sketches the current state of affairs with regard to arbitral disclosures, third-party participation and the publication of arbitral awards.

---

[51] M. Moses, *The Principles and Practice of International Commercial Arbitration* (Cambridge University Press, 2017), p. 6.

[52] Equal Representation in Arbitration (the pledge), www.arbitrationpledge.com/take-the-pledge.

[53] Ibid.

[54] Ibid.

[55] M. Waibel, ICSID Arbitrators: The Ultimate Social Network, www.ejiltalk.org/icsid-arbitrators-the-ultimate-social-network/.

[56] C. Rogers, 'Transparency in International Commercial Arbitration' (2006) 54 *University of Kansas Law Review* 1301, 1314.

[57] Ibid.

First, AIs have introduced stricter standards for arbitral disclosures: 'the disclosure obligations … are principally directed at substantive information and are designed to benefit those receiving the relevant information'.[58] AIs require arbitrators to affirm that the arbitrator has 'no close relationship – financial, professional, or personal – with a party or its counsel'.[59] Most AIs set a standard of 'justifiable doubts' for this purpose. For example, the LCIA Rules require an arbitrator to submit declarations about circumstances 'which are likely to give rise in the mind of any party to any justifiable doubts as to his or her impartiality or independence'.[60] The Stockholm Chamber of Commerce (SCC) Rules specify that '[b]efore being appointed, a prospective arbitrator shall disclose any circumstances that may give rise to justifiable doubts as to the prospective arbitrator's impartiality or independence'.[61] The ICC Rules follow this example: '[t] he prospective arbitrator shall disclose in writing to the Secretariat any facts or circumstances which might be of such a nature as to call into question the arbitrator's independence in the eyes of the parties, as well as any circumstances that could give rise to reasonable doubts as to the arbitrator's impartiality'.[62] The ICSID Arbitration Rules do not mention 'justifiable doubts' as a standard for disclosure. Instead, they require the arbitrator to sign a declaration that discloses '(a) [their] past and present professional, business and other relationships (if any) with the parties and (b) any other circumstance that might cause [their] reliability for independent judgment to be questioned by a party'.[63]

---

[58] Ibid., 1309.

[59] *Commonwealth Coatings Corp v. Continental Casualty* 393 US 145 (1968) 149 (stating 'we can perceive no way in which the effectiveness of the arbitration process will be hampered by the simple requirement that arbitrators disclose to the parties any dealings that might create an impression of possible bias').

[60] The London Court of International Arbitration Rules, www.lcia.org/dispute_resolution_services/lcia-arbitration-rules-2014.aspx, Art. 5.5.

[61] Arbitration Rules of the Arbitration Institute of the Stockholm Chamber of Commerce 2017, http://sccinstitute.com/media/169838/arbitration_rules_eng_17_web.pdf, Art.18.2.

[62] International Chamber of Commerce Arbitration Rules (2017), https://iccwbo.org/dispute-resolution-services/arbitration/rules-of-arbitration/, Art. 11.2. See also L. Shore, 'Disclosure and Impartiality: An Arbitrator's Responsibility vis-a-vis Legal Standards' (2002) 57 *Dispute Resolution Journal* 32.

[63] Rules of Procedure for the Institution of Conciliation and Arbitration Proceedings, ICSID Basic Documents 55, ICSID Doc.ICSID/15(Jan.1985), Arts. 6.2 and 13.2 of the Additional Facility Arbitration Rules (hereafter ICSID Rules). ICSID Secretariat, Possible Improvements of the Framework for ICSID Arbitration (2004) Discussion Paper, https://icsid.worldbank.org/en/Documents/resources/Possible%20Improvements%20of%20the%20Framework%20of%20ICSID%20Arbitration.pdf, para. 17.

Second, AIs have encouraged third-party participation by amending their arbitration rules. For example, the ICSID Arbitration Rules 'created, for the first time, procedures and standards by which tribunals shall consider requests from third parties to file amicus briefs to address issues that may not adequately be addressed by the parties'.[64] Under the ICSID Rules, the tribunal rules on the acceptability of third-party submissions after consulting with the parties to the dispute. The SCC Rules permit a third person to 'apply to the Arbitral Tribunal for permission to make a written submission in the arbitration'.[65] Third-party participation permits the voices of constituencies (other than the parties) to be heard under the institutional framework of the investment regime. Such feature enhances public accountability of the arbitrators and shapes a perception of greater transparency among the stakeholders.[66]

With regard to publishing the arbitral awards, the progress is modest but AIs are hard to blame. AIs cannot publish awards without the consent of the parties. For example, the SCC Rules indicate that '[u]nless otherwise agreed by the parties, the SCC, the Arbitral Tribunal and any administrative secretary of the Arbitral Tribunal shall maintain the confidentiality of the arbitration and the award'.[67] The ICSID Convention also stipulates that the ICSID Centre may publish the awards, the records of the proceedings and the reports of the conciliation commission if 'parties to a proceeding consent to the publication'.[68] The SIAC Arbitration Rules require 'a party and any arbitrator, including any Emergency Arbitrator, and any person appointed by the Tribunal, including any administrative secretary and any expert' to 'treat all matters relating to the proceedings and the Award as confidential', unless otherwise agreed by the parties.[69] Accordingly, the current default position is to maintain the confidentiality

---

[64] C. Rogers and R. Alford, *The Future of Investment Arbitration* (Oxford University Press, 2009), p. 30.

[65] SCC Arbitration Rules 2017 note 61 above, Appendix III at art.3(1).

[66] M. Dimsey, 'Submission By a Third Person' in D. Euler, M. Gehring and M. Scherer, (eds.), *Transparency in International Investment Arbitration: A Guide to the UNCITRAL Rules on Transparency in Treaty-Based Investor-State Arbitration* (Cambridge: Cambridge University Press, 2015), pp.132–33.

[67] SCC Arbitration Rules 2017 note 61 above, art.3

[68] Convention on the Settlement of Investment Disputes Between States and Nationals of Other States (ICSID Convention), 18 March 1965, in force 14 October 1966, 575 UNTS 159; 4 ILM 524 (1965), Art. 48.5 Administrative and Financial Regulations, ICSID, Regulation 22; ICSID Administrative and Financial Regulations Art. 22.2, https://icsid .worldbank.org/en/Documents/icsiddocs/ICSID%20Convention%20English.pdf.

[69] SIAC Arbitration Rules 2016, www.siac.org.sg/our-rules/rules/siac-rules-2016, Rule 39.1.

of proceedings and awards. The reason for this may be that AIs avoid alienating parties from institutional arbitration. Their fear is that an obligation to publish the awards may result in a situation in which users will avoid institutional arbitration in general or have recourse to competing arbitral institutions that are less concerned with transparency. There are legal constraints as well: for example, if the ICSID Centre were to publish the full awards without the parties' consent, it would act in breach of the ICSID Convention, unless the latter were to be amended.

AIs selectively publish awards or sanitized extracts of the key holdings of the awards.[70] For instance, the ICSID Arbitration Rules state that '[t]he Centre shall not publish the award without the consent of the parties. The Centre shall, however, promptly include in its publications excerpts of the legal reasoning of the Tribunal'.[71] The ICSID Centre also makes public information about the disputes via its registers by publishing 'information on procedural developments in all of the cases pending before the Centre'.[72] If the Centre cannot release an award, one of the parties can publish it unilaterally.[73] Antonio Parra explains that '[i]n short, all ICSID arbitral awards, or at least their key legal holdings, are now published'.[74] According to Parra, in the case of ICSID 'the question of the timeliness of publication' remains particularly pressing because '[i]t occasionally is not until several months have passed that ICSID receives the consent of both parties for it to publish an award'.[75] The publication of awards is important for a number of reasons; the freely accessible awards permit participants of the regime to make informed choices when they appoint the arbitrators and understand the parameters of the applicable law.[76]

---

[70] C. Drahozal and R. Naimark, *Towards a Science of International Arbitration: Collected Empirical Research* (Kluwer Law International, 2005), p. 6. E. Zlatanska, 'To Publish or Not to Publish Arbitral Awards: That is the Question' (2015) 81 *International Journal of Arbitration, Mediation and Dispute Management* 25, 26.

[71] ICSID Rules, Rule 48.4.

[72] ICSID Administrative and Financial Regulation 23. ICSID Secretariat, Possible Improvements of the Framework for ICSID Arbitration (2004) Discussion Paper (hereafter ICSID Discussion Paper), https://icsid.worldbank.org/en/Documents/resources/Possible%20Improvements%20of%20the%20Framework%20of%20ICSID%20Arbitration.pdf, para. 11.

[73] L. Reed, J. Paulsson and N. Blackaby, *Guide to ICSID Arbitration* (Kluwer Law International, 2011), p. 16.

[74] ICSID Discussion Paper, para. 11.

[75] Ibid., para. 12.

[76] J. Karton, 'A Conflict of Interests: Seeking a Way Forward on Publication of International Arbitral Awards' (2012) 28(3) *Arbitration International* 447, 461–464.

Accordingly, AIs' activities show their commitment to balancing the interests of the parties in maintaining the confidentiality of proceedings with deeper concerns over the legitimacy deficits that such secrecy can generate in the context of investment disputes.[77]

19.2.3   Expedition

Arbitral institutions have the authority to make changes in arbitration rules to enhance the expedition of dispute resolution. In recent years, AIs have introduced a number of provisions to address concerns over a lack of expedition. Among others, they have adopted rules and practices limiting the rounds of submissions, expedited rules for arbitration, the option to have an entirely written procedure without hearings, so-called 'emergency' arbitration rules, the early dismissal of manifestly meritless claims and stricter timelines for the parties to file their submissions. To illustrate the commitment of AIs to enhance expedition, this section will review the provisions on stricter timelines, emergency arbitration and the early dismissal of claims.

First, AIs have promoted stricter timelines for the parties to file their submissions. For example, Article 2.1 of the LCIA Rules requires a respondent to submit to the Registrar a written response within 28 days from the commencement date of a dispute.[78] The LCIA Court may determine a 'lesser or greater period' for delivering a written response to the Registrar.[79] The Court can make such determination 'upon application by any party or upon its own initiative'.[80] Rule 25.1 of the ICSID Arbitration Rules sets a time limit of 30 days for the parties to file a written statement,[81] but the president of the tribunal may fix a longer period.[82]

Second, arbitration rules provide for the availability of so-called emergency arbitrators. Dipen Sabharwal and Rebecca Zaman explain that '[t]he availability of an emergency arbitrator enables parties to apply for relief and have it ordered within an exceptionally short

---

[77] Warwas, The Liability of Arbitral Institutions, p. 109; D. Caron, 'Regulating Opacity: Shaping How Tribunals Think' in D. Caron, S. Schill, A. Cohen Smutny, E. Triantafilou (eds.), *Practising Virtue: Inside International Arbitration* (Oxford University Press, 2015), pp. 379–380.

[78] LCIA Arbitration Rules, Art. 2.1.

[79] Ibid.

[80] Ibid.

[81] ICSID Rules, Rule 25.1.

[82] Ibid.

period'.[83] For example, Rule 5 of the SIAC Rules permits a party to file for an expedited procedure if any one of three criteria is met; first, 'the amount in dispute does not exceed the equivalent amount of S$6,000,000, representing the aggregate of the claim, counterclaim and any defence of set-off',[84] the parties agree to the expedited procedure[85] or the case is of 'exceptional urgency'.[86] The SCC was one of the first AIs to introduce emergency arbitrator provisions,[87] requiring the parties, the register and the arbitrator to 'act in an efficient and expeditious manner'.[88] The SCC Rules set a ten-day period for the parties to appoint an emergency arbitrator. Similar provisions exist under the LCIA,[89] SIAC[90] and ICC Arbitration Rules.[91] In contrast, the ICSID Arbitration Rules do not establish provisions for conducting emergency arbitration.[92]

The emergency arbitration procedure is available by default if the conditions under the applicable arbitration rules are met and the parties did not agree otherwise prior to the dispute.[93] The emergency procedure has been increasingly used in the past two years. According to the SCC, parties triggered the emergency arbitration procedure only once in 2015,[94] but no less than 13 times in 2016.[95] ICC statistics show a similar trend.[96]

---

[83] D. Sabharwal and R. Zaman, 'Vive la difference? Convergence and Conformity in the Rules Reforms of Arbitral Institutions: The Case of the LCIA Rules 2014' (2014) 31 *Journal of International Arbitration* 701, 703.

[84] SIAC Arbitration Rules, Rule 5.1.a.

[85] Ibid., Rule 5.1.b.

[86] Ibid., Rule 5.1.c.

[87] R. Schütze (ed.), *Institutional Arbitration: A Commentary* (Bloomsbury Publishing, 2013), p. 447. Other AIs introduced the emergency arbitration provisions in subsequent years: ICC (2012), SIAC (2013), LCIA (2014).

[88] Arbitration Rules of the Arbitration Institute of the Stockholm Chamber of Commerce, http://sccinstitute.com/media/169838/arbitration_rules_eng_17_web.pdf, Art..2.

[89] LCIA Arbitration Rules, Art. 9B., para. 9.8

[90] SIAC Arbitration Rules, Schedule 1.

[91] ICC Arbitration Rules 2017, Art. 29, Appendix V.

[92] See J. Cullbord, 'Emergency Arbitrators in Investment Treaty Disputes', Kluwer Arbitration Blog, http://arbitrationblog.kluwerarbitration.com/2015/03/10/emergency-arbitrators-in-investment-treaty-disputes/.

[93] R. Bose and I. Meredith, 'Emergency Arbitration Procedures: A Comparative Analysis' (2012) 5 *International Arbitration Law Review* 186, 194.

[94] Stockholm Chamber of Commerce 2015 Statistics, www.sccinstitute.com/media/181705/scc-statistics-2015.pdf, 2.

[95] Stockholm Chamber of Commerce 2016 Statistics, www.sccinstitute.com/statistics/.

[96] ICC, Full 2016 ICC Dispute Resolution Statistics Published in Court Bulletin, https://iccwbo.org/media-wall/news-speeches/full-2016-icc-dispute-resolution-statistics-published-court-bulletin/.

Such an increase presumably relates to the fact that parties become more familiarized with the procedure.

Third, arbitration rules allow manifestly non-meritorious claims to face an early dismissal. For example, ICSID Rule 41.5 states that a party may raise a preliminary objection to dismiss a claim if the claim manifestly lacks legal merit. In addition, the ICSID Rules stipulate that the Secretary General has the power to dismiss a claim if it is manifestly outside the jurisdiction of the Centre.[97] The newly amended SIAC Rules, in particular Rule 29.1, contain provisions for the early dismissal of claims and defences if 'a claim or defence is manifestly without legal merit' or if 'a claim or defence is manifestly outside the jurisdiction of the Tribunal'.[98] In 2016, the ICSID Centre registered 597 cases under the Convention and the Additional Facility Rules; only in 1 per cent of cases did the tribunal decide that the claim manifestly lacked merit pursuant to the procedure under Rule 41.5.[99] SIAC's statistics are silent on how often users employ the early dismissal procedures, but SIAC Rules have only been equipped with such provisions since 2017.

Accordingly, it can be said that AIs already undertake steps to ensure an expeditious arbitration process. In a recent survey by the International Council for Commercial Arbitration, the representatives of prominent AIs indicated that AIs review and modernize arbitration rules in consultation with the system's users to reflect the best available practices.[100] For instance, John Beechey of the ICC has indicated that to foster expedition, the ICC has introduced the 'case management conference' and 'specific time limits for rendering an award'.[101] Meg Kinnear of ICSID has observed that the Centre follows the 'internal service standards … addressing delay' in the arbitration process.[102] According to Kinnear, the Centre 'works closely' and follows up with the President of the Tribunal 'if an award is outstanding for too long'.[103] Kinnear, however, has acknowledged that delays continue to be 'a difficult challenge for arbitral institutions'.[104] The

---

[97] C. Schreuer, *The ICSID Convention: A Commentary* (Cambridge University Press, 2001), p. 933.

[98] SIAC Arbitration Rules, Rule 29.1.a–b.

[99] ICSID Report, note 40 above, p. 37.

[100] 'Survey: Arbitral Institutions Can Do More To Foster Legitimacy: True or False?' in Albert Van Den Berg (ed.), *Legitimacy: Myths, Realities, Challenges* (Wolters Kluwer, 2015), p. 685.

[101] Ibid., p. 694.

[102] Ibid., p. 676.

[103] Ibid.

[104] Ibid.

reason is that the arbitrators as well as the parties are responsible for the conduct of proceedings; and if the users of the process are not sensitive to the deadlines, the process can be unjustifiably delayed.

It appears that the rules on timelines for written submissions by the parties are default rules that may be altered when a tribunal approves a request from the parties. Parties do not have to explain why they want to deviate from the default rule. In practice, a request without any explanation can result in a refusal of the tribunal to satisfy such request. Yet the tribunal has full discretion in the matter and the explanation of the party may be nominal, i.e., a party may not provide any extensive reasoning or proof justifying such a delay. The provisions on early dismissal of claims, on the other hand, are strict provisions that cannot be altered upon request of the parties. The emergency arbitration provisions apply by default unless the parties have agreed otherwise; they must, however, show that the specified conditions in the applicable rules are satisfied before the emergency arbitration procedure is triggered. Thus, insofar as the efforts of AIs to increase expedition are concerned, AIs appear to have already started developing the necessary default rules, concerning for example emergency arbitration procedures and timelines.

The sections above outline the role of AIs and the steps they have taken to improve diversity, transparency and expedition. The next section will discuss which other measures AIs could take and describe from a procedural standpoint how AIs could respond to the backlash against the investment regime via the choice architecture model.

19.3   Choice Architecture: Explaining the Concept

The term 'architecture of choice' is best explained through a simple example from everyday life. Imagine that the owner of a coffee shop has to arrange their stand with goods and beverages.[105] There are several ways to approach such an arrangement. The owner may decide to display the goods with high added sugar up front to make it easier for the customers to access. Alternatively, the owner can choose to locate the low sugar goods at the front stand where they are easily accessible. The owner can also place all goods with a high level of added sugar at the second floor of the cafeteria to force customers to climb the stairs to get a chocolate chip cookie. Finally, the owner may make an absolutely random choice in

---

[105] Thaler and Sunstein, *Nudge*.

displaying goods without taking into account the preferences or interests of the customers. In any scenario, whatever choice the owner makes, he or she in fact creates an architecture of choice. In behavioural economics, the architecture of choice has a profound impact on the everyday choices of customers, employees and citizens. Users can opt out, i.e. there are other choices available and accessible to them. The architecture of choice, however, helps to steer individuals into making particular choices by setting up default options. AIs also can be 'choice architects' with 'responsibility for organizing the context in which people make decisions'.[106]

19.3.1   Choice Architecture, Default Rules and Arbitratal Institutions

Choice architecture could be built by means of default rules. In the investment regime, the model of choice architecture is valuable to conceptualize the possible role of AIs and their inputs within the investment regime. Arbitral institutions may play the role of 'choice architects' by establishing the default provisions and by changing arbitration rules in a way that 'steers' other participants into making certain choices, i.e. to advance diversity, transparency and expedition. In pursuing these goals, AIs do not advance pro-investor or pro-state interests. Instead, AIs promote the systemic interest of the investment regime which, for the purpose of this chapter, is defined as the long-term survival of the regime. More diversity, greater transparency and a more expeditious arbitration process contribute to the greater legitimacy of the investment regime, ensuring its long-term existence and acceptance of its decisions by the regime's participants. AIs have a particular interest in preserving the regime because it provides a significant market share of arbitral services and contributes to revenue generation.

The creator of the choice architecture establishes the default rules for the users in the system. The default rules 'matter enormously' because they influence the participants of the system to follow the default setting.[107] Omri Ben-Shahar and John Pottow explain that the users tend to do so even when the alternative option or provision is more beneficial to them.[108] Defaults are employed broadly in areas such as contract and

---

[106]   Ibid., p.3.
[107]   O. Ben-Shahar and J. Pottow, 'On the Stickiness of Default Rules' (2006) 33 *Florida State University Law Review* 651, 652.
[108]   Ibid.

company law.[109] Listokin underscores that 'only 20 percent of companies incorporated in states without fair price statutes choose to write fair price protection into their corporate charters ... almost all companies (almost 98 percent) in states where fair price protection is the default rule have fair price protection.'[110] Korobkin concludes that 'parties ... prefer terms identified as legal defaults to those that are not legal defaults.'[111] Companies often prefer to 'stick' to defaults to avoid switching costs.[112]

Alan Schwartz identifies the so-called transformative defaults that are 'adopted to persuade parties to prefer the result the rule directs.'[113] If AIs change their arbitration rules by establishing transformative defaults, they can create a choice architecture for the participants of the investment regime that advances 'fairness' without the risk of losing business and ultimately failing in their competition with other AIs. Admittedly, there may be a strong first-mover disadvantage for the AI that starts building the choice architecture, but preserving the parties' ability to reverse a default may minimize this disadvantage.

There are two possible objections to the transformative possibility of default rules. The first relates to the meaning of fairness and the question of who is to determine what is 'fair' in the given context. 'Fairness' is narrowly defined to reflect functions of legal norms in the investment community. According to this view, legal norms are not intended to regulate the conduct of the parties by expressly banning or prescribing certain behaviour but are rather intended to alter and shape the preferences of the participants. Accordingly, 'rules can teach what good actions or states of affairs are.'[114] Second, one may argue that the participants must be ready to accept defaults, otherwise the defaults will do little to change their preferences.[115] As such, the environment appears to matter greatly for ensuring that the transformative defaults are functional. Given the current political momentum, it is submitted that the environment for

---

[109] Y. Listokin, 'What Do Corporate Default Rules and Menus Do? An Empirical Analysis' (2009) 6 *Journal of Empirical Legal Studies* 284.

[110] Ibid.

[111] R. Korobkin, 'Inertia and Preference in Contract Negotiation: The Psychological Power of Default Rules and Form Terms' (1998) 51 *Vanderbilt Law Review* 1586, 1595.

[112] M. Kahan and M. Klausner, 'Standardization and Innovation in Corporate Contracting or "The Economics of Boilerplate"' (1997) 83 *Virginia Law Review* 713, 727.

[113] A. Schwartz, 'The Default Rule Paradigm and the Limits of Contract Law' (1993) 3 *Southern California Interdisciplinary Law Journal* 389, 390–391.

[114] Kahan and Klausner, 'Standardization and Innovation in Corporate Contracting', 727–28.

[115] Ibid.

default rules that enhance transparency, diversity and expedition is favourable.

Admittedly, some may argue that such momentum exists only on paper. For example, the statistics of AIs in Section 19.2.1 show that investors and co-arbitrators do not appoint female arbitrators as often as AIs. Sometimes, parties do not wish to disclose any information concerning the nomination of the arbitrators or to consent to the publication of the award. Nevertheless, the field of arbitration cannot be seen as a static legal structure. The Dupont and Schultz lens of the political system is useful to understand the dynamic character of the investment regime and its evolvement over time. New trends are shaped by the participants of the regime: AIs and States have shown their commitment to change by increasing the number of female appointees. Parties expect more expeditious and less costly arbitration services.[116] The growing commitment to the United Nations Commission on International Trade Law (UNCITRAL) transparency rules demonstrates that some States at least aspire to achieve greater transparency.[117] Private parties hope to have better access to information about arbitrators as well as a clearer understanding of how the governing law is interpreted and applied.[118] This is achievable only if the awards are available for public scrutiny.[119]

19.3.2 Outlining Some Initial Proposals Based on the Choice Architecture Model

This section puts forward a number of proposals on how AIs could utilize the framework of choice architecture to improve diversity, transparency and expedition. These proposals are only a starting point and a subject for further discussion and conceptual development. Arbitral institutions may amend arbitration rules by incorporating default options concerning arbitral appointments. A default arbitral rule to promote diversity might

---

[116] Survey 2018, note 16 above, p. 2.

[117] J. Ketcheson, 'Investment Arbitration: Learning from Experience', in S. Hindelang and M. Krajewski (eds.), *Shifting Paradigms in International Investment Law: More Balanced, Less Isolated, Increasingly Diversified* (Oxford University Press, 2016), p.112.

[118] Survey 2018, note 16 above, p. 22. The survey states 'the suggestion that institutions should publish awards in a redacted form (and/or as summaries) was accordingly not only favoured for its academic value and usefulness when arguing a case, but also often named as a method to gain more insight into arbitrator performance and to encourage arbitrators to write high-quality awards'.

[119] Ibid.

require the parties to appoint an arbitrator from an underrepresented group; the parties will have to choose their arbitrators from the list prepared by the AI. The parties can opt out from this but they would then be required to report and explain why they have decided to refuse the candidates on the AI list. A default rule could set a minimum number of candidates from underrepresented groups that must be presented on such a list. AIs could choose to publish the proposed list on their websites to make the appointment procedure more transparent. This way AIs could promote diversity in the arbitral appointments made by the parties and co-arbitrators. The default provisions on appointments may be developed further by offering co-arbitrators the option to appoint a president from the list of candidates composed by the AI.

The default rule on transparency could provide that AIs always publish the arbitral awards in full without mentioning the parties' names or other confidential information. Currently, ICSID can only publish the key holdings of awards, but it cannot release the full award unless the parties consent thereto. However, to acquire consent may take months. Accordingly, a default option could be introduced so that the Centre would publish awards unless the parties file a written notice of confidentiality within a certain timeframe. Similarly, the default provisions could establish that investor-State arbitration proceedings are public and available for publication unless the parties require otherwise in their written statement filed prior to the proceedings.

Some arbitration rules already provide for strict rules on timelines for the parties to submit their materials to the tribunal. These rules also establish the opportunity for the parties to address the tribunal to extend the timelines for filing submissions. To enhance the expedition of the arbitration process, an additional default rule could require that parties must request such extension of timelines within a certain timeframe (for example, 20 days after the constitution of the tribunal). If parties did not follow this default rule, they would lose the opportunity to obtain an extension.

In addition, default rules may be helpful when the parties intentionally delay the proceedings by requesting '[e]xtension after extension, postponing a hearing because a witness or client "somehow" accepted a conflicting engagement, jettisoning the timetable to instruct "necessary" new or additional counsel; [s]tubbornly pursuing a virtual death march of document disclosure disputes – each document more "critical" to presenting its case than the last'.[120] These actions are not exhaustive and

[120] L. Reed, 'Ab(use) of Due Process: Sword vs Shield' (2017) 33 *Arbitration International* 361, 375.

simply represent an example of how a party can bamboozle the process and cause significant delay in the proceedings. By taking an action, the tribunal is put in jeopardy, i.e. '[i]f the tribunal says no, the applicant's due process flag goes up'; the party can even challenge the arbitrators (although, as Lucy Reed puts it, this would be rather a 'nuclear option').[121] In this context, AIs could set up default rules that 'switch on' when the tribunal faces such conduct, for example by limiting the number of possible extensions, fixing the permissible time period within which the parties can bring in a new counsel. After this window has closed, the default option may prescribe that no further extensions are possible.

Of course, the strength of the choice architecture model is that it shapes the incentives that guide the behaviour of different stakeholders. Accordingly, the parties always have an opportunity to opt out from the default rules if they so wish. The 'opt out' procedure may follow the 'report-and-explain' model whereby parties are required to explain to the relevant AI why they are opting out from the default option. This way, choice architecture preserves party autonomy, which is fundamental for international arbitration. In conclusion, the choice architecture model can be useful for AIs to alter users' incentives and respond to the recurring legitimacy concerns, in particular that the system lacks diversity, transparency and expedition.

[121] Ibid.

Identifying the Voices of Unseen Actors in Investor-State Dispute Settlement

DAMIEN CHARLOTIN

20.1 Introduction

International law literature has recognised that data science methods and tools, together with the empirical analysis they facilitate, can fruitfully assist the study of international law. In an important paper, Urska Sadl and Henrik Palmer Olsen introduce methods such as network and citation analysis to conclude that '[q]uantitative techniques or citation network approach are relevant for the study of international case law primarily because (contrary to many methods used by political scientists) they clearly shift the focus from legal/doctrinal questions to the content of judicial decisions, meaning the law itself'[1] – and therefore, its formation and evolutions.

These tools, as applied in recent literature, have offered instructive views concerning some pressing issues of international law, from the systematic study of international judicial bodies' citation practice,[2] and the networks of arbitrators and appellate bodies' judges,[3] to the influence of litigants' language on a case's final outcome.[4] Data methods allow for new insights into already-existing theories, and provide ways to confirm (or deny) the conclusions reached by traditional legal scholarship. By allowing legal researchers to observe international law through mathematical and

---

[1] U. Sadl and H.P. Olsen, 'Can Quantitative Methods Complement Doctrinal Legal Studies? Using Citation Network and Corpus Linguistic Analysis to Understand International Courts' (2017) 30 *Leiden Journal of International Law* 327.

[2] W. Alschner and D. Charlotin, 'The Growing Complexity of the International Court of Justice's Self-Citation Network: Institutional Achievement or Access-to-Justice Concern?' (2018) 29 *European Journal of International Law* 1.

[3] S. Puig, 'Social Capital in the Arbitration Market' (2014) 24 *European Journal of International Law* 2, at 407.

[4] M. Daku and K. Pelc, 'Who Holds Influence over WTO Jurisprudence?' (2017) 20 *Journal of International Economic Law* 233–255.

statistical abstractions, they offer a different lens of analysis – a lens as worthy of research time as the classic method of examining the meaning of a judicial decision through textual and doctrinal analysis.

This chapter aims to add one argument in favour of such data-oriented methods and approaches in international law: as with most 'big data' applications, an approach rooted in the empirical features of international law can allow researchers to discern what is invisible, or barely perceptible, to the observer's unassisted eyes. Such an approach can unveil (to some extent) the hidden aspects of international dispute settlement – and therewith its 'hidden actors', their role and influence(s), and their impact on how international justice is being served. This, in turn, relates to the legitimacy of international dispute settlement, of international courts and tribunals' findings and pronouncements.

International dispute settlement can indeed be described as a 'black box':[5] while the input and outcome of international disputes are broadly known,[6] what happens inside the black box remains mostly shrouded in mystery. Yet, it is in this black box that the role, power and influence of some of these hidden actors are the most potent. It does not take much imagination to expect that arbitral institutions and secretariats have some leeway on managing how a dispute is conducted;[7] that tribunal secretaries relieve arbitrators of some drafting duties and thereby arrogate themselves some adjudicative powers; that experts and *amici curiae* can have a greater impact on a judicial body's reasoning than the parties; and so on. Yet, to what extent do these commonly shared intuitions hold true? Besides anecdotal observations, it is hard to tell.

Enter empirical methods, which can help shed light on these issues – and in fact, have already done so. One of the main headlines in international arbitration news in recent years bore on the (alleged) role of a tribunal's secretary in drafting substantial parts of a billion-dollar award in the *Yukos* case.[8] That role is now part of the arguments being used to set aside the awards in this case, whereby the alleged covert action of the alleged 'fourth arbitrator' gives fodder to the attacks on the legality (if

---

[5] B. Berger and M.E. Schneider (eds.), *Inside the Black Box: How Arbitral Tribunals Operate and Reach Their Decisions* (Juris, 2014).

[6] That is, except when they are confidential.

[7] D. Caron, 'Towards a Political Theory of International Courts and Tribunals' (2007) 24 *Berkeley Journal of International Law* 401, at 416, noting the possible 'critically important' role of secretariats.

[8] J. Hepburn, 'Battling $50 Billion Yukos Awards on two Fronts, Russia Focuses on Claimants' Alleged Fraud and Linguistic Analysis of Tribunal Assistant's Alleged Role

not the legitimacy) of the outcome.[9] While the news did not shock out of proportion the habitués of international arbitration, the forensic linguistics used to prove it elicited some surprise. These methods are, however, within the reach (at least in a simplified form) of any researcher; they only require the use of a computer. International law is thus ripe for this kind of empirical analysis.

This chapter reviews some easily accessible and useful tools at the disposal of international law scholars interested in working with corpus of (text) data related to international law and international dispute settlement. Section 20.2 provides the reader with a short primer on a selection of computer tools helpful to collect, manage and analyse datasets. Section 20.3 takes a step back to analyse the relationship between the legitimacy of an adjudicative body and the identity of the decision-maker – and the legitimacy issues entailed in delegating the drafting of decisions to assistants. Section 20.4 returns to the empirical tools introduced earlier and applies some of them in a case study that investigates the role of secretaries and assistants (20.4.1),[10] and the role of the ICSID's Secretariat in allegedly 'streamlining' the language of ICSID awards (20.4.2).

20.2   A Primer on Empirical Tools and Methods

This part introduces the use of computer tools and languages (most notably R and Python) to collect, store, manage and analyse a text-based dataset, and thus assist legal scholars in their research.[11] This part also identifies a few specific python modules that underpin the growing 'Digital Humanities' movement.[12] To illustrate the potential uses of these tools, this section will also explain how the data later analysed in Section 20.4 was collected and pre-processed.

---

in Drafting Awards' *IAReporter*, 3 November 2015; see also Ministry of Finance of the Russian Federation press release dated 6 February 2015, available at https://web.archive .org/web/20150328213321/http://old.minfin.ru/en/news/index.php?id_4=24358.

[9] This is notably one of the grounds recently offered by Gazprom to set aside an award in favour of Ukraine before the Stockholm Court of Appeal: see L. Young, 'Gazprom Attacks Tribunal Secretary Role in Naftogaz Award' (29 May 2018) *Global Arbitration Review.*

[10] As explained further below, the word 'secretaries' encompasses different names and categories, but this chapter will use it as a general term for the assistants to a given tribunal.

[11] Those already familiar with computer science methods and technics should skip to Section 20.3.

[12] See, for example, the lessons available on *The Programming Historian*, available at https:// programminghistorian.org/lessons/.

20.2.1 *Python*

Computer-based tasks can be performed, roughly, at two levels: using a specific dedicated program suited to one's needs (for example, a computer's calculator to compute; a web browser to go online, etc.), or programming a dedicated function directly in computer language.[13] The former is usually easier and more intuitive to use, and more predictable in its results; it is, however, lacking in flexibility: if a calculator has no function to compute a cosine value, there is little than can be done beyond acquiring a more sophisticated one. An alternative is to program one's own calculator, and endow it with the user's or programmer's desired features. Learning computer languages allows for this second alternative.

Python is one of the most popular computer languages in social sciences,[14] or indeed in any field.[15] Python's strengths lie in its vibrant community of users and developers, who constantly answer users' needs by adding novel functions and tools ('modules') to Python's core functions,[16] such modules being then generally freely available. The sections below demonstrate how some of these Python-based modules can prove helpful to collect and manipulate 'international law'-related data.[17]

---

[13] Of course, the former is itself written in computer language. And there are various levels of what is commonly called 'computer language', with the most commonly used relying on an interpreter (compiler) to translate them into deeper instructions closer to pure machine language.

[14] See the post from Berkeley's Institute for Data Science's blog, describing Python as 'the best of both worlds' (that is, highly general capacities supplemented by dedicated packages for specific subjects or tasks): https://bids.berkeley.edu/news/what%E2%80%99s-big-deal-about-python. Python's name is a tribute to the TV series *Monty Python*.

[15] See the results of a 2017 survey by Stackoverflow, a popular programming forum: https://insights.stackoverflow.com/survey/2017.

[16] Another way to think about modules is that they provide a shortcut: instead of developing the hundreds of lines of code that would allow the manipulation of a *date* object (different from another computer variable in that you could, for example, manipulate it with reference to its features in terms of years, days, hours, etc.), Python users may use several 'date' modules already in existence.

[17] This chapter assumes that the reader has Python installed and knows how to start using it, including how to download modules. For Windows, a good tutorial to install Python is available at: www.howtogeek.com/197947/how-to-install-python-on-windows/. Learning Python is straightforward, and an embarrassment of tutorials is available online. Highly recommended, especially for social sciences, law and humanities scholars, is A. Sweigart, *Automate the Boring Stuff with Python: Practical Programming for Total Beginners* (No Starch Press, 2015), also available at: https://automatetheboringstuff.com/.

20.2.2   Collecting Datasets

Collecting data from the internet is commonly known as scraping. This section explains the basic process of collecting data from webpages using scraping methods available with Python-based methods and modules.

Imagine a scholar looking for the names of all arbitrators in the (publicly disclosed) investor-State arbitrations administered by the Permanent Court of Arbitration ('PCA').[18] A straightforward way to collect this information in an automated manner could comprise the following steps:

- Find a list of all PCA webpages with relevant information. In this example, such information is readily accessible: all case-specific webpages from the PCA website take the form https://pca-cpa.org/en/cases/XX/, with XX being a number starting from 1 to the number assigned to the most recently registered arbitration.
- Locate, in the PCA's pages, the relevant html[19] element in the webpage's html structure, assuming that all case webpages adopt the same structure (this is normally the case for this kind of data-oriented content). The easiest way to locate the relevant html element is with a browser: for example, on Google Chrome, right-clicking on the row that says 'Arbitrator(s),' and selecting 'Inspect,' will unveil the page's html structure. This word turns out to be a '<td></td>' html element enclosing the text 'Arbitrator(s)'; according to the html structure, the names of the arbitrators are given in the next html element in the webpage's structure.[20]
- Connect in turn to every URL (for instance, with Python's Requests module),[21] and gather the html structure of the webpage in a Python object.

---

[18]   The list of all cases publicly disclosed by the PCA with a – limited – amount of information on each is available at https://pca-cpa.org/en/cases/.

[19]   'HTML,' an acronym of 'Hypertext Markup Language' is the most commonly used web-oriented language. It typically takes the form of a hierarchical structure, whereby any part of a webpage is represented by elements (of various types) in this structure. For example, a search field on a webpage is usually an <input> element inserted into another element representing the search-box area, itself typically a <div> element of the webpage's <body> element. An introduction to html can be found at: www.w3schools.com/html/.

[20]   An even easier method here would be to convert the PCA's '<table>' element to a DataFrame with the python module pandas.

[21]   Requests is a module facilitating the access to webpages and the download of their content in a format easily exploitable in Python; see more at http://docs.python-requests.org/en/master/.

- Use the BeautifulSoup module to manipulate this object,[22] and then to find the '<td></td>' html element enclosing the words 'Arbitrator(s)'; once this element is found, as per the html structure identified above, the next html element yields the arbitrators' names.
- Add these names, webpage after webpage, to a database.[23]

This method can be roughly replicated on most websites containing data in an html format.[24] Even considering the time to code the scraping scripts, and providing for the inevitable exceptions, this process allows for a considerable gain of time (and accuracy) compared to manual data collection. As a further example, the online annex also includes code to scrape the (slightly more complicated) data available on ICSID's website.

Note, however, that, when it comes to judgments and awards (not mere metadata[25]), most publicly available documents are.pdf files, which are not exploitable as such and need to be converted to another format (for example, .txt or .xml files). Converting .pdf documents is not an accurate science, to say the least. It is advisable to collect such data when available in text format (for example, within html elements), such as is the case for many judgments available on www.worldcourts.com.

20.2.3   Regexes

In keeping with the dataset studied in Section 20.4, this chapter will focus on investment arbitration awards and other written decisions by investment tribunals and ICSID ad hoc annulment committees. However, rather than scraping all data on italaw.com anew, this chapter relies on the excellent efforts of Wolfgang Alschner and Aleksander Umov in creating an 'international economic law disputes' database that already contains these decisions in an exploitable form.[26]

---

[22] The BeautifulSoup module allows for the easy reading and manipulation of html code by creating a 'soup' object, whose content is that of the scraped webpage, but whose associated methods, architecture, etc., are optimised for researching and manipulating this content.

[23] An easy format to use here is CSV;.csv files are rows-based data containers that can be opened in Excel but are typically easier to handle with computer languages.

[24] Some online resources, such as ICSID's case database, are made of more sophisticated web structures, which require more ingenuity in elaborating a parsing script.

[25] 'Metadata' denotes the characteristics and features of a particular data element, such as its date, author, type, etc.

[26] See, more generally, Alschner and Umov, 'Towards an Integrated Database of International Economic Law (IDIEL) Disputes for Text-As-Data Analysis', CTEI Working Papers No. 2016-08, http://repository.graduateinstitute.ch/record/294805/files/CTEI-2016-08.pdf.

Regexes, short-hand for 'regular expressions', are rules-based search terms that allow for powerful ways to parse and search a corpus of texts, by looking for flexible patterns rather than given features or words. For example, the regular expression '\db.t' includes the symbols '\d' and '', which respectively mean (to the regex-based search module's eyes) 'any number' and 'any character'. Applied to a piece of text, this regex would catch the terms '3bit' or '4bot,' but not 'rabbit'. Regexes allow for exceptions and conditions,[27] and can even accommodate a pre-set number of mistakes, deletions or substitutions (using so-called 'fuzzy' logic) – a highly relevant feature in dealing with texts that have been obtained from scans and, therefore, often include typographical mistakes.

Regexes are especially useful when variations in searched-for material can be expected. Because Section 20.4.1 focuses on tribunal secretaries, whose identification varies ('secretary', 'assistant', etc.),[28] regexes were used to find out their names in investment disputes, without having to painfully open all documents and note down the information manually. Parsing over all documents one at a time, the Python script would collect the sentence where the regex module matches the regex terms,[29] as well as the preceding and following sentence for context. All sentences were collected in a .csv file, which were then manually checked for correct identification.[30]

A unique ID was assigned to all secretaries and assistants, following the form 'SEC-XXXX,' with XXXX being a four-digit number.[31] At the end of this process, the dataset comprised 65 'institutional secretaries'

The data has already been converted into .xml documents and comes with a lot of helpful metadata.

[27] For example, the regex '(?<=Holy)Grail' would capture the word 'Grail' only when preceded by 'Holy' (an admittedly common occurrence).

[28] A point further elaborated upon further below, at p. 13.

[29] The search checked for the following alternative wordings and was not case-sensitive: 'Tribunal Secretary|(Secr.ta.?ry?e?|Assistant)(of|to|du)(the)?(tribunal|president|chair|Co mm?itt?| (Administrative|Legal) Secretary|its Secretary.'

[30] The names of assistants and secretaries were recorded only when it was certain that they had participated in the drafting of the document bearing their name. Thus, the mention of an assistant that 'served for a time' did not make the cut (see, for example, *Garanti Koza LLP v. Turkmenistan*, ICSID Case No. ARB/11/20, Award (19 December 2016), at §10). An additional, manual check into awards allowed me to plug the gaps where the regexes had been unable to detect any trace of a secretary (for example, when the underlying text had been badly OCR-ed).

[31] For anonymity purposes, no names of secretaries will be disclosed in this chapter; the data only includes the ID assigned to the individuals studied.

(ICSID- or PCA-employed), and 77 'assistants' (as indicated above, the terminology in this respect varies a lot), for some 300 different disputes for which a decision was available.[32] 'Assistants' appeared (or rather, were explicitly acknowledged) in only one dispute, whereas institutional secretaries were involved in an average of eight disputes.

No similar dataset is currently publicly available, despite its usefulness in terms of researching, for example, ICSID's practice in appointing secretaries to the disputes administered under its rules. It can also shed a helpful empirical light on some controversies regarding these appointments: one investment arbitration practitioner wrote an article decrying several 'elephant(s) in the room' with respect to ICSID cases, one of which was that ICSID's Secretary-General would sometimes assign the same secretary to the original proceedings *and* to the annulment proceedings.[33] This was described as both 'objectionable' and 'inappropriate' for a number of reasons. While there could be good reason to support this practice (be it in terms of familiarity with the case, 'institutional memory', etc.), absent empirical evidence, there is a question over the actual prevalence of this practice.

Based on the dataset collected for the purposes of this chapter, ICSID secretaries have been appointed in original proceedings *and* annulment proceedings in the same case in slightly half (40) of the ICSID cases that included an annulment phase (n=93). In other words, in 53 of these cases, the secretary in the annulment proceedings is/was different from the secretary appointed in the case's original proceedings,[34] or the identity of the secretary was unreported; when the cases where no secretary name can be found (in the original or annulment proceedings) are subtracted, however, there would seem to be only 15 cases where it is certain that ICSID assigned a different secretary between the original proceedings and the entire annulment phase.[35]

---

[32] This is to be compared with more than 500 arbitrators.

[33] H. Gharavi, 'ICSID Annulment Committees: The Elephant in the Room', *GlobalArbitrationReview.com*, 24 November 2014; an ungated version is available at www .derainsgharavi.com/2014/11/icsid-annulment-committees-the-elephant-in-the-room/.

[34] However, ICSID secretaries tend to change quite often, and it is not uncommon to see that an annulment case might start with the same secretary as the original proceedings, only to have a replacement later.

[35] A possible extension of this phenomenon would be the instances where the same secretary also stays for the resubmitted proceedings, or for concurrent proceedings brought by the same claimant: for example, in the two ICSID arbitrations opposing Caratube to Kazakhstan, the same secretary officiated in the first arbitration, the annulment

The data collected concerning these secretaries is further exploited below in Section 20.4.1.

20.2.4   NLTK

'NLTK' stands for 'Natural Language Tool Kit' and is a suite of tools available in Python to perform a broad range of text analysis over a corpus, be it an original one or one of the dozens of pre-loaded corpora available in the NLTK library. NLTK typically work as follows:

- Divide the words in a corpus into as many 'tokens' (that is, unique words) and check their frequency; word frequency is in turn useful in a range of analyses, including authorship attribution – as seen in more detail below in Section 20.2.6 – or text similarity;
- Parse a text to find its PoS elements (for 'Parts of Speech', such as adjectives, proper nouns, etc.); or
- Recognise named entities ('ConocoPhillips', 'Eureko', 'Yves Fortier', 'Paris', etc.).

Among its many functions, NLTK offers the opportunity to engage in 'sentiment analysis'. Sentiment analysis allows computation of the positivity or negativity of a text, relying on the expected values of a set of words (for example, 'thrilled' is positive, 'disappointed' negative, etc.). Several threads of research could, in the future, rely on this type of analysis, for instance to check the influence of a party's general tone in its pleadings on the decision-maker's ultimate disposition towards this party; or if judgments and awards follow a particular 'emotional' trajectory as novels and fictional works seemingly do.[36]

At a less ambitious level (and for illustration purposes), sentiment analysis can be applied to check the intuitive assumption that dissenting opinions would be, on average, more 'negative' (since they would use more critical vocabulary) than concurring opinions. For the purposes of this chapter, sentiment analysis tools were tested over a dataset of 45 dissenting opinions and 21 separate opinions in investment arbitration. The average sentiment score of dissenting opinions, as expected, tended more to the negative side than to the positive side, but only slightly: on a scale of -1 to 1 (negative to positive), dissenting opinions had a score of

---

proceedings and the second arbitration filed by the disappointed claimants (the latter two being contemporaneous).

[36] Andrew J. Reagan, L. Mitchell, D. Kiley, C. Danforth and Peter Sheridan Dodds, 'The Emotional Arcs of Stories Are Dominated by Six Basic Shapes' (2016), available at https://arxiv.org/pdf/1606.07772.pdf.

0.10, while concurring opinions scored 0.15. More informative, however, is the ranking: out of the 25 most 'negative' opinions, only four were concurrent opinions, all others were dissenting opinions.

20.2.5   Network Analysis

Network analysis refers to the study of links and relationships between individual items as though they belong to a 'network', whereby these individual items (such as awards) are the nodes, and the links between these nodes (such as the citations from one award to another) are the 'edges'. Network analysis tools such as Gephi apply algorithms to these links with the aim of forming cluster of nodes that exhibit the closest relationships, be it because they exhibit many links to each other (for example, when an award relies heavily on one precedent), or if they have links with common neighbours (for example, when two awards are cited by a third in the same context).

In a previous paper, I 'mapped' international law disputes using the citations and cross-citations between international law awards and judgments.[37] The method is straightforward: it consists in identifying citations in a corpus of texts (notably using regexes, as discussed above); noting the source of the citation and identifying its target (that is, the decision cited); and lastly compiling these source–target couples in a row-based database (such as a .csv file).

Network analysis tools typically distinguish between two elements: nodes (here, the elements that cite or are cited) and edges (the source–target couples just mentioned). Nodes can be accompanied by further information corresponding to the context of the decision citing or cited (for example, underlying treaty, dispute phase, presiding arbitrator, etc.). Gephi allows users to display such metadata using colours. One end result is a network visualisation where things speak for themselves.

For instance, the map at Figure 20.1 shows all collected citations between majority decisions from the following major international fora. Node size is dependent on the number of times the case has been cited. Only cases that have at least one connection with another case are displayed.[38]

---

[37] D. Charlotin, 'The Place of Investment Awards and WTO Decisions in International Law: A Citation Analysis' (2017) 20 *Journal of International Economic Law* 2.

[38] Gephi's algorithm 'Force Atlas 2' was used for the maps in this chapter: M. Jacomy, T. Venturini, S. Heymann and M. Bastian, 'ForceAtlas2, a Continuous Graph Layout Algorithm for Handy Network Visualization Designed for the Gephi Software' (2014) 9(6) *PLoS ONE* e98679.

Figure 20.1 Network of international judgments and awards

- Investment arbitration cases (top right);
- The International Court of Justice ('ICJ') and its predecessor the Permanent Court of International Justice ('PCIJ') (centre);
- The International Criminal Tribunal for the former Yugoslavia ('ICTY') and its sister the International Criminal Tribunal for Rwanda ('ICTR') (bottom left);
- The Iran-US Claims Tribunal (top left);
- The World Trade Organization's ('WTO') dispute settlement system, and those cases decided under its predecessor the General Agreement on Tariffs and Trade ('GATT') (bottom right);
- Black nodes represent all cited decisions from national and EU courts and legal systems; and

- White nodes represent older arbitrations, such as the cases decided under mixed commissions in the nineteenth and early twentieth centuries.

The usefulness of network analysis – as with most data visualisation methods – lies in its displaying relationships and phenomena that otherwise rely mostly on qualitative assessments and/or intuitions. Figure 20.1, for example, clearly illustrates the division of international law – at least with respect to citations – in different specialised legal areas, although the map also shows the existing links between sub-regimes. Notably, the network graph confirms that the ICJ is the central reference for all sub-regimes.[39] The investment 'galaxy' is closer to the ICJ one than is the WTO/GATT bloc, and includes more links to older arbitrations, whereas criminal tribunals cite a lot more domestic decisions.

Further examples of the use of network analysis tools can be found in Section 20.4 below.

20.2.6   Stylometry

Stylometry refers to a range of methods rooted in linguistics that are used to study the stylistic features of a text. Authorship attribution is one of the main applications of stylometry, be it to assign a known author to a corpus of texts of unknown authorship, or (and more relevant for our purposes) classifying a corpus of texts as being authored by as many probable authors based on the varying stylistic features found in the corpus. As judicial opinions and writings often take the form of texts signed by a single (or, at least, lead), identified author, stylometry can be relevantly applied to a corpus of international legal decisions.[40]

One very efficient stylometry module is freely available and easy to use: Stylo()[41] is a module in R (a computer language designed especially

---

[39] The author further elaborates on this map, and in particular on whether (or not) it supports the idea of the 'fragmentation' of international law, in Charlotin, 'The Place of Investment Awards'.

[40] As with every bit of legal empirical research, it has already been conducted with respect to the US Supreme Court: see J. Rosenthal and A. Yoon, 'Judicial Ghostwriting: Authorship on the Supreme Court' (2016) 96 *Cornell Law Review* 1307.

[41] https://sites.google.com/site/computationalstylistics/home. See also M. Eder, J. Rybicki and M. Kestemont 'Stylometry with R: A Package for Computational Text Analysis' (2016) 8(1) *R Journal* 107–121, https://journal.r-project.org/archive/2016-1/eder-rybicki-kestemont.pdf.

for statistical analysis),[42] whose use lies within the reach of any neophyte, as it includes a Graphical User Interface ('GUI').[43] On the basis of a pre-prepared corpus of text (pre-stored in a folder named 'corpus'), Stylo() offers an exhaustive choice of stylometric tools and algorithms to perform stylometric analyses. The GUI allows a selection of several different features in terms of input (language of the text, encoding, etc.) and output (distance tables, graphs, etc.).

The results would often 'speak for themselves,' either as self-produced dendrograms, or transformed into network-analyses maps (introduced above in Section 20.2.5). These dendrograms and maps will indicate the 'stylistic' proximity of two different texts or passages that served as input for Stylo().[44] The module also produces 'distance tables' that assess the stylistic proximity between each pair of documents in the corpus. Stylometric tools are further discussed below, in Section 20.4.

20.3   Legitimacy: Who Writes, Who Decides?

20.3.1   Legitimacy in (and of) International Adjudicative Bodies

The tools and methods introduced above allow for further data-based inquiry into international law decisions, and, as will be seen below in Section 20.4, give a better view of the role of the various actors (secretaries, parties, decision-makers) involved in any given case. Section 20.4 will indeed use these tools to shed light on (i) the role of presidents of tribunals, institutional secretaries and assistants in drafting the text of investment awards; and (ii) the alleged 'streamlining' efforts of the ICSID secretariat on the awards and decisions that pass through its hands.

Why, however, would such greater knowledge be important? In short, for reasons of legitimacy, taking into account the four following observations:

1.   Legitimacy is 'a quality that leads people (or states) to accept authority – independent of coercion, self-interest, or rational

---

[42] See the explanations at www.r-project.org/.

[43] In addition, a comprehensive 'how-to' guide is available on the Stylo()'s webpage and does not presume any prior knowledge of R.

[44] In particular, Stylo()'s 'consensus tree' method performs several analyses at several degrees of precision (that is, using different lists of most-frequent words) and, from the result of these analyses, performs a 'consensus' image that is supposed to better retrace the relationships between the texts in the corpus and eliminate part of the noise. See further M. Eder, 'Visualization in Stylometry: Cluster Analysis Using Networks' (2017) 32 *Digital Scholarship in the Humanities* 1.

persuasion – because of a general sense that the authority is justi-fied'.[45] Legitimacy is especially important in the context of interna-tional adjudicative bodies that, contrary to municipal courts, are not provided with an apparatus allowing for the exercise of state power and the prompt executions of their decisions, and must thus rely on other sources of authority for compliance. Legitimacy, however, is often in the eye of the beholder;[46] it does not mean the same thing for the same set of actors, and can shift when the context evolves.[47]

2. Legitimacy is, at least partly, related to the expectations of the dis-puting parties – and one of these expectations is that the international adjudicative body will resolve a dispute in 'a manner acceptable to both parties, based on law or *ex aequo et bono*'.[48] In this respect, it can be expected that the more compelling or robust the legal reasoning of the decision, the greater the likelihood that it will find grace in the eyes of the disputing parties[49] – which in turn boosts the adjudicative body's legitimacy.

3. The identity of the decision-maker is relevant to the legitimacy of an adjudicative body: not everyone can judge a dispute, or will be selected to this end.[50] Hence debates about the selection of adjudicators,[51] the role of diversity in the composition of international courts and

---

[45] D. Bodansky, 'The Legitimacy of International Governance: A Coming Challenge for International Environmental Law?' (1999) 93 *American Journal of International Law* 596, at 600.

[46] Y. Shany, *Assessing the Effectiveness of International Courts* (Oxford University Press, 2014), at p. 138: 'legitimacy is a nebulous concept, meaning different things to different people'. Besides, the determinants of legitimacy might differ between different adjudicative bodies, depending, for instance, on the different audiences they serve.

[47] 'Introduction' in H. Grant Cohen, A. Føllesdal, and N. Grossman (eds.) *Legitimacy and International Courts* (Cambridge University Press, 2018), available at https://papers.ssrn .com/sol3/papers.cfm?abstract_id=2926591, at p. 18, with the example of ICSID.

[48] Ibid., at p. 10.

[49] Taking correct decisions also furthers the 'norm support' goal of international courts and tribunals (that is, their role in upholding the legal obligations upon which they adjudi-cate): Shany, Assessing the Effectiveness of International Courts, at p. 41. 'Norm support' is also often another expectation of the state disputing parties, who usually are, at the same time, the founding parties to the adjudicative body before which they later litigate their disputes.

[50] J. Pauwelyn, 'The Rule of Law without the Rule of Lawyers? Why Investment Arbitrators Are from Mars, Trade Adjudicators from Venus' (2015) 109 *American Journal of International Law* 761: '*Who* decides – as much as what law applies – may then guide forum choice, liti-gation outcomes and even the longer term legitimacy and future of international trade and investment law.'

[51] M. Waibel, 'Arbitrator Selection – Towards Greater State Control' (2016) Cambridge Law Faculty Paper No. 30/2016, at 10.

tribunals,[52] or the requirements that judges be endowed with some particular qualities, such as 'high moral character'.[53] That increasingly parties and institutions in arbitral proceedings ask to know of assistants and secretaries[54] indicates that the identity of some 'hidden actors' matters as well.[55]

4.   Abiding by predetermined rules matters for the legitimacy of judicial proceedings.[56] A corollary of this proposition is that an institution's legitimacy is likely to suffer when the rules are not complied with,[57] or when they are merely *de façade* and in contradiction with the expectations of the parties: '[i]f an institution exhibits a pattern of egregious disparity between its actual performance, on the one hand, and its self-proclaimed procedures or major goals, on the other, its legitimacy is seriously called into question'.[58] However, the discrepancy between rules and realities often stems from the fact that rules can yield to the reality of practice, such as the power structures that can circumscribe them.[59]

If these four propositions hold true (even partially), then one conclusion can be drawn: if the expected decision-maker covertly delegates part of

[52] G. Kaufmann-Kohler and M. Potestà, 'The Composition of a Multilateral Investment Court and of an Appeal Mechanism for Investment Awards' (2017) *CIDS Supplemental Report*, at §49: 'diversity on adjudicatory bodies is necessary in its own right to enhance the legitimacy of a dispute settlement system in the public perception'; C. Giorgetti, 'Is the Truth in the Eyes of the Beholder? The Perils and Benefits of Empirical Research in International Investment Arbitration' (2014) 12 *Santa Clara Journal of International Law* 263, at 272.

[53] ICJ Statute, Article 2.

[54] See the most recent amendment to the LCIA's Note to arbitrators, at §74: 'An Arbitral Tribunal can only obtain assistance from a tribunal secretary once the tribunal secretary has been approved by the parties.'

[55] Z. Douglas, 'The Secretary to the Arbitral Tribunal', in Berger and Schneider (eds.), *Inside the Black Box*, at p. 87, for whom such transparency is key.

[56] Shany, *Assessing the Effectiveness of International Courts*, at p. 143: 'specific judicial decisions would be typically regarded as legitimate if they are issued by a properly established international court, applying its legal procedures in a regular manner'.

[57] T. Treves, 'Aspects of Legitimacy of Decisions of International Courts and Tribunals' (2017) 75 *Seqüência (Florianópolis)* 28, describing 'adherence' (for example, to pre-existing rules) as the fourth factor of legitimacy according to Thomas Frank.

[58] A. Buchanan and R. Keohane, 'The Legitimacy of Global Governance Institutions' (2006) 20 *Ethics & International Affairs* 405, at 44.

[59] See, for instance, Caron, 'Towards a Political Theory of International Courts and Tribunals', at 417, explaining how WTO panels might be structurally disadvantaged in contesting the secretariat's analysis of the case, despite the panel members' exclusive decision-making power.

his or her work to a third party, in breach of the rules and the expectations of the parties, then the legitimacy, not only of the decision but also of the institution in which it takes place,[60] is put into question.

Is this more than a simple hypothetical? It is hard to say: few adjudicators would readily confess to having delegated their decision-making power. As Section 20.4 will attempt to show, however, it is now possible to lift the veil (if only partly) over this question, by trying to identify the roles of the various stakeholders behind the text of an international decision.

20.3.2   Writing International Legal Decisions

One objection to this conclusion, however, is that drafting a decision is not the same as deciding it; the reasons supporting judgments or awards are distinct from their operative part, which suffices to settle the case between the parties and accomplish the court or tribunal's judicial function. A model where a decision-maker reviews the case and takes a decision before assigning the material embodiment of this decision (that is, the written judgment or award) to an assistant or a secretariat could remain in line with the expectations of the parties, provided they are aware of it.[61]

Yet, this model forgets that the written medium is one of the primary ways through which an adjudicative body expresses itself and builds up its legitimacy for its particular audience.[62] Besides, the model is alien to the reality of decision-making and decision-drafting. Writing a decision is certainly part of *deciding* in itself, and a way to ensure the best of judgments[63] – in accordance with the parties' expectations. As explained by the Honourable Frank Kitto, former judge of the High Court of Australia:

> The main justification for believing that written reasons serve so much better than oral reasons the purposes for which judgment is reserved is, I suggest, that all the travail of making the necessary preparations for the task, knuckling down to the sheer toil of it, enduring the soul-searing tedium of it, going over the first draft, the seventh draft if need be, and

---

[60] Douglas, 'The Secretary to the Arbitral Tribunal', at 88: 'Such a challenge [based on the alleged participation of a secretary in drafting an award] would be very damaging – and I am talking of the perfect storm – to the reputation of international arbitration.'

[61] Ibid.; see also ibid., at 89, for the hypothesis that extensive participation of secretaries behind the scenes might be the parties' preference, if this involves a swifter resolution of the dispute.

[62] Grant Cohen et al., 'Introduction', at p. 13.

[63] S. Gageler 'Why Write Judgements?' (2014) 36 *Sydney Law Review* 189.

making all the necessary corrections and improvements with the crossings out, the balloons and the marginal scribblings that provide the test of a good associate – all these add up to discipline; and an adjudication that is not disciplined cannot but be more or less of a travesty, however facile its language, however impressive the voice that pronounces it.[64]

In this context, it matters that the expected decision-maker holds the pen of the international legal decision: not only because the parties often chose the decision-maker on an *intuitu personae* basis (notably in arbitral proceedings),[65] but also because they expect the decision-maker to reach the most compelling judicial outcome. '[T]he act of writing,' it has been held, 'is the ultimate safeguard of intellectual control over the decision-making process.'[66]

In this context, delegating drafting tasks to an assistant, even instructed with guidelines to justify a pre-determined outcome, fails to play the disciplinarian role identified by Sir Kitto. An assistant, out of deference to the delegating adjudicator, will be less inclined to question the adequacy of the outcome with the facts and the law as restated in the draft, or may be reluctant to point out the holes he or she perceives in the analysis, once put on paper. Certainly, some international decision-makers seem to agree: Terris et al. learned from interviews with international judges that there is in some quarters strong opposition to the practice of leaving drafting duties to assistants: 'I would never allow anybody else than myself to draw up the judgment,' an ICJ judge is quoted as saying.[67]

Yet, as the next section hopes to prove, there are indications (although no definite proof) that the non-delegation principle is not always observed in some fields of international dispute settlement.

---

[64] Sir Frank Kitto, 'Why Write Judgments?' (1992) 66 *Australian Law Journal* 787; he continued: 'What we think that we think on the spur of the moment often undergoes a remarkable change when we go through the discipline of putting it down on paper and looking at it. Only after much refining and reforming in the process of writing are our first vociferations likely to yield the crystals of our final thoughts, propositions freed from the impurities of our innate prejudices and from the distortions and the fuzziness around the edges that are the too-frequent products of our emotions, our sympathies, our dislikes and our predilections.'

[65] Swiss Federal Tribunal, decision 4A_709/2014.

[66] Douglas, 'The Secretary to the Arbitral Tribunal', at 89, although he also recognises that 'this is not the only legitimate way to serve the parties' interests in an arbitration.'

[67] D. Terris, C. Romano and L. Swigart, *The International Judge: An Introduction to the Men and Women Who Decide the World's Cases* (Brandeis, 2007), p. 57.

20.4   Two Applications

20.4.1   *Secretaries and Assistants in Investment Arbitration*

20.4.1.1   Introduction: A Lack of Clarity

The topic of secretaries and assistants in international arbitration has recently became a popular one: *Arbitration Station* (an arbitration-focused, excellent podcast series) dedicated its first episode to, inter alia, administrative secretaries.[68] The controversy surrounding the *Yukos* awards has served as a catalyst for the debate on the use of secretaries, in turn having repercussions in at least one further case, where parties have battled around 'the proper scope of a tribunal's assistant'.[69] In January 2017, the news broke that another case had had its own secretary-related issues, where the whole tribunal was being challenged for an alleged lack of impartiality after the ICSID secretary in the case joined the law firm advising the respondent while the dispute was ongoing.[70] As another sign of the times, the 2017 Jessup problem includes a fact pattern about a tribunal secretary who allegedly wrote a contested award.[71] An increasing number of papers and chapters,[72] or even judicial decisions,[73] try to

---

[68] Joel Dahlquist Cullborg and Brian Kotick, *About the Arbitration Station*, www.thearbitrationstation.com/about/.

[69] *ConocoPhillips Petrozuata B.V., ConocoPhillips Hamaca B.V. and ConocoPhillips Gulf of Paria B.V. v. Bolivarian Republic of Venezuela*, ICSID Case No. ARB/07/30, Decision on the Proposal to Disqualify a Majority of the Tribunal (1 July 2015), §55, where Venezuela argued that 'Mr. Valasek's role in the Yukos arbitrations "did not fit with the description of administrative assistant" to which Mr. Fortier had referred' earlier.
Investment arbitration is not the only context where the role of assistants has elicited controversies: Terris et al., The International Judge, at p. 57 write: 'This issue of having legal assistants at international courts involved in judgment writing is somewhat controversial.'

[70] *Supervision y Control S.A. v. Republic of Costa Rica*, ICSID Case No. ARB/12/4, Original proceedings (18 January 2017), Final Award, at §§36–41. See also L.E. Peterson and V. Djanic, In New Award, Arbitrators Disagree Whether Claims Should Be Nixed due to Overlap with Local Cases', *IAReporter*, 1 February 2017, at: www.iareporter.com/articles for the proposition that the challenge might have had additional reasons.

[71] Available at www.ilsa.org/Jessup/Jessup18/2018%20Combined%20Compromis%20and%20CandC%20final.pdf.

[72] See, for example, M. Polkinghorne and C.B. Rosenberg, 'The Role of the Tribunal Secretary in International Arbitration: A Call for a Uniform Standard' (2014) 8 *Dispute Resolution International* 107; B. Meyer and J. Baier, 'The Swiss Federal Supreme Court's View on Arbitrator Consultants and Secretaries, and Its Practical Implications' (2017) 14 *Transnational Dispute Management* 1.

[73] Swiss Federal Tribunal, decision 4A_709/2014; Popplewell J, *P v. Q* [2017] EWHC 194 (Comm) at 68; Italian Court of Cassation, *Sacheri v. Robotto* ('Decision', excerpt available

delineate the proper role of assistants to tribunals; arbitral institutions are updating their rules to clarify it,[74] when they are not proposing new training programmes for secretaries.[75]

Yet, despite this recent surge in interest, the exact role and remit of secretaries remain unclear. This uncertainty is illustrated in two particular respects: the lack of precise typology to categorise these 'assistants', and the fuzzy boundaries of what they can (or should) and cannot (or should not) do.

Typology

First, there is an acute lack of clarity in the terminology at play, as 'secretaries' are not always reported as such in the dataset collected for this chapter – if they are reported at all. A common alternative is 'assistant', yet this label is sometimes further qualified by 'legal',[76] as opposed to 'administrative' (with a few 'administrative secretaries' as well), not to mention at least one instance of one 'Counsel assisting the *ad hoc* Committee'.[77]

'Assistants/Secretaries' can also be reported as being attached not necessarily to the tribunal per se, but to a member of the tribunal: most often to the President,[78] but sometimes to a named co-arbitrator.[79] Some have their name listed with the arbitrators' on the decision's first page; others are just mentioned as appearing at the hearing, and others (if not most) are never mentioned at all.[80]

---

in Yearbook Commercial Arbitration, Volume 16, Kluwer Law International 1991, pp. 156–157.

[74] LCIA, 'LCIA Implements Changes to Tribunal Secretary Processes' (26 October 2017), available at: www.lcia.org/News/lcia-implements-changes-to-tribunal-secretary-processes.aspx.

[75] See the workshop 'Institute Training for Tribunal Secretaries', proposed for the first time in April 2017 by the International Chamber of Commerce, available at https://web.archive .org/web/20170415221259/https://iccwbo.org/event/icc-institute-training-for-tribunal-secretaries/.

[76] *Tulip Real Estate and Development Netherlands B.V. v. Republic of Turkey*, ICSID Case No. ARB/11/28, Award, at §38.

[77] *Enron Corporation and Ponderosa Assets, L.P. v. Argentine Republic*, ICSID Case No. ARB/ 01/3, Decision on the Application for Annulment of the Argentine Republic (30 July 2010), although the 'counsel' is also later introduced as an 'assistant' (§12) or a 'legal assistant' (at §30).

[78] *TECO Guatemala Holdings, LLC v. Republic of Guatemala*, ICSID Case No. ARB/10/23, PO No. 1, at §20.1.

[79] *Caratube International Oil Company LLP v. The Republic of Kazakhstan*, ICSID Case No. ARB/08/12, Award, at §100.

[80] In this respect, discretion was used to count a given assistant as involved in a dispute or not, most of the time checking for the relevant time-frame of the arbitrator/assistant

The fact that there exist cases with both 'secretaries' and 'assistants' on the side of the tribunal, however, indicates that the distinction is at least partly meaningful. In the ICSID context, the label 'secretary' is usually reserved for the staff attached to the Centre[81] as opposed to the tribunal or one of its members (persons assisting these are then usually labelled as 'assistants').[82] Yet, some cases have only one 'secretary' and no assistant, and there are indications[83] that ICSID secretaries still perform the same tasks expected of assistants in general, casting into doubt the extent of the distinction.[84] On the other hand, coming back to the discussion on legitimacy above in Section 20.3, it seems that most ICSID secretaries are appointed by the Centre with the knowledge but not necessarily the input or even prior approval of the parties.

Two (non-exclusive) assumptions can be made, to be tested below: the first is that institutional secretaries are a default mechanism and that their role in a case decreases as the assistant specially designated by a tribunal takes over the secretary's task (there is explicit support for this relationship in some procedural orders).[85] The second, related supposition is that, on a spectrum between mundane administrative tasks and work more closely related to the substance of the dispute,[86] institutional secretaries can be presumed to be usually concerned with the former, 'assistants' with the latter.

---

collaboration. For example, if a second, contemporaneous award recorded the role of the assistant in conjunction with an arbitrator, the assistant's role in the first award was accounted for even if that person is just mentioned in passing.

[81] With 'assistant secretaries' in some cases.

[82] In what follows, for clarity purposes, 'institutional' secretaries (be they attached to ICSID or the PCA) are distinguished from non-institutional ones.

[83] *Compañiá de Aguas del Aconquija S.A. and Vivendi Universal S.A. v. Argentine Republic* (II), ICSID Case No. ARB/97/03, Second Annulment proceedings, Dissenting Opinion of Jan-Hendrik Dalhuisen, §§3–4, which can be found at the end of the ad hoc committee's decisions, itself available at www.italaw.com/sites/default/files/case-documents/ita0221 .pdf.
   In Prof. Dalhuisen's recounting, the role of the Secretariat in drafting decisions goes from the 'recitals' (which presumably mean the procedural history) to the summary of the parties' arguments.

[84] See Ibid., at §8, where Prof. Dalhuisen explains that some 'busy' arbitrators farm out the drafting of awards to ICSID's secretariat.

[85] *China Heilongjiang et al. v. Mongolia*, UNCITRAL, Procedural Order No. 1 (2 November 2010): 'The Tribunal expects that in light of the appointment of a Secretary, the PCA's administrative assistance will consist only of the handling of the financial aspects of the proceeding and, possibly, assistance with hearings.'

[86] A spectrum observable in the answers to a survey about arbitral secretaries: see Young ICCA, Young ICCA, 'Young ICCA Guide on Arbitral Secretaries,' Preface by

Role

The second conundrum, closely related, lies in the role of assistants and secretaries – a role whose boundaries are unclear and yet crucial for the legitimacy issues identified in Section 20.3.

A Queen Mary University survey from 2015 records that close to nine
in ten arbitrators surveyed[87] thought that secretaries should not work on
any task too closely related to the merits, or to 'substantive' matters in a
case. The *Arbitration Station* podcast mentioned above returned at several
junctures to what we might call the 'ideal' role of the Secretary: involved
in the case but severed from the decision-making process.[88] A decision
from the Swiss Federal Tribunal opined that assistants to international
tribunals are prevented from 'exercising functions of a judicial nature,'[89]
sometimes also described as the functions relevant to the arbitrators'
'decision-making power'.[90] There remains, however, an 'enormously grey
area'[91] of possible activities. As the preface to the Young ICCA Guide
on Arbitral Secretaries puts it: '[u]nsurprisingly, the major area of disagreement lies in the nature of the tasks properly assigned to arbitral
secretaries.'[92]

This is only partly remedied by the information available on record.
While documents that mention secretaries do so in bland, boilerplate
terms that give some credence to the view that secretaries are usually
restricted to non-substantial tasks,[93] the awards' procedural record is

---

G. Aguilar-Alvarez, available at: https://pca-cpa.org/wp-content/uploads/sites/175/2016/
01/ICCA-Reports-No.-1_Young-ICCA-Guide-on-Arbitral-Secretaries.pdf, at 2.
[87] White & Case, LLP, and Queen Mary University of London, '2015 International Arbitration
Survey: Improvements and Innovations in International Arbitration' (2016), at 43, available
at www.arbitration.qmul.ac.uk/docs/164761.pdf: '89% of arbitrators consider that tribunal
secretaries should not be allowed to prepare drafts of substantive parts of awards and 92%
think that the secretary should not discuss the merits of the dispute with the arbitrators.'
[88] Dahlquist Cullborg and Kotick, *About the Arbitration Station.*
[89] Swiss Federal Tribunal, Arrêt, 4A_709/2014 (21 May 2015), at 3.2.2.
[90] Meyer and Baier, 'The Swiss Federal Supreme Court's View', at 6.
[91] Polkinghorne and Rosenberg, 'The Role of the Tribunal Secretary'.
[92] Young ICCA, 'Young ICCA Guide on Arbitral Secretaries'.
[93] See, for example, Model Letter from Arbitral Tribunal to Parties on the Appointment of
an Arbitral Secretary or Assistant, in G. Kaufmann-Kohler and A. Rigozzi, *International
Arbitration: Law and Practice in Switzerland* (Oxford University Press, 2015), p. 312.
This language can sometimes be even more vague and equivocal, however; see *Lion Mexico
Consolidated L.P. v. United Mexican States*, ICSID Case No. ARB(AF)/15/2, Procedural
order No. 1 (14 October 2016), at §8.2: 'The Assistant to the Tribunal shall undertake to
facilitate the arbitral process and complete such tasks as are placed under his purview or
specifically assigned to him by the Arbitral Tribunal or the President.'

sometimes (yet, still rarely) more verbose, and indicates that the tasks trusted to secretaries include activities ranging from flipping coins to decide on procedural matters,[94] to holding informal discussions with parties on matters of procedure,[95] or communicating to the parties on behalf of the tribunal.[96] Institutional rules are characterised by a 'significant divergence of practice'.[97]

Presumably, then, secretaries of all stripes are more likely to be drafting the procedural parts of an award, as well as the factual background and similar introductory parts. They might also be involved in summarising the arguments of the parties, in awards that record those. The truly substantive parts of an award, where the tribunal elaborates on its approaches and findings, should be the place where we are less likely to find their trace.

As reasonable as these assumptions are, in the black box that dispute settlement proves to be, no one can really be sure of the part of a secretary in a given decision. This is why, in what follows, the data science tools and methods introduced above in Section 20.2 are applied to investigate the extent of the secretaries' role in drafting investment awards or decisions, and to check if the alleged distinction between institutional and non-institutional secretaries holds according to the data.

20.4.1.2 Methodology

The following section describes in more detail the methodology followed to try to cast light on the questions discussed.

Corpus Preparation

From the above discussion, it can be expected that secretaries have different levels of input on different parts of investment awards and decisions. To be able to investigate this angle, the various parts of the awards and decisions that entered the dataset were annotated according to their content. The tagging process was semi-automatised, using a Python script.

---

[94] *Société Abidjan et al. v. Republic of Côte d'Ivoire*, ICSID Case No. ARB/16/11, Decision on Jurisdiction (1 August 2017), at § 23.

[95] *Glamis Gold, Ltd. v. The United States of America*, UNCITRAL, Award (8 June 2006), at § 263.

[96] See, for example, *Oko Pankki Oyj, VTB Bank (Deutschland) AG and Sampo Bank Plc v. The Republic of Estonia*, ICSID Case No. ARB/04/6, and the several letters sent by the (institutional) secretary to the parties in that case.

[97] See S. Maynard, 'Laying the Fourth Arbitrator to Rest: Re-Evaluating the Regulation of Arbitral Secretaries' (2018) 34 *Arbitration International* 173, at 176–177 for a review of the existing rules.

The tags differentiated between introduction-type sections ('I'), procedural records ('P'), facts ('F'), jurisdiction-related sections ('J'), merits
('M'), quantum ('Q') and the operative part of a decision ('OPER'). In
addition, parts could be qualified as embodying the arguments of the
parties ('ARGS', and then further 'RES' or 'CL' for 'Respondent(s)' and
'Claimant(s)' respectively) or the analysis of the tribunal ('T'). Given that
not all awards and decisions had the same profile (some awards do not
summarise the arguments of the parties, or the factual background, etc.),
and that Stylo() works best with texts that are not too short, the number
n of elements in the dataset varied depending on the sections analysed.

Before proceeding to the results, one caveat needs to be made explicit: the
data records only the names of the secretaries and assistants that were
publicly disclosed; that is, the analysis is limited to 'unseen' actors in
investment arbitration that are, actually, visible. This might or might not
be the tip of the iceberg; certainly, many other undisclosed *petites mains*
work in the back-kitchen of the international investment restaurant, and
the analysis performed below has little to say about them.[98] Yet, working
on this subset of 'seen' secretaries is a first step in having a clearer view of
what is going on behind the scenes.

Features

The wealth of stylometric methods identified above (Section 20.2.6) reflects
a threshold issue, however, in that a given method might not be appropriate
for every dataset it is applied to. Legal writing, including international legal
writing, has its own style and inherent features that distinguish it from other
types of writing, requiring a carefully selected approach.

The first methodological aspect to be tackled concerned the number
and type of features to use in the analysis. Since there is so far little
precedent in using these tools over a legal dataset, part of the preparatory work consisted in devising the most efficient features of the model.
Efficiency here is assessed with respect to how the stylometric tools fare in
reproducing the ex-ante relationship between two texts, that is, whether,
knowing that X wrote Y and Z, how did Stylo() fare in calculating the
proximity score between Y and Z?

In order to find the best approach under this criterion (through a process of trial and error), the analysis started with similar international legal

---

[98] Although the high stylistic variations from one award to another, supposedly written by
the same chair, could indicate the influence of these truly unseen actors.

writings whose authorship was, in theory, less contentious: individual separate and dissenting opinions of ICJ judges.[99]

The approach that offered the best results was to focus on a few features only (that it, most-frequent words, or 'MFW'). 100 MFWs[100] tended to show very good results. However, the most important factor proved to be the 'culling' parameter – that is, the choice of which words entered the analysis. A culling value of 20 (out of 100) will mean that the stylometric analysis would consider only those (most-frequent) words that are present in at least 20 per cent of all texts in the corpus.[101]

This makes sense: legal writing opposes two named parties in each case, relying heavily on citations – the analysis can be misled in classifying two texts as close or similar merely because they cite the same proper names (for example, 'Maffezini'), representing parties or past cases,[102] or because they belong to the same case (and then would tend to share the same vocabulary). A culling value starting at 30, climbing up to 60, proved relatively helpful in remedying this issue,[103] although the links between two cases in the same dispute (in terms of proximity scores, or 'edges' between two decisions)[104] were also excluded from the analysis.

---

[99] Of course, ICJ judges also have clerks, but (at least) four factors support the assumption that this dataset could be more reliable (in terms of authorship) than the dataset of investment awards: (i) notwithstanding individual cases, ICJ judges are likely to be less prone than investment arbitrators to delegate drafting to their clerks; (ii) these individual opinions span a longer time-frame than investment awards, and then cover a period where such delegating was likely to be less common, be it only because ICJ judges had fewer clerks at their disposal; (iii) as their name indicates, 'individual' opinions are more related to the individual writing it; and (iv) given the Court's docket, ICJ judges are unlikely to be working on more than one or two opinions at a given time, while arbitrators must often handle several cases at once.

With reference to (ii) and (iii) above, see also Rosenthal and Yoon, 'Judicial Ghostwriting', who found that (i) there is a likely upward chronological trend in the US Supreme Court's judges' delegation of drafting tasks to their clerks; and (ii) dissenting and concurrent opinions of the same US Justice tended to display less stylistic variability between themselves than majority opinions.

[100] These words are often the 'function' words at the heart of the analysis in Rosenthal and Yoon, 'Judicial Ghostwriting', such as 'the', 'a', 'what', etc.

[101] That is, not only function words but also those words that are very common in this kind of text: 'tribunal', 'claimant', 'law', 'international', etc.

[102] But also the name of the home and host state, or that of the lawyers involved; an alternative would be to root out all these proper names and 'neutralise' the texts studied – a task fit for NLTK tools, as introduced above in Section 20.2.4.

[103] This 'climbing' takes place in the framework of the 'consensus' method introduced above, at note 44.

[104] In the context of the network analysis figures below, therefore, if two nodes are close to each other, it is not because they relate to the same case, but truly because the author is

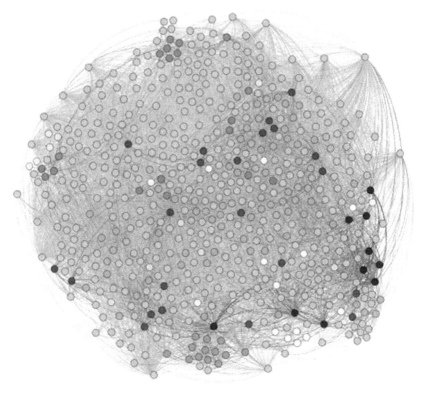

Figure 20.2 Network of ICJ Individual Opinions

The results of the analysis of ICJ individual (not joint) opinions are observable on the network 'map' shown in Figure 20.2. The hubs of opinions written by a given judge are immediately noticeable as nodes representing opinions written by the same judge that are close to each other, and located in the same part of the graph (only opinions by the top 12 most active judges, measured over the court's life, were coloured).

Stylo() also computes proximity scores, indicating the stylistic proximity between a pair of documents. In this training example, a pair of opinions with a common author had an average rank[105] of 29, on a scale

---

similar (if two texts share similar stylistic features, the stylistic relationship they will have with third-party nodes will tend to be similar, prompting the network analysis algorithms to group these two nodes together even though there is no edge between them).

[105] I used ranks to normalize Stylo()'s scores, which otherwise tend to be very close to one another and highly dense.

going from 0 – full similarity – to 100, or full dissimilarity (all other pairs had an average rank of slightly above 50).

20.4.1.3   Findings

The analysis started with an 'ideal' scenario, where every text would be written by the presiding arbitrator.[106] Does this fit the data? Figure 20.3 shows a map of 415 decisions from investment tribunals on merits, jurisdiction, provisional measures and rectification, as well as ICSID annulment and stay of enforcement rulings.

Although we can readily observe some 'hubs' of a few arbitrators, the accuracy in clustering is relatively low compared to other stylometric studies, or even to Figure 20.2 above (for instance, there are fewer identifiable hubs on the borders of the map, whereas the algorithm is supposed to push stronger hubs there). While the quality of the data might be a partial culprit (not all texts mined from the .pdfs are of pristine quality), one fair inference is that awards are subject to external inferences, but which ones?

While this could be the co-arbitrators, it could also be the secretaries and/or assistants. The map in Figure 20.4 starts from the same assumptions as Figure 20.3 above, but this time with nodes shaded by secretaries (the 12 most common, all of them of the 'institutional' variety). It is much harder to discern any cluster of cases whose style would indicate the role of one given secretary in different cases or decisions.

This is, however, but one part of the story, as we can further distinguish between institutional secretaries and assistants. The distinction is pursued in Table 20.1, which uses the proximity scores between pairs of awards, ranked (to normalise the scores) from 0 to 100: a rank of 0 means perfect similarity of the underlying texts, 100 perfect dissimilarity; in-between ranks represent the degree of stylistic similarity. The scores are means over the whole dataset.

As explained above, the procedural/factual/introductory parts of an award are the more likely to be susceptible of being written by an assistant

---

[106] There is of course nothing wrong in having the co-arbitrators writing parts of the award, but the lead role of the President in this activity is generally acknowledged. See, for example, T. Tucker, 'Inside the Black Box: Collegial Patterns on Investment Tribunals' (2016) 7 *Journal of International Dispute Settlement* 1, describing several types of presiding and wings arbitrators in investment arbitration; M. Scherer, 'Drafting the Award' in Berger and Schneider (eds.), *Inside the Black Box*, at p. 27: 'In my view, [drafting] is the task and prerogative of the chairman'.

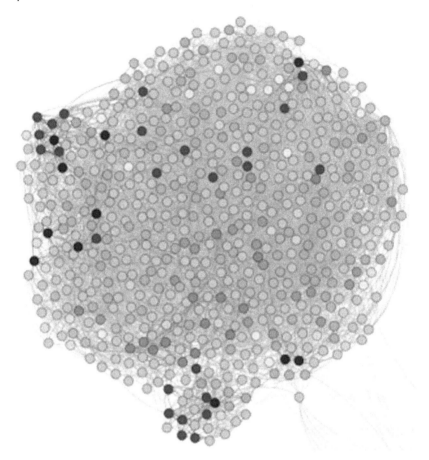

Figure 20.3 Investment decisions, full text, shaded according to presidents

Note: Only the decisions of the 12 most common presidents have been coloured.

or secretary. The analysis was then repeated to study the style of procedural sections of the awards (n=485), the facts (n=275), and then over the parts corresponding to the summary of the arguments of the parties (n=417), as well as the sections corresponding to the analysis of the tribunal on the substance of the claims (n=500). In addition, a distinction is made between ICSID-related secretaries and others (meaning, mostly, PCA-related secretaries), keeping in mind that the number of pairs of decisions sharing the latter is very low, skewing somewhat the results. These are observable in Table 20.1.

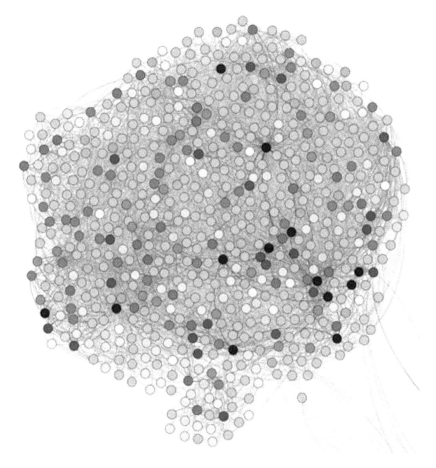

Figure 20.4 Investment decisions, full text, shaded according to secretaries and assistants

As the table shows, the mean proximity score of a pair of decisions that share a president is always lower (that is, those pairs have on average a lower ranking) than the mean of pairs that do not share a president (which would have a score of 50), proving the likelihood of the president's involvement in drafting these awards. This score is also slightly lower when it comes to the substantial part of the award. This role is, however, never as clear as that of ICJ judges in their individual opinions (as seen above), but this is not surprising given the higher potential number of quills involved in drafting an award compared to an individual opinion.

Table 20.1 *Proximity scores of sections of awards and decisions, ranked, in per cent*

Section(s)	President	Secretaries		Assistants
		ICSID	Others	
Introduction + Procedure	40	46	42	38
Facts	40.8	53	36	41.6
Arguments	41	49	38	35
Substance	39	48	46	42

In this respect, it bears repeating that it is common that co-arbitrators participate in the drafting of decisions.[107]

What is really striking, however, are the consistently lower scores of assistants and non-ICSID institutional secretaries (as opposed to ICSID secretaries), even when it comes to substantial parts of awards and decisions. Non-ICSID secretaries score, in turn, lower than assistants. This could mean that non-ICSID secretaries and assistants have, on average, an influence in drafting the decision, while ICSID secretaries are more aloof in this respect.[108] This result should not be over-interpreted, especially when contrasted with the scores of presidents: the sample of decisions that share an assistant is but a tiny share of all pair of decisions. But it is striking that this very small share exhibits the scores we could have expected – and even further than that, since substantial parts of awards display high similarity scores.

Meanwhile, the only part of awards where we see a very slight influence in cases sharing an institutional, ICSID secretary is, as expected, the procedural and introductory parts. This must be qualified (as all the numbers introduced in this part) by the fact that we are talking here of mean scores. Some institutional secretaries exhibit average individual proximity scores that resemble those of assistants; others are likely to have very little influence on a decision's wording.

---

[107] This also might explain why the average proximity scores of awards sharing a president is only marginally lower when it comes to substantial parts of awards: this is, arguably, the part where the co-arbitrators would be the most eager to participate, be it only because they might have more experience on a given legal point.

[108] This would comport with anecdotal evidence that indicates that ICSID secretaries do *revise* and *correct* awards and decisions: as Stylo()'s analysis relies on syntax – and not merely on vocabulary – whoever writes down the first draft would have more impact on the results, even if this draft is later amended lightly.

Yet, as explained above, it might be that institutional secretaries operate as default assistants (that is, their involvement and tasks increase when there is no assistant otherwise appointed). To check for this inference, I repeated the analysis over those cases that had no assistant at all, but only a secretary assigned by ICSID; there was no, or only a very slight variation in the scores recorded in Table 20.1, meaning that this theory (that the role of an institutional secretary is greater when they don't share it with an assistant) does not hold (although, once again, it is likely the case that many assistants are not recorded in the award, and the number of cases with only a secretary is hard to assess).

Before concluding this section, a last point needs to be strongly stressed: these analyses do not conclusively prove anyone's involvement, but offer clues and measures of likelihood. That the numbers comport (to an extent) with the initial assumptions and intuitions might mean that these are (partly) true; or that another mechanism is at play. The mean proximity score of awards sharing an assistant *might* be explained because presidents with assistants are much more active and take a larger part than usual in drafting awards, pushing the similarity scores between the decisions where assistants are recorded. Their style might also be more easily discernible in the corpus, compared to the less recognisable style of other arbitrators.

Yet, despite their limits, the data at least offer further support for what was mainly anecdotal observations before that: secretaries are likely to have a role in drafting investments awards and decisions, and the *Yukos* case was not necessarily an outlier in this respect. Given the issues involved in such likely participation of assistants in international dispute settlement, and absent any move to regulate it or make it more transparent, the increasing empirical evidence in this respect is likely to impact the legitimacy of international judgments and awards.

20.4.2   Alleged 'Streamlining' of Awards by the ICSID Secretariat

20.4.2.1   Introduction

The second problem is based on an intriguing, seemingly one-off opinion penned by an ad hoc committee member, Prof. Jan-Hendrik Dalhuisen, in 2012 in the second annulment proceedings concerning the long-running *Vivendi v. Argentina* case.[109] In this opinion, Prof. Dalhuisen fiercely criticised

---

[109] See above, note 83.

the ICSID Secretariat for attempting to 'involve itself in the drafting of the decisions'. The reason for this was, according to Prof. Dalhuisen, that the Secretariat was keen to ensure a greater coherence in case law, indeed a true '*jurisprudence constante*', by 'streamlin[ing]' the text drafted by the Committee.[110]

It is hard to assess the truth of these accusations, but this is not the first time the ICSID Secretariat allegedly used its influence to achieve a greater coherence of case law;[111] in the past, the Secretariat reappointed the same ad hoc committee members in different disputes.[112] Following Prof Dalhuisen's Opinion some stakeholders have sought further clarification from the Secretariat,[113] but whether there was any actual change in ICSID practice is unclear. Notably, however, several arbitrators and stakeholders have explained that Prof. Dalhuisen's comments did not reflect their own experience with ICSID,[114] further blurring the picture of the extent of ICSID's alleged meddling in the arbitration and annulments it oversees.

20.4.2.2   Methodology

Not all investment awards pass through the hands of ICSID's Secretariat, allowing us to investigate to some extent the phenomenon. The extent to which ICSID-based decisions and awards differ, in any significant respect, from the ones rendered under UNCITRAL Rules with no link with ICSID

---

[110] Ibid., at §9. One particular criticism raised in this respect was that the Secretariat's requests and attempts at intervening were mostly informal: Prof. Dalhuisen left a role open for the Secretariat to spot 'clear mistakes or oversight', but then communication from the Secretariat should take a more formal form.

    Prof. Dalhuisen also noted that, when it comes to delegating part of the drafting, the task might be better entrusted to an assistant chosen by the tribunal itself, rather than to the Secretariat.

[111] This discussion does not take a side on whether such coherence is welcome, although it might be in line with the wishes of the parties (state parties, notably). Indeed, hopes for a more coherent jurisprudence can often be witnessed in the mooted propositions of an International Investment Tribunal and/or an Appellate Body. Yet, as noted above in Section 20.3, the issue of legitimacy in these matters – and notably of deciding what shape the jurisprudence should take – is strongly related to the ability to identify easily and accurately the decision-maker.

[112] L.E. Peterson, 'ICSID Committee Confirms Egypt's Lack of Treaty Breaches in Hotel Dispute, but Takes Issue with Tribunal's Comment on Recourse to Local Courts', *IAReporter*, 2 July 2010, talking of a past 'unwritten policy' in this respect.

[113] L.E. Peterson, 'Argentina Calls for Discussion at Upcoming World Bank Meeting Following Annulment Committee Member's Allegation of Meddling by ICSID Secretariat in Annulment Process' *IAReporter*, 15 September 2010.

[114] Ibid.

whatsoever (thus excluding those UNCITRAL-rules arbitrations that are indeed conducted with ICSID's Additional Facility) might offer a key to the question prompted by Prof. Dalhuisen's opinion – providing that other arbitral institutions do not, themselves, engage in a similar streamlining exercise. The analysis focuses on 297 ICSID-arbitration decisions against 93 non-ICSID-arbitration ones.[115]

If ICSID's Secretariat really tried to 'streamline' the language of awards, this might mean two things: (i) that the Secretariat seeks a coherence between the decisions taken in the cases it oversees and other investment decisions, and then merely tries to remedy the arbitrators' idiosyncrasies; or rather (ii) that it is developing its own 'investment-arbitration' language, concepts, terms, etc., making it distinct from non-ICSID awards (unless those try later to follow ICSID's choices).[116]

If (i) is right, then ICSID awards should display a greater coherence compared to non-ICSID awards where such 'streamlining' does not take place. We could expect a greater variation between proximity scores of non-ICSID awards, as embodied in the set of scores' standard deviations.

As for (ii), if ICSID and non-ICSID awards differed to some extent in their choice of 'investment-arbitration' language, then ICSID awards and decisions should be marginally closer stylistically, and thus systematically closer in terms of network analysis. In this respect, 'assortativity' (or *homophily*) is the measure of how well a common characteristic predicts the proximity between nodes in a network:[117] tested with the condition 'ICSID or non-ICSID', the assortativity score will indicate how much closer ICSID decisions are to each other.

20.4.2.3   Findings

Starting with the variation between cases (i), the average standard deviations in proximity scores (obtained following the method of Section 20.4.1) was compared for pairs of awards belonging to the same group (ICSID or non-ICSID).

---

[115] Annulment decisions are not treated because they have no equivalent under non-ICSID rules or proceedings. Although it is possible that ICSID's alleged interventions would be more naturally directed at annulment proceedings, the comments of Prof. Dalhuisen concerned all phases of ICSID arbitrations.

[116] Of course, a third possibility is that ICSID's alleged actions resort to both categories in turn, depending on the awards and the terms used.

[117] See M. Newman, 'The Structure and Function of Complex Networks', at 16, available at https://arxiv.org/pdf/cond-mat/0303516.pdf.

By contrast with the analysis performed in Section 20.4.1, the focus is not on the style of a given presumed author(s), but on how much these styles vary within one group, the (challengeable) assumption being that arbitrators are roughly the same in both groups of decisions, and that therefore there should not be too much of a difference in the average proximity scores of the two sets (indeed, the mean proximity scores of all ICSID pairs and of all non-ICSID pairs does not depart much from the mean proximity scores of all pairs).

In this respect, there is some evidence that ICSID decisions are slightly more likely to differ stylistically between themselves, over the full text of the decisions, than are non-ICSID decisions (or the whole set of decisions)[118] – bearing in mind that there are three times more ICSID decisions in the dataset. The results are similar, but still likely to be statistically insignificant, when only the parts of the decisions dealing with substantial issues substance are considered.[119]

Turning to the second hypothesis,[120] a network of 508 full-text investment awards and decisions similar to those built above[121] displays an assortativity score of 0.16 – which means that the fact that two decisions are both ICSID and non-ICSID has some bearing on the probability of them being linked together in the network (assortativity varies between 0 and 1, with the latter occurring when all nodes are connected with each other). Albeit slight, this is higher that the assortativity score associated with presidents of tribunals (0.07) for the same network.

Overall, however, these results are not enough to conclude in one way or the other that the Secretariat is (or has been) engaged in a systematic 'streamlining' of awards' language. The weak signals in this direction might be no more than the expected similarity between decisions rendered under the same framework,[122] and not the evidence of a heavy,

---

[118] Standard Deviations: all awards (100); ICSID (101.1); non-ICSID (99.2).

[119] Standard Deviations: all awards (100); ICSID (101.7); non-ICSID (97.4).

[120] A second way to check the distinction between ICSID and non-ICSID decisions is by looking at the most frequent words (MFW) used by the tribunals in the two sets of decisions. According to the results, at any given number of MFWs considered, the two corpora share around three-quarters of the MFWs – indicating that all these decisions share a common vocabulary to a significant extent. The symmetric difference between the two sets (that is, the words that appear in one of the two sets but not both) mostly includes words typical to one dispute ('Venezuela', 'Perenco'), and seemingly no word that would indicate stark divergences in investment-law lexicology.

[121] That is, with Stylo() creating directly the 'Nodes' and 'Edges' files for Gephi.

[122] For instance, there is no such thing as a 'provisional,' or 'Partial' award in the ICSID context, whereas they are common outside this context.

streamlining hand. At most, they would indicate that, if the ICSID's Secretariat does (or did) attempt to do such a thing, it is not obviously perceptible in the data and might operate in a subtle manner. (This does not, however, discard the possibility that comparisons following other methods might reveal a different picture.)

20.5   Conclusion

The broad assumption underlying this chapter is the following: if the 'hidden actors' of international dispute settlement cannot be seen, it does not mean they cannot be heard. As the two analyses in Section 20.4 tried to demonstrate, their presence can be detected – to an extent – in the text produced in the process of rendering justice. More sophisticated analyses could go further and pinpoint with greater certainty what part of any given decision should be attributed to whom, or what words, meaning, expressions or legal grammar seem to have been superimposed on the text by an eager 'streamlining' force. In this respect, the constant improvement of empirical tools and methods and their ever-broader diffusion in the community of legal scholars are pushing us closer to a situation where these actors will no longer be hidden – with implications for tribunals' legitimacy.[123]

Hidden actors (at least in the realm of investment arbitration) have thus some degree of (covert) influence in the way international decisions are being written,[124] and then some degree of power. As observed in Section 20.3, this influence entails consequences for the legitimacy of the eventual awards and judgments, if not for the entire system of international arbitration and litigation. The participation of those hidden actors in deciding a case can therefore be used as a weapon by a disappointed party to challenge the legitimacy of a dispute's outcome, and an increasing number of disputes, such as those surrounding the fate of the *Yukos* or *Gazprom* awards, bear witness to this conclusion.

As this chapter has demonstrated, these incidents are unlikely to be isolated instances, and absent some significant changes to the way tribunals and parties deal with the role of these hidden actors, this threat to the legitimacy of international awards and judgments will remain – if not

---

[123] See Section 20.3 above.

[124] Although the role of ICSID itself in 'streamlining' awards cannot be proven at that point, some ICSID secretaries are likely to have an input in drafting awards, at least with respect to the procedural sections.

increase – as methods to detect the influence of secretaries and assistants improve. As such, the solution might lie in proactively increasing the level of transparency related to the conduct of these actors,[125] and thereby, hopefully, the legitimacy of their role.

---

[125] See Maynard, 'Laying the Fourth Arbitrator to Rest', who does, however, also warn against *too much* transparency.

PART V

Ethics and Accountability

Physicians' Impact on the Legitimacy of the International Criminal Court

GIOVANNA MARIA FRISSO

21.1 Introduction

Writing about the judiciary, Voermans asserts that its authority and legitimacy are no longer self-evident in democratic states.[1] Nowadays, the independent role of a judge as an arbiter operating under the rule of law seems insufficient to ensure the judiciary's legitimacy. Transparency, openness, efficiency, and new forms of interaction between politics and the law have been considered more essential in current debates.[2] The authority of international criminal tribunals, nonetheless, has never been self-evident and their legitimacy has been questioned in light of their wide-ranging and sometimes concurrent objectives. They have embraced goals usually related to punishment: retribution, deterrence, incapacitation, and rehabilitation.[3] In addition, they have been attributed objectives such as promoting social reconciliation, giving victims a voice, or making a historical record of mass atrocities.[4] As such objectives are better achieved through the trial procedure, the emphasis has shifted from punishment to trials in international criminal tribunals.[5]

---

[1] Wim Voermans, 'Judicial Transparency Furthering Public Accountability for New Judiciaries' (2007) 1 *Utrecht Law Review* 3, 148.
[2] Gar Yein Ng, 'Quality of Judicial Organisation and Checks and Balances', unpublished PhD thesis, University of Utrecht (2007), p. 17.
[3] David Luban, 'Fairness to Rightness: Jurisdiction, Legality and the Legitimacy of International Criminal Law', in Samantha Besson and John Tasioulas (eds.), *The Philosophy of International Law* (Oxford University Press, 2010), p. 575.
[4] Ibid. See also: Eric Stover, *The Witnesses: War Crimes and the Promise of Justice in The Hague* (University of Pennsylvania Press, 2007), p. 14; Mark Klamberg, 'What Are the Objectives of International Criminal Procedure? Reflections on the Fragmentation of a Legal Regime' (2010) 79 *Nordic Journal of International Law* 279.
[5] Luban, 'Fairness to Rightness', p. 575.

Therefore, the debates about the legitimacy of international criminal tribunals have concentrated on the fairness of their proceedings to their main stakeholders: the defence, the prosecutor, and the judge. Nonetheless, there are many other actors whose conduct can interfere with the overall legitimacy of an international criminal tribunal. This chapter is concerned with the involvement of physicians in international criminal trials and, consequently, the impact of the interplay between law and medicine on the legitimacy of international criminal tribunals. Within the context of international criminal trials, the debate on this interplay reached one of its climaxes on 11 March 2006, when Slobodan Milošević, the former Yugoslav president, was found dead in his prison cell while being tried at the International Criminal Tribunal for the former Yugoslavia (ICTY). The impact of a defendant's health on the proceedings has been discussed in various international criminal tribunals, such as the International Tribunal for Rwanda,[6] the Extraordinary Chambers in the Courts of Cambodia,[7] the Special Tribunal for Sierra Leone[8] and the International Criminal Court (ICC).[9]

This chapter focuses on the ICC, as the only international criminal tribunal whose rules specifically provide for physician-patient privilege,[10] acknowledging that medical information might become relevant during the criminal procedure. In particular, this chapter focuses on aspects directly related to a defendant's health and their effect on the ICC's legitimacy.[11] Three cases are relevant for this analysis: *Prosecutor v. Bosco Ntaganda*, *Prosecutor v. Laurent Gbabgo* and *Prosecutor v. Dominic Ongwen*.[12] These cases have highlighted that, during an international

---

[6] See, for instance, ICTR, *Prosecutor v. Rutaganda*, Case No. ICTR-96-3-T, Decision on the Request Filed by the Defence for Provisional Release of Georges Rutaganda, 7 February 1997; ICTR, *Prosecutor v. Karemera et al.* (ICTR-98-44-T), Decision on Remand Regarding Continuation of Trial, 10 September 2009.

[7] Spencer Cryder, *Implications of the Age and Health of the Charged Persons and Accused Before the Extraordinary Chambers in the Courts of Cambodia* (Documentation Center of Cambodia, 2009).

[8] SCSL, *Prosecutor v. Sankoh*, Case No. SCSL-03-02-PT, Ruling on the Motion for a Stay of Proceedings Filed by the Applicant, 22 July 2003.

[9] Ian Freckelton and Magda Karagiannakis, 'Fitness to Stand Trial under International Criminal Law' (2014) 12 *Journal of International Criminal Justice* 707.

[10] The phrase *physician-patient privilege* embraces both physician-patient privilege and psychiatrist-patient privilege.

[11] The word *defendant* is used in this article to refer to both the suspect and the accused in the proceedings before the ICC.

[12] ICC, *Prosecutor v. Bosco Ntaganda*, Transcript, ICC-01/04-02/06-T-130-Red-ENG WT, 13 September 2016, pp. 4 and 8; ICC, *Prosecutor v. Dominic Ongwen*, Public Redacted Version of 'Defence Request for a Stay of the Proceedings and Examinations Pursuant to Rule 135

criminal trial, the involvement of physicians is, even if indirect, practically continuous, as the defendant usually remains detained during the trial. In the ICC, the continuous involvement of a physician is provided for in Regulation 104 of the Regulations of the Court (RoC), which stipulates that a qualified medical officer with experience in psychiatry and a nurse must be available at the detention centre, ensuring the defendant's right to health. The right to medical care of persons in detention is guaranteed under human rights law. The UN Human Rights Committee, for example, has indicated that the right to health of all detained persons is protected under Articles 6 and 7 of the International Covenant on Civil and Political Rights, which refer to the right to life and the prohibition of torture.[13]

The defendants' health is directly related to the possible administration of justice, as the meaningful exercise of defendants' fair trial rights requires not only their physical presence, but also their mental presence. In this context, the notion of fitness to stand trial gains particular relevance, as it is 'rooted in the idea that whenever the accused is, for reasons of ill health, unable to meaningfully exercise his or her procedural rights, the trial cannot be fair and criminal proceedings must be adjourned until the obstacle ceases to exist'.[14] By ensuring the defendants' health and, ultimately, their fitness to stand trial, Regulation 104 of the RoC creates a context in which the ICC Detention Unit (ICC DU) medical officer is committed to other objectives than the health of his or her patient.[15]

In the medical field, dual relationships have received a great deal of attention,[16] but in the legal context, the issue has raised far less debate, despite the lack of clear guidance.[17] This chapter argues that this lack of guidance is also felt in the ICC, posing great challenges to its legitimacy.

of the Rules of Procedure and Evidence', ICC-02/04-01/15-620-Red, 5 December 2016; ICC, *Prosecutor v. Laurent Gbagbo*, Version publique expurgée de la requête de la Défense en report de l'audience de confirmation des charges prévue le 18 juin 2012, ICC-02/11-01/11-140-Red, 7 June 2017.

[13] Human Rights Committee, 'Concluding Observations: Georgia' (2002) UN Doc A/57/40, vol. I, 53, para. 78(7).

[14] ICC, *Prosecutor v. Laurent Gbagbo*, Decision on the fitness of Laurent Gbagbo to take part in the proceedings before this Court, ICC-02/11-01/11-286-Red, 20 November 2012, para. 43.

[15] International Dual Loyalty Working Group, *Dual Loyalty and Human Rights in Health Professional Practice* (2003). Available at: http://physiciansforhumanrights.org/library/reports/dual-loyalty-and-human-rights-2003.html.

[16] Sara G. Gordon, 'Crossing the Line: Daubert, Dual Roles, and the Admissibility of Forensic Mental Health Testimony' (2016) 37 *Cardozo Law Review* 1360.

[17] Ibid.

To develop this argument, the ICC's legitimacy is examined in light of Franck's work,[18] according to which legitimacy is related to the notions of determinacy, symbolic validation, coherence, and adherence.[19] Among these notions, this chapter will focus primarily on determinacy and coherence.[20] To Franck, determinacy relates to the enactment of clear messages and coherence relates to the degree to which a rule is applied consistently within the framework of the existing legal order. In this perspective, the ICC's legitimacy requires the clear and due application of procedural rules concerning the interactions between physicians, the parties, and the judges. The relevance of these aspects to the legitimacy of international courts has been acknowledged in the Oslo Recommendations for Enhancing the Legitimacy of International Courts, which outlines that 'judges should remain aware that producing well-reasoned judgments, based on the applicable law, remains their central role and the lynchpin of their institution's legitimacy'.[21]

To examine the impact that the relationship between law and medicine can have on the ICC's legitimacy, Section 21.2 introduces the regulation of patients' right to privacy. Section 21.3 explores the impact of the specific reference to physician-patient privilege on the interpretation of the defendant's right to privacy within the ICC framework. Section 21.4 suggests that a broader consideration of the views of the physicians involved in the proceedings could improve the reasoning in decisions that balance the confidentiality of medical information and the transparency of the proceedings, increasing the perceived fairness of the proceedings and the overall legitimacy of the ICC.

21.2   Patients' Privacy in International Criminal Trials

21.2.1   Patients' Privacy

Respect for patient privacy and confidentiality has been affirmed as a professional responsibility of physicians since antiquity. In the famous oath attributed to Hippocrates, ancient Greek physicians pledged to respect confidentiality in these words: 'What I may see or hear in the course of

---

[18] Thomas M. Franck, 'Legitimacy in the International System' (1988) 82 *American Journal of International Law* 705.
[19] Ibid., 712.
[20] Symbolic validation and adherence are not considered in this chapter.
[21] Brandeis Institute for International Judges, Oslo Recommendations for Enhancing the Legitimacy of International Courts, 26 July 2018, p. 2, para. B.

the treatment or even outside of the treatment in regard to the life of men, which on no account one must spread abroad, I will keep to myself, holding such things shameful to be spoken about.'[22] Nowadays, privacy and confidentiality are no less significant, and contemporary medical oaths continue to echo the Hippocratic principle of respect for confidentiality. One of the physicians' pledges as a member of the World Medical Association's Declaration of Geneva reads: 'I will respect the secrets which are confided in me, even after the patient has died.'[23]

Although privacy and confidentiality have overlapping meanings and are sometimes used synonymously, they are distinct concepts in medical ethics. Allen distinguishes four major usages of the term privacy: physical privacy, property privacy, decisional privacy, and informational privacy.[24] Physical privacy refers to freedom from contact with others or exposure of one's body to others.[25] In contemporary health care, physical privacy is unavoidably limited. Patients grant their carers access to their bodies for medical examination and treatment, but expect caregivers to protect them from any unnecessary or embarrassing bodily contact or exposure. Proprietary privacy embraces concerns related to the appropriation and ownership of 'a repository of personal identity',[26] such as patients' photographs and DNA. This notion of privacy mainly relates to developments in the field of medical research. Decisional privacy refers to 'the ability to make one's own decision and to act on those decisions free from governmental or other unwanted interference.'[27] Decisional privacy is closely linked to the principle of respect for an individual's autonomy and the doctrine of informed consent to treatment.[28] Informational privacy refers to prevention of disclosure of personal information. This type of privacy is limited in health care by the need to communicate information about one's condition and medical history to one's caregivers. In disclosing this information, however, patients expect that access to it will be

[22] John C. Moskop, C. Marco, G. Larkin, J. Geierman and A. Derse, 'From Hippocrates to HIPAA: Privacy and Confidentiality in Emergency Medicine – Part I: Conceptual, Moral and Legal Foundations' (2005) 4 *Annals of Emergency Medicine* 1, 53.
[23] World Medical Association. Declaration of Geneva, in Stephen G. Post (ed.), *Encyclopedia of Bioethics*, vol. 5 (Macmillan, 1995), pp. 2646–2647.
[24] Anita Allen, 'Privacy in Healthcare', in Stephen G. Post (ed.), *Encyclopedia of Bioethics*, vol. 4 (Macmillan, 1995), p. 2120.
[25] Ibid., 2121.
[26] Ibid.
[27] Ibid., 2222.
[28] Moskop et al., From Hippocrates to HIPAA, 54.

carefully restricted. This use of the term 'privacy' is most closely related to the concept of confidentiality.[29]

Despite its relevance, confidentiality is not an absolute principle. There are circumstances in which exceptions do and ought to exist. Within the legal framework, the duty of confidentiality is related to the notion of privileged communications. The regulation of privileged communications by the Rules of Procedure and Evidence (RPE) of international criminal tribunals has been dealt with in a variety of ways. The following subsection compares the RPEs of the ICTY and the ICC.

21.2.2   Patients' Privacy in International Criminal Tribunals

The ICTY's normative framework has not specifically addressed physician-patient confidentiality. Nonetheless, the ICTY's RPE contain several provisions relating to non-disclosure of certain information. Rule 53(A) states that 'in exceptional circumstances, a Judge or a Trial Chamber may, in the interests of justice, order the non-disclosure to the public of any documents or information until further order'. Rule 70(d) provides that 'if the Prosecutor calls a witness to introduce in evidence any information provided under this Rule, the Trial Chamber *may not compel* that witness to answer any question relating to the information or its origin, if the witness declines to answer *on grounds of confidentiality*'. The only privileged communications recognized by the ICTY's RPE are those made in the context of the professional relationship between a person and his or her legal counsel. In accordance with ICTY Rule 97, these communications cannot be the subject of a disclosure order unless '(i) the client consents to such disclosure; or (ii) the client has voluntarily disclosed the content of the communication to a third party, and that third party then gives evidence of that disclosure'.

Lacking a specific rule on physician-patient privilege, the ICTY was confronted with the issue of medical privilege in *Prosecutor v. Furundžija*. In *Furundžija*, a women's therapy centre in Bosnia was subpoenaed to disclose the medical records of prosecution Witness A.[30] The Trial Chamber also ordered the proceedings to be reopened to allow the defence to recall prosecution Witness A for cross-examination strictly on any medical,

---

[29] Ibid.
[30] ICTY, *Prosecutor v. Furundžija*, Case No. IT-95-17/1-T, Decision, 16 July 1998, para. 18.

professional, or psychiatric treatment or counselling received and ordered the prosecution to disclose any other documents in its possession relating to the certificate and relevant to Witness A's treatment.[31] The decision was questioned in light of the problems and prejudices facing women who are victims of sexual violence, and also the need to enhance the protection afforded to counselling relationships.[32] In this regard, Patricia Wald, a former ICTY Judge, remarked:

> This seems paradoxical in view of the special protections afforded rape and sexual abuse victims in the Tribunal rule which excludes evidence of past sexual conduct rules out the need for corroboration of the victim's testimony and severely circumscribes the occasions on which the defense of consent can be used … Because witnesses are so vital to the success of any international criminal tribunal, we must be scrupulously protective of their rights, as well as the rights of the accused.[33]

The privilege for communications between physicians and defendants has also arisen before the ICTY. Rule 74 *bis* of the ICTY provides that 'a Trial Chamber may, *propio motu* or at the request of a party, order a medical, psychiatric or psychological examination of the accused'. The ICTY has generally allowed the parties to have access to defendants' medical information when issues related to their fitness to stand trial are raised. In *Prosecutor v. Jovica Stanišić*, for instance, the ICTY Trial Chamber held that transparent medical reporting should not unnecessarily encroach on the privacy rights of the accused or third persons.[34] Nonetheless, redactions of medical reports were only considered in relation to the public, maintaining the full information available to the parties and the Chamber.[35] The ability of the public to examine how the reasoning followed by the parties as well as the Chamber was limited by the redactions, restricting the scope of possible contributions to a consistent

---

[31] Ibid., para. 19.
[32] See ICTY, *Prosecutor v. Furundžija*, Case No. IT-95-17/1-T, Amicus Curiae Brief Respecting the Decision and Order of the Tribunal of 16 July 1998 requesting that the Tribunal Reconsider its Decisions having regard to the Rights of Witness A to Equality, Privacy and Security of the Person and to Representation by Counsel.
[33] Patricia M. Wald, 'The International Criminal Tribunal for the Former Yugoslavia Comes of Age: Some Observations on Day-To-Day Dilemmas of an International Court' (2001) 5 *Journal of Law & Policy* 113.
[34] ICTY, *Prosecutor v. Jovica Stanišić and Simatović*, IT-03-69-T, Decision on Urgent Defence Request for Further Submission of Psychiatric Medical Expert and Decision on Defence Motion to Redact Medical Reports, 6 July 2009.
[35] Ibid.

and clear development of the notion of fitness to stand trial by the overall public, including doctors and lawyers.

ICC Rule 73(1) contains the same provision on lawyer-client privilege as found in the Rules of the ad hoc criminal tribunals. Rule 82(3) reiterates that the ICC's Trial Chamber may not compel a person to testify about a privileged communication. Unlike the ad hoc tribunals, ICC Rule 73(3) expressly recognizes the confidentiality of communications between patients and their doctors, establishing both physician-patient and psychiatrist-patient privileges.[36] As with lawyer-client privilege, physician-patient privilege is not subject to disclosure unless the person consents to disclosure or voluntarily discloses the communications to a third person who in turn gives evidence.

Even though the ICC Rule seems to have been informed by the debate surrounding the decision in Prosecutor v. Furundžija related to a witness's medical record, it has provided for a clearer protection of the communications between defendants and their physicians. In the ICC, the scope of physician-patient privilege has been discussed primarily in relation to patients who are in the position of defendants in the legal proceedings. The establishment of physician-patient privilege in the ICC RPE acknowledges that defendants' health is best ensured when there is a relationship of trust between them and their physicians. The importance of this relationship to therapeutic treatment has been articulated as follows: 'patients who are aware that the information they disclose to a therapist might be later used in a legal proceeding are much more likely to self-censor and withhold damaging information from the therapist.'[37] This attitude could have a negative impact on the patient's further treatment[38] and, ultimately, on the trial.

To create an environment favourable to the development of a relationship of trust between the defendant and the ICC DU medical officer, Regulation 156 of the Regulations of the Registry (RoR) provides that the medical record of each detained person must be kept strictly confidential. The limitations to the confidentiality of the medical record stipulated in the RoR are related primarily to the medical care of the defendant. In this context, RoR 156(2) states that the medical record can be consulted by any medical staff directly involved in the detained person's treatment *without the express written consent of the detained person.* RoR 156(7)

---

[36] Further reference will be made only to physician-patient privilege.
[37] Gordon, 'Crossing the Line', 1369.
[38] Ibid.

provides that the 'medical officer shall inform the external medical practitioner about the health of the detained person. The medical officer shall also be informed of the findings of any external medical practitioner.'

Within the medical care framework, not only medical staff might have access to medical information related to a defendant. RoR 157(2), for instance, provides that if 'a detained person wishes to be visited by or consult an external medical practitioner but lacks the financial means to do so, he or she shall inform the Chief Custody Officer, who in turn shall inform the Registrar thereof'.[39] Another situation that might further limit the confidentiality of the detained person's medical record concerns possible conflicts between the ICC DU medical officer and the external medical practitioner. In this context, RoR 157(10) states that the Registrar and the Chief Custody Officer need to be informed by the ICC DU medical officer if he or she refuses to administer the treatment or medication prescribed by an external medical practitioner and the reasons for refusing it. The provision about the confidentiality of the medical record is, therefore, limited in light of the practical need to ensure the defendant's health and, ultimately, the administration of justice.

The interpretation of these provisions by the judges must not, in accordance with Rule 73(2), rely on 'national laws governing evidence, other than in accordance with Article 21' of the Rome Statute. This reference acknowledges the different forms through which privileged communications and confidentiality have been regulated domestically.[40] The different regulations of these topics might pose a problem to the ICC when granting privileged status to physician-patient communications, as Rule 73(2)(a) requires such communications to be made 'in the course of a confidential relationship producing a reasonable expectation of privacy and non-disclosure'. A reasonable expectation can be created by the laws of the state where the relationship takes place: a 'specific class of relationships may hold a 'reasonable expectation of privacy' in one state due to the fact that the law in that state protects that class of relationship,

---

[39] The sub-regulations of Regulation 157 indicate that the identification of a suitable external medical practitioner by the Registrar will follow a procedure similar to that of an expert. The selected medical doctor will go through a security check in accordance with sub-regulation 157(6) and be paid by the ICC. Information about the payment of the experts is available at www.icc-cpi.int/get-involved/Pages/Experts.aspx.

[40] For a comparison of different national standards see: Amanda J. White, 'Cognitive Abilities and Expert Assessment Practices in Fitness to Stand Trial Evaluations: An Australian Study Based on the Legal Standard of Presser', unpublished Master's dissertation, Macquarie University (2015).

while in another state the laws do not protect that class of relationships and therefore they do not produce a 'reasonable expectation of privacy'.[41]

Reference to Article 21 of the Rome Statute in Rule 73(2) brings to the fore the opportunity to explore these topics in light of the defendants' rights to privacy, to health, and to a fair trial. The first has been recognized in the ICC Rules, the last mentioned in the Rome Statute.[42] Even though the defendant's right to health has not been incorporated in the founding instruments of the ICC, the notion of fitness to stand trial, which is clearly related to defendants' right to health, has been viewed 'as an aspect of the broader notion of a fair trial'.[43] The right to health is, therefore, ensured by the recognition of defendants' right to a fair trial in the Rome Statute.

21.3   Coherence and Patients' Privacy in International Criminal Trials

Current debates about the legitimacy of the ICC have been dominated by procedural aspects.[44] In these debates, coherence is a relevant indicator of legitimacy in accordance with Franck.[45] When applied to the analysis of international judicial decisions, it requires 'that decisions are in some measure predictable in light of previous decisions because like cases are treated alike'.[46] When distinctions are made, 'they must themselves be explicable by reference to generally applied concepts of differentiation'.[47] In the ICC legal framework, coherence requires, for instance, that the application of a rule be connected with the Rome Statute, with previous applications of such a rule, and with the general principles underlying the rule's application and those implicated in other relevant rules. The following subsections will examine whether ICC decisions

---

[41] Notburga K. Calvo-Goller, *The Trial Proceedings of the International Criminal Court: ICTY and ICTR Precedents* (Brill, 2006), p. 261.

[42] ICC, *Prosecutor v. Laurent Gbagbo and Charles Blé Goudé,* Order to provide Appointed Expert with access to Mr Gbagbo's medical record, ICC-02/11-01/15–302, 20 October 2015, para. 17.

[43] ICC, *Prosecutor v. Laurent Gbagbo,* Decision on the fitness of Laurent Gbagbo to take part in the proceedings before this Court, ICC-02/11-01/11-286-Red, 20 November 2012, para. 43.

[44] Hitomi Takemura, 'Reconsidering the Meaning and Actuality of the Legitimacy of the International Criminal Court' (2012) 4 *Amsterdam Law Forum* 2, 8.

[45] Franck, 'Legitimacy in the International System'.

[46] Tullio Treves, 'Aspects of Legitimacy of Decisions of International Courts and Tribunals' (2017) 75 *Sequência*, 26, 26.

[47] Ibid.

have consistently dealt with defendants' consents and the differentiation between the roles attributed to the ICC DU medical officer and medical experts, promoting the overall predictability of the proceedings related to a defendant's health.

21.3.1   Coherence and the Defendants' Consent

Most ligation regarding the alleged poor health of a defendant and its legal consequences has taken place in *Prosecutor v. Laurent Gbagbo*. The initial assessment of Mr Gbagbo's health by a medical expert was requested during the pre-trial phase of the proceedings by his lawyer. Pre-Trial Chamber I considered the request in accordance with Rules 113 and 135.[48] Rule 113 states that the Chamber must 'consider the nature and purpose of the examination and *whether the person consents to the examination*'. It ensures the decisional privacy of the defendant, indicating that his or her consent to be examined needs to be considered by the judges. Even though Rule 135 provides for medical examination during the trial, Pre-Trial Chamber I understood that it is applicable during the pre-trial phase of the proceedings.[49] In accordance with Article 64(8)(a), which is referred to in Rule 135, 'the Trial Chamber shall satisfy itself that the accused understands the nature of the charges'.[50] Even though Rule 135 does not expressly refer to the consent of the defendant to be examined, Rule 135(1) refers to the conditions set out in Rule 113. Therefore, the overall normative framework of the ICC seems to provide for the decisional privacy of the defendant throughout the proceedings.

Mr Gbagbo's fitness to stand trial was raised again during the trial phase of the proceedings. Following a literal interpretation of Rule 113, Trial Chamber I stated that the consent of the defendant to be examined is not required.[51] This interpretation allows the ICC to deal with situations in which it is alleged that the health of the defendant impedes a fair trial,

[48] ICC, *Prosecutor v. Laurent Gbagbo*, Decision on the fitness of Laurent Gbagbo to take part in the proceedings before this Court, ICC-02/11-01/11-286-Red, 20 November 2012, para. 42.
[49] Ibid., para. 55.
[50] Sub-rule 135(4) provides that 'where the Trial Chamber is satisfied that the accused is unfit to stand trial, it shall order that the trial be adjourned. If necessary, the Trial Chamber may order further examinations of the accused. When the Trial Chamber is satisfied that the accused has become fit to stand trial, it shall proceed in accordance with rule 132.'
[51] ICC-02/11-01/15-206, Decision granting in part the Prosecution request for an examination of Mr Gbagbo pursuant to Rule 135 of the Rules and instructing the parties to file supplemental submissions concerning the selection of expert(s) 2015, para. 12.

but the defendant opposes being examined. It, nonetheless, might pose serious challenges to the legitimacy of the proceedings, as, acknowledged by Judge Schmitt, the accused cannot be compelled to participate in a psychiatric examination.[52] To achieve a more calibrated response, a more detailed analysis of each case and the broader normative framework is required. A consistent and reasonable application of Rule 113 needs, therefore, to be sought by the ICC.

Conducting a medical assessment without the defendant's consent might also present a challenge to the medical expert. Even though the medical literature acknowledges that a defendant's autonomy is restricted by loss of liberty and that the detention can affect his or her ability to make an informed choice, Wadee suggests that if a detainee refuses to be examined after having been informed of the consequences of his or her conduct, that decision should be respected.[53] The defendant's refusal to be examined might lead not only to different, but to contradictory medical and legal consequences, posing a risk to the ICC's ability to enforce a medical examination order. Without the development of convincing reasoning by the ICC, the achievement of a consistent approach to medical assessment might end up being restricted by the individual views and defence strategies of each defendant.

Another aspect that requires further analysis is the disclosure of the defendant's medical record kept by the ICC DU medical officer. In *Prosecutor v. Laurent Gbagbo,* the decisional privacy of the defendant was restricted by the ICC, as Mr Gbagbo attempted to limit the access of Mr Lamothe, the expert who considered him fit to stand trial at an earlier evaluation, to his medical record.[54] Trial Chamber I, nonetheless, ordered the disclosure of the medical record to Mr Lamothe so that he could fulfil the terms of his appointment as a medical expert.[55] As the

---

[52] ICC-02/04-01/15-902, para. 5. In this case, Mr Ongwen consented to be examined by experts approved, appointed, instructed, and paid for by the Chamber, but not by any expert retained by the prosecutor. Defence Response to the Prosecution Application to Conduct a Medical Examination on Mr Ongwen (ICC-02/04-01/15-860-Conf), ICC-02/04-01/15-883-Red (redacted version notified 21 June 2017).

[53] Shabbir Ahmed Wadee, 'Examination of Detainees' (2006) 24 *Continuing Medical Education* 2, 69.

[54] ICC, *Prosecutor v. Laurent Gbagbo and Charles Blé Goudé,* Notification par la Défense de l'absence de consentement de Laurent Gbagbo à ce que son dossier médical soit transmis à M. Lamothe ICC-02/11-01/15-285, 12 October 2015.

[55] ICC, *Prosecutor v. Laurent Gbagbo and Charles Blé Goudé,* Order to provide Appointed Expert with access to Mr Gbagbo's medical record, ICC-02/11-01/15-302, 20 October 2015, paras. 20, 21.

ICC DU medical officer is the person responsible for the medical record of the defendant, this decision puts that official in a difficult position, as he or she is compelled not only to disclose the defendant's medical record without the defendant's written consent, but also to do so against the defendant's expressed will, contrary to RoR 156, the only provision that regulates this issue in the normative framework of the ICC. Even if, from a strictly legal perspective, RoR 156 does not bind the judges, but the ICC DU medical officer, a decision not to apply it creates a context in which the relationship between the ICC DU medical officer and the defendant is marked by uncertainty and, therefore, cannot be fully transparent.

The disclosure of the medical records kept by the ICC DU medical officer has also been discussed in *Prosecutor v. Bosco Ntaganda*. In this case, the medical files relating to Mr Ntaganda's physical and mental health in the context of his hunger strike were provided to the Chamber and the defence without his written consent.[56] After this initial disclosure, the Registry pointed out that further disclosure would require the written consent of the defendant in accordance with RoR 156(2). In its file the Registry indicated the ICC DU medical officer's obligation towards his national deontological code as one of the reasons for requiring the written consent of the defendant.[57] The reference to the medical officer's national deontological code is particularly interesting when contrasted with Rule 73(2) that proscribes reliance on national law. The relationships between law and medicine as well as the ICC normative framework, national law, and medical ethics require, therefore, more attention.

Within the framework of the trial, the RoR regarding the confidentiality of the medical record provides exclusively for the relationship between physicians, the defendant, and the judges, disregarding other interested parties, including the defence. In *Prosecutor v. Dominic Ongwen*, the lack of a clear regulation regarding the disclosure of the medical record to the defence was brought to the fore. Believing that the ICC DU medical officer was hindering the defence's efforts to review Mr Ongwen's medical files, even though a waiver was signed by Mr Ongwen authorizing the

---

[56] ICC, *Prosecutor v. Bosco Ntaganda*, Decision on Defence request for independent medical evaluation and related matters, ICC-01/04-02/06-1598, 28 October 2016, para. 7.

[57] The Registry's observation was made on a confidential basis. The reference to the medical officer's national deontological code is found in ICC, *Prosecutor v. Bosco Ntaganda*, Decision on Defence request for independent medical evaluation and related matters, ICC-01/04-02/06-1598, 28 October 2016, para. 7.

release of these files to the defence, the defence emailed the Chamber.[58] The Chamber notified the defence that it had forwarded the email to the Registry to enable that body to fully resolve the matter. Only after this minimal interference by the Chamber was the defence made aware of alleged defects in Mr Ongwen's waiver with respect to the release of his medical records.[59] Any alleged unwillingness by the ICC DU medical officer to grant the defence access to the medical report might negatively impact not only the proceedings, which could be delayed, but also the trust relationship between the defendant and the medical officer, as the defendant might perceive the medical officer's action as an attempt to impede his or her legal claims. The Chamber's reliance on the ability of the Registry and the defence 'to liaise with each other to 'ensure the disclosure of relevant documents'[60] might not, therefore, be sufficient to ensure the development of a consistent approach regarding the disclosure of the medical records to the defence, due to the particularities of this type of document, the current lack of consistency in the ICC's jurisprudence, and the reduced accessibility to the discussion between the Registry and the defence.

21.3.2   Coherence and the Attributions of Medical Experts and the ICC DU Medical Officer

Despite the limitations imposed by the jurisprudence on the informational and decisional privacy of the defendants, the ICC has attempted to maintain an environment of trust between them and the ICC DU medical officer through the differentiation between the ICC DU physician, 'the treating doctor', and the experts, 'the reporting doctors'. In *Prosecutor v. Dominic Ongwen*, Judge Tarfusser authorized the visits to Mr Ongwen by the medical experts to take place in a confidential setting, without monitoring.[61] He stressed, nonetheless, that 'the purpose of these visits is ... to generate evidence that could eventually be disclosed to the parties and the Court and used in the proceedings'.[62] Judge Tarfusser's decision

---

[58] See reference to an email in ICC, *Prosecutor v. Dominic Ongwen,* Public Redacted Version of 'Defence Request for a Stay of the Proceedings and Examinations Pursuant to Rule 135 of the Rules of Procedure and Evidence', ICC-02/04-01/15-620-Red, 5 December 2016, paras. 21, 22.

[59] See reference to ICC-02/04-01/15-Conf-Exp, para. 12 in ibid., para. 31.

[60] Email from Pre-Trial Chamber II to Defence, 1 February 2016 at 16h24 CET, in ibid., para. 34.

[61] See reference to an email exchange in ibid., para. 15.

[62] Ibid.

was later confirmed by Trial Chamber IX,[63] which also decided not to grant privileged telephone conversations between Mr Ongwen and the medical expert for the purpose of seeking medical advice for his mental condition.[64] This situation illustrates the challenges that the differentiation between the ICC DU medical officer and the medical expert might present to the development of a coherent jurisprudence, as medical advice had been asked for from a medical expert, whose appointment by the court aimed at reporting on the impact of the medical conditions of Mr Ongwen on his ability to exercise his fair trial rights. It also questions the scope of the relationship between the defendant and the medical expert as well as the possible impact in the proceedings of preconceptions related to the role of doctors.

The attributions of the ICC DU medical officer and the medical expert have also failed to be clearly differentiated in *Prosecutor v. Bosco Ntaganda*. In this case, Trial Chamber VI relied on the evaluation of Dr Paulus Falke, the ICC DU medical officer, to continue with the trial. The ICC DU medical officer stated that Mr Ntaganda showed fatigue, 'due to the ongoing voluntary protest fast and due to the psychological stress'.[65] Despite that, Dr Falke concluded that Mr Ntaganda was 'fit for transport and fit to attend Court'.[66] There are, therefore, situations in which the ICC DU medical officer might be asked to report to the judges. Nonetheless, this kind of involvement of the ICC DU medical officer is neither specifically provided for in the normative instruments of the ICC nor justified in the jurisprudence, leaving the basis of its legitimacy unclear. Additionally, the scope of the contribution of the ICC DU medical officer to the ICC becomes imprecise. From the ICC DU medical officer's perspective, the delivery of a forensic assessment of the defendant can lead to an ethical dilemma, as its legal outcome might impinge on the physician's ethical obligation to do no harm to the patient. His forensic assessment might, therefore, compromise the trust relationship between the ICC DU medical officer and the defendant and, ultimately, the defendant's right to health.

The differentiation between the roles of the ICC DU medical officer and the medical expert is further complicated by their expected attributes.

---

[63] Ibid.
[64] See reference to ICC-02/04-01/15-450-Conf, para. 8, in ibid., para. 18.
[65] ICC, *Prosecutor v. Bosco Ntaganda*, Transcript, ICC-01/04-02/06-T-134-Red-ENG, 18 September 2016, p. 7.
[66] Ibid.

The defence of Mr Gbagbo, for instance, stressed the importance of a relationship of trust between the defendant and any expert appointed.[67] This position could reinforce a context of dual relationships, allowing a forensic assessment of a defendant's health to be asked for from the ICC DU medical officer. In addition to the ICC DU medical officer's relationship of trust with the concerned defendant, that official's ability to quickly produce a report and the reduction of the costs related to hiring an expert could further promote this practice. This choice, nonetheless, presents various risks to the legitimacy of the court proceedings:

> Testimony arising out of dual relationships causes harm to the patient by subjecting her to potentially negative legal outcomes, and to the therapeutic relationship by impairing the patient's trust in the therapist. Furthermore, this type of dual relationship creates a conflict of interest for the clinician. This conflict may render the clinician unable to eliminate bias from her judgment, bias that may ultimately make her an unreliable witness.[68]

It is essential to have a broader understanding of the challenges that the dual relationship characterizing the work of the ICC DU medical officer presents to the defendant's right to a fair trial, his health, and the overall legitimacy of the proceedings before the ICC. For this purpose, the ICC could benefit from a broader interaction with physicians, which could facilitate a consistent approach to the disclosure of medical records and the stipulation of clear attributions to the ICC DU medical officer and the medical experts. The following section focuses on the medical experts.

21.4   Ensuring the Determinacy of the Decisions Informed by Physicians' Reports in the Trial

Determinacy, according to Franck, concerns 'the ability of a text to convey a clear message.'[69] As Treves stated, 'decisions of international courts and tribunals may fail this test if their operative part is unclear, avoids answering the questions addressed to the adjudicating body or if the reasons given are difficult to understand or may be subject to different interpretations'.[70] The overall legitimacy of decisions concerning the legal

---

[67] ICC, *Prosecutor v. Laurent Gbagbo and Charles Blé Goudé*, Order to conduct an examination of Mr Gbagbo under Rule 135 of the Rules, ICC-02/11-01/15–253, 30 September 2015, para. 8.
[68] Gordon, 'Crossing the Line', 1366.
[69] Franck, 'Legitimacy in the International System', 713.
[70] Treves, 'Aspects of Legitimacy', 25.

impact of a defendant's health in the trial relates, therefore, to the comprehensibility for the parties, participants, and the public of a specific version of the facts and their proposed legal interpretation. For this purpose, the legal appropriation of the information provided by a medical report needs to be carefully explained by the ICC.

Franck has used determinacy to indicate, in particular, 'the clarity of the message transmitted ... to those at whom it is directed as a command'.[71] As various decisions related to a defendant's health enact an order not only to the parties, but also to the ICC DU medical officer or medical expert, the message needs to be clear to all of them. The relevant physician needs to know precisely what is expected of him or her and how the principles of confidentiality and transparency are balanced out in relation to his role. As the order might, in some cases, contradict medical ethics, it needs not only to be clear, but also to follow from a legal reasoning capable of persuading that physician. For this purpose, a broader engagement with medical knowledge might be required.

In relation to the medical experts, such engagement might be relevant to their selection. In the ICC, contrary to the procedure established at the ICTY, the judges, not the parties, appoint the experts. To Boas, this procedure has the potential to produce more trustworthy information than the adversarial procedure adopted by the ICTY.[72] To select the medical experts, the relevant Chamber considers the views of the parties and the suggestions of the Registry.[73] The submissions made by the Registry until now do not indicate whether the ICC DU medical officer's views have been asked for and considered during this process. Nonetheless, the ICC DU medical officer might be one of the most suitable officers in the ICC to assist with this task due to his or her specialized knowledge. The ICC DU medical officer could suggest medical specialties and training to be sought by the ICC or prioritized when selecting the candidates. His or her views could inform both the judges and the parties, facilitating their evaluation of the relevance of the experience of each candidate to that specific proceeding. The ICC DU medical officer could provide a transparent framework against which the appointments of experts by a relevant Chamber could be assessed.

---

[71] Franck, 'Legitimacy in the International System', 721.
[72] G. Boas, 'A Code of Evidence and Procedure for International Criminal Law: The Rules of the ICTY', in G. Boas and W.A. Schabas (eds.), *International Criminal Law Developments in the Case Law of the ICTY* (Martinus Nijhoff, 2003), p. 26.
[73] The consultation of the Registry is based on RoC 44(1). No provision requires the judges to consult the parties.

The relevance of a broader understanding of the medical field has indeed been felt in *Prosecutor v. Laurent Gbagbo*. In this case, Pre-Trial Chamber I appointed three experts 'to provide different types of expertise in light of their specific areas of competence, in the expectation that they would complement each other'.[74] Nonetheless, this expectation was not fulfilled, as the assessment led to different conclusions in relation to the impact of the post-traumatic stress disorder and the hospitalization syndrome suffered by Mr Gbagbo on his capacity to participate meaningfully in the proceedings. Dr Chuch and Dr Daunizeau concluded that the defendant was not fit to participate in the proceedings, whilst Dr Lamothe reached a different conclusion.[75] Pre-Trial Chamber I understood that Mr Gbagbo was fit to stand trial.[76] Nonetheless, the decision of Pre-Trial Chamber I did not address the relationship between the experts' different specialties nor the weight accorded to each of them. This clarification is particularly relevant in light of the jurisprudence of the ICTY, which has required doctors and experts to comment only with respect to issues that fall within their area of expertise[77] and indicated that a primary care physician's report and a medical specialist's report should not be accorded the same weight.[78] The silence of the Pre-Trial Chamber I opens the space for debates related to the overall weight given to the defendant's health in light of other procedural concerns, such as the extension of the trial.

Courts' assessment of expert testimony is an acknowledged challenge.[79] Divergence among experts intensifies this challenge, as not only will the expert medical reports need to be assessed, but also the reasons for following a specific view among various alternatives. In this context, the

---

[74] ICC, *Prosecutor v. Laurent Gbagbo*, Decision on the fitness of Laurent Gbagbo to take part in the proceedings before this Court, ICC-02/11-01/11-286-Red, 20 November 2012, para. 68.

[75] Ibid., para. 67.

[76] ICC, *Prosecutor v. Laurent Gbagbo*, Decision on the fitness of Laurent Gbagbo to take part in the proceedings before this Court, ICC-02/11-01/11-286-Red, 20 November 2012.

[77] ICTY, *Prosecutor v. Jovica Stanišić and Franko Simatović*, IT-03-69-PT, Decision on Prosecution Motion for Revocation of Jovica Stanišić's Provisional Release and Re-Assessment of his Health and Revocation of Franko Simatović's Provisional Release, 24 April 2009, para. 40; ICTY, *Prosecutor v. Popović et al.*, IT-05-88-T, Decision on Defence Rule 94 bis Notice regarding Prosecution Expert Witness Richard Butler, 19 September 2007, para. 30.

[78] ICTY. *Prosecutor v. Jovica Stanišić and Franko Simatović*, IT-03-69-PT, Decision on Start of Trial and Modalities for Trial, 29 May 2009, para. 20.

[79] See Melanie Klinkner, 'Forensic Science Expertise for International Criminal Proceedings: an Old Problem, a New Context and a Pragmatic Resolution' (2009) 13 *The International Journal of Evidence and Proof* 102.

judges might need to pay attention to the adequacy of the theories and techniques used by the experts as well as whether the physicians' testimonies reflected current medical thought and standards of care.[80] Their assessment of experts' testimonies should articulate arguments that would allow not only the parties, but also the experts whose views have not been followed and other interested physicians to understand the decision. For this purpose, the judges would benefit from an opportunity to explore how different medical specialties relate to each other and how they can contribute to the assessment of the legal impact of the defendant's health on his or her fair trial rights.

Another element that could contribute to the enactment of clearer decisions by the ICC regards the unambiguous design of the instructions and questions that will inform a defendant's health examination. The judges should ensure that the meaning of the capacities required by a defendant to stand trial and the standard for evaluation are understood by all experts.[81] It should be clear, for instance, whether the defendant's capacity to communicate with counsel embraces his or her ability to act in his or her own best interests or if the defendant needs only to be able to recount to counsel the necessary facts pertaining to the offence, so that counsel will then be able to present a proper defence. The existence of clear criteria would provide a common framework to the work of the experts and, consequently, to the judges' evaluation of the medical assessments produced.

The clarification of the meaning attributed to the capacities required by a defendant to stand trial would facilitate the analysis of the medical reports by the judges. In addition, it would allow the identification of possible biases within the medical field.[82] As explained by Gordon, 'in the criminal context, if a defendant is accused of a serious or heinous crime, this could evoke a strong negative emotional response in the mental

---

[80] Gordon, 'Crossing the Line', 1358.

[81] The lack of a common frame of reference was identified in *Prosecutor v. Strugar*. In this case, the ICTY noted that the defence expert applied incorrect standards to her diagnostic findings, examining the defendant under the misapprehension that English common law required that an accused fully comprehend the proceedings. This initial error led her to continue to measure other capacities at an excessively high standard. ICTY, *Prosecutor v. Strugar*, Case No. IT-01-42-T, Decision on the Defence Motion to Terminate Proceedings, 26 May 2004, para. 48.

[82] Virginia G. Cooper and Patricia A. Zapf, 'Predictor Variables in Competency to Stand Trial Decisions' (2003) 27 *Law and Human Behavior* 4; Klinkner, 'Forensic Science Expertise', 110.

health professional performing the forensic examination and bias any resulting testimony against the defendant'.[83] Even if there is a positive bias towards the defendant, the objectivity of the final forensic evaluation is affected. Such bias can only be identified if the criteria that inform the assessment of the defendant's health are clear. The broader availability of these criteria to the public could also contribute to the development of the notion of fitness to stand trial, as it would facilitate their scrutiny within the legal and medical fields. The contribution of the medical field to the development of the notion of fitness to stand trial is illustrated by the various tests that have informed the assessment made by medical experts of defendants' health[84] as well as the acknowledgement that some disorders might leave some capacities intact while seriously affecting others.[85]

A broader interaction with appointed medical experts might also facilitate the communication between the parties, the judges, and the experts, creating an initial opportunity to deal with any language barrier. Writing in 1960, Broderick stated that 'the language barrier between the lawyer and the psychiatrist is a serious one in the trial of a case'.[86] There is, he continued, the problem of translating medical jargon into plain English. In this regard, the Australian Medical Association Ethical Guidelines for Doctors Acting as Medical Witnesses state that the medical expert should 'use simple terms wherever possible and explain technical terms or jargon'.[87] The Guidelines continue:

> your advice and evidence will be used to assist the determination of the medical and legal position by people who are not medically qualified … Your report should be clear and explained in lay terminology, with explanations provided for any medical abbreviations, technical terms or processes referred to.[88]

Nowadays forensic physicians are expected to know legal definitions, policies, procedures, and precedents and to possess an ability to communicate their findings clearly and to be able to do so under the difficult situation

---

[83] Gordon, 'Crossing the Line', 1379.
[84] Freckelton and Karagiannakis indicate the need to rely on well-regarded psychometric instruments as well as neuropsychological assessments. Freckelton and Karagiannakis, 'Fitness to Stand Trial', 727.
[85] Ibid., 726.
[86] John J. Broderick, 'Role of the Psychiatrist and Psychiatric Testimony in Civil and Criminal Trials' (1960) 35 Notre Dame Law Review 4, 518.
[87] Australian Medical Association, Ethical Guidelines for Doctors Acting as Medical Witnesses (2011), guideline 6.5.
[88] Ibid.

of cross-examination.[89] Nonetheless, this expected previous knowledge might not be suitable in the case of the ICC, as the ICC encompasses features of both common and civil law and, as a recent institution, it is still establishing its jurisprudential precedents in this area. In this context, both the judges and the parties need to be attentive to the possible impact that a physician's previous legal knowledge and experience might have on the medical assessment of a defendant. Furthermore, one might consider the challenges of translating not only medical jargon into plain English, but also legal and medical jargon into a language understood by all and, in particular, the defendant.

A broader interaction with the medical field might also contribute to a more consistent application of the physician-patient privilege provision by the ICC as it can assist in the adoption of measures aimed at ensuring that the defendant clearly understands the different roles attributed to the ICC DU medical doctor, medical experts, and other practitioners. It is crucial that defendants comprehend that the expert is required to objectively evaluate the impact of their health conditions on their ability to meaningfully exercise their right to a fair trial. Therefore, the expert is in no position to reassure them on matters of confidentiality or privacy. Additionally, the expert's findings might endanger the defendants' legal strategies. Actually, the experts themselves have to have a precise understanding of their role in the proceedings and the limitations that such role imposes on their overall position as a doctor.

As demonstrated by a study from 2003,[90] it might not be reasonable to expect that a defendant understands the notion of confidentiality and its limits. More importantly, it cannot be assumed that a defendant can clearly distinguish between the ICC DU medical officer and the medical expert in terms of their right to confidentiality and privilege. The case of *Prosecutor v. Dominic Ongwen* illustrates this risk, as Ongwen asked the expert, appointed by the judges, for clinical advice. The due respect for the rights of the defendant requires that efforts to breach the general assumption that the practice of medicine is meant to serve only the needs of the patient are made by, at least, the defence, the medical experts, and the judges. This joined endeavour has to further consider that the defendants are in a vulnerable situation and under a great deal of stress.

---

[89] Julio Arbodela-Florez, 'Forensic Psychiatry: Contemporary Scope, Challenges and Controversies' (2006) 5 *World Psychiatry* 2, 89.

[90] Pamela Sankar et al., 'Patient Perspectives of Medical Confidentiality: A Review of the Literature' (2003) 18(8) *Journal of General Internal Medicine* 660.

21.5   Conclusion

The analysis of ICC jurisprudence indicates the existence of significant room for conflict within the legal framework created to regulate the role of physicians during the trial. This conflict can be perceived in the indeterminacy of ICC decisions as well as in the lack of a consistent application of various provisions related to the evaluation of a defendant's health. Indeterminacy and inconsistency affect the overall legitimacy of the ICC. They limit predictability, as they create a context in which conflicting views coexist about what is expected from a physician. As a result, the physician can become an actor whose actions instead of contributing to the administration of justice can end up raising different legitimacy concerns.

As dual relationships have not received a great degree of attention in the legal field, a lack of coherence and determinacy in the provisions that regulate the relationship between medicine and law and in the jurisprudence of the ICC could be expected. This context does not mean that the ICC's legal framework and the decisions examined in this chapter are illegal. It, nonetheless, indicates an area that deserves more attention, as it infringes directly on the right to fair trial and, ultimately, on defendants' right to health. It is, therefore, worth nourishing the notions of determinacy and consistency.

To do so, this chapter has argued that a broader understanding of the medical field and ethics is necessary. It has suggested that physicians should have a greater degree of involvement in the proceedings before the ICC. Orders that do not refer to a defendant's medical information should be as accessible as possible to the public, allowing the discussion of the criteria that inform legal concepts such as fitness to stand trial as well as the definition of clearer boundaries between the role of the medical experts and the ICC DU medical office. Physicians' involvement could contribute not only to the enactment of clear decisions, but also to the development and maintenance of an environment that is favourable to a relationship of trust between the ICC DU medical officer and the defendant.

This chapter has also pointed out that the coherence and determinacy of the decisions related to the attributions of the ICC DU medical officer require a clearer understanding of the challenges posed by the notion of dual relationships and their impact on the principles of transparency and confidentiality. As these principles also inform medical practice, it is important to have a broader understanding of their relationship, an understanding that takes into account the medical context.

Such an understanding would allow the ICC to expand on the reasons why, on certain occasions, the ICC DU medical officer might need to state whether a defendant is capable of attending trial and, on other occasions, why that official's view is not required, providing a more precise indication of what can be expected by different stakeholders from the ICC DU medical officer.

The reasoning of the ICC should, therefore, be attentive not only to the relationship between the ICC DU medical officer and the ICC, but also to his or her relationship with the defendants and the long-term consequences of its decisions. Similarly, the due consideration of the relationship between the ICC DU and the defendants would facilitate the design of a procedure related to the disclosure of the medical records that would not violate medical ethics or current regulations, allowing for a greater degree of consistency.

Input from medical experts could also contribute to the analysis of the medical reports by the ICC. They could provide information regarding the various medical specialties that can inform the assessment of a defendant's health as well as how they relate to each other. This information could contribute to the enactment of clearer decisions when opposing expert reports have to be considered. They could also draw attention to the most recent developments in the medical field that have a direct impact on the notion of fitness to stand trial. In particular, the broader involvement of the medical experts could offer an opportunity to clarify the criteria that need to be assessed, allowing the ICC to establish clear guidelines for the medical assessment. The determinacy of the decisions that instruct the medical experts ensures that the work of all medical experts is equally valuable to the ICC. It also allows a more informed scrutiny of the medical reports, facilitating the identification of possible biases in the medical assessments.

Whilst a broader interaction between physicians and the ICC can take place during the proceedings, the ICC might also want to consider the discussion of specific issues in the abstract, in order to have an overall understanding of the medical issues that might become relevant. The views of the physicians should be taken into account, not only because they are the addressees of various orders, but also because they can contribute to the development of a procedure capable of safeguarding the defendants' rights during the trial. The establishment of clearer and more transparent interactions between physicians, the parties, and the judges has the potential to increase the consistency and determinacy of the ICC's decisions and, consequently, the overall legitimacy of the ICC.

22

Screening Powers in Investment Arbitration

Questions of Legal Change and Legitimacy

RELJA RADOVIĆ*

22.1 Introduction

The evolution of investment treaty arbitration has proved that the practice of investment tribunals is an important source of law.[1] This certainly applies to the jurisdictional framework governing that dispute resolution system. By virtue of their *compétence de la compétence* power, arbitrators create standards meant to guide the implementation of ambiguous treaty provisions pertaining to their jurisdiction. A crucial notion in such developments, which is placed at the heart of this chapter, is legal change. Many of the jurisdictional 'products' of arbitral practice have been seen as new, or unexpected.[2] Arbitral tribunals have become fora where demands for legal change regarding jurisdictional standards are advanced and sometimes enforced by virtue of an arbitral decision.

Such demands do not appear automatically before arbitrators. In one form or another, all the major arbitral institutions provide for mechanisms of administrative examination of requests initiating arbitrations. Some

---

* The author is grateful to Professor Freya Baetens, the editor of this volume, and to Johannes Hendrik Fahner for their comments on an earlier version of this chapter. This work is supported by the National Research Fund, Luxembourg.
[1] See generally, among many others, S.W. Schill, 'System-Building in Investment Treaty Arbitration and Lawmaking', in A. von Bogdandy and I. Venzke (eds.), *International Judicial Lawmaking. On Public Authority and Democratic Legitimation in Global Governance* (Springer, 2012), p. 133; A.K. Bjorklund, 'Investment Treaty Arbitral Decisions as *Jurisprudence Constante*', in C.B. Picker, I.D. Bunn and D.W. Arner (eds.), *International Economic Law: The State and Future of the Discipline* (Hart, 2008), p. 265; G. Kaufmann-Kohler, 'Arbitral Precedent: Dream, Necessity or Excuse?' (2007) 23 *Arbitration International* 357, 368–373.
[2] For example, the application of most-favoured-nation clauses to dispute resolution, arbitrating contract claims under broad jurisdictional treaty clauses, arbitrating treaty claims outside the scope of narrow jurisdictional clauses etc.

of them are set as regular 'screening' powers of secretariats over every request,[3] while others are conceptualised as exceptional powers and meant to be exercised very rarely.[4] Some mechanisms are not explicitly regulated, although factually they do exist.[5] This chapter will commonly refer to them as 'screening powers', because of their common feature of being exercised by administrative organs of arbitral institutions, disqualifying requests which do not satisfy certain minimum jurisdictional requirements.[6] Screening powers, however, carry prospective undesired effects beyond taking cases off the list in exceptional circumstances. Can they filter the demands for legal change that will be heard before tribunals? And can they impact future 'production' of arbitrator-made jurisdictional rules and standards? If so, is the legitimacy of screening powers somehow negatively affected?

This chapter argues that the answer to all these questions is affirmative. Although screening powers have been conceptualised with much caution so as not to limit the *compétence de la compétence* power of arbitral tribunals, they still offer possibilities of setting arbitrators' agenda in terms of which demands for legal change will be heard. The negative aspect of such possibilities is that some demands might end up disqualified without being considered by arbitral tribunals. This may affect the legitimacy of screening powers, but it does not mean that they have completely lost justification. Rather, screening powers must be exercised with an extreme level of diligence, requiring an almost complete elimination of legal considerations, in order to safeguard their legitimacy.

Section 22.2 of this chapter discusses the justifications of screening powers, their theoretical conflict with the powers of arbitral tribunals, and their increasingly adversarial character. Section 22.3 examines the applicable standards in screening procedures and the risk of censorship towards demands for legal change. Section 22.4 concludes by discussing

---

[3] As under the framework of the International Centre for Settlement of Investment Disputes ('ICSID').
[4] As under the auspices of the International Chamber of Commerce ('ICC') and Stockholm Chamber of Commerce ('SCC').
[5] As within the framework of the Permanent Court of Arbitration ('PCA').
[6] Screening powers of these various institutions have also been compared in the past: A.R. Parra, 'The Screening Power of the ICSID Secretary-General' (1985) 2 *News from ICSID* 10, 10–11; A.R. Parra, 'Provisions on the Settlement of Investment Disputes in Modern Investment Laws, Bilateral Investment Treaties and Multilateral Instruments on Investment' (1997) 12 *ICSID Review-FILJ* 287, 303–304.

whether this risk affects the legitimacy of screening powers of arbitral institutions, and how these powers should be exercised to safeguard their justifications.

22.2   Problematizing Screening Powers

The term 'screening powers' is commonly associated with the ICSID Convention, which instructs the ICSID Secretary-General to refuse to register a request for arbitration if 'the dispute is manifestly outside the jurisdiction of the Centre'.[7] Other notable fora for the settlement of investment disputes contain similar mechanisms. The Secretary General of the ICC International Court of Arbitration ('ICC Court') can refer a case to the ICC Court, which can decide to proceed with arbitration if it finds prima facie that an arbitration agreement may exist.[8] The Board of Directors of the Arbitration Institute of the Stockholm Chamber of Commerce ('SCC Board') may dismiss a case if 'the SCC manifestly lacks jurisdiction over the dispute'.[9] The PCA, on the other hand, does not provide for any similar procedure in its Arbitration Rules. Still, when acting as an appointing authority, or when designating one, it will check prima facie whether there is an arbitration agreement between the parties.[10] These powers have their rationales and justifications (Section 22.2.1). However, their use can bring administrative organs into a clash with arbitral tribunals (Section 22.2.2), particularly when the exercise of such powers is seen as another opportunity for addressing jurisdictional issues (Section 22.2.3).

---

[7] Art. 36(3) of the Convention on the Settlement of Investment Disputes Between States and Nationals of Other States, Washington DC, 18 March 1965, in force 14 October 1966, 575 UNTS 159 ('ICSID Convention') ('The Secretary-General shall register the request unless he finds, on the basis of the information contained in the request, that the dispute is manifestly outside the jurisdiction of the Centre'). See also Art. 6(1)(b) of the Rules of Procedure for the Institution of Conciliation and Arbitration Proceedings, in force 1 January 2003 ('ICSID Institution Rules').

[8] Art. 6(3)–(4) of the Rules of Arbitration of the International Chamber of Commerce, in force 1 March 2017 ('ICC Rules').

[9] Art 12(i) of the Arbitration Rules of the Arbitration Institute of the Stockholm Chamber of Commerce, in force 1 January 2017 ('SCC Rules'). The SCC Board takes its decision after obtaining a recommendation from the Secretariat: F. Mutis Tellez, 'Prima Facie Decisions on Jurisdiction of the Arbitration Institute of the Stockholm Chamber of Commerce: Towards Consolidation of a 'Pro Arbitration' Approach' (2013), p. 2, available at: www.sccinstitute .com/media/29996/felipe-mutis-tellez_paper-on-scc-challenges-on-jurisdiction.pdf.

[10] B. Daly, E. Goriatcheva and H. Meighen, A Guide to the PCA Arbitration Rules (Oxford University Press, 2014), pp. 23, 84.

22.2.1   *Justifying Screening Powers*

Screening powers are justified on multiple grounds. The central concerns that are observed within the ICSID framework are two-fold: avoiding the embarrassment of the non-consenting party, and saving resources when it is obvious that a case does not deserve to proceed.[11] It has been said that screening should ensure *bona fide* use of the ICSID mechanism,[12] and similar rationales have been advanced as regards other systems.[13] But these concerns are not as 'ethical' as they might seem at first. The under-lying rationales play primarily a protective role towards States as future respondents. The fact that a State is always the respondent to disputes brought under ICSID auspices has been invoked in defence of the man-datory nature and a high passing threshold of the screening process.[14] Safeguarding the consensual basis of international adjudication appears as the principal rationale behind the screening power within the ICSID system. Broches notes that the decision to confer the Secretary-General with the screening power was inspired by the wish to ensure that State consent to arbitration was secured prior to the establishment of a tribunal, which practically eliminated the possibility of basing jurisdiction on the *forum prorogatum* doctrine.[15] One concern was that investors could gain advantages from making the non-consenting State appear 'in an unfa-vorable light as having avoided by a mere technicality a decision on the merits of the case'.[16] The aim was to fortify the centrality of State consent as the basis of arbitral jurisdiction.

This conclusion is supported by the drafting history of the ICSID Convention. The introduction of the screening procedure was explained by fear of the negotiating States being sued by investors for the sake of

[11] 'Report of the Executive Directors on the Convention on the Settlement of Investment Disputes Between States and Nationals of Other States, 1965' (1993) 1 *ICSID Reports* 23, para. 20; A. Broches, 'A Guide for Users of the ICSID Convention' (1991) 8 *News from ICSID* 5, 7. See also A. Carlevaris, 'Preliminary Matters: Objections, Bi-Furcation, Request for Provisional Measures', in C. Giorgetti (ed.), *Litigating International Investment Disputes: A Practitioner's Guide* (Brill, 2014), p. 175.

[12] Parra, 'Screening Power', 10.

[13] Parra, 'Provisions', 303 (besides ICSID, mentioning ICC and SCC mechanisms).

[14] C.N. Brower, 'The Initiation of Arbitration Proceedings: 'Jack Be Nimble, Jack Be Quick ...!' (1998) 13 *ICSID Review-FILJ* 15, 16; E. Obadia and F. Nitschke, 'Institutional Arbitration and the Role of the Secretariat', in C. Giorgetti (ed.), *Litigating International Investment Disputes: A Practitioner's Guide* (Brill, 2014), p. 85.

[15] A. Broches, 'The Convention on the Settlement of Investment Disputes: Some Observations on Jurisdiction' (1966) 5 *Columbia Journal of Transnational Law* 263, 273.

[16] Ibid. (but noting that this view was seen as exaggerated).

'intimidation' without having obtained State consent.[17] When the formulation of what is now Article 36(3) was changed from a positive to
a negative one, a concern was raised by the Chinese representative that
this would facilitate reaching the constitution of an arbitral tribunal,[18]
even suggesting a double screening procedure.[19] However, that proposal
was not supported.[20] Another protective aspect of the screening procedure and its rigid time limits[21] was said to be preventing investors from
commencing arbitrations without giving an opportunity to the State to
settle the dispute amicably, which is often a condition precedent to arbitral jurisdiction.[22] It was suggested in the drafting process that investors
should provide information on the exhaustion of local administrative
remedies in their requests, because States could condition their consent
with such exhaustion,[23] but that suggestion was not welcomed either.[24]
That would, perhaps, be a step too far, requiring investors to exhaust
domestic remedies even when that was not required in the consent instrument. Nevertheless, it is hard to ignore the *leitmotif* of the screening process under the ICSID Convention: the exceptionality of international
adjudication and the protection of States in that respect.

The situation should not be different as regards the mechanisms which are
subject to the control of domestic courts. Arguably, the tougher screening
test under the ICSID Additional Facility Rules[25] could be explained by the
wish to prevent the exposure of awards to domestic setting aside.[26] This
rationale fits well within the context of safeguarding the consensualism of
international adjudication when it comes to private arbitration frameworks
which are used for the settlement of investment disputes such as the ICC
and SCC.[27] The validity of arbitral awards can be challenged before domestic

---

[17] *History of the ICSID Convention*, 4 vols. (ICSID, 1968), vol. II, p. 772 (Broches).
[18] Ibid., p. 774 (Tsai).
[19] Ibid., p. 775 (Tsai).
[20] Ibid., (Broches).
[21] The ICSID Secretary-General should register the request or refuse to do so 'as soon as possible.' See Rule 6(1) of the ICSID Institution Rules.
[22] S. Puig and C. Brown, 'The Secretary-General's Power to Refuse to Register a Request for
Arbitration under the ICSID Convention' (2012) 27 *ICSID Review-FILJ* 172, 182.
[23] *History of the ICSID Convention*, pp. 771–772 (Perez).
[24] Ibid., p. 774 (Broches).
[25] See discussion in Section 22.3.1 below.
[26] Puig and Brown, 'Power to Refuse', 188.
[27] ICC and SCC screening powers target arbitration agreements exclusively: A. Reiner and
C. Aschauer, 'ICC Rules', in R.A. Schütze (ed.), *Institutional Arbitration. Article-by-Article
Commentary* (C.H. Beck, 2013), p. 52; K. Hobér, *International Commercial Arbitration in
Sweden* (Oxford University Press, 2011), pp. 195–196.

courts on the ground that the tribunal has overstepped its mandate.[28] The prospect of such an error should be eliminated as soon as recognised.

22.2.2   Conflict with Arbitral Tribunals

A theoretical conflict between administrative screening powers and the tribunals' competence to resolve the questions of their own jurisdiction has been recognised from the outset of their formulation. When the ICSID Convention was drafted, some delegates observed that the Secretary-General would thus interfere in jurisdictional determinations,[29] and for that reason some thought that screening should be left to tribunals themselves.[30] Interestingly, the caution not to jeopardise the tribunals' *compétence de la compétence* power prompted many suggestions to subject the Secretary-General's refusal to register a case to some form of review,[31] although this was not accepted.[32]

From the beginning, a crucial notion behind the ICSID screening process was to preserve the tribunal's status as 'the sole judge of its competence.'[33] It was precisely with that aim that the change in the wording of Article 36(3) was made from a positive to a negative one: instructing the Secretary-General to register each case, *unless* he finds that the dispute is manifestly outside the ICSID jurisdiction, instead of requiring prima facie establishment of arbitral jurisdiction.[34] It has been argued that the Secretary-General's decision to register or to refuse the registration of a case does not amount to a jurisdictional determination.[35] Formalistically speaking, that is true, particularly observing the principle that the Secretary-General's decision should not have any influence whatsoever on the tribunal's findings regarding its jurisdiction.[36] The Secretary-General's screening power is

---

[28] Art. V(1) of the Convention on the Recognition and Enforcement of Foreign Arbitral Awards, New York, 10 June 1958, in force 7 June 1959, 330 UNTS 38.

[29] *History of the ICSID Convention*, p. 772 (Guarino).

[30] Ibid., p. 771 (Agoro).

[31] Ibid., p. 770 (Heth, Lokur, Tsai).

[32] Ibid., p. 773 (Broches).

[33] Ibid., p. 769 (Broches).

[34] Ibid., p. 774 (Ghachem, Broches).

[35] M. Polasek, 'The Threshold for Registration of a Request for Arbitration under the ICSID Convention' (2011) 5 *Dispute Resolution International* 177, 179; Carlevaris, 'Preliminary Matters', p. 176.

[36] *American Manufacturing & Trading, Inc. v. Republic of Zaire*, ICSID Case No. ARB/93/1, Award (21 February 1997), para. 5.01; C.H. Schreuer, L. Malintoppi, A. Reinisch and A. Sinclair, *The ICSID Convention: A Commentary*, 2nd edn (Cambridge University Press, 2009), pp. 471–472.

limited in all its aspects: from a very narrow scope of its review, to no value given to its decisions in the further arbitral proceedings.[37]

However, factually, the conclusion might be different. The Secretary-General's decisions to register or to refuse registration of requests directly determine the possibilities to access investment treaty arbitration within the ICSID framework.[38] One commentator observed that, at the time of his writing, it was 'becoming more difficult to persuade the "gatekeeper" of ICSID, the Secretary-General, to register a request for arbitration than it [was] to persuade an arbitral tribunal to exercise jurisdiction over a claim'.[39] That was probably an exaggeration. Statistics do not show a defeating effect of screening processes on the number of arbitrated investment claims, either within the ICSID[40] or commercial arbitration frameworks.[41] However, those requests that are disqualified in a screening process presumably have their jurisdictional constructions.[42]

---

[37] See particularly 'Report of the Executive Directors', para. 38 ('Article 41 reiterates the well-established principle that international tribunals are to be the judges of their own competence … It is to be noted in this connection that the power of the Secretary-General to refuse registration of a request for conciliation or arbitration … is so narrowly defined as not to encroach on the prerogative of Commissions and Tribunals to determine their own competence and, on the other hand, that registration of a request by the Secretary-General does not, of course, preclude a Commission or Tribunal from finding that the dispute is outside the jurisdiction of the Centre.'). See also Parra, 'Screening Power', 12.

[38] Parra, 'Screening Power', 12 (commenting that 'if the screening of a request reveals that it should be rejected, the screening authority will in effect assume a role normally reserved to the tribunals').

[39] S.D. Sutton, '*Emilio Augustin Maffezini v. Kingdom of Spain* and the ICSID Secretary-General's Screening Power' (2005) 21 *Arbitration International* 113, 126.

[40] By 1997, ICSID had registered 45 cases and rejected four requests: Brower, 'Initiation', 17. By 2011, ICSID had rejected 13 requests: Polasek, 'Threshold', 187. By that year, ICSID had already registered more than 300 arbitration cases: 'The ICSID Caseload – Statistics 2011–2', ICSID, 2011, p. 8. By the end of 2013, the number of rejected requests (for both arbitration and conciliation) was 18, while there was only one refusal of access to the Additional Facility: Obadia and Nitschke, 'Institutional Arbitration', pp. 93, 96. However, these numbers should be viewed with some caution. For example, already in 1999 Shihata and Parra reported 'about fifteen' unregistered requests: I.F.I. Shihata and A.R. Parra, 'The Experience of the International Centre for Settlement of Investment Disputes' (1999) 14 *ICSID Review-FILJ* 299, 307.

[41] It is estimated that the ICC Court has dismissed some 3 per cent of requests, but this number primarily concerns commercial arbitrations: Reiner and Aschauer, 'ICC Rules', p. 52. The number of investment arbitrations dismissed by the SCC Board for manifest lack of jurisdiction is unknown; but for one partial dismissal see *Limited Liability Company Amto v. Ukraine*, SCC Case No. 080/2005, Final Award (26 March 2008), para. 4.

[42] As required by all the rules on the institution of arbitration: Rule 2(1)(c) of the ICSID Institution Rules; Art. 4(3)(e) of the ICC Rules; Art. 6(iv) of the SCC Rules; Art. 3(3)(c) of the Arbitration Rules of the Permanent Court of Arbitration, in force 17 December 2012.

Furthermore, as discussed in Section 22.3, screening organs occasionally engage in legal interpretations, potentially conflicting with arbitral tribunals.

A theoretical conflict with arbitral tribunals becomes obvious particularly in light of the fact that arbitral tribunals give effect to legal changes concerning their jurisdiction. The jurisdictional standards governing investment treaty arbitration have been seen *in principle* as unsettled and subject to change. For example, the ICSID Convention does not define the notion of an 'investment'. The failure to define that notion was caused by the reluctance to impose absolute limits on the jurisdiction of the ICSID, and by the preference for a more flexible approach allowing States to draw such definitions in their consent instruments.[43] Such a move has often been characterised as 'wise', primarily because it defers that definition to States and their needs, but also because it 'permits the Convention to be adapted to changes in the form of cooperation between investors and host States'.[44] The lack of absolute jurisdictional limits is not an original feature of investment arbitration. In the commercial arbitration context, strict limits of screening powers have been defended on the grounds that the law governing arbitration agreements is in constant development.[45] The ideals of stability and objectivity, which are implied in the power to dismiss or refuse to register requests because they do not meet certain standards, contradict the changing character of jurisdictional rules.

At least on one occasion the outcome of a screening process was given a definitive value. A US district court refused to compel arbitration, which was then upheld by a Court of Appeal, on the ground that the submitted request contradicted an earlier notification of the PCA Secretary-General to the plaintiff of the failure to find prima facie an arbitration agreement providing for UNCITRAL arbitration.[46] This sort of *res judicata* value given to the PCA Secretary-General's screening determination was clearly wrong, because it ignored its prima facie nature.[47] The US courts could have reached their own decision on the interpretation of the arbitration

---

[43] A. Broches, 'The Convention on the Settlement of Investment Disputes between States and Nationals of Other States', in A. Broches (ed.), *Selected Essays. World Bank, ICSID, and Other Subjects of Public and Private International Law* (Martinus Nijhoff, 1995), p. 208.

[44] Ibid.; 'ICSID 1984 Annual Report', 3 September 1984, p. 9.

[45] Reiner and Aschauer, 'ICC Rules', p. 52 (mentioning the development of oral arbitration agreements, the extension of arbitration agreements to third parties or other contracts, the expansions of the concept of arbitrability etc.).

[46] *Marks 3-Zet-Ernst Marks Gmbh Co. Kg v. Presstek Inc.* [2006] 455 F.3d 7 (1st Cir.), paras. 36–38.

[47] Daly, Goriatcheva and Meighen, *Guide to the PCA*, p. 25.

agreement.[48] That interpretation should determine the prospects of arbitration.

The language of the ICSID Convention implies deference to tribunals regarding questions of jurisdiction,[49] which is also implicit in the ICC and SCC Rules.[50] The question arises at which point an administrative organ should defer to the arbitral tribunal. One suggestion is that whenever the jurisdictional question is a complex one, the ICSID Secretary-General should register the case and defer to the tribunal.[51] Another proposal is that whenever the ICSID Secretary-General has a 'slightest doubt' he should register the request and defer to the tribunal.[52] Such subjective criteria, however, cannot establish a clear boundary between the competences of administrative organs and tribunals.

22.2.3   Screening Procedures as a Forum for Debate

Arbitration rules differ significantly in terms of who should be heard in a screening process. The ICSID Convention provides that the Secretary-General will consider only the request and the information provided by the claimant.[53] Other frameworks, however, such as the ICC and SCC, require an objection from the respondent, or at least its inaction, to enter a screening process.[54] The PCA Rules are silent on this issue, but bearing in mind that the PCA will commence its screening only if acting as or

---

[48] Ibid.

[49] Art. 36(3) of the ICSID Convention instructs the Secretary-General to register each case, unless the dispute is manifestly outside ICSID jurisdiction, which means that any jurisdictional uncertainty should be resolved by the tribunal.

[50] See Art. 6(4) of the ICC Rules (requiring that an arbitration agreement prima facie may exist to proceed with the case); Art. 12(i) of the SCC Rules (requiring a manifest lack of jurisdiction for dismissal of a case by the SCC Board).

[51] Sutton, 'Maffezini', 123.

[52] Broches, 'Guide', 7. See also Schreuer et al., *ICSID Convention*, p. 469.

[53] Art. 36(3) of the ICSID Convention ('on the basis of the information contained in the request'). See also Parra, 'Provisions', 305.

[54] Art. 6(3) of the ICC Rules ('If any party against which a claim has been made does not submit an Answer, or if any party raises one or more pleas concerning the existence, validity or scope of the arbitration agreement ...'). It should be noted that in both situations the Secretariat can, but it is not obliged, to start the screening procedure: T.H. Webster and M.W. Bühler, *Handbook of ICC Arbitration: Commentary, Precedents, Materials*, 3rd edn (Sweet & Maxwell, 2014), pp. 109–110. The SCC commences a screening process only upon an objection from a party: Hobér, *Arbitration in Sweden*, p. 196. However, Hobér notes two possible *ex officio* screening instances: inactivity of the respondent, and non-arbitrability of the matter.

designating an appointing authority, and where the parties do not agree on the applicable procedural rules, the same conditions probably apply.[55] The rationale of the ICSID's independent assessment of the request is an obvious one: ICSID is the only system discussed here with a limited jurisdiction defined in its constitutive treaty, the ICSID Convention.[56] Furthermore, unlike ICSID, other fora allow jurisdiction of an arbitral tribunal to be established by a subsequent agreement concluded by the lack of the respondents' objection.[57]

However, even within the ICSID framework the screening process has become a forum for debate. The Secretary-General receives spontaneous comments from respondents, which he then transmits to claimants.[58] Early attitudes within ICSID were quite sceptical towards giving any significance to such comments.[59] But later on, the Secretary-General integrated respondents' replies into the screening process by allowing claimants to comment, and sometimes he even allows a few rounds of such exchanges of comments prior to rendering his decision.[60] One reason for the submission, and possibly acceptance, of respondents' replies is the fact that some of them consider – wrongly – the registration of the request as an endorsement of jurisdiction.[61] Another possibility might be that respondents wish to eliminate cases on the first occasion.

This development should not be overemphasised. The ICSID Secretary-General is unlikely to refuse to register a request because of the respondent's objections.[62] One suggestion is that such a reluctance arguably aims 'at balancing the potential for undue influence against the registration of a case under the ICSID Convention'.[63] But policy aims should

---

[55] See Daly, Goriatcheva and Meighen, *Guide to the PCA*, pp. 23, 84.

[56] Its jurisdiction is regulated in Article 25(1) of the ICSID Convention. Shany uses the term 'foundational jurisdiction' to refer to jurisdiction as defined in courts' constitutive instruments, which determines their potential to adjudicate certain classes of cases: Y. Shany, *Questions of Jurisdiction and Admissibility before International Courts* (Cambridge University Press, 2016), pp. 22–23.

[57] Regarding the ICC framework: W.L. Craig, W.W. Park and J. Paulsson, *International Chamber of Commerce Arbitration*, 3rd edn (Oceana, 2000), p. 21. As for the Swedish law applicable to SCC arbitrations: Hobér, *Arbitration in Sweden*, p. 96.

[58] Polasek, 'Threshold', 180.

[59] Parra, 'Screening Power', 12.

[60] A.R. Parra, 'The Institution of ICSID Arbitration Proceedings' (2003) 20 *News from ICSID* 12, 13. The same is the case with the ICC: Webster and Bühler, *Handbook*, p. 110.

[61] Polasek, 'Threshold', 180.

[62] Ibid., 181.

[63] Puig and Brown, 'Power to Refuse', 178.

not be overstated either. The mechanism refers any doubt regarding jurisdiction of a tribunal to the tribunal itself. Any objection raised by the
respondent can cause only that: a doubt. A refusal to register solely on the
basis of such doubt would be inconsistent with the concept and purpose
of screening.

The ICSID Secretary-General has also been the addressee of comments
and petitions from civil society organisations. For example, after the
Bolivian withdrawal from the ICSID Convention, NGOs have pressured
against the registration of cases initiated against that country during
the six-month withdrawal period.[64] There is an opinion that the specific
nature of ICSID proceedings, which includes various stakeholders, might
justify hearing different voices and their arguments against registration.[65]
There is a danger, however, in such an approach: giving any significance
to 'other voices' could transform the screening process and distort its
concept. The Secretary-General was never meant to be a jurisdictional
decision-maker. Legitimising public debates in the screening stage might
assign him that role.

22.3   The Applicable Standards and the Risk of Censorship

The ICSID Convention requires refusal of registration if 'the dispute is
manifestly outside the jurisdiction of the Centre'. 'Manifest' was said to
mean 'easily recognizable',[66] or 'beyond reasonable doubt whatever evidence or argument might be produced subsequently'.[67] The ICC Rules set
a positive formulation, requiring prima facie finding that an arbitration
agreement may exist.[68] Although the SCC Rules adopt wording similar
to the ICSID Convention ('manifestly lacks jurisdiction'), the screening
conducted by the SCC Board is often qualified as prima facie finding
on jurisdiction.[69] The PCA Secretary-General will also look prima facie

---

[64] See 'Petition protesting Telecom Italia's case against Bolivia at World Bank tribunal, ICSID',
     21 March 2008, available at: www.tni.org/en/archives/act/18079.
[65] Puig and Brown, 'Power to Refuse', 179.
[66] Schreuer et al., *ICSID Convention*, p. 470.
[67] Note C to Rule 6 at 'Rules of Procedure for the Institution of Conciliation and Arbitration
     Proceedings (Institution Rules)', in *ICSID Regulations and Rules* (ICSID, 1975), p. 34.
[68] Art. 6(4) of the ICC Rules.
[69] See generally D. Ramsjö and S. Strömberg, 'Manifest Lack of Jurisdiction? A Selection
     of Decisions of the Arbitration Institute of the Stockholm Chamber of Commerce
     Concerning the *Prima Facie* Existence of an Arbitration Agreement' (2011), available at:
     www.sccinstitute.com/media/61989/prima_facie_decisions_-by_the_scc.pdf; and Mutis
     Tellez, '*Prima Facie* Decisions'.

for an arbitration agreement.[70] The practice in screening processes is discussed first (Section 22.3.1), followed by a discussion on the burden of proof imposed on claimants (Section 22.3.2).

22.3.1   Screening in Action

Because the screening procedures and standards under the ICSID Convention, on the one hand, and the ICC, SCC, and PCA frameworks, on the other, differ significantly, their screening practices will be discussed separately.

22.3.1.1   The ICSID Convention

The ICSID framework contains the most complex set of criteria that should be verified in a screening process. The ICSID Secretary-General should conduct a 'double review' of requests, observing provisions of both the ICSID Convention and the investment treaty that carries the jurisdictional clause.[71] Regarding the ICSID Convention, the Secretary-General must consider the requirements of Article 25(1), that is the existence of a legal dispute, its proximity to an investment, the quality of the parties as a contracting State and a national of another contracting State, and the parties' consent.[72] The last requirement refers to the relevant investment treaty. Its examination, including the fulfilment of its criteria for coverage,[73] forms the second part of such 'double review'.

The examination of the requirements of the ICSID Convention bears some connotation of objectivity. The Secretary-General should firstly observe whether there is a legal dispute, which should not be an issue 'as long as the requesting party invokes the existence or scope of a legal right or obligation, as opposed to a mere conflict of interest or threat of a future dispute'.[74] The Secretary-General should observe the criteria developed in judicial and arbitral practice.[75] Indeed, an analysis of that practice has

---

[70] Daly, Goriatcheva, and Meighen, *Guide to the PCA*, pp. 23, 84.

[71] Parra, 'Institution', 13.

[72] A.A. Escobar, 'Three Aspects of ICSID's Administration of Arbitration Proceedings' (1997) 14 *News from ICSID* 4, 5; Polasek, 'Threshold', 178.

[73] Polasek, 'Threshold', 184; Puig and Brown, 'Power to Refuse', 181.

[74] Polasek, 'Threshold', 187. See also 'Report of the Executive Directors', para. 26. It has been argued that a failure to indicate clearly the questions in disagreement between the parties might lead to a refusal to register: Puig and Brown, 'Power to Refuse', 184.

[75] Puig and Brown, 'Power to Refuse', 183.

concluded that objections to the existence of a dispute are very unlikely to succeed.[76] But it would be wrong to regard the standard of 'dispute' as a static one, with a necessarily low threshold.[77] Furthermore, the inquiry into the elements of a dispute becomes complex by virtue of the fact that the Secretary-General may examine whether the acts or facts have occurred after the entry into force of the investment treaty, relying on the rules of the temporal application of treaties.[78] This can be an intricate interpretive process, because treaties contain various temporal limitation clauses subject to different interpretations,[79] and in any event the fact that a treaty applies to disputes after its entry into force does not mean that earlier acts and facts are excluded.[80]

In practice, the ICSID Secretary-General has requested clarifications concerning the legal basis of a dispute.[81] A lack of such basis would make the claim unmeritorious but not manifestly outside the ICSID jurisdiction.[82] While this might be only a verification that claimants have provided all the information required by the ICSID Institution Rules, too much emphasis on the basis of the dispute might not be so wise,[83] because an examination of the suitability of the legal basis and the stated facts for adjudication in ICSID arbitration resembles the *Oil Platforms* test.[84] That appears hardly

---

[76] C. Schreuer, 'What Is a Legal Dispute?', in I. Buffard, J. Crawford, A. Pellet and S. Wittich (eds.), *International Law between Universalism and Fragmentation. Festschrift in Honour of Gerhard Hafner* (Brill, 2008), pp. 978–979.

[77] For an example of the sharpening of this standard, by inquiring whether the respondent 'was aware, or could not have been unaware' of an allegation of breach, see *Obligations concerning Negotiations relating to Cessation of the Nuclear Arms Race and to Nuclear Disarmament (Marshall Islands v. United Kingdom)* ICJ Reports (2016), paras. 44–52. See further L. Palestini, 'Forget About Mavrommatis and Judicial Economy: The Alleged Absence of a Dispute in the Cases Concerning the Obligations to Negotiate the Cessation of the Nuclear Arms Race and Nuclear Disarmament' (2017) 8 *Journal of International Dispute Settlement* 557; V.-J. Proulx, 'The World Court's Jurisdictional Formalism and Its Lost Market Share: The *Marshall Islands* Decisions and the Quest for a Suitable Dispute Settlement Forum for Multilateral Disputes' (2017) 30 *Leiden Journal of International Law* 925.

[78] Parra, 'Institution', 13. The claimant should also provide evidence that the treaty has entered into force: Polasek, 'Threshold', 187.

[79] See generally S. Blanchard, 'State Consent, Temporal Jurisdiction, and the Importation of Continuing Circumstances Analysis into International Investment Arbitration' (2011) 10 *Washington University Global Studies Law Review* 419.

[80] Schreuer, 'Legal Dispute', pp. 974–978.

[81] Puig and Brown, 'Power to Refuse', 183–184.

[82] Ibid.

[83] Contrary to the suggestion of Puig and Brown, who recommend caution: ibid.

[84] See, for example, *SGS Société Générale de Surveillance S.A. v. Republic of the Philippines*, ICSID Case No. ARB/02/6, Decision of the Tribunal on Objections to Jurisdiction (29

justifiable in the application of the 'manifestly outside the jurisdiction' standard. The Secretary-General has also been willing to check whether the dispute concerned particular issues, like expropriation, that is the *ratione materiae* jurisdiction.[85] Bearing in mind all the issues arising in connection to the scope of consent in investment treaties,[86] this seems an inappropriately detailed inquiry for the purposes of registering the request.

A closely related question is whether the dispute arises directly out of an investment.[87] Two occasions have been reported in which registration was refused because of the manifest lack of an investment.[88] Both cases concerned supply contracts for the sale of goods.[89] Crucially, in regard to one of them registration was refused 'despite the fact that the request had been made on the basis of a BIT providing for arbitration under the Convention in respect of disputes arising out of investments which, as defined in the BIT, could be understood as including sale of goods transactions'.[90] Some caution is needed here, because of the diverse practice of investment tribunals in interpreting the notion of an 'investment'. It has been suggested that registration should be refused only if the request concerns 'a simple commercial transaction that clearly falls outside the broadest interpretation identified by ICSID jurisprudence'.[91] But investment tribunals have been sometimes willing to qualify sales contracts as investments.[92] The advice that this issue should generally be left to tribunals should be supported.[93]

January 2004), para. 26. This jurisdictional test inquires whether there is an international obligation between the parties capable of being breached by the alleged conduct of the respondent.

[85] *Telenor Mobile Communications A.S. v. The Republic of Hungary,* ICSID Case No. ARB/04/15, Award (13 September 2006), paras. 3–4.

[86] In particular, tribunals have been struggling with various questions of scope of consent, like whether a narrow jurisdictional clause which allows arbitrating only issues surrounding the amount of compensation for expropriation could be extended to include the issue of occurrence of expropriation. There are no clear answers to these questions, and the practice remains divided.

[87] For the requirement of 'directness', also known as 'proximity' to investment, see Schreuer et al., *ICSID Convention,* pp. 106 *et seq.*

[88] Polasek, 'Threshold', 188.

[89] Puig and Brown, 'Power to Refuse', 184; 'ICSID 1985 Annual Report', 6 September 1985, p. 6; Shihata and Parra, 'Experience', 308.

[90] Shihata and Parra, 'Experience', 308.

[91] Polasek, 'Threshold', 188.

[92] *Petrobart Limited v. The Kyrgyz Republic,* SCC Case No. 126/2003, Arbitral Award (29 March 2005), pp. 69–72. Although not an ICSID case, the tribunal relied on previous ICSID practice in reaching its conclusions.

[93] Puig and Brown, 'Power to Refuse', 185.

Refusals to register concerned also the quality of the parties, for example
if the claimant was a national of the host State, or if the respondent State
agency had not been designated or its consent had not been approved by
the State.[94] The ICSID Convention does not generally allow arbitrations
to be initiated by nationals of the State in dispute.[95] This might contradict
the definition of an 'investor' in the applicable investment treaty. In such
circumstances, the Secretary-General has refused to register a request if
the requesting party had the nationality of the respondent State.[96] The
Secretary-General basically conducts again a two-fold examination, and
checks whether the claimant is a party to the dispute, and whether he
has the proper nationality.[97] Locally incorporated companies who wish
to commence arbitration under the exception of Article 25(2)(b) of the
ICSID Convention are in a more difficult position,[98] because they must
prove foreign 'control' and that they are recognised as foreign by the host
State.[99] On the one hand, because of the lack of definition of 'control'
in the ICSID Convention, it would be hard to deny registration in such
cases.[100] On the other, the Secretary-General has been willing to question
registration, holding that there was no agreement treating the investor as
'foreign',[101] although the issue of what forms such an agreement was open
to debate.[102]

Outside these 'objective' criteria of the ICSID Convention, another
question is whether the Secretary-General should deny registration

[94] Polasek, 'Threshold', 188.
[95] Art. 25(1)–(2) of the ICSID Convention.
[96] Polasek, 'Threshold', 185–186; Parra, 'Institution', 13.
[97] Puig and Brown, 'Power to Refuse', 186.
[98] Which provides that the term 'national of another Contracting State' includes 'any juridical person which had the nationality of the Contracting State party to the dispute on that
date [that is, the date of consent] and which, because of foreign control, the parties have
agreed should be treated as a national of another Contracting State for the purposes of
this Convention'.
[99] Puig and Brown, 'Power to Refuse', 186–187.
[100] Ibid.
[101] *Tokios Tokelés v. Ukraine,* ICSID Case No. ARB/02/18, Award (26 July 2007), para. 19. Cf.
*Cable Television of Nevis, Ltd and Cable Television of Nevis Holdings, Ltd v. Federation of
St. Kitts and Nevis,* ICSID Case No. ARB/95/2, Award of the Tribunal (13 January 1997),
paras. 5.22–24 (where that question was deferred to the tribunal).
[102] ICSID tribunals have been willing to find such agreements elsewhere or by implication.
See *Amco Asia Corp. and others v. The Republic of Indonesia,* ICSID Case No. ARB/81/1,
Award on Jurisdiction (25 September 1983), para. 14(ii); *Klöckner et al. v. United Republic
of Cameroon and Société Camerounaise des Engrais (SOCAME),* in 'Legal Rules Applied
by ICSID Arbitral Tribunals' (1984) 1 *News from ICSID* 5, 10–11.

because the claimant has not fulfilled some condition precedent to the institution of arbitration. In *Tokios Tokelés v. Ukraine*, the Secretary-General informed the requesting parties that the condition of prior negotiations had not been fulfilled, which led the requesting parties to withdraw and resubmit the request after the fulfilment of this condition.[103] On another occasion, the claimant admitted that a similar requirement had not been met, and requested the registration of the request after its satisfaction, which the Secretary-General was unable to do.[104] The requesting party must indicate in the request the fulfilment of all conditions precedent, as imposed by the investment treaty both expressly or implicitly.[105] But what happens if the claimant aims to bypass a certain requirement, or maintains that it need not be fulfilled, for example using a most-favoured-nation clause? One suggestion is that an argument to that effect would suffice for registration, but under the condition that the most-favoured-nation clause is not manifestly inapplicable.[106] The crucial question in such constructions, however, is precisely the applicability of the most-favoured-nation clause to the jurisdictional clause, to which answers are rarely 'manifest'.[107] A possibility is that the Secretary-General should not interpret the most-favoured-nation clause, if the investment treaty refers to ICSID arbitration and both instruments are investment protection treaties, 'provided that the reference may indeed be read, to the Secretary-General's satisfaction, as the manifestation of consent to the arbitral mechanism invoked.'[108] However, even such contextual conclusions, like on the subject matter of the treaties invoked, amount to treaty interpretation and the application of the rules governing the scope of most-favoured-nation clauses.[109]

[103] *Tokios Tokelés v. Ukraine*, para. 18.
[104] Polasek, 'Threshold', 185.
[105] Escobar, 'Three Aspects', 6.
[106] Polasek, 'Threshold', 184.
[107] The fact that a case is registered implies the Secretary-General's position that the most-favoured-nation clause might be applicable to dispute resolution in the instant case, or at least that the contrary is not obvious. Some tribunals, however, advanced arguments implying manifest inapplicability of most-favoured-nation clauses to dispute resolution clauses: *Telenor v. Hungary*, para. 92; *Kılıç İnşaat İthalat İhracat Sanayi Ve Ticaret Anonim Şirketi v. Turkmenistan*, ICSID Case No. ARB/10/1, Award (2 July 2013), para. 7.3.9.
[108] Puig and Brown, 'Power to Refuse', 182.
[109] Such as the *ejusdem generis* rule. See Arts. 9 and 10 of ILC, 'Draft Articles on Most-Favoured-Nation Clauses', in *Yearbook of the International Law Commission* (1978), vol. II, Part Two, p. 16.

The most important findings of the Secretary-General concern the existence of consent to arbitrate. In *Biwater v. Tanzania*, the ICSID Secretary-
General informed the claimant of his doubts as to the existence of an
arbitration agreement, asking for clarifications.[110] This was an interpretation of the provision alleged to constitute an offer to arbitrate. As can be
seen in the tribunal's award, such a conclusion could be reached only in a
thorough interpretive process.[111] In *SPP v. Egypt*, despite noticing an error
in the submitted translation of the relevant act, the Secretary-General registered the request, but anticipated a possible objection to the existence of
State consent to arbitration to be raised by the respondent.[112] Although
these precautionary statements are said to be unlikely in the future, due to
certain changes within the ICSID framework,[113] their significance should
not be underestimated. They illustrate that the Secretary-General is not
conducting merely administrative checks, but engages in a substantive
analysis of the submitted documents and arguments.

The ICSID Additional Facility provides wider discretion of the Secretary-
General, by empowering him to approve every arbitration agreement that
makes reference to those rules.[114] An analogy with the standard of the
ICSID Convention has been suggested,[115] but that was criticised on the
ground that, unlike the Convention, the Additional Facility provides discretionary space in the Secretary-General's approval.[116] The difference
between positive and negative formulations is central in this criticism.[117]

[110] *Biwater Gauff (Tanzania) Ltd. v. United Republic of Tanzania,* ICSID Case No. ARB/05/22, Award (24 July 2008), para. 327.
[111] Ibid., paras. 329–333.
[112] *Southern Pacific Properties (Middle East) Limited v. Arab Republic of Egypt,* ICSID Case No. ARB/84/3, Award (20 May 1992), para. 3 ('I have, thus, registered the request of SPP without prejudice to the question whether said Article eight constitutes consent for the purposes of the ICSID Convention or merely includes a reference to this Convention in the cases where consent for ICSID jurisdiction is issued separately. This matter, if raised, will be for the Arbitral Tribunal to decide.')
[113] Polasek, 'Threshold', 183 ('Because of the recent streamlining of the registration process and the possibility of raising objections to be heard on an expedited basis, ICSID is now unlikely to make any statements of this kind').
[114] Art. 4(1) of the Rules Governing the Additional Facility for the Administration of Proceedings by the Secretariat of the International Centre for Settlement of Investment Disputes (Additional Facility Rules), in force 10 April 2006 ('Additional Facility').
[115] See *Nova Scotia Power Incorporated (Canada) v. República Bolivariana de Venezuela,* UNCITRAL, Decision on Jurisdiction (22 April 2010), para. 133.
[116] Puig and Brown, 'Power to Refuse', 188.
[117] Art. 4(2)–(3) of the Additional Facility uses a positive formulation, requiring the Secretary-General to approve arbitration agreements 'only if he is satisfied' that certain

Moreover, since the Secretary-General does not approve requests initiating arbitrations but arbitration agreements, it has been argued that this power does not amount to screening.[118] Both conclusions contradict factual aspects: by approving arbitration agreements the Secretary-General filters future disputes administered by ICSID, and he does so observing similar jurisdictional notions as in the regular screening process (nationality, proximity of the dispute to an investment etc.). Furthermore, just as the Convention's negative formulation of the screening power did not stop the Secretary-General from making detailed inquiries, it should not be necessarily expected that the language of the Additional Facility Rules will have drastic effects in practice.

22.3.1.2   Other Frameworks

Commercial arbitration frameworks unfortunately do not offer clear insights into their screening practices regarding investment disputes, but some parallels can be drawn from the commercial sphere. Within the SCC mechanism, containing a similar standard as ICSID ('manifestly lacks jurisdiction'), a jurisdictional construction referring to the SCC should suffice for screening.[119] In practice, the SCC Board has left issues like invalidity of arbitration clauses and their modifications to tribunals.[120] It has also done so as regards multi-tiered arbitration clauses and prior negotiations.[121] On the other hand, the SCC Board was willing to find a manifest lack of jurisdiction by giving priority to a storage agreement over the standard for contract to which the former was referring.[122] On another occasion it found a manifest lack of jurisdiction because the arbitration agreement referred to 'a Court of Arbitration in Stockholm', reading it as a reference to ad hoc arbitration.[123] As for the ICC mechanism, the ICC Court seeks 'to determine whether the Tribunal may decide that it has

---

conditions are met (that is that one of the States concerned is not a contracting State, or that the dispute does not arise directly out of an investment).

[118] Sutton, 'Maffezini', 124–125.

[119] Ramsjö and Strömberg, 'Manifest Lack of Jurisdiction?', p. 2.

[120] SCC Arbitration V 010/2005 and SCC Arbitration F 037/2007 reported in Ramsjö and Strömberg, 'Manifest Lack of Jurisdiction?'; SCC Arbitration V 028/2010 reported in Mutis Tellez, 'Prima Facie Decisions'.

[121] SCC Arbitration V 005/2011 and SCC Arbitration V 026/2011 reported in Mutis Tellez, 'Prima Facie Decisions'.

[122] SCC Arbitration F 067/2007 reported in Ramsjö and Strömberg, 'Manifest Lack of Jurisdiction?'.

[123] SCC Arbitration F 086/2010 reported in Mutis Tellez, 'Prima Facie Decisions'.

jurisdiction',[124] although it seems willing to make more substantive legal examinations.[125] Such findings, by the SCC Board and the ICC Court, are a form of contract interpretation, and therefore these inquiries go beyond purely administrative examinations.

The PCA follows these practices. A jurisdictional construction suffices to pass the prima facie control of the agreement to arbitrate.[126] Similarly to ICSID, the PCA Secretary-General was willing to inquire about the authorisation of the claimant to commence arbitration and to refuse to act if it found that the claimant had not properly passed its internal procedures.[127] And similarly to the SCC, the PCA Secretary-General was reluctant to designate an appointing authority when faced with vague arbitration clauses, such as those referring to 'arbitration in the Hague under the International Arbitration rules'.[128]

22.3.2   Burden of Proof and Compelling Requests

The standards that are observed in screening processes raise an important question: does the requesting party bear the burden to prove the satisfaction of such standards, in order to achieve the registration of the request? In theory, at least within the ICSID system, the answer should be 'no'. The drafting history of the ICSID Convention shows that the screening power of the Secretary-General was formulated in such a way as to liberate the claimant of any burden in this process.[129] The Secretary-General should take the facts alleged by the claimant as true, unless there is serious doubt to the contrary.[130] The approach that places burden rather on the

---

[124] Webster and Bühler, *Handbook*, p. 112.
[125] See Brower, 'Initiation', 18 (reporting a disqualified ICC case, where it was argued that non-signatories to an arbitration agreement were bound by it).
[126] It has been reported that in *DS Construction FZCO v. Libya* the PCA Secretary-General was willing to designate the appointing authority, facing the claimant's argument that jurisdiction of an UNCITRAL tribunal could be established through a most-favoured-nation clause in the investment treaty of the Organization of Islamic Cooperation: S. Perry, 'PCA Ends Standoff over Islamic Treaty Claim', *Global Arbitration Review*, 3 April 2017, available at: globalarbitrationreview.com/article/1138857/pca-ends-standoff-over-islamic-treaty-claim.
[127] Brower, 'Initiation', 19 (reporting a case where the PCA Secretary-General declined to designate the appointing authority, because the claimant, an unincorporated joint venture, had failed to obtain authorisation to institute arbitration from the joint venture parties, as required by their agreement). As for ICSID, see Polasek, 'Threshold', 187.
[128] *Marks v. Presstek Inc.*, paras. 18–19.
[129] *History of the ICSID Convention*, pp. 774–775 (Ghachem, Broches, Tsai).
[130] Puig and Brown, 'Power to Refuse', 178; Schreuer et al., *ICSID Convention*, p. 470.

Secretary-General's work is also, at least declaratively, pursued in practice.[131] But factually, there is at least some burden on the claimant and
the information it provides in the request.[132] This is supported by the
Secretary-General's practice to consult with the requesting party. The
ICSID Convention and Rules do not contain any provisions to that effect,
but it has been the Secretary-General's practice to ask the claimant for
clarification or to supplement the request if necessary.[133] Such requests
differ, from those concerning quite basic information such as consent
to arbitration,[134] to those concerning detailed information forming a
jurisdictional construction.[135] The Secretary-General has also requested
additional information about the fulfilment of detailed conditions of the
applicable investment treaty.[136] In some instances, the requesting party
responded by modifying the initial request because of the failure to meet
some requirements.[137] Therefore, it appears that some burden of proof is
imposed on the requesting party by the mere fact that its request must be
screened.

Other frameworks might be more open about the imposition of such
a burden. Firstly, this could be so because of the differences in the applicable screening standards. As seen above, the ICC Rules require finding
prima facie that an arbitration agreement may exist. This is potentially a
tougher test, because 'something may not be shown *prima facie* that could

[131] *Plama Consortium Limited v. Republic of Bulgaria*, ICSID Case No. ARB/03/24, Decision on Jurisdiction (8 February 2005), para. 232 (the Secretary-General said: 'I do not find with the required degree of certainty ("beyond reasonable doubt") that the request is unregistrable under the provisions of the Energy Charter Treaty').

[132] Parra argued that the requesting party 'need only provide information showing that the dispute is not "manifestly outside the jurisdiction of the Centre"'. Parra, 'Screening Power', 12.

[133] Ibid.

[134] *Parkerings-Compagniet AS v. Republic of Lithuania*, ICSID Case No. ARB/05/8, Award (11 September 2007), para. 13 (requesting information concerning the claimant's consent and evidence of the entry into force of the relevant BIT).

[135] For example, *Eudoro Armando Olguín v. Republic of Paraguay*, ICSID Case No. ARB/98/5, Award (26 July 2001), paras. 5, 7; *Sempra Energy International v. The Argentine Republic*, ICSID Case No. ARB/02/16, Award (28 September 2007), para. 7; *EDF (Services) Limited v. Romania*, ICSID Case No. ARB/05/13, Award (8 October 2009), para. 4.

[136] *Joy Mining Machinery Limited v. Arab Republic of Egypt*, ICSID Case No. ARB/03/11, Award on Jurisdiction (6 August 2004), para. 3 (requesting further information 'on the investment of Joy Mining "in the territory" of Egypt as envisaged by Article 8(1) of the BIT').

[137] For example, *Tokios Tokelés v. Ukraine*, para. 19 (removing one entity as a requesting party after the Secretary-General's notification that the nationality requirement was not fulfilled).

be shown'.[138] The ICC also has a practice of asking for clarifications and exchanging comments between the parties before referring the matter to the ICC Court.[139] The SCC framework sets a similar standard to the ICSID, but its rules still explicitly allow the SCC Board to request further details from the parties.[140] However, the imposed burden can be significantly mitigated, if not completely lost, by the low standards applied in screening processes.

In any event, requests should make an impression: every request should 'tell a compelling story, so that the person reading it reaches the end of the narrative convinced that justice requires that something be done for the claimant'.[141] Surely this advice would be useful in a screening process. Another significant question is whether requests should anticipate defences,[142] which certainly arises in the context of screening. A screening process should result in an administrative decision to register or to refuse registration of a request. The requesting party should not weaken its case. However, screening processes have become more adversarial or even multi-voiced fora. If anticipation can bring advantage, claimants could consider it even in the context of screening procedures. This is even more so in the context of legal change, when an arbitral activity in the formation of jurisdictional standards is sought.

22.4   Conclusion: Legitimacy Preserved?

There is no uniform attitude towards the justification of screening powers. In the context of the ICSID framework, the benefits of a Secretary-General's broad screening power have been seen in the mitigation of costs and the avoidance of possible State party embarrassment.[143] At the same time, that power has problematic aspects, like transparency,[144] and possible redefinition of its unclear limits in practice.[145] Other fora, like the SCC, have been said to pursue pro-arbitration policies by maintaining a

---

[138] Brower, 'Initiation', 18.

[139] Webster and Bühler, *Handbook*, p. 110.

[140] Art. 10(1) of the SCC Rules.

[141] J.M. Townsend, 'The Initiation of Arbitration Proceedings: "My Story Had Been Longer"' (1998) 13 *ICSID Review-FILJ* 21, 24.

[142] Ibid., 25.

[143] I.F.I. Shihata, *The World Bank in a Changing World*, 3 vols. (Kluwer Law International, 2000), vol. III, p. 808.

[144] Sutton, 'Maffezini', 126.

[145] Ibid.

low standard for proceeding with arbitrations.[146] Such approaches could be reasonable for commercial arbitration mechanisms: they might favour 'the more the merrier' policies in their competition for leadership. All these suggestions are only theorising, without clear answers about the practical impact of screening powers.

The legitimacy of screening powers should rather be assessed from a factual perspective. This chapter advances four major conclusions. First, despite being conceptualised as administrative, preliminary review, screening processes have been taken much more seriously by many actors: administrative organs, disputing parties, civil society, and, on some occasions, courts. Arbitral tribunals refrain from giving any value to the registration process, because this would diminish their own *compétence de la compétence*.

Second, the extent and intensity of screening depend on the applicable jurisdictional requirements. Contrary to common beliefs, the extent and intensity do not necessarily depend on the positive or negative wording of the rules granting screening powers. Furthermore, a burden is imposed on the requesting party by the mere existence of a screening process.

Third, in exercising their screening powers, administrative organs might encounter complex jurisdictional issues, which require engaging in interpretive exercises. The theory, of course, says that in such situations administrative organs must defer to arbitral tribunals. But it would be naïve to believe that that is always the case. The question arises whether a requesting party can avoid screening by artificially increasing the complexity of a jurisdictional question, expecting the administrative organ to defer that question to the tribunal.[147] If the answer is affirmative, that would probably encourage those who argue for thorough screenings.

Fourth, the resolution of jurisdictional issues in screening processes can affect the prospects for legal change effected before arbitral tribunals. Although unintended, screening powers of administrative organs imply the objectivity and stability of the applicable jurisdictional standards. Furthermore, administrative organs enjoy discretion in the exercise of their screening powers. This is best evidenced by the lack of a uniform correlation between the written standards of review (that is, their positive or negative definition) and the screening practice. For example, the

---

[146] Mutis Tellez, '*Prima Facie* Decisions', p. 20.
[147] For example, it has been argued that the requesting party can legitimately bypass ICSID screening if it includes in its request only a translation of a treaty, and not its original text containing an ambiguous arbitration clause: Brower, 'Initiation', 17.

ICSID framework prescribes a low standard, but it has applied arguably high criteria in practice; the PCA Secretary-General looks prima facie for an arbitration agreement on a regular basis without any written empowerment; the SCC Rules prescribe a very low standard, and the SCC Board arguably takes the same approach in practice.

While these conclusions do not affect the main idea behind screening processes, they raise serious concerns about their possible, undesired effects on arbitral practice, and the development of investment treaty arbitration. In order to avoid such effects, and to safeguard the legitimacy of screening powers, they must be exercised with an extreme level of diligence. Screening powers should be exercised in a more administrative (as opposed to judicial) manner.[148] To put this in more concrete terms, administrative organs should not engage in any interpretations of the law, and should only verify whether the requesting party has submitted the required information. Any further legal considerations, such as whether the transaction qualifies as an investment or whether the dispute falls within the scope of consent, should be left to tribunals. Such an approach was already supported in early ICSID practice, when a tribunal went through a checklist of all the information that should be indicated in a request for arbitration, concluding that the Secretary-General was right to register the case.[149] Tribunals should not be expected to do the same in every arbitration, but administrative organs should consider adopting this more technical approach. In order to at least mitigate the danger of censorship towards legal change, and to safeguard the justification of screening powers, their reasonable use should be secured by focusing on the administrative role played by screening organs within arbitral institutions.

---

[148] In support of this argument see Sutton, 'Maffezini', 126.
[149] *Cable Television of Nevis v. St. Kitts and Nevis,* para. 5.02.

23

Legitimacy and the Role of Legal Officers in Chambers at International and Hybrid Criminal Courts and Tribunals

MARKO DIVAC ÖBERG[*]

23.1 Introduction

Legal officers in chambers at international and hybrid criminal courts and tribunals are legally trained staff recruited to assist the judges in their judicial work. They are unseen actors par excellence. The cover page to any judgment issued by such a court or tribunal presents prominently the names of the judges sitting on the case, as well as that of the registrar. The name or names of the accused are also generally conspicuously placed, typically in the name of the case. Then follows a list of the names of prosecution, defence and, where applicable, witness or victim counsel. The names of the legal officers assisting the judges are nowhere to be found.

This state of affairs is entirely justified. The judges are chosen by States to exercise judicial powers. They are the public face of the chambers and are authorised to speak on the official record of the oral proceedings and issue written filings such as judgments, decisions and orders. Similarly, the other actors whose names figure on the cover page are allowed, under certain conditions, to make submissions in court and in their written filings. The legal officers in chambers, in contrast, have no such rights. Their role in court is limited to behind-the-scenes communication and other work. They cannot make any submissions on the record.

[*] I thank Jonas Nilsson and Sandesh Sivakumaran for their comments on previous versions of this article. The opinions expressed in it are mine alone and do not necessarily correspond to those of the Special Tribunal for Lebanon, or the United Nations in general. For correspondence: marko.divac.oberg@nyu.edu.

Nevertheless, legal officers in chambers are sometimes suspected of exercising influence and wielding power beyond their formal role. The suspicions can go as far as alleging that the legal officers are making decisions for and instead of the judges. If this were true, the legal officers would clearly be acting outside their remit. While the judges may delegate certain tasks to the legal officers, including research and drafting, all decision-making must rest firmly in the hands of the judges.[1] If this is clear in theory, in practice the distinction between assistance in research and drafting, on the one hand, and judicial decision-making, on the other hand, might not always be crystal clear. Depending on one's definition of 'decision-making' it may therefore appear problematic that actors who are vested with legitimacy delegate such work to unseen actors, who are not.

This touches upon the legitimacy of the judicial process. Applying a normative conception of legitimacy, this chapter will ask whether things are done, and in particular decisions are made, in accordance with the applicable principles and rules, and by the persons who are legally empowered to act and decide. From the perspective of sociological legitimacy, it will ask whether the addressees of international criminal decisions and judgments consider that the role of legal officers is justified.[2] The main addressees in question are the accused, represented by the defence, the prosecution, and the victims of the international crimes, in some cases represented by a legal representative.

In trying to answer these questions, this chapter will examine a number of legal challenges that have been brought alleging undue influence by legal officers on the judicial decision-making process. In addressing these challenges, the judges have publicly defined the contours of the legal officers' contributions to the work of the chambers, as well as the limits of what they can do. This chapter will present and evaluate this case law,

---

[1] See ICTY and United Nations Interregional Crime and Justice Research Institute, *ICTY Manual on Developed Practices* (UNICRI Publisher, 2009), p. 116; H. Thirlway, 'The Drafting of ICJ Decisions: Some Personal Recollections and Observations' (2006) 5 *Chinese Journal of International Law* 15, pp. 20–23; P.M. Wald, 'The International Criminal Tribunal for the Former Yugoslavia Comes of Age: Some Observations on Day-to-Day Dilemmas of an International Court' (2001) 5 *Washington Journal of Law and Policy* 87, 93; M.D. Oberg, 'Processing Evidence and Drafting Judgments in International Criminal Trial Chambers' (2013) 24 *Criminal Law Forum* 113, 114.

[2] On these two conceptions of legitimacy, see Freya Baetens's chapter 'Unseen Actors in International Courts and Tribunals: Challenging the Legitimacy of International Adjudication' in the present volume.

focusing successively on: (1) the respective roles of the judges and the legal officers; and (2) how the borders of these roles are enforced.

23.2 The respective roles of the judges and the legal officers

The role of judges is generally defined in the founding instruments of each international criminal court or tribunal. Ever since the creation of the International Criminal Tribunal for the Former Yugoslavia (ICTY) revived international criminal law, judges in international and hybrid criminal courts and tribunals are required to be persons of high moral character, impartiality and integrity who possess the qualifications required in their respective countries for appointment to the highest judicial offices.[3] Starting with the Special Court for Sierra Leone (SCSL), it was further specified that the judges shall be independent in the performance of their functions and shall not accept or seek instructions from any Government or any other source.[4] As reflected in the rules of procedure and evidence of each court or tribunal, the judges control the court proceedings, receive evidence, deliberate, decide motions and issue a judgment in which they determine the guilt or innocence of the accused as well as a sentence in the case of guilt.

No equivalent provisions exist for legal officers in chambers. Thus, it is not clear from the applicable rules what their role should be. Nevertheless, as early as 1999, the Appeals Chamber of the ICTY recognised that the work of a legal officer assigned to a trial chamber 'is integral to the operation of the Tribunal which must be protected by confidentiality.'[5] In practice, providing legal advice, research and drafting are the three main functions of legal officers (setting aside administrative tasks and

---

[3] ICTY Statute, Art. 13; ICTR Statute, Art. 12; ICC Statute, Art. 36(3)(a); SCSL Statute, Art. 13(1); ECCC, Agreement between the United Nations and the Royal Government of Cambodia Concerning the Prosecution under Cambodian Law of Crimes Committed during the Period of Democratic Kampuchea, 6 June 2003, Art. 3(3); Statute of the Special Tribunal for Lebanon, Art. 9(1); Statute of the Mechanism for International Criminal Tribunals, Art. 9(1); Kosovo Law on Specialist Chambers and Specialist Prosecutor's Office, Art. 27(1).

[4] SCSL Statute, Art. 13(1); ECCC, Agreement between the United Nations and the Royal Government of Cambodia Concerning the Prosecution under Cambodian Law of Crimes Committed during the Period of Democratic Kampuchea, 6 June 2003, Art. 3(3); Statute of the Special Tribunal for Lebanon, Art. 9(1); Kosovo Law on Specialist Chambers and Specialist Prosecutor's Office, Art. 27(1).

[5] *Prosecutor v. Zejnil Delalić et al.* ('*Čelebići* case'), Decision on Motion to Preserve and Provide Evidence, Case No. IT-96-21-A, Appeals Chamber, 22 April 1999, p. 4. See ibid., p. 3.

managerial duties). A typical vacancy announcement for a mid-level legal officer position (P-3) in chambers describes his or her responsibilities as follows:

> The incumbent will provide specialized legal and judicial administrative support to a Trial or the Appeals Chamber of the Tribunal through the P-4 Legal Officer or Senior Legal Officer. The duties include conducting and supervising legal research, particularly on international humanitarian and criminal law; supervising the preparation of draft memoranda, decisions and judgments; providing leadership to teams that provide support at the trial or appeal phase; providing legal support to the P-4 Legal Officer or Senior Legal Officer and Judges of the Chamber; undertaking legal analysis of judgments and evidence; assessing trial and appeal briefs and authorities submitted by parties; maintaining files on Tribunal practice and development and monitoring relevant developments in international law.[6]

The lack of clarity in the rules on the respective roles of judges and legal officers was ripe ground for legal challenges. The first challenge came in 2006 in the *Lubanga* case before the International Criminal Court (ICC). The prosecution, joined by the defence, made a request to Pre-Trial Chamber I to prevent the senior legal officer of the pre-trial division from rendering advice in the case because of his past involvement in the same case when he used to work for the prosecution. All judges of the pre-trial division requested the President of the ICC to convene a special plenary in order to deal with the issue because they considered that the request raised a question with regard to their own impartiality.[7] As a result, Pre-Trial Chamber I found that it was not the appropriate organ of the court to deal with the issue and held that it lacked jurisdiction to entertain the request. As a provisional measure, the President of the Pre-Trial Division also separated the senior legal advisor from the case.[8]

The *Lubanga* decision provided very little guidance for future cases, considering that a special plenary had been convened and that Pre-Trial Chamber I therefore found that it lacked jurisdiction. Nevertheless, it is noteworthy that the judges took it very seriously and separated the legal officer from the case. It is also notable that the issue was framed as concerning an alleged appearance of bias of the judges, rather than

---

[6] www.icty.org/sites/icty.org/files/vacancy/160920_lo_p3.pdf.

[7] *Prosecutor vs. Thomas Lubanga Dyilo*, Decision on the Prosecutor's Application to Separate the Senior Legal Adviser to the Pre-Trial Division from Rendering Legal Advice regarding the Case, Case No. ICC-01/04-01/06, Pre-Trial Chamber I, 27 October 2006, p. 2, referring to Art. 41(2) of the ICC Statute and Rule 4(2) of the ICC Rules of Procedure and Evidence.

[8] Ibid., p. 3.

the senior legal officer himself.[9] This would become a recurring theme in the ensuing case law on the role of legal officers in chambers. It reflects a vision of the judges as the decision-makers by virtue of their legitimacy.

At the ICTY, the role of a senior legal officer in chambers was challenged in 2009 by the defence for Florence Hartmann, former spokesperson for the ICTY Prosecutor, in the context of the contempt proceedings against her for disclosing confidential information.[10] The defence requested that the senior legal officer be removed from the case, arguing that he provided 'assistance and advice of an unspecified sort' to the *amicus curiae*, amounting to direct and *ex parte* participation in the investigation and preparation of the case, and that his continued involvement in the case casts an apprehension of bias over the chamber.[11] The defence also argued that the impartiality of a judge may be prejudiced by his or her association with chambers staff, who fall within the ambit of ICTY Rule 15(A) according to which a judge should be disqualified if (s)he has 'any association which might affect his or her impartiality'.[12] The panel of judges appointed to consider the motion held that Rule 15 clearly applies only to judges, not legal officers. It also noted that the disqualification of chambers staff is not contemplated in the ICTY's jurisprudence. Finally, the panel did not consider the conduct of a staff member to be relevant to a judge's impartiality.[13]

By limiting the application of Rule 15 to judges and seemingly rejecting the idea of disqualifying staff, the panel introduced a clear distinction between judges and legal officers, allowing challenges only to the former. This in combination with the holding that the conduct of a staff member is not relevant to a judge's impartiality set up a firewall between legal officers and judges, which might have put an end to further litigation on this issue. However, subsequent case law examined below did contemplate that the behaviour of chambers staff could go too far and did consider that the conduct of a staff member may be relevant to a judge's impartiality.

---

[9] Ibid., p. 2.

[10] *In the Case Against Florence Hartmann*, Report of Decision on Defence Motion for Disqualification of Two Members of the Trial Chamber and of Senior Legal Officer (public redacted version), Case No. IT-02-54-R77.5, Panel, 27 March 2009, para. 2.

[11] Ibid., para. 18. Specifically, the defence claimed that the senior legal officer 'authorised' the *amicus curiae* to disclose confidential decisions to the defence and to interview Hartmann's publisher. Ibid., para. 18.

[12] Ibid., para. 19.

[13] Ibid., para. 54.

Later in 2009, Ieng Sary requested the pre-trial chamber of the Extraordinary Chambers in the Courts of Cambodia (ECCC) to dis-qualify a legal officer in the Office of the Co-Investigating Judges from all legal, analytical or investigative tasks on his case.[14] The defence alleged that the legal officer's publicly expressed opinions concerning the ECCC gave the impression that he harboured prejudgments and biases.[15] Mr. Sary argued that Rule 34 of the ECCC's Internal Rules, entitled 'Recusal and Disqualification of Judges', applied to the legal officer because the judicial obligation of impartiality must equally apply to those people who work closely with the judges and carry out judicial functions on their behalf.[16] Mr. Sary also argued that the fundamental importance of the right to an independent and impartial tribunal shall lead to a broad appli-cation of Internal Rule 34.[17] The legal officer received a notification pur-suant to a provision of this Rule according to which the impugned 'judge' was entitled to present written submissions to the chamber. However, true to his nature as an unseen actor, the legal officer did not make any such submission.[18]

The Pre-Trial Chamber was not impressed by Mr. Sary's arguments, holding that Internal Rule 34 referred only to specific judges and did not apply to staff members.[19] The Pre-Trial Chamber also canvassed the relevant rules and jurisprudence of international courts and tribunals, observing that they apply exclusively to judges and do not extend to staff members whose impartiality may be a cause for disqualification of the judge with whom they are associated but not of the officer him or her-self.[20] Finally, regarding the argument in favour of a broad application of Internal Rule 34, the Pre-Trial Chamber held that the role and functions of legal officers are distinct from those of the judges, who have sole authority

---

[14] *Prosecutor v. Ieng Sary*, Case No. 002/08-07-2009-ECCC-PTC, Decision on the Charged Person's Application for Disqualification of Drs. Stephen Heder and David Boyle, 22 September 2009, paras. 1, 6.

[15] *Prosecutor v. Ieng Sary*, Case No. 002/19-09-2007-ECCC-OCIJ (PTC), Ieng Sary's Application for Disqualification of OCIJ Investigator Stephen Heder and OCIJ Legal Officer David Boyle in the Office of the Co-investigating Judges, 8 July 2009, para. 4.

[16] *Prosecutor v. Ieng Sary*, Case No. 002/08-07-2009-ECCC-PTC, Decision on the Charged Person's Application for Disqualification of Drs. Stephen Heder and David Boyle, 22 September 2009, paras. 7–8.

[17] Ibid., para. 8.

[18] Ibid., para. 3, referring to Internal Rule 34(7).

[19] Ibid., para. 14.

[20] Ibid., para. 15.

and responsibility to conduct the judicial investigation and determine on what they will rely in their decisions and orders.[21]

This decision of the Pre-Trial Chamber relied and built on the approach taken in previous cases, notably by making a fundamental distinction between, on the one hand, the role and functions of legal officers and, on the other hand, those of the judges. Only the latter, as the legitimate actors, can exercise judicial functions such as determining on what they will rely in their decisions and orders. This expression could be understood to refer to the legal authorities on which they wish to rely, or to the arguments that they wish to adopt. The latter interpretation seems more reasonable as the construction of legal argument is more central to judicial decision-making than the choice of the specific legal authorities that underpin the argument. By implication, legal officers, being unseen actors, may advise the judges in this regard but not usurp their decision-making authority. The distinction between the role and functions of judges and legal officers would become a central tenet of the case law pertaining to legal officers in chambers.

The issue of the role of legal officers in chambers came before the International Criminal Tribunal for Rwanda (ICTR) in 2009, leading to the most seminal decision yet to be issued on the matter. The defence in the *Bizimungu et al.* case argued before Trial Chamber II that it should refrain from engaging a legal consultant who previously held the position of Deputy Registrar of the tribunal, arguing that it would create an appearance of bias.[22] The defence argued that Rule 15 of the ICTR Rules of Procedure of Evidence (which provides, in Rule 15(A): 'A Judge may not sit in any case in which he has a personal interest or concerning which he has or has had any association which might affect his impartiality') applied to the prospective legal consultant and that his alleged bias or appearance of bias may be imputed to the judges.[23] Relying on the *Hartmann* report and the similarity between the relevant ICTY and ICTR rules, the trial chamber held that ICTR Rule 15 did not apply to chambers legal officers or consultants.[24] The trial chamber also held that a chambers

---

[21] Ibid., para. 20. See also ibid., paras. 16–19, 21–22.
[22] *The Prosecutor v. Casimir Bizimungu et al.*, Decision on the Objections of the Mugiraneza and Bicamumpaka Defence Teams to the Engagement of Mr. Everard O'Donnell as a Chambers Consultant, Case No. ICTR-99-50-T, Trial Chamber II, 28 August 2009, paras. 1, 4.
[23] Ibid., paras. 7–8.
[24] Ibid., paras. 11–14.

legal officer or consultant did not enjoy the same presumption of impartiality as the judges.[25]

The defence appealed the matter.[26] One defence team argued that Article 22 of the ICTR Statute[27] entitled the accused to a judgment free of actual bias or the appearance of bias and that legal staff cannot have such bias, as their association with a judge may prejudice his or her impartiality.[28] Another defence team argued that Rule 15(A), although not directly applicable to consultants or legal officers, should serve as a test for the disqualification of these persons.[29] The Appeals Chamber found no error in Trial Chamber II's reliance on *Hartmann* to conclude that ICTR Rule 15 did not apply to chambers legal officers or consultants.[30] It went on to make the most significant holding yet:

> The Appeals Chamber further notes that the submissions of [the defence] are premised on the erroneous notion that legal officers or consultants play a central role in the Judges' deliberations. Judicial decision-making is the sole purview of the Judges and legal officers and consultants play no role in it. Rather, they merely provide assistance to the Judges in legal research and preparing draft decisions, judgements, opinions, and orders in conformity with the instructions given to them by the Judges. Accordingly, there is no merit in [the defence's] assertions that legal officers and consultants must be subject to the same standards of impartiality as the Judges of the Tribunal.[31]

Nevertheless, in an *obiter dictum*, the Appeals Chamber qualified this statement by holding that: 'In some cases, a prospective staff member's statements or activities may be so problematic as to either impugn the perceived impartiality of the Judges or the appearance thereof, or, even if

[25] Ibid., para. 17.
[26] See *The Prosecutor v. Casimir Bizimungu et al.*, Decision on Appeals Concerning the Engagement of a Chambers Consultant or Legal Officer, Case No. ICTR-99-50-AR-73.8, Appeals Chamber, 17 December 2009, paras. 1–3.
[27] Article 22(1) provides: 'The Trial Chambers shall pronounce judgements and impose sentences and penalties on persons convicted of serious violations of international humanitarian law.' Article 22(2) provides: 'The judgement shall be rendered by a majority of the judges of the Trial Chamber, and shall be delivered by the Trial Chamber in public. It shall be accompanied by a reasoned opinion in writing, to which separate or dissenting opinions may be appended.'
[28] *The Prosecutor v. Casimir Bizimungu et al.*, Decision on Appeals Concerning the Engagement of a Chambers Consultant or Legal Officer, Case No. ICTR-99-50-AR-73.8, Appeals Chamber, 17 December 2009, para. 5.
[29] Ibid., para. 6.
[30] Ibid., para. 8.
[31] Ibid., para. 9. See also ibid., paras. 15–16.

this were not the case, the Tribunal's fundamental guarantees of fair trial.' The Appeals Chamber added that the facts before it fell far short of this test.[32]

The Appeals Chamber's holdings are notable in several ways. First, it recognises a practical reality sometimes deemed sensitive, namely that the legal officers prepare draft decisions, judgments, opinions and orders for the judges, while downplaying another important function of legal officers, namely providing legal advice to the judges. Regardless, this is a significant step in rendering the role of legal officers less opaque. In the view of this author, it enhances the legitimacy of both the actors who chose to be transparent, i.e. the judges, and of those whose role they have validated, i.e. the legal officers. At the same time, it raises the question of where the border lies between carrying out these functions for a judge and usurping his or her judicial power. For instance, if a legal officer prepares a draft decision without first consulting the judge and the judge then quickly reads and approves the decision with no or almost no edits, does the judicial decision-making in effect still lie with the judge? Second, the Appeals Chamber answers this question in the affirmative by setting a clear distinction between judges and legal officers, giving the latter 'no role' in judicial decision-making. Indeed, the judges alone carry the burden of judicial obligations and hold the international legitimacy to determine the guilt or innocence of the accused. Third, the Appeals Chamber nevertheless opened a breach in the firewall between judges and their legal staff by acknowledging that there might be cases in which staff's statements or activities may be 'so problematic' as to impugn the perception or appearance of judicial impartiality (not mentioning their actual impartiality) or affect the fairness of the trial. This holding would appear to contradict, or at least qualify, the ICTY finding that the conduct of a staff member is not relevant to a judge's impartiality.[33]

The issue of the role of legal officers in chambers reappeared in the *Butare* case before ICTR Trial Chamber II, which discovered in July 2009 that the then-chief of the Chambers Support section at the ICTR had participated in the same case as an employee of the prosecution a decade earlier. Before the chief of the Chambers Support section participated in any deliberations relating to the guilt or innocence of the accused in the *Butare* case and as an immediate precautionary measure, Trial Chamber

---

[32] Ibid., para. 11.
[33] See *In the Case Against Florence Hartmann*, Report, para. 19.

II *proprio motu* excluded him from the judgment drafting process. In November 2009, upon closer examination, Trial Chamber II confirmed this measure out of an abundance of caution and in the interest of justice and the appearance of justice.[34]

The defence appealed the matter, submitting that the chief of the Chambers Support section's participation in the preparation of the trial judgment affected their right to a fair trial. One defence team argued that his participation in the work of Trial Chamber II in this case prior to his exclusion in November 2009 constituted a serious conflict of interest or, at least, an appearance of conflict of interest. The defence team added that the trial chamber erred in failing to take precautionary measures when the person was hired as the Chief of the Chambers Support Section to avoid this situation, in not providing sufficient details about the extent of his participation in the work of the trial chamber, and in allowing the prejudice to persist even though it became aware of the situation in July 2009. Another defence team submitted that, as a party to the proceedings, the chief of the Cambers Support section should not have participated in the drafting of the trial judgment.[35]

The Appeals Chamber, relying heavily on its holdings in the *Bizimungu et al.* case, observed that the defence had not pointed to any element suggesting that the Chief of the Chambers Support Section had participated in the judicial decision-making process or had exercised any undue influence on this process. To the contrary, the Appeals Chamber emphasised that Trial Chamber II had excluded the person from participating in any deliberations relating to the guilt or innocence of the accused and had excluded him from all aspects of the trial judgment drafting process from July 2009. As a result, it found that the defence had failed to provide support for the assertion that the impartiality or appearance of impartiality of the judicial decision-making process and, consequently, their fair trial rights might have been affected by his limited involvement in this case prior to July 2009.[36]

While the *Butare* case adds little to the *Bizimungu et al.* case in terms of the applicable law, it is nonetheless notable for a couple of reasons. First, by stating that it excluded the chief of the Chambers Support from the

---

[34] *The Prosecutor v. Pauline Nyiramasuhuko et al.* ('*Butare* case'), Judgement and Sentence, Case No. ICTR-98-42-T, Trial Chamber II, 24 June 2011, para. 204.

[35] *The Prosecutor v. Pauline Nyiramasohuko et al.* ('*Butare* case'), Judgement, Case No. ICTR-98-42-A, Appeals Chamber, 14 December 2015, para. 271.

[36] Ibid., paras. 273–274.

judgment drafting process before he had participated in any deliberations relating to the guilt or innocence of the accused, the trial chamber seemed to suggest that he would otherwise have been involved in such deliberations. If so, it would have been in a role of assisting the judges, not directly partaking in the deliberations, which is within the sole purview of the judges. Second, by approving of Trial Chamber II's swift action upon discovering the issue, the Appeals Chamber showed the way forward for other trial chambers that discover similar conflicts of interest.[37] It remains to be seen what course of action should be taken where a similar conflict of interest is discovered at a stage too advanced to prevent negative effects on justice and the appearance of justice.

In the *Hategekimana* case, some children's drawings that had been entered into a competition were displayed at the ICTR. According to the defence, one of the first prizes in the competition was awarded to a drawing in which Mr. Hategekimana admitted guilt. The defence contended that this drawing, which was exhibited in the corridors of the tribunal before the delivery of the trial judgment, could be viewed by the judges of the trial chamber and that a legal officer involved in the drafting of the trial judgment was part of the competition's jury. At the pronouncement of the trial judgment, the defence complained about the exhibition of the drawing and the trial chamber ordered that it be placed under seal.[38] The defence submitted that the accused's rights to be presumed innocent and to be tried by impartial judges were violated by the legal officer's involvement in the judgment drafting process and by the display of the drawing at the tribunal. It also contended that the judges violated his presumption of innocence and exhibited bias by posing in front of the drawing for a photograph and by allowing a member of the competition's jury to assist in the judgment-drafting process.[39]

The Appeals Chamber acknowledged that it was highly improper to display such a drawing in the tribunal during the trial. However, it found that the defence had failed to provide support for the allegation that the judges saw the drawing or posed for a photograph in front of it. It held that, even if the judges had viewed the drawing, this would not be sufficient to show an appearance of bias or to rebut the presumption of impartiality of the judges.[40] To the contrary, the Appeals Chamber held that

---

[37] See also above, footnote 8.
[38] *The Prosecutor v. Ildephonse Hategekimana*, Judgement, Case No. ICTR-00-55B-A, Appeals Chamber, 8 May 2012, para. 13.
[39] Ibid., para. 14.
[40] Ibid., para. 17.

the trial chamber's prompt reaction upon hearing the defence's complaint contradicted any appearance of bias.[41] Relying heavily on the *Bizimungu et al.* decision, the Appeals Chamber dismissed the argument that the trial chamber violated the accused's rights by accepting the legal officer's contribution to the drafting of the trial judgment, as it was based on the erroneous premise that legal officers play a controlling role in judicial decision-making.[42] The Appeals Chamber also found that the role of the legal officer in the competition was not 'so problematic' as to impugn the impartiality of the judges or the appearance thereof.[43]

The *Hategekimana* judgment re-affirmed the *Bizimungu et al.* decision as a leading authority on the issue of the role of legal officers in chambers. While acknowledging that displaying the drawing at the tribunal was highly improper, the Appeals Chamber used, like in the *Butare* case, the swift action of the trial chamber as an indicator of lack of bias. The Appeals Chamber also applied the *obiter dictum* in the *Bizimungu et al.* case, finding that the role of the legal officer in the competition was insufficient to break down the firewall between judges and their staff.[44] In doing so, it clarified the *Bizimungu et al.* precedent in that the behaviour of a legal officer might affect not only the perception of impartiality of the judges but also their actual impartiality.

In the *Mladić* case at the ICTY, the defence filed a motion before Trial Chamber I, alleging that Mr. Mladić's fair trial rights had been violated by the trial chamber integrating staff who had previously worked for another trial chamber seised of the *Karadžić* case.[45] The defence argued that the staff had drafted the trial judgment in that case, which contained findings in effect convicting Mr. Mladić, and therefore were no longer impartial towards him. Their influence on the judges might therefore affect the judges' impartiality under Rule 15(A).[46] The defence also argued that the idea that judicial decision-making is solely within the purview of the judges did not apply to the *Mladić* trial chamber, which had issued decisions by emails sent by staff.[47]

---

[41] Ibid., para. 18.

[42] Ibid., paras. 19–20.

[43] Ibid., para. 20.

[44] One wonders, however, what the chamber would have found if the staff member had been the artist of the drawing on display.

[45] *Prosecutor v. Ratko Mladić*, Decision on Defence Motion for a Fair Trial and the Presumption of Innocence or, in the Alternative, a Mistrial, Case No. ICTR-09-92-T, Trial Chamber I, 4 July 2016, para. 1.

[46] Ibid., para. 2.

[47] Ibid., para. 5.

Trial Chamber I noted that the defence erroneously assumed that it was the staff rather than the judges who made findings in the *Karadžić* case.[48] Relying on the ICTR and ICTY case law outlined above, the trial chamber held that the staff merely assist the judges, who retain all decision-making power, that the conduct of the staff is irrelevant to the impartiality of the judges and that the disqualification of staff is not envisaged under the relevant rules and jurisprudence.[49] The trial chamber noted that the judges would rule fairly on the issues before them by virtue of their professional training and experience, relying exclusively on the evidence in the *Mladić* case, even if their staff had been exposed to evidence in both cases.[50] The findings in the *Karadžić* trial judgment that Mr. Mladić identified as having 'convicted' him neither established the criteria to constitute a criminal offence, nor drew conclusions on his responsibility.[51] The trial chamber also explained that while chambers staff informally communicated decisions to the parties on time-sensitive matters until formal decisions could be placed on the record, this was done pursuant to explicit instructions from the judges.[52]

The defence appealed Trial Chamber I's decision.[53] It argued that the trial chamber erred when stating that the bias of staff did not affect Mr. Mladić's right to be presumed innocent and that it implicitly acknowledged that chambers staff do not have to be impartial. According to the defence, it would be unreasonable to think that the staff would completely reanalyse the evidence without relying on preconceived conclusions that they drew from the *Karadžić* case.[54] Relying on the ICTY and ICTR jurisprudence outlined above, the Appeals Chamber agreed with the trial chamber that Mr. Mladić's argument was misconceived as it presumed that legal officers were subject to the same standards of impartiality as the judges.[55] The Appeals Chamber therefore disagreed that the trial chamber had acknowledged that staff are allowed to be biased. It also upheld the trial chamber's conclusion that the assistance of the staff does

---

[48] Ibid., paras. 18, 24.
[49] Ibid., paras. 18, 20, 26.
[50] Ibid., para. 23.
[51] Ibid., para. 24.
[52] Ibid., paras. 19–20.
[53] *Prosecutor v. Ratko Mladić*, Decision on Interlocutory Appeal against Decision on Defence Motion for a Fair Trial and the Presumption of Innocence, Case No. IT-09-92-AR73.6, Appeals Chamber, 27 February 2017, para. 1.
[54] Ibid., para. 15.
[55] Ibid., paras. 29–30.

not influence the decision-making ability of the judges.[56] The Appeals Chamber held that case law relating to the impartiality of judges sitting in overlapping judicial proceedings involving co-accused does not apply to legal officers.[57] It concluded that staff's previous work on an overlapping case is not, in and of itself, sufficient to impugn the judges' impartiality or appearance of impartiality.[58]

The *Mladić* case cemented the prior jurisprudence on the topic of the role and functions of legal officers in chambers. In doing so, it added further clarifications. For instance, chambers staff may informally communicate decisions to the parties pursuant to instructions from the judges. In addition, case law relating to the impartiality of judges sitting in overlapping judicial proceedings involving co-accused does not apply to legal officers. Finally, staff's previous work on an overlapping case does not suffice to impugn the judges' impartiality or appearance of impartiality. Apart from such refinements, it seems unlikely that future case law will diverge significantly from the precedents laid down so far.

In conclusion, the case law of international and hybrid criminal courts and tribunals draws a clear distinction between the judges and the legal officers. The latter are not subject to the same impartiality standards or disqualification procedures as the judges. However, a legal officer's statements or activities may be so problematic as to affect the impartiality or appearance of impartiality of the judges or the right to fair trial. So far, the only indication in the case law of what might be problematic enough to meet this test is if the legal officer has a conflict of interest such as having previously worked for one of the parties on the same case. As to their respective tasks, judicial decision-making is the sole purview of the judges, while legal officers merely assist them in performing legal research, preparing draft decisions, judgments, opinions and orders, and communicating decisions to the parties, in conformity with the judges' instructions. The case law thus reflects that all judicial powers, responsibility and legitimacy lie with the judges. Finally, it is noteworthy that, apart from a bit of evolution in the case law, all courts and tribunals, whether they are hybrid or international and follow a predominantly adversarial or inquisitorial procedure, rely on each other's case law and have adopted a uniform approach to the role of legal officers in chambers.

---

[56] Ibid., para. 30.
[57] Ibid., para. 33.
[58] Ibid., para. 39.

23.3   Enforcing the Borders of the Role of the Legal Officer

Enforcing the borders of the role of legal officers starts with the legal officers themselves. It is their professional responsibility to ensure that they are advising and assisting the judges, rather than usurping any of their judicial functions. For instance, if a judge tasks a legal officer with drafting a decision based on a general indication of the direction to follow, it is the duty of that legal officer to indicate to the judge in case the drafting process reveals an unforeseen difficulty in the outlined solution. Similarly, if the drafting process reveals that there is a different and more convincing outcome to a matter under litigation, then the legal officer should inform the judge. If, on the other hand, the judge tasks the legal officer with drafting a decision without any guidance as to its outcome then the legal officer should apply the applicable law as strictly and neutrally as possible and advise the judge to the existence of any alternative approaches meriting consideration. By taking such a course of action, the legal officers can enhance rather than damage the legitimacy of their court or tribunal.

Senior chambers staff who are very familiar with the judges' preferences can review the decisions drafted by junior staff to ensure that they duly present all relevant issues and can form the basis for deliberations between the judges. Senior chambers staff can also assist the judges in advising on assigning chambers staff by examining their curriculum vitaes so as to avoid conflicts of interest. For instance, a legal officer should not be assigned to a case on which he or she has previously worked for the prosecution or the defence, or on which his or her partner is working for the prosecution or the defence. Nor should the legal officer be assigned to a case on appeal if he or she performed any substantive work on the case at trial. Careful scrutiny of this kind can prevent difficult reassignments of staff and litigation from occurring at a later stage. In other words, it can help safeguard the legitimacy of the judicial institution.

The judges also have a role to play. Aware of their judicial responsibilities, they will have to consider what can properly be delegated and what cannot. Ultimately, it is for the judges, deliberating independently, to decide which arguments to adopt and which conclusions to reach.[59] The judges will also have to consider whether assistance from certain legal

---

[59] See above, footnotes 1, 20, 30.

officers would create a reasonable apprehension of bias in the mind of a properly informed observer.[60] For instance, if it comes to their attention that a legal officer assisting them on a case had previously worked for the prosecution or the defence on the same case, they should immediately take measures to preserve their own appearance of impartiality. In some circumstances it may be sufficient to swiftly remove the legal officer from the case.[61] It is important how the judges, as the legitimate decision-makers, are seen to act in these situations.

If it gets to the point where the parties initiate litigation that questions the role of a legal officer in chambers, then the burden of proof is on the moving party,[62] and the competent body is the chamber whose legal officer is in issue.[63] It is up to the judges themselves to settle the matter based on the applicable law of their specific court or tribunal, as well as the generally relevant jurisprudence examined above.[64] Thus, it is the judges who determine their own bias or appearance of bias. While this might seem surprising at first blush, judges are generally keen to preserve their own appearance of impartiality. This serves to protect their legitimacy. Basing a decision on the appearance of bias rather than actual bias allows the judges to make a finding in favour of the moving party without stating that they as judges are no longer impartial. It is submitted, however, that the drafting of such a decision should not be delegated to the legal officer whose role is litigated. To protect the legitimacy of the court or tribunal, this legal officer should rather be isolated from the litigation in question and have no role in it.

What is the applicable standard of appellate review when a decision is appealed? This question was first dealt with in the seminal *Bizimungu et al.* decision of the ICTR Appeals Chamber. It held that a trial chamber's determination of whether the engagement of a legal officer would lead

[60] See *Prosecutor v. Anto Furundžija*, Judgement, Case No. IT-95-17/1-A, Appeals Chamber, 21 July 2000, para. 189. See also T. Meron, 'Judicial Independence and Impartiality in International Criminal Tribunals' (2005) 99 *American Journal of International Law* 359, 366–367.

[61] See above, footnotes 8, 34.

[62] *The Prosecutor v. Casimir Bizimungu et al.*, Decision on the Objections of the Mugiraneza and Bicamumpaka Defence Teams to the Engagement of Mr. Everard O'Donnell as a Chambers Consultant, Case No. ICTR-99-50-T, Trial Chamber II, 28 August 2009, para. 17.

[63] See cases examined above in Section 23.2, with the exception of the *Lubanga* decision which has not been followed in this respect by any other chamber. See above, footnote 8.

[64] See above, Section 23.2.

to actual bias or the appearance of bias is a *discretionary decision*.[65] This essentially means that the Appeals Chamber has a narrower margin for finding error in what a trial chamber did or found. Indeed:

> Where a discretionary decision is appealed, the issue is whether the Trial Chamber correctly exercised its discretion and not whether the decision was correct, in the sense that the Appeals Chamber agrees with it. Consequently, the Appeals Chamber will only reverse an impugned decision where it is demonstrated that a Trial Chamber committed a discernible error, based on an incorrect interpretation of the governing law, a patently incorrect conclusion of fact, or where the impugned decision was so unfair or unreasonable as to constitute an abuse of the Trial Chamber's discretion.[66]

It is easy to accept that a trial chamber's hiring decisions lie within its discretionary powers. It is arguably less obvious that the same holds true for its determination of whether such a decision would lead to actual bias or the appearance of bias. Perhaps that is why, as seen above, the Appeals Chamber added a warning that chambers staff's statements or activities could be so problematic as to either impugn the perception or appearance of judicial legitimacy or affect the right to fair trial.[67]

In the *Mladić* case, the defence argued that the denial of his motion relating to the presumption of innocence is not a discretionary decision since the right to the presumption of innocence is absolute. Instead, he argued, the applicable standard of review should be whether the trial chamber committed errors of law or of fact.[68] The Appeals Chamber repeated the holding from the *Bizimungu et al.* case that a trial chamber's determination of whether the engagement of a legal officer would lead to actual bias or the appearance of bias is a discretionary decision to which the Appeals Chamber must accord deference.[69] However, perhaps recognising some merit in Mr. Mladić's argument, the Appeals Chamber also emphasised that trial chambers must exercise their discretion

---

[65] *The Prosecutor v. Casimir Bizimungu et al.*, Decision on Appeals Concerning the Engagement of a Chambers Consultant or Legal Officer, Case No. ICTR-99-50-AR-73.8, Appeals Chamber, 17 December 2009, para. 4. See also ibid., para. 11.

[66] Ibid., para. 4 (internal references omitted).

[67] Ibid., para. 11.

[68] *Prosecutor v. Ratko Mladić*, Decision on Interlocutory Appeal against Decision on Defence Motion for a Fair Trial and the Presumption of Innocence, Case No. IT-09-92-AR73.6, Appeals Chamber, 27 February 2017, para. 12.

[69] Ibid., paras. 8, 23.

consistently with the statutory provisions requiring trial chambers to ensure that a trial is fair and expeditious.[70]

The Appeals Chamber's decision in the *Mladić* case brings to the forefront the tension that was left unresolved in the *Bizimungu et al.* decision. On the one hand, it seems logical that a trial chamber's hiring decisions should be within its discretionary powers, largely shielded from the interference of the Appeals Chamber. On the other hand, if fundamental rights of the accused are at stake, the Appeals Chamber cannot refuse to intervene on the basis of according deference to the trial chamber's discretion. With the *Mladić* decision, the Appeals Chamber clearly recognised this tension and set a precedent, albeit in the form of an *obiter dictum*, which will allow future appeals chambers to interpret the *Bizimungu et al.* holding in a way that lets them intervene when necessary. This provides the appeal judges with a tool to potentially safeguard judicial legitimacy in the face of a legal officer who has gone too far.

In conclusion, legal officers and judges must monitor the statements and acts of the legal officers to ensure they do not throw doubt on the fairness of the proceedings. The judges have discretion in deciding whether engaging a certain legal officer would lead to actual bias or the appearance of bias, and appeals chambers must accord deference to their decision. However, this discretion must not be exercised in a way that renders the trial unfair. A legal officer's statements or activities could either directly compromise the fairness of the trial or do so indirectly by casting doubt on the impartiality of the judges.

23.4   Conclusion

The introduction to this chapter raised the question of how to define 'decision-making'. On one conception, the more the judges rely on the legal research, advice and drafting of their legal officers, the less they are the ones actually making the decisions. If so, it becomes necessary to define the minimum core that the judges need to decide. Limiting their decision-making to overall findings of guilt or innocence would give too much influence to legal officers, who lack judicial legitimacy. It would infringe on the right to be tried before an independent and impartial tribunal, i.e. by *judges* who are independent and impartial.[71] However,

[70] Ibid., para. 23.
[71] See *The Prosecutor v. Ferdinand Nahimana et al.* ('*Media* case'), Judgement, Case No. ICTR-99-52-A, Appeals Chamber, 28 November 2007, para. 28; *Prosecutor v. Augustin*

expecting the judges to deliberate on every detail in every draft would place an unrealistic burden on their shoulders and threaten the expeditious conduct of proceedings and the right of the accused to be tried without undue delay.[72] One solution might be for the judges to focus on which arguments to grant or deny, on what basis, which legal precedents to set and whether each and every factual and legal element required to establish the commission of crimes and the existence of individual criminal liability has been proven beyond reasonable doubt. Legal officers may draft for the judges and advise them on these matters but should be careful not to usurp their responsibility to make the decisions.[73]

On another conception of decision-making, it remains entirely with the judges, as only they are qualified to make decisions. Regardless of the ways in which and the extent to which the legal officers assist them, ultimately the judges take all decisions by putting their name to the work of the Chambers and making the end product their own. For instance, a busy judge may choose to rely entirely on an experienced and trusted legal officer's legal research, advice and/or drafting with regard to an uncontroversial matter. The judge trusts the work product enough to make it his or her own without examining it in depth. The decision to adopt the work of the legal officer is exclusively that of the judge and no issue arises with regard to the statements or activities of the legal officer. This conception of decision-making was implicitly endorsed by the ICTR Appeals Chamber in the *Bizimungu et al.* case when it held that legal officers have 'no role' in judicial decision-making despite drafting decisions, judgments, opinions and orders for the judges.

Applying to the *Bizimungu et al.* precedent a normative conception of legitimacy, one can conclude that the judicial decisions are indeed made in accordance with the applicable principles and rules and by the persons who are legally empowered to act and decide. But from the perspective of sociological legitimacy, do the addressees of international criminal decisions and judgments consider that the role of legal officers is justified? Arguably, the recurring challenges examined above by the prosecution and especially the defence to the role of legal officers suggest that this is not necessarily so. However, the lawyers who decided to bring the

---

Ngirabatware, Order to the Government of the Republic of Turkey for the Release of Judge Aydin Sefa Akay, Case No. MICT-12-29-R, Pre-Review Judge in the Appeals Chamber, 31 January 2017, para. 11.

[72] See Oberg, 'Processing Evidence and Drafting Judgments', 115–119.

[73] Ibid., 140–141.

challenges may simply have been motivated by the desire to seize a chance to further the interests of the party for whom they were working.

In this regard, it is notable that international and hybrid criminal courts and tribunals have so far rejected all challenges to the role of legal officers. One can imagine a number of reasons for this. First, legal officers and judges may in general be effective in regulating the behaviour of legal officers so as to avoid situations in which a challenge would be successful. The cases examined above reveal instances in which a trial chamber reacted swiftly when discovering that the participation of a legal officer in its work was problematic. Similarly, in the personal experience of the present author, senior chambers staff will monitor carefully whether chambers staff have a conflict of interest before engaging them on a specific case. Second, there may be a disconnect between how the parties perceive the role and influence of the legal officers from the outside and how the judges perceive them from the inside. In the cases examined above the parties and in particular the defence often subscribe great influence and power to the legal officers, which the judges reject in their analysis. Third, the standard set at trial and on appeal for making a successful application for relief is even higher and more difficult to meet than the standard for disqualification of judges.[74] This may be compounded by a reluctance to remove a legal officer from a case in the name of a possible perception of impartiality that is difficult to measure, especially if the work of the legal officer is quite valuable to the trial chamber and if the removal would be detrimental to the morale of the remaining legal officers. In sum, the sociological legitimacy of the role of legal officers appears to be open to debate.

Be that as it may, it is submitted that the case law on the role of legal officers in chambers strikes the right balance between pragmatic realism, acknowledging the necessary role of legal officers, and higher concerns of judicial integrity and legitimacy. In fact, the combination within chambers of legitimate actors chosen at the highest level based notably on their morals, impartiality, integrity and independence, and unseen actors hired on the basis of their technical expertise may be a wise balancing of legitimacy and pragmatism. Looking to the future, it is likely that litigation on

---

[74] See *Prosecutor v. Anto Furundžija*, Case No. IT-95-17/1-A, Judgement, Appeals Chamber, 21 July 2000, paras. 189–191; *Prosecutor v. Mićo Stanišić and Stojan Župljanin*, Case No. IT-08-91-A, Judgement, Appeals Chamber, 30 June 2016, paras. 32–33.

this issue will continue before international and hybrid criminal courts and tribunals. Even if the challenges to the role of legal officers remain unsuccessful, they will serve as helpful reminders for judges and legal officers to constantly ensure that the latter remain within their limited role so as not to tarnish the legitimacy of the judicial process.

The Référendaire as Unseen Actor

A Comparative Look at the Court of Justice of the EU, the US Supreme Court and International Arbitral Tribunals

GILLIAN CAHILL[1]

24.1   The Unseen Référendaire – An Introduction

The role of the Court of Justice of the European Union (the Court or CJEU) in the development of Europe since the mid-twentieth century cannot be overstated. The CJEU is the guarantor of the stability of the architecture of the European project. Its founding was intrinsically connected with the idea of creating a new European spirit in law, justice and politics, underpinned by the idea that conflicts in a future Europe should be solved not by war but by common institutions.[2] The Court achieves this, largely, via its role in determining appeals, preliminary reference procedures, direct actions between the actors of the Union and, of course, infringement proceedings. As the European Union grew, so inevitably did the issues of EU law. More issues of EU law led, again inevitably, to more cases arriving at the CJEU. More countries acceding to the Union meant a larger court, which in turn required a bigger administration and more support staff. For example, each new accession brought with it a need for more linguistic capabilities within the institution, new translators and interpreters being necessary to deal with cases from accession countries. Thus, the structure of the CJEU itself has been required to adapt to the demands that the development of the European project has created.

---

[1] The views expressed in this chapter are strictly personal.
[2] D. Tamm, 'The History of the Court of Justice of the European Union Since its Origin', in A. Rosas, E. Levits, Y. Bot and Court of Justice of the European Union (eds.), *The Court of Justice and the Construction of Europe: Analyses and Perspectives on Sixty Years of Case-Law* (Asser Press, 2013), pp. 9–35.

At present the CJEU as an institution has a staff of over 2,000, comprised of various professionals: translators and interpreters, legal researchers and librarians, along with a significant number of administrative and support staff. A smaller number of these staff act as *référendaires*, known in English as 'legal secretaries'. These actors, who are all lawyers or academics, act essentially as agents for the Members of the Court of Justice and General Court they serve. Despite playing a significant part in the functioning of the CJEU, the role of these actors remains relatively hidden and low profile, at the very least to those without an in-depth knowledge of the CJEU system. By way of contrast, whilst many Americans may be aware that the justices of their Supreme Court have law clerks to assist them, and some might even be aware of the potential significance of that role, the same cannot be said of the référendaires who serve the judges and advocates general of the CJEU.

Who, then, are these unseen actors and what precisely is their role in the functioning of the CJEU system? Most importantly, what are the limits of this role and how is the legitimacy of both the actor and the institution preserved? Have there been controversies surrounding the exercise of this actor's functions similar to those that have arisen for law clerks and, in particular, for tribunal secretaries in international arbitrations? The present chapter seeks to examine these questions on a comparative basis.

24.2 The CJEU Architecture

24.2.1 The Role of the Référendaire Within the CJEU Architecture

The role of *référendaire* has existed since the enactment of the first Coal and Steel Communities Treaty in 1952. Initially each of the seven judges and two advocates general, that then comprised the Court, had his or her own legal assistant.[3] In the 1960s this developed to two assistants and as the caseload and role of the Court evolved, so too did the number of référendaires, increasing to three per chambers of any given member of the Court.[4]

At present, judges of the CJEU maintain three référendaires, but may also engage a 'fourth référendaire' or legal assistant. The latter actors are

---

[3] D. Sarmiento, 'The Legal Secretary (CJEU)', in *Max Planck Encyclopedia of Procedural Law*, p. 3 (forthcoming).
[4] Ibid.

often younger lawyers, whose tasks may vary depending on the member for whom they work. Chambers of the advocates general at the CJEU have four référendaires. Certain judges with special functions within the CJEU system such as the President of the Court or the judge charged with responsibility for urgent preliminary procedures may also engage, at least, four référendaires in their chambers. Similarly, the chambers of judges at the General Court are staffed with three référendaires. Most recently, these judges have had the option of using a référendaire from an additional floating pool of lawyers where needs require.

Most people familiar with the functioning of the CJEU agree that référendaires form an important part of any given member's chambers. However, look for evidence of this role and at first glance it will be hard to find. The status of the référendaire is not defined by the Treaties. There is no mention of the référendaire in the Rules of Procedure of the CJEU. There are, in effect, no external rules governing the status of this actor. Where then does it fit within the EU system and if this actor is as hidden as it may first appear, from where does it derive its legitimacy?

In essence, as agent for the member of the Court they work for, the référendaire is subject to the Staff Regulations of the Court, an internal document of the institution. They do not (in general) form part of the permanent civil service that makes up the core staff of the CJEU. Rather, they are hand selected by the member they work for and their tenure depends precisely on the tenure of that member. They serve at the member's will and, for the purposes of EU staff regulation rules, they are deemed contractual agents. However, the role may also be filled by someone who is a permanent member of the EU Civil Service. In such cases, once the tenure of the member ends or once their time as référendaire is over, the permanent civil servant may then return to their previously held or similar position, which is often in an alternative service of the CJEU. Thus, the référendaire operates from within the CJEU employment structure, but at the same time slightly apart from it.

24.2.2 Ethical Standards and Supervision of référendaires

Despite the somewhat unusual place where référendaires sit within the CJEU system, they do not operate in a vacuum. All employees of the CJEU are obliged upon taking up their functions to comply with the staff rules of the EU institutions and in particular take an oath of loyalty and discretion to the CJEU itself. Moreover, in 2009, référendaires became subject to the 'Code de Bonne Conduite of Référendaires'.[5] These rules, effectively an ethical code, were enacted in order to avoid conflicts of interest and to ensure that référendaires were behaving in accordance with consistent and high ethical standards. The rules address issues such as how référendaires may conduct themselves, the limitations on what they can write and how they can express opinions and/or publish work whilst they are engaged at the CJEU and prevents them from receiving payment for speaking engagements. However, these rules do not have the same status as, for example, the staff rules of the EU institutions. Accordingly, a breach of them amounts to a breach of trust of the member they work for and would therefore be dealt with by the judge or advocate general in question, as he or she deems appropriate.

The issue of such a breach of trust also highlights a further difference between other permanent employees of the CJEU and référendaires, in that the référendaire is under the direct supervision of the member and not someone from the institution further up its hierarchy. Accordingly, decisions on hiring and firing and satisfactory performance are not determined by the EU institutional rules, as otherwise would be the case, but rather by the relevant judge or advocate general according to the criteria they so choose.

24.3 The Precise Role of the Référendaire

Given the intimate link between the référendaire and the member they work for, the precise confines of the référendaire's role are variable and member dependent. Much depends on how the given member of the CJEU they work for wishes to run his or her cabinet. As agent of that member, référendaires are there to serve, assist and advise the member in his or her exercise of judicial power. They are, in effect, the judge or advocate general's right hand in any given case. However, the precise nature of what that right hand looks like can vary quite considerably from member to member and even from case to case. A consequence of

---

[5] 'The Rules of Good Behaviour of Référendaires'.

the nature of the role is that there must be a great deal of trust between the référendaire and the member they work for, if the relationship is to function well.

Further, as the role of the référendaire has not been specifically set out, as is the case for all other roles within the CJEU's permanent civil service, there are no specific rules governing their tasks or qualifications. However, almost invariably référendaires tend to be highly qualified and experienced lawyers, very often specialised in EU law, and drawn from a wide range of backgrounds including both academics and practitioners. Référendaires may also be drawn from the ranks of national judges. Unlike clerks in the US Supreme Court, they are very rarely younger lawyers, fresh out of law school. Instead the average age of référendaires is currently around 39 years. How long a référendaire will stay at the CJEU tends to fall generally into two camps. In the first camp, many référendaires stay between three and six years, the latter being a full mandate for a member of the Court. Others recruited mid-mandate may stay for less time, although it is rare for a référendaire to stay for less than two years as a certain degree of time is required to familiarise and integrate oneself into the internal CJEU system.

In the second camp, and in sharp contrast to actors such as US Supreme Court clerks (recruited for a one-year term only) and to arbitral secretaries (where the role lasts essentially as long as the case does), some référendaires undertake the role as a career for life. A number of factors may explain this difference. Of most significance is perhaps the nature of the work at the CJEU, as will be described in more detail below. The role, in general, permits a référendaire substantive involvement in some of the most significant issues in EU law and is therefore attractive for many lawyers, particularly those interested and with a practice in EU law. The breadth of the issues that the CJEU deals with and the impact that the decisions made by the Court have on those living in the EU should therefore not be underestimated as a draw for lawyers wishing to make their career as a référendaire.

24.3.1   The Influence of the Volume of Cases?

Before turning to look at the functions of the référendaire in more detail, this actor's role should also be examined against the backdrop of how the CJEU works. One distinguishing feature pertaining to the CJEU that is absent from both the US Supreme Court and arbitral tribunals is the high volume of cases that the CJEU deals with each year. In 2017, the CJEU completed 699 cases. Of these, 447 concerned preliminary ruling requests.[6]

On the other side of the Atlantic, the US Supreme Court hears, on average, 65 to 70 cases per year. This significant divergence can be put down, in large part, to the filtering system used by the US Supreme Court, of which its clerks are an integral and important part. One of the main, and most important, tasks of the Supreme Court law clerk is to read and provide summaries of the petitions for certiorari that the US Supreme Court frequently receives.[7]

By contrast, the majority of the cases dealt with by the CJEU are preliminary reference procedures, which are not technically a litigious proceeding at all, but rather a dialogue between the CJEU and the national courts of the EU Member States, which facilitates the uniform interpretation and application of EU law within the EU. Indeed, the CJEU frequently mentions the importance of this dialogue and of the reference procedure as the keystone to the maintenance of the EU legal system. In a recent seminal case, the CJEU reiterated its position that:

> the judicial system as thus conceived has as its keystone the preliminary ruling procedure provided for in Article 267 TFEU, which, by setting up a dialogue between one court and another, specifically between the Court of Justice and the courts and tribunals of the Member States, has the object of securing uniform interpretation of EU law …, thereby serving to ensure its consistency, its full effect and its autonomy as well as, ultimately, the particular nature of the law established by the Treaties[8]

Thus, despite an increasing caseload, the Court is, in reality, eager to continue fostering dialogue between it and the national courts of the Member States of the EU. Accordingly, a filtering system such as that present used in the US system would not be appropriate in the CJEU system. A consequence of this is that the Court has much less direct control than the US Supreme Court over the number of cases it must deal with annually. This

---

[6] See the 2017 Annual Report of the Court of Justice, p. 105: https://curia.europa.eu/jcms/upload/docs/application/pdf/2018-04/_ra_2017_en.pdf.

[7] R.C Black, C.L. Boyd and A.C. Bryan, 'Revisiting the Influence of Law Clerks on the U.S. Supreme Court's Agenda-Setting Process' (2014) 98 *Marquette Law Review* 75.

[8] Opinion 2/13 of the Court (Full Court), 18 December 2014, ECLI:EU:C:2014:2454, concerning the accession of the EU to the European Convention on Human Rights.

is particularly so as a preliminary reference procedure is absent from the US system and the Supreme Court acts as the Court of last resort only.

Clearly, from a purely practical perspective, it would be an impossible task for the 28 judges that currently make up the full bench of the CJEU to deal with such a significant volume of cases, as the Court deals with annually, (i.e., over 700) were they not assisted in some form or another. Yet, the continued volume of cases is of paramount importance to ensure the smooth dialogue between EU Member State national courts and the CJEU. Judges of the CJEU must therefore be facilitated in their work by the very architecture of the institution in order to enable them to deliver judgments and justice in such a high volume of cases. Therein lies, at least one factor, that contributes to the functional necessity of the role of référendaire.

24.3.2   The Influence of Language

A further factor that contributes greatly to this issue is language. In both the US Supreme Court and in any well-constituted arbitral tribunal, it is assumed that the working language of the judges and arbitrators would be one in which they are extremely comfortable. Within the CJEU, the working language is French. French is used for all steps of the CJEU's internal proceedings, from the language in which judgments are drafted, the manner in which judges and advocates general formally communicate with each other in cases, to the actual deliberations in any particular case. For members of the CJEU who may not have worked in French prior to joining the CJEU, this can prove a challenge during an initial period. In this regard, an experienced référendaire, at ease drafting in French, can be of considerable assistance at the start of a judge's mandate in the CJEU as they may be able to guide a new member of the Court through the initial process of adjusting to working in French. Whilst there are some differences here in relation to référendaires working for advocates general, who may draft opinions in a language they choose, it would be, at the very least initially, extremely hard for a judge not used to working in French to adjust to the CJEU system without some assistance from lawyers in his or her chambers who are accustomed to working and drafting in French.

24.3.3   Particular Tasks

Against this backdrop, the functions of the référendaire make more sense. As stated previously, each member of the CJEU may define the extent of a référendaire's involvement and tasks in a case as they see fit. However, the most common functions of a référendaire may be broadly categorised into three main groups.

The first set of functions revolve around the initial case analysis when a case is assigned to a given reporting judge (being the judge responsible for drafting a first draft of the eventual decision) and advocate general, who will then each assign one of their référendaires to assist them in that case. It is at this stage in the CJEU internal procedure that the reporting judge will need to determine, in agreement with the advocate general assigned to the case, a proposal for the procedural treatment of the case. Thus, the reporting judge will need to determine what formation of judges is warranted. Should the case be dealt with by 3 judges, 5 judges, the Grand Chamber (15 judges) or exceptionally the full Court (presently 28 judges)? The significance of the case and where it lies in relation to the CJEU's previous jurisprudence will influence the type of formation required. At the same time the reporting judge must determine whether the case merits requesting an opinion from the advocate general, who, normally, would agree to any proposal that an opinion be drafted or not. In addition, it must be determined whether a hearing is required and/or whether any additional information or clarification is required from a national court (if the case is a preliminary reference) to enable the CJEU to make its decision.

For these decisions to be properly taken by the reporting judge and approved by all members of the CJEU, référendaires are often tasked with drafting a report that analyses the case from the above perspective for the reporting judge, enabling him or her to decide how the case should be dealt with procedurally. This document is generally an in-depth analysis of issues raised by the case and may contain considerable research into the substantive legal issues to be determined. Once the reporting judge has made his or her assessment, a liaising process occurs with the assigned advocate general to ensure that he or she is in agreement with the proposed treatment of the case. Thereafter, the full members of the Court will have the opportunity at their weekly meeting to examine this report and the proposed treatment of the case.

The second set of functions revolves around the drafting of the judgments, orders or advocate general's opinions. As highlighted, the CJEU deals with a huge volume of cases per year. Whilst not all of these cases will require a full written decision by a member as reporting judge, référendaires will likely assist their member in the drafting of judgments or opinions where necessary. That process may vary considerably depending on how a member, be they judge or advocate general, likes to work. One suggested trend comes from an empirical study based on interviews with a number of Advocates General dating from 2006, which found that whilst there were stylistic differences in working patterns in the chambers of a given advocate general, in most chambers the drafting was left to the référendaires, upon the advocate general's instruction as to the direction to take, whilst the advocate general undertook edits.[9] Chambers of judges can often operate similarly. Thus, the member and the référendaire must work closely during the drafting process in order to ensure that the draft correctly reflects what the member decides.

The third set of functions involves a sub-set of mixed tasks that ranges from assisting a member to prepare for the hearing, organising and welcoming visitors to the CJEU, and crucially, liaising with référendaires from other cabinets on draft judgements or orders and preliminary reports where a member wishes to raise issues or comments on a draft.

Interestingly, the legitimacy of the référendaire's involvement in the drafting process of CJEU decisions has been the subject of some, although not yet extensive, criticism.[10] This criticism has focused on a dependence on the référendaire for linguistic and experiential reasons. It has not yet, however, gone as far as to allege that the role of référendaire involves an impermissible delegation of powers from the decision-maker (judge or advocate general) to the référendaire. Given the controversies surrounding other unseen actors, it may be asked whether the lack of controversy is linked to the fact that no such line is crossed still by the CJEU system or could it be, in part, due to the hidden nature of the référendaire's role? A brief look below at the role of law clerks and arbitral tribunal secretaries highlights that their roles have engendered much greater visibility and, with that visibility, criticism.

24.4   Similarities with the Clerks in the US Supreme Court?

By contrast to référendaires, law clerks in the US Supreme Court have been placed on a legal footing since the 1922 Appropriations Act, which allowed each Supreme Court justice to have a paid clerk, thus ensuring their legitimacy in the Supreme Court architecture. By 1980 that number

---

[9] Iyiola Solanke, '"Stop the ECJ?" An Empirical Analysis of Activism at the Court' (2011) 17(6) *European Law Journal* 764.

[10] Zhang, 'The Faceless Court' (2016) 38(1) *University of Pennsylvania, Journal of International Law*, 103.

had gone up to four clerks per justice. One judge in the US Supreme Court has therefore the same number of legal assistants as a member of the CJEU, and this, despite the fact that the CJEU has a caseload almost 9 or 10 times higher than the US Supreme Court. As mentioned above, in 2017, the CJEU closed 699 cases[11] whereas in the same year the US Supreme Court heard 69 cases, of which 63 were disposed of in 59 signed opinions.[12]

The hiring of clerks for the Supreme Court would also appear to take place in a more predictable manner than in the CJEU. In the US Supreme Court, there is, as in the CJEU, a personal method for choosing a clerk, who are typically recently graduated law students and the clerks change every year. Many Supreme Court Justices rely on what is commonly known as 'feeder judges' sitting on the US Court of Appeals to propose candidates, or on the recommendations of certain law school deans.[13] This fact highlights one of the most significant differences with the CJEU, where référendaires tend to be experienced lawyers whose term at the Court, as mentioned earlier, can last up to the six-year mandate of a CJEU member or even longer and is not therefore easily comparable to a one-year period for a recent law school graduate. However, similar to the CJEU, the exact duties and responsibilities of the US Supreme Court clerks are determined by their hiring justice.[14] It is clear though that clerks have an important role in reviewing the thousands of petitions for certiorari that come before the Supreme Court each year and in thus filtering what cases are ultimately heard.

24.5   From Unseen Référendaires to Seen Arbitral Tribunal Secretaries

Perhaps not surprisingly, the legitimacy of tribunal secretaries in international arbitration has given rise to more debate than that of référendaires and law clerks combined. This may stem from a number

---

[11] See 2017 Annual Report of the Court of Justice, p. 105.
[12] Note also that 6,315 cases were filed before the Supreme Court in the 2017 period. See further the Supreme Court 2017 year-end report: www.supremecourt.gov/publicinfo/year-end/2017year-endreport.pdf.
[13] M.C. Miller, 'Law Clerks and Their Influence at the US Supreme Court: Comments on Recent Works by Peppers and Ward: Influence of Supreme Court Clerks' (2014) 39 *Law & Social Inquiry* 741–757, 742.
[14] Ibid., 743.

of factors, including the distinct nature of the arbitral process. No uniform standard exists in international arbitration as to the practice of using a tribunal secretary or as to what that role should be. The most controversial question raised is whether such secretaries are ever impermissibly delegated the powers of the arbitral tribunal. For example, can a tribunal secretary ever legitimately draft any parts of an award, as a référendaire might draft an initial draft of a judgment? If the secretary is merely summarising the factual positions of the parties as set out in their written submissions, would that be permissible? Or does even that simple task involve an exercise of discretion insofar as certain facts may be summarised with a certain emphasis and were the arbitrator to do it himself or herself, he or she may emphasise different elements than those chosen by the tribunal secretary?[15] And what of the decision to engage a tribunal secretary in the first place? Where should the impetus for the decision to use a tribunal secretary come from? Given the consensual nature of the arbitral process, should it be party driven and at their request? Or is it sufficient for the Tribunal itself to decide they wish to engage a secretary? In such a case, is party consent to the engagement ever or always required?

Criticism of tribunal secretaries has focused on some of these questions. Professor Jan Hendrik Dalhuisen rendered a highly critical Additional Opinion in the ICSID case of *Campañia de Aguas v. Argentina*[16], dealing precisely with this issue and arguing that a tribunal secretary, in that case one provided by the ICSID secretariat, should not draft any portion of an award. In his view:

> What are the key facts and relevant arguments and how they should be presented in the final decision or award is for the Arbitrators or ad hoc Committee Members to select and decide... For the Secretariat also to draft part or all of the decisions and reasoning would appear wholly inappropriate, even if following basic instructions of Arbitrators or ad hoc

---

[15] See for example the criticisms raised by US Appellate Court judge Richard Posner who has asserted in relation to clerks in the US system that a loss occurs when judgments are ghostwritten by law clerks, as clerks are bright but inexperienced and 'judges fool themselves when they think that by carefully editing, they can make a judicial opinion their own'. See further, R. Posner, *How Judges Think* (Harvard University Press, 2008), p. 34.

[16] *Compañía de Aguas del Aconquija SA & Vivendi Universal SA v. Argentine Republic*, ICSID Case No ARB/97/3 (Annulment Proceeding), Additional Opinion of Professor J.H. Dalhuisen under Art. 48(4) of the ICSID Convention, 30 July 2010.

Committee Members whilst the final version would naturally still be left to them for approval. This would not appear to be sufficient to legitimise the text.

Professor Dalhuisen's point can be easily understood in the context of the international arbitration system. Where the parties have effectively elected to have their dispute settled outside the jurisdiction of a national court and have themselves very often chosen, presumably with care, the arbitrator that they will themselves pay to determine their case, it seems at the very least counter-intuitive to permit any delegation of that arbitrator's powers. This point arguably remains valid even where this delegation may be superficially inconsequential or where the Tribunal themselves would ultimately 'approve the text', precisely because of the uniquely personal nature of the arbitrator's mandate.[17] This personal mandate factor is absent from proceedings before the CJEU and litigation before the US Supreme Court.

The issue as to delegation of an arbitrator's powers is also intrinsically linked to who the tribunal secretary is supposed to be serving. Whereas référendaires serve their members but owe duties to the institution that is the CJEU, the situation with tribunal secretaries is more opaque. Is the arbitral secretary engaged and serving for the benefit of the parties in the case? If so, it should be immediately obvious and apparent to the parties what the precise role of the secretary is and how this benefits them. Or is the arbitral secretary engaged ultimately for the benefit of the Tribunal, but whose appointment may (or possibly may not) have knock-on corresponding benefits for the parties? Thus, the argument is regularly made that if the secretary assists the Tribunal, it may enable it to decide the case quicker, saving time and costs to the parties and possibly even improving the quality of the work product.

Not inconsequentially, however, it cannot be overlooked that, unlike judges in either the CJEU or the US Supreme Court, the use of an arbitral secretary may arguably also free up very busy arbitrators to manage more appointments as arbitrator. In essence, a tribunal secretary may permit a certain amount of the time consuming and/or administrative part of the arbitrator's role to be effectively outsourced. And if the latter is perhaps an unacknowledged factor, then not only does it potentially call the legitimacy of the appointment of the tribunal secretary into question but it also raises a more fundamental question as to whether that is desirable

---

[17] In this regard, Professor Dalhuisen appears to join Justice Posner's criticism levied against clerks drafting any portion of an award cited at footnote 17.

in international arbitration at all, given that the arbitral process is essentially to be a party-driven process. The question therefore remains as to whether the potential benefits of using a secretary are sufficient to outweigh the doubts that the use of arbitral secretaries may cast on the arbitral process.

Nowhere have these issues been more forcefully thrown into the spotlight than in the recent annulment action taken on 28 January 2015 by the Russian Federation in the Hague District Court alleging, inter alia, that the arbitrators did not fulfil their mandate personally because the tribunal secretary played a significant role in analysing the evidence and legal arguments, in the Tribunal's deliberations, and in drafting the award.[18] Essentially, the argument was advanced that the tribunal secretary acted as a fourth arbitrator and evidence for this was drawn from the fact that the tribunal secretary carried out not only administrative but also substantive tasks and that the tribunal secretary carried out almost 1,000 hours more work than the arbitrators during the merits phase of the case.

On 20 April 2016, the Hague District Court set aside these awards on the grounds that the Russian Federation was not bound by the offer to arbitrate contained in Article 26 of the Energy Charter Treaty. The District Court annulled the interim awards on jurisdiction, as well as the final awards, but did so without having to address any of the other grounds for annulment that the Russian Federation had raised, including the allegation that the Arbitral Tribunal had impermissibly not personally fulfilled its mandate having delegated substantive tasks to the secretary of the Arbitral Tribunal. Whilst the District Court's decision is currently under appeal, the issue of impermissible delegation to the tribunal secretary will not be settled by this case given the District Court did not address the issue. However, the fact that the argument was raised at all, indicates that, first, the tribunal secretary is not an unseen actor and second, the legitimacy of the tribunal secretary is not a given and may be called into question. It remains to be seen how long it will take before a similar argument is made and dealt with by another court in another case.

It is also worth noting that a similar situation had been dealt with in an old case arising out of a commercial arbitration, in a decision by the Italian

---

[18] Writ filed by the Russian Federation before the Hague District Court, seeking to annul the awards which resulted from arbitral proceedings commenced by the former shareholders of Yukos Oil Company against the Russian Federation, paras. 15(b), 21(c), 363(3), 509.

Supreme Court rendered on 7 June 1989 in the case *Sacheri v. Robotto*.[19] In that case the arbitrators were not lawyers and thus did not draft the award, having hired a lawyer who was appointed as an expert to draft the award for them. The Italian Supreme Court had no difficulty finding that this was an impermissible delegation of power: '[d]ue to the arbitrators' professed incapacity to decide issues other than technical construction problems, it amounted to delegating a third person to formulate the final decision, which the arbitrators were not able to conceive and which they could not critically examine once it had been drafted'.[20] Essentially, for the Italian Supreme Court, legal decision-making was a task that could not be delegated to persons other than the arbitrators[21] and this despite the fact that the arbitrators were not themselves lawyers. Given the peculiarities of this case, though, it is difficult to extract from it a wider precedent concerning the role of tribunal secretaries in general.

Against the backdrop of these legitimacy issues, calls for a uniform standard for tribunal secretaries have been made.[22] In the absence of court guidance as to where the line between permissible and impermissible delegation should be drawn, arbitral institutions appear to be taking some steps themselves to, at the very least, manage better the issue. Whilst certain arbitral institutions have codified rules or guidance as regards the use of tribunal secretaries, others offer no guidance at all. Most recently, the International Chamber of Commerce (ICC) has, as of 1 January 2019, updated its guidance on the use of what it deems 'administrative secretaries' in its 'Note to the Parties and Arbitral Tribunals on the conduct of the Arbitration under the ICC Rules of Arbitration'.[23] Crucially, this updated guidance note now permits the parties to object to the proposal of an administrative secretary by the Tribunal, should a party so wish and states that the secretary may not be appointed if such an objection is raised.[24] The note also explicitly states the confines of the role that the

---

[19] *Sacheri v. Robotto*, Case No. 2765, Corte di Cassazione, Supreme Court, 7 June 1989, excerpt available in Yearbook Commercial Arbitration, Volume 16, Kluwer Law International 1991, pp. 156–157.

[20] Ibid., para. 1.

[21] Ibid., paras. 3 and 4.

[22] Michael Polkinghorne and Charles B. Rosenberg 'The Role of the Tribunal Secretary in International Arbitration: A Call for a Uniform Standard', 5 March 2015, available at www.ibanet.org/Article/NewDetail.aspx?ArticleUid=987d1cfc-3bc2-48d3-959e-e18d7935f542.

[23] See Article XIX of this Note at: https://cdn.iccwbo.org/content/uploads/sites/3/2017/03/icc-note-to-parties-and-arbitral-tribunals-on-the-conduct-of-arbitration.pdf.

[24] Ibid., Article 184.

secretary may undertake.[25] Clarification by the ICC on both the parties' right to object to the secretary's appointment and on the scope of tasks that the secretary may perform is to be welcomed. However, given that this Note has issued so recently, further time will be required before its full effect on the current practice regarding tribunal secretaries is to be seen. Likewise, the London Centre for International Arbitration (LCIA) has issued a note on the use of arbitral secretaries.[26] The Hong Kong International Arbitration Centre (HKIAC)[27] also expressly provides in its Rules that the tribunal may appoint a secretary *after* consulting with the parties. Thus, both the LCIA Note to Arbitrators and the HKIAC Rules expressly requires consultation with the parties on the issue.

On the other end of the spectrum and bypassing the issue of express party consent to the use of a secretary, the ICSID Administrative and Financial Regulations provide that a secretary 'shall' be appointed to each ICSID tribunal[28] and specify that the secretary shall 'keep summary minutes of hearings' and 'perform other functions with respect to the proceeding at the request of the President of the ... Tribunal ... or at the direction of the [ICSID] Secretary-General'.[29] The ICSID Arbitration Rules also clarify in Article 15(2) that secretaries are precluded from attending deliberations unless the tribunal consents. Interestingly, neither Articles 25 nor 15(2) define what the parties *have* consented to in terms of the secretary's involvement. Thus, if a party objects to the tribunal secretary's presence in deliberations they may find the argument raised too late as consent to the ICSID Rules is implicit consent to, inter alia, Article 15(2).

---

[25] Point 185 of the Guidance Note states that '(t)he tasks entrusted to an administrative secretary shall in no circumstances release the arbitral tribunal from its duty to personally review the file' and that '(u)nder no circumstances may the arbitral tribunal delegate its decision-making functions to an administrative secretary'. The arbitral tribunal is also prohibited from relying on an administrative secretary to perform on its behalf any of the essential duties of an arbitrator.

[26] See Notes to Arbitrators, Section 8 published on 26 October 2017 and 'Frequently Asked Questions' London Court of International Arbitration website: www.lcia.org/Frequently_Asked_Questions.aspx#Secretaries.

[27] Hong Kong Administered Arbitration Rules (2013), Art. 13.4 and see also 'Guidelines on the Use of a Secretary to the Arbitral Tribunal', Hong Kong International Arbitration Centre, 1 June 2014, para. 1.1: www.hkiac.org/images/stories/arbitration/HKIAC%20Guidelines%20on%20Use%20of%20Secretary%20to%20Arbitral%20Tribunal%20-%20Final.pdf.

[28] ICSID Financial and Administrative Regulations, Art. 25.

[29] Ibid., Art. 25(c), (d).

Whilst various ideas have been floated as regards how to safeguard the legitimacy of the role of the tribunal secretary (such as ensuring the secretary remains impartial and independent, determining what tasks they may or may not undertake and whether they can attend deliberations or draft portions of the award), one crucial criterion should be borne in mind. In order to ensure that the use of the tribunal secretary is essentially for the benefit of the parties, it would seem highly desirable that the parties' consent should be given not just to the appointment of the secretary in the first instance, but also to the precise nature of the secretary's permissible tasks. Not only would such a conversation between parties and the tribunal safeguard an award from any eventual *Yukos*-type tribunal secretary arguments in annulment proceedings, but it would also ensure much greater transparency in the arbitral process as regards the confines of the role of the secretary, thus guaranteeing the legitimacy of this actor. Whilst this may mean that a tribunal cannot always lean as heavily on a tribunal secretary as they might like, it should not be forgotten that the parties' consent to the arbitrators personally determining the outcome of the dispute is at the heart of the arbitral process. It therefore seems only fitting that it be also the parties that define the scope of the role they wish the arbitrators and correspondingly any tribunal secretary to undertake.

Such a step would go a long way to safeguarding the legitimacy of the role of this actor.

24.6 The CJEU Safeguard?

Curiously, and as stated above, the role of the référendaire has not yet generated the same level of controversy as other unseen actors. In general, the role has yet to be the subject of extensive academic scrutiny, though some writings do exist[30] and with the exception of those involved in the EU law sphere, the role of the référendaire receives considerably less attention than the importance of the role would potentially merit.

---

[30] See, for some examples, S. Kenney, 'Beyond Principals and Agents: Seeing Courts as Organisations by Comparing Référendaires at the European Court of Justice and Law Clerks at the U.S. Supreme Court', (2000) 33(5) *Comparative Political Studies*, 593; D. Edward, 'How the Court of Justice Works' (1995) 20 *European Law Review*, 539; Zhang, 'The Faceless Court'.

Arguably, however, the CJEU system would easily withstand any such discussion because of the safeguard found in the collective judgment.

Unlike an international arbitral tribunal or the US Supreme Court, when the CJEU rules it speaks in one voice and one voice only, with no provision for dissenting opinions. The judges of the CJEU meet for deliberations alone without référendaires. At that meeting, the judges work from a modified draft judgment that has already had the collective influence of not only the reporting judge (and his or her référendaire), but also the other members of the formation and potentially their référendaires, depending, as always, on how a given member wishes to work. The draft text of a judgment is then discussed, often with considerable reworking and discussion of modifications to the text until there is a group consensus amongst the judges deciding the case as to the judgment. If no group consensus is found, the judges' deliberation meeting can be adjourned to allow further consideration of the treatment of particular issues. The modifications to the draft text are agreed by the judges alone and when an agreed text is reached, it is signed off by the judges alone with one voice. Whilst the lack of dissenting opinions within CJEU procedure can be scrutinised for other reasons, the fact that the system is organised in this manner adds a safeguard to the deliberation process and therefore removes a potential criticism that could be levied at référendaires. Once the deliberation has occurred, the référendaire's role will be to simply ensure that modifications dictated by the formation of judges in their deliberation are correctly reflected in the judgment and that linguistically all is as it should be. It is therefore clear that in the CJEU system, the ultimate decision is one made by the judges in deliberations alone. Arguably, it is that aspect that adds to the legitimacy of the référendaire, despite its status as a (somewhat) hidden actor within the CJEU system.

24.7   Conclusion

The only way to ensure there is zero risk of impermissible influence on a judge or an arbitrator is to remove recourse to assistants of any kind. Whilst this may be an option in an international arbitration, the institution of the CJEU is intimately bound up in access to and the administration of justice within the EU. Thus, requiring members of the CJEU to work without any assistants would at best delay the rendering of judgments and at worst require the architecture of the CJEU system to be fundamentally changed. Moreover, the current functioning of the CJEU system utilising the largely unseen référendaire appears to work, at least to a very large degree, without the controversies that have arisen in relation to other comparable actors and, particularly, as regards to tribunal secretaries in international arbitration. This is arguably because the CJEU's internal processes work to ensure and guarantee that the exercise of judicial power is made by the judges of the Court alone. The fact that so little controversy has surfaced in relation to the référendaire's role suggests therefore that both the current CJEU system functions well and as 'unseen actor' is fulfilling its unseen role very successfully indeed.

PART VI

External Influences and Activities

'Outside Activities' and Workload Management as Unseen Actors (and Factors) in International Adjudication

CATHERINE H. GIBSON*

25.1 Introduction

International jurists pride themselves on keeping busy, and between permanent tribunal seats, ad hoc arbitral appointments, speaking engagements, writing, and teaching (among other activities), many do keep their calendars full. But how busy is too busy for members of permanent international courts and tribunals? While some institutions, such as the International Court of Justice (ICJ) and the International Criminal Court (ICC), provide guidance for members on outside activities, such guidance tends to be broad and focused on issues such as conflicts of interest, judicial independence, and the appearance of impropriety, rather than workload management. Groups at the United Nations, the International Law Association, and elsewhere have also prepared guidance on judicial conduct with provisions on competence, diligence, and efficiency, but largely lacking considerations of workload management. Academic literature on the outside activities of international judges likewise tends to focus on conflicts of interest and ensuring judicial independence and impartiality, rather than on workload management.[1]

---

* The opinions expressed in this chapter belong to the author alone and do not reflect those of Covington & Burling LLP or its clients.

[1] See, e.g., Paul Mahoney, 'The International Judiciary – Independence and Accountability' (2008) 7 *Law & Practice of International Courts and Tribunals*, 313; Yuval Shany, 'Squaring the Circle? Independence and Impartiality of Party-Appointed Adjudicators in International Legal Proceedings' (2008) 30 *Loyola Los Angeles International & Comparative Law Review*, 473; Nigel Rodley, 'The *Singarasa* Case: *Quis Custodiet* ...? A Test for the Bangalore Principles of Judicial Conduct' (2008) 41 *Israel Law Review*, 500.

This chapter analyses outside activities and workload management for members of permanent international courts and tribunals, with the aim of determining what factors a judge should consider when weighing up whether to undertake a particular outside activity. Outside activities – and the reasons judges might or might not undertake them – relate to the legitimacy of international adjudication as such activities may affect the decision-making of permanent international courts and tribunals. These permanent institutions are created to play particular roles, and the judges that serve there are selected to carry out these roles, and perhaps to fulfil certain regional, professional, or other criteria. If a particular international jurist is overworked with outside activities, however, and is not able to contribute as planned to the work of his or her permanent tribunal, the perceived legitimacy of that tribunal's decisions may be negatively affected. On the other hand, experience that an international jurist may gain through outside activities may enhance the decision-making of that judge's permanent institution and improve the institution's perceived legitimacy.

Section 25.2 compares members' outside activities in various international institutions and suggests advantages and disadvantages of such activities, particularly for the perceived legitimacy of the jurist's permanent institution; Section 25.3 discusses standards for judicial conduct applied by certain international courts and tribunals, particularly as to workload management; Section 25.4 describes the guidance on judicial conduct provided by various international groups; and finally, Section 25.5 offers suggestions as to what reasonable additional guidance might be provided – either by international tribunals, national bar associations, or other groups – regarding the advisability of an international judge taking on particular outside activities in light of workload management and the potential effects on the legitimacy of the permanent courts or tribunals the judge serves.[2]

25.2   Comparing the Advantages and Disadvantages of Outside Activities

For members of some international courts and tribunals, participation in outside activities is common and almost expected. At certain times,

---

[2] This chapter leaves aside the more frequently considered questions of such outside activities and judicial independence or impartiality.

members of the International Court of Justice (ICJ), for example, have engaged in activities outside those directly connected with the Court, including participating in commissions or arbitral tribunals, publishing books or articles, or teaching and attending conferences.[3] For members of other institutions, however, participation in such activities is less common.

25.2.1   Advantages

Judges' outside activities may benefit judicial decision-making and permanent courts by assisting members in keeping abreast of current developments, raising the profile of the permanent institutions they serve, and promoting international courts and international law. Outside activities may also facilitate cross-fertilisation among international courts and tribunals, particularly in procedural matters – such as the standards for admission of evidence, or the propriety of granting interim relief – that may arise in a variety of fora.

Indeed, to some extent, international judges may be expected to undertake activities outside their core judicial function of deciding cases before the courts they serve, as international judges play broad leadership roles. Importantly, even deciding disputes before a tribunal requires life experience outside the courtroom, for example in order to appropriately determine the conduct of a 'reasonable person'. If judges in international courts and tribunals are more effectively able to make such determinations because they have engaged in outside activities, then outside activities may enhance the perceived legitimacy of international courts and tribunals. Accordingly, a number of advantages may be gained from judges engaging in certain activities outside the core judicial function of deciding the cases before his or her permanent institution.

25.2.2   Disadvantages

Engaging in outside activities may also have drawbacks, however, such as introducing conflicts of interest or interfering with a member's availability to participate in hearings or deliberations. Of particular interest in this article are problems of workload management that may be caused by

---

[3] See Chiara Giorgetti, 'The Challenge and Recusal of Judges of the International Court of Justice', in Chiara Giorgetti (ed.), *Challenges and Recusals of Judges and Arbitrators in International Courts and Tribunals* (Brill, 2015), p. 8.

outside activities. That is, even if an extra-judicial activity does not give rise to a conflict of interest or create the appearance of impropriety, an individual jurist may simply become so busy with outside activities that he or she cannot afford adequate attention to an individual dispute before his or her permanent institution.

Indeed, commentators have recognised this potential problem, outside the context of specific conflicts of interest. As one commentator wrote, 'when a judge dedicates himself to activities other than adjudication, the time afforded to adjudication is reduced' and '[t]he judge devotes less time to his judicial duties and that leads to a build-up of cases and a slowing of the mechanism for the resolution of disputes'.[4] Such a slow-down in the resolution of disputes before international courts and tribunals can detract from their perceived legitimacy, as parties or colleagues may feel that a judge is distracted by outside work.

Despite the recognition of potential problems of excessive outside activities, international tribunals appear to provide relatively little guidance for judges seeking to harmonise their outside activities with the needs of the permanent institutions they serve. As set forth below, international courts and tribunals provide some guidance for judges regarding their potential outside activities, but this guidance is primarily focused on related – but distinct – issues such as avoiding conflicts of interest and maintaining the dignity of judicial office. International bodies have also drafted guidance on judicial conduct, but such guidance is likewise general and typically focused on conflicts, independence, or impartiality.

As set forth in Section 25.5, in light of the dearth of guidance for international jurists particular to workload management, international tribunals and judges may benefit from additional considerations regarding the advisability of taking on additional outside activities, even if these activities do not introduce conflicts of interest or related problems.

25.3 Existing Regulation of Outside Activities by International Courts

The guiding documents of some international courts and tribunals already speak to the advisability and scope of members' outside activities.

---

[4] Shimon Shetreet, 'Standards of Conduct of International Judges: Outside Activities' (2003) 2 *Law & Practice of International Courts and Tribunals*, 160.

Some institutions prohibit members from exercising political or administrative functions, which has led members to resign other positions upon
appointment. Some tribunals remain permanently in session and require
members to remain available at short notice, which could serve to limit
members' outside activities. Some institutions encourage members to
consult with colleagues regarding the advisability of taking on outside
activities. Such considerations are not specific to workload management,
however, but rather focus on other issues.

The following sections describe relevant rules of a variety of international institutions, chosen to provide a sampling of existing approaches
to outside activities in institutions established at different times and with
differing mandates. The institutions considered are (1) the International
Court of Justice, (2) the International Tribunal for the Law of the Sea,
(3) the International Criminal Court, (4) the European Court of
Human Rights, and (5) tribunals established in international investment
instruments.

25.3.1   International Court of Justice

The Statute of the International Court of Justice[5] contains several provisions
relevant to members' outside activities, many of which are reinforced
in the Registry's ICJ Handbook.[6] Regarding the judges' availability, the
Statute provides that the Court 'shall remain permanently in session'
except during established judicial vacations, and requires that members
'hold themselves permanently at the disposal of the Court' unless they are
on leave or prevented from attending due to illness or other reasons 'duly
explained' to the President.[7] The current ICJ Handbook reinforces these
requirements.[8]

---

[5] Statute of the International Court of Justice, 26 June 1945, in force 24 October 1945, 3
Bevans 1179; 59 Stat 1031; TS 993; 39 AJIL Supp. 215 [hereinafter 'ICJ Statute'].

[6] The International Court of Justice Handbook, available at www.icj-cij.org/files/publications/
handbook-of-the-court-en.pdf [hereinafter 'ICJ Handbook']. This handbook was first
published in 1976, and has been updated several times since then. The handbook available
on the ICJ website at the time this chapter was written is the sixth edition, last updated on
31 December 2013. The ICJ Handbook states that it does not constitute an official publication of the ICJ and has been prepared by the Registry, which alone is responsible for its
content. Ibid. at 5.

[7] ICJ Statute, Article 23.

[8] ICJ Handbook, p. 24.

The Statute also forbids members from exercising political or administrative functions, or any other occupation of a professional nature.[9] This provision leads ICJ judges to resign from previous academic, civil service, or other positions upon joining the Court.[10] The ICJ Handbook states further that members may 'investigate, conciliate or arbitrate in certain cases not liable to be submitted to the ICJ,' so long as 'the exigencies of his or her Court duties so allow'.[11] Under the same contingency, ICJ members may participate in learned bodies, or may give lectures or attend academic meetings.[12] After stating these requirements, the ICJ Handbook observes that members are 'subject to particularly strict rules with regard to questions of incompatibility of functions'.[13]

To determine which activities are inconsistent with ICJ membership, the Court has at times established internal committees or commissions to examine the compatibility of functions and draw up reports and recommendations.[14] After the establishment of the first such committee in 1947, it was agreed that whenever a judge was in doubt as to whether it would be advisable to undertake certain functions, that judge 'might ask for advice from the President of the Court, and if necessary, the full Court'.[15] In 1967, 'in the light of present conditions and recent experience', the Court again convened a committee to re-examine this practice.[16] This second committee made particular recommendations relating to (1) other forms of peaceful settlement of disputes; (2) scientific activities; (3) public functions and occupations of a professional nature; and (4) private activities.[17] The report is considered a guideline only, so that individual members retain discretion to determine the propriety of their outside activities and may consult the President as to any doubts.[18]

---

[9] ICJ Statute, Article 16.
[10] See Giorgetti, 'The Challenge and Recusal of Judges', p. 10 (describing judges who have recently stepped down from academic or civil service positions after becoming members of the ICJ).
[11] ICJ Handbook, p. 24.
[12] Ibid.
[13] Ibid.
[14] Philippe Couvreur, 'Article 16', in Andreas Zimmermann, Christian Tomuschat, Karin Oellers-Frahm and Christian J. Tams (eds.), *The Statute of the International Court of Justice*, 2nd edn (Oxford University Press, 2012), paras. 21–23.
[15] 1967–68 ICJ Yearbook, pp. 91–92.
[16] Ibid., p. 92.
[17] Ibid.
[18] Couvreur, 'Article 16', para. 23.

Before taking up their ICJ duties, members must declare in open court that they will exercise their powers 'impartially and conscientiously'.[19] Although requiring members to exercise their powers conscientiously could be construed as setting some limits on outside activities, this declaration is seen as ensuring the impartiality of judges.[20] Finally, the ICJ Statute also addresses conflicts of interest, and provides that '[n]o member may participate in the decision of any case in which he has previously taken part as agent, counsel, or advocate for one of the parties, or as a member of a national or international court, or of a commission of enquiry, or in any other capacity'.[21]

The particular issue of outside activities carried out by ICJ members came into focus in the 1990s in light of questions raised by the United Nations General Assembly Advisory Committee on Administrative and Budgetary Questions.[22] In the concluding lines of a report that focused on the pension scheme for ICJ members, this committee requested that this 'broader review of the conditions of service should also include an analysis of the practice of the Court with respect to article 16, paragraph 1 of its statute, which provides that "no member of the Court may exercise any political or administrative function, or engage in any other occupation of a professional nature"'.[23] The responsive report states that members of the Court were barred from holding commercial positions, practising law, rendering legal or expert opinions, or holding permanent teaching or administrative positions at a university or faculty of law.[24] That report also clarified the Court's view of the ICJ Statute as 'not debarring a limited participation of Judges in other judicial or quasi-judicial activities of an occasional nature, as well as scholarly pursuits in the sphere of international law as members of learned societies or as occasional lecturers'.[25] This responsive report further stated that the ICJ members were explicitly permitted to serve as arbitrators in third-party settlements of disputes.[26]

---

[19] ICJ Statute, Article 20.

[20] See Daniel-Erasmus Khan, 'Article 20', in Andreas Zimmermann, Christian Tomuschat, Karin Oellers-Frahm and Christian J. Tams (eds.) *The Statute of the International Court of Justice*, 2nd edn (Oxford University Press, 2012).

[21] ICJ Statute, Article 17.2.

[22] UNGAOR, 49th Sess., Suppl. 7, Add. 11, p. 3, A/49/7/Add.11 (9 March 1995).

[23] Ibid.

[24] A/C.5/50/18 (2 November 1995), pp. 12, 30.

[25] Ibid., p. 31.

[26] Ibid., p. 32.

ICJ judges' ability to undertake such activities is limited, however, as the responsive report makes clear. In particular, undertaking such activities is subject to two conditions: (1) members must give 'absolute precedence' to their obligations as ICJ members, and (2) they should not accept appointment in an arbitral case that is subject to being submitted to the ICJ.[27] As discussed below, requiring ICJ members to give precedence to the Court's work in considering their participation in outside activities echoes the recommendations set forth in the Bangalore Principles of Judicial Conduct.

Moreover, the ICJ has recently expanded upon these considerations of outside activities and workload management, as announced by the President of the Court in October 2018.[28] Specifically, members of the ICJ decided in September 2018 that, in light of the Court's 'ever-increasing workload', ICJ judges will not 'normally' participate in international arbitration.[29] Although ICJ judges might undertake such activities 'exceptionally', they would do so only under limited circumstances, with prior authorisation and 'subject to the strict condition that their judicial activities [at the ICJ] take absolute precedence'.[30]

25.3.2   International Tribunal for the Law of the Sea

Members of the International Tribunal for the Law of the Sea (ITLOS) are subject to provisions similar to those that have governed ICJ members. In a provision entitled '[i]ncompatible activities', the ITLOS Statute prohibits members from exercising political or administrative functions, or associating actively with or being financially interested in any of the operations of any enterprise concerned with the exploration for or exploitation of the resources of the sea or the seabed, or any other commercial use of the sea or seabed.[31] The ITLOS Statute also forbids members from acting as agent, counsel, or advocate in any case.[32] Finally, any doubt as to these

---

[27] Ibid.
[28] Speech by H.E. Mr. AbdulQawi A. Yusuf, President of the International Court of Justice, on the Occasion of the Seventy-Third Session of the United Nations General Assembly (25 October 2018), www.icj-cij.org/files/press-releases/0/000-20181025-PRE-02-00-EN.pdf.
[29] Ibid.
[30] Ibid.
[31] Statute of the International Tribunal for the Law of the Sea, Article 7, available at www.itlos.org/fileadmin/itlos/documents/basic_texts/statute_en.pdf [hereinafter 'ITLOS Statute'].
[32] Ibid.

incompatible activities 'shall be resolved by decision of the majority of the other members of the Tribunal present'.[33]

Like ICJ members, ITLOS members must make a solemn declaration that they will 'perform [their] duties and exercise [their] powers as judge honourably, faithfully, impartially and conscientiously'.[34] The ITLOS Statute also includes provisions on conflicts of interest, which forbid members from taking part in decisions of any case in which that member has previously taken part as agent counsel or advocate for one of the parties, or as a member of a national or international court or tribunal, or in any other capacity.[35] Like doubts about issues related to incompatible activities, doubts related to the conditions of a member's participation in a particular case 'shall be resolved by decision of the majority of the other members of the Tribunal present'.[36] Notably, the ITLOS Statute appears to lack provisions stating explicitly that the tribunal remains permanently in session, and that members must be available at all times and at short notice.[37]

25.3.3   International Criminal Court

The Code of Judicial Ethics of the International Criminal Court[38] goes further than the provisions governing other international courts and tribunals in providing guidance on issues regarding outside activities and workload management. In particular, the ICC's Code of Judicial Ethics provides some limitations on the extra-judicial activity of members and

---

[33] Ibid.
[34] Ibid., Article 11; International Tribunal for the Law of the Sea, Rules of the Tribunal, ITLOS/ 8 (17 March 2009), Article 5, available at www.itlos.org/fileadmin/itlos/documents/basic_ texts/Itlos_8_E_17_03_09.pdf.
[35] ITLOS Statute, Article 8(1).
[36] ITLOS Statute, Article 8(4).
[37] In fact, Article 25 of the ITLOS Statute sets out the particular procedures to be followed if provisional measures are sought and the tribunal is not in session or a sufficient number of members is not available to constitute a quorum.
[38] International Criminal Court, Code of Judicial Ethics, ICC-BD/02-01-05, www.icc-cpi.int/ NR/rdonlyres/A62EBC0F-D534-438F-A128-D3AC4CFDD644/140141/ICCBD020105_ En.pdf [hereinafter 'ICC, Code of Judicial Ethics']. This Code was agreed by the judges themselves, pursuant to its Regulation 126, which permits the ICC president to draw up a code of ethics after consulting with the judges, and to transmit that code to the judges meeting in plenary session for the purpose of adoption by the majority of judges. See ibid., Pmbl. and Article 1; International Criminal Court, Regulations of the Court, ICC-BD/ 01-02-07, at Regulation 126, available at www.icc-cpi.int/NR/rdonlyres/DF5E9E76-F99C- 410A-85F4-01C4A2CE300C/0/ICCBD010207ENG.pdf.

establishes expectations of their conduct while on the bench. For example, the ICC's Code of Ethics requires judges to 'act diligently in the exercise of their duties' and to 'devote their professional activities to those duties'.[39] Judges must perform their judicial duties 'properly and expeditiously' and 'deliver their decisions and any other rulings without undue delay'.[40] Such provisions speak much more directly to workload management than the provisions governing the actions of members at other international tribunals.

The ICC Code also explicitly speaks of 'extra-judicial activity' seemingly with an eye towards avoiding conflicts of interest or the appearance of impropriety. For example, the ICC Code forbids judges from engaging in extra-judicial activity that 'is incompatible with their judicial function or the efficient and timely functioning of the Court, or that may affect or reasonably appear to affect their independence or impartiality'.[41] The ICC Code forbids judges from exercising any political function[42] and more generally forbids judges from engaging in any activity which 'is likely to interfere with their judicial functions or to affect confidence in their independence'.[43] The ICC Code of Judicial Ethics likewise admonishes judges to avoid conflicts of interest, or situations that might reasonably be perceived as such.[44] Finally, the ICC Code advises that judges must exercise their freedom of expression and association 'in a manner that is compatible with their office and that does not affect or appear to affect judicial independence or impartiality'.

The ICC Code of Judicial Ethics does not wholly forbid extra-judicial activity, however, and in fact contemplates that judges will engage in certain types of outside activities. Specifically, the ICC Code contemplates that judicial activity will include more than just deciding individual cases, and requires that judges 'take reasonable steps to maintain and enhance the knowledge, skills and personal qualities necessary for judicial office'.[45] The inclusion of such a provision is valuable as it may serve to encourage members of the ICC to take part in conferences or other activities that would enhance their judicial functions, and potentially also enhance the

[39] ICC, Code of Judicial Ethics, Article 7(1).
[40] Ibid., Article 7(3) & (4).
[41] Ibid., Article 10(1).
[42] Ibid., Article 10(2).
[43] Ibid., Article 4(2).
[44] Ibid.
[45] Ibid., Article 7(2).

perceived legitimacy of the institutions they serve, by increasing the basis of knowledge on which these judges decide the cases before them.

25.3.4   European Court of Human Rights

Like similar instruments at other courts and tribunals, the Resolution on Judicial Ethics of the European Court of Human Rights[46] also emphasises general principles of independence, impartiality, integrity, and discretion, and forbids judges from accepting 'any gift, favour or advantage that could call their independence or impartiality into question'.[47] Like the ICC Code, the Resolution on Judicial Ethics recognises judges' freedom of expression, but admonishes that this freedom must be exercised 'in a manner compatible with the dignity of their office' and that judges must refrain from expressions that 'may undermine the authority of the Court or give rise to reasonable doubt as to their impartiality'.[48] The Resolution on Judicial Ethics also requires that judges must perform the duties of their office diligently, and that continuing to develop their professional skills is necessary 'to maintain a high level of competence'.[49]

As to outside activities in particular, called '[a]dditional activity' here, the Resolution on Judicial Ethics forbids judges from engaging in any additional activity 'except insofar as this is compatible with independence, impartiality and the demands of their full-time office'.[50] Judges at the European Court of Human Rights must declare 'any' additional activity to the President in the Court, as provided in Rule 4 of the Rules of the Court.[51] Rule 4 of the Rules of the Court relates to 'incompatible activities' and provides that, similar to ITLOS procedures, if the president of the court and a judge disagree as to whether a particular activity is compatible with that judge's role in the court, the plenary court shall decide

---

[46] Council of Europe, European Court of Human Rights, *Resolution on Judicial Ethics* (adopted 23 June 2008), available at www.echr.coe.int/Documents/Resolution_Judicial_Ethics_ENG.pdf. This Resolution on Judicial Ethics was adopted by the plenary court having regard to relevant provisions of the European Convention on Human Rights and certain Rules of the Court, and taking into account that the principles articulated in this Resolution 'should enhance public confidence in the Court'. Ibid., Pmbl.
[47] See ibid. at 2–3.
[48] Ibid. at 3.
[49] Ibid. at 2.
[50] Ibid. at 3.
[51] Ibid.

the matter.[52] Neither the Resolution on Judicial Ethics nor the Rules of Court define precisely what activities may be considered 'additional' or potentially 'incompatible', however, apparently leaving some ambiguity as to what activities exactly must be reported to the president of the court, and potentially to the plenary court as well.

25.3.5   International Investment Instruments

Some recent treaties and proposals include provisions establishing permanent investment courts, as well as accompanying guidelines for arbitrators. For example, using language that recalls provisions of the ICJ rules, the EU-Vietnam Free Trade Agreement (FTA)[53] requires that individuals serving as members of a tribunal resolving potential FTA disputes 'shall be available at all times and on short notice, and shall stay abreast of dispute settlement activities under this Agreement'.[54] Although FTA disputes will be ad hoc, the agreement seeks to secure arbitrator availability through payment of a monthly retainer fee.[55] For State-to-State dispute settlement, the FTA includes a code of conduct for arbitrators, which requires that those chosen to decide State-to-State disputes must perform their duties 'thoroughly and expeditiously throughout the course of the proceeding and shall do so with fairness and diligence'.[56] Similar provisions on permanent investment tribunals were included in the EU-Singapore Free Trade Agreement,[57] and the Comprehensive Economic and Trade Agreement between the European Union and Canada (CETA).[58]

---

[52] European Court of Human Rights, *Rules of Court* (14 November 2016), available at www .echr.coe.int/Documents/Rules_Court_ENG.pdf.

[53] EU-Vietnam Free Trade Agreement, available at http://trade.ec.europa.eu/doclib/press/ index.cfm?id=1449.

[54] Ibid., Section 3, Article 12(13).

[55] Ibid., Section 3, Article 12(14). Questions have been raised, however, regarding whether this retainer fee will be sufficient to tempt international jurists to give up their positions on permanent international institutions, and the propriety of permitting judges to receive remuneration from States that may later appear as parties before them. Such questions fall outside the scope of the present chapter.

[56] Ibid., Annex 29-B(7).

[57] EU-Singapore Free Trade Agreement, available at http://trade.ec.europa.eu/doclib/press/ index.cfm?id=961.

[58] Comprehensive Economic and Trade Agreement between the European Union and Canada, Article 8.27(2), (11), & (12), available at http://trade.ec.europa.eu/doclib/docs/ 2014/september/tradoc_152806.pdf.

25.4   Guidance on Judicial Conduct in Instruments Prepared by International Bodies

International bodies have also prepared a number of instruments with guidance relevant to outside activities of international judges. Such instruments by international bodies include the Bangalore Principles of Judicial Conduct,[59] the Universal Charter of the Judge,[60] and the Burgh House Principles on the Independence of the International Judiciary.[61] As set forth below, these instruments typically require that judges afford primacy to judicial duties, while also acknowledging potential benefits of outside activities. A number of instruments provide some guidance for determining whether to undertake an outside activity specifically through reporting or consultation with other members of the judiciary. Like the documents governing international courts and tribunals, however, instruments prepared by international organisations primarily seek to avoid conflicts of interest and maintain judicial independence, and do not provide significant guidance on judicial workload management.

25.4.1   Bangalore Principles of Judicial Conduct

Significant guidance on the proper scope of outside activities may be gleaned from the Bangalore Principles of Judicial Conduct (Bangalore Principles), drafted in the early 2000s by the Judicial Group on Strengthening Judicial Integrity, under the auspices of the United Nations Office on Drugs and Crime. Although the Bangalore Principles were developed in connection with efforts to combat corruption in the domestic judiciary,[62] they also provide general guidance that has been

---

[59] United Nations Office on Drugs and Crime, Commentary on the Bangalore Principles of Judicial Conduct, available at www.unodc.org/documents/corruption/publications_unodc_commentary-e.pdf [hereinafter 'Bangalore Principles'].

[60] Universal Charter of the Judge, available at www.iaj-uim.org/universal-charter-of-the-judges/ [hereinafter 'Universal Charter of the Judge'].

[61] Burgh House Principles on the Independence of the International Judiciary, available at www.ucl.ac.uk/laws/cict/docs/burgh_final_21204.pdf [hereinafter 'Burgh House Principles'].

[62] See United Nations Office on Drugs and Crime, Strengthening the Integrity of the Judiciary, www.unodc.org/unodc/en/corruption/judiciary.html.

more broadly accepted,[63] including with respect to judicial workload and activities outside the core judicial functions.

In particular, these principles provide guidance on six 'values', including independence, impartiality, integrity, and – most relevant for present purposes – propriety, competence, and diligence. The Bangalore Principles contain general statements regarding competence and diligence, and characterise these qualities as 'prerequisites to the due performance of judicial office.'[64] As the Bangalore Principles make clear, competence and diligence obligations require that judicial duties 'take precedence over all other activities.'[65] Further, judicial duties must be performed 'efficiently, fairly, and with reasonable promptness'[66] and judges 'shall not engage in conduct incompatible with the diligent discharge of judicial duties.'[67]

Despite this focus on diligence and the primacy of judicial duties, the Bangalore Principles also contemplate that judges will participate in certain activities outside their judicial duties. For example, the Bangalore Principles explicitly permit judges to write, lecture, teach, and participate in activities concerning the law, so long as these activities are consistent with 'proper performance of judicial duties.'[68] The Bangalore Principles also permit judges to serve as members of an official body or other government commission, so long as such membership is not inconsistent with the perceived impartiality and political neutrality of a judge.[69] The Bangalore Principles also permit judges to engage in other outside activities, so long as such activities do not detract from the dignity of the judicial office or otherwise interfere with judicial duties.[70]

---

[63] As stated in the 2007 Commentary on the Bangalore Principles, this instrument has 'increasingly been accepted by the different sectors of the global judiciary and by international agencies interested in the integrity of the judicial process'. Bangalore Principles, preface.

[64] Ibid., Value 6 (Competence and Diligence), Principle and Application 6.1.

[65] Ibid.

[66] Ibid., Value 6.5.

[67] Ibid., Value 6.7. A commentary to the Principles acknowledges that the efforts required to ensure proper diligence in judicial work may depend on a number of other factors, such as 'the burden of work, the adequacy of resources ... and time for research, deliberation, writing and judicial duties other than sitting in court.' Ibid., Commentary, para. 193.

[68] Ibid., Value 4.11. Regarding publications, commentaries on the Bangalore Principles provide that when judges write or contribute to publications, the judge should not permit anyone associated with the publication to exploit the judicial office including through advertising. Ibid., Commentary, para. 151.

[69] Ibid., 4.11.3.

[70] Ibid., 4.11.4.

Certain activity outside the core functions of deciding individual disputes is required, however, so that judges may stay abreast of legal developments. To this end, the Bangalore Principles – like the ICC Code of Ethics – provide that judges must 'take reasonable steps to maintain and enhance' not only the knowledge and skills necessary to perform their judicial duties, but also the necessary personal qualities.[71] According to the commentary on this provision, faith in the judiciary may be affirmed 'if a judge possesses the kinds of personal skills and understanding (in and outside the courtroom) that enable him or her to manage cases and deal with all persons involved appropriately and sensitively'.[72] The Bangalore Principles also require that judges keep themselves 'informed about relevant developments of international law' including international human rights norms.[73]

With these provisions, the Bangalore Principles indicate that outside activities may enhance the perceived legitimacy of international courts and tribunals. In particular, outside activities may help ensure that judges possess the type of personal skills and understanding that enable him or her to deal appropriately and sensitively with cases and all persons involved. In addition, outside activities may help judges keep informed about developments in international law, thereby enhancing their decision-making.

As a general matter, the Bangalore Principles provide that outside activities should be organised to minimise the possibility of disqualification from judicial decision-making, through conflicts of interest, for instance.[74] The Bangalore Principles also make clear that judges are entitled to the same freedoms of expression, belief, association, and assembly as other citizens – but that in exercising these rights, judges should conduct themselves so as to preserve the dignity of the judicial office, and the impartiality and independence of the judiciary.[75]

The Bangalore Principles admonish judges not to become involved in public controversies, however, so as not to compromise the 'detached, unbiased, unprejudiced, impartial, open-minded, and even-handed approach which is the hallmark of a judge'.[76] Judges may speak on

---

[71] Ibid., Value 6.3.
[72] Ibid., Commentary, para. 200.
[73] Ibid., Value 6.4.
[74] Ibid., Value 2.3 & Commentary, para. 66.
[75] Ibid., Value 4.6.
[76] Ibid., Commentary, para. 136.

matters that affect the judiciary or discussions of the law, so long as those discussions are within reason.[77] Judges may participate in community, non-profit organisations, so long as – among other limits – the organisation does not make 'excessive demands' on the judge's time.[78]

With such statements the Bangalore Principles acknowledge ways in which outside activities may detract from the perceived legitimacy of international courts and tribunals, particularly as related to questions of workload management. In particular, if outside activities demand excessive amounts of a judge's time, that judge's decision-making in his or her permanent tribunal may suffer, thus undermining the perceived legitimacy of the tribunal itself.

In some situations, the Bangalore Principles encourage judges to consult with colleagues or otherwise seek authorisation when considering outside activities. Under the Bangalore Principles, when a judge is called upon to undertake a task that would detract from his or her regular work, the judge may consult with the presiding members of his or her permanent tribunal or other judicial colleagues. Such consultations are intended to ensure that acceptance of the extra-curricular assignment will not 'unduly interfere with the effective functioning of the court or unduly burden its other members'.[79] The Bangalore Principles further provide that when a judge has accepted such extra-curricular activities, a judge should resist the temptation to devote 'excessive' attention to these activities, particularly if doing so 'reduces the judge's capacity to discharge the judicial office'.[80] With such references to limiting excessive demands on a judge's time and resisting the temptation to devote excessive attention to extra-judicial activities, the Bangalore Principles again explicitly acknowledge concerns relating to workload management for international judges, and the perceived legitimacy of international courts and tribunals.

25.4.2   Other Instruments Contemporaneous with the Bangalore Principles

Around the same time that the UN Office on Drugs and Crime prepared the Bangalore Principles, other international groups put forth similar instruments. The Universal Charter of the Judge ('Universal Charter'),

---

[77] Ibid., Commentary, paras. 138–139.
[78] Ibid., Commentary, para. 167.
[79] Ibid., Commentary, para. 195.
[80] Ibid.

for example – approved in 1999 by the member associations of the International Association of Judges – touches on several themes also present in the Bangalore Principles. These themes include judicial independence, status, and personal autonomy, as well as security in office, judicial selection, and remuneration and retirement.

In language that recalls the competence and diligence requirements of the Bangalore Principles, the Universal Charter provides that judges must 'diligently and efficiently' perform their duties 'without any undue delays'.[81] The Universal Charter of the Judge also advises some limits on activities outside the core judicial function, and states in particular that judges must not carry out other functions, whether public or private, paid or unpaid, which are 'not fully compatible with the duties and status of a judge'.[82] The Universal Charter does not elaborate on how to determine whether extra-judicial activities are fully compatible with the duties and status of a judge.

Standards that are more specific than those provided in the Bangalore Principles are set forth in the European Charter on the Statute of Judges (European Charter), particularly as to the broader scope of 'judicial' activities and whether outside activities are paid or unpaid. The European Charter was developed from 1997 to 1998 and arose out of the Council of Europe's activities on the organisation of justice in democratic states, governed by the rule of law.[83] These principles do not have a formal legal status, but instead are intended to provide guidance to judges, lawyers, politicians, or others with an interest in the judiciary.

The European Charter limits when and to what extent judges should undertake activities outside their core judicial functions. Notably, like the ICJ and ITLOS governing documents, the European Charter requires judges to show 'availability' among other characteristics in the discharge of their duties.[84] In this provision, 'availability' refers to both the time required to judge a case properly and the attention and alertness required for such duties.[85] Like the ICC Statute and the Bangalore Principles, the European Charter encourages judges to engage in training and ' the

---

[81] Universal Charter of the Judge, Article 6.
[82] Ibid., Article 7.
[83] See The European Charter on the Statute of Judges, available at www.coe.int/t/dghl/cooperation/ccje/textes/Avis_en.asp.
[84] Ibid., para. 1.5.
[85] Ibid., Commentary, para. 1.5.

maintenance and broadening of their knowledge, technical as well as social and cultural, needed to perform their duties'.[86]

Unlike the Bangalore Principles, however, the European Charter suggests that the propriety of outside activities may differ, depending on whether these activities are paid or unpaid. Under the European Charter, when a judge would receive remuneration for outside activities, other than literary or artistic pursuits, the judge must obtain express prior authorisation from the court or tribunal on which the judge serves.[87] Commentary on this provision calls for a 'pragmatic' assessment of any negative effects that the contemplated outside activities could have on the conditions for exercising judicial duties.[88] This pragmatic approach suggests that this provision was intended to allow judges to weigh competing considerations such as the consequences of outside activities for the perceived legitimacy of the international courts and tribunals they serve.

Additional guidance, particularly for international courts and tribunals, is set forth in the Burgh House Principles on the Independence of the International Judiciary (Burgh House Principles), prepared in the early 2000s by the Study Group of the International Law Association on the Practice and Procedure of International Courts and Tribunals.[89] The Burgh House Principles do not speak to diligence or availability of judges specifically, but rather prohibit judges from exercising political functions or any 'extra-judicial' activities that are 'incompatible with their judicial function or the efficient and timely functioning of the court'.[90] In addition, the Burgh House Principles prohibit judges from engaging in extra-judicial activities 'that may affect or reasonably appear to affect their independence or impartiality'.[91] Like other instruments, the Burgh House Principles confirm that judges enjoy freedom of expression and association, but advise that these freedoms 'must be exercised in a manner that is compatible with the judicial function and that may not affect or reasonably appear to affect judicial independence or impartiality'.[92]

---

[86] Ibid., para. 4.4
[87] Ibid., para. 4.2. As that charter provides, '[t]he exercise of an outside activity, other than literary or artistic, giving rise to remuneration, must be the object of a prior authorization on conditions laid down by the statute'.
[88] Ibid., Commentary, para. 4.2.
[89] See Philippe Sands and Campbell McLachlan, 'The Burgh House Principles on the Independence of the International Judiciary' (2005) 4 *Law & Practice of International Courts and Tribunals*, 247.
[90] See Burgh House Principles, para. 8.1.
[91] Ibid.
[92] Ibid., para. 7(1).

The Burgh House Principles provide more specific guidance than other instruments for international courts and tribunals seeking to advise members on the proper scope of outside activities. Specifically, the Burgh House Principles advise that international courts should establish mechanisms to provide guidance to judges in relation to undertaking 'extra-judicial activities' and to ensure that parties have the ability to raise any concerns in proceedings.[93] With this guidance, the Burgh House Principles recognise the role that international courts and tribunals may play in guiding members' conduct.

25.4.3   More Recent Guidance on Judicial Conduct

More recent guidance on the outside activities of international judges is set forth in the Bologna and Milan Global Code of Judicial Ethics ('Global Code'), which was approved at the International Conference of Judicial Independence in June 2015.[94] Under the Global Code, international judges are forbidden from exercising political functions or activities that are 'incompatible with their judicial function or the efficient and timely functioning of the court of which they are members'.[95] Like its predecessor instruments, the Global Code admonishes that outside activities should be avoided if they would affect or reasonably appear to affect judicial independence or impartiality.[96] The Global Code also echoes the Burgh House Principles in advising international courts and tribunals to establish 'an appropriate mechanism' to guide judges regarding outside activities and to permit parties to raise concerns about such activities.

Like the other instruments discussed above, the Global Code confirms that international judges enjoy freedom of expression and association, and that such freedoms must be exercised in a manner that is compatible with the judicial function. The Global Code also echoes the conflicts of interest provisions of other instruments and forbids judges from serving in cases in which they have previously served as agent, counsel, expert, or in another capacity, or in a case on which the judge had previously commented or expressed an opinion. The inclusion of such provisions in this more recent instrument indicates their importance and some degree

---

[93] Ibid., para. 8.3.
[94] See Bologna and Milan Global Code of Judicial Ethics, available at www.jiwp.org/global-code-of-judicial-ethics.
[95] Ibid.
[96] Ibid.

of acceptance in the international community, but also indicates a certain lack of progress in the development of guidelines to assist international judges and their institutions in issues of workload management.

25.4.4   International Instruments Lacking Guidance on Judicial Workload

Notably, a number of international instruments – both recent and more dated – lack any meaningful guidance on judicial workload considerations and the role of outside activities of judges. For example, such guidance is absent from the Magna Carta of Judges of the Consultative Council of European Judges, which was developed in 2010 by the Consultative Council of European Judges of the Council of Europe.[97] This instrument highlights the importance of the rule of law and justice, ensuring judicial independence, and access to justice and transparency.[98] This instrument does not, however, speak more directly to the propriety of outside activities and judicial availability, or set specific standards regarding the diligence or competence with which judges must carry out their functions.

Similarly, the United Nations Basic Principles of Independence of the Judiciary, adopted in 1985, generally affirms judges' freedom of expression, belief, association, and assembly, and advises that judges 'shall always conducted themselves in such a manner as to preserve the dignity of their office and the impartiality and independence of the judiciary'.[99] These Basic Principles do not, however, contain significant guidance on the propriety of undertaking activities outside the core judicial function. The absence of guidance relevant to judicial workload from such instruments indicates that these issues call for consideration separate from the more commonly discussed issues of conflict of interest, transparency, and independence.

25.5   Recommendations

In light of the variety of practices and needs in international courts and tribunals, a flexible approach should be applied to considerations of

---

[97] CCJE (2010)3 Final, available at www.icj.org/wp-content/uploads/2014/06/MagnaCarta.pdf.
[98] Ibid.
[99] Basic Principles on the Independence of the Judiciary, paras. 8 and 9, available at www.ohchr.org/EN/ProfessionalInterest/Pages/IndependenceJudiciary.aspx.

workload management for members of these international institutions. Existing standards on issues of judicial workload management are relatively sparse, however, indicating that both international institutions and their members could benefit from incorporating additional guidance into such a flexible standard. As set forth below, a number of additional factors could be incorporated into such an analysis, as conducted by individual judges alone or in collaboration with their colleagues. The factors set forth below are very likely to be ones that particular judges and their institutions already consider. Interests of transparency and legitimacy, however, might be better served if such considerations were set forth in a more systematic manner.

25.5.1 Outside Activities Should Be Permitted, Within Reason

First, as made clear by existing rules of international courts and tribunals, as well as guidelines prepared and adopted by international organisations, certain outside activities of international jurists are desirable and should be encouraged. Such activities include those that allow a judge to remain abreast of developments in the law and can permit certain cross-fertilisation among various international organs. Encouraging judges to engage in such activities may promote the perceived legitimacy of international courts and tribunals by furthering the knowledge and experience on which judges base their decisions. Allowing members of international tribunals to take part in such outside activities is also consistent with maintaining their freedom of expression and association, as recognised by the Bangalore Principles, the Burgh House Principles, the Global Code of Judicial Ethics, and other instruments.

In particular, as confirmed in the ICC Code of Judicial Ethics as well as in the Bangalore Principles and other instruments, international courts and tribunals should encourage their members to take part in outside activities that allow them to maintain and expand the knowledge, expertise, and personal skills required for their core judicial activities of deciding individual cases. Such outside activities might include participation in conferences, activities to maintain membership in national bar associations, and activities that would connect international judges with the communities concerned in their judgments. Depending on the work of the international tribunal itself, such activities might also include additional scientific or technical training that would enhance a judge's understanding of the particular work of the permanent institution on which the judge sits. By encouraging judges to engage in such activities, international tribunals may promote their perceived legitimacy.

25.5.2 Conferring with Colleagues Should Be Encouraged

Second, members of international courts and tribunals should be encouraged to confer with colleagues to discuss the advisability of undertaking particular outside activities when they are sitting judges. More generally, similar discussions could also take place before an individual judge joins or seeks to join an institution, in order to avoid surprises as to the ability to undertake such activities while on the bench. Conferring in this manner – as to specific outside activities for sitting judges and as a general matter before taking office – would permit frank conversations about the expected workload of the permanent institution concerned, as well as the potential additional work that an outside activity would entail.

Establishing internal mechanisms to address workload questions is not only consistent with the existing practices of international courts, but is also encouraged in related commentary on this topic. As one commentator recently observed, '[t]he publishing of individual statistics and names to the outside world is not necessary' to police the international judiciary.[100] Instead, such policing should take place – as it apparently does already – '[w]ithin the confines of some sort of internal control under a case-management system' and in particular 'it could appropriately be the responsibility of presidents of international courts or tribunals (including chamber, section or panel presidents) to tackle unproductive and lazy judges, if they are unlucky enough to have any such colleagues.'[101] Conferring in this manner could assist international courts and tribunals in ensuring that their members bear in mind the effect that their outside activities may have on the perceived legitimacy of the institution.

25.5.3 Relevant Considerations

Finally, an individual tribunal member – perhaps in connection with his or her permanent institution and colleagues on that institution – may consider a number of workload-related factors when weighing up whether to

---

[100] Paul Mahoney, 'The International Judiciary – Independence and Accountability' (2008) 7 *Law & Practice of International Courts and Tribunals*, 346.
[101] Ibid.

undertake a particular outside activity. As set forth below, these factors include: (1) the existing workload of the judge's permanent institution; (2) the type of activity concerned and whether it is teaching, writing, ad hoc arbitration, or another activity; (3) the subject-matter of the activity and whether it is within the judge's existing areas of expertise; (4) whether remuneration would be provided for the outside activity; (5) the duration of the activity; and (6) the resources and other support available to the judge in carrying out the outside activity.

25.5.3.1   Existing Workload of the Permanent Institution

Of primary importance in workload management considerations for members of permanent international courts and tribunals is the existing docket of that member's permanent institution. The number of cases pending with the institution may provide some indication of the institution's workload, but the complexity of those existing cases and the stage of development must also be considered, as well as the expectation and likelihood of additional cases being filed. Also of relevance is whether existing cases are likely to lead to additional work for tribunal members through the filing of counterclaims, preliminary or jurisdictional objections, requests for provisional measures, or review proceedings.

Although the amount of work that an individual case will entail – and the likelihood of additional cases being filed – will be difficult to determine with certainty, an individual member of a tribunal could benefit from discussing such considerations with the presiding member of the tribunal or other colleagues. Such discussions, while speculative, would permit an individual tribunal member to benefit from colleagues' views as to the work that the existing caseload will require, and the advisability of undertaking a particular outside activity in light of that workload.

25.5.3.2   Type of Activity Concerned

The type of activity concerned – whether it is teaching, writing, lecturing, or serving on an ad hoc arbitral tribunal or commission – is also relevant in workload management considerations for members of permanent international courts and tribunals. In particular, different types of activity will have different impacts on the physical availability of individual jurists for hearings, deliberations, meetings, and other aspects of judicial activity at their permanent institutions.

While activities related to external writing may be flexible in that they can be carried out at any location, activities related to regular teaching engagements or participation in international arbitrations are more likely to require the individual jurist's presence away from his or her permanent institution, and may be more likely to limit that member's availability for hearings, deliberations, or other meetings of the permanent institution. Activities that require a judge's absence from his or her permanent institution may be more likely to adversely affect that institution's perceived legitimacy, as the judge's divided attentions will be more obvious and activities that require a judge's presence away from his or her permanent institution are more likely to involve greater demands on the judge's time.

A related consideration is the role that the international jurist will play in the outside activity. Serving as president of an ad hoc arbitral tribunal, for example, may require a greater time commitment than serving as a party-appointed member, particularly to the extent that the president of the tribunal may be expected to organise hearings and deliberations of an ad hoc tribunal, undertake communications with the parties, and play the primary role in drafting resulting awards.

25.5.3.3   Subject-matter of the Activity

Another consideration relevant to judicial workload and outside activities is the subject-matter of the outside activity, and in particular whether it will require significant new study by the international jurist. An international jurist may require little time or preparation to deliver lectures or prepare publications on aspects of their existing or prior work. Such outside activities may also support the perceived legitimacy of the judge's permanent court or tribunal, particularly if the activity allows the jurist to showcase his or her expertise to a new audience, or promote the work of the court or tribunal on which he or she serves.

If a speaking engagement or writing project will require the international jurist to take on a new area of law or a significant new development in the law, however, a greater time commitment from the judge may be required. With such a greater time commitment, other considerations may become relevant in determining the advisability of undertaking this outside activity, such as the extent to which the tribunal member will receive external resources or support for the activity, as discussed below.

25.5.3.4   Remuneration for the Activity

Another relevant consideration, as referred to in the European Charter on the Statute of Judges is whether the activity is paid or unpaid. While the receipt of payment in itself may be unlikely to persuade an international jurist to spend more or less time on an activity, the level of remuneration may indicate the commitment expected by the party demanding the time of the jurist concerned. Remuneration is not a binary issue, however, as parties may simply be paying for having the privilege of an international jurist's name on their conference programme or faculty website. Thus, while the potential difference in expectations between paid and unpaid activities supports at least some consideration of this factor when determining the advisability of undertaking outside activities, the pragmatic approach to this issue suggested by the European Charter on the Statute of Judges may be the best way to consider any remuneration received for outside activities.

25.5.3.5   Duration of the Activity

Also of relevance is whether the outside activity is an ongoing obligation, even if intermittent, or whether it involves only a single occasion. While delivering a lecture for a single occasion, for example, may be unlikely to cause workload management problems for an international jurist, delivering an ongoing course that may entail weekly or monthly preparations may be a different matter. For an ad hoc arbitration, relevant considerations may include whether the parties envision bifurcating the jurisdictional and merits phases of the dispute, and whether preliminary proceedings are contemplated, such as a request for provisional measures.

25.5.3.6   Resources and Other Support

Finally, the resources and other support that an international jurist may have available to assist with any contemplated outside activities are also relevant to workload management issues. This aspect of 'outside activities' is not explicitly mentioned in the documents governing international institutions discussed above or in the guidelines prepared by international bodies. Nevertheless, considerations of whether an international jurist will receive additional support for his outside activities may have a significant impact on the amount of time that such activities take, and consequently on the extent to which such outside activities affect the time an individual jurist may devote to the activities of his or her permanent institution.

For example, whether a university or law faculty provides teaching assistants or similar support may significantly affect the time commitment required for an individual jurist to deliver a course. Similarly, for ad hoc arbitrations, the role a tribunal secretary may play in the case may affect the time commitment required for international jurists serving as arbitrators in that dispute. Similarly, the extent to which an ad hoc tribunal may rely on the work of technical or other experts in reaching their decisions may also be of relevance. To the extent that such external support may be lacking, an additional consideration is whether the tribunal member envisions using the resources of his or her permanent institution in support of these outside activities, or whether the tribunal member will enlist his or her own external support in these activities. Depending on the workload of the permanent institution itself, as discussed above, determining whether the outside activity will involve the use of institutional resources may be of particular importance when deciding the advisability of undertaking outside activities.

25.6   Conclusions

Documents governing international courts and tribunals and existing judicial conduct guidelines developed by international organisations do not provide significant guidance to address issues related to outside activities and workload management for members of permanent international courts and tribunals. Although some of these documents contain general guidance on the efficient operation of the tribunal and the diligence and availability of its members, such general guidance does not provide institutions or their members with a specific framework for considering whether it is advisable for an individual member to undertake a particular outside activity. In light of the sparseness of existing guidance, international courts and tribunals or other international bodies should consider adopting more explicit guidance that would include consideration of factors such as the nature of the outside activity, the workload of the permanent institution, and the degree of outside support that a tribunal member might expect in undertaking an outside activity. Having access to such particularised guidance, members of international courts and tribunals would be better able to consider the advisability of undertaking outside activities.

Providing such additional guidance may also serve to promote the legitimacy of the permanent international courts and tribunals themselves. In some circumstances, outside activities may enhance an individual judge's ability to serve a permanent institution, such as by assisting the judge in staying abreast of new developments in the law or by increasing the profile of the permanent institution. In other circumstances, such activities could negatively affect the legitimacy of these permanent institutions, for example, if an individual judge – chosen to serve that permanent institution to achieve geographic representation or to fulfil the requirement for a particular professional qualification – is unable to devote adequate time to his activities at that institution. Providing more transparent and comprehensive guidance to international jurists who are considering whether to undertake these activities could ensure that outside activities are undertaken in ways that promote, rather than detract from, the legitimacy of permanent international courts and tribunals.

The Legitimacy of Private Lawyers Representing States Before International Tribunals

ANDREAS R. ZIEGLER AND KABRE R. JONATHAN

26.1 Introduction

International adjudication, i.e. the use of international tribunals and arbitral bodies to decide international disputes, has experienced a rapid growth since World War II. While traditional arbitration may have experienced its heyday in the period between the Peace Conferences of 1899 and 1907, and thereafter until World War II, the number of international courts and tribunals has increased in the last 70 years and they are deciding more cases than ever before. This is particularly true in the area of international trade law, but to a lesser extent also in other fields such as border disputes and the law of the sea.[1]

This growth has been accompanied by a rise in challenges and difficulties for those courts and tribunals. One of these challenges is their legitimacy,[2] which has been neglected for many years in the context of international law, for many reasons.[3] We use a simple concept of legitimacy where the justification of the process and the acceptance of the actor are of primary importance, as discussed in more detail in Section 26.2. In recent years, however, the *raison d'être* of international adjudicative bodies

---

[1] We have deliberately not included arbitral procedures in so-called Investor-State Dispute Settlement (ISDS) in this chapter. While this may be one of the most interesting areas of the use of private lawyers (and especially large international law firms) we have limited the scope of this contribution to procedures involving States only. Future work will certainly be undertaken to see to what extent the presence of non-State actors as parties to a dispute alters the finding of this contribution. The same is true for the dispute settlement system of the World Trade Organization (WTO), where many (developing) States are using highly specialized law firms. Where useful, specific references to this system have been included in this chapter without an in-depth analysis that would go beyond its scope.

[2] For a definition of how this term is used in this contribution see below Section 26.2.2.

[3] See Christopher A. Thomas, 'The Uses and Abuses of Legitimacy in International Law' (2014) 24(4) *The Oxford Journal of Legal Studies* 730–732.

and their (dis)advantages are increasingly debated.[4] This debate affects the acceptance of international tribunals,[5] their functioning,[6] and the behaviour of some of their key actors. Among those actors, only the role of private counsel is the object of analysis in this contribution. Although these lawyers cannot be properly described as 'unseen actors' (because they are 'seen' performing some roles for litigant parties and their function of assistance to litigant parties is expressly enshrined in international texts), the legitimacy of assigning them certain 'unseen' roles merits discussion.[7]

As Jean-Pierre Cot (a Member of the International Tribunal of the Law of the Sea (ITLOS) since 2002) has stated, private counsel 'have always played an important role in international litigation'.[8] Nonetheless, their role has been subject to many criticisms,[9] the main one being their

---

[4] An international adjudicative body can be defined as 'a dispute resolution mechanism that decides disputes between litigants, at least one of whom is a state'; see, for example, Nienke Grossman, 'Legitimacy and International Adjudicative Bodies' (2009) 41 *The George Washington International Law Review* 107, 111.

[5] This is particularly true for more complex international tribunals that go beyond State-to-State dispute settlement. For instance, Bolivia, Ecuador, and Venezuela denounced the Convention on the Settlement of Investment Disputes between States and Nationals of Other States (ICSID Convention), 18 March 1965, into force 14 October 1966 (1967), See Grossman, 'Legitimacy and International Adjudicative Bodies', 107–108. In addition, the Republic of Burundi and the Republic of the Philippines withdrew their membership from the Rome Statute of the International Criminal Court, 17 July 1998, into force 1 July 2002 (37 ILM (1998) 999; UN doc. A/CONF.183/9 of 17 July 1998), which is the founding treaty of the International Criminal Court, see www.icc-cpi.int/Pages/item.aspx?name=pr1371 (27 July 2018). The WTO Appellate body is also facing a crisis as the USA is blocking the appointment and reappointment of this body's members. Consequently, the Appellate Body is currently composed of only four members instead of seven and, if nothing is done, this Body will be unable to operate by 10 December 2019, see www.wto.org/english/tratop_ e/dispu_e/ab_members_descrp_e.htm (27 July 2018).

[6] This issue has already been addressed, in a more general way, by various scholars, notably Grossman, 'Legitimacy and International Adjudicative Bodies'; Susan D. Franck, 'The Legitimacy Crisis in Investment Treaty Arbitration: Privatizing Public International Law Through Inconsistent Decisions' (2005) 73 *Fordham Law Review* 1521; Nienke Grossman, 'The Normative Legitimacy of International Courts' (2013) 86 *Temple Law Review* 61; Tullio Treves, 'Aspects of legitimacy of International Courts and Tribunals' in Rüdiger Wolfrum and Volker Röben (eds.), *Legitimacy in international law* (Springer, 2008), pp.169–188.

[7] In their unseen role, we are talking about the representation of a litigant State by a private lawyer. This role is not expressly enshrined in international texts, see below pp. 7–8.

[8] Jean-Pierre Cot, 'Appearing "for" or "on Behalf of" a State: The Role of Private Counsel Before International Tribunals', in Nisuke Nando, Edward McWhinney, Rüdiger Wolfrum and Betsy Baker Röben (eds.), *Liber Amicorum Judge Shigeru Oda*, vol. II, (Kluwer Law International, 2002), p. 835.

[9] See WTO, Panel Report, *European Communities – Regime for the Importation, Sale and Distribution of Bananas*, adopted 22 May 1997, WT/DS27/R/GTM, p. 294, para. 7.12; see also criticisms examined in Section 26.3.1.1.

legitimacy. The question is normally not whether those lawyers possess the necessary legitimacy to assume a specific role on behalf of a State but rather, what measures need to be undertaken to enhance their legitimacy. This chapter addresses this issue with particular attention to private counsel who act on behalf of developing countries,[10] who use private lawyers more frequently than developed ones. Developing countries also regularly entrust private lawyers with more extensive tasks than developed States do, as the latter have large groups of specialized lawyers within their own administrations.[11]

Among international adjudicative bodies, this chapter surveys only tribunals adjudicating disputes between States and, more specifically, the International Court of Justice (ICJ) and ITLOS. This choice may be explained by the following methodological reasons. Firstly, the ICJ has a specific place in international adjudication given its position as an organ of the United Nations and as the only permanent court whose jurisdiction is not limited to a specific area of international law or specific region of the world and given its influence on the development of international law. As this inquiry may involve public international law interests, it would seem inconceivable to not include the most important public international court, also referred to as the World Court. Secondly, the ICJ and ITLOS clearly distinguish between the function of judges and the function of litigants' representatives.[12] As this chapter investigates how international tribunals perceive the legitimacy of private lawyers representing States, this distinction may be very important. Thirdly, the transparency of tribunals' proceedings was a selection criterion. Before some tribunals, such as the WTO Dispute Settlement Body (DSB), proceedings are confidential.[13]

---

[10] This expression has not received an official definition. For this study, developing countries are considered to be those that have become members of the Advisory Centre on WTO Law (ACWL) and Least Developed Countries (LDCs) that are entitled to the services of ACWL, making a total of 79 countries; see www.acwl.ch/download/ql/Services_of_the_ACWL.pdf (03 July 2017).

[11] See below

[12] See Statute of the International Court of Justice, 26 June 1945, in force 24 October 1945, 3 Bevans 1179; 59 Stat 1031; TS 993; 39 AJIL Supp. 215, Article 17 (ICJ Statute); see also Statute of the International Tribunal for the Law of the Sea, United Nations Convention on the Law of the Sea, 10 December 1982, 1833 UNTS 396 X, Annex VI, Article 7(2) (ITLOS Statute). This is not the case in ICSID arbitration, for example, where States' representatives may act also as arbitrators.

[13] See, however, the interesting contribution by Jessica C. Pearlman, 'Participation by Private Counsel in World Trade Organization Dispute Settlement Proceedings' (1999) 30(2) *Law and Policy in International Business* 399–416.

The same is traditionally true for arbitral proceedings. In contrast, the ICJ and ITLOS are characterized by the transparency of their proceedings as well as the availability of their reasoned decisions. References to other tribunals are included where relevant.

In their judgments, international courts and tribunals do not tend to refer to any discussions concerning the role of a private counsel representing a State, unless they perceive a specific problem. Whenever international adjudicative bodies do include such references, these form useful sources to identify the factors that influence the perception of whether the exercised authority of private counsel is legitimate. We suggest examining criticisms made by international adjudicative bodies, in their judgments, regarding private counsel's presence and participation in international dispute settlement proceedings (usually alongside official State representatives). Reviewing these criticisms serves to identify and discuss standards that could be used to enhance a private lawyer's legitimacy.

For methodological reasons, the present analysis first clarifies the framework of the study by defining the key terms at issue (Section 26.2) before looking at (Section 26.3) factors that may challenge or enhance private counsel's legitimacy (with a particular focus on how accountability can influence legitimacy and what needs to be done in order to clarify this liability and, consequently, enhance private lawyers' legitimacy). Section 26.4 summarizes the findings and suggests areas for further research.

26.2   Terminology

26.2.1   Private Lawyers

In this section, we define the term 'private lawyer', i.e. identify who appears as private counsel or agent in inter-State litigation, and explain why private lawyers are employed by developing States – sometimes even as agents and not simply as (additional) counsel. The term 'private counsel' is sometimes used in the literature as a synonym for 'private lawyer' (without clear differentiation as to the exact authority he or she has in specific proceedings). In this chapter, we clearly distinguish those situations where we think the exact powers make a difference, in particular, when it comes to the use of agents before certain international courts and tribunals.

The term 'counsel' has not been clearly defined in international texts, but is in practice often used as a synonym for 'advocate'. For example, according to Article 42(2) of the ICJ Statute, 'counsel or advocates before the Court' may assist the agents of States, whereby the use of the conjunction 'or' implies an equivalence between those two terms.[14] The Study Group of the International Law Association (ILA) on the Practice and Procedure of International Courts and Tribunals proposed to consider as counsel,

> any person discharging the functions of counsel by representing, appearing on behalf of, or providing legal advice to a party in proceedings before an international court or tribunal, however such person may be described, and whether or not the person has professional legal training or is admitted as a member of a bar association or other professional body[15]

According to this definition, the affiliation with a bar association or professional legal training is not a mandatory requirement. Rather, the focus lies on the functions performed: to be qualified as counsel, the person must represent, appear on behalf of, or provide legal advice to one of the parties to the dispute. This wide definition seems in the interest of State parties given the diversity of people who have appeared as counsel before internationals courts and tribunals, notably lawyers affiliated with a national bar, lawyers who are not affiliated with a national bar,[16] and law professors.[17] For the purpose of this chapter, only the case of private counsel (i.e. lawyers operating in private practice, to the exclusion of those working in the public administration) who are retained by foreign States other than their own governments is examined.

---

[14] 'The uniform current practice is to use the two terms interchangeably, or even conjointly. The distinction in kind is rather between "counsel and advocates", on the one hand, and "advisers" on the other', Sir Franklin Berman, 'Article 42' in Andreas Zimmermann, Christian Tomuschat, Karin Oellers-Frahm and Christian J. Tams (eds.), *The Statute of the International Court of Justice, a Commentary*, 2nd edn (Oxford University Press, 2012), pp. 1083–1084 (note 33).

[15] Article 1 of The Hague Principles on Ethical Standards for Counsel Appearing before International Courts and Tribunals adopted 27 September 2010 (hereinafter The Hague Principles), available at www.ucl.ac.uk/laws/cict/docs/Hague_Sept2010.pdf (20 August 2017).

[16] For a definition of 'lawyer', see Arman Sarvarian, *Professional Ethics at the International Bar* (Oxford University Press, 2014), pp. 121–127.

[17] According to Alain Pellet, the ICJ bar is composed 'almost exclusively of university professors', see Alain Pellet, 'The Role of the International Lawyer in International Litigation' in Chanaka Wickremasinghe (ed.), *The International Lawyer as Practitioner*, (British Institute of International and Comparative Law, 2000), p. 150.

In inter-State adjudication, lawyers in private practice have expressly been charged to 'assist' litigant States and not to represent them.[18] The main difference between 'assistance' and 'representation' lies in the binding powers of the State representative (also called agent): while the government needs to endorse the assistant's actions in order for the latter to be valid, the agent possesses the power to bind the represented State.[19] It is the agent who receives communications on behalf of the litigant States,[20] signs pleadings,[21] and reads a party's final submissions.[22] An agent may also appear as counsel and but not vice versa.[23]

Some international texts provide the counsel with a representative role but only for non-State actors (this contributes to the confusion that sometimes exists in the literature and statements made in public)[24]. Although private lawyers have not been expressly granted the role of State representative in legal documents,[25] some (mainly developing) countries, based on the principle of free representation, have selected private lawyers instead of public servants or political figureheads as their representatives (agents).[26] At the same time, the roles of the agent and counsel may

[18] Article 42(2) ICJ Statute, Article 53 ITLOS Rules of the Tribunal (ITLOS/8) as adopted on 28 October 1997 and amended on 15 March 2001, 21 September 2001, and 17 March 2009, available at www.itlos.org/fileadmin/itlos/documents/basic_texts/Itlos_8_E_17_03_09.pdf (8 December 2017).

[19] Sir Franklin Berman, 'Article 42', p. 1080 (note 10).

[20] Article 40(1), ICJ Rules.

[21] Article 52, ICJ Rules, Article 65, ITLOS Rules.

[22] Article 60(2), ICJ Rules, Article 75(2), ITLOS Rules; see also *Case concerning the Northern Cameroons (Cameroon v. United Kingdom), Oral arguments,* ICJ Reports 1963, 15 (250).

[23] For an overview of the agent's role, see Michael J. Matheson, 'Practical Aspects of the Agent's Role in Cases Before the International Court' (2002) 1 *Law and Practice of International Courts and Tribunals* 467–479; see also Shabtai Rosenne, 'The Agent in Litigation in the International Court of Justice', in William Kaplan and Donald McRae (eds.), *Law, Policy and International Justice: Essays in Honour of Maxwell Cohen* (McGill-Queen's University Press, 1993), pp. 41–68.

[24] Article 19 of the Statute of the Court of Justice of the European Union, Consolidated version of Protocol (No 3) on the Statute of the Court of Justice of the European Union, annexed to the Treaties, as amended by Regulation (EU, Euratom) No 741/2012 of the European Parliament and of the Council of 11 August 2012 (OJ L 228, 23.8.2012, p. 1).

[25] This statement must be qualified if appearing 'on behalf of' a State (according to Article 292 of United Nations Convention on the Law of Sea, signed 10 December 1982, into force 16 November 1944, it is considered to be State representation. One author distinguishes between 'acting as a State representative' and 'acting on behalf of a State'; see Cot, 'Appearing "for" or "on behalf of" a State', pp. 835–848.

[26] Under international law, it is improper to consider as representation the fact that a State sends someone who will defend its interests before an international tribunal. The

sometimes overlap in terms of their real influence on the dispute settlement proceedings and the representation of the States involved.

In contrast to developed countries, which usually possess sufficient legal capacity to take part in international proceedings in an effective manner, developing countries often lack the specific legal expertise necessary to successfully participate in those proceedings.[27] Unfortunately, 'there is no systematic survey, both qualitative and quantitative, of the availability of international legal expertise in the foreign policy machinery of States in general, not to speak of developing countries'.[28] Nonetheless, it would seem that most developing States lack the required international legal expertise,[29] so they need to call upon external resources to address this lack of human resources. Those external resources are usually found in private practice (international law firms) or among specialized academics offering their services; exceptionally an institutional mechanism may exist. For example, developing countries can have recourse to the legal aid services of a purpose-built international organization, such as the WTO's Advisory Centre on WTO Law (ACWL).[30] Otherwise, they must turn to international law firms.

Many governments have chosen this last option for counsel and sometimes even as agents. In proceedings before ITLOS, for instance, the majority of developing countries retain foreign lawyers also as agents. This has been the case of countries such as Saint Vincent and the Grenadines,[31]

---

proper representation in international law implies that the State's representative, the State represented and third persons are subjects of international law, see Angelo Piero Sereni, *La représentation en droit international* (Brill/Nijhoff, 1948), p. 80. However, many international texts use the word 'representation' to characterize the relationship between a country and its organ or employees who must defend its interests before international tribunals. Rosenne suggests using this expression in its 'accepted diplomatic sense', see Rosenne, 'The Agent in Litigation in the International Court of Justice', p. 61.

[27] It seems that developed countries even tend to influence the awards of those adjudicative bodies, see Mark Daku and Krzysztof Pelc, 'Who Holds Influence over WTO Jurisprudence?' (2017) 20(2) *Journal of International Economic Law* 245–249.

[28] Cesare P.R. Romano, 'International Justice and Developing Countries (Continued): A Qualitative Analysis' (2002) 1(3) *The Law and Practice of International Courts and Tribunals*, 539–611, 557.

[29] As noted in the preamble of the Agreement establishing the WTO ACWL. This remark, made in the context of the WTO DSB, may be extended to other international tribunals.

[30] Certain WTO members established the ACWL in order to 'provide developing countries and LDCs with the legal capacity necessary to enable them to take full advantage of the opportunities offered by the WTO', www.acwl.ch/acwl-mission/ (3 August 2017).

[31] The M/V 'SAIGA' Case (Saint Vincent and the Grenadines v. Guinea), Prompt Release, Judgment, ITLOS Report 1997, p. 16; The M/V 'SAIGA'(N°2) Case (Saint Vincent and the Grenadines v. Guinea), Prompt Release, Judgment, ITLOS Report 1999, p. 10; 'Juno Trader' (Saint Vincent and the Grenadines v. Guinea-Bissau), Prompt Release, Judgment, ITLOS

Guinea,[32] Guinea-Bissau,[33] Seychelles,[34] Belize,[35] and Panama.[36] Before the ICJ, for example, Ethiopia,[37] Liberia,[38] Djibouti,[39] and the Democratic Republic of Congo[40] have been represented by private counsel.

Aside from the lack of legal capacity, the presence of private lawyers within governmental delegations is also due to the complexity of international courts' proceedings. To illustrate this complexity, 'WTO law consists of a complex web of over 20 agreements, which – together with the attached Member-specific schedules of concessions and commitments – cover more than 20,000 pages'.[41] Procedural rules are often not sufficiently detailed to ensure that those who are not familiar with them can use those rules in an efficient way. This leads to the perception that opacity surrounds international proceedings.

In the case of international arbitration, for example, procedural rules can even be established on an ad hoc basis and officials of developing countries may often feel disoriented if they do not have prior experience in dealing with these kinds of issue. Against this background, private counsel who knows the 'rules of the game, the usual practice and even the layout'[42] of those courts and tribunals appears to have a comparative advantage over developing States' civil servants and other private practitioners.

Reports 2004, p. 17; *M/V 'Louisa' (Saint Vincent and the Grenadines v. Kingdom of Spain), Judgment*, ITLOS Reports 2013, p. 4.

[32] *The M/V 'SAIGA' Case (Saint Vincent and the Grenadines v. Guinea), Prompt Release, Judgment*, ITLOS Report 1997, p. 16; *The M/V 'SAIGA'(N°2) Case (Saint Vincent and the Grenadines v. Guinea), Prompt Release, Judgment*, ITLOS Report 1999, p. 10.

[33] *'Juno Trader' (Saint Vincent and the Grenadines v. Guinea-Bissau), Prompt Release, Judgment*, ITLOS Reports 2004, p.17; *M/V 'Virginia G' (Panama/Guinea-Bissau), Judgment*, ITLOS Reports 2014, p. 4.

[34] *The 'Monte Confurco' Case (Seychelles v. France), Prompt Release*, Judgment of 18 December 2000, p. 86.

[35] *The 'Grand Prince' Case (Belize v. France), Prompt Release*, Judgment of 20 April 2001, p. 17.

[36] *The 'Camouco' Case (Panama v. France), Prompt Release*, Judgment of 7 February 2000, p. 10; *The 'Chaisiri Reefer 2' Case (Panama v. Yemen), Prompt Release*, 13 July 2001, p. 82; *M/V 'Virginia G' (Panama/Guinea-Bissau), Judgment*, ITLOS Reports 2014, p. 4.

[37] *'South West Africa Cases (Ethiopia v. South Africa; Liberia v. South Africa)*, Preliminary Objections, Judgment of 21 December 1962: ICJ Report, 1962, p. 319.

[38] Ibid.

[39] *Certain Questions of Mutual Assistance in Criminal Matters (Djibouti v. France)*, Judgment, I.C.J. Reports 2008, p. 177.

[40] *Armed Activities on the Territory of the Congo (Democratic Republic of the Congo v. Uganda)*, Judgment, ICJ Reports 2005, p. 168.

[41] See www.acwl.ch/acwl-mission/ (20 August 2017).

[42] Pellet, 'The Role of the International Lawyer in International Litigation', p. 149.

26.2.2   *Legitimacy*

The concept of 'legitimacy' is not easy to define,[43] even though many scholars have attempted over time to identify its constitutive elements.[44] For the purpose of this chapter, legitimacy stands for the justification and the acceptance of a political authority.[45] The private lawyer serving as counsel in international proceedings can be regarded as such a political authority because he or she plays an active role in inter-State proceedings. Through this assignment, the private lawyer is given a specific role in the representation of the State, including with regard to the outcome that will affect the State as such.

This authority may be legitimized by its source, its procedure, the outcomes it has produced, or a combination of these elements.[46] In the case of counsel acting on behalf of a State, the question of legitimacy arises, in particular, in the case of private lawyers acting as agents, rather than as State counsel. In fact, the agent benefits from an important delegation of authority and can bind the represented country with his or her actions.[47] Is the authority of the agent-lawyer perceived as legitimate? But even a simple counsel may play a very active role and a significant part in specific proceedings that justify the questions of his or her legitimacy.

---

[43] Legitimacy may be described as a 'nebulous concept', see Yuval Shany, *Assessing the Effectiveness of International Courts* (Oxford University Press, 2014), p. 138; see also Thomas, 'The Uses and Abuses of Legitimacy in International Law', 733; Alain Pellet, 'Legitimacy of Legislative and Executive Actions of International Institutions' in R. Wolfrum and V. Röben (eds.), *Legitimacy in International Law*, p. 63.

[44] Grossman, 'Legitimacy and International Adjudicative Bodies', 115–122; Thomas, 'The Uses and Abuses of Legitimacy in International Law', 734–742; Mattias Kumm, 'The Legitimacy of International Law: A Constitutionalist Framework of Analysis' (2004) 15 *EJIL* 907, 917.

[45] Many scholars use this term in that way, see Grossman, 'Legitimacy and International Adjudicative Bodies', 115; see also various contributors in Wolfrum and Röben, *Legitimacy in International Law*, pp. 1–24, 25–62, 309–317; Nienke Grossman, Harlan Grant Cohen, Andreas Føllesdal and Geir Ulfstein, 'Legitimacy and International Courts – A Framework' in Nienke Grossman, Harlan Grant Cohen, Andreas Føllesdal, and Geir Ulfstein (eds.), *Legitimacy and International Courts*, (Cambridge University Press, 2018), p. 3.

[46] Rüdiger Wolfrum, 'Legitimacy in International Law from a Legal Perspective: Some Introductory Considerations' in Wolfrum and Röben (eds.), Legitimacy in International Law, p. 6.

[47] See Berman, 'Article 42', pp. 1080–1083; see also Matheson, 'Practical Aspects of the Agent's Role in Cases before the International Court', 467–479; Rosenne, 'The Agent in Litigation in the International Court of Justice', pp. 41–68.

In the context of international law, there are some important arguments in favour of the legitimacy of private lawyers being used as counsel (or even agent). The first argument is the consent of the represented State.[48] The moment a private person is assigned by the State to represent this State before an international adjudicative body, this lawyer is 'legitimized' to exercise this authority on behalf of that State.[49] Assuming that this is the free will of the competent State organs, this decision benefits from the same legitimacy as the appointing authority has under domestic law.

In addition, the specific expertise of the appointed counsel provides a strong argument in favour of the legitimate authority of private council (outcome-based legitimacy). Only the appointment of (foreign) private persons (experts) can assure the correct representation of certain States and the defence of their best interests[50].

However, the present discussion is not focused on the actual legitimacy of the counsel but rather on the perception of this legitimacy. Is the authority of the agent-lawyer perceived as legitimate? Who must perceive the agent-lawyer's authority as legitimate in the context of international adjudication? In the case of private counsel, the relevant constituencies are first and foremost States, but also international adjudicatory bodies, potential litigants, and even the population (citizens) of the State appointing such a counsel.[51] This chapter focuses exclusively on how international courts and tribunals perceive the exercise of public authority by lawyers on behalf of States, though the wider question on the legitimacy as perceived by other actors definitely deserves attention in future research.

26.3   Factors Influencing Legitimacy

Several criticisms regarding private counsels' legitimacy acting on behalf of governments are based on their supposed lack of proximity to the

---

[48] Rüdiger Wolfrum, 'Legitimacy in International Law from a Legal Perspective: Some Introductory Considerations', in Wolfrum and Röben (eds.), Legitimacy in International Law, pp. 6–10.

[49] Ibid., pp. 10–24. This State consent tends to be insufficient as the base of the legitimacy in some aspects of international law and must be completed with other elements such as the test of democratic governance, for example; ibid., pp. 20–24.

[50] WTO, Appellate Body Report, European Communities – Bananas, adopted 9 September 1997, WT/DS27/AB/R, p. 7, para. 12; Permanent Court of Arbitration (PCA) Case No. AA 227, Yukos Universal Limited (Isle of Man) v. The Russian Federation, Final award, 18 July 2014, p. 577.

[51] Shany, Assessing the Effectiveness of International Courts, p. 139.

represented State (Section 26.3.1) and the vagueness of rules regulating their accountability (Section 26.3.2).

26.3.1   Proximity with the Represented State

26.3.1.1   Private Counsel's Proximity to the Represented State

As an introduction to this factor, we would like to give two examples: in a dispute between Belize and France, one member of ITLOS noted 'an unusual feature':

> The Agent appointed by Belize is not well placed, as a non-Belizean lawyer in private practice in Spain, to explain to the Tribunal the seeming inconsistencies in the statements of different government departments and agencies in Belize.[52]

In another case, an ICJ judge, made the following statement:

> Furthermore, in the present case, I note that a State appearing before the Court is not represented by a person holding high office in the Government acting as Agent, but by a private lawyer from another, highly developed, country. This has rarely been the case in the history of the Court and reinforces my feeling that a question arises as to whether the case is brought to the Court in the interest of the State involved or for some other reason.[53]

In those two cases, lawyers were criticized for being of a nationality other than that of the country for which they were acting and for not holding highest office in the local government[54]. An aggravating factor seemed to be that they were not only acting as counsel but also as agent for the States concerned. A legitimacy-influencing factor may be derived from those reproaches: the proximity of a legal representative with the represented country. The underlying idea is that the more the counsel (or at least the agent) has a close relationship with the represented country, the stronger his or her legitimacy. This proximity can be assessed using criteria such

---

[52] *The 'Grand Prince' Case (Belize v. France), Prompt Release*, Judgment, Separate Opinion of Judge Anderson, 20 April 2001.

[53] *Armed activities on the territory of the Congo (Democratic Republic of the Congo v. Uganda)*, Provisional Measures, Order of 1 July 2000, I.C.J. Reports 2000, Declaration of Judge Oda, at 132.

[54] In a recent case, the representativeness of a private lawyer acting as the State's representative was also questioned, see *M/V 'Norstar' (Panama v. Italy), Preliminary Objections*, Judgment, ITLOS Reports 2016, pp. 18–26; see also Declaration of Judge Cot, ITLOS Reports 2016, p. 2.

as nationality or participation in the performance of a public interest mission or the exercise of highest office in the country.

This standard could, however, simply have been influenced by governments' past practice (i.e. tradition) in terms of representation.[55] In fact, in their relations with others States and international organizations, States used to send delegations that included a head of delegation, other delegates, diplomatic staff, and administrative, technical, and service staff.[56] Ministers or other persons holding high office in the represented governments used to be part of such delegations.[57] Even if a State has the sovereign right to do so, the appointment of persons who do not possess its nationality seems more the exception than the rule.[58] This practice could simply have led to the belief that State representation should be assumed by (high) government officials whose mission is to work on a daily basis for the safeguarding of a government's public interests. In the United States, for example, there is a difference in the traditional understanding between the role of governmental entities' attorneys and private parties' attorneys. In this traditionally 'adversarial' system both functions are described as attorneys but characterized differently. The first serve the public interest while the second, primarily, defend individual self-interests of their private clients.[59]

In support of this legitimacy factor, it has been suggested that the absence of proximity between the agent and its government could result in improper consequences for the conduct of the international proceedings. This may be less true for other legal systems (such as those on the European continent), where many legal systems attribute specific duties in the public interest to private lawyers when defending private parties against the State.

---

[55] In the years of the General Agreement on Tariffs and Trade (GATT), for instance, only government lawyers or government trade experts were representing governments in dispute settlement proceedings, see WTO, Appellate Body Report, *European Communities – Bananas*, adopted 9 September 1997, WT/DS27/AB/R, pp. 5–6, paras. 8–9.

[56] Article 45 of the Vienna Convention on the Representation of States in their Relations with International Organizations of a Universal Character, 14 March 1975 (hereinafter 'Vienna Convention') (Un Doc. A/Conf. 67/16; 1975 Digest of US Practice in International Law 40). 'Although this Convention has not yet entered into force, its Part 111 (Delegations to Organs and to Conferences) particularly represents a reflection of customary international law in this area', see Rutsel Silvestre J. Martha, 'Representation of Parties in World Trade Disputes' (1997) 31(2) *Journal of World Trade* 86.

[57] Article 50, Vienna Convention.

[58] Article 73, Vienna Convention; see also Shabtai Rosenne, *The Law and the Practice of the International Court 1920–2005* (Brill, 2006), pp. 1120–1121.

[59] Steven K. Berenson, 'Public Lawyers, Private Values: Can, Should, and Will Government Lawyers Serve the Public Interest?' (2000) 41(4) *Boston College Law Review* 796 ff.

26.3.1.2   Consequences of the Lack of Proximity Between the Represented Government and its Counsel/Agent

The problems arising from non-proximity between authorities of represented government and counsel or agent are numerous. Only two of them are to be analysed here. Firstly, the private counsel can provide the tribunal with inaccurate information. As representative, the agent (and to a lesser degree the counsel) is the link between the court and the litigant State. Given this position, the agent is expected to be highly reliable.[60] This requires legal expertise but also a good knowledge of local realities. When the agent is not a national (or at least resident) of the represented country, he or she may give the international tribunal incorrect information or be unable to provide all the information requested, notably when this information relates to the government's domestic affairs. In the *Grand Prince* Case, the agent appointed by Belize provided 'incomplete and contradictory information concerning the registration of the vessel and the position of Belize as to the nationality of the Grand Prince'.[61] Additionally, Judge Anderson 'would have favoured asking for more information about the legal status of the Grand Prince at the material times'.[62] But given the fact that the agent was not familiar with local practices of different government departments and agencies in Belize, the Tribunal decided 'not to seek further information from the Applicant'.[63] In the *Juno Trader* Case, it seems that there was a divergence between information provided by the agent and 'the view of the law as it emerges from the decision of the Regional Court of Bissau.[64]

Judge Cot summed up the situation (under the particular circumstances typical for the application for release of a vessel under Article 292 of the UN Convention on the Law of the Sea): 'The lawyer-agent is not necessarily in close contact with the authorities of the flag State. The credibility and reliability of the information he provides as to the legal position of the flag State may be questionable'.[65]

---

[60] See Cot, 'Appearing "for" or "on behalf of" a State', p. 842. Another author adds that the agent has to 'understand and faithfully reflect the national policy decisions of its government', see Matheson, 'Practical Aspects of the Agent's Role in Cases Before the International Court', 473.

[61] 'Grand Prince', Declaration of Judge *ad hoc* Cot, para. 14.

[62] 'Grand Prince', Separate Opinion of Judge Anderson.

[63] Ibid.

[64] 'Juno Trader', Joint Separate Opinion of Judges Mensah and Wolfrum, 59.

[65] 'Grand Prince', Declaration of Judge *ad hoc* Cot, para. 14.

Nevertheless, the proximity with national authorities does not guarantee that the information provided is credible and reliable. Even civil servants have provided false information in some proceedings[66] or were unable to adequately defend the interests of their State.[67] If the civil servant does not possess relevant experience in international litigation, his or her knowledge of local matters may be insufficient to properly defend the interest of the government. Adding civil servants to a State delegation who will provide the international lawyer (possibly leading the delegation) with correct factual information might form a workable compromise. This may avoid contradictions between the information provided to a court and the facts (as occurred in the 'Juno Trader' case).[68]

Secondly, the lack of permanent association between the agent-lawyer and the State he or she is representing can lead to a conflict of interests. Judge Oda underlined the risk of conflict of interests in at least one situation.[69] Judge Cot also expressed his concern of 'a proliferation of applications that are manifestly unfounded inspired by law firms for reasons having nothing to do with the interests of the Applicant State'.[70]

Those conflicts can derive from multiple sources. Only a limited number of them can be discussed here. Firstly, besides the recourse to the judicial mode, States may use other amicable modes of international dispute settlement with a view to finding a diplomatic solution to a dispute: this is the obligation to negotiate.[71] They have various means to fulfil this obligation,

---

[66] In one case (*Maritime Delimitation and Territorial Questions between Qatar and Bahrain (Qatar v. Bahrain)*, Merits, Judgment, ICJ Reports 2001, p. 40), Qatar's representatives produced 82 false documents during the written proceedings. However, those documents were withdrawn after an objection from Bahrain. In this affair, Qatar was represented by the Secretary-General of the Cabinet of the Government of the State of Qatar and it seems that the outside counsel, retained by Qatar, had not been aware of any fraud, see *M/V 'Louisa'*, Separate Opinion of Judge Cot, ITLOS Reports 2013, 114.

[67] In the *CDC Group* Case, the governmental agents of the Republic of Seychelles have demonstrated their incompetence to defend their State's interests, notably with counter-memorial incorrectly drafted and poor management of witness, see *CDC Group PLC v. Republic of Seychelles*, ICSID Case N° ARB/02/14, 17 December 2003, 8.

[68] The *'Juno Trader'*, Joint Separate Opinion of Judges Mensah and Wolfrum, 59.

[69] *Armed Activities on the Territory of the Congo (Democratic Republic of the Congo v. Uganda)*, Provisional Measures, Order of the 1 July 2000, ICJ Reports 2000, Declaration of Judge Oda,132.

[70] *'Grand Prince'*, Declaration of Judge *ad hoc* Cot, para. 13.

[71] '(a) the parties are under an obligation to enter into negotiations with a view to arriving at an agreement, and not merely to go through a formal process of negotiation as a sort of prior condition for the automatic application of a certain method of delimitation in the absence of agreement; they are under an obligation so to conduct themselves that the

notably 'negotiation, enquiry, mediation, conciliation, arbitration, judicial settlement, resort to regional agencies or arrangements'.[72] Depending on the type of dispute, it may be helpful to make use of other means and not only (ab)use of judicial means because the judicial settlement of international disputes 'is simply an alternative to the direct and friendly settlement of such disputes between the parties.[73] In this situation, the private lawyers assisting a State may be confronted with conflicting interests since their expertise is mainly sought in the context of the judicial resolution and not the diplomatic resolution of the dispute. The private counsel, thereupon, may be tempted by 'abuse of the right to institute proceedings before the Court' without 'first exhausting diplomatic channels'.[74]

Secondly, in the case of ITLOS prompt release disputes (Article 292 of the UN Convention on the Law of the Sea), the agent-lawyer may be tempted to give priority to private interests (those of the shipowner) at the expense of the represented government's interests. This special procedure is a form of diplomatic protection that provides shipowners, via the flag State, a fast-track procedure and direct access to ITLOS.[75] The dispute remains intergovernmental but the interests of the shipowner are also involved. It is not unusual that the agent appointed by the State, appears to be, in reality, the shipowner's counsel.[76] In such a case, it is reasonable to assume that this agent-lawyer will prioritize the interests of the shipowner over those of the flag State should those two interests conflict.

Thirdly, counsel fees are another potential source for a conflict of interests. The underlying idea is that some agent-lawyers can seek to let the procedure drag on as long as possible in their own economic interest. The WTO Panel in the *EC – Bananas* case underlined the risk of high counsel fees.[77] The

---

negotiations are meaningful', see *North Sea Continental Shelf, (Federal Republic of Germany v. Denmark)*, Judgment, ICJ Reports 1969, 48.

[72] Article 33 of United Nations Charter.

[73] *Free Zones of Upper Savoy and the District of Gex*, Order of the 19 August 1929, PCIJ, Serie A, No. 22, p. 13.

[74] Shigeru Oda, 'The Compulsory Jurisdiction of the International Court of Justice: A Myth? – A Statistical Analysis of Contentious Cases' (2000) 49 *The International and Comparative Law* 265.

[75] Tullio Treves, 'Article 292', in Alexander Proelss (ed.), *United Nations Convention on the Law of the Sea, A Commentary* (Beck/Hart/Nomos, 2017), p. 1882.

[76] In the *'Louisa'* case, the personal lawyer of the shipowner was solely in charge of Saint-Vincent and the Grenadines' representation, given the withdrawal of governmental employees, *M/V 'Louisa'*, Separate Opinion of Judge Cot, 117.

[77] 'There was a question in our minds whether the admission of private lawyers to Panel meetings, if it became a common practice, would be in the interest of smaller Members

ACWL is trying to solve this problem by offering services similar to those of law firms at a relatively low cost.[78] However, the WTO-ACWL example is hard to transpose to other international adjudicative bodies given the difference in prices that may exist between lawyers' fees for disputes before different international courts and tribunals. For the time being, the WTO-ACWL remains unique, despite suggestions to use similar mechanisms, for example, in ISDS.[79] Philippe Sands (who is himself very actively assisting governments in international proceedings) gives an interesting example of:

> a case in which the lawyer [is] acting as counsel for a State but where the legal fees are being paid by a private actor with an interest in the case. The interests of private actor and of State are different. The lawyer gets different instructions, one set of instructions from the person paying the legal fees, and another set of instructions from the State that appears as the party before the proceedings. What is counsel to do?[80]

There is no clear answer from the outset. All those problems revive the debate on counsel regulation at the international level, which is the second legitimacy-influencing factor.

26.3.2   Clarity of Accountability Rules

Our purpose is to establish a link between legitimacy and accountability, and to enhance this legitimacy through accountability. To do so, we examine the influence of accountability on the perception of legitimacy and establish the current situation of counsel accountability both in term of binding rules and regulatory authorities. Then, we conclude the examination by suggesting some ways of enhancing counsel liability.

In the analysis of a private counsel's legitimacy, accountability tends to be a key element for it is assumed that a legitimate actor is necessarily an accountable actor. Many scholars have underlined the relationship

---

as it could entail disproportionately large financial burdens for them', see Panel Report, *European Communities – Bananas*, p. 294, para. 7.12.

[78] For an overview of ACWL's charges, see ACWL's website, www.acwl.ch/download/basic_documents/management_board_docs/ACWL-MB-D-2007-7.pdf (6 August 2017).

[79] For example, 'Investment treaty cases are within a range of 5 to 10 times more expensive than trades disputes', see Anna Joubin-Bret, *Establishing an International Advisory Centre on Investment Disputes? E15Initiative* (International Centre for Trade and Sustainable Development (ICTSD) and World Economic Forum, 2015), p. 2.

[80] Philippe Sands, 'Interaction between Counsel and International Courts and Arbitral Tribunals: Ethical Standards for Counsel', in Rüdiger Wolfrum and Ina Gätzschmann (eds.), *International Dispute Settlement: Room for Innovations?* (Springer, 2012), p. 128.

between accountability and legitimacy. The main argument is that the absence of clarity in accountability rules could result in a crisis of confidence that may reflect negatively on legitimacy.[81]

Furthermore - and from the point of view of democratic legitimacy - national law seems to have more legitimacy than international law, given the presence of accountable institutions at national level.[82] This clarity may materialize with accountability rules that offer predictability and help counsel, litigant States, and other actors involved in international adjudication to plan their conduct accordingly.

26.3.2.1   The Lack of Transparency of Counsel Accountability Rules

Unlike the situation at the national level, there is no International Bar.[83] The principal consequence is the lack of a clear normative framework for the regulation of private lawyers' actions before international courts.[84] Nonetheless, there are some principles related to counsel conduct before certain tribunals.[85] Do those principles also apply to agent-lawyers given

---

[81] This WTO Panel was criticizing the lack of 'disciplinary rules' private lawyers have to comply with, see Panel Report, *European Community – Bananas*, p. 294, para. 7.12; see also Doak Bishop, 'Ethics in International Arbitration', in Albert Jan van den Berg (ed.), *Arbitration Advocacy in Changing Times, International Council for Commercial Arbitration (ICCA) Congress Series No. 15* (Kluwer Law International, 2011), p. 383; Franck, 'The Legitimacy Crisis in Investment Treaty Arbitration', 1584; Grossman, 'Legitimacy and International Adjudicative Bodies', 153.

[82] Kumm, 'The Legitimacy of International Law', 924.

[83] Judge James Crawford distinguishes between the situation of international criminal tribunals with an emerging international criminal law bar, the situation of courts and tribunals hearing inter-State disputes where it seems to be an invisible bar, and the situation of international investment tribunals where there is need of an international investment law bar, see James Crawford, 'The International Law Bar, Essence before Existence?' (January 2014) The University of Cambridge Faculty of Law Research Paper No. 19/2014, pp. 343–354.

[84] The International Criminal Court's *Code of Professional Conduct for Counsel* stands out as an exception (annexed to Resolution ICC-ASP/4/Res.1, and adopted at the third plenary meeting on 2 December 2005, by consensus, available at www.icc-cpi.int/resource-library/Documents/COPCEng.pdf (10 August 2017). It has limited relevance for our study given the fact that States are not litigants before this court, but this Code can provide basic principles for international lawyers' accountability.

[85] Those principles may be found in texts such as the Code of Conduct for European Lawyers and the Charter of Core Principles of the European Legal Profession, adopted by the Council of Bars and Law Societies of Europe (CCBE), The Hague Principles on Ethical Standards for Counsel Appearing before International Courts and Tribunals adopted by the International Law Association (ILA), and the International Bar Association's (IBA) Guidelines on Party Representation in International Arbitration.

the specific nature of the agent's function? 'As the agent is the representative of a sovereign State, is it conceivable that he be subject to the authority of a court whose jurisdiction depends upon the consent of that State?'[86] Agents are not, by definition, responsible under international law. They do not engage their personal responsibility for acts performed within the framework of their mandate of representation. The represented State is responsible for the actions of its agent.[87] However, some authors take exception to this conclusion and claim that agent-lawyers should face individual liability for their conduct[88]. We are also of the opinion that individuals acting before international courts and tribunals should be subject to specific rules and that their violations should lead to specific sanctions.

Nevertheless, at least one question remains. Which institution should be in charge of regulating private lawyers' behaviour before an international adjudicative body? Is it the international tribunal before which the private lawyer appears?[89] Are the lawyer's national disciplinary bodies (public prosecutor, local court, bar association, and the like) well positioned?[90] Is it the represented State?[91] Is it a system of self-regulation with

---

[86] 'Grand Prince' Case, Declaration of Judge ad hoc Cot, para. 48.

[87] Riad Daoudi, Notion de représentation en droit international public (Librairie Générale de Droit et de Jurisprudence, Paris, 1980), pp. 65–66.

[88] 'Grand Prince' Case, Declaration of Judge ad hoc Cot, para. 49; see also Stephan Wilske, 'Sanctions against Counsel in International Arbitration – Possible, Desirable or Conceptual Confusion?' (2015) 8(2) Contemporary Arabian Asian Journal 141, 164.

[89] Those courts have no explicit powers to apply the basic principles identified above. Moreover, those tribunals are reluctant to use their inherent powers to challenge agent-lawyers' accountability. It seems that such powers do not include the power to take disciplinary action against a lawyer, Fraport AG Frankfurt Airport Services Worldwide v. Philippines, ICSID Case No. ARB/03/ 25, Decision on Application for Disqualification of Counsel, 18 September 2008, para. 39. See also see Crawford, 'The International Law Bar, Essence before Existence?', p. 353.

[90] Of course, they have a role to play in the regulation of counsel at international level. However, entrusting those bodies with the exclusive power to control lawyers appearing before international adjudicative bodies may give rise to confidentiality concerns, additional costs, interference with international process, etc., see Wilske, 'Sanctions against Counsel in International Arbitration', 149–153.

[91] For international adjudicative bodies, it appears that agent-lawyers' accountability does fall under the authority of the represented government, see 'Grand Prince' Case, Declaration of Judge ad hoc Cot, para. 15. The represented State has some means to sanction counsel misconduct, notably by bringing that misconduct before its own domestic courts, but States rarely uses those means. But it is safe to assume that a government that relies on a private lawyer for the defence of its interests before an international court may not be able to properly regulate this counsel and sanction him/her in case of wrongdoing.

advocates regulating themselves?[92] Another institution?[93] Usually, none of these has been provided expressly with the mission of regulating lawyers' actions at the international level.

The absence of any institution clearly in charge of regulating counsel behaviour, coupled with the lack of coordination between these different potential regulatory authorities, results in an 'ethical no man's land' in which counsel operate with total freedom.[94]

This all contributes to blurring counsel accountability and reinforces concerns regarding lawyers with almost unlimited powers that are not sufficiently counter-balanced and/or controlled. Personally, we are of the opinion that the existence of an 'International Bar' is not a necessary pre-requisite for the regulation of counsel accountability. In fact, we would rather suggest that international adjudicative bodies' inherent powers are sufficient to deal with this issue. The appeal of entrusting international tribunals with the determination of the accountability of counsels or agents acting before them is twofold: to clarify their accountability and thereby enhance their legitimacy.

26.3.2.2   Clear Accountability Rules for Enhanced Legitimacy?

Legitimizing the public authority of international institutions, organs, and norms is one of the goals international courts are expected to attain (external legitimization).[95] Their capacity to achieve this goal is directly linked to their own legitimacy in the eyes of their constituencies (internal legitimization).[96] International lawyers may contribute to this internal legitimacy given their expertise (even more so due to the fact that they may subsequently be retained as judges especially in international arbitration).[97]

---

[92] Before the ICJ, it appears that there is an acceptable system of self-regulation of the invisible bar, see Crawford, 'The International Bar, Essence before Existence?', pp. 349–350.

[93] For example, the president of the Swiss Arbitration Association, Elliott Geisinger has called for the creation of a truly transnational body for the regulation of counsel appearing before international arbitral tribunals; see Elliott Geisinger, 'President's Message: Counsel Ethics in International Arbitration – Could One Take Things a Step Further?' (2013) 32(3) *ASA BULL 2014* 455.

[94] Catherine Rogers, 'Fit and Function in Legal Ethics: Developing a Code of Conduct for International Arbitration' (2002) 23(2) *The Michigan Journal of International Law* 341, 341–342.

[95] Shany, 'Assessing the Effectiveness of International Courts', pp. 44–46.

[96] Ibid., p. 137.

[97] This appointment may enhance the image of international tribunals and their professionalism and provide additional justifications to support their authority, ibid., p. 147.

This legitimacy-conferring capacity could be extended to counsel acting before international courts and tribunals because these lawyers form part of the regime to which international courts are meant to contribute[98] and may be seen as having a contractual or quasi-contractual commitment vis-à-vis these courts.[99]

In addition, a detailed regulation, such as 'judicial formation governed by public international law',[100] imposed by international public institutions may not be seen as favouring the private interests of law firms but rather the public interest of the international community in the administration of justice.[101] This would also enhance the image of counsel appearing before these courts and provide additional justifications to support lawyers' authority as States' representatives.

Moreover, making international adjudicative bodies responsible for counsel's conduct at the international level may resolve many practical problems: it will resolve concerns about breaches of confidentiality, as well as restoring equal treatment among international lawyers since not all international lawyers are affiliated with national bars. Those who are affiliated with national bars may be subject to different rules of conduct given differences among legal traditions. International bodies will apply the same rules to all lawyers appearing before them. However, there is a risk of fragmentation of accountability rules because of the differences between international courts and tribunals but this could be minimized through a dialogue between these institutions.

Finally, international tribunals' inherent powers include not only the power to adopt rules of conduct for counsel (or agents if they are private

---

[98] According to Principle (i) of 'The Charter of Core Principles of the European Legal Profession', adopted on 24 November 2006, the lawyer is an 'officer of the Court' or a 'minister of justice'.

[99] Wilske, 'Sanctions against Counsel in International Arbitration', 163.

[100] *Hrvatska Elektroprivreda, d.d. v. Slovenia*, ICSID Case No. ARB/05/24, Ruling regarding the participation of David Mildon QC in further stages of the proceedings, 6 May 2008, para. 33.

[101] See also Stephan Schill, 'The Case for Public Regulation of Professional Ethics for Counsel in International Arbitration', Kluwer Arbitration Blog, 7 July 2017. International adjudicative bodies have a public function that goes beyond the private function to settle a dispute between litigant parties. In particular, those tribunals have to ensure the proper administration of international justice and to play a role in the clarification and the progressive development of international law, see Chester Brown, 'Inherent Powers in International Adjudication', in Cesare P.R. Romano, Karen J. Alter and Yuval Shany (eds.), *The Oxford Handbook of International Adjudication* (Oxford University Press, 2014), pp. 842–844.

lawyers)[102] but also the power to sanction.[103] The latter is a more delicate matter, but it seems that international tribunals' reluctance to exercise this control is mainly due to political reasons.[104] However, the public function of those tribunals means they need to take into consideration interests other than those of the parties to the dispute; an international case usually involves not only interests of the litigant States but also those of the international community in a whole.[105]

26.4   Conclusions

A private lawyer's legitimacy (especially when acting as an agent) is heavily dependent on his or her knowledge of the facts and the law as applicable to the State by which he or she was appointed. The lawyer must be competent to represent the State, which this chapter has defined in terms of 'proximity with the represented State'. In cases where this proximity does not exist, this may have a negative impact on the defence of the interests of the represented government. This finding seems not particularly surprising and is also known from domestic law (lawyer-client relationship) but problems in this respect have arisen in recent years before the international tribunals studied in this chapter.

Accountability is also important for the analysis of the legitimacy of the use of private lawyers before international courts given the fact that the more transparent the normative framework of counsel regulation is, the more these lawyers' legitimacy as State representatives will be enhanced. International tribunals can be entrusted with regulating counsel since, as international public actors, they possess the legitimacy and the inherent competence to do so. Some of them have already exercised control over

---

[102] International Criminal Court paved the way with the adoption of a code for counsel. The ICJ took a step in that direction with the adoption of its Practice Direction that contains some rules for counsel's conduct.

[103] International courts sanctioned counsel many times, see for example the *Hrvatska Elektroprivreda, d.d. v. Slovenia* case. The ICJ rebuked counsel in three cases, see Crawford, 'The International Bar, Essence before Existence?', pp. 349–350. In *The Rompetrol Group N. V. v. Romania*, ICSID Case No. ARB/06/ 3, Decision of the Tribunal on the Participation of a Counsel, 12 January 2010, para. 16, the Tribunal did not deny this power of control but rather restricted its scope.

[104] See *Fraport AG Frankfurt Airport Services Worldwide v. Philippines*, para. 39; see also Cot, 'Appearing "for" or "on behalf of" a State', 847; Crawford, 'The International Bar, Essence before Existence?', p. 350.

[105] Brown, 'Inherent Powers in International Adjudication', p. 844.

counsel behaviour but a more widespread debate about the existing rules and necessary improvements would enhance the perception of private lawyers' legitimacy In turn, this could contribute to improving the legitimacy of international dispute settlement as a whole.

We agree with Judge Cot when he says '[t]hat these are difficult questions', continuing that '[i]t falls primarily to the States parties to a dispute to answer them. They, acting in sovereign fashion, organize their representation and the defence of their interests. They do so at their own risk.'[106] In sum, this chapter concludes that common international rules to safeguard the integrity and thereby the legitimacy of international dispute settlement are needed when it comes to the use of private lawyers as counsels and agents.

---

[106] 'Grand Prince', Declaration of Judge *ad hoc* Cot, para. 15.

Online Reporters and Databases

Four Narratives of Their Roles in Investor-State Dispute Settlement

PIETRO ORTOLANI

There is competition in the chaos.

Emanuel Carnevali, *Almost a God*

27.1   Introduction

Any topic of study is identified by certain core tensions and unresolved dilemmas, around which the debate develops. These foundational questions are, perhaps, even more important than basic definitions: whilst the latter point towards what we conventionally agree on about a given topic, the former unveil the unsettled regions of knowledge we do not yet fully master. In a way, they constitute the current plan of our future intellectual explorations.

One of the defining dilemmas for international courts and tribunals is the question of their identity and role. What are they? And what is it, exactly, that they do? For a relatively long time, these questions have constituted the focal point of a wealth of legal research and international lawmaking. The work of scholars such as von Bogdandy and Venzke reinforces the centrality of the questions at hand, demonstrating the usefulness of a multifunctional approach to international courts and tribunals.[1]

In the specific case of investor-State dispute settlement (hereinafter 'ISDS'), the identity dilemma is particularly relevant and complex, because the system has developed over time in an uncoordinated and

---

[1] A. von Bogdandy and I. Venzke, *In Whose Name? A Public Law Theory of International Adjudication* (Oxford University Press, 2014), pp. 5–17. According to this approach, international adjudication is best understood as performing more than one function at the same time, and namely not only settling disputes, but also stabilising normative expectations, making law and controlling and legitimising public authority.

partially unforeseen manner. Originally grounded in a 'procedure before substance' approach, whereby a successful mechanism of dispute resolution was to be borrowed from transnational commercial relations and adapted to contract-based investor-State relations,[2] ISDS has progressively morphed into a partially different reality, where the applicable law and the consent to arbitrate are both often found in instruments of public international law. It is hence unsurprising that one of the main strands of ISDS scholarship focuses on the question of identity, trying to determine whether investment arbitration is 'public' or 'private'.[3]

To be sure, the public/private divide is only one of the ways in which the ISDS identity quest may be cast. One may also see the problem at hand as one of the variables affecting the trilateral interaction between deep economic integration, democratic politics and the centrality of the nation-State as a set of architectures of control and power.[4] Whatever the preferred theoretical framework may be, one thing is certain: the debate surrounding ISDS is increasingly clustering around the question of its identity.

There are two main reasons why the identity of ISDS is particularly difficult to grasp. Firstly, international investment law developed through a network of mainly bilateral investment treaties rather than through a comprehensive multilateral agreement. Despite the many similarities among these treaties, hence, the reality of ISDS is unavoidably the result of incremental and not necessarily coordinated initiatives of multiple actors, operating under conditions of growing economic interconnectedness.[5]

---

[2] R. Dolzer and C. Schreuer, *Principles of International Investment Law* (Oxford University Press, 2012), Ch. 1; A.R. Parra, *The History of ICSID* (Oxford University Press, 2012), pp. 17, 26.

[3] J.E Alvarez, 'Is Investor-State Arbitration "Public"?' (2016) 7(3) *Journal of International Dispute Settlement* 534; A. Roberts, 'Clash of Paradigms: Actors and Analogies Shaping the Investment Treaty System' (2013) *American Journal of International Law* 45; S.W. Schill (ed.), *International Investment Law and Comparative Public Law* (Oxford University Press, 2010).

[4] D. Rodrik, *The Globalization Paradox. Democracy and the Future of the World Economy* (Norton, 2011), pp. 200–201. For an exchange of views concerning the core arguments of the book, from an international law perspective, see R.M. Lastra, 'The Globalization Paradox: Review of Dani Rodrik, The Globalization Paradox: Democracy and the Future of the World Economy' (2013) 11(3) *International Journal of Constitutional Law* 809; R. Howse, 'Further Considerations on Dani Rodrik, The Globalization Paradox' (2013) 11(3) *International Journal of Constitutional Law* 813; D. Rodrik, 'The Globalization Paradox: A Response to Rosa Lastra and Robert Howse' (2013) 11(3) *International Journal of Constitutional Law* 816.

[5] The current face of ISDS, hence, can be seen as a product of network power, rather than of a single deliberate sovereign decision: see D. Singh Grewal, *Network Power: The Social Dynamics of Globalization* (Yale, 2008).

Secondly, the task of adjudicating investment disputes is entrusted upon arbitral tribunals, rather than upon a standing court. Given the ever-changing composition of these tribunals, and the sudden confluence of different epistemic communities in international investment law, no single conception of the identity and function of investment arbitrators has yet solidified.

In light of this, if we want to understand the development of ISDS as a system, we need to consider the influences of a liquid multitude of actors (not only the States that enter into the treaty, but also arbitral tribunals with no fixed composition, arbitration institutions and secretaries, NGOs and the civil society, and academics). The institutionalisation of ISDS is best understood as a never-ending collective work in progress, where each of the actors adds or substitutes a piece of machinery influencing its overall functioning, without being able to unilaterally shape it entirely: a peculiar, somewhat chaotic blend of competition and cooperation, whose contours determine the constantly shifting answers to the ISDS identity dilemma. In sum, ISDS evolves in the same way as languages do: as a result of different social and cultural forces, without anybody being able to force the change singlehandedly.

Despite the importance of understanding the influence of different stakeholders on the current reality and future evolution of ISDS, one important category of actors has been understudied so far: online reporters and databases (hereinafter 'ORDs'). For the purposes of this article, ORDs are broadly defined as those Internet-based services that provide information on ISDS. This information can be offered in a wide range of different methods, such as by publishing awards and other documents relevant to ISDS cases, collecting investment treaties, reporting on ongoing proceedings, pre-paring summaries of cases and offering insights on the social and professional structures underlying the ISDS system. The definition is purposely vague, this being a first exploration of the topic; as such, it benefits from a broad scope of analysis. Needless to say, not all ORDs are identical and perform the same functions; this chapter, therefore, could pave the way for future research with a more specific focus and, accordingly, narrower definitional premises. The chapter devotes particular attention to the roles played by Italaw,[6] IAReporter,[7] Global Arbitration Review,[8] Investor-State

---

[6] www.italaw.com
[7] www.iareporter.com
[8] www.globalarbitrationreview.com

Law Guide[9] and the UNCTAD website.[10] The list is by no means exhaustive, but it constitutes a meaningful sample of ORDs playing an important role in shaping the ISDS system and influencing its perceived legitimacy.

The chapter proceeds as follows. Section 27.2 presents four different narratives, describing the role of ORDs in the ISDS system. These narratives are not mutually exclusive or necessarily complementary – they are 'lenses', or heuristic tools through which specific features of the contribution of ORDs to the development of ISDS can be highlighted and magnified.[11] Section 27.3 tests these narratives against empirical data gathered through an online survey and secondary desk research concerning Internet traffic and inbound links. Finally, Section 27.4 concludes.

27.2 Narratives

The following sub-sections observe the role of ORDs from four different points of view. Firstly, we look at ORDs as clerks, managing the invisible archive of ISDS. Secondly, we consider their function as gatekeepers and allocators of symbolic value within the ISDS social system. Thirdly, we scrutinise their contribution as an informal liaison office, providing cultural mediation services and enabling a flow of information between the ISDS system and its environment. Fourthly, we reflect on the unintended effects they may bring about, in terms of procedural strategy and arbitration 'guerrilla'.

27.2.1 The Archivists

One of the obvious consequences of the decentralised institutional architecture of the ISDS system is the absence of a single archive where information about cases can be retrieved. ORDs fill this gap and perform archival functions by publishing not only arbitral awards, but also a wide range of other documents and information related to ISDS cases. From

---

[9] www.investorstatelawguide.com
[10] http://unctad.org/en/
[11] In a similar fashion, Dupont and Schultz use a heuristic approach to investigate investment arbitration: C. Dupont and T. Schultz, 'Towards a New Heuristic Model: Investment Arbitration as a Political System' (2016) 7(1) *Journal of International Dispute Settlement* 3. In social sciences, the tendency to sketch out a plurality of different (and not necessarily compatible) readings of the same sets of social phenomena has recently proved to be a valuable approach, through which different aspects of reality can be contextualised and given meaning: see e.g. P. Frase, *Four Futures: Life After Capitalism* (Verso, 2016).

this point of view, hence, ORDs can be seen as invisible clerks, enhancing the transparency of the ISDS system.

The relatively wide availability of awards constitutes one of the main aspects in which ISDS diverges from commercial arbitration, where confidentiality often prevails and only a small amount of awards are published in redacted form.[12] By acting as archivists of the system, hence, ORDs enhance the peculiarity of ISDS, as opposed to other types of arbitration. It is precisely because of the relatively wide availability of investment awards that ISDS tribunals tend to refer to arbitral precedents and to the notion of *jurisprudence constante* much more than tribunals adjudicating international commercial cases.[13] Many ISDS tribunals, when citing past awards, make express reference to ORDs like Italaw, where the text of the relevant decision can be retrieved.[14] This practice clearly suggests that ORDs are a fundamental archival source for both parties and tribunals, hence playing a significant role in shaping the development of arbitral case law. However, despite their best efforts, ORDs are unavoidably never complete, and it would be misleading to portray them as all-encompassing archives of past decisions: to date, a certain portion of investment case law is still outside the public domain, and confidentiality constraints may limit the tribunals' ability to rely on these decisions as precedents. The relevance of this problem has been recently demonstrated in the *Eiser* case,[15] where the respondent State sought to rely on the previous and not publicly available *Isolux* award. Spain was eventually prevented from adding

---

[12] For an example of this practice see J.-J. Arnaldez, Y. Derains and D. Hascher, *Collection of ICC Arbitral Awards, 2008–2011* (International Chamber of Commerce, 2013).

[13] G. Kaufmann-Kohler, 'Arbitral Precedent: Dream, Necessity or Excuse? The 2006 Freshfields Lecture' (2007) 23(3) *Arbitration International* 357. Interestingly, Kaufmann-Kohler distinguishes between commercial arbitration, on the one hand, where no constant practice of referring to precedents exists, and investment, sports and domain names arbitration, on the other hand, where on the contrary arbitral precedent has a significant influence. In a nutshell, the same procedural mechanism of dispute resolution (arbitration) can ramify into factually different 'systems', depending on the different level of availability of information.

[14] *Orascom TMT Investments S.à r.l. c. La République algérienne démocratique et populaire*, ICSID Case No. ARB/12/35, para. 292, n. 312; *Isolux Infrastructure Netherlands, B.V. c. Reino de España*, SCC V2013/153, Laudo, para. 231, nn. 237 and 238; *Oxus Gold v. The Republic of Uzbekistan*, Final award, para. 892, n. 33; *Daimler Financial Services AG v. The Argentine Republic*, ICSID Case No. ARB/05/1, Award, para. 271, n. 460; *El Paso Energy International Company v. The Argentine Republic*, ICSID Case No. ARB/03/15, Award, para. 357.

[15] *Eiser Infrastructure Limited and Energia Solar Luxembourg S.à.r.l. v. Kingdom of Spain*, ICSID Case No. ARB/13/36.

the *Isolux* award to the record, as it was unable to show that the submission would not breach the confidentiality instructions of the *Isolux* tribunal.[16] ORDs, hence, facilitate references to past awards, but the body of investment case law that is made available to parties and tribunals through these channels is far from complete.

In addition to publishing awards, ORDs provide information on pending cases, thus ensuring the possibility of public scrutiny on proceedings that may otherwise remain confidential, or even entirely secret. The importance of this function can hardly be overstated: the investigative focus of services such as IAReporter keeps external observers informed of the current developments taking place in the ISDS system, and plays a key role in making investment arbitration more transparent.

To gauge the importance of the archival role of ORDs in shaping ISDS, let us consider the counterfactual scenario of an ISDS system operating in the absence of any ORD performing archival tasks. The system would be much more similar to the one of commercial arbitration: it could often be difficult for parties and tribunals to refer to past awards in their submissions and decisions, and it would be almost impossible to imagine the development of conceptual categories such as *jurisprudence constante*. In some cases, it may even be impossible to know that certain cases are pending at all. The arbitral tribunals' perception of their own role would probably change as well: consider all those cases where a tribunal has stated that reliance on past awards can help advance the development of the law.[17] If these awards were not easily available, tribunals would be more likely to theorise their function as one of *una tantum* dispute resolution service providers, adjudicating a specific case on the basis of the parties' mandate, without any major repercussion on other cases or on the general development of the law.[18]

---

[16] *Eiser v. Spain* (n. 15), award of 4 May 2017, paras. 88–92.

[17] See e.g. *Fireman's Fund Insurance Company v. United Mexican States*, ICSID Case No. ARB(AF)/02/01, Award, 17 July 2006, para. 172; *International Thunderbird Gaming Corporation v. United Mexican States*, UNCITRAL, Separate Opinion, 01 December 2005, paras. 15–16; *Canfor Corporation and others v. United States of America*, UNCITRAL, Order of the Consolidation Tribunal, 7 September 2005, paras. 131–133; *ADC Affiliate Limited and ADC & ADMC Management Limited v. Republic of Hungary*, ICSID Case No. ARB/ 03/16, Award, 2 October 2006, para. 293; *Saipem S.p.A. v. People's Republic of Bangladesh*, ICSID Case No. ARB/05/07, Award, 30 June 2009, para. 90; *Cargill, Incorporated v. Republic of Poland*, ICSID Case No. ARB(AF)/04/2, Award, 5 March 2008, para. 224; *Tza Yap Shum v. Republic of Peru*, ICSID Case No. ARB/07/6, Decision on Jurisdiction and Competence, 19 June 2009, para. 173.

[18] S.W. Schill, 'W(h)ither Fragmentation? On the Literature and Sociology of International Investment Law' (2011) 22(3) *European Journal of International Law* 875, 890 notes that,

The documents available through ORDs are not only orders, decisions and awards issued by arbitral tribunals, but also (inter alia) written statements and submissions by the parties. Such a level of transparency is not common in domestic justice systems, where the general public normally has the possibility to access the court's decision, but not the parties' pleadings. From this point of view, some ISDS cases are more open to external scrutiny than domestic litigation: ORDs, it could be argued, sometimes decline transparency in its more pervasive form, going even beyond what the 'open court principle' generally requires in national legal systems.[19]

While ORDs have played a central role in ensuring the transparency of ISDS throughout the second decade of the twenty-first century, they have not been alone. The push towards transparency in ISDS (and international adjudication in general) is a widespread trend,[20] resulting in the development of the UNCITRAL Rules on Transparency in Treaty-based Investor-State Arbitration (hereinafter, the 'Transparency Rules').[21] Not only do the Transparency Rules require that a wide range of ISDS documents be made available to the public,[22] they also foresee that such documents should be accessible through a repository of published information, pursuant to Article 8. According to the logic of the Transparency

---

because of the relatively widespread availability of awards, 'inconsistencies bec[o]me apparent much more easily in investment arbitration as compared to commercial arbitration'. From a behavioural perspective, the high likeliness that inconsistencies will be detected nudges arbitrators to devise consistency-oriented solutions.

[19] The relevance of the open court principle in domestic jurisdiction is not an entirely settled issue, especially in light of the trends towards privatisation and settlement of claims: see J. Resnik, 'Bring Back Bentham: "Open Courts," "Terror Trials," and Public Sphere(s)' (2011) 5 *Law & Ethics of Human Rights*, 226; Dame H. Genn, 'Why the Privatization of Civil Justice is a Rule of Law Issue', 36th FA Mann Lecture, Lincoln's Inn, 19 November 2012, available at www.laws.ucl.ac.uk/wp-content/uploads/2014/08/36th-F-A-Mann-Lecture-19.11.12-Professor-Hazel-Genn.pdf.

[20] A. Bianchi, 'On Power and Illusion: The Concept of Transparency in International Law', in A. Bianchi and A. Peters (eds.), *Transparency in International Law* (Cambridge University Press, 2013), p. 1 notes how transparency 'has become one of the fundamentally distinctive traits of contemporary Western culture'.

[21] UNCITRAL Rules on Transparency in Treaty-based Investor-State Arbitration, www.uncitral.org/pdf/english/texts/arbitration/rules-on-transparency/Rules-on-Transparency-E.pdf.

[22] See Arts. 2 and 3, referring to the notice of arbitration, the response to it, the statements of claim and defence, any further written statements and submissions by the disputing parties, a table listing all exhibits, any written submissions by non-disputing parties to the treaty and third persons, transcripts of hearings and orders, decisions and awards of the tribunal.

Rules, hence, the Transparency Registry[23] should to a large extent take over the archival tasks currently fulfilled by ORDs: in a hypothetical future where the Transparency Rules would always be applicable, there would be little need for ORDs collecting and publishing treaty-based ISDS awards and documents. For the time being, however, there are two main reasons why the Transparency Registry does not, by itself, have the capacity to discharge this archival function: the limited applicability of the Transparency Rules and the fragmentation of the regulatory framework within which ISDS proceedings are conducted. Let us briefly consider these two factors.

From the first point of view, obviously, many of the currently pending ISDS cases are initiated pursuant to a treaty concluded before 1 April 2014, and in the absence of an agreement pursuant to Article 1(2) of the Transparency Rules. To date, the United Nations Convention on Transparency in Treaty-based Investor-State Arbitration (Mauritius Convention) has only been signed by twenty-three States and ratified by four of them.[24] Such limited applicability, in itself, curtails the practical relevance of the Transparency Registry as a repository of information, at least for the time being. A simple comparison between the amount of information publicly available on the Transparency Registry and the wealth of data published by ORDs such as Italaw is a good measure of the current gap.

From the second point of view, not all ISDS cases are conducted under the UNCITRAL Arbitration Rules: investor-State proceedings may be held under a variety of different rules, and investment treaties containing a standing offer to arbitrate frequently leave the claimant free to choose among multiple options of fora and rules. In the absence of a centralised institutional ISDS architecture, any transparency obligation dependent on the application of a specific set of rules cannot, by itself, lead to the development of an exhaustive archive. ORDs like Italaw and IAReporter provide a solution to this problem, by offering a repository where a wide range of ISDS documents and information is available, irrespective of the institutional setting and the framework of rules within which the arbitrations take place. From this point of view, ORDs undoubtedly enhance the legitimacy of ISDS, injecting transparency and 'open courts' guarantees into a decentralised and uncoordinated adjudicative system.

---

[23] www.uncitral.org/transparency-registry/registry/index.jspx.

[24] Cameroon, Canada, Mauritius and Switzerland: for an up-to-date status of the Convention, see www.uncitral.org/uncitral/en/uncitral_texts/arbitration/2014Transparency_Convention_status.html.

One final archival role performed by ORDs concerns the retrieval and comparison of investment treaties.[25] Not only do these instruments constitute an invaluable tool for anybody with an interest in investment policy and treaty-making; they can also have an influence on the way treaty provisions are interpreted. By making the comparison among different treaty formulations easy, these treaties encourage a systemic interpretative approach to international investment law, whereby the meaning of a treaty may be elucidated by the similarities or differences with other treaties.[26] By facilitating such comparison, these tools contribute to the multilateralisation of international investment law, providing the technical background against which legal observers can visualise the network of BITs as one 'system'.[27] Furthermore, these tools may also have the effect of creating some kind of separation between the relevance of investment treaties, retrievable through the ORDs, and the relevance of other international treaties, which may be more easily disregarded.[28]

27.2.2   The Gatekeepers

Online reporters and databases can also be seen as invisible gatekeepers of the ISDS system. In order to introduce this narrative, it is useful to refer to the sociology of law and, in particular, to the idea of the 'legal field'. In his groundbreaking 1986 article 'La force du droit', Pierre Bourdieu theorised law as an independent 'field', largely immune from external constraints

---

[25] See, in particular, UNCTAD's IIA Navigator (http://investmentpolicyhub.unctad.org/IIA) and IIA Mapping Project (http://investmentpolicyhub.unctad.org/IIA/mappedContent).

[26] An interesting factor in this respect could be the emergence of sophisticated algorithmic tools, treating treaty text as data, as demonstrated by the 'Mapping BITs' project: http://mappinginvestmenttreaties.com. See W. Alschner and D. Skougarevskiy, 'Mapping the Universe of International Investment Agreements' (2016) 3(1) *Journal of International Economic Law*, 561.

[27] For the purposes of treaty interpretation, direct comparison among treaties should mainly be relevant when the state parties to the treaties to be compared are the same, given the rules of interpretation set forth in Art. 31 of the Vienna Convention on the law of treaties. However, in the practice of treaty interpretation, it may be difficult to entirely disregard the existence of another agreement with different parties, but identical wording. In addition, from an academic point of view, these comparison-enabling tools also allow the identification of general treaty-making trends.

[28] M. Hirsch, 'The Sociological Dimension of International Arbitration: The Investment Arbitration Culture', in T. Schultz and F. Ortino (eds.), *Oxford Handbook of International Arbitration* (Oxford University Press, 2018) puts forth a similar argument, illustrating how the socio-cultural features of the investment arbitration community has an effect on the way arbitral tribunals interpret human rights obligations. The existence of tools facilitating the comparison between investment treaties, while at the same time not including

and responding to its own internal relations of power and authority.[29] According to Bourdieu, the self-sufficiency of the legal field is ensured by a strict division between laypeople and professionals:[30] the former are external to the field, as they do not master the technical knowledge of the law, while the latter are internal, as they have the ability of transforming social relations and conflicts into legal ones.[31] Within the legal field, the social relations among professionals are shaped by the distribution of symbolic value, i.e. by internal mechanisms for the valorisation of personal capital.[32]

Arbitration can productively be seen as a legal field, as demonstrated by Dezalay and Garth in their 1995 book *Dealing in Virtue*.[33] Online reporters and databases fulfil a fundamental function in the field, contributing to the determining of standards by which symbolic value is distributed. Arbitration, in a nutshell, never happens in isolation: it is an intrinsically social activity, taking place in a hierarchically organised field.[34] Controlling the circulation of symbolic value within the field, hence, can constitute a significant source of power. Before observing in detail the different mechanisms through which ORDs can exert such power, however, let us briefly consider two reasons why a sociologically oriented reading of the gatekeeping role of ORDs can advance the understanding of ISDS as a whole.

The first, obvious value of adopting a law and society approach is the ability to go beyond over-simplified characterisations of ISDS as a mere instrument in the hands of powerful investors and capital-exporting

---

different types of agreement, could be a factor contributing to the socio-cultural distance of investment lawyers from 'general' public international law.

[29] P. Bourdieu, 'La force du droit: Eléments pour une sociologie du champ juridique' (1986) 64 *Actes de la recherche en sciences sociales* 3.

[30] Ibid., 4.

[31] Ibid., 10.

[32] Y. Dezalay and M.R. Madsen, 'The Force of Law and Lawyers: Pierre Bourdieu and the Reflexive Sociology of Law' (2012) 8 *Annual Review of Law and Social Science* 433.

[33] Y. Dezalay and B.G. Garth, *Dealing in Virtue: International Commercial Arbitration and the Construction of a Transnational Legal Order* (University of Chicago, 1998); for recent reflections on the book see T. Schultz and R. Kovacs, 'The Rise of a Third Generation of Arbitrators? Fifteen Years after Dezalay and Garth' (2012) 28(2) *Arbitration International* 161; Thomas Schultz, 'Celebrating 20 Years of "Dealing in Virtue"' (2016) 7(3) *Journal of International Dispute Settlement* 531.

[34] This circumstance, in itself, has a significant impact on the behavioural incentives of the individuals operating within the field. For a contextual approach to arbitration and psychology see T. Cole, P. Ortolani and S. Wright, 'Arbitration from a Law and Psychology Perspective' in Schultz and Ortino (n. 28) forthcoming.

States.[35] In other words, a sociological approach unveils insights relevant to the debate concerning the legitimacy of ISDS and allows us to go beyond unreliable caricatures of international investment law and arbitration. Whatever one's opinion of the ISDS system may be, it is undeniable that understanding it as a Bourdieusian field adds an important layer of complexity to the analysis: ISDS is, first and foremost, a self-contained network of relations, operating according to its own mechanisms rather than simply channelling external influences or demands. Those who *make* ISDS, in brief, primarily aim at the maximisation of their own symbolic value within the system. From this first point of view, hence, locating the gatekeeping role of ORDs within the field can provide us with a fuller and more nuanced understanding of ISDS as a whole.

The second advantage of viewing ISDS as a 'field' is the possibility of recasting the debate concerning the cohesiveness of international investment law as a unified normative system. It has been convincingly argued that, despite its formal fragmentation and bilateralism, international investment law has effectively evolved into a relatively homogeneous regime, with some distinctive and recurring features.[36] Among the arguments supporting this thesis, it has been observed that investment treaty-making tends towards uniformity[37] and, in any case, most favoured nation ('MFN') clauses allow the export of treaty provisions from one agreement to another, thus leading to a *de facto* uniformity of the international regime protecting investments.[38] While the aforementioned factors indeed play a fundamental role in shaping the current reality of international investment law, the debate concerning the systemic coherence of BITs cannot be conclusively resolved by relying exclusively on positivistic

---

[35] See, e.g. P. Eberhardt and C. Olivet, 'Profiting from Injustice: How Law Firms, Arbitrators and Financiers Are Fuelling an Investment Arbitration Boom', Corporate Europe Observatory, www.tni.org/files/download/profitingfrominjustice.pdf. The report attracted significant attention within the community of ISDS specialists: see, e.g., The Honorable C.N. Brower and S. Blanchard, 'What's in a Meme? The Truth about Investor-State Arbitration: Why It Need Not, and Must Not, Be Repossessed by States' (2014) 52 *Columbia Journal of Transnational Law* 689; R. Howse, 'International Investment Law and Arbitration: A Conceptual Framework', IILJ Working Paper 2017/1, www.iilj.org/wp-content/uploads/2017/04/Howse_IILJ_2017_1-MegaReg.pdf.

[36] S.W. Schill, *The Multilateralization of International Investment Law* (Cambridge University Press, 2010).

[37] Ibid., pp. 65–120.

[38] Ibid., pp. 121–196.

approaches.[39] To the contrary, it is useful to complement the attention to formalistic data-points with the sociological reality of ISDS: the emergence of investment arbitration as a self-standing network of relations, responding to its own internal logic, reinforces the narrative of investment law as a consistent 'system', rather than as a more or less chaotic multitude of bilateral agreements. Understanding how ORDs contribute to the establishment of ISDS as a legal field, hence, helps us gauge to what extent investment law has been effectively 'multilateralised' over time.

Let us now turn to consider the different ways in which ORDs act as gatekeepers, allocating symbolic power within the ISDS legal field. Online reporters and databases such as Global Arbitration Review (hereinafter 'GAR') perform the function at hand in multiple ways: they report on individual career progressions and developments concerning law firms, they award annual prizes,[40] they organise conferences and networking-oriented social gatherings[41] and sometimes they provide an avenue for what has been defined by Schill as 'investment community gossip'.[42] Through such activities, ORDs array individuals along a visibility spectrum, determining who is a leader, who is emerging and who is invisible. In doing so, they act as gatekeepers in two complementary fashions.

Firstly, by generating social narratives shared among ISDS specialists, ORDs create a separation between the field and its environment. One could informally say that ORDs contribute to making ISDS 'a thing', i.e. to legitimising its value as a topic of study and a career to be pursued, rather than a mere subset of international law with no real identity and autonomy. By developing this identity-building narrative, ORDs structurally tend towards the development of systemic boundaries. In a similar vein, Schill has argued that the creation of online communities has kept the social circle of international investment lawyers 'close-knit', preventing it from drifting apart.[43] Interestingly, similar insights can be found (with

[39] A similar point with reference to arbitration in general is made by J.-B. Racine, 'Éléments d'une sociologie de l'arbitrage: Actes de la Journée d'étude du Groupe Sociologie de l'Arbitrage du Comité Français de l'Arbitrage' (2012) 4 *Revue de l'arbitrage* 709.

[40] The sociological relevance of prizes in international arbitration has been highlighted by E. Gaillard, 'Sociology of International Arbitration' in D.D. Caron, S.W. Schill, A. Cohen Smutny and E.E. Triantafilou, *Practising Virtue: Inside International Arbitration* (Oxford University Press, 2015), pp. 187, 197.

[41] For an analysis of the relevance of social networks in arbitration see S. Menétrey, 'Le réseau associative: Un exemple de marketing arbitral' (2012) 4 *Revue de l'arbitrage* 741.

[42] Schill, 'W(h)ither Fragmentation?' 887.

[43] Ibid., 886.

reference to law in general) in Bourdieu's article theorising the legal field, back in 1986: according to Bourdieu, the establishment of a 'legal space' hinges on the imposition of a boundary between those who are willing to embrace a system-specific mindset and everybody else, who is conversely excluded.[44] In sum, the first gatekeeping function of ORDs is to separate the social field of investment law from the outside. Establishing an external boundary means, unavoidably, building an internal identity.

Secondly, within the ISDS legal field, ORDs act as allocators of symbolic value, inasmuch as they can influence career progression patterns and personal or organisational success. In brief, through their activities, ORDs manage (to a certain extent) the gates which separate different tiers within the field, thus consolidating internal social hierarchies. Typical activities through which this function can be performed are the awarding of prizes, the development of ranking charts for lawyers and law firms and, more generally, the publication of reports detailing the achievements and successes of a given individual or group acting within the field. However, in the close future, one ORD function is likely to be particularly important: arbitrator matchmaking.

The expression 'arbitrator matchmaking' refers to those services through which information about arbitrators is made publicly available, with the purpose of facilitating the selection of arbitrators for future cases. By injecting transparency in the process of arbitrator appointment, platforms such as Arbitrator Intelligence[45] and GAR's Arbitrator Research Tool (hereinafter 'ART')[46] aim to facilitate a satisfactory match before the offer (on the arbitrators' side) and the demand (on the users' side) of private adjudication services. While these tools all aim to create a better mechanism for arbitrator appointment and ultimately enhance the legitimacy of arbitration as a whole, they are not identical in nature and functioning. Arbitrator Intelligence, for instance, is based on an extensive data-collection exercise: the platform aggregates information concerning the past behaviour and preferences of arbitrators, for the purpose of helping parties, counsels and institutions compare prospective arbitrators and make an informed choice. ART, by contrast, is mainly based on arbitrator-curated profiles, through which the adjudicators advertise their areas of expertise to potential users. In a nutshell, these instruments

---

[44] Bourdieu, 'La force du droit', 9.
[45] www.arbitratorintelligence.org
[46] www.globalarbitrationreview.com/arbitrator-research-tool

should make it easier to 'find the right arbitrator'.[47] While current arbitrator matchmaking tools are primarily geared towards commercial arbitration, they may in the future be relevant for ISDS too. ISDS has been criticised for the lack of diversity in the group of repeat arbitrators,[48] and the steady increase in the ISDS caseload[49] could be a valuable occasion for appointing authorities to diversify the pool of investment arbitrators, relying inter alia on the aforementioned online tools.

By enhancing or decreasing the visibility of arbitrators, arbitrator matchmaking instruments can exert significant power, similarly to what Uber does with cabdrivers or Yelp does with restaurants. As a result, these tools may face new regulatory challenges, since ranking choices based on artificial intelligence and algorithmic decision-making may have significant real-life effects on the career of tomorrow's arbitrators. From this point of view, tools like ART or Arbitrator Intelligence open the field to a new conceptualisation of platform-to-business relations in the arbitration market. In a future where most arbitrators are selected on the basis of information aggregated and published online, ORDs would effectively become market-makers, just like e-commerce platforms already are. Given the prominence that platform-to-business disputes are gaining in the current EU lawmaking agenda,[50] it is not unreasonable to foresee a future where the gatekeeping function of ORDs is (at least partially) regulated by the law.

27.2.3 The Liaison Office

The two narratives we have considered so far (the archivists and the gatekeepers) describe functions that ORDs perform *within* the ISDS

---

[47] Such tools, which are still at the embryonic stage in international arbitration, are already existing and functioning in other types of private adjudication. A good example, in this respect, is private adjudication based on blockchain technologies: see P. Ortolani, 'Self-Enforcing Online Dispute Resolution: Lessons from Bitcoin' (2016) 36(3) *Oxford Journal of Legal Studies* 595 and 'The Three Challenges of Stateless Justice' (2016) 7(3) *Journal of International Dispute Settlement* 596.

[48] C. Dolinar-Hikawa, 'Beyond the Pale: A Proposal to Promote Ethnic Diversity Among International Arbitrators' (2015) 4 *Transnational Dispute Management*; S. Puig, 'Social Capital in the Arbitration Market' (2014) 25(2) *European Journal of International Law* 387.

[49] R.L. Wellhausen, 'Recent Trends in Investor-State Dispute Settlement' (2016) 7(1) *Journal of International Dispute Settlement* 117, 121.

[50] European Commission, 'Communication from the Commission to the European Parliament, the Council, The European Economic and Social Committee and the Committee of the Regions: Online Platforms and the Digital Single Market: Opportunities and Challenges for Europe', COM (2016) 288 final.

system. However, ORDs also act as mediators between ISDS and the external environment: they are the invisible liaison office of investment arbitration.

In establishing themselves as the ISDS cultural mediators, ORDs meet a twofold demand. First of all, as international investment law solidifies and increases its internal complexity, it becomes increasingly difficult for external observers to grasp the reality of the phenomenon without the help of a liaison officer who is conversant enough in the field. Secondly, the rise in the visibility of ISDS triggers an increase in the need for external mediation: as a result of high-profile cases such as *Vattenfall*[51] and *Philip Morris*,[52] which have put investment arbitration in the spotlight of generalist media and political debate, the pool of external observers has grown in size. Descriptive attempts by non-specialists, such as journalistic outlets and blogs, have recently proliferated.[53] In a nutshell, as more people are interested in understanding the functioning of a system whose inner complexity tends to increase over time, the need arises for channels of cultural mediation and information exchange between internals and externals. ORDs address this need.

The new critical observers of the ISDS system may be unable to delve directly into the reality they want to address, analysing arbitral awards and other ISDS documents, as they may not master the 'code' of investment arbitration. International investment law, after all, is a highly specialist topic, whose technicalities cannot always be grasped by observers without a very special set of epistemic tools. Online reporters and databases resolve this problem by providing a host of descriptive shortcuts, i.e. resources that offer an overview of the system while at the same time de-complexifying it.

Online reporters and databases perform the task at hand in several different ways. First of all, they provide information on pending cases.

---

[51] *Vattenfall AB and others v. Federal Republic of Germany*, ICSID Case No. ARB/12/12 and *Vattenfall AB, Vattenfall Europe AG, Vattenfall Europe Generation AG v. Federal Republic of Germany*, ICSID Case No. ARB/09/6.

[52] *Philip Morris Asia Limited v. The Commonwealth of Australia*, UNCITRAL, PCA Case No. 2012-12; *Philip Morris Brands Sàrl, Philip Morris Products S.A. and Abal Hermanos S.A. v. Oriental Republic of Uruguay*, ICSID Case No. ARB/10/7.

[53] While it is impossible to provide an account of the enormous amount of recent newspaper articles and blog posts describing ISDS, it is useful to note that not all of these attempts are necessarily comparable in nature: some of them are informed and rather sophisticated opinion pieces, while others mainly seek some form of *succès de scandale*. See, inter alia, C. Hamby, 'Secrets of a Global Super Court', *BuzzFeed*, www.buzzfeed.com/ globalsupercourt.

Section 27.2.1 above has already argued that this activity, carried out by ORDs such as IAReporter, is important from an archival point of view, as it ensures that the existence of a given case be communicated to the public, rather than being kept confidential. Now, we can observe this activity through a different lens: by publishing overviews of pending cases, ORDs act not only as archivists, but also as liaison officers, or *traits d'union* between the inner reality of investment arbitration and the outside world. Journalists reporting on pending cases can rely on these services to obtain the data feeding into their articles.[54] Along similar lines, non-governmental organisations can integrate these reports into their communications and political strategies. By describing the contents of currently pending cases, the investigative efforts of ORDs create a significant flow of information towards the general audience.

Another fundamental category of descriptive shortcuts provided by ORDs are summaries of past cases. These summaries typically offer a synthetic overview of the facts of the case, the procedural development of the arbitration and the decision issued by the tribunal. Unlike the scenario of pending proceedings, where ORDs publish information that may otherwise be unavailable, in this case the information (e.g. the award) is typically already available: the added value of the service provided by ORDs consists in condensing the reality of ISDS in a more accessible form. This service is obviously beneficial for external observers without a background on international investment law, as it allows them to absorb the basic contents of a case without having to deal with technical materials. However, there may be a significant benefit for ISDS specialists as well: given the ever-growing size of investment case law, those practising and/or studying ISDS can undoubtedly benefit from an accessible entry point into the details of cases they may not be familiar with.

Interestingly, by providing this repository of descriptive shortcuts, ORDs indirectly enhance their own relevance. Every act of curatorship is an act of creation, and no description is ever objective;[55] therefore, by assuming the task of describing the system, ORDs acquire more power within the system itself. More specifically, this power consists in the ability to influence the system's legitimacy by portraying it for an ever-growing audience of observers. Just like art curators and merchants are sometimes

---

[54] For an empirical assessment of this claim see below, Section 27.3.
[55] Bianchi aptly notes that any description of legal phenomena exists not in an objective vacuum, but is rather situated in the context of the intellectual schemes of its authors: A.

as influential as the artist they work with (if not more), the importance of the liaison office function described in this section renders ORDs important stakeholders within the ISDS field.

27.2.4   The Guerrilla Tools

Before turning to analyse the available empirical evidence, let us briefly consider one last narrative. This last scenario differs from the previous three in a fundamental way: while the previous sections have outlined activities that ORDs perform willingly and consciously, this section hypothesises a function that ORDs may be performing *unwillingly* or *unconsciously*. More specifically, by making more information on ISDS cases available, ORDs may sometimes indirectly affect the way in which these cases are litigated and decided.[56] We might say that ORDs can, sometimes, become *guerrilla tools*, i.e. instruments of procedural warfare.

Some of the ways in which ORDs influence the defensive strategy of the parties to investment proceedings are relatively uncontroversial. The most evident is the publication of past awards, which (as already illustrated) makes it common for arbitral tribunals to refer to precedents. In turn, hence, the parties are expected to refer to past awards, rather than just supporting their case with an abstract line of reasoning. From this point of view, it can be argued that ORDs contribute to determining the expected quality standard for litigating investment claims. This influence, however, should not be seen as an undue interference in the proceedings, but rather as a dependent variable of the development on international investment law into a relatively cohesive legal regime.

A second, potentially more problematic aspect is the publication of information on ongoing cases. This could have an influence on the proceedings in multiple ways. For instance, it could attract public attention, with the consequence that the parties' submissions speak also to the public, rather than to the arbitrators. Furthermore, it may indirectly elicit *amicus curiae* submissions, and therefore change the body of

---

Bianchi, 'Reflexive Butterfly Catching: Insights from a Situated Catcher', in J. Pauwelyn, R.A. Wessel and J. Wouters, *Informal International Lawmaking* (Oxford University Press, 2012), pp. 200, 202. Any case report prepared by an ORD, hence, unavoidably reflects the situated point of view of those who have prepared it.

[56] For a general overview of the ways in which the Internet changes the life of arbitration practitioners, see G. Decocq, 'L'influence d'internet sur la pratique de l'arbitrage' (2014) 4 *Revue de l'arbitrage* 769.

materials itself submitted for consideration to the tribunal. In addition, and most importantly, the case overview developed by an ORD could suggest a way to frame and decide the dispute, and could thus generate a cognitive bias for the arbitrators.[57] The influence of the commentary provided by ORDs on arbitral reasoning has been recently demonstrated in the *Nova Group Investments B.V. v. Romania* case.[58] In that case, the tribunal stressed the importance of detailed reasoning justifying a decision on provisional measures by making reference to IAReporter's criticism against the approach adopted by a different tribunal in a previous case.[59] While referring to commentary published by an ORD is not, in essence, different from citing an academic publication, online commentary may be more incisive in practice, because of its timeliness and higher responsiveness to recent developments.

A third, crucial aspect is the publication of party submissions. As a consequence of the public availability of party submissions, the arguments put forth by a counsel in a given case remain available, for potential future scrutiny. This circumstance could be relevant, were the counsel advocating a certain interpretation of the law in a given case to be appointed as arbitrator in a subsequent, unrelated dispute: in this scenario, the arbitrator may be challenged on grounds of 'issue conflict'. The expression 'issue conflict' does not designate an actual conflict of interest on the part of the challenged arbitrator, but rather a situation of pre-judgment, in which the arbitrator is deemed to be incapable of approaching a disputed issue with an open mind, given the views she or he has expressed on the topic in the past.[60]

---

[57] For an experimental study of cognitive biases and arbitral decision-making see S.D. Franck, A. van Aaken, J. Freda, C. Guthrie and J.J. Rachlinski, 'Inside the Arbitrator's Mind' (2017) 66 *Emory Law Journal* 1117.

[58] *Nova Group Investments, B.V. v. Romania* (ICSID Case No. ARB/16/19).

[59] Ibid., Procedural Order No. 7: Decision on Claimant's Request for Provisional Measures, para. 289, n. 403, with reference to L.E. Peterson, 'Arbitrators Order Albania to Halt Extradition Bid, But Don't Offer Much Proof for Conclusion That "Procedural Integrity" of Arbitration Was in Peril', Investment Arbitration Reporter, 9 March 2016. The previous case on which the website commented was *Hydro S.r.l. and others v. Republic of Albania* (ICSID Case No. ARB/15/28), Order on Provisional Measures of 3 March 2016. See also R. Kabra, 'Analysis: In a Welcome Development, an ICSID Tribunal Acknowledges the Importance of Offering Comprehensive Reasoning When Ordering Provisional Measures – and Explains Why Procedural Integrity of Arbitration Might Be in Peril', *IAReporter*, 18 October 2017.

[60] International Council for Commercial Arbitration, 'Report of the ICCA-ASIL Joint Task Force on Issue Conflicts in Investor-State Arbitration', The ICCA Reports no. 3, 17 March 2016, www.asil.org/sites/default/files/ASIL_ICCA.pdf.

The practical relevance of the phenomenon at hand has recently become evident in *Tethyan Copper Company v. Pakistan*.[61] In this case, the respondent State challenged the arbitrator nominated by the claimant, arguing the existence of an 'issue conflict' concerning the choice of the most appropriate valuation method. More specifically, the experts appointed by the claimant in the case at hand advocated the adoption of a specific variation of the discounted cash flow valuation method,[62] whose application the claimant-appointed arbitrator had previously requested in a different case, *Bear Creek v. Perú*,[63] acting as counsel for the respondent State.[64] Such a motion to disqualify the arbitrator would have probably been impossible to formulate had the parties' submission in the previous *Bear Creek* case not been available online.[65] In addition, the *Tethyan* challenge has indirectly originated a motion to disqualify the same arbitrator in a third unrelated case, *SolEs v. Spain*,[66] and a motion to annul the award in *Eiser v. Spain*.[67] In *SolEs*, the party putting forth the challenge argued that it only learned of the circumstances justifying its motion as a result of the previous *Tethyan* challenge.[68]

In sum, the ease of information retrieval brought about by the Internet can lead to an increase in the frequency of challenges against arbitrators, with potentially significant effects on the practice of investment arbitration and on its perceived legitimacy. In this context, the information published by ORDs could be made into an instrument by parties attempting to 'raise the heat' on the arbitrator appointed by their counterpart. Needless to say, this is not an intended goal of ORDs, but rather a spillover effect of the publication of information and documents concerning ISDS cases.

---

[61] *Tethyan Copper Company Pty Limited v. Islamic Republic of Pakistan*, ICSID Case No. ARB/12/1.

[62] L.E. Peterson, 'Pakistan's Effort to Disqualify Stanimir Alexandrov in Tethyan Copper Case Proves Unsuccessful', *IAReporter*, 7 September 2017.

[63] *Bear Creek Mining Corporation v. Republic of Perú*, ICSID Case No. ARB/14/21.

[64] J. Hepburn, 'Peru's Defence in Bear Creek Arbitration Alleges Illegality of Mining Investment, and Debates Scope of Key Protections in Canada-Peru Trade Pact', *IAReporter*, 20 November 2015.

[65] The submissions are available on the ICSID website, in accordance with Article 835 of the Canada-Perú Free Trade Agreement: see *Bear Creek v. Perú*, Procedural Order no. 1, para. 24.

[66] *SolEs Badajoz GmbH v. Kingdom of Spain*, ICSID Case No. ARB/15/38.

[67] *Eiser v. Spain*; see L.E. Peterson, 'As Spain Seeks to Annul Energy Charter Treaty Award Government Hires Outside Law Firm and Complains about Arbitrator's Relationship with Damages Experts', *IAReporter*, 27 July 2017.

[68] L.E. Peterson, 'Spain Follows Up on its Annulment Strategy by Filing a Request to Disqualify Arbitrator', *IAReporter*, 18 September 2017.

27.3 Testing the Narratives

To what extent do the four narratives outlined above correspond to the reality of ISDS? Each of us, of course, is free to assess the aptness of the proposed 'lenses', on the basis of personal experiences and opinions. To go beyond the anecdotal, however, it is useful to consider the available empirical data concerning ORDs. This section attempts to test the narratives against two categories of empirical data:

1) the results of an online survey aimed at ISDS practitioners and academics (hereinafter 'the survey');[69] and
2) publicly available data concerning the Internet traffic of ORDs.[70]

One preliminary *caveat* is in order: given the relatively small size of the survey sample and its main focus on European academics, the data presented below can by no means be relied upon to draw definitive conclusions on the roles played by ORDs in the ISDS system. This section is best understood as a first attempt at covering a heavily under-researched aspect of investment arbitration through empirical methods, so it only aims at providing some general, broad-stroke indications on the current state of affairs. Hopefully, it will pave the way for further investigations on the topic, leading to more detailed results.

One first indication emerging from the survey is that users generally consider ORDs to be useful, with Italaw and IAReporter being central in the opinion of most respondents (Table 27.1). IAReporter was also indicated as the subscription-only ORD to which the respondents most commonly had access.[71]

---

[69] The survey was conducted via SurveyMonkey and disseminated through social media and personal invitations. As of 26 September 2017, it had been taken by 34 participants. When asked to identify their professional background, 64.71 per cent of respondents described themselves as full-time academics working on ISDS, 8.82 per cent qualified themselves as part-time academics also working as ISDS counsels or arbitrators; 8.82 per cent reported being counsels or arbitrators; 8.82 per cent described themselves as governmental advisors and 5.88 per cent reported working in publishing. The remaining 2.95 per cent reported no involvement with ISDS at all, and were for this reason disqualified from the sample. When asked to identify their main geographical location, 8.82 per cent of respondents answered 'Asia', 2.94 per cent 'Africa', 67.65 per cent 'Europe', 11.76 per cent 'North America', 2.94 per cent 'South America' and 5.88 per cent 'Australia/Oceania'.

[70] The data was generated through MOZ Open Site Explorer.

[71] When asked whether their institution/firm had a subscription to IAReporter, 75 per cent of respondents answered positively. For the sake of comparison, only 50 per cent of respondents reported having an institutional/firm subscription to the Investor-State Law Guide, and 44.83 per cent to GAR.

Table 27.1 *Survey results on usefulness of online reporters and databases in ISDS*

	Very useful	Useful	Not particularly useful	Not useful at all	I don't know/ I don't use this resource
Italaw (Italaw.com)	68.97%	27.59%	3.45%	0.00%	0.00%
Investment Arbitration Reporter (iareporter.com)	51.72%	27.59%	13.79%	3.45%	3.45%
UNCTAD websites	37.93%	48.28%	6.90%	3.45%	3.45%
Investor State Law Guide (investorstatelawguide.com)	34.48%	17.24%	6.90%	6.90%	34.48%
Arbitral Institutions websites (e.g. ICSID; PCA)	13.79%	58.62%	27.59%	0.00%	0.00%
GAR - Global Arbitration Review (globalarbitration review.com)	13.79%	41.38%	24.14%	3.45%	17.24%
Academic blogs (e.g. EJIL: Talk!)	10.34%	55.17%	20.69%	10.34%	3.45%

The survey results support the view that ORDs effectively act as archivists and liaison officers. When asked what type of information concerning ISDS they look for (Table 27.2), respondents overwhelmingly indicated arbitral awards: this result suggests that the archival role of ORDs is central to their functioning. Interestingly, however, the second most commonly sought type of information is the one on the existence and content of pending cases: this data-point corroborates the argument that ORDs ensure the transparency and outreach of the ISDS system, ensuring an outbound flow of information and thus indirectly enhancing the legitimacy of the system.

Summaries of cases are the third most commonly sought type of information. This result is particularly interesting, as the vast majority of the survey respondents are ISDS specialists, rather than external observers. In other words, the size of the ISDS case law is such that even some specialists rely to a certain extent on summaries as a source of information, to cover the field and track the developments of international

Table 27.2 *Survey results on type of information searched online in ISDS*

	Very often	Often	Rarely	Very rarely	Never
Arbitral awards	82.76%	17.24%	0.00%	0.00%	0.00%
Information on the existence and content of pending cases	37.93%	51.72%	3.45%	3.45%	3.45%
Summaries of cases	27.59%	37.93%	20.69%	3.45%	10.34%
Opinion pieces	13.79%	55.17%	10.34%	13.79%	6.90%
Information on arbitrators	13.79%	37.93%	34.48%	10.34%	3.45%
Information on counsels/law firms	10.34%	17.24%	41.38%	24.14%	6.90%
Other documents from cases	3.45%	34.48%	41.38%	20.69%	0.00%
Party submissions	0.00%	34.48%	58.62%	6.90%	0.00%

investment law.[72] This observation, of course, also reinforces the hypothesis that ORDs are powerful cultural mediators, providers of descriptive shortcuts and narrators of the ISDS system.

Section 27.2.1 has argued that the archival function of ORDs helps observers to construe and visualise ISDS as a coherent regime whose case law grows and evolves over time, rather than as a more or less random sequence of *una tantum* arbitral procedures. The survey results offer some support to this argument: when asked to describe their preferred search method to retrieve an award, the vast majority of respondents reported either using Italaw, or simply Googling the name or number of the case (see Figure 27.1). This data-point suggests that, for users, it is important to have a unified entry point, through which all requests for information

---

[72] This observation could also explain why the results concerning summaries of cases are significantly more polarised than the ones regarding the other types of information: while 27.59 per cent of the survey respondents reported looking for such summaries 'very often' and 37.93 per cent claimed that they look for this type of information 'often', there is a not inconsiderable portion of respondents (10.34 per cent) who reported never looking for summaries. In fact, summaries are the source of information that the largest minority of respondents reported 'never' looking for. This result may be interpreted as meaning that some ISDS specialist consider summaries as a useful way to learn some basic facts about a case before reading the relevant case documents, while others see summaries as mainly a source of information for outsiders.

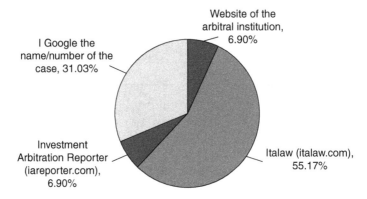

Figure 27.1 Survey results on preferred/first search method to retrieve an arbitral award online

can be satisfied irrespective of the institutional framework within which a given arbitration takes place. Given the absence of a centralised institutional ISDS architecture, the websites of arbitral institutions cannot, by themselves, adequately satisfy this need. By contrast, ORDs, and Italaw in particular, seem to be able to fill this gap satisfactorily. Such a conclusion is confirmed by the publicly available Internet traffic data for Italaw, which indicates Google searches as the primary traffic source for the website.[73] Italaw, hence, seems to have established itself as the 'go-to' ORD for investment awards, either because users browse the website directly, or because they conduct Google searches that lead them to the website.

Despite the significant wealth of information concerning ISDS made available through ORDs, the survey respondents did not show a uniform level of satisfaction regarding the exhaustiveness of the data at their disposal. When asked to estimate how often they are unable to find an ISDS document they need online, 27.59 per cent answered 'very rarely', 34.48 per cent answered 'rarely' and 37.93 per cent answered 'often'. Along similar lines, when asked whether they were satisfied with the amount of information available online for free, the results were scattered: 6.90 per cent answered that they were 'very satisfied', 37.93 per cent answered 'satisfied', 27.59 per cent reported having a neutral opinion, 20.69 per cent answered 'dissatisfied' and 6.90 per cent

---

[73] According to the SimilarWeb statistics for August 2017, the traffic sources for Italaw.com were searches (75.78 per cent), direct access (14.36 per cent), referrals from other websites (7.85 per cent), email messages (1.35 per cent) and social networks (0.65 per cent).

answered 'very dissatisfied'.[74] The main lesson that can be drawn from the data is that dissatisfied users exist, but seem to be a minority. All in all, ORDs are successful archivists, despite the secrecy constraints still characterising a non-negligible minority of ISDS cases.

One final, useful data-point can be found in the Internet traffic data for IAReporter. Interestingly, IAReporter has more inbound links than Italaw,[75] despite the fact that the latter was described by the survey respondents as the most useful ORD. In other words, other websites refer to IAReporter more frequently than to Italaw. One possible explanation for this result is that, while 'insiders' (i.e. the members of the ISDS social field, such as the ones who took the survey) particularly appreciate Italaw for its archival role, IAReporter is often referred to by external observers, such as online news outlets and blogs, which link to the website as a source. According to this theory, journalists and bloggers would be more likely to refer to case overviews edited by IAReporter, rather than simply linking to ISDS documents available on Italaw. Were this explanation confirmed, the narrative of ORDs as a liaison office that influences the legitimacy of the system by providing descriptions of it would be corroborated.

27.4 Conclusions

This chapter has presented four narratives of ORDs covering the field of ISDS. By magnifying different aspects of the current reality of ISDS, it was argued that these online services can be understood as archivists, gatekeepers, liaison offices and/or guerrilla tools. Each of these roles has a potential effect on the perceived legitimacy of ISDS as a whole. The available empirical evidence corroborates at least some of these narratives, namely highlighting the importance of the archival and liaising roles performed by ORDs. Users rely on ORDs as a single entry point to

---

[74] The survey also evinces the existence of different opinions as to how information gaps can be filled. The respondents who described themselves as either 'dissatisfied' or 'very dissatisfied' were requested to answer an additional question, asking whether they were more satisfied with subscription-only ORDs, as compared to the freely accessible ones. Of the relevant sub-set of respondents 31.25 per cent argued that subscription-only websites entirely fill the gaps of the freely accessible ones, 62.50 per cent answered that they find subscription-only services are more satisfactory, but there is still information they cannot retrieve, and 6.25 per cent reported not having access to any subscription-only service.

[75] According to MOZ Open Site Explorer, as of 26 September 2017, 2,422 links refer to Italaw, while 10,589 links refer to IAReporter. Furthermore, according to the same source, over the 60 days before 26 September 2017, 31 new links referring to IAReporter have been created, while only 1 new link referring to Italaw has been detected.

retrieve information and documents on ISDS cases, and they frequently make use of the descriptive shortcuts (such as case summaries) provided by the specialised websites covering the field.

As every uncoordinated and largely spontaneous social reality, the activities of ORDs may apparently come across as chaotic, heterogeneous and difficult to constrain into an overarching theory. Behind this appearance of chaos, however, ORDs actually perform a host of meaningful activities. They provide a user-friendly interface for the retrieval of documents that would, otherwise, be at best scattered across multiple sources. They allocate symbolic value within the field of ISDS, partially keeping its gates. They constitute a decomplexifying interface between ISDS and the external world. Sometimes, they may also become an arsenal of guerrilla tools. In short, they compete and cooperate in shaping the reality of ISDS.

As unseen actors of the ISDS system, ORDs effectively influence its legitimacy in different ways. By enabling the retrieval of past awards they facilitate reliance on precedent, thus contributing to the development of investment law as a coherent and legitimate field of law, enjoying a certain degree of autonomy. By helping the construction of a social field they enhance the inner cohesiveness of investment arbitration, thus also impinging upon the legitimacy of the system from the point of view of external observers. By narrating the system, they make it more understandable, and they influence the way in which it is perceived. By changing the way in which cases are litigated and adjudicated they have the potential to make the regime more transparent, but also more vulnerable to guerrilla tactics.

Bilateral Committees in EU Trade and Investment Agreements

Platforms for the Reassertion of State Control Over Investor-State Adjudication?

HANNES LENK

28.1 Introduction

Investor-State arbitration is at the centre of an intensely polarized debate in academia and civil society. Although the negotiation of international agreements for the purpose of protecting the interests of investors abroad is no novelty,[1] the structure of the modern investment protection regime that is characterized by the emergence of an extensive network of more than 3,500 bilateral investment treaties, bilateral and regional free trade agreements (FTAs) with comprehensive chapters on foreign investment,[2] as well as a number of plurilateral and (quasi) multilateral treaties[3] is a distinct phenomenon of the post-war period. Investor-State dispute settlement (ISDS) provisions, which empower investors to

---

[1] The protection of foreign property in international treaties can be traced back as far as the fourteenth century, but relevant practice under friendship and navigation treaties was generally a result of early trends in globalization and international economic integration during the colonial era, see Kenneth J. Vandevelde, *Bilateral Investment Treaties: History, Policy and Interpretation* (Oxford University Press, 2010), p. 19 *et seq*; On the origins of international investment law, see Kate Miles, 'International Investment Law and Universality: Histories of Shape-Shifting' (2014) 4(3) *Cambridge Journal of International and Comparative Law* 986.

[2] e.g. the North American Free Trade Agreement (NAFTA), ASEAN, CARICOM, MERCOSUR and ECOWAS.

[3] e.g. Energy Charter Treaty; even the EU – ACP Cotonou agreement is sometimes referred to as providing a multilateral framework, see Thomas W. Wälde, 'Improving the Mechanism for Treaty Negotiation and Investment Disputes: Competition and Choice as the Path to Quality and Legitimacy' in Karl P. Sauvant (ed.), *Yearbook on International Investment Law & Policy 2008–2009* (Oxford University Press, 2009).

HANNES LENK

vindicate interferences with their investments directly before international tribunals, are central to these investment agreements (IIAs), and
have become an attractive procedural avenue for aggrieved investors.[4]

Since the mid-1990s ISDS has attracted much criticism that broadly
gravitates around a common theme, i.e. the potential influence of ISDS
on the domestic regulatory policy space.[5] Described as a 'mechanism for
the control of governmental discretion and not merely a system of international commercial disputes settlement',[6] ISDS is criticized for lacking
fundamental traits to legitimize its extensive judicial authority.[7] These
concerns address in particular the (perceived and actual) impartiality of
arbitrators,[8] but also institutional biases, various procedural shortcomings,
and the scope of investment protection standards.[9] Although empirical

---

[4] As of 31 December 2016 nearly 600 cases have been registered with ICSID alone, ICSID
Caseload Statistics (2017-1), 7, available at https://icsid.worldbank.org/en/Documents/
resources/ICSID%20Web%20Stats%202017-1%20(English)%20Final.pdf.

[5] Stephan Wilske and Martin Raible, 'The Arbitrator as Guardian of International Public
Policy? Should Arbitrators Go Beyond Solving Legal Issues?' in Catherine A. Rogers
and Roger P. Alford (eds.), *The Future of Investment Arbitration* (Oxford University
Press, 2009), 249, 252; notably Tietje and Baetens have not found empirical evidence to
support a 'chilling effect', see Christian Tietje and Freya Baetens, *The Impact of Investor-
State-Dispute Settlement (ISDS) in the Transatlantic Trade and Investment Partnership*,
Report (2014), available at www.rijksoverheid.nl/documenten/rapporten/2014/06/24/
the-impact-of-investor-state-dispute-settlement-isds-in-the-ttip.

[6] Peter T. Muchlinski, *Multinational Enterprises and the Law*, 2nd edn (Oxford University
Press, 2007).

[7] Gus Van Harten, *Investment Treaty Arbitration and Public Law* (Oxford University
Press, 2008), 208; Frederick M. Abbott, 'The Political Economy of NAFTA Chapter
Eleven: Equality Before the Law and the Boundaries of North American Integration
(Investment, Sovereignty, and Justice: Arbitration Under NAFTA Chapter 11)' (2000) 23(3
4) *Hastings International and Comparative Law Review* 303–309, 308; Wilske and Raible,
'The Arbitrator as Guardian of International Public Policy?' p. 260.

[8] Yves Dezalay and Bryant G. Garth, *Dealing with Virtue: International Commercial Arbitration
and the Construction of a Transnational Legal Order* (University of Chicago Press, 1996);
Malcom Langford, Daniel Behn, and Runnar Lie, 'The Revolving Door in International
Investment Arbitration' (1 June 2017) *Journal of International Economic Law* 301; Jan
Paulsson, 'Moral Hazard in International Dispute Resolution' (2010) 25(2) *ICSID Review*
339–355; Thomas Schultz and Robert Kovacs, 'The Rise of a Third Generation of Arbitrators?
Fifteen Years after Dezalay and Garth' (2012) 28(2) *Arbitration International* 161–171; Audley
Sheppard, 'Arbitrator Independence in ICSID Arbitration' in Christina Binder, U. Kriebaum,
A. Reinisch and S. Wittich (eds.), *International Investment Law for the 21st Century: Essays
in Honour of Christoph Schreuer* (Oxford University Press, 2009), p. 131; Michael Waibel,
'Arbitrator Selection: Towards Greater State Control' in Andreas Kulick (ed.), *Reassertion of
Control over the Investment Treaty Regime* (Cambridge University Press, 2016).

[9] Albert Jan van den Berg, 'Dissenting Opinions by Party-Appointed Arbitrators in
Investment Arbitration' in Mahnoush H. Arsanjani, J. Cogan, R. Sloane and S. Wiessner
(eds.), *Looking to the Future: Essays on International Law in Honor of W Michael Reisman*

data does not support all of these claims,[10] the persistent aura of illegitimacy surrounding investor-State arbitration has already prompted political reactions.[11] Of particular relevance for the present chapter is the tendency amongst States to exert greater influence over the application of investment protection by investor-State tribunals, i.e. a reassertion of state control.[12]

States can avail themselves of a great variety of strategies and tactics in this respect. Prior to a dispute arising, States can change their policy objectives and adjust their negotiating strategies,[13] or withdraw from

(Martinus Nijhoff, 2011; Susan D. Franck, 'The Legitimacy Crisis in Investment Treaty Arbitration: Privatizing Public International Law Through Inconsistent Decisions' (2005) 73(4) *Fordham Law Review* 1521–1625; Gus Van Harten, 'Investment Treaty Arbitration, Procedural Fairness, and the Rule of Law' in Stephan W. Schill (ed.), *International Investment Law and Comparative Public Law* (Oxford University Press, 2010); Gus Van Harten, Investment Treaty Arbitration and Public Law.

[10] Daniel Behn, 'Legitimacy, Evolution, and Growth in Investment Treaty Arbitration: Empirically Evaluating the State-of-the-Art' (2015) 46 *Georgetown Journal of International Law* 363; Susan D. Franck, 'Conflating Politics and Development? Examining Investment Treaty Arbitration Outcomes' (2014) 55(1) *Virginia Journal of International Law* 13; Susan D. Franck, 'Empirically Evaluating Claims About Investment Treaty Arbitration' (2007) 86 *North Carolina Law Review* 1; Susan D. Franck, 'Development and Outcomes of Investment Treaty Arbitration' (2009) 50 *Harvard International Law Journal* 435; Emilie M. Hafner-Burton and David G. Victor, 'Secrecy in International Investment Arbitration: An Empirical Analysis' (2016) 7(1) *Journal of International Dispute Settlement* 161–182; Sergio Puig, 'Social Capital in the Arbitration Market' 25(2) *European Journal of International Law* (2014) 387–424; Michael Waibel and Yanhui Wu, 'Are Arbitrators Political? Evidence from International Investment Arbitration' (2017), available at www .researchgate.net/publication/256023521_Are_Arbitrators_Political.

[11] Lauge N. Skovgaard Poulsen and Emma Aisbett, 'When the Claim Hits: Bilateral Investment Treaties and Bounded Rational Learning' (2013) 65(2) *World Politics* 273–313; Louis T. Wells, 'Backlash to Investment Arbitration: Three Causes' in Michael Waibel, A. Kaushal, K. Chung and C. Balchin (eds.), *The Backlash against Investment Arbitration: Perceptions and Reality* (Wolters Kluwer, 2010) 341.

[12] Lise Johnson and Merim Razbaeva, 'State Control over Interpretation of Investment Treaties', VALE Columbia Center on Sustainable International Investment (2014); Malcom Langford, Daniel Behn, and Ole Kristian Fauchald, 'Backlash and State Strategies in International Investment Law,' in Thomas Gammeltoft-Hansen and Tanja E. Aalberts (eds.), *The Changing Practices of International Law: Sovereignty, Law and Politics in a Globalising World* (Cambridge University Press, 2017); Martins Paparinskis, 'Masters and Guardians of International Investment Law: How to Play the Game of Reassertion,' in Andreas Kulick (ed.), *Reassertion of Control over the Investment Treaty Regime* (Cambridge University Press, 2016), p. 30.

[13] E.g. India's termination of all existing BITs following its new Model BIT of 2015, which makes access to ISDS conditional on the exhaustion of local remedies; or in Australia the "Gillard Government Trade Policy Statement: Trading our Way to More Jobs and Prosperity" of April 2011 vowing no longer to include ISDS provisions in their FTAs and IIAs; the statement is no longer available. For a discussion see Ashique Rahman

arbitration institutions such as the International Centre for Settlement of Investment Disputes (ICSID).[14] As respondents, States may attempt to influence the outcome of particular disputes by issuing authoritative interpretations, use existing mechanisms to present novel challenges for arbitrators and the tribunals' jurisdiction,[15] delay proceedings, or refuse the enforcement of procedural orders and even the final award. The balance between legitimate control and abuse of due process is evident.

Against this backdrop the present chapter analyses the design and function of the bilateral trade committee (hereinafter referred to as the 'committee' or 'bilateral committee') in EU trade and investment agreements as instruments for the exercise of State control over various aspects of investor-State adjudication. This discussion takes place in the context of the EU investment court system (ICS), a concrete proposal of ISDS reform that has already been incorporated in the Comprehensive Economic and Trade Agreement (CETA),[16] the EU-Vietnam Investment Protection Agreement (EUVIPA),[17] and the EU-Singapore Investment Protection Agreement (EUSIPA)[18]. Despite significant divergences between the individual agreements, this chapter concludes that bilateral

and Chester Brown, 'Regional Economic Integration in Southeast Asia' in Christoph Herrmann, Markus Krajewski, and Jörg Philipp Terhechte (eds.), *European Yearbook of International Economic Law 2013* (Springer, 2013), p. 365.

[14] Bolivia, Ecuador, and Venezuela denounced the ICSID Convention in accordance with Article 71 of the Convention respectively in 2007, 2009, and 2012; for a discussion, see Christoph Schreuer, 'Denunciation of the ICSID Convention and Consent to Arbitration,' in Michael Waibel et al. (eds.), *The Backlash against Investment Arbitration* (Wolters Kluwer, 2010), p. 353.

[15] Germany recently challenged all three arbitrators shortly after the panel rejected any implications of the *Achmea* (Case C-284/16, EU:C:2018:158) judgment, where the Court of Justice of the European Union declared ISDS provisions in intra-EU BITs to be incompatible with the EU Treaties. On the *Vattenfall v. Germany* (ICSID Case No. ARB/12/12) dispute, see Luke Eric Peterson, 'Germany Lodges Request To Disqualify All Three Arbitrators in Vattenfall Nuclear Arbitration', *IAReporter*, 14 November 2008, http://tinyurl.com/y6vv4bau.

[16] Council Decision 2017/38 of 28 October 2016 on the provisional application of the Comprehensive Economic and Trade Agreement (CETA) between Canada, of the one part, and the European Union and its Member States, of the other part, OJ L 11, 14.1.2017, 1080.

[17] Authentic text as of August 2018.

[18] Authentic text as of April 2018; European Commission, Proposal for a Council Decision on the signing, on behalf of the European Union, of the Investment Protection Agreement between the European Union and its Member States, of the one part, and the Republic of Singapore of the other part (COM/2018/195 final), 18 April 2018; the text of the EUSIPA is available on the Commission's website (http://trade.ec.europa.eu/doclib/press/index.cfm?id=961).

committees present an important platform through which State Parties can exercise influence over the structure of tribunals as well as procedural and substantive aspects of adjudication and, thus, exert influence and control over their obligations vis-à-vis foreign investors. This chapter hopes to contribute to a better understanding of the role of treaty bodies in trade and investment agreements, which has thus far attracted relatively little scholarly attention.

28.2 Treaty Bodies as Instruments for the Exercise of State Control

The depth and ambition of the European Union's comprehensive trade and investment agreements is only matched by its impotence to bring them into operation. The EU-Singapore FTA (EUSFTA) and the Comprehensive Economic and Trade Agreement between the EU and Canada (CETA) have taken little less than a decade to negotiate and their full implementation is still hanging in the balance. In its recent Opinion 2/15 the CJEU concluded that the EU cannot negotiate investment agreements with ISDS provisions without the participation of its Member States.[19] A severe blow to the Commission, the judgment triggered major adjustments to the EU's foreign investment policy.[20] The FTAs with Singapore and Vietnam now no longer contain provisions on investment protection, instead these are contained in separate agreements, i.e. the EUSIPA and EUVIPA.

These agreements are illustrations of how quickly political objectives are subjected to a change in public sentiment. Following resistance to the inclusion of ISDS provisions in the Transatlantic Trade and Investment Partnership (TTIP) between the EU and United States, the European Parliament (EP) adopted a non-binding resolution urging the Commission to replace investor-State arbitration with a system that would reflect more democratic accountability.[21] The Commission, which is dependent on the

---

[19] The Court of Justice of the European Union has recently confirmed that the EU does not enjoy the requisite exclusive competences to conclude the EUSFTA alone (Opinion 2/15 *Free Trade Agreement between the EU and Singapore*, ECLI:EU:C:2017:376).

[20] Draft Council conclusions on the negotiation and conclusion of EU trade agreements (ST 8549 2018 INIT), 7 May 2018, available at, www.consilium.europa.eu/register/en/content/out?&typ=ENTRY&i=LD&DOC_ID=ST-8549-2018-INIT.

[21] European Parliament resolution of 8 July 2015 containing the European Parliament's recommendations to the European Commission on the negotiations for the Transatlantic Trade and Investment Partnership (2014/2228(INI)).

consent of the EP to conclude IIAs, swiftly presented a more judicialized system for CETA.[22] In its remarkable journey since the Lisbon Treaty took effect in 2009, institutional ISDS reform has become the hallmark of the EU's foreign investment policy.[23]

Policy preferences may also change throughout the lifetime of an agreement. Indeed, key moments in the development of international relations often demonstrate the need to manage international commitments in light of a constantly changing environment. What modern IIAs require is 'a "toolbox" of legal mechanisms that the State Parties can call upon to help construct lasting and effective international managerial regimes'.[24] Broad and generically phrased standards of investment protection already provide investment tribunals with interpretive flexibility to apply treaty provisions to factual circumstances that were unforeseen at the time of negotiation. States, on the other hand, are furnished with little influence over IIAs subsequent to their ratification. Bilateral treaty bodies play an important role in this respect as they institutionalize platforms for States to shape the development of investor-State adjudicative processes without having to engage in formalized political processes of amendment and modification. Notably, although transaction costs and the lack of political constraints facilitate the efficient management of IIAs through treaty bodies,[25] this of course requires effective checks and balances that safeguard demands for legitimacy and due process. For the ensuing discussion it is helpful to distinguish between expert or specialized committees and plenary bodies comprising representatives of the State Parties.[26]

---

[22] European Commission Press Release, 'CETA: EU and Canada agree on new approach on investment in trade agreement', (29 February 2016), accessed 21 September 2017 at http://trade.ec.europa.eu/doclib/press/index.cfm?id=1468.

[23] European Commission Concept Paper, 'Investment in TTIP and beyond – the path for reform. Enhancing the right to regulate and moving from current ad hoc arbitration towards an Investment Court' (5 May 2015), accessed 21 September 2017 at http://trade.ec.europa.eu/doclib/docs/2015/may/tradoc_153408.PDF.

[24] Eric J Pan, 'Authoritative Interpretation of Agreements: Developing More Responsive International Administrative Regimes' (1997) 38(2) *Harvard International Law Journal* 503–535, 505.

[25] Ibid., 507.

[26] On the classification of international organs, see Henry G. Schermers and Niels Blokker, *International Institutional Law: Unity within Diversity*, 4th edn (Martinus Nijhoff, 2005), pp. 285 *et seq.*

28.3 Committees in EU Trade and Investment Agreements

The present chapter focuses in particular on the role of bilateral committees within the framework of EU investment agreements. It is important to reiterate at this point that at the time of writing none of the agreements under discussion here has come into operation. Discerning the influence of treaty bodies over parts of the agreement, and specifically with respect to the ICS, is, thus, a markedly abstract undertaking. This section aims at situating bilateral trade committees within the broader political context of bilateral relations (Section 28.3.1). Subsequently, Section 28.3.2 discusses the composition and decision-making process of bilateral committees. Section 28.3.3 emphasizes some of the checks and balances in place.

28.3.1 Framework Agreements and the Common Institutional Framework

Trade agreements do not exist in isolation, but constitute an integral part of broader political ambitions. It is common practice in EU external relations to negotiate framework agreements, association agreements, or Partnership and Cooperation Agreements (PCAs), which set out larger political objectives. The PCAs concluded with Singapore and Vietnam stipulate in nearly identical terms:

> Existing agreements relating to specific areas of cooperation falling within the scope of this Agreement shall be considered part of the overall bilateral relations as governed by this agreement and as forming part of a *common institutional framework*.[27]

The EUSIPA and EUVIPA, therefore, ultimately operate under the broader umbrella of their respective framework agreements and the common institutional framework these purport to establish.[28] The EU–Canada Strategic Partnership Agreement, on the other hand, purports not to 'affect or prejudice the interpretation or application of other agreements between the Parties'.[29] Rather than subsuming CETA under the umbrella of a strategic

---

[27] Article 55(3), EU – Vietnam PCA (emphasis added).
[28] This is achieved either by generically phrased 'future development clauses' (Article 54, EU – Vietnam PCA), or by way of specific reference to trade and investment agreements (Article 9(2), Draft EU – Singapore PCA).
[29] Article 28(8), EU – Canada Strategic Partnership Agreement.

partnership, this approach envisages EU–Canada trade and investment relations to develop in parallel with a broader political cooperation.

The relationship between the framework agreement and the respective trade agreements likewise determines the relationship between their respective institutions. The examples of Vietnam and Singapore are reminiscent of vertical hierarchical structures, which makes bilateral committees in the EUSIPA and EUVIPA politically accountable to high-level political bodies established under the PCAs. This is not the case in the horizontal model underlying EU–Canada relations.

28.3.2 Composition and Decision-making

The bilateral committees comprise representatives of both Contracting Parties[30] and are co-chaired by a representative of the Parties at ministerial level, referring on the part of the EU to the Trade Commissioner.[31] Decisions are generally taken by consensus.[32] The size and composition will determine the spectrum of potentially diverging interests for which a political compromise will need to be negotiated.[33] Whether participation in the committee is limited to a small number of representatives of the EU institutions, or comprises Member State representatives in addition to the EU is therefore of great relevance. Whereas bilateral committees function as platforms for the implementation of trade and investment policy, the framework agreements establish an institutional structure that is aimed at political dialogue. Representation at the highest political level is guaranteed either through the creation of Joint Committees,[34] or in the case of CETA through the establishment of a Joint Ministerial Council.[35]

Certain aspects of the ICS are subject to special procedures, including the power to appoint the Presidents of the Tribunal and the Appellate Tribunal, which is explicitly reserved to the chairs of the committee;[36] and

---

[30] Article 21.1(1), CETA; Article 4.1(1), EUSIPA; Article 4.1(1), EUVIPA.
[31] Minister for International Trade in Canada (Article 26.1(1) CETA); Minister for Trade and Industry of Vietnam (Article 4.1(2), EUVIPA); Minister for Trade and Industry of Singapore (Art. 4.1(2), EUSIPA).
[32] Article 26.3(3), CETA; Article 4.2(3), EUSIPA; Article4.2(3), EUVIPA.
[33] Pan, 'Authoritative Interpretation of Agreements', 512.
[34] Article 41(1), Draft EU – Singapore PCA; Article 52(1), EU – Vietnam PCA.
[35] Article 27(2)(b)(ii), EU – Canada Strategic Partnership Agreement.
[36] Article 8.27(8), CETA; Articles 3.9(6) and 3.10(6), EUSIPA; Articles 3.38(8) and 3.39(6), EUVIPA.

the removal of members from the ICS due to ethical violations, where the committee acts upon the 'reasoned' recommendation from the president of the Appellate Tribunal or upon joint initiative of the parties.[37] Notably, CETA also provides for the establishment of a specialized sub-committee[38] with extensive powers within the framework of the ICS.[39] Similar arrangements existed in the FTAs with Singapore and Vietnam, but were abandoned in the recent restructuring. The EUSIPA and EUVIPA no longer provide for sub-committees.

In order to understand the political nature of decisions taken by the bilateral committee, the power balances behind these decisions, and the relative decision-making autonomy of committees it is pivotal to take into account the composition of the bilateral committee, as well as its relationship with Joint Committees and, where applicable, sub-committees. The following section problematizes the degree of relative autonomy that underlies decision-making in the bilateral committee and the sub-committee.

28.3.3   The Relative Autonomy of Committees and Sub-committees: Procedural Dependency, Accountability, and Safeguards

Interdependencies between the bilateral committee and other bodies in the committee structure are created through a system of checks and balances. Although the CETA sub-committee is clearly subordinate to the bilateral committee, whose work it functionally supports without affecting the committee's relative decision-making autonomy,[40] it is nonetheless furnished with important powers of initiation. More specifically, this concerns amendments regarding the fair and equitable treatment (FET) standard[41] and the adoption of authoritative interpretations.[42] Indeed, powers of initiation curtail the decision-making autonomy of the committee and thereby depoliticize the implementation of two politically charged areas under the agreement.

---

[37]   Article 8.30(4), CETA); Article 3.11(5), EUSIPA; Article 3.40(5), EUVIPA.
[38]   Article 26.2(1), CETA.
[39]   Article 8.44, CETA.
[40]   With the exception of the amendment of the FET chapter and the adoption of authoritative interpretations.
[41]   Articles 8.10(3) in combination with Articles 26.1(5)(c) and 8.44(3)(e), CETA.
[42]   Article 8.31(3) in combination with Articles 26.1(5)(c) and 8.44(3)(a), CETA.

Although in all other aspects of the agreement the power of initiation remains in the hands of the bilateral committee,[43] the sub-committee enjoys certain decision-making powers with respect to, for instance, the adoption of a code of conduct for the members of the Tribunal,[44] and amendments to applicable arbitration rules and rules of transparency.[45]

CETA furthermore establishes a formal chain of accountability that charges the committee with supervising the work of the sub-committee.[46] To this end, the committee may change or undertake the tasks assigned to the sub-committee, dissolve the sub-committee,[47] and request extraordinary meetings.[48] The sub-committee, on the other hand, is under an obligation to inform the committee of its agenda and report the results of the meetings,[49] but is also tasked to review the functioning of the Appellate Tribunal – an area where the CETA Joint Committee enjoys extensive decision-making autonomy – and can recommend a revision of the committee's decisions.[50] Canada and the EU furthermore enjoy the option to override the substantive issue allocation to the sub-committee and bring an issue directly to the bilateral committee.[51]

The bilateral committee's power vis-à-vis structural aspects of the ICS is furthermore subject to external checks and balances. Accordingly, if the committee fails to appoint the members of the tribunal, the Secretary-General of the ICSID shall appoint a three-member division of the Tribunal by random selection from amongst the existing nominations.[52] Another example is the procedure for the adoption of working procedures for the EU–Vietnam ICS tribunals, which are drawn up by their respective presidents but require formal adoption by the bilateral committee.[53] Notably, where no consensus is obtained within three months, the working procedures are to be revised, taking consideration of the views expressed by the parties. The method for adoption under these circumstances becomes negative-consensus, i.e. the working procedures are deemed

---

[43] Article 8.10(3) and 8.44(3)(d), CETA.
[44] Article 8.44(2), CETA.
[45] Article 8.44(3)(b), CETA.
[46] Article 26.1(4)(b), CETA.
[47] Article 26.1(5)(g), CETA.
[48] Article 26.2(4), CETA.
[49] Article 26.2(6), CETA.
[50] Articles 8.28(8) and 8.44(3)(e) in combination with Article 8.28(7), CETA.
[51] Article 26.2(6), CETA.
[52] Article 8.27(17), CETA.
[53] Articles 3.38(10) and 3.39(10), EUVIPA.

adopted unless the parties reject the revised rules by mutual consent. This solution reflects a pragmatism that protects the functioning of the dispute settlement mechanism from being halted by political interests.

Unlike the committees established under the new FTAs with Singapore and Vietnam,[54] the EUSIPA and EUVIPA no longer explicitly require that the bilateral committee keeps the Joint Committee informed of its activities. Be that as it may, they are nonetheless an 'integral part' of the common institutional framework and, thus, cannot entirely escape political oversight and accountability.[55]

28.4   The Role of Bilateral Committees in the Context of Investor-State Dispute Settlement

It transpires from the above discussion that although the institutional set-up of bilateral committees in all post-Lisbon agreements displays certain common features, their level of political accountability, the level of decision making, as well as the relative autonomy of decision-making authority varies significantly across these agreements. The bilateral committee is generally responsible for the implementation and proper operation of the agreement[56] and fulfils in this respect a number of political functions, including the assessment and development of bilateral investment relations,[57] the implementation of broader strategic goals,[58] the adoption of recommendations for amendments to the agreement,[59] as well as responsibilities vis-à-vis the engagement with civil society and stakeholder dialogues.[60] The committee also acts as a platform to facilitate amicable solutions if disagreements arise,[61] and fulfils an important role in the multilateralization of the investment court system by way of deciding on transitional arrangements.[62] Notably, the EU–Vietnam committee may even extend the transitional period, during which automatic enforcement

---

[54] Article 16.1(5), EUSFTA; Article 17.1(5), EUVFTA.
[55] Article 4.12(1), EUSIPA; Article 4.20(2), EUVIPA.
[56] Article 26.1(3), CETA; Article 4.1(3)(a) and (b), EUSIPA; Article 4.1(3)(a) and (b), EUVIPA.
[57] Article 26.1(5)(d) and (f), CETA; Article 4.1(3)(c), EUSIPA.
[58] Article 26.1(4)(a), CETA; Article 4.1(3)(b), EUSIPA; Article 4.1(3)(b), EUVIPA.
[59] Article 26.1(5)(c), CETA; Article 4.1(4)(b), EUVIPA.
[60] Article 26.1(5)(b), CETA; Article 4.1(4)(a), EUVIPA.
[61] Article 26.1(4)(c), CETA; Article 4.1(3)(d), EUSIPA; Article 4.1(3)(h), EUVIPA.
[62] Article 8.29, CETA; Article 3.12, EUSIPA; Article 3.41, EUVIPA.

of awards against Vietnam is suspended in favour of the application of the
New York Convention.[63]

This section, however, is concerned with concrete powers over aspects
of the agreement that have a direct impact on investor-State disputes. For
analytical purposes, these are categorized into structural (Section 28.4.1),
procedural (Section 28.4.2), and substantive (Section 28.4.3) powers.

28.4.1   Structural Powers

The ICS introduces powers for the bilateral committee to influence
the structure and composition of the Tribunal and Appellate Tribunal.
In particular, the committee decides on the retainer fees and expenses
for Tribunal and Appeal Tribunal members, as well as daily fees for the
presidents and vice-presidents of ICS tribunals[64] and of Tribunal and
Appeal Tribunal members, and is empowered to transform appointments
on the ICS into full-time employment subject to a fixed salary.[65] The
committee may increase or decrease the number of Tribunal and Appeal
Tribunal members,[66] remove members from the Tribunal for ethical
violations,[67] and lay down procedures for the replacement of members
and the filling of vacancies on Appeal Tribunal divisions.[68] Under CETA
the committee may also decide on the administrative support for the
Appeal Tribunal.[69]

The chair of the committee appoints the President and Vice-President
of the Tribunal by lot from amongst the third-country Members of the
Tribunal, providing the Contracting Parties with direct influence over key
positions in the ICS.[70] Notably, the EUVIPA provides the trade committee
with powers to decide whether Article 3(3) of the UNCITRAL Rules on
Transparency in Treaty-based Investor-State Arbitration shall apply to the

---

[63] Article 3.57(4), EUVIPA.
[64] Article 8.27(12), CETA; Articles 3.9(12), 3.10(15), and 4.1(4)(b), EUSIPA; Articles 3.38(14), 3.39(15) and 4.1(5)(d), EUVIPA.
[65] Article 8.27(15), CETA; Articles 3.9(15), 3.10(13), and 4.1(4)(c), EUSIPA; Articles 3.38(17), 3.39(17), and 4.1(5)(d), EUVIPA.
[66] Articles 8.27(3) and Article 8.28(7)(f), CETA; Articles 3.9(3), 3.10(3), and 4.1(4)(a), EUSIPA; Articles 3.38(3), 3.39(4), and 4.1(5)(a), EUVIPA.
[67] Article 8.30(4), CETA; Articles 3.11(5) and 4.1(4)(a), EUSIPA; Articles 3.40(5) and 4.1(5)(a), EUVIPA.
[68] Article 8.28(7)(c), CETA.
[69] Article 8.28(7)(a), CETA.
[70] Article 8.27(8), CETA; Articles 3.9(6) and 3.10(6), EUSIPA; Articles 3.38(8) and 3.39(6), EUVIPA.

transparency of the proceedings instead of Article 20(3), which operates as the default.[71]

Most importantly, however, the committees control the appointment of members to the Tribunal and Appellate Tribunal.[72] The ICS differs in this respect markedly from traditional investor-State arbitration. Indeed, the selection process of members to individual divisions is completely withdrawn from the influence of the disputing parties and is, thus, no longer governed by party autonomy. However, the influence on the appointment of ICS members through the bilateral committee furnishes the Contracting Parties with indirect control over the composition of Tribunal and Appeal Tribunal divisions. This is perpetuated by the fact that one member of the division is always affiliated to the respondent State.[73] Only the investor, who is left without any direct or indirect influence over the composition of the ICS and its divisions, remains entirely excluded from the selection process. State control over this structural element of the ICS is most pronounced in the EUSIPA, which allows contracting parties to directly nominate the share of ICS members with national affiliation and requires consensus only for two of the six members.[74] Both CETA and the EUVIPA subject the appointment of all members to consensus in the bilateral committee, and the political compromise that such a decision represents.[75]

28.4.2 Procedural Powers

The bilateral committee also exercises control over procedural aspects of the adjudication. This is particularly pronounced under CETA, which lacks significant detail regarding the appellate process. Instead, far-reaching powers are transferred to the CETA Joint Committee, which is charged with deciding whether and under what circumstances a case is referred back to the Tribunal, and whether or not the Appellate Tribunal enjoys jurisdiction to complete the legal analysis.[76] The committee furthermore enjoys competence to decide on any other elements it determines

---

[71] Article 3.46(6), EUVIPA.
[72] Articles 8.27(2) and 8.28(3), CETA; Article 4.1(4)(a), EUSIPA; Article 4.1(5)(a), EUVIPA.
[73] Articles 3.9(7) and 3.10(7), EUSIPA; Articles 3.38(6) and 3.39(8), EUVIPA.
[74] Articles 3.9(2) and 3.10(2), EUSIPA.
[75] Articles 8.27(2) and 8.28(3), CETA; Articles 3.38(2) and 3.39(2), EUVIPA.
[76] Article 8.28(7)(b), CETA.

necessary for the effective functioning of the appellate tribunal.[77] The EUVIPA and EUSIPA endow the committee with powers to supplement the applicable arbitration rules.[78] Notably, CETA allocates this power to a sub-committee that enjoys autonomous decision-making authority in this respect.[79]

28.4.3   Substantive Powers

Bilateral committees exercise significant powers over substantive aspects of investor-State adjudication. This chapter has already briefly touched upon the power to amend the scope of the FET standard, which in all three agreements is determined by reference to a list of prohibited treatments.[80] Whereas this list can only be extended in accordance with the formal amendment procedure under the EUSIPA[81] and the EUVIPA,[82] CETA has delegated this power entirely to the committee, but reserves the power of initiation to the sub-committee.[83] Notably, the EUSIPA empowers the committee to recommend amendments. Consequently, control over the FET standard under the agreements with Singapore and Vietnam is exercised through lengthy political processes, whereas CETA utilizes the bilateral committee to provide the contracting parties with flexibility to adjust the FET standard more dynamically. Indeed, the extensive powers of the sub-committee largely isolate this aspect of the agreement from political interests.

As pragmatic as this method may be, removing quasi-amendments of the agreement from democratic oversight raises obvious legitimacy concerns. However, even in CETA it is the committee that ultimately retains decision-making authority, and the sub-committee is required to act 'on agreement of the Parties, and after completion of their respective internal requirements and procedure'.[84] CETA, therefore, harnesses most of the efficiency gains of functional delegation while maintaining some level of State control over a relevant part of the agreement. This residual

---

[77] Article 8.28(7)(g), CETA; in a similar fashion, see Article 4.1(4)(g), EUSIPA; and Article 4.1(3)(i), EUVIPA.

[78] Article 4.1(f), EUSIPA; Article 4.1(5)(b), EUVIPA.

[79] Article 8.44(3)(b), CETA.

[80] Article 8.10(2), CETA; Article 2.4(2), EUSIPA; Article 2.5(2), EUVIPA.

[81] Article 2.4(4), EUSIPA.

[82] Article 2.5(3), EUVIPA.

[83] Article 8.10(3) in combination with Articles 8.44(3)(d) and 26.1(5)(c), CETA.

[84] Article 8.10(3), CETA.

involvement of political authority bestows the decision with a certain level of procedural legitimacy. These variations amongst CETA, the EUSIPA, and EUVIPA aptly illustrate the difficult choices in balancing the need for flexible and responsive IIAs with increased State control vis-à-vis politically sensitive issues.

Even more importantly, bilateral committees are endowed with broad powers to adopt authoritative interpretations of the agreement, which are deemed binding on the Tribunal and Appellate Tribunal.[85] The contracting parties enjoy certain rights under customary international law to influence the interpretation of their agreements.[86] Accordingly, Article 31(3)(a) and (b) of the Vienna Convention on the Law of Treaties stipulates that subsequent agreements and subsequent practice need to be taken into account in the interpretation of an international agreement. State parties are, therefore, at liberty to agree on the interpretation of certain aspects of the investment agreement without being exposed to the political risk that is inherent in constitutional ratification procedures that formal amendment or modification of the agreement could entail.[87] Although the evidentiary threshold for subsequent agreement is lower than what is required for subsequent practice,[88] both are ultimately based on objective proof of the shared understanding amongst the treaty parties with respect to the meaning of certain aspects of the agreement.[89]

[85] Articles 8.30(3) in combination with 8.44(3)(a) and 26.1(5)(e), CETA; Articles 16(4) in combination with 34(2)(b), Investment Chapter, Articles 3.13(3) and 4.1(4)(f), EUSIPA; Articles 3.42(5) and 4.1(4)(c) EUVIPA.

[86] Thomas W. Wälde, 'Interpreting Investment Treaties: Experiences and Examples' in Christina Binder et al. (eds.), *International Investment Law for the 21st Century: Essays in Honour of Christoph Schreuer* (Oxford University Press, 2009), pp. 724, 765.

[87] Kirsten Schmalenbach and Oliver Dörr, *Vienna Convention on the Law of Treaties: A Commentary* (Springer, 2012), pp. 554–555; for an example of a subsequent agreement through the exchange of diplomatic notes see Johnson and Razbaeva, 'State Control over Interpretation of Investment Treaties'.

[88] Johnson and Razbaeva, 'State Control over Interpretation of Investment Treaties'; on the role of human rights bodies as 'producers' of subsequent practice, see Kerstin Mechlem, 'Treaty Bodies and the Interpretation of Human Rights' (2009) 42 *Vanderbilt Journal of Transnational Law* 905–948, 920–921.

[89] Generally see Julian Arato, 'Subsequent Practice and Evolutive Interpretation: Techniques of Treaty Interpretation over Time and Their Diverse Consequences' (2010) 9(3) *The Law & Practice of International Courts and Tribunals* 443–494; for a discussion of authoritative context of the IMF see Pan, 'Authoritative Interpretation of Agreements'; for a discussion of the WTO context, see Claus-Dieter Ehlermann and Lothar Ehring, 'The Authoritative Interpretation Under Article IX:2 of the Agreement Establishing the World Trade

Alternatively, the contracting parties may also formalize this process in the agreement,[90] including delegating this power to treaty bodies. In the context of human rights treaties the endowment of treaty bodies with interpretive functions plays an important role. Melchem observes that because these agreements are particularly tailored towards the benefit of individuals, they must be interpreted in a manner that achieves an effective protection of individual rights. The delegation of interpretive powers to expert bodies protects against political opportunism and has, therefore, a depoliticizing effect.[91] The further away from the political centre of bilateral relations the power to adopt authoritative interpretations is exercised, the less political interests are likely to influence the particular interpretation that is being adopted.[92]

This is reminiscent of the international investment law discourse, where depoliticization is recognized as an existential *raison d'être* of ISDS.[93] Indeed, the transfer of interpretive authority to treaty bodies is no novelty to IIAs.[94] The exercise of State control over the agreement for the purpose of establishing a sovereignty-protective interpretation could easily be perceived as an improper tactic to escape liability for the violation of rights that have particularly been designed for the protection of investors, rather than a legitimate attempt to clarify ambiguous provisions of the agreement.[95] This view, however, ignores the fact that bilateral committees are ultimately designed to protect the interests of State Parties. As Crawford observed:

> [T]here is a certain tendency to believe that investors own bilateral investment treaties, not the States parties to them. So, for example, when the

Organization: Current Law, Practice and Possible Improvements' (2005) 8(4) *Journal of International Economic Law* 803–824.

[90] e.g. Article 21.1 and 21.2(e), US–Australia FTA of 2005; Article 832, Canada–Colombia FTA of 2011; Article 30(3), US Model BIT of 2012.

[91] Mechlem, 'Treaty Bodies and the Interpretation of Human Rights', 912.

[92] On the delegation of interpretive authority to joint administrative commissions for the purpose of enhancing procedural legitimacy, see Anne van Aaken, 'Delegating Interpretative Authority in Investment Treaties: The Case of Joint Administrative Commissions' in Jean E. Kalicki and Anna Joubin-Bret (eds.), *Reshaping the Investor-State Dispute Settlement System: Journeys for the 21st Century* (Brill Nijhoff, 2015), pp. 21, 33.

[93] Franck, 'The Legitimacy Crisis', 1538; Rainer Geiger, 'The Multifaceted Nature of International Investment Law' in Karl P. Sauvant (ed.), *Appeals Mechanism in International Investment Disputes* (Oxford University Press, 2008), pp. 17, 19.

[94] e.g. Article 1131, NAFTA; Article 10.23, CAFTA-DR.

[95] Georg Nolte, 'Jurisprudence under Special Regimes Relating to Subsequent Agreements and Subsequent Practice' in Georg Nolte (ed.), *Treaties and Subsequent Practice* (Oxford University Press, 2013), p. 237; Lise Johnson and Razbaeva, 'State Control over Interpretation of Investment Treaties', 11; Wälde, 'Interpreting Investment Treaties', pp. 765–767.

NAFTA provides for interpretation of its provisions by a Commission of States parties, this is regarded as somehow an infringement on the inherent rights of investors under the NAFTA. That is not what international law says. International law says that the parties to a treaty own the treaty and can interpret it. One might say within reason, but one might not question the application of reason as they see fit.[96]

Interpretation, by its very nature, does not affect the constitutive agreement in the same manner as modification or amendment,[97] but merely narrows the range of acceptable interpretations.[98] This view is also supported by the conclusions of the International Law Commission, which confirmed that joint interpretive declarations, despite being authoritative, do not outrank other means of interpretation under the Vienna Convention on the Law of Treaties.[99] Arguably, therefore, by redefining the boundaries of interpretive flexibility, an authoritative interpretation affects the jurisdiction of a competent court or tribunal, but cannot determine the outcome of a particular dispute in the context of which that court or tribunal exercises its jurisdiction subject to the accepted tenets of interpretation. This is also supported by the experience under NAFTA, where the joint interpretive declaration of the FTC is accepted as one of the relevant aspects in interpreting the FET standard.[100]

Authoritative interpretations have some significant advantages over formal amendment and modification, because they provide a high level of flexibility and responsiveness in the implementation of the agreement. Efficiency benefits accompanied by the delegation of decision-making power to treaty bodies are, however, premised on a limited rather than elevated role of the State, i.e. the circumvention of more lengthy and costly

---

[96] James Crawford, 'A Consensualist Interpretation of Article 31(3) of the Vienna Convention,' in Georg Nolte (ed.), *Treaties and Subsequent Practice* (Oxford University Press, 2013), pp. 29, 31.

[97] Pan, 'Authoritative Interpretation of Agreements', 505.

[98] On how to draw the line between interpretation and amendment, see Michael Ewing-Chow and Junianto J. Losari, 'Which Is To Be the Master? Extra-arbitral Interpretive Procedures for IIAs' in Jean E. Kalicki and Anna Joubin-Bret (eds.), *Reshaping the Investor-State Dispute Settlement System* (Brill Nijhoff, 2015), pp. 107–112.

[99] United Nations, Report of the International Law Commission on its sixty-fifth session: held at the United Nations Office, Geneva, from 6 May to 7 June 2013 and from 8 July to 9 August 2013, A/68/10 (2013), 21–22.

[100] e.g. *ADF Group Inc. v. United States*, ICSID No. ARB(AF)I00I1, para. 177; notably, the response of tribunals on the authoritative interpretation of the NAFTA Free Trade Commission has been markedly divergent; for a discussion see Anthea Roberts, 'Power and Persuasion in Investment Treaty Interpretation: The Dual Role of States' (2010) 104(2) *The American Journal of International Law* 179–225.

political negotiations. Likewise, a depoliticization or, indeed, legitimizing effect, only occurs where interpretive authority is delegated away from the political centre.[101] In the context of the ICS, therefore, authoritative interpretations are primarily relevant as instruments that help to effectively exercise the Contracting Parties' right to regulate. Unlike adjudication, which locks respondent states into a mantra of defensive self-interests, the benefit of joint interpretations is that they facilitate progressive development through mutually agreed solutions.[102] Arguably, CETA adopts a balanced approach. While the details are worked out in the specialized sub-committee, the decision-making authority rests with the committee. Under both the EUSIPA and the EUVIPA this task falls exclusively on the committee and results in the direct exercise of state control over the interpretation of the agreement. Whereas this is not generally problematic, the EUSIPA and EUVIPA bestow on the committee the power to determine the specific date from which that interpretation shall have binding effect on the ICS tribunals[103] and the Parties.[104] If this power were utilized to influence the outcome of pending disputes it would violate fundamental principles of due process[105] and equality of arms.[106] Consequently, whereas CETA makes use of the bilateral committee to insulate authoritative interpretation from political opportunism, the EUSIPA and EUVIPA incorporate maximum state control over the normative formulation of treaty commitments as well as their effects on State Parties.

28.5   Concluding Remarks: Bilateral Committees as Unseen Actors in International Adjudication

This chapter has demonstrated the significance of bilateral committees in EU trade and investment agreements as instruments for the exercise of

---

[101] Indeed, Pan recognizes that plenary bodies charged with authoritative interpretations may avoid formalized political processes of treaty amendment and modification, but would not eliminate the political barrier of having to build consensus, see 'Authoritative Interpretation of Agreements', 527.

[102] Ibid., 518.

[103] Article 3.13(3), EUSIPA; Article3.43(5), EUVIPA.

[104] Article 4.1(4)(f), EUSIPA.

[105] Rudolf Dolzer and Christoph Schreuer, *Principles of International Investment Law* (Oxford University Press, 2012), pp. 89–90; Tomoko Ishikawa, 'Keeping Interpretation in Investment Treaty Arbitration "on Track": The Role of State Parties' in Jean E. Kalicki and Anna Joubin-Bret (eds.), *Reshaping the Investor-State Dispute Settlement System* (Brill Nijhoff, 2015), pp. 115–149, 142.

[106] UNCTAD, *Interpretation of IIAs: What States Can Do* (2011), p. 4.

State control over structural, procedural, and substantive features of the ICS. Exercising relative decision-making authority, bilateral committees partake as unseen actors in investor-State adjudication. Although this is largely a reflection of the contracting parties' ownership of the agreement, it represents an important power shift in comparison to traditional investor-State arbitration. This is particularly problematic where political actors utilize the committee to interfere with pending disputes, violating fundamental principles of due process and equality of arms.

It is notable, however, that the agreements reflect significant divergences in the design of committees, both with respect to their institutional features as well as the extent of their specific powers. The latest version of the ICS in the EUSIPA is undoubtedly more sophisticated and well drafted than CETA, which was in large part a reaction to the rising criticism and the unequivocal rejection of ISDS in the context of negotiations on the EU–US TTIP Agreement,[107] and these might explain some of the variations. Others, such as the decision to subject extension of the FET standard to formal amendment and modification procedures rather than delegating that authority to the committee, are clear examples of diverging interests underlying the agreement.

The extent of control that the CETA contracting parties exercise over the ICS is in this respect first and foremost dependent on the decision-making autonomy of the committee that is limited through powers of initiation of the specialized sub-committees. With the move towards investment protection agreements, the establishment of sub-committees appears to be a thing of the past. However, the involvement of specialized committees over politically sensitive issues guarantees a high level of flexibility while addressing some of the legitimacy concerns that are accompanied by the delegation of far-reaching powers that shape the normative content of IIAs. Under CETA, therefore, the use of sub-committees isolates decisions with an impact on the ICS from political opportunism. From this perspective, sub-committees are, indeed, a desirable feature. Pan advocated the use of empowered treaty bodies to equip international agreements with the requisite flexibility and responsiveness that complex global economic interdependencies require. These efficiency gains are premised on the delegation of discretionary powers to a centralized

---

[107] Commission Staff Working Document, 'Report on Online public consultation on investment protection and investor-to-state dispute settlement (ISDS) in the Transatlantic Trade and Investment Partnership Agreement' (SWD(2015) 3 final), in particular see pt. 3.1

administrative body with as little exposure to the need for politically negotiated compromise as necessary.[108]

However, the empowerment of technocratic sub-committees over politically sensitive issues is likely to deepen the democratic deficit by removing the electorate from the decision-making process.[109] The IPAs with Singapore and Vietnam are interesting in this respect. Unlike CETA, they reserve a high level of direct State control over aspects related to investor-State adjudication. More importantly, these agreements form an integral part of broader political framework agreements and the accountability structure these agreements purport to establish. As the decision-making process within bilateral committees remains highly politicized, it appears that these committees have primarily been designed with the objective of optimizing mechanisms that allow contracting parties jointly to exert control over investor-State adjudication. It is in light of these inherent conflicts that the role of bilateral committees as unseen actors in investor-State adjudication ought to be understood, and why more research is needed to better understand this phenomenon.

---

[108] Pan, 'Authoritative Interpretation of Agreements', 505.
[109] Ibid., 529.

Epilogue

An Unseen Actor Speaks

Smile at us, pass us or greet us; then, if you like, forget,
For we are the unseen actors, who have not spoken yet.
The interns, law clerks, jurists, of less than judicial rank,
Whom judges and arbitrators have nonetheless reason to thank.
We are the unobtrusive – we could almost be said to 'lurk';
But make no mistake about it, we're doing important work.
We stand well back in the shadows (except for the Registrar),
If you meet us around the building you may not know who we are,
But still it seems that we're valued: this volume tells us so;
We don't get many plaudits, so at least that's nice to know.
We are the backroom people, who are neither heard nor seen,
But we help the judges with language, to say what they really mean,
And we summarise the facts, too, a job that needs much patience,
But it has to be done – and carefully – when you're bringing peace between nations;
We have to deal with the Agents, which is sometimes not much fun
When it's we who get the reaction to what the Court has just done.
We keep tribunals running; we see that deadlines are met;
And once our judges start arguing, they would still be arguing yet,
If they could not agree at some stage it is time for the Court to adjourn,
And that of course is the moment when it's good to be able to turn
To the staff for their willing assistance; though they say it's not open to doubt
That deciding's a judicial duty, not something that can be farmed out.
See, the judgment's judiciously worded, each sentence clear and exact,
With State susceptibilities all handled with highly suitable tact,
So that even the losing party is bound to be persuaded . . .
You don't think it was the judges, then, who wrote all that, unaided?
But with dissenting and separate opinions, we leave judges to have their say;
(Though if they did ask us to write them, they might be better that way).
We have to be ready and able to work in more languages than one,
And be equally tactful in each of them, that's sometimes not easily done.
But still we do usually manage to make everything clear to the Bench,
Though we find that what's specious in English sounds no more convincing
   in French.
Then preparing the minutes of meetings, we don't just transcribe, but instead

We write what we think that each judge who spoke will be thinking he *ought* to
have said.
We're not called 'Excellency'; we don't wear a formal gown,
We're not invited to parties in the embassy part of the town,
We don't hobnob with ambassadors and such, but all the same,
We have our own entertainments: spectators see most of the game.
The judges you see get the kudos, but the actors unseen have their fun,
And once the decision's delivered, we take pride in a job well done.

INDEX